IMMANUEL KANT

Notes and Fragments

The purpose of the Cambridge Edition is to offer translations of the best modern German edition of Kant's work in a uniform format suitable for Kant scholars. When complete (sixteen volumes are currently envisioned), the edition will include all of Kant's published works and a generous selection of his unpublished writings, such as the *Opus postumum*, *handschriftliche Nachlaß*, lectures, and correspondence.

This volume provides the first-ever extensive translation of the notes and fragments that survived Kant's death in 1804. These include marginalia, lecture notes, and sketches and drafts for his published works. They are important as an indispensable resource for understanding Kant's intellectual development and published works, casting new light on Kant's conception of his own philosophical methods and his relations to his predecessors, as well as on central doctrines of his work such as the theory of space, time, and categories; the refutations of skepticism and metaphysical dogmatism; the theory of the value of freedom and the possibility of free will; the conception of God; the theory of beauty, and much more.

Paul Guyer is Professor of Philosophy and Florence R. C. Murray Professor in the Humanities at the University of Pennsylvania.

Curtis Bowman has taught at the University of Pennsylvania, Bryn Mawr College, and Haverford College.

Frederick Rauscher is Assistant Professor of Philosophy at Michigan State University.

THE CAMBRIDGE EDITION OF THE WORKS OF IMMANUEL KANT

General editors: Paul Guyer and Allen W. Wood

Theoretical Philosophy, 1755–1770
Critique of Pure Reason
Theoretical Philosophy after 1781
Practical Philosophy
Critique of the Power of Judgment
Religion and Rational Theology
Anthropology, History, and Education
Natural Science
Lectures on Logic
Lectures on Metaphysics
Lectures on Ethics
Opus postumum
Notes and Fragments
Correspondence
Lectures on Anthropology
Lectures and Drafts on Political Philosophy

IMMANUEL KANT

Notes and Fragments

EDITED BY

PAUL GUYER
University of Pennsylvania

TRANSLATED BY

CURTIS BOWMAN

PAUL GUYER

FREDERICK RAUSCHER

CAMBRIDGE
UNIVERSITY PRESS

CAMBRIDGE UNIVERSITY PRESS
Cambridge, New York, Melbourne, Madrid, Cape Town, Singapore, São Paulo

Cambridge University Press
40 West 20th Street, New York, NY 10011-4211, USA

www.cambridge.org
Information on this title: www.cambridge.org/9780521552486

First published 2005

Printed in the United States of America

A catalog record for this publication is available from the British Library.

Library of Congress Cataloging in Publication Data

Kant, Immanuel, 1724–1804.
[Selections. English. 2005]
Notes and fragments : logic, metaphysics, moral philosophy, aesthetics / edited by
Paul Guyer ; translated by Curtis Bowman, Paul Guyer, Frederick Rauscher.
p. cm. – (The Cambridge edition of the works of Immanuel Kant in translation)
Includes bibliographical references and index.
ISBN 0-521-55248-6
1. Philosophy. I. Guyer, Paul, 1948– II. Title.
B2758 2005
193 – dc22 2004051946

ISBN-13 978-0-521-55248-6 hardback
ISBN-10 0-521-55248-6 hardback

Contents

General editors' preface

Within a few years of the publication of his *Critique of Pure Reason* in 1781, Immanuel Kant (1724–1804) was recognized by his contemporaries as one of the seminal philosophers of modern times – indeed as one of the great philosophers of all time. This renown soon spread beyond German-speaking lands, and translations of Kant's work into English were published even before 1800. Since then, interpretations of Kant's views have come and gone and loyalty to his positions has waxed and waned, but his importance has not diminished. Generations of scholars have devoted their efforts to producing reliable translations of Kant into English as well as into other languages.

There are four main reasons for the present edition of Kant's writings:

1. Completeness. Although most of the works published in Kant's lifetime have been translated before, the most important ones more than once, only fragments of Kant's many important unpublished works have ever been translated. These include the *Opus postumum*, Kant's unfinished *magnum opus* on the transition from philosophy to physics; transcriptions of his classroom lectures; his correspondence; and his marginalia and other notes. One aim of this edition is to make a comprehensive sampling of these materials available in English for the first time.

2. Availability. Many English translations of Kant's works, especially those that have not individually played a large role in the subsequent development of philosophy, have long been inaccessible or out of print. Many of them, however, are crucial for the understanding of Kant's philosophical development, and the absence of some from English-language bibliographies may be responsible for erroneous or blinkered traditional interpretations of his doctrines by English-speaking philosophers.

3. Organization. Another aim of the present edition is to make all Kant's published work, both major and minor, available in comprehensive volumes organized both chronologically and topically, so as to facilitate the serious study of his philosophy by English-speaking readers.

4. Consistency of translation. Although many of Kant's major works have been translated by the most distinguished scholars of their day, some of these translations are now dated, and there is considerable terminological disparity among them. Our aim has been to enlist some of the most accomplished Kant scholars and translators to produce new translations, freeing readers from both the philosophical and literary preconceptions of previous generations and allowing them to approach texts, as far as possible, with the same directness as present-day readers of the German or Latin originals.

In pursuit of these goals, our editors and translators attempt to follow several fundamental principles:

1. As far as seems advisable, the edition employs a single general glossary, especially for Kant's technical terms. Although we have not attempted to restrict the prerogative of editors and translators in choice of terminology, we have maximized consistency by putting a single editor or editorial team in charge of each of the main groupings of Kant's writings, such as his work in practical philosophy, philosophy of religion, or natural science, so that there will be a high degree of terminological consistency, at least in dealing with the same subject matter.

2. Our translators try to avoid sacrificing literalness to readability. We hope to produce translations that approximate the originals in the sense that they leave as much of the interpretive work as possible to the reader.

3. The paragraph, and even more the sentence, is often Kant's unit of argument, and one can easily transform what Kant intends as a continuous argument into a mere series of assertions by breaking up a sentence so as to make it more readable. Therefore, we try to preserve Kant's own divisions of sentences and paragraphs wherever possible.

4. Earlier editions often attempted to improve Kant's texts on the basis of controversial conceptions about their proper interpretation. In our translations, emendation or improvement of the original edition is kept to the minimum necessary to correct obvious typographical errors.

5. Our editors and translators try to minimize interpretation in other ways as well, for example, by rigorously segregating Kant's own footnotes, the editors' purely linguistic notes, and their more explanatory or informational notes; notes in this last category are treated as endnotes rather than footnotes.

We have not attempted to standardize completely the format of individual volumes. Each, however, includes information about the context in which Kant wrote the translated works, a German–English glossary, an English–German glossary, an index, and other aids to comprehension. The general introduction to each volume includes an explanation of specific principles of translation and, where necessary, principles of selection of works included in that volume. The pagination of the standard German edition of Kant's works, *Kant's Gesammelte Schriften*, edited by the Royal Prussian (later German) Academy of Sciences (Berlin: Georg Reimer, later Walter de Gruyter & Co., 1900–), is indicated throughout by means of marginal numbers.

Our aim is to produce a comprehensive edition of Kant's writings, embodying and displaying the high standards attained by Kant scholarship in the English-speaking world during the second half of the twentieth century, and serving as both an instrument and a stimulus for the further development of Kant studies by English-speaking readers in the century to come. Because of our emphasis on literalness of translation and on information rather than interpretation in editorial practices, we hope our edition will continue to be usable despite the inevitable evolution and occasional revolutions in Kant scholarship.

PAUL GUYER
ALLEN W. WOOD

Introduction

THE CONTENTS OF THIS VOLUME

This volume offers a selection of Kant's surviving notes and fragments on topics in logic, metaphysics, moral philosophy, and aesthetics, drawn almost entirely from the material presented in the third division of *Akademie* edition[1] of his works as the *handschriftliche Nachlaß*, or "handwritten remains." These materials supplement Kant's published works, his surviving correspondence, and surviving transcriptions of his classroom lectures in providing evidence about Kant's philosophical development through almost all of his career, from the 1750s through the 1790s. They are an unparalleled source for investigation of the genesis, development, and revision of Kant's views and his published works. This is the first extensive selection of them to be translated from German.

The *handschriftliche Nachlaß* in the *Akademie* edition comprises ten volumes, divided into two main parts: volumes 14 through 19 contain notes and fragments organized into volumes representing the subjects of Kant's main lecture courses, and in many cases coming from his annotations in his own copies of the textbooks he used for those courses, while volumes 20 through 23 contain drafts for published or planned works, mostly from Kant's later years, as well as transcriptions from Kant's notes in two of his own works, namely the early *Observations on the Feeling of the Beautiful and Sublime* (1764) and the first edition of the *Critique of Pure Reason* (1781). In the first group, volume 14 contains notes on mathematics, physics and chemistry, and physical geography, all of which Kant lectured on at some point in his career; volume 15 contains notes on anthropology, on which Kant lectured regularly beginning in 1772–73, and forty pages of notes on medicine; volume 16 contains notes on logic, on which Kant lectured throughout his career; volumes 17 and 18 contain notes on metaphysics, on which Kant likewise lectured throughout his career; and volume 19 contains notes on moral philosophy and political and legal philosophy (*Naturrecht* or "natural right"), on the former of which Kant lectured regularly and on the latter of which he lectured at least occasionally, as well as some notes on religion. In the second group, volume 20 contains Kant's notes in his copy of the *Observations on the Feeling of the Beautiful and Sublime*, his first draft of the introduction to the

Critique of the Power of Judgment, his drafts for a submission to an essay competition on the question *What Real Progress Has Metaphysics Made in Germany since the Times of Leibniz and Wolff?* which he never finished but which were published shortly after his death, as well as a few smaller items; volumes 21 and 22 contain the voluminous notes and drafts for a final work on the transition from the metaphysical foundations of natural science to physics, now referred to as the *Opus postumum*, on which he worked during his final five or so years of activity but never completed; and volume 23 contains Kant's notes (*Nachträge*) in his own copy of the first edition of the *Critique of Pure Reason*, some brief drafts (*Vorarbeiten*) for the *Prolegomena to any Future Metaphysics* (1783), *Critique of Practical Reason* (1788), *Religion within the Boundaries of Mere Reason* (1793), the essay "On the Common Saying: That may be correct in theory but it is of no use in practice" (1793), *Toward Perpetual Peace* (1795), and several other essays, and, finally, more than two hundred pages of drafts for the *Metaphysics of Morals* (1797).

The present volume begins, in Chapter 1, with Kant's notes on the *Observations on the Feeling of the Beautiful and Sublime*, which are datable to 1764–65 and provide the earliest evidence of the outlines of Kant's emerging moral philosophy.[2] The selection here focuses on these early notes in moral philosophy rather than on the other matters that Kant also discusses, and while they could have been integrated into the chapter of "Notes on Moral Philosophy," they are presented together at the outset of the volume both because they constitute such a distinct group from an early period in Kant's career and because they are a reminder of the ultimately moral objective of Kant's philosophizing throughout so much of his career. The translation here is not based on the text in volume 20, however, but on the more recent and more helpful edition by Marie Rischmüller.[3] With a few small exceptions, that is all of the material from volumes 20 through 23 that is included here, for much of the material from these volumes has been or will be translated elsewhere in the Cambridge edition. From volume 20, a translation of the first draft of the introduction to the *Critique of the Power of Judgment* is included in the Cambridge edition of that work,[4] and the other main item, the drafts for the essay on the *Real Progress* of metaphysics, has been translated in *Theoretical Philosophy after 1781*.[5] Selections from volumes 21 and 22, the *Opus postumum* properly so called, have been translated in the Cambridge volume with that title.[6] From volume 23, the *Nachträge* to the first edition of the *Critique of Pure Reason* have been included *in situ* in the Cambridge edition of the *Critique*,[7] while selections from Kant's extensive drafts for the "Doctrine of Right" in the *Metaphysics of Morals* as well as for several other of Kant's political essays will be included in a newly planned volume of the Cambridge edition, *Lectures and Drafts on Political Philosophy*.[8] Notes on political philosophy from volume 19 will also be included in *Lectures and Drafts on Political Philosophy* rather than in the present volume.

Chapters 2 through 5 of the present volume, therefore, come primarily from the first division of the *handschriftliche Nachlaß*. Nothing from the scientific notes in volume 14 has been included here, because those notes are highly specialized as well as accompanied by lengthy annotations that could hardly have been included here. So it is largely material from volumes 15 through 19 that makes up these chapters. Chapter 2, "Notes on Logic," draws its material from volume 16; Chapter 3, "Notes on Metaphysics," draws largely from volumes 17 and 18; Chapter 4, "Notes on Moral Philosophy," draws mostly from the first half of volume 19 but includes a few relevant passages from elsewhere among these volumes; and Chapter 5, "Notes on Aesthetics," uses material from volumes 15 and 16, the *Akademie* edition volumes on anthropology and logic.

There were two main sorts of sources for the materials included in volumes 15 through 19: Kant's annotations in his own copies of the textbooks on which he lectured, which Kant had often had bound with interleaved blank sheets in order to leave himself room for such annotations; and unbound papers, or "loose sheets" (*lose Blätter*), which survived his death and subsequently became known to posterity, especially through a collection formed in the Königsberg university library during the nineteenth century. The heading to each note translated in this volume indicates whether it came from one of Kant's textbooks or from the *lose Blätter* (abbreviated "*LBl* "). For his textbook in logic, Kant used Georg Friedrich Meier, *Auszug aus der Vernunftlehre* (Halle: Johann Justinus Gebauer, 1752); Kant's notes on this book are thus included in Chapter 2. For his textbook in metaphysics, Kant used primarily Alexander Gottlieb Baumgarten, *Metaphysica*, fourth edition (Halle: Carl Hermann Hemmerde, 1757),[9] and he also used the chapter on psychology in this volume as the basis for his lectures on anthropology, including a section on aesthetics; notes on this volume are thus included in volume 15 as well as volumes 17 and 18 of the *Akademie* edition, and are here included in both Chapter 3 and Chapter 5. Volume 18 of the *Akademie* edition also includes notes Kant made in his copy of Johann August Eberhard, *Vorbereitung zur natürlichen Theologie* (Halle: im Waisenhause, 1781), which he used for lectures on philosophy of religion in 1783–84 and 1785–86, and a selection of those notes is also included here in Chapter 3. For his lectures on moral philosophy, Kant used another book by Alexander Gottlieb Baumgarten, *Initia philosophiae practicae primae* (Halle: Carl Hermann Hemmerde, 1760), and Chapter 4 includes a selection of Kant's notes in that volume. Kant also used a further book in ethics by Baumgarten, *Ethica Philosophica* (Halle: Carl Hermann Hemmerde, 1751), for the second half of his moral philosophy course, the part dealing with duties to God, self, and others rather than with the foundations of "universal practical philosophy,"[10] but Kant's copy of this book has not survived, so volume 19 includes no notes from it.[11] Many other copies of textbooks that Kant did or may have used during his career have also not survived. The rest of the material translated in Chapters 2 through 5 comes from *lose Blätter*. We have aimed to be as inclusive as possible in the translation of the *lose Blätter*, which are often substantial, relatively self-contained sketches several pages in length, while being more selective in the choice of the marginalia from Kant's textbooks, which are sometimes intelligible as well as important on their own, but sometimes too closely tied to the text to which they are attached to be separated from the latter, and sometimes, of course, not as interesting as Kant's more free-floating sketches and reflections.

II.
THE HISTORY OF KANT'S
HANDSCHRIFTLICHE NACHLAß

The present volume, as just explained, is based largely although not entirely on volumes 15 through 19 of the *Akademie* edition of *Kant's gesammelte Schriften*. But the *Akademie* edition was not the first *locus* for the publication of Kant's handwritten remains. The history of these materials prior to their inclusion in the *Akademie* edition and the history of the *Akademie* edition itself are complicated. What follows is a brief sketch of these histories.

When the German philosopher Wilhelm Dilthey (1833–1911) formulated the plan for a complete and critical edition of Kant's writings and presented it to the Royal Prussian Academy of Sciences in 1895, he conceived of the fourfold division of the edition into Kant's published work, his correspondence, the surviving notes, sketches, and drafts in Kant's own hand, and transcriptions of Kant's lectures that was adopted and that has governed the effort to complete the edition that continues to this day. Dilthey's decision to include whatever could be found of Kant's unpublished materials was influenced by his own hermeneutical approach to philosophy, according to which any of a philosopher's works could only be understood in the larger context of his intellectual career and indeed his life as a whole, to be understood through the psychological insight of the interpreter. Dilthey's view was not universally shared: for example, Hermann Cohen (1842–1918), the founder of the Marburg school of neo-Kantianism and an immensely accomplished interpreter of Kant in his own right, held that true works of genius are "unities that do not grow through additions" and are not made "more comprehensible by probing among putative parts, pieces, and attempts,"[12] and was not in favor of the inclusion of posthumous materials in the edition. But Dilthey's proposal was accepted by the Royal Prussian Academy of Sciences in Berlin, and a "Kant Commission" headed by Dilthey was established to oversee publication of the edition. With the optimism that would seem to be essential to anyone who would undertake such a project, Dilthey thought the edition would be completed within a decade. Instead, in the remaining fifteen years of his life, Dilthey saw the partial publication only of the first two divisions of the edition, Kant's published works (volumes 1 through 9) and his correspondence (volumes 10 through 13), and none of the handwritten remains or lectures that were so central to his own vision of the project. The edition remains incomplete more than a century after Dilthey first conceived it.[13]

Dilthey and the Kant Commission did not foresee any special problems in the editing of Kant's published works; the bulk of Kant's correspondence was thought to have already been collected at the university libraries of Königsberg and Dorpat, in the Courland (now Tartu, Estonia), and the initial plan for the publication of Kant's lectures was modest, foreseeing chiefly the reprinting of transcriptions of lectures on metaphysics, theology, and anthropology that had been published during the first part of the nineteenth century. The greatest challenge from the outset was that of finding someone to edit Kant's handwritten remains.

Kant did not save or organize his books and papers for posterity. He never had a personal secretary to copy and file his papers, although he would, at least in later years, hire a copyist to prepare a clean copy of a manuscript about to be sent to a publisher, and what we have of his correspondence was saved by its recipients rather than its author. If he ever received the manuscripts of his published works back from the publishers – which would not have been the usual practice at the time – he did not keep them. And in at least one will that he wrote, Kant directed that any papers that survived him be destroyed after his death, although in 1798 he seems to have superseded that with instructions that his books, his desk, and all the papers in it be given to his executor, Johann Friedrich Gensichen (1759–1807), to be used or distributed – but not sold at public auction – as Gensichen saw fit, and these were apparently the instructions that were followed upon Kant's death on 12 February 1804.[14] Subsequently, much of the material in that desk seems to have made its way into the Königsberg university library, although perhaps not all of it, since some was apparently distributed among Kant's friends as souvenirs, and Kant had earlier given some books to his disciple Gottlob Benjamin Jäsche (1762–1842), who had edited Kant's handbook on logic, the so-called *Jäsche Logic*,[15] in 1800, and had then taken them with him when he went to teach at the newly established German-Russian university at Dorpat in 1802. These books included the two textbooks from which Kant had lectured on anthropology, logic, and metaphysics for much of his career, and which he had heavily annotated, namely Meier's *Auszug aus der Vernunftlehre* and Baumgarten's *Metaphysica*.

These two volumes eventually made their way into the Dorpat university library.

In spite of Kant's own indifference to the fate of his books and papers and their consequent dispersal after his death, there were several publications of materials from the *Nachlaß* during the course of the nineteenth century. In preparation for the first collected edition of Kant's works, edited by the Königsberg historian Friedrich Wilhelm Schubert (1799–1868) and the Hegelian philosopher Karl Rosenkranz (1805–1879), and published in twelve volumes in Königsberg from 1838 to 1842, Schubert had organized the various unbound manuscripts in Kant's hand (*lose Blätter*) in the Königsberg library into a series of thirteen folders, designated "A" through "N" (there was no folder "I"), but then included only a small number of them in the edition. Only later in the century were these *lose Blätter* published in their entirety by the university librarian, Rudolf Reicke (1825–1905), first in a series of articles in the *Altpreussische Monatsschrift* from 1882 to 1889 and then in three freestanding volumes, *Lose Blätter aus Kants Nachlaß*, in 1889, 1895, and 1898. Reicke preserved Schubert's assignment of the papers to lettered folders and his numbering of the items within each folder, and those letters and numbers remained the designations for the *lose Blätter* from the Königsberg collection; they are the designations used in this volume as well. The folders were as follows:

A. 18 sheets on physics and mathematics.
B. 12 sheets on topics related to the *Critique of Pure Reason*.
C. 15 sheets on logic.
D. 33 sheets on metaphysics, including the "Refutation of Idealism."
E. 78 sheets on moral philosophy and the "Doctrine of Right."
F. 23 sheets on general matters of politics from 1785 to 1799.
G. 28 sheets on the philosophy of religion and the *Conflict of the Faculties*.
H. 59 sheets on anthropology.
J. 6 sheets on physical geography.
K. 15 pieces labelled "Little concepts from Kant's hand purchased from the auction of the books of Prof. Gensichen."
L. 61 pieces labelled "Little cards of thoughts from the final period of his life," also purchased from the auction of Gensichen's books, together with three memoir books from Professor Buck.
M. General biographical notices (36 pieces).
N. 63 letters to Kant, also from the Gensichen auction, and six other letters.[16]

Folders B through E provided much of the material from the *lose Blätter* that is included here, while E through G would provide much of the material that ultimately made its way into volume 23 of the *Akademie* edition. Folder N was obviously a major source for Kant's correspondence.

Meanwhile, the young philosopher Benno Erdmann (1851–1921), professor at Kiel from 1878 (he would move to Halle in 1890 and to Bonn in 1898),[17] had become interested in Kant's philosophical development, first publishing critical editions of the *Critique of Pure Reason*, the *Prolegomena*, and the *Critique of the Power of Judgment* from 1878 to 1880, then a detailed transcription of Kant's annotations in his own copy of the *Critique of Pure Reason*, preserved in the Königsberg university library, in 1881,[18] and finally a first edition of Kant's notes in his copy of Baumgarten's *Metaphysica*, which, as noted above, had been taken to Dorpat by Jäsche and subsequently belonged to the university library there. As already noted, Kant used Baumgarten's textbook as the basis for his lectures on anthropology as well as metaphysics, and Erdmann consequently published his edition of these notes in two volumes of *Reflexionen Kants zur kritischen Philosophie*, namely, *Reflexionen Kants zur Anthropologie* and *Reflexionen Kants zur Kritik der Reinen Vernunft* (Leipzig: Fues's Verlag, 1882 and 1884).[19]

But who would edit the *handschriftliche Nachlaß* for the *Akademie* edition? In spite of his advanced age, the librarian Reicke was assigned the task of editing Kant's correspondence. Reicke had in fact begun working on an edition of the correspondence, his lifelong ambition, ten years before the *Akademie* edition was begun, and was ready to move quickly: the first volume of correspondence (volume 10) was in fact the first volume of the *Akademie* edition to be published, in 1900.[20] But Reicke could not possibly also undertake the task of editing the notes and fragments, in spite of his familiarity with the materials in the Königsberg library. Dilthey did approach Erdmann, but by 1895–96 Erdmann, although still in the prime of life, was more interested in his own philosophical work than in such a consuming task of scholarship as editing this material would necessarily be, and after some discussion he turned Dilthey down.[21] (He did, however, edit the *Critique of Pure Reason* in volumes 3 and 4 of the *Akademie* edition.) Dilthey then approached Hans Vaihinger (1852–1933), also a professor at Halle, who had made his mark with an incredibly detailed commentary on the *Critique of Pure Reason*;[22] but Vaihinger chose instead to devote his energies to getting the newly established journal *Kant-Studien* off the ground.[23] However, Dilthey was not out of options, for by 1896 an extraordinary scholar even younger than Erdmann and Vaihinger had appeared on the scene. This was Erich Adickes (1866–1928), who earned his Ph.D. at Berlin at the age of twenty-one with a dissertation on nothing less than the systematic structure of Kant's whole philosophy, at twenty-three published his own edition of the *Critique of Pure Reason*, and, most remarkably, between the ages of twenty-seven and thirty (1893–96), while employed as a high school teacher in Kiel, published, in the *Philosophical Review* and *in English*, a 622-page, exhaustive and extensively annotated bibliography of writings by and on Kant published in Germany through 1804 (although the title of the first installment promised it would be taken up through 1887!).[24] This volume remains an unparalleled resource on the early reception of Kant. Although published only in the American journal, it had come to Dilthey's attention, and after being turned down by Erdmann, Dilthey invited the young Adickes to undertake the task of editing the third division of the *Akademie* edition.[25]

Adickes – who would continue as a high school teacher until receiving a professorial appointment at the new Prussian state university at Münster in 1902[26] (he would become professor at Tübingen two years later, and remain there for the rest of his career) – quickly accepted Dilthey's invitation and came up with a scheme for the organization of the *handschriftliche Nachlaß*. He made a number of key decisions that received the approval of Dilthey and his associates at the Academy of Sciences. First, he decided upon a rigorous separation between all of Kant's notes, fragments, and freestanding sketches on the one hand and everything that could be securely classified as an actual draft (or *Vorarbeit*) of an eventually published work on the other hand, with the notes and fragments to comprise the first volumes of the section and the *Vorarbeiten* the final volumes – with the exception of drafts for the *Critique of Pure Reason*, which would be included with the notes on metaphysics.[27] Thus, Adickes decided upon the division between the contents of volumes 14 through 19 on the one hand and what eventually became volumes 20 and 23 on the other. (The inclusion of the *Opus postumum* manuscripts in volumes 21 and 22 could not be foreseen in 1896, because it belonged to a private owner, the Krause family, who had inherited it through a line of succession going back to the son-in-law of Kant's brother Johann Heinrich, and they were not willing to grant permission for its publication. They would agree to do so only under the pressure of the German financial crisis of 1922–23, when they finally sold the rights to de Gruyter, not the Academy of Sciences, for the sum of $750.)[28] Second, he decided that the notes and fragments in the first section should be divided into volumes corresponding to Kant's lectures on natural science and physical geography, anthropology, logic, metaphysics and natural theology, and moral and political philosophy, since a great deal of the material that would be published – the annotations in Kant's textbooks – had presumably been intended for use as notes in those lectures. And third, he would publish all the material in chronological order: an easy task in the case of the *Vorarbeiten*, since they could be ordered in the chronological sequence of the published works,[29] but a monumental challenge in the case of the almost entirely undated notes and sketches coming from the Königsberg and other collections of *lose Blätter*, from the two textbooks from Dorpat, one of which had previously been edited by Erdmann, and from two of Kant's copies of his own books also in the Königsberg library, the copy of the first *Critique* already used by Erdmann and Kant's extensively annotated copy of his much earlier work *Observations on the Feeling of the Beautiful and Sublime* (1764).[30] But Adickes was nevertheless confident that he could finish the work, which he originally foresaw as comprising six parts, in a decade. Inevitably, the work took him the rest of his life, and remained unfinished at the time of his death from cancer at the age of sixty-two.

Adickes's intentions for the presentation of the notes and fragments in the first half of his division of the *Akademie* edition was altogether more ambitious than the earlier publications of the *lose Blätter* by Reicke and of the *Reflexionen* by Erdmann. First, of course, Erdmann had only published Kant's notes in his own copy of the first edition of the first *Critique* and in his copy of Baumgarten, whereas Adickes's edition would include those notes but also the notes in Kant's copy of Meier's *Vernunftlehre*, as well as the notes in Kant's own copy of the *Observations on the Feeling of the Beautiful and Sublime*, his notes in Eberhard's *Vorbereitung zur natürlichen Theologie*, his notes in the textbook for his moral philosophy lectures, Baumgarten's *Initia philosophiae practicae primae*, notes in a copy of the text that Kant used for his lectures on *Naturrecht*, namely Gottfried Achenwall, *Juris naturalis pars posterior complectens jus familiae, jus publicum, et jus gentium*, fifth edition (Göttingen: Victor Bossiegell, 1763) – and then all of this would be integrated with the Königsberg library papers previously edited by Reicke, as well as whatever else could be found. Second, while in his volume of "Reflections for the *Critique of Pure Reason*" Erdmann had arranged Kant's notes in correspondence with the chapters and topics of the *Critique*, and then only within them in a chronological order based on his own conception of the four main periods of Kant's philosophical development,[31] and Reicke had not attempted to impose a chronological ordering on the *lose Blätter* at all, Adickes aimed at a far more detailed as well as in his view objective chronological ordering of all of Kant's notes and fragments: in the end, he would divide Kant's notes into no fewer than thirty-three strata, as he liked to think of them in geological fashion.

We will return to the matter of Adickes's chronology in the next section; this section will conclude with an account of Adickes's progress in the task.[32] Having signed on in 1896, Adickes spent the next several years investigating the materials as well as many of the transcriptions of Kant's lectures, which he would not be editing for the *Akademie* edition but which he would use for comparative dating of the notes and fragments. His progress was slowed by his relocations to the university at Münster in 1902 and then to Tübingen in the fall of 1904. He began the final editing of the manuscript for the first volume, volume 14, the notes on natural science, in the fall of 1906, and typesetting began the following summer; but between delays at the publisher and Adickes's own desire to delay publication until he could also publish his own scholarly studies of the material,[33] the volume did not actually appear until 1911. While Adickes spent much time in the next several years working on a new edition of Kant's lectures on physical geography, which in the end was not published,[34] he continued to make steady progress on the notes and fragments: volume 15, on anthropology, was completed in 1913 and published in 1914, and volume 16, on logic, was also completed in 1914. Adickes was also finished with the metaphysics material – his student Theodor Haering had been able to use the particularly important *lose Blätter* from 1775 known as the *Duisburg Nachlaß* for his doctoral dissertation as early as 1910,[35] and typesetting for volume 17 began in 1914, but it was broken off in 1915 because of the war.[36] Work on the volume would not resume until 1924, and it was only published in 1926. The delay was by no means due only to the war: in the meantime, Adickes had been able to spend time with the *Opus postumum* manuscripts owned by the Krause family, and he devoted much of his time between 1915 and 1924 to a book on that material, *Kants Opus postumum dargestellt und beurtheilt* (*Kant-Studien Ergänzungsheft* 50, Berlin, 1920), to his massive work on Kant and the natural sciences, *Kant als Naturforscher* (two volumes, Berlin, 1924–25), and his controversial work on "the thing in itself," *Kant und das Ding an sich* (Berlin, 1924) – the works for which he remains best known apart from his edition of the *Nachlaß* itself. All this work done, Adickes returned to the *Nachlaß* and completed the work on volume 18, the second metaphysics volume, by the first of October, 1927 – the book was published in 1928 – and then turned to volume 19 on moral and political philosophy. He had apparently done much of the work necessary to prepare this volume for the press when he learned in April 1928 that what he had thought was arthritis was actually cancer of the spine and pelvis, and that he had only a few more months to live. He had indeed only a short time to live, and died on 8 July 1928.[37] But even in his final months, he was able to devote attention to the Kant edition, and spent time preparing a Tübingen *Privatdozent*, Friedrich Berger, to complete volume 19. Berger was appointed to do so by the Kant Commission in November 1928,[38] and was apparently finished with the work in 1929: as he states in the Preface to the volume, "The reflections were in their entirety already transcribed by Erich Adickes and also provisionally chronologically ordered" (19:vi). However, the publication of the volume was once again delayed at the publisher, de Gruyter, this time not due to military or financial exigency but rather apparently due to the intervention of the two de Gruyter employees, Arthur Buchenau and Gerhard Lehmann, who would from this time and, in the case of Lehmann, through 1979, take over the editing of the *Akademie* edition, and who may have made changes to Berger's manuscript.[39] Volume 19 finally appeared in 1934.

Thus Adickes did not live to complete the six volumes of the notes and fragments, let alone the two volumes of *Vorarbeiten* that he had planned, although he had apparently already done much work on them. Nor did he live to edit the two volumes of *Opus postumum*, although de Gruyter had finally acquired the rights to do so by the beginning of 1924,[40] and Adickes had determined the chronology of that material. All of the Kantian materials that Adickes had as well as his own work toward the remaining volumes was turned over by his family to the Academy of Sciences in Berlin, and Buchenau and Lehmann would edit the two volumes of the *Opus postumum*, published in 1936 and 1938, on principles very different from those Adickes would have used,[41] while Lehmann would edit the *Vorarbeiten* in volumes 20 and 23, finally published in 1942 and 1955. Finally, Adickes's unexpected death meant that he was not able to write the extensive explanation and justification of his determination of the chronology of the materials that he had always planned to include in the final volume of the *handschriftliche Nachlaß* (see 14:xlii–xliv). Nevertheless, what Adickes did accomplish was, in the moving words of his successor Friederich Berger, a "grand accomplishment of the most self-abnegating detail work, to which for more than thirty years he sacrificed his finest energies. Ruthlessly hard on himself, he here completed a heroic life in the service of scholarship" (19:v).

The present volume, then, consisting in very large part of material from volumes 15 through 19 of the *Akademie* edition, is based on the work of Erich Adickes, Friedrich Berger, and, in the case of Chapter 1, Marie Rischmüller. The continuing controversy about the quality of the work done by Arthur Buchenau and Gerhard Lehmann on volumes 21 and 22, and then by Lehmann on volumes 20 and 23 as well as the lectures volumes 24, 27, 28, and 29 does not affect this volume.[42]

III.
CHRONOLOGY AND STYLE

Adickes did not live to produce the detailed justification of his chronological method that he always intended, but he explained the general principles as well as some of the factual bases for it in the Introduction to volume 14, the first of the volumes of the *handschriftliche Nachlaß* that he published. There were two main elements to his dating: first, *ordering* the materials into distinct strata (*Schichten*) – having long studied Kant's physical geography, Adickes liked to use this geological metaphor – and second, *attaching* enough of these strata to specific dates or periods to allow for the dating of the intervening strata as well. The latter could be done when a clearly identifiable stratum could be conclusively assigned to a date or contained a datable item: for example, the notes in the *Observations on the Feeling of the Beautiful and Sublime* could only have been written after the publication of the book, and most give every indication of having been written at much the same time, so they can be assigned to the period 1764–68, or even more probably 1764 to 1765 or 1766 (14:xxxviii); one note in the *Duisburg Nachlaß* and another on page 432 of the *Metaphysica* explicitly refer to Kant's intention to enter an essay competition that was announced in several journals in February and March 1770, so those notes and everything that can be securely associated with them can be dated to 1770 (14:xxxix); Kant makes related notes on four letters dated from 3 July 1773 to 20 May 1775, so those notes and everything securely related to them can be dated to the period 1773–75 (14:xl); and so on. With enough such fixable dates and clear enough strata to associate with them or place between them, the outlines of a chronology could be established.

But how did Adickes establish the separate strata themselves? Here he relied on visual evidence: similarities in handwriting, for while Kant's *Reinschrift*, or handwriting for finished documents, did not undergo much change during his mature years, his style of taking notes did; changes in ink, because Kant mixed his own, and the mixture and thus the appearance of the ink changed over the years; and, an element on which Adickes placed great emphasis, the position of the notes on the page and relative to each other: a note placed right next to a paragraph in the textbook would clearly be earlier than one evidently concerning the same paragraph but written in a more remote location; a note surrounding another or written between its lines would clearly be later than the other, and so on (14:xxx–xxxi).

These considerations too sound reasonable. But on the basis of the two kinds of criteria mentioned, Adickes divided all of Kant's handwritten remains into no fewer than thirty-two strata, identified with the letters of the Greek alphabet and the addition of numerical superscripts for some periods, especially "psi" (1780–89) and "omega" (from 1790 until Kant's death). Although Adickes did not live to provide the detailed description of his method that he promised, he described the scheme itself, with some information about the visual criteria he used and references to the dated materials with which the strata could be associated, in the Introduction to volume 14 (14:xxxvi–xliii), and the original editions of the volumes came with a handy little card correlating the Greek letters with the dates so that the reader would not have to turn back to volume 14 until the scheme was memorized.[43] Adickes emphasized that his thirty-two strata were not each distinct chronological periods, because sometimes two strata separated by his visual indices were nevertheless assigned to the same year or period of years or overlapping years or periods on the basis of their external correlations with dated material. So in the end Adickes recognized something like twenty-two distinct periods for Kant's notes and fragments. But even twenty-two chronological periods are a great many, compared for example to the four that Erdmann proposed. Could Adickes really have had sufficient grounds for dividing the material up so finely?

The first thing that should be said is that Adickes did not always pretend that he could assign a note conclusively to a single stratum or associated chronological period. Where he was completely confident about the stratum and date of a note, he would print only a single Greek letter in its heading. But if he was uncertain, he would provide a sequence of Greek letters, using their sequence, question marks, and parentheses to indicate decreasing certainty about the date. This system works as follows. A single Greek letter or pair of letters connected by a dash, without any further modification, indicates an unequivocal assignment to a single stratum or range of strata. Two or more Greek letters each followed by a single question mark indicates equal probability for each stratum. There could then follow a pair of parentheses enclosing one or more Greek letters each followed by a question mark; this would indicate a lower level of probability than the unbracketed letters preceding. Further sets of parentheses would indicate decreasing probability that the note belongs to that period. Further Greek letters followed by two question marks would be even more unlikely, and so on. Adickes describes the system at 14:lx–lxi.

So Adickes was confident that some notes could be conclusively assigned to a single stratum and period, and was less certain about others. Nevertheless, he was confident about his chronological scheme as a whole. But how confident can we be about it? The simple answer is that in the absence of direct acquaintance with the originals from which he worked – many of which have not been found since the end of World War II – as well as in the absence of the years of study it would take to be able even to decipher Kant's crowded and crabbed handwriting, full of abbreviations and signs, let alone to learn to recognize different strata in it, no one could have any particular basis for challenging Adickes's system, as opposed to general skepticism about it (except where the content of a particular note might seem obviously incompatible with what we know about Kant's views from a conclusively dated published work or letter). So there are really only two choices: make no pretense to date the fragments at all, except for those particular ones that were actually on a dated piece of paper or make direct reference to a precisely datable event; or accept Adickes's scheme, even if with the general reservation that such an elaborate scheme for the transcription, enumeration, and dating of so much often barely legible material could hardly be correct in every detail. In this volume, Adickes's proposed date or range of dates for each note will be reported in its heading. There will be one change, however: instead of out supplying Adickes's Greek letters, they have been converted directly into dates. We trust this will make the volume easier to use for the great majority of its readers, while since we retain Adickes's numberings for the fragments and also provide the *Akademie* edition pagination for every note drawn from that source, any reader who wants the sometimes even more fine-grained discrimination provided by Adickes's system of Greek letters can readily locate the notes in the *Akademie* edition and retrieve that information.

Following the number of the note and the proposed date or dates for it, the third item in our heading of the notes will be a reference to its source. For those notes that were originally annotations in Kant's textbooks, this reference will take the form of the abbreviation for the title of the book (the abbreviations are explained in the introductions to the chapters below), the roman or Arabic number of the page or pages on which the note was found, and, where Adickes provided one, the section or paragraph number (marked by "§") with which the note was associated. Adickes added a prime to the page number to indicate that a note was on the side of an interleaved sheet facing the numbered page or a lowercase cursive letter (*a*, *b*, etc.) where several blank pages followed a numbered page; we have omitted those marks, since we have not had, nor do we expect readers of this volume to have, access to Kant's original textbooks. (The two volumes originally from the Dorpat university library, which had been in Adickes's possession since 1896, were returned to the Berlin academy after his death in 1928, but did not make their way back to Dorpat (now Tartu) for more than sixty years: in 1993, the copy of Baumgarten's *Metaphysica* was in the Lower Saxon State Library in Göttingen, where it had been since 1949, while the copy of Meier's *Auszug aus der Vernunftlehre* was in the collection of the Academy of Sciences in Berlin as of 1993.[44] The volumes now appear in the Tartu university library catalogue, and so presumably have finally been returned. The location of the other volumes Adickes used is unreported and apparently unknown; they may have been among the papers that Gerhard Lehmann removed from Berlin toward the end of World War II for safekeeping, but which were not found after the war.) For the *lose Blätter*, Adickes provided either the original folder and item number from the Königsberg library or another owner's name and number for items that had not been part of that collection; we reproduce that. Where notes had previously been printed, either in Erdmann's volumes or Reicke's volumes, Adickes also provided those locations (using "*E*" for Erdmann and "*R*" for Reicke); we have not reproduced those references, although again they may easily be retrieved from the *Akademie* edition. (Adickes provided a table correlating the *Akademie* edition number for each of the 1,779 notes that had previously been published by Erdmann with Erdmann's numbers at 18:x–xxiii, and Lehmann provided a catalogue of Reicke's *lose Blätter* and their numbers as reprinted in the *Akademie* edition at 23:534–42. In an appendix to his volume, Werner Stark lists all the *lose Blätter* in the sequence of the original Königsberg folders or the other sources, and then correlates that list with their *Akademie* edition number and location.)[45]

As for the texts of the notes themselves, Adickes aimed to provide a diplomatic edition reproducing every aspect of the original text. He used *Fraktur* type to show what Kant had written in German handwriting and roman type to show what Kant had written in Latin letters, showing that he regarded the words as in a foreign language (typically Latin, occasionally French).[46] Adickes used spaced type (*Sperrdruck*) to show Kant's emphasis, and reserved cursive (italics) for his own editorial material. We have followed the model of the Cambridge editions of the first and third critiques, using normal roman type for Adickes's *Fraktur* type, italics for his roman, and boldface for his *Sperrdruck* (which would have been set as *Fettdruck* or heavier type in the original editions of Kant's published works). Adickes also used two typefaces in punctuation, "round" or ordinary roman type punctuation for punctuation Kant himself had provided, and "square" or *Fraktur* type punctuation for punctuation that Adickes added to the text. (Kant himself provided very little punctuation in these private notes.) We have not attempted to reproduce this distinction. In Adickes's transcription, new sentences or sentence fragments do not always begin with a capital letter. We have started every sentence with a capital letter. Sometimes Kant appears to have written a clause, typically starting with "E.g.," as a new sentence, but we have treated it as a dependent clause of the previous sentence.

Adickes also used a complicated system to show additions and deletions that Kant made in his notes. Where Kant himself used parentheses in his text, Adickes reproduces those without any special marking, and we likewise always reproduce Kant's own parentheses. Where Kant made an addition or insertion that Adickes assigned to the same period as the original composition of the note, Adickes placed this material in parentheses prefixed with a superscript "g," for *gleichzeitig* (simultaneous). We have integrated these additions into the text without any remark and without parentheses, except where the syntax requires parentheses. Where Kant made what Adickes determined to be a later addition to a note, Adickes placed that in parentheses prefixed with a superscript "s," for *später* (later); we have retained Adickes's parentheses for that material, and prefix the contents of the parentheses with the words "*later addition.*" Where Kant attached a separate footnote or other addendum to a passage, Adickes put the attached material in parentheses prefixed by one or more asterisks; we have reproduced both the asterisks and the parentheses. Finally, where Adickes could decipher words or passages that Kant had crossed out, he placed that material between square brackets and printed it in smaller type. Here we have exercised judgment: where Kant crossed out something simply because he changed his mind about the syntax of his sentence and used the same word a few words later, we have not reproduced it; but where he did not simply use the crossed-out word or phrase a few words later, but clearly changed his mind about what to write, then we have included the material he crossed out, enclosed in square brackets and prefixed with the words "*crossed out.*" Occasionally Adickes described crossed-out material in a footnote rather than presenting it in the text; we have generally followed our standard procedure for such material. Adickes also noted possible variant readings of Kant's writing in his footnotes; with very few exceptions, we have not included that information. Again, the reader of our translation interested in that level of detail will in any case want to consult our sources in the *Akademie* edition.

We have left Latin words or phrases occurring in notes otherwise written in German in Latin, but provided translations in our footnotes where the meaning of the Latin is not self-evident to any reader of English; where Kant wrote a whole note in Latin, we have indicated that fact but translated the note in our main text. We have also used our footnotes to indicate the German words being translated where the translation departs from our general practice or masks something interesting about the terminology of the German original, but we have tried to keep those notes to a minimum. We have used endnotes for editorial material, including descriptions of the contents of the sections in Kant's texts to which he appends his notes, cross-references among the notes, cross-references to relevant passages in Kant's published works or sometimes lectures as well as to passages in other authors whom Kant mentions in his notes, biographical and bibliographical references, and so on.

We have tried to follow the glossaries of the rest of the Cambridge edition, especially those of the *Critique of Pure Reason*, *Practical Philosophy*, and the *Critique of the Power of Judgment*, but have made some changes. We have restricted the glossaries included at the end of this volume to philosophically significant terms.

Our principle throughout has been to try to provide the reader of the translation as much evidence about the development of Kant's thought as would be available to the reader of Adickes's edition, but not to burden the translation with information about the appearance or sources of Kant's originals – from which we are in any case at one remove – that could not possibly bear on any hypothesis about that development.

Acknowledgments

This volume has been a long time in the making, and I have a number of debts to discharge.

First, I would like to thank Dieter Henrich for introducing me to the use and importance of Kant's *handschriftliche Nachlaß* during a visit he made to Harvard during my final semester of graduate study in the spring of 1973 – as well as for his interest in and support of my work for many years later. Several scholars writing in English had made use of the *Nachlaß* shortly after its publication in the *Akademie* edition in the 1920s and 1930s, notably H. J. Paton in his *Kant's Metaphysic of Experience* (two volumes, London: George Allen & Unwin, 1936) and Paul Arthur Schilpp in his *Kant's Pre-Critical Ethics* (Evanston: Northwestern University Press, 1938); but their example did not become a model for subsequent British and American scholarship – the *Nachlaß* was definitely ignored in the exciting analytical work on Kant done during the 1960s by philosophers such as Graham Bird, Robert Paul Wolff, Peter Strawson, and Jonathan Bennett that was so formative for students of my vintage – and I doubt that I would have discovered the treasures in the *Nachlaß* as soon as I did had it not been for the example and tutelage of Henrich.

I would like to thank Allen Wood and Jonathan Sinclair-Wilson, then the philosophy editor in the New York office of Cambridge University Press, for inviting me to coedit the Cambridge Edition in 1986 and for entrusting me with the present volume. I would like to thank Terence Moore, who succeeded Sinclair-Wilson the following year, for his support of all my work and for his patience in waiting for the completion of this volume, which was inevitably delayed after the untimely death of Eva Schaper and the decision that I should replace her as the editor of the *Critique of the Power of Judgment*. Every philosopher and student of philosophy in the English-speaking world owes Terry Moore gratitude for his energy and imagination in the creation and support of so many publishing projects ranging from the present edition to the Cambridge Companions to Philosophy. His premature death in 2004, while this volume was in press, was a personal loss for me as well as a professional loss throughout the philosophical community. I would like to thank Deans Samuel Preston and Rebecca Bushnell of the School of Arts and Sciences of the University of Pennsylvania for their generosity with teaching relief, which has facilitated the completion of this volume. And I would like to thank Gertrud Grünkorn of Walter de Gruyter & Co. for her generous permission to use so much material from the *Akademie* edition.

But above all I would like to thank my collaborators, Curtis Bowman and Frederick Rauscher, who had both just completed their Ph.D.s at Penn almost a decade ago when this project got seriously under way. I made the initial selection of materials to be translated in 1995. Bowman did the first drafts of the initial selections on logic and part of the notes on metaphysics, while Rauscher did the first drafts of the initial selections on moral philosophy, as well as of some notes on political philosophy that we eventually decided would appear in the separate volume of *Lectures and Drafts on Political Philosophy*. I did the initial drafts of the notes on the *Observations on the Feeling of the Beautiful and Sublime*, of the remainder of the notes on metaphysics, and of the notes on aesthetics. Both Bowman and Rauscher made many suggestions about additions and deletions to my original selection of materials that were of great value in my final determination of the contents of the volume. Bowman had finished his drafts by 1999 and Rauscher finished his not much later, and both have been patient in waiting for me to complete the volume. I am responsible for the final selection of materials, the final form of all translations, and for the introductions to the volume and to each chapter as well as the annotations. So this is a case in which I can sincerely say that I alone am responsible for the errors that inevitably remain.

Frederick Rauscher would like to thank Eastern Illinois University for a Summer Research Award in 1997, Gary Aylesworth, Robert Louden, Mark Mikkelsen, and Hilde Nelson for advice on translation, and Joseph Slowik for his painstaking assistance with editing and proofreading his drafts.

December 2004   PAUL GUYER

Selections from the Notes on the Observations on the Feeling of the Beautiful and Sublime

This chapter presents a selection of the notes that Kant made in 1764–65 in his own interleaved copy of his 1764 work *Observations on the Feeling of the Beautiful and Sublime (Beobachtungen über das Gefühl des Schönen und Erhabenen)*. This popular work, organized around the division of aesthetic responses into the feelings of the beautiful and of the sublime that Edmund Burke had made canonical in his 1757 book *A Philosophical Enquiry into the Origin of Our Ideas of the Sublime and Beautiful*, is primarily devoted to an exploration of differences in the aesthetic preferences between the two genders and among different nationalities and races; it offers no analysis of the concepts or experiences of the beautiful and sublime themselves and therefore foreshadows nothing of the distinctive theories of the beautiful and the sublime that Kant would offer many years later in the *Critique of the Power of Judgment* (1790). But the work does explore connections between the different preferences for the beautiful and the sublime and differences in moral sentiment and character, and that may be why Kant was prompted to use this volume in the months following its publication to write some of the first notes that reflect his emerging moral theory. These reflections on morality no doubt reflect the influence of Kant's reading of the recently published chief works of Jean-Jacques Rousseau, especially the tract *On the Social Contract* and the novel *Émile*, both published in 1762 (see especially notes 8, 13, 17, 46, and 50), but they are also our first evidence of the emergence of some of the most distinctive and important themes and theses of Kant's mature moral philosophy, including his conception of the intrinsic value of the good will (2, 3, 34, 35), the fundamental value of freedom (9, 22, 24, 25, 26, 27, 36, 45), the categorical rather than hypothetical character of moral commands (39, 42), the moral requirement of the universalizability of maxims (19, 44), and the dependence of religion on morality rather than vice versa (16, 41). At the same time, Kant is still clearly inclined to explain the immediate value of morality in terms of a fundamental moral sentiment, as he did in his *Inquiry concerning the Distinctness of the Principles of Natural Theology and Morality*, written for the Berlin Academy of Sciences essay competition of 1762 and published by the Academy, as the winner of the second prize, in 1764, but had not yet developed an alternative account of the source of the unconditional value of the free will (if he ever did). The prize essay is translated in Immanuel Kant, *Theoretical Philosophy, 1755–1770*, translated and edited by David W. Walford in collaboration with Ralf Meerbote (Cambridge: Cambridge University Press, 1992), pp. 243–75. The following selection from the notes on the *Observations* emphasizes those that deal with these themes from Kant's moral philosophy, but also includes the small number of them that touch upon taste and the beautiful and the sublime as central concepts of aesthetics (20, 28, 29, 30, 31). A few scattered notes concerning Kant's scientific concerns in this period are omitted.

These notes were included in the *Akademie* edition in volume 20, edited by Gerhard Lehmann (Berlin: Walter de Gruyter, 1942), at pp. 1–192. However, the present translation is based on the more recent edition by Marie Rischmüller, Immanuel Kant, *Bemerkungen in den "Beobachtungen über das Gefühl des Schönen und Erhabenen,"* Kant-Forschungen, Band 3 (Hamburg: Felix Meiner, 1991). Rischhmüller's edition is preferable to Lehmann's because it carefully describes the location of each note in relation to the text of the *Observations* itself, as well as providing an extensive apparatus, including translations of those notes written in Latin, cross-references to parallel passages within the notes, and annotation on persons, books, and authors referred to by Kant. The present translation follows Rischmüller in providing the location of each passage translated in the original edition of the *Observations* followed by the location of that passage of the *Observations* as printed in the *Akademie* edition, where it appears in volume 2. The location of the texts translated here in Rischmüller's own volume is then given parenthetically by the abbreviation "Ri" followed by the relevant page number or numbers. Since we are not using Lehmann's text, we do not provide the pagination of the passage being translated from volume 20 of the *Akademie* edition. As Rischmüller's numbering of these notes has not become standard, however, the numbers assigned to the passages translated here are our own, not hers. Each paragraph in the translation represents a complete paragraph in the transcription, unless an elision at the end of a paragraph indicates otherwise. Elisions will not be used at the beginning and end of a paragraph to indicate that what is being translated is part of a larger series of paragraphs, but will be used between paragraphs from the same note if intervening paragraphs have been omitted.

The full text of Kant's notes on the *Observations* has been translated into French, as Emmanuel Kant, *Remarques touchant les Observations sur le Sentiment du Beau et du Sublime*, translated by Brigitte Geonget with a preface by Bernard Bourgeois (Paris: J. Vrin, 1994), and into Italian, as Immanuel Kant, *Bemerkungen: Note per un diario filosofico*, edited and translated by Katrin Tenenbaum (Rome: Meltemi, 2001), a bilingual edition based on and presenting Lehmann's *Akademie* edition text rather than Rischmüller's edition. Both of these editions include useful annotation. There has been no prior publication of these notes in English.

* *
*

1. On the reverse of the cover, opposite 2:205 (Ri 7).

Sympathy with the natural misfortune of another is not necessary, but that with an injustice that another has suffered is.

The feeling from which I act is so constituted that I do not need to be taught [*crossed out*: to engage in subtle argument] in order to sense it.

2. Sheet inserted at *Ob* 2, obverse, at 2:207–8 (Ri 15).

The common duties do not need as their motivating ground the hope of another life, rather great sacrifice and self-denial have an inner beauty; but our feeling of pleasure in that can never be so strong in itself that it will outweigh the oppression of discomfort, unless the representation of a future condition of the duration of such a moral beauty and of the happiness that will thereby be increased comes to its assistance, so that one will thereby find oneself more capable of so acting.

. . .

Rousseau. He proceeds synthetically and begins from the natural human being; I proceed analytically, beginning from the civilized[a] human being.

3. Sheet inserted between *Ob* 4 and *Ob* 5, reverse, at 2:208–9 (Ri 19).

The threat of eternal punishment cannot be the immediate ground of morally good actions, although it may be a strong counterweight against temptations to evil so that the immediate sensation of morality is not outweighed.

4. Sheet inserted after *Ob* 8, obverse, at 2:210 (Ri 23–4).

Those who would make a doctrine of virtue into a doctrine of piety would make a whole out of a part, for piety is only a kind of virtue.

It often seems to us that the human race would have almost no value if it did not contain great artists and scholars; hence the countryfolk, the peasants seem to be nothing even to themselves and to be something only as the means for the support of the former. The injustice of this judgment already indicates that it is false. . . .

There is a great difference between overcoming one's inclinations and eradicating them, that is, losing them; this is also different from restraining one's inclinations . . .

[a] *gesitteten*

There is thus a great difference between being a good human being and a good rational being. Being perfect as the latter has no limits except for finitude; being perfect as the former has many limits.

5. Sheet inserted after *Ob* 8, reverse, at 2:210–11 (Ri 24–5).

It takes great art to avoid lies among children. For since they are much too wanton and much too weak to tolerate denials or punishments, they have very strong inducements to lie that older people never have. Especially since they cannot do things on their own as older people do, but rather everything depends on how they represent the impression that they will make on others. One must therefore punish them only for that which they cannot deny, and not approve of something on the basis of excuses.

If one would [*crossed out*: approve] develop morality then one must not introduce any motivating grounds that would not make the action morally good, e.g., punishments and rewards. Hence one must also depict the lie as immediately hateful, as it is in fact, and not subordinate it to any other rule of morality, e.g., that of duty toward others.

(One has no duties toward oneself, rather one has absolute duties, i.e., an action is good in and for itself. It is also absurd that in our morality we should be dependent upon ourselves.)

. . .

The universal love of mankind has something elevated and noble in it, but among human beings it is chimerical. If one aims for that, one becomes accustomed to deceive oneself with longings and idle wishes. As long as one is so dependent on how things are, one cannot participate in the happiness of others.

6. Sheet inserted after *Ob* 10, obverse, at 2:211 (Ri 25).

The simple person very early has a sentiment of what is right, but only quite late or not at all a concept of it. That sentiment must be developed much more than the concept. If one teaches him according to rules too early then he will never have a sentiment of it.

7. Sheet inserted after *Ob* 10, reverse, at 211–12 (Ri 26–7).

It must be asked how far internal moral grounds can bring a person. They can perhaps bring him to be good if, in a condition of freedom, he does not have great temptations, but if the injustice of others or the force of mania does him violence, then this internal morality will not have sufficient power. He must have religion and be encouraged by the rewards of the future life; human nature is not capable of an immediate moral purity. But if purity were somehow supernaturally brought about in him, then the future rewards would no longer have the property of being motivating grounds.

The difference between false and healthy morals is that the former seeks only assistance against evil, while the latter is concerned that the causes of this evil not exist at all.

8. Sheet inserted after *Ob* 12, obverse (Ri 27–8).

It is unnatural that a person should spend the greater part of his life in teaching one child how it should live. A tutor like *Jean Jacques* is therefore artificial.[1] In an isolated condition little service is done to one child; as soon as it has a little power it will itself perform little useful adult actions, as by a countryman or a hand-worker, and will gradually learn the rest.

It is therefore seemly that a person spend his life teaching so many how to live that the sacrifice of his own is by contrast not to be considered. Hence schools are necessary. But for them to be possible one must draw [on] *Émile*. It were to be wished that Rousseau had shown how schools could arise from it.

. . .

It is a burden for the understanding to have taste. I must read Rousseau so long that the beauty of his expressions no longer disturbs me, and only then can I first investigate him with reason.

9. Sheet inserted after *Ob* 12, reverse opposite *Ob* 13, 2:212–13 (Ri 28–9).

If I would place myself in a great although not complete independence from people, then I must be able to be poor without feeling it and to make do with little without paying attention to it. But if I were a rich man then I would above all introduce freedom from things and from people into my enjoyments. I would not be weighed down with things like guests, horses, and servants, about the loss of whom I would have to be concerned. I would not have any jewels, because I can lose them. I would not [*crossed out*: arrange my clothing] according to the whims of another, so that he would not really injure me, e.g., diminish my relations with others, but not so that my comfort would depend upon him.

How freedom in the proper sense (moral not metaphysical) is the supreme *principium* of all virtue and of all happiness.

10. Sheet inserted after *Ob* 14, obverse, at 2:213 (Ri 30).

I can never convince another person except by means of his own thoughts. I must therefore presuppose that the other has a good and correct understanding, otherwise it is in vain to hope that he could be won over by my reasons. Likewise I cannot touch another morally except by his own sentiments; I must therefore presuppose that the other has a certain goodness of the heart, otherwise he will never feel abhorrence at my depictions of vice nor feel incentives in himself from my praises of virtue. But since it would be impossible for there to be any morally correct sentiments in him or for him to be able to suspect that his sentiment could be harmonious with that of the entire human race if his evil were complete and he was evil through and through, I must concede partial goodness to him, and must depict the slippery similarities of innocence and crime as deceptive.

11. Sheet inserted after *Ob* 20, obverse, at 2:215–16 (Ri 35).

One could promote one's welfare by allowing one's desires to expand and striving to satisfy them; one could promote one's rectitude if one allowed the inclinations of whim and luxuriousness to grow and then tried to resist them for the sake of moral incentives. But there is another solution to both of these problems, namely, not allowing these inclinations to arise. Finally, one could promote good conduct by setting aside all immediate moral goodness and merely grounding one's actions on the commands of an overlord who issues rewards and punishments.

What is evil about science for humans is above all this, that the greatest part of them would adorn themselves with it not for any improvement of their understanding but only as a perversion of it, not to mention that for most of them it serves only as an instrument of vanity. The utility that the sciences have is either for excess, e.g., mathematics, or for a hindrance of the evil that they have themselves brought on, or also a certain kind of good behavior as a by-product.

The concepts of civil and of natural justice and the sense of obligation that arise from them are almost completely opposite. If I beg from a rich man who has won his fortune through the oppression of his peasants and then give what I have received as a gift to the very same poor people, then in a civil sense I perform a very generous action, but in the natural sense I merely fulfill a common obligation.

12. Sheet inserted after *Ob* 20, reverse, opposite *Ob* 21, at 2:216 (Ri 36).

The greatest concern of the human being is to know how he should properly fulfill his station in creation and rightly understand what one must be in order to be a human being. But if he learns gratifications that are above or beneath him, that may flatter him but [*crossed out*: for which] he is not organized and which conflict with the arrangements that nature has made for him, or when he learns ethical qualities that shimmer there, then he will himself disturb the beautiful order of nature and only be ready to damage it, for he will have left his post [*crossed out*: he knows that he cannot be content with that which is noble], since he is not content to be that for which he is destined, where he has left the sphere of a human being he is nothing, and the hole that he has made spreads its own damage to the neighboring members.

13. Sheet inserted after *Ob* 22, obverse, at 2:216–17 (Ri 37–9).

The first impression that an intelligent reader who does not read merely out of vanity or to pass the time acquires of the writings of Mr. *J. J. Rousseau* is that he has encountered an uncommon acuity of spirit, a noble impetus of genius, and a feeling soul combined in such a high degree as has perhaps never before been possessed by a writer of any age or any people. The impression that follows next is alienation from odd and contrasensical opinions, that depart so far from what is common that one could readily form the suspicion that with his extraordinary talents the author would only demonstrate [*crossed out*: the force of an enchanting wit] and the magical power of his oratory and make himself an eccentric who would stand out among all competitors in wit as something invitingly newsworthy. The third thought which one will reach only with difficulty, because it seldom occurs [*breaks off*]

One must teach youth to honor the common understanding on the basis of moral as well as logical grounds.

I am myself by inclination an investigator. I feel a complete thirst for knowledge and an eager unrest to go further in it as well as satisfaction at every acquisition. There was a time when I believed that this alone could constitute the honor of mankind, and I had contempt for the rabble who know nothing. *Rousseau* brought me around. This blinding superiority disappeared, I learned to honor human beings, and I would find myself far more useless than the common laborer if I did not believe that this consideration could impart to all others a value in establishing the rights of humanity.

It is quite ridiculous to say that you should love other people, rather one must say that you have good ground to love those who are closest to you. This is valid even for your enemy.

Virtue is strong, thus what weakens and makes one soft for pleasures and dependent upon whim is opposed to virtue. What makes life contemptible or even hateful to us does not lie in nature. What makes vice easy and virtue difficult does not lie in nature.

. . .

It is not compatible with happiness to let the inclinations become excessive, for since there are uncommonly many cases where circumstances are unfavorable for these inclinations, when things are not as desired, they become a source of oppression, misery, and worry, of which the simple person knows nothing.

It also does not help here to preach great-hearted patience.

14. Sheet inserted after *Ob* 22, reverse, opposite *Ob* 23, at 2:217 (Ri 39).

If there is any science that the human being needs it is that which teaches him properly to fulfill the position that has been assigned to him in the creation, and from which he can learn what one must be in order to be a human being. Suppose he had unwittingly become familiar with deceptive temptations above or beneath him that would bring him from his proper position, then this instruction would bring him back again to the station of a human being, and then even if he finds himself ever so small or lacking, still he would do well by remaining at the post to which he has been assigned, because he [*crossed out*: is neither more nor less than] is exactly what he ought to be.

15. Sheet inserted after *Ob* 24, reverse, opposite *Ob* 25, 2:218 (Ri 43).

Moral taste is inclined to imitation; moral principles rise above this. Where there are courts and great distinctions among people, everything is given over to taste; it is otherwise in republics. Hence taste in social gatherings is more refined in the former, and coarser in the latter. One can be very virtuous and have little taste. If social life is to increase then taste must be extended, since the agreeableness of social gatherings must be easy, but principles are difficult. Among women this taste is easiest. Moral taste is not readily united with the appearance of principles. . . .

16. Sheet inserted after *Ob* 28, obverse, at 2:219 (Ri 46).

About compassion it is only to be noted that it must never rule, but must rather be **subordinated** to the capacity and the rational desire to **do** good. He who himself cannot do without very much or is lazy has an idle compassion.

The natural person without religion is much to be preferred to the civilized person with merely natural religion. For the latter must have a high degree of morality if it is to be a counterweight to its corruption.

Meanwhile, a civilized person without any religion is much more dangerous.

Namely, no correct concept of God can arise at all in the natural condition, and the false conception that is formed there is injurious. Consequently the theory of natural religion can be true only where there is science; thus it cannot obligate all human beings.

Natural theology, natural religion. A supernatural theology can nevertheless be combined with a natural religion. Those who believe the Christian [*crossed out*: religion] theology nevertheless have only a natural religion insofar as the morality is natural. The Christian religion is supernatural with regard to the doctrine and also the power to exercise it. How little do the usual Christians have cause to pause over the natural.

The cognition of God is either *speculative*, and this is uncertain and liable to dangerous errors, or moral, through beliefs, and this conceives of no other qualities in God except those that are aimed at morality. . . .

17. Sheet inserted after *Ob* 28, reverse, opposite *Ob* 29, at 2:219–20 (Ri 48).

Newton saw for the first time order and regularity combined with great simplicity, where before him was found disorder and barely paired multiplicity; and since then comets run in geometrical courses. Rousseau discovered for the first time beneath the multiplicity of forms human beings have taken on their deeply buried nature and the hidden law by the observation of which providence is justified. Before that the objection of Alphonsus and Manes[2] still held. After Newton and Rousseau, God is justified and Pope's theorem is true.[3]

18. Sheet inserted after *Ob* 36, obverse, at 2:222–3 (Ri 52–3).

Good consequences are to be sure marks of morality, but not the only ones, because they cannot always be known with certainty. Many a lie could have good consequences.

The ground of the *potestatis legislatoriae divinae*[a] is not in the good, for then the motivating ground would be gratitude (a *subjective* moral ground, a kind of feeling) and hence not strict duty. The ground of the *potestatis legislatoriae* presupposes inequality, and causes one person to lose a degree of freedom to another. This can only happen if he sacrifices his will itself to another; if he does this with regard to all of his actions, then he makes himself into a **slave**. A will that is subject to another is imperfect and contradictory, because the human being has *spontaneitatem*;[b] if he is subjected to the will of another (when he himself can already choose) then he is hateful and contemptible, but if he is subjected to the will of God then he is in accordance with nature. One must not perform actions from obedience to another person that one could do out of internal motivating grounds, and to do everything out of obedience where it could have been done from internal motivating grounds makes **slaves**.

The body is mine because it is a part of my self and is moved by my capacity for choice. The whole living or non-living world which does not have its own capacity for choice is mine insofar as I can compel it and move it in accordance with my capacity of choice. The sun is not mine. The same thing is true for another person, thus no possession is a property[c] or exclusive possession. However, insofar as I would appropriate something to myself exclusively, I must presuppose that the other's will or his deed is at least not opposed to mine. I will therefore perform the actions that designate what is mine, i.e., cut down the tree or make it into lumber. The other person says to me that that is his,

---

[a] divine legislative power
[b] spontaneity
[c] *Proprietat*

9

for it belongs through the actions of his faculty of choice as it were to his self.

19. Sheet inserted after *Ob* 36, reverse, opposite *Ob* 37, at 2:223 (Ri 53).

That will must be good which does not cancel itself out[a] if it is taken universally and reciprocally; on this account the other will not take as his what I have worked upon, for otherwise he would presuppose that his will has moved my body.

Thus when a person calls things his own he thereby *tacite* promises that in similar circumstances through his will he will not...

20. Sheet inserted after *Ob* 40, obverse, at 2:225 (Ri 56).

In everything that pertains to beautiful or sublime sentiment, we do best if we allow ourselves to be led by the example of the ancients: in sculpture, architecture, poetry, and oratory, by ancient mores, and the ancient political constitution. The ancients were closer to nature; between ourselves and nature we have much in the way of frivolous or excessive or servile corruption. Our age is the *Seculum* of beautiful trivialities, *Bagatelles*, or sublime *Chimaera*.

21. Sheet inserted after *Ob* 42, reverse, opposite *Ob* 43, at 2:225–6 (Ri 60).

A person's contentment arises either from satisfying many inclinations with many agreeable things, or from not letting many inclinations sprout, and thus by being satisfied with fewer fulfilled needs. The state of him who is satisfied because he is not familiar with agreeable things is simple sufficiency, that of him who is familiar with them but who voluntarily does without them because he fears the unrest that arises from them is wise sufficiency. The former requires no self-compulsion and deprivation, the latter however demands this; the former is easily seduced, while the latter has been seduced and is therefore more secure for the future. The condition of the person without a lack of gratification[b] because he is not familiar with greater possible gratification and therefore does not desire it.

Virtue does not at all consist in overcoming acquired inclinations in particular cases, but in seeking to be free of such inclinations and thus learning to do without them gladly. It does not consist in conflict with the natural inclinations, but rather in making it the case that one has none except for the natural ones, because these can always be satisfied.

22. Sheet inserted after *Ob* 50, obverse, at 2:229 (Ri 68).

The human being has his own inclinations, and by means of his capacity of choice has a clue from nature to conduct his actions in accordance

---

[a] *sich selbst aufheben*
[b] *Misvergnügen*

with these. Nothing can be more appalling than that the action of one human stand under the will of another. Hence no abhorrence can be more natural than that which a person has against servitude. On this account a child cries and becomes bitter if it has to do what another wants without one having made an effort to make that pleasing to him. And it wishes only to become a man quickly and to operate in accordance with its own will. What new servitude to things must it arouse in order to introduce that.

23. Sheet inserted after *Ob* 50, reverse, opposite *Ob* 51, at 2:229 (Ri 68).

The sweetness that we find in attending to beneficence to others is an effect of the feeling of the general well-being that would occur in the condition of freedom.

24. Sheet inserted after *Ob* 52, obverse, at 2:230 (Ri 70–1).
On freedom
Find himself in what condition he will, the human being is dependent upon many external things. [*crossed out*: On means of nourishment, the impressions of the air, the sun] He always depends on some things because of his needs, on others because of his concupiscence, and because he is the administrator of nature but not its master he must [*crossed out*: often submit to the yoke of necessity and bow to the order of nature and accommodate himself to its laws] often accommodate himself to its compulsion, since he does not find that it will always accommodate itself to his wishes. But what is harder and more unnatural than this yoke of necessity is the [*crossed out*: dependence] subjection of one human being under the will of another. No misfortune can be more terrifying to one who is accustomed to freedom, who has enjoyed the good of freedom, than to see himself delivered [*crossed out*: under] to a creature of his own kind who can compel him to do what he will (to give himself over to his will).

It [*crossed out*: necessarily] requires a very long habituation to make the [*crossed out*: horrible] terrifying thought of servitude tolerable, for everyone must always feel that even when there are many adversities that one might not be pleased to shed at the risk of one's life, still in the choice between slavery and the risk of death one will have no reservation about preferring the latter.

25. Sheet inserted after *Ob* 52, reverse, opposite *Ob* 53, at 2:230 (Ri 71).

The cause of this is also very clear and rightful. All other evils of nature are nevertheless subject to certain laws that one learns to know in order subsequently to be able to choose how far one will give in to them or be subject to them. The heat of the burning sun, the raw wind, the motions of the water always afford a person something to consider about how to protect himself from them or at least [*breaks off*]

But the will of another person is the effect of his own drives [and] inclinations and agrees only with his own true or imagined welfare. But if I was previously free, then nothing can open a grimmer prospect of misery and desperation to me than that in the future my condition should not lie in my own will but in that of another. If it is very cold today then I can go out or stay at home as I alone prefer, but the will of another determines not what on such an occasion would be most agreeable to me but to him. I would rest or play, and he forces me to work. The wind that rages outside may well force me to flee into a hole but here or elsewhere it finally leaves me in peace, but my master seeks me out, and since the cause of my misfortune has reason he is far more skillful at torturing me than all the elements. Even if I suppose that he is good, nothing stands in the way of his sometime thinking otherwise. The motions of matter hold to a certain determinate rule, but the obstinacy of the human being is without any rule.

26. Sheet inserted after *Ob* 54, obverse, at 2:230 (Ri 72–3).

There is in subjection not only something externally dangerous but also a certain ugliness and a contradiction that at the same time indicates its injustice. An animal is not yet a complete being because it is not conscious of its self, and whether its drives and inclinations be resisted by another or not, it certainly feels its ills, but these are forgotten in a moment, and it knows nothing of its own existence. But that a human being should as it were need no soul himself and have no will of his own, and that another soul should move my limbs, that is absurd and perverse: Also in our constitutions every person is contemptible to us who is to any great degree subjected [*breaks off*]

. . .

Instead of freedom elevating me above the cattle, it places me beneath them, since I can more easily be coerced.

Such a person is to himself as it were nothing but the houseware of another. I could just as well indicate my respect to the boots of the master as to his lackey. In short, the person who is dependent in this way is no longer a person, he has lost this rank, he is nothing but a belonging of another person.

Subjection and freedom are commonly mixed together to a certain degree, and one depends on the other. But even a small degree of dependency is much too great an evil for it not to be naturally terrifying. This feeling is very natural although one can also greatly weaken it. The power to resist the evils of others can become so small that slavery seems a lesser evil than adversity. Yet it is certain that in human nature it stands above [*breaks off*]

The ox is coerced by the human, but the human by the whim of another human.

The momentary power of an attack is much smaller than servitude.

27. Sheet inserted after *Ob* 54, reverse, opposite *Ob* 55, at 2:312 (Ri 73).

There may well be attractions that a person prefers to freedom for a moment, but this must make him sorry in the end.

Society makes one esteem oneself merely comparatively. If others are not better than me then I am good, and if everyone else is worse then I am perfect.

Yet comparative esteem is to be distinguished from honor.

Chastity cannot be a lack of passion in love because then it is really a failing, namely if this passion is too small for its whole end then it is good insofar as it is appropriate to one's age and means, only this goodness is not moral.

. . .

We have all sorts of drives that should serve us as means to serve others and we often immediately dominate them. First, [a drive] to compare ourselves with others and thereby to esteem ourselves; from that arises the falsehood of estimating one's worth comparatively, of pride, and of estimating one's happiness on the basis of envy. Second, [a drive] to put ourself into the position of another in order thereby to know what he feels. From this arises the blind compassion which brings justice into disorder. Third, [a drive] to investigate the judgments of others because this can correct the truth in our own morally as well as logically. From this arises the desire for reputation. Fourth, [a drive] to acquire everything and to save it for enjoyment; from this arises the greed that is parsimonious.

28. Sheet inserted after *Ob* 68, obverse, at 2:237 (Ri 88–9).

The capacity for pleasure and displeasure in general is feeling. Lack of feeling [*breaks off*]

The capacity for pleasure and displeasure in things that do not belong among our needs is taste. It is coarse taste insofar as it is close to needs; refined[a] taste is taste in that which is well distanced from needs. [*Crossed out*: The feeling for things that presupposes the perfections of a greater understanding is *ideal*.]

Insofar as the powers of the soul must not be merely passive but active and inventive[b] taste is called spiritual[c] and ideal (when the foremost feeling is moved not by external sensation but by that which has been invented for that purpose).

[a] *feine*
[b] *dichtend*
[c] *geistig*

With regard to morality, feeling either merely remains at the level of needs, i.e., obligation, or it goes farther; in the latter case it is sentiment.[a]

The beautiful and the sublime in the highest degree are closely related. To be felt, both presuppose that the soul is at peace. Yet they are so different that if it is busyness, cheerfulness, and liveliness that dominate them, then it is beauty that shines forth, while if they come to a stop and peaceful contentment shows through, then the sublime stands out. The former is early morning, the latter is the evening.

In its lesser forms, beauty is related to the change of variable novelty. The sublime, with constancy, oneness, and unalterability. With beauty, manifoldness, with the noble, unity.

29. Sheet inserted after *Ob* 68, reverse, opposite *Ob* 69, at 2:237 (Ri 89–90).

Only that which is dispensable is beautiful, but the noble can be combined with utility. Yet in moral matters, the noble must not be considered from the viewpoint of utility. Blossoms are beautiful, fruit is useful. In these refined sentiments it is presupposed that the person is not dependent on things because of need, otherwise the refined taste is ridiculous. Enchanted by beauty, astonished by sublimity.

The beautiful in a lesser degree is agreeable and pretty, when sublimity disappears, it is cute.[b] If beauty is imitated, it is decorated, like golden hens.

In the feeling of the sublime, the powers of a person are as it were stretched; in that of the beautiful, they contract.

. . .

There are moral and nonmoral necessities (obligations), which are presupposed before there is talk of beauty. Sciences inside the head are for many people as useless as powder on top. And as it would be quite ridiculous to have flour on one's curls and none in one's soup, it is likewise absurd to have knowledge of the dispensable sciences but none of those that constitute the welfare of life.

30. Sheet inserted after *Ob* 74, obverse, at 2:239 (Ri 94).

Taste always depends on that which is not an actual need. From this it follows that in painting when similarity with nature is called for, e.g., landscapes and portraits,[c] then this nature must be captured, but otherwise it is ideal gratification which is best. Nature is not good enough for our gratification. For that the softness and tenderness of our organs,

---

[a] *Sentiment*
[b] *niedlich*
[c] *Naturalien, Portraite*

indeed our imagination is required. Hence painting can very well depart from nature, like poetry and theatrical action.

Truth is more of an obligation than beauty. One must therefore hide one's obligations in order to be beautiful.

. . .

Harmony arises from the concordance of the manifold, as in music so in poetry and painting. Those are resting points for some nerves.

31. Sheet inserted after *Ob* 80, obverse, at 2:242 (Ri 100).

Beauty is without utility because the latter is the pressing of an object into the service of other ends, thus indicates no perfection complete in itself. Hence the more useful things are, the more corners, so to speak, do they display, as means to fit into other connections; the roundness of a sphere is perfect in itself.

32. Sheet inserted after *Ob* 89, reverse, opposite *Ob* 81, at 2:243 (Ri 101).

Benevolence is a calm inclination toward the happiness of others as an object of one's joy, and is to be regarded as a motivating ground of one's actions. Compassion is an affect of benevolence toward those who suffer, by means of which we represent to ourselves that we would do what is in our power to help them; it is thus often chimerical, because to help them is neither always in our power nor in our will. The citizen is compassionate toward others who are oppressed by the prince. The nobleman is compassionate toward another nobleman, but is himself hard on the peasants.

33. Sheet inserted after *Ob* 82, obverse, at 2:243 (Ri 102).

The will is perfect insofar as in accordance with the laws of freedom it is the greatest ground of the good in general. The moral feeling is the feeling of the perfection of the will.

34. Sheet inserted after *Ob* 82, reverse, opposite *Ob* 83, at 2:244 (Ri 103–4).

The free will (of someone with needs) is good for itself if it wills everything that contributes to its perfection (gratification), and good for the whole if at the same time it desires all perfection. However lacking in capacity*[a]* the person who has this will may be, the will is still good. Other things may be useful; other people may do much good in a certain action with a lesser degree of will but with more power; yet the ground of willing to do the good is uniquely and solely moral.

The mathematician and the philosopher: they differ in that the former requires *data* from others while the latter examines them himself. Hence the former can construct proofs from any revealed religion.

---

[a] *unvermögend*

15

35. Sheet inserted after *Ob* 86, reverse, opposite *Ob* 87 (Ri 107–8).

The capacity to recognize something as a perfection in others does not at all have the consequence that we will find gratification in it ourselves. But if we feel gratification in it, then we will also be moved to desire it and to apply our powers to it. Thus the question arises, whether we feel gratification immediately in the well-being of another or whether the immediate pleasure actually lies in the promotion of the possible application of our power. Both are possible, but which is actual[?] Experience teaches that in a simple condition a person regards the good fortune of another with indifference, but that if he has promoted it then it pleases him infinitely more. Likewise, the ill fortune of another is usually equally indifferent, but if I have caused it then it sickens me more than if another had done it. And as far as the sympathetic instincts of compassion and being well disposed are concerned, we have cause to believe that these are merely great efforts to ameliorate the ills of others derived from the self-approbation of the soul that brings forth these sentiments.

We have gratification in certain of our perfections, but far more if we ourselves are the cause. We have the most if we are the freely acting cause. To subordinate everything to the free capacity for choice is the greatest perfection. And the perfection of the free capacity for choice as a cause of possibility is far greater than all the other causes of the good even if they produce actuality.

36. Sheet inserted after *Ob* 88, obverse, at 2:246 (Ri 108–9).
Habit.
Action from the singular will is moral solipsism.
Action from the communal will is moral justice.[a]
The feeling of pleasure and displeasure concerns either something with respect to which we are passive or our self as an active *principium* of good and evil through freedom. The latter is moral feeling. Past physical evil makes us joyful, but past moral evil depresses us, and the kind of joy that we take in the good that befalls us is entirely different from that we take in what we do.

We have little feeling for whether the condition of another is evil or good except insofar as we feel able to alleviate the former or promote the latter. Sympathy is an instinct that is operative only on rare and very important occasions; its other effects are artificial.

Since the greatest inner perfection and the perfection that arises from that consists in the subordination of all of our capacities and receptivities to the free capacity for choice, the feeling for the goodness of the free

---

[a] These three lines are in Latin in the original.

16

capacity for choice must immediately be much different and also greater than all of the good consequences that can thereby be effected.

Now this capacity for choice contains either the merely individual will as well as the universal will, or it considers the person at the same time in *consensu* with the universal will.

37. Sheet inserted after *Ob* 88, reverse, opposite *Ob* 89, at 2:246 (Ri 109).

Since the human being requires little of nature, and the more he requires the more miserable he is, the human being is perfect insofar as he can do without but yet has much power left to promote the needs and happiness of others; thus he has a feeling of a will that is active in behalf of a good outside of himself. Since the capacity for choice, insofar as it is also useful to the acting subject, is physically necessary with regard to good, it has no immediate goodness. Hence the moral goodness of action does not consist in utility to the self.

38. Sheet inserted after *Ob* 90, obverse, at 2:247 (Ri 110).

The inner sense of pleasure and displeasure precedes desire and aversion, since the receptivity to enjoyment and aversion lies in the subject, even if it, the subject, does not have any knowledge of the object of this sense, as there cannot be a desire for something unknown. Desire is either original or derived; the former also varies with respect to quality. The inner sense, if it is held to be a logical principle for the judgment of the moral law, is an occult quality; if it is a faculty of the soul whose ground is unknown, then it is a phenomenon.[a]

A *pactum*[b] is not possible between a *domino*[c] and a *mancipio*.[d] God enters into a union with humans because they do not have an adequate **practical** concept of his *dominio*[e] and therefore are led by an analogy with the *pacto* among men and do not abhor his strength to command.

All conditional goodness of an action stands under either a possible condition (as in problems) or under an actual one (as in the rules of prudence, [e.g.] everyone wants to be healthy), but in mediate or conditional goodness the absolute will is not good if the powers and circumstances of time and place are lacking. And it is a good if the will is effective, but one will also be able to consider this goodness with respect to the will alone; even if the powers should be lacking, the will is still

[a] This paragraph is in Latin in the original.
[b] contract
[c] lord
[d] slave
[e] lordship

praiseworthy.[4] In great things it suffices to have had the will.[5] And this absolute perfection, whether something is effected by it or not, is called moral.[a]

39. Sheet inserted after *Ob* 92, obverse, at 2:248 (Ri 111–12).

[b]The objective goodness of a free action or, what is the same, its objective necessity, is either conditional or categorical; the former is the goodness of an action as a means, the latter as an end; the former is therefore mediate, the latter immediate; the former contains problematic practical necessity, the latter [*breaks off*]

A conditionally good free action is therefore not categorically necessary, e.g., my generosity is useful to another who is in need, therefore one must be generous. By no means. But if one wants to be useful to someone else, then one must be generous. But if the action of an open-hearted generosity is not merely good for others but is good in itself, then it is an obligation.

On the moral feeling and the possibility of its opposite. Providence has so connected the moral feeling with public and universal utility that the goodness of the will[c] is not judged as highly as it should be.

[d]If I say that this action would bring me more honor than another, I mean that I appeal to the general judgment in order to ground the judgment that I make about my own action.

Controversies in philosophy have the utility that they promote the freedom of the understanding and arouse distrust against the doctrine that has itself been constructed on the ruins of another. One is still happy with a refutation.

40. Sheet inserted after *Ob* 92, reverse, opposite *Ob* 93, at 2:248 (Ri, 112–13).

One talks so much about virtue. But one must first eliminate injustice before one can be virtuous. One must first set aside the luxuries of excess and everything that elevates me by oppressing others in order that I should not be one of those who all oppress their own kind. All virtue is impossible without this decision.

All virtue is grounded on ideal feeling. Hence in the state of excess no virtue will be found in the person who has merely corporeal feeling, but in the state of nature simplicity in straightforward sentiments and simplicity in mores[e] are quite consistent.

---

[a] This passage is in Latin in the original.
[b] This paragraph and the two following it are in Latin.
[c] *arbitrii*
[d] Here Kant reverts to German.
[e] *Sitten*

41. Sheet inserted after *Ob* 94, obverse, at 2:249 (Ri 113–14).

We can see other worlds in the distance, but gravity forces us to remain on the earth; we can see other perfections in spirits above us, but our nature forces us to remain human beings.

Since in society all property^a comes down to *pacta*, but these depend on keeping one's word, the love of truth is the foundation^b of all social virtue, and lying is the chief sin against others, alongside robbery, murder, and *stuproviolatio*.^c

If humans subordinate morality to religion (which is also only possible and necessary among the oppressed rabble), they will be hostile, insincere, and backhanded; but if they subordinate religion to morality, they will be goodly, benevolent, and just.

. . .

The human being in his perfection is not in the state of sufficiency nor in the state of excess but rather in the return from the latter state to the former. The admirable constitution of human nature. This most perfect state rests on a hair's breadth. The state of simple and original nature does not last long, the state of reconstituted nature is more durable but not so innocent.

42. Sheet inserted after *Ob* 96, obverse, at 2:250 (Ri 115–16).

^dThe objective necessity (goodness) of actions is either conditional (under the condition of some desired good) or categorical. The former is problematic, and, if the drives that are considered to be the necessary conditions of the action are regarded not only as possible but as actual, then it is the necessity of prudence. In order to know them, it will be necessary to diagnose all of the desires and instincts of human nature, so that a computation can be performed of what is best for the inclination of the subject, and this not only in its present but also in its future state. The categorical necessity of an action does not require so much effort, but merely the application of the matter to the moral feeling.

In certain situations in life a lie is apparently necessary and hence in accordance with the rule of prudence lying seems the thing to do, but for this there is required great acuity and sagacity concerning the consequences. But if one considers things morally, then on the ground of moral simplicity it will immediately be known what is to be done.

Even if a false assertion may sometimes be useful for others, it is still a lie if no strict obligation necessitates it. From this one can see

---

^a *alles Mein und Dein*
^b *Fundament* (italicized in the original)
^c rape
^d This note is entirely in Latin.

that truthfulness does not depend on philanthropy, but on the sense of justice, from which we learn to distinguish what may be done from what may not be done. This sense, however, has its origin in the nature of the human spirit, through which it judges what is categorically good (not useful), not in accordance with utility to oneself or others, but rather by considering the same action in others: if in that case there arises opposition and contrariety, then the action displeases, but if there arises harmony and consensus, then it pleases. Hence the capacity to put oneself into the position of others is a heuristic means to morality. For we are by nature sociable and cannot call that good in ourselves which we blame in others. The common sense for the true and the false is nothing other than human reason, taken in general as the criterion of the true and the false, and the sense of good and evil is the criterion thereof. Heads that are in opposition cancel out logical certainty; hearts that are in opposition cancel out moral certainty.

The goodness of the will is derived from the effects of private or public utility and from the immediate pleasure in them, and the former has its basis in need, the latter in the power for the good; the former is related to one's own utility, the latter to general utility; both feelings conform to natural simplicity. But the goodness of the will as a free principle is recognized not insofar as such forms of utility arise from it, but rather it is possible to cognize it in itself. And the happiness of others in accordance with reason.

43. Sheet inserted after *Ob* 96, reverse, opposite *Ob* 97, at 2:250 (Ri, 116–17).

Natural obligation toward other persons has a determinate measure, the duty of love has none. The former consists in nothing more happening than what I myself would allow another, and in giving him only what is his; consequently following such an action everything is equal. (Sympathy is an exception to this.)

If I promise something to him then I rob him of something, for then I have raised a hope that I do not fulfill. If he is hungry and I do not help him, then I have not overstepped any obligation. But if in the case in which I myself should be hungry and would gladly desire the help of another on the condition of returning it, then it is an obligation for me to satisfy him. A robber may well wish that he would be pardoned, but he well knows that if he were the judge he would not grant a pardon. The judge punishes although he well knows that if he were the delinquent he would not want to be punished, but with punishment it is otherwise. It is not the judge who robs the criminal of his life, but the criminal himself, on account of his misdeed. No one in need can represent to himself that if he were rich he would help everyone in need.

44. Sheet inserted after *Ob* 98, reverse, opposite *Ob* 99, at 2:251 (Ri 119–20).

[a]An action considered from the point of view of the universal will of human beings, if it contradicts itself, is morally impossible (impermissible). Let me have the idea of taking possession of the fruits of another. As I then see that no person would acquire anything under the condition that what he has required can be ripped from him, I would from a private point of view want that which belongs to another, but from a public point of view decline it.

Insofar, namely, as something is entirely dependent on the will of a subject, to that extent it is impossible that it contradict itself (objectively). Nevertheless, the divine will would contradict itself if it willed that there exist human beings whose will was opposed to its own. The will of human beings would contradict itself if it willed that it abhor the universal will.

In the case of a conflict, the universal will is more important than the individual will.

The [*crossed out*: hypothetical] conditional necessity of an action as a means to a possible end is **problematic**, as a means to an actual goal it is a necessity of **prudence**, categorical necessity is **moral**.

45. *Ob* 102, at 2:252 (Ri 123).
Upper margin:
The drive for honor is grounded on the drive for equality and the drive for unity, as it were, two forces that move the animal world. The instinct for unity is either unity in judgments and thoughts or also in inclinations. The former brings about logical perfection, the latter, moral perfection.
Left-hand margin:
The sole naturally necessary good of a human being in relation to the wills of others is equality (freedom) and, with respect to the whole, unity. Analogy: Repulsion – by its means the body fills its space, just as everybody fills his own. Attraction, through which all parts are bound into one.

The truth of a perfection consists in the magnitude of the pleasure, which is greater if it is not exclusive with regard to oneself and others. If falsehood could be durable and more enjoyable than truth, then the pleasure from this deception would be a true pleasure but a false cognition.
Bottom margin:
The natural instincts of active benevolence toward others consists in love toward the [opposite] sex and toward children. That toward other persons concerns merely equality and unity.

---

[a] The following paragraphs are in Latin.

There is unity in the sovereign state but not equality; if this is combined with the unity of all, then it constitutes the perfect republic.

46. Sheet inserted after *Ob* 102, obverse, at 2:252 (Ri 124).

The drive to esteem oneself merely comparatively, with regard to both one's worth as well as one's welfare, is far more extensive than the drive for honor, and contains the latter. It does not lie in nature, and is a side effect of the use of comparison with others as a means to come to know oneself better. The desire for honor, which is a spur to science, arises from the comparison of our judgment with the judgment of others as a means, and thus presupposes a high valuation on the judgment of others.

. . .

A reason why Montesquieu was able to say so many excellent things is that he presupposed that those who introduced customs or gave laws always had a rational ground.

The chief intention of Rousseau is that education be free and also make a free human being.

47. Sheet inserted after *Ob* 102, reverse, opposite *Ob* 103, at 2:253 (Ri 125).

It is to be noted that we do not esteem the goodness of an action because it is useful to another, otherwise we would not esteem it more highly than the utility that it creates.

48. Sheet inserted after *Ob* 106, obverse, at 2:254 (Ri 128).

Moral delusion consists in one taking the opinion of a possible moral perfection to be actual.

We have sentiments that are selfish and those that are unselfish. The former are older than the latter, and the latter are first generated in sexual inclination. The human being is needy, but also powerful over these needs. A person in the state of nature is more capable of sentiments that are useful to all and active; a person who lives in excess has imaginary needs and is selfish. One sympathizes more with the evil that others have suffered from injustice than with their welfare. The sympathetic sentiment is true if it is equal to the unselfish forces, otherwise it is chimerical. It is universal in an indeterminate way insofar as it is directed to one among all those whom I can help, or in a determinate way, toward helping everyone who suffers; the latter is chimerical. Good-heartedness arises through the cultivation of moral but inactive sentiments, and is moral delusion. From private good-heartedness, to do no evil and to fulfill one's obligation out of justice.

That morality is chimerical which wills pure unselfishness and which is sympathetic to imaginary needs. That morality is crude which asserts only one's selfish good.

The *officia beneplaciti*[a] can never entail that one must rob one's own needs, but the *officia debiti*[b] can, because these are moral needs.

Virtue brings with it a natural reward, not in goods of excess but in sufficiency.

One can think of a human being most perfect in nature, but not in art.

49. Sheet inserted after *Ob* 106, reverse, opposite *Ob* 107, at 2:255 (Ri 130).

The doubt that I assume is not dogmatic, but a doubt of postponement. Zetetics (ζητεῖν), seekers. I will raise the grounds for both sides. It is marvelous that anyone should be concerned about the danger of that. Speculation is not a matter of necessity.[c] Our knowledge with regard to the latter is secure. The method of doubt is useful because it preserves the mind, not for speculation, but for acting in accordance with the healthy understanding and sentiment. I seek the honor of *Fabius Cunctator.*[6]

Truth has no value in itself; whether an opinion about the habitation of other worlds is true or false is indifferent. One must not confuse it with truthfulness. Only the way in which one arrives at truth has a determinate value, since a way that leads to error can also do so in practical matters.

If gratification from the sciences is to be the motivating ground, then it is indifferent whether it is true or false. In this case, the ignorant and the hastily clever have an advantage over those who are more knowledgeable and cautious. The final end is to determine the vocation of mankind.

50. *Ob* 107, lower margin, at 2:255 (Ri 130).

The opinion of inequality also makes people unequal. Only the doctrine of Mr. *Rousseau* can make it the case that even the most learned philosopher with all his knowledge and without the help of religion is as upright and no better than the common man.

51. On the inside of the back flyleaf (Ri 134–5).

Simplicity is either ignorant simplicity or rational and wise simplicity. In all moral definitions the expression *mediocritas*[d] is quite miserable and indeterminate, e.g., *in parsimonia,*[e] because it says only that there must be a degree the magnitude of which is not good, without saying how large the good degree is.

This *mediocritas aurea* is a *qualitas occulta.*[f]

---

[a] duties of benevolence
[b] duties of obligation
[c] *Nothdurft*
[d] the mean
[e] in thriftiness
[f] The golden mean is an occult quality.

. . .

One could say that metaphysics is a science of the limits of human reason.

Doubt about metaphysics does not cancel out useful certainty, but only useless certainty.

Metaphysics is useful in that it cancels out appearance, which can be harmful.

In metaphysics, not to think of the opposite side is partiality, and not to say it is also a lie; in actions it is otherwise.

One merely falls in love with appearance,[a] but one loves the truth. If one were to reveal appearance to most people they would be stunned, as the lover was with his bride when she removed her pretty silken eyebrows, a few ivory teeth, the handkerchiefs that propped up her bosom and her beautiful locks of hair and washed off her make-up.

Appearance requires refinement and art, truth simplicity and peace. According to Swift, everything in the world is mere dress.[7]

What is most ridiculous is this, that one maintains the appearance against others so long that one imagines it is truth, just as children do with religion. When one who intends it takes appearance to be the thing in itself, that is madness.

[a] *Schein*

2

Notes on Logic

This chapter presents notes drawn from Volume XVI of the *Akademie* edition, edited by Erich Adickes and originally published in 1914. As Adickes reports (16:v), these notes were drawn from Kant's interleaved copy of Georg Friedrich Meier's *Auszug aus der Vernunftlehre* (Halle: Johann Justinus Gebauer, 1752), the textbook for Kant's logic lectures (Meier's textbook is reproduced in volume XVI). Adickes provides the page and, after the Introduction, the numbered section in Meier's textbook to which Kant's notes were appended. Those will be provided here with the abbreviation "*V*" followed by the page and, when given, section number. We present here only a small selection of the almost two thousand notes that Adickes transcribed. Many of these notes are very brief comments on Meier's paragraphs, reminders to Kant of what he wanted to say in his lecture, examples he might use, and so on, and are uninformative or of little interest by themselves; others are paralleled by more extensive passages in Kant's lectures on logic, a selection of which has been published in the Cambridge edition as Immanuel Kant, *Lectures on Logic*, edited and translated by J. Michael Young (Cambridge: Cambridge University Press, 1992).

Although compact, Meier's textbook covered topics well beyond what one would find in a modern logic textbook. He covered the traditional topics of concepts, judgments, and inferences, the trichotomy around which logic books from the middle ages through the eighteenth century were organized and which lived on in the organization of the *Critique of Pure Reason* and beyond, for example, in the structure of Hegel's *Science of Logic*. But Meier also discussed the relation between logic and other disciplines of thought, particularly, following his own mentor Alexander Gottlieb Baumgarten, the distinction between logical and aesthetic thought and judgment. In this chapter, we first present a selection of Kant's notes on Meier's introduction, concerning the scope of the discipline of logic (1578, 1579, 1599, 1601, 1602, 1603, 1604, 1605, 1606, 1608, 1612), and then focus on Kant's notes that clarify central concepts employed in the *Critique of Pure Reason*, such as his conceptions of representations (1676, 2394, 2835, 2836), concepts (2279, 2280, 2281, 2282, 2283, 2286, 2287, 2288), and judgments (3042, 3043, 3044, 3045, 3046, 3047, 3051, 3053, 3054, 3055, 3063, 3068, 3069), his theories of the degrees of belief and knowledge (2450, 2451, 2452, 2789), his theory of definitions (2920, 2925, 2936, 2947, 2950,

2951, 2962, 2994, 2995, 3004, 3005), his conceptions of hypotheses (2675, 2678), analogies and induction (3276, 3277, 3280, 3281, 3282, 3294), his theory that logic provides only necessary but not sufficient conditions for the knowledge of truth (2132, 2133, 2142, 2147, 2155, 2161, 2162, 2173, 2174, 2176, 2177), the difference between analytic and dialectic (1579, 1601, 1602), and his eventual contrast between determining and reflecting judgment (3200, 3287). As part of his discussion of belief and knowledge, Kant included notes on the contrast between theoretical and practical belief, and a selection of those notes is included in the present chapter (2454, 2460, 2462, 2470, 2503, 2714, 2716, 2788, 2793, 2794, 3115, 3116, 3118, 3133), although of course they are also relevant to the notes on ethics that will be presented in Chapter 4. Following Baumgarten, Meier used the contrast between logic and aesthetics to define the very nature of the discipline of logic and devoted an entire chapter to the contrast between the "logical and aesthetic perfection of cognition" (V, §§19–35). Kant's notes on Meier's text therefore include a number that would now be classified as concerning the discipline of aesthetics more than logic (1747 through 1935), and our selection from those notes will be reserved for Chapter 5, on aesthetics, although some of Kant's notes on Meier's Introduction included here also touch briefly upon aesthetics as part of their discussion of the division of intellectual disciplines (e.g., 1578 and 1579).

* *
*

I.
NOTES ON MEIER'S INTRODUCTION[1]

16:16   1578. 1760–64? 1764–68? 1769? 1769–1770? (1771? 1773–75?) V, iv.
      We can convince someone only on the basis of his own healthy understanding. If I deny this to him, then it is foolish to reason with him.
      Common and healthy reason ascends from *a posteriori* experience to what is general.
      Learned reason, from the general to experiences.
      The *sensus communis*[2] forms general laws out of individual experiences and subsumes only in proportion to the experiences from which it has abstracted them. In morals the general rule is also abstracted only from what we judge in individual cases, and the general rule is not blindly obeyed in every application but is tested and often improved. The philosophy of healthy reason does not mean philosophy that judges merely by means of the *sensum communem*, for then it is not philosophy, or philosophy that agrees with the *sensum communem*, for every philosophy must do this, but rather philosophy in which common sense provides

the criteria of philosophy. Only morals is this (for taste indicates the correctness of aesthetic rules, but these are not philosophical *dogmata*). The logic of the rules and limits of healthy reason is an *organon*, but morals is a doctrine. Now healthy reason in morals is not empirical, yet in it the universal *in abstracto* is determined only through the universal considered *in concreto*.

1579. 1760–64? 1764–68? 1769–1770? 1773–1775?? *V*, v–vi.　　16:17

The rule either necessarily precedes practice and is called a prescription, *praeceptum* [*breaks off*].

Common use of powers

Natural use of powers.　　(Through testing; according to a norm.*)

Artificial use.

*(The artificial use is either by means of empirically cognized rules and allows for a discipline, or by means of rules cognized *a priori* and becomes a doctrine, a science.)

All our powers proceed according to rules, thus understanding and reason as well.

(*Later addition*: Because a common ground exists, all the effects of a power are in accordance with it, namely the nature of this power.)

Either one is aware of these rules before practice, or practice precedes the rules.

(*Later addition*: Natural or acquired rules, i.e., prescriptions, *praecepta*.)

These rules are either borrowed from practice or only accompany practice: common arts, chores. Economics. Crafts. Common speech. An eye for distance. Morals.

Or they precede practice: Navigation. Astronomy. Grammar. Geometry. Jurisprudence. Calculation.

Art and science.

(*Later addition*: The faculty of cognizing the universal *in abstracto*.)　　16:18

The faculty of general cognitions (*later addition*: of judging, of subsuming and judging (inferring) *a priori*) is called the understanding (*later addition*: reason *a priori* (or *in abstracto*)).

If general cognitions are borrowed from particular ones, it is **common understanding** (*Later addition*: sensus communis. *Universale in concreto*, consequently in experience or individual cases. *Sensus communis*.)

If the particular cognitions are borrowed from general ones, it is **science**. (*Later addition*: Concretum ab abstracto.)[a]

In the first case one proceeds according to rules of which one is not conscious, and the rules are abstracted from practice. Natural use of rules.

---

[a] The concrete from the abstract.

In the second case one must be conscious of the rules prior to practice. Artificial use of rules.

(*Later addition*: The use of the understanding according to form or content.

The material or formal doctrine of the understanding; the latter is metaphysics.)

[*Crossed out*: The science of the rules of understanding is logic; the science of the common understanding is criticism; the science of the use of the understanding in sciences is doctrine.]

The science of the objective rules of the correct use of reason in general is logic.

The science of the objective rules of the correct use of pure reason is metaphysics.

The science of the subjective rules of our cognition and the other powers of the soul is psychology.

The logic of healthy reason: critique; of learned reason: doctrine.

The science of the rules in the common use of reason is the *critica sensus communis*.

16:19 The science of the rules in the learned use of reason is *logica proprie dicta, doctrina*.

The former serves as a *catarcticon*[a] like grammar, the latter as an *organon*.

(*Later addition*: Common understanding cognizes the *universale in concreto*. The healthy understanding does this according to the grounds of the understanding, not of sensory illusion, prejudice.

The rules of a common cognition serve only as the discipline of drawing everyone's attention to the rules which one already knows in advance and preventing our deviating from them, or producing cognition; then it is called doctrine.

The artificial use of the understanding (in accordance with precepts) is either as discipline or doctrine; the former use **is negative** (preventing mistakes: aesthetics); 2, **positive**: producing cognitions; the former serves as critique, the latter as *organon*.

Logic as critique and discipline of healthy reason;[3] and as a doctrine of learned reason: an *organon*. Its principles are *a priori* (because they contain the rules of the understanding). Thus it is philosophy and a science.

Logic serves as discipline and as doctrine; the former as critique and as *organon*. Naming all actions artificially, as in grammar, aesthetics.

Aesthetics serves as critique because its principles are discovered *a posteriori*, and thus not **genetically**, logic serves as *organon*.

---

[a] purgative

Common and speculative reason: the former *in concreto* (the *criterium*), the latter *in abstracto*. The boundaries of the former are determined by means of the field of experiences. Restriction to these conditions and expansion into the field of speculative reason according to the *analogon* of healthy reason.

Common reason: also according to rules which, however, are not precepts, i.e., the learning of which practice depends upon. Speculative   16: 20
reason: in which general cognitions precede *in abstracto*.

Logic in its common use is the critique of common reason; in the sciences, critique of the sciences.

Logic as *canon* (analytic) or *organon* (dialectic); the latter cannot be treated generally because it is a doctrine of the understanding not according to its form but rather its content.

The use of the understanding accompanied by the consciousness of the rules of this use is science.

The discipline that contains the rules of the proper use of the understanding in general is logic.)

All logic contains either merely rules of adjudication[a] and is theoretical: it indicates the conditions under which a cognition is complete;

or of execution: it teaches how to bring about these conditions.

(*Later addition*: Doctrine can be cognized *a priori* and the rules can be demonstrated.)

Logic is a philosophy of the universal laws (rules) of the **correct** use of our understanding and reason (in healthy or learned understanding).

(*Later addition*: **Objective** logic. How the understanding **should** be used.

Whether there is a practical logic?

Critique of healthy understanding or *organon*.)

Moral philosophy is a philosophy of the universal laws (rules) of the proper use of our will.

Materia.

1. Names of logic: (*Later addition*: *a priori*) science of reason. Not because of its form but rather because of its object. (*Later addition*: Because of its matter. Object. Reason in general, not applied to a particular object. The form must be philosophical, and the object is itself philosophy.)

2. Science: [*crossed out*: cannot be historical, but must be philosophy,   16: 21
because it is part of the latter] *canon* on account of its form because its rules can be proven *a priori*. Taste allows only critique of the beautiful sciences; not merely critique, not merely doctrine, but *scientia*.

3. Not subjective laws: how the understanding thinks (this belongs to psychology, as do subjective laws of the will), but: how it should think.

---

[a] *diiudication*

29

Education. (*Later addition*: Not its nature, but precept. Of its good use; correctness is not the only thing.)

4. Not the particular laws of pure reason, but also of applied reason. (*Later addition*: 4. Not of the particular use (*organon*) with respect to an object, but of the understanding in general. *Propaedetica philosophiae.* Logic: a. of the *sensus communis*; b. of the sciences. Critique (discipline). *Organon.* What is the *sensus communis*? Its logic is not *cognitio sensus communis*, but *scientia.* d'Argens.⁴)

It is the *catarcticon* of common understanding. (*Later addition*: It is a theory and a science, namely, of the rules of reason themselves proven from reason. The difference from the critique of taste, whose *principia* are borrowed from their distinctions *in concreto* and are *a posteriori. Analysis* of common understanding serves as *catarcticon* and critique. *Dialectica* is the *disciplina apparentiae logicae.ᵃ*)

16:22   The theory of all rational cognition, both of healthy understanding and of science.

(*Later addition*: Either of all sciences in general or particular ones.)

The *organon* of the sciences (*later addition*: in particular).

As a *catarcticon* it is most useful; as critique (*later addition*: discipline) of the sciences it serves as aesthetics through terminologies.

As an *organon* it is still quite incomplete. It is more the fruit than a means of the rational sciences. Doctrine of method.

It is theoretical or practical. The former contains rules of **adjudication** and prescribes the conditions of a complete cognition. The latter contains rules of **execution** and prescribes the means for attaining these conditions.

(*Later addition*: This is partly the general: dialectic, partly the *organon.*

This cannot be taught; for the application of rules requires not another rule but rather healthy understanding. One can, however, consider the subjective conditions *in concreto* and become acquainted with both the instrument of execution and the obstacles.

16:23   1. Analytic: of the elements of reason.

2. Dialectic: of the production of cognitions in accordance with the rules of reason (of its use).

The former is precept; the latter, application; the first: the *criterium* of truth; the latter, the attempt.)

It has two parts: the logic of healthy reason, which is actually a critique of application *in concreto*, and the logic of learning: *organon.*

Dialectic is the doctrine of the subjective laws of the understanding insofar as they are taken for* objective. It is either sophistical or critical; the former is the practice of leading us astray.

ᵃ discipline of logical appearance

*(Psychology treats of the subjective grounds of practice which are taken for objective. For it belongs under that which is contingent.)

General practical logic is the logic of assertion or of illusion: dialectic;* because application permits no more rules, it only allows for critique: it is sophistical and skeptical.

*(The particular practical logic is the doctrine of method or *organon*.))

1599. 1769–1770? (1771–72?) (1760–64? 1764–68?) 1773–75?? *V*, 4.   16:29

1. In logic we deal not with the origin of concepts, whether from the senses or other grounds (and the powers in which each of them has its ground): that belongs to metaphysics.

2. Not with subjective rules (psychological laws or *phaenomenis* of   16:30
thought): how the understanding in us thinks, but with objective ones: how it should think, i.e., what is to be thought in accordance with the rules of the **understanding in general**. Psychology.

3. *Not with (cognitions insofar as they distinguish themselves by means of things) the relations and determinations of things, but with the relations of concepts. Therefore, logic pertains to all sciences because, after all, concepts are found in them, and is like arithmetic, although it comprehends such things within itself.

The relation which logic considers is that of comparison. For it cannot be that of connection, neither objective: n. 3, nor subjective: n. 2.

*(Not with regard to the objects of pure reason: metaphysics, but rather with the use of understanding in general and thus with the form of the understanding, which one can ascribe to all given representations in general. One does not thereby learn to use the understanding correctly so much as to observe its use and misuse.)

1601. 1773–75. *V*, vii   16:31
Logic contains either merely the critique of reason or the *canon*, or the *organon*. Logic is never an *organon*, rather if it is used as such it is dialectic. Experience is the *substratum* of logic, but never the *principium*.

1602. 1773–75. *V*, vii, viii.   16:31
There are two types of rules: the first, which are necessarily derived from use and are [*crossed out*: critical] rules; the other, which necessarily precede [*crossed out*: use and are *praecepta*: precepts.] or both at the same time. The first: healthy understanding; the second: science. Critique and *organon*. The former are derived either from natural use, e.g., the understanding, or from contingent use: language.

Logic is necessarily derived from use because it contains the first actions of the understanding, and we cannot think it without thereby using the understanding (*in concreto*, examples); we would not, however, have learned this without practice and thus would know it as little as

16: 32   we would know language without practice. It is the linguistic art of our representations.[a] Thus it does not precede use, but its rules are still clear on their own, once they are cognized, because they contain the ground of all judgments, namely, their form. Thus its rules are *a priori* and not derivative; consequently, there is a *canon*. Mathematics does not contain rules abstracted from use; rather, they are self-sufficient. Hence mathematics does not need a *canon*, that is, a guiding principle for its propositions. It also requires no *organon*. Transcendental logic requires a *canon* because it too has principles borrowed from common reason. They give rise to a natural *dialectic*; formal logic has an artificial one.

Logic provides a guiding principle, not a precept. The former, for judging actions of the understanding; the latter, for producing them.

Dialectic arises when the *organon* of critique is taken for the *organon* of doctrine.

Natural rules provide a *canon* for doctrine,

Artificial rules provide a norm for critique.

General logic, considered as *canon*, is the analytic of common understanding; considered as *organon*, it is dialectic. Logic, which should be an *organon*, is not general, but it follows the critique of science, not merely the *analysin* thereof. For not every *analysis* provides a *canon*, but only that of the essential and elementary actions of the understanding and of reason.

Pure general logic serves only for the critique, and thus not for the production, of the understanding and of rational cognition in general, and is no *organon* of science, but rather of the critique thereof. But if it is considered an *organon*, then it is the logic of illusion. Syllogistic forms.

But even pure logic, in terms of its content, is only a *canon* and analytical; it serves not as an *organon* but only as critique.

16: 33   **1603.** 1773–75. *V*, vii.

Logic is an *a priori* science of the [*crossed out*: general] pure laws of the understanding and reason in general, not of the particular use.[5]

Thus, as it is applied in **common cognition** and in the sciences **without distinction of object**.

It is a *canon* but not an *organon*, namely an *a priori* demonstrable rule for the judging (adjudication) but not the construction of our cognition.

(**abstracted** from experience but not **derived** from it)

On the objective [*crossed out:* laws of correct cognition in general with regard to possible cognition] and possible use of the understanding,

---

[a] The antecedent of the subject *Es* is unclear. Presumably, though, it refers to "Logic" from the previous sentence, although *Logik* is feminine and thus requires the pronoun *sie*.

not the subjective and actual (no empirical *principia*; psychology). I.e., on the conditions of possible perfected cognition, not actual cognition.

It is an *organon* not of *doctrine* (it produces nothing) but of *critique*. For it is **undetermined with regard to all objects**. Hence it is only an *organon* concerning the form of the understanding's cognition, not its content.

1604. 1773–75. *V*, viii.   16: 33

Logic cannot derive any *principia theoretica* (of adjudication) from experience, hence not from psychology, although it can thus derive *principia practica* (of construction).

Theoretical logic is merely the *canon* of adjudication and asserts the conditions under which the use of the understanding would be perfect.   16: 34 Practical logic should provide rules for the means by which to attain to these conditions; they are subjective and empirical.

1605. 1773–75. *V*, viii.   16: 34

Psychology can provide no *principia* other than those for the empirical use of the understanding, consequently those for clarifying the common understanding.

1606. 1773–75. *V*, viii.   16: 34

The *principia* of the *canon* must be *a priori*, but those of the *organon* can be *a posteriori*.

1608. 1773–75. *V*, viii.   16: 34

The *canon* of all formal use of the understanding is logic.

The *canon* of all real use of the understanding is transcendental philosophy.[6]

This real use is determined with regard to the object, when it pertains to experience, and undetermined, when it pertains to things in general. But because it therefore pertains to things insofar as they are given through experience, it is predetermining, in that it contains the conditions under which all appearances can be cognized in accordance with a rule. For here it is first necessary to bring every appearance under a title of the understanding: *realitas, substantia*.[7] This title always signi-   16: 35 fies a condition of apprehension in accordance with some moment of sensibility. The second thing is the function of the rule of apperception under which, etc.[8] This apprehension is the *general* ground for becoming conscious of appearance in its relation. Hence the rule of the consciousness of the conjugation (association) of sensation. This rule is merely the condition of time in which the appearance stands in relation, as 1. the *perpetuum (fixum)* in contrast to the variable, 2. the consequence in every time, 3. the connection of everything into one time, thus the omnipresence of time.

16:35 **1609.** 1773–75. *V*, viii.

In every relation what is perceived is *a posteriori* unity; this is always connected with *a priori* unity, i.e., what is determined *a posteriori* is also determined *a priori* under the same conditions.

16:36 **1612.** 1773–75? 1775–77? *V*, ix.

An *a priori* science is called a doctrine, not a discipline.

1. Logic is a science of reason concerning both matter and form. As far as the latter is concerned, as a *canon* of reason it has clear *principia a priori* and not empirical principles, thus it borrows nothing from psychology. It is **abstracted** from the **empirical** use of the understanding, but not **derived** from it. This is theoretical logic.

2. Not subjective laws: how one thinks; but objective laws: how one should think.

3. Not of particular and determinate, but of general use. Precisely because it is not determined with respect to any object it is therefore a *principium* only of **adjudication**, not of the **construction** of cognition, a *canon* and not an *organon*. General logic has no **practical** part (except for the critique of common reason). The *canon* of reason in general is analytic; the *organon* of the use of the understanding **in general** would be dialectic (where without distinction of content one produces merely the form of understanding and reason, which can be given true as well as false cognitions, and therefore [*breaks off*])

The *organon* of the sciences can only be found in accordance with acquaintance with their nature, object, and sources of cognition.

II.
NOTES TO THE BODY OF MEIER'S *AUSZUG AUS DER VERNUNFTLEHRE*

16:76 **1676.** 1753–59. *V*, 4, §§10, 11.[9]

Repraesentatio est determinatio mentis (interna), quatenus ad res quasdam
16:77 *ab ipsa (nempe repraesentatione) diversas refertur.*[a] It is that determination of the soul that is related to other things.[10] But I call it related if its constitution is suitable to the constitution of the outer things, *sive si rebus externis conformis est.*[b]

---

[a] representation is the (internal) determination of the mind insofar as it refers to something as it were outside of it (not a representation).
[b] or if it is in conformity to the external things

34

The author purports that the representation of a thing that is to be found in the soul has the same sort of similarity with the represented thing as a painting has with the depicted object. But I assert that this is false, and prove it thus. When I see a house, then according to this opinion there is a depiction of the house in my soul which is similar to the represented house. Now since similar things differ only with regard to their magnitude, a tiny house is depicted in my soul which, however small it is, must still occupy some space – which is impossible. Likewise, when I feel the vibration of the air, the sensation of which I call sound, I can well say that [crossed out: in the substance] within my soul there is also such a vibration – but what could be vibrating there [?] We can prove the same thing from experiences. Can somebody who tastes something sour say that his representation depicts for him pointed and cone-shaped particles of salt, which stimulate his gustatory nerves? Yet with a microscope one sees that they are really thus constituted. Etc.

What is it then in the representation that is in agreement with the represented things? Since the representation borrows its ground from the represented thing, it agrees with the latter in that it is composed out of its partial concepts in the same way that the whole represented thing is composed out of its parts. E.g., one can say that the notes of a musical piece are a representation of the harmonic combination of the tones – not as if a note were similar to a tone, but because the notes have a combination among themselves like that of the tones themselves. Yet if the soul attends to itself, then it still seems to observe that a representation within it presents itself in the same way as a painting that it sees with its eyes. This cannot be otherwise. A painting is made to resemble the object; just as the object moves us, so does the painting move us, and this idea or determination of the soul, which is produced by the painting, can be produced by means of the imagination; therefore it must [crossed out: be related to the object] just as [breaks off]

16: 78

1683. 1769? 1770–71? 1773–77? 1764–68?? *V* 4, at §10.[11]   16: 81

(*Later addition*:

Sensation,	*relata ad objectum*,	*objectivum*,	*intuitus*)
repraesentatio,	*perceptio*,	*cognitio*,	*conceptus*,

(*Later addition*:

to represent something,	to represent something to oneself,	*conscius*,	*cogitatio*

conceptus non empiricus)   16: 82
notio, (*later addition: idea**
Exemplary idea, *dessein*,
cognitio exemplaris pertains to an aim)

*(Later addition: we have no idea of plants or of the entirety of creatures.)

16:247 **2131.** 1772–75? 1771–72? *V*, 23.[12]

In logic one can expound not the characteristic of the cognition of the understanding in general, but rather the actions of the understanding in general in judging. I.e., it is merely analytical. A cognition can be logically correct, yet still not therefore be true; thus where nothing more than logical form exists to act as a guarantee, there cognition is only dialectical.[13]

16:247 **2132.** 1772–75? (1771–72?) *V*, 23.

Agreement with an object, without there being something determined with regard to this object, cannot be provided, i.e., cannot determine anything with regard to the object. Thus, with regard to cognition in general, logic is merely analytical.

16:247 **2133.** 1772–75 (1771–72?) *V*, 23.

Characteristics of truth in general cannot be provided, because these must always be related to objects, but only the conditions of cognition in the understanding in general, i.e., of judgments in general, that they do not contradict themselves. (I.e., the understanding cannot itself determine generally whether it has judged in accordance with its laws, but that must be determined *in casu*[a] by the faculty of judgment.)

16:250 **2142.** 1773–78? (1770–71?) *V*, 23.

Error and truth exist only in judgments (*later addition*: namely, if they are thought of as **propositions**. The geometer says: Assume that in a Δ there is more than an *angulus rectus*.)

Judgments are actions of the understanding and reason.

Truth is the correspondence of the understanding and reason.

The understanding by itself does not err* (*later addition*: because it cannot conflict with its own laws). Neither do the senses (*later addition*: because they do not make any judgments). The grounds of error must lie in other powers. Pure reason does not err. Human understanding, however, can have no cognition without intuition that is sensible. (*Later addition*: In logic, sensibility is merely the subjective element of cognition, insofar as it does not agree with the objective element, as hastiness, confusion, habit, miscalculation. Logic concerns itself only with the harmony of cognition with itself, in accordance with the *principio contradictionis* as well as *rationis*.)

*(It also does not judge by itself, i.e., independently; for in it are mixed all the conditions which submit it to some cognition or other. In human

---

[a] in the individual case

beings it is partly passive. Some things are supplied to it; others are held back. Subjective conditions. One must be aware of what one thinks by means of concepts; and this stems from the state of inner sense, whether its horizon is clear or clouded. Stimulus for the senses.

16:251

Thus sensibility is a power that is always required for judging; the understanding is the other; both make the skewed movement through the diagonal, in which there is something true as well as something false.)

(Like good rules in calculation, but overlooked in practice.)

2147. 1773–78? (1770–71?) *V*, 24.

16:252

Inessential marks of truth consist not in the agreement of reason with its own laws, be it according to internal or external marks, but in the agreement with another's reason. The latter produces no sign (*later addition*: proof), but rather the presumption of truth; thus others have a *votum consultativum*, not *decisivum*.[a] Therefore, the drive to communicate is combined with the thirst for knowledge because our own judgment must be rectified by another's point of view. Even reason which thinks about and attends to itself. Egoist and pluralist, in the logical sense; in contrast to it is timid reason which entrusts others with the decision about the truth; it is often also servile.

2155. 1776–78? (1778–1780s?) *V*, 23.

16:254

The matter of cognition is the object. Agreement with that is truth. Logic abstracts from the matter; consequently it provides no *criterium* of truth except for that without which cognition would not be cognition at all, i.e., the harmony of cognition with itself. This is the formal and propaedeutic *criterium* of truth (negative); the material *criterium* is the agreement of judgments with intuitions, thus not formal tautology and identity.

The material *criterium* of truth should pertain to the difference among objects, consequently not abstract from these. There can therefore be a general formal but not a material *criterium* (neither generally sufficient nor generally necessary) of truth.

It is absurd to demand a *criterium* of truth which would be sufficient for its determination in all judgments; for if it is to be general, it can determine nothing about truth with regard to content.

2161. 1776–78? (1790s?) *V*, 23, §§92, 93.

16:255

The material *criteria* of truth consist in the agreement of cognition with the representations that are immediately related to the object, thus in agreement with the intuitions and perceptions.

[a] an advisory vote, not a decisive one

Whether we may not distinguish reason from illusion, i.e., the subjective in judgment from what is objective, even without experiment with others, e.g., in religious beliefs?

16:256 **2162.** 1776–78? (1790–1804?) *V*, 23, §§93, 94.

In logic we can only state formal *criteria* of truth, i.e., the conditions of the agreement of cognition as cognition in general without reference to the object (as matter); these criteria are negative: namely, that one find no errors in the form. If one also speaks of cognition in general, nothing more than form can be at issue. (In transcendental logic the matter is determined and differentiated generally; hence criteria of truth but no *organon*.)

16:258 **2173.** 1776–78? (1778–89?) *V*, 24.

Logic can indeed provide us with general criteria for the correct use of the understanding; not, however, for the power of judgment, because it only provides rules, yet not simultaneously how one is to decide what belongs under them (the error of legislators who make laws suited to particular cases. *Jus certum*, mere *casus in terminis*[a]). The mark of the correct use of the power of judgment is external and consists in the assent of others who verify or reform ours. All conditions must be drawn into a rule, as in the case of the mathematician, in order to determine the faculty of judgment. In *jure*[b] this is of no concern because the most insignificant circumstances provide rights and obligations. Therefore, jurists cite the *sententias* of other *juris consultorum*.[c]

16:258 **2174.** 1780–89? (1776–79?) *V*, 24.

Logical judging of truth and falsity (in itself for the understanding in general). 1. From cognition in itself; 2. connection with other cognition: a. with grounds, b. with consequences. Here logic considers only formal rules. The external mark of truth is the understanding of others, thus not internally but relatively true.

16:259 **2176.** 1780–89? (1776–79?) *V*, 24.

The internal (logical) criteria of truth. 1. Possibility as problematic judgments; 2. that they are grounded as assertoric judgments; 3. that it must be judged necessarily so and not otherwise, i.e., the contrary is false, for apodictic judgments. The external mark of truth (after one has previously judged for oneself) is, in order to avoid deception through illusion, a judgment that agrees with someone else's.

---

[a] Law is certain, a mere case of explication.
[b] jurisprudence
[c] the opinions of other jurists

2177. 1780–89? (1776–79?) *V*, 24. 16: 259

A universal material *criterium* of truth is impossible because it would have to contain the agreement of cognition with the object regardless of the difference among the objects. But objective truth just consists in the distinction of the object. A universal *criterium* of truth can thus only be formal, i.e., consist in the logical marks of the agreement of cognition with the general laws of the understanding and of reason, i.e., of the agreement of cognition with itself. But this is not sufficient for objective truth. *Conditio sine qua non.* Mere agreement of cognition with itself as a sufficient *criterium* produces dialectic.

2244. 1760–64? 1764–68? 1769? *V*, 27, at §109.[14] 16: 283

We can only become aware of error through our understanding, and thus we can err only when the understanding acts contrary to its own laws. This, however, is impossible. No force of nature can act contrary to its own laws if it acts alone. But just as bodies in empty space indeed 16: 284
fall in accordance with the laws of gravity or describe perfect parabolas but deviate from this rule on account of air resistance: so other activities of the soul, such as stimulus, imagination, *etc.*, are connected with the judgments of the understanding, and one errs if one takes this mixed effect to be a judgment of the understanding. E.g., we have a propensity to compare concepts *qua identitatem et diversitatem*, which is mother-wit, but also a propensity to combine them positively or negatively, which is the understanding; the one action mixes with the other. The imagination combines formerly connected concepts; hence imitation as well.

Matters are the same with the moral element in actions. We do what we disapprove of. Only here there is this difference: here the disapproval can coexist with the action; there, however, it can only follow upon the perverted judgment.

2246. 1769–70? 1771? *V*, 27. 16: 284

If we had a pure reason and pure understanding, we would never err; and if we had a pure will (without inclination), we would never sin.

2269. 1780–89? 1776–79? *V*, 28.[15] 16: 292

One does not turn directly from error toward truth, but first to consciousness of one's ignorance and suspension of judgment. One is made wary by experience, but does not become more insightful from this alone.

Crude mistake: that which demonstrates ignorance in common cognition (of the *sensus communis* or of science) or mistake in the face of common attention. Tactless mistake: that for which nothing, not even 16: 293
illusion, serves as an excuse. Dangerous mistake: that which draws many other mistakes, chiefly practical ones, in its wake. (*Later addition*: Consequence in *ius*.)

Participating in the shortcomings (*homo sum* etc., etc. Chremes)[a] of universal human reason. Leniency in the judging of the same.

Bearable mistake. Difficult to avoid. Way of thinking: problematic, not judging decisively. (*Later addition*: Asserting irrevocably.)

(*Later addition*: Orienting oneself in thought (for popular writing).)

Touchstone

The external mark of error is* the incompatibility of other judgments with our own. This is a hint to investigate our procedure, not to reject it. (*Later addition*: Even where we have our own experience, we are still to seek counsel in the experience of others, but not in the case of mere truths of reason, except with regard to application.) One can be correct about the matter and incorrect about the manner, i.e., the exposition. General illusion is the greatest obstacle to the truth, and he who errs with the great crowd relates to common human understanding. This in itself is also a touchstone for discovering the mistakes of artificial use. Test, counter-test. (*Later addition*: Orientation by means of common understanding.)

*(*Later addition*: The internal mark: that judgments do not follow from the same principles. Logical danger.)

16:294 **2271.** 1790–1804. *V*, 28.

To distinguish the subjective from the objective determining ground of judgment requires not only the judgment of others, but also the comparison of our judgment with other truths as grounds or consequences.

16:294 **2272.** 1790–1804. *V*, 28.

The external, non-logical mark of truth is comparison with the judgments of others; because that which is subjective is not present in all others in the same way, illusion can thus be uncovered thereby. *Citatio autorum*. Jurists.

16:297
16:298 **2279.** 1770–78. *V*, 29, at §115.[16]

That in a thing which constitutes part of the cognition of it, *cognition partialis*, is the mark. We cognize things only through marks.

16:298 **2280.** 1770–1780s. *V*, 29.

That which is considered to belong like a part to the whole (possible) representation of a thing is called a mark.

---

[a] Presumably a reference to the famous saying "I am human, nothing human is alien to me," spoken by the character Chremes in Terence, *Heautontimorumenos* ("The Self-Tormenter"), I, 1, 25.

2281. 1780s? 1770–79?? *V*, 29.   16: 298

We cognize things only through marks; that is, to cognize[a] comes precisely from to be acquainted.[b] For the understanding is a faculty for thinking, i.e., for cognizing discursively through concepts; but concepts are marks for general use.

Intuition comes from the senses; through marks the understanding dissolves intuitions and puts them together. Reason subsequently goes from that which the marks contain to that which the whole concept contains.

2282. 1780s? 1770–79?? *V*, 29.   16: 298

A mark is not always a concept of a thing, but often only of part of a thing. E.g., the hand is a mark of a human; but having hands is only this mark as a concept of a human. Thus the partial concept serves by means of its generality to bring the thing under a ground of differentiation even without comparison.

A partial representation as a ground of cognition for the whole representation is a mark.

2283. 1780s? 1770–79?? *V*, 29.   16: 299

The partial concept as the ground of cognition of the whole representation is the mark. The ground of cognition is of twofold use, either internal, for derivation, or external, for comparison. This either of identity or diversity.

2286. 1780s. *V*, 29.   16: 299

A mark is a partial representation, which as such is a ground of cognition. It is either intuitive (synthetic part): a part of the intuition, or   16: 300
discursive: a part of the concept, which is an analytical ground of cognition. *vel intuitus vel conceptus partialis*.

2287. 1790s. *V*, 29.   16: 300

All of our concepts are marks and all thinking is representation by means of them.

We talk here only of marks as concepts.

2288. 1790s? 1776–78?? *V*, 29.   16: 300

Human cognition is discursive on the side of the understanding, i.e., it takes place by means of representations which make that which is common to several things into the ground of cognition, hence through marks as such.

---

[a] *erkennen*
[b] *kennen*

16:342 **2394.** 1769? 1769–70? 1764–66? *V*, 37, at §140.[17]

The following degrees are to be distinguished:

16:343 1. Representing something to oneself.

2. Knowing something. Representing with consciousness. (*Later addition*: representing to oneself with consciousness. [*Crossed out*: perceive] *percipere*. *Apprehendere* [*crossed out*: grasp]: the beginning of *percipere*.)

3. Being acquainted with something. Distinguishing from others in this way in comparison.

4. Understanding something. (*Later addition*: What I **am acquainted with** and **understand**, that I **cognize**. Being able to expound and communicate to others.) Cognizing something through the understanding. (*Later addition: Concipere*: cognizing through a concept. *Intelligere*: through a judgment.)

(*Later addition*: Knowing – opining.)

5. Having insight into something. (*Later addition: Perspicere*.) Cognizing through reason. (*Later addition*: Understanding something *a priori*. Through grounds: either possible or even actual ones.)

6. *Comprehending something. Having insight sufficient for some aim. (*Later addition*: Even being able to make. Having insight entirely through reason.)

*(*Later addition*: I comprehend what I can determine (relatively) *a priori*, and thus also would have cognized from *datis* or would have been able to cognize, if it were not given, e.g., an eclipse of the moon, but not warmth from friction. The rest is called having insight into explanations.)

16:344 One can explain something that experience provides, i.e., make a concept of its possibility without having any insight into it, i.e., cognize *a priori* its necessity, and consequently that the object will be so. E.g., one explains the dissolution of salt in water by means of the same attractive force whereby water causes wetness; but one would not be able to say it in advance, if experience had not shown that a piece of salt can be entirely dispersed in a fluid in this way. We have insight into nothing except what we can produce.

Hypothesis is sufficient for explanation (principle of possibility), – insight – certainty of the ground.)

16:373 **2450.** 1764–68? 1769–70? (1772–75?) *V*, 43, at §157.[18]

(*Later addition*:

To suppose	To expect)	
To hold opinions,	To believe,	To know
To take something to be true	To wager	To swear

(*Later addition*: Having more grounds on one side than on the other

| To suppose | To assume | To assert) |

Knowledge and belief are decided, opinion is undecided.

Certainty is the subjective *completudo* of affirming something to be true.

To believe: subjective necessity of affirming something to be true; that affirming of something to be true which determines the truth from grounds (which are communicable) that are independent of the constitution of the subject is (*later addition*: logically) objectively necessary (*later addition*: adequate).

To belief there belongs not only subjective *sufficientia* but also subjective necessity.

He who holds opinions reserves for himself the retraction of his judgment. God knows this better. *Salvis melioribus,*[a] in the case of him who believes: not with inalterability, but with the freedom of everyone else.

A consciously inadequate affirmation of something as true is opinion. An adequate affirmation of something as true is conviction. If it is (practically) subjectively necessary: believing (wagering); if it is (logically) objectively necessary: knowing (swearing).

In speculative philosophical cognition one can indeed hold opinions, but not believe. In mathematical cognition one can neither hold opinions nor believe, but only know. In empirical or historical cognition, all three. In practical cognition, only belief.

2451. 1764–68? 1769–70? (1772–75?) *V*, 43, opposite §§157, 158.　　16: 374

Practical belief is decided and completely certain, so that its affirmation of something as true is complete *in sensu practico* and cannot receive any supplement even through the grandest grounds of speculation.

To hold an opinion is contradistinguished not from believing but from knowing.

Believing is more properly opposed to knowing, as only historical cognition is opposed to rational cognition; for* we also say of historical cognitions, e.g., where Madrid is, that we know it, although we have it on the basis of the accounts of others.

In the case of actions in conformity with believing everything happens honorably, but not in the case of making mistakes, protesting, and complaining, except when one swears that one sincerely believes this.　　16: 375

The difference in affirming something to be true really seems to be merely practical, namely, how much one could stake on it.

*The subjectively adequate affirmation of something as true which is at the same time objective is conviction; if it is not: persuasion. (*Later addition*: Lottery prize.)

---

[a] saving the better ones

16: 374

16:375 **2452.** 1769? 1769–70? (1764–68?) *V*, 43, opposite §156.
If the grounds for affirming something to be true are only a part of a sufficient ground, then it is called probability.
If the affirmation of something as true is considered only *subiective* and is thus not universally valid, then it is called plausibility.
If the cognition is plausibly certain, then it is called persuasion.
If the objective certainty is intuitive, then it is called evidence.

16:375 **2454.** 1769–70? 1771–75? *V*, 44, opposite §162.
(*Later addition*: All conviction is either logical (the object is certain) or (practical: belief versus knowledge) moral (I am certain).)
Certainty is either empirical* or rational (*later addition*: of common understanding or speculative reason.)
16:376 Rational certainty is either apodictic (*later addition*: knowledge) (speculative) or (*later addition*: rational faith) moral (practical).**
Apodictic certainty is mathematical or philosophical; the former is intuitive, the latter discursive.
*(*Later addition*: One can also know, and not merely believe, historically; e.g., geography; a good many things, however, pass from this into belief.
**(*Later addition*: Consequently, that is morally certain the denial of which is prohibited by morality.* Something can be morally certain only for the jury.)
*(Moral certainty is, subjectively, the greatest among all forms of certainty, and if (something according to legal precept) a judge can be juridically certain that someone is the debtor, he is not yet for that reason morally certain, that is, he cannot assert it with the most painstaking conscientiousness. Moral certainty holds, however, only for someone who should do something; he can and must presuppose it in accordance with all conscientiousness. But for this reason he cannot objectively assert it before others in all conscientiousness. The *argumentum a tuto* is not conscientious.
Moral certainty is not objective, i.e., a thing is certain, but rather objective: I am, etc.)

16:379 **2460.** 1773–75? (1770–71?) (1769?) (1764–68?) 1776–78?? *V*, 43, at conclusion of §157.
All certainty finally resolves itself into a sensible certainty.
Practical certainty* is firm belief.
1. Apodictic certainty (*later addition*: logically adequate. Belief: practical. 2. Empirical certainty.)
*Either from grounds without which no *praxis* would take place, or: whose denial would contradict universal practical laws.

(*Later addition*: Moral certainty does not refer to cognition objectively but to right and wrong; it is negative.)

2462. 1773–75? (1770–71?) (1769?) (1764–68?) 1776–78?? *V*, 43.　　16: 380

Belief is a provisional assumption of a cognition.

One must assume something even though one does not know it for certain because of the usefulness of presuppositions in finally confirming something by means of their consequences. What one has first believed, one knows afterwards. Worthy of being assumed.

The complete affirmation of something as true in accordance with practical laws (not from practical grounds) is belief. I believe that America exists (not: I know it from logical grounds); for if I were not yet willing to assume it on such testimony, what would I then be willing to assume as regards my actions or decisions[?] Here the grounds are, to be sure, merely theoretical, but if they are considered on analogy with practical grounds, then they are adequate in accordance with practical laws. This assumption is then a complete resolve if it must be assumed in accordance with practically necessitating laws. E.g., I believe that there is another world. This belief would not be legitimate if it were based merely on reports. For then more grounds for its credibility would be required. Moral belief is that belief which is necessary in accordance with moral laws, either as a consequence or as a ground of morality. Here is a ground　　16: 381　which, by means of morals, determines for me what I should assume.

With practical laws in general it is like this: if I were not willing to assume this, then I would not be able to do anything prudent by means of such a way of judging. I do not need to answer for my opinion (unless someone disagrees with the correctness of my grounds), for I have assumed it. What I believe, however, I must answer for.

One can indeed carry out an investigation of a *facti*[a] on the basis of a mere opinion, but an accusation requires the belief that the other person is guilty. In chemistry, propositions which are believed.

(*Later addition: Quod dubitas, ne feceris.*[b] Moral certainty.)

2470. 1776–78? (1775–77?) *V*, 43.[19]　　16: 383

Historical [*crossed out*: affirmation] belief is only opinion; for otherwise we can also know historically. Moral certainty is what I can assert in all conscientiousness. One can even believe mathematical propositions, but not philosophical ones. Practical belief rests on the subjective grounds of willing; it can possess practical adequacy for all human beings, but the affirmation of it as true is, of course, logically inadequate if I abstract

---

[a] in this context, a deed
[b] "What you doubt may not be done by you." From Pliny, *Epist.* I, 18,5: see **2504.**

from all subjective grounds. If I considered the human being solely in terms of his understanding and as practically indifferent, then the proof of God's existence and the other world is not speculatively sufficient. But he has an interest here, and with regard to this sees himself *in absurdo practico* if he does not assume it. The conviction is not less but rather greater in the practical sense, but of another kind.

16: 384   Stories are not the proper objects of belief, for they are knowledge. Nor are truths of reason (one cannot hold opinions regarding them); but the presupposition* of theoretical conditions for moral use is [the proper object of belief].

    *Which can only be made subjectively adequate, not objectively clear. E.g., the perpetrator of a crime.

16: 395   **2503.** 1790s. *V*, 45.

    Belief – I would **gladly** believe what I wish for, if only I had a reason for it. (*Later addition*: but it is not on that account **easy**, rather I seek to **convince** myself that I can hope for that which is good from a practically necessary point of view.) – If, however, it is a duty to wish for something (for there is no duty to believe), then I am right to believe it if I can. – If, however, I cannot believe it (e.g., a future life), then I have reason

16: 396 enough to act as if such a thing were the case. – Thus there is a reason that is adequate from a practical point of view, although the theoretical reason is inadequate for me; and, as concerns the latter, I may well doubt it.

16: 418   **2564.** 1764–68? 1769? *V*, 46, opposite the beginning of §170.[20]

    Because the universal validity of our judgments for reason in everyone is a sign of objective truth, there follows (*later addition*: that the judgment of others is an external *criterium* of truth) the necessity of a participatory reason, which is opposed to egoism; likewise, the right to make one's judgments known, and the love of honor as the incentive of the sciences. A participatory understanding and a participatory will are always good; healthy reason is always bound up with probity, at least the converse.

    A provisional judgment for the advantage of others consists in the fact that if others obviously seem to have erred, one prefers to believe that one does not understand them.

    (*Later addition*: A person's prejudice: his own or someone else's.* Reputation is valid only in that which is historical. Truth must be valid anonymously. One must not ask whether it is begotten by noble parents.)

    * (*Later addition: Egoism*: the prejudice of indifference toward the judgment of others as one of the *criterii* of the truth of our judgment.

16: 419   First, thinking from one's own point of view. Thinking from everyone else's point of view. Thus testing one's judgment on others.)[21]

2565. 1764–68? 1769–70? (1771–1772?) *V*, 46.   16:419

Because we find it neccesary to instruct others about our judgments, we must not merely be communicative but also participatory; and the drive to communication which directs our understanding is present in us only so that we should verify our own judgments by means of those of others.

What has survived from antiquity must be good, just like the Russians who can survive their harsh upbringing. (*Later addition*: But the deficiencies have also disappeared.

The ancients have already invented everything.

The harm that great men have done by means of their greatness. It is not good to make oneself into an idol or to think a man great.

Envy of others makes a man excessively great. The spirit of imitation dies out. Reform becomes difficult.)

2566. 1769–76. *V*, 46.   16:419

The communicative inclination of reason is appropriate only on the condition that it is at the same time combined with the participatory one. Others are neither pupils nor judges, but rather colleagues in the great council of human reason and have a *votum consultativum*; and *unanimitas*   16:420
votorum est pupilla libertatis. Liberum veto.[a]

2667. 1790s. *V*, 50, at §§178–80.[22]   16:459

Dogmatism is the [*crossed out*: principle] prejudice* of being able to do without the critique of the faculty of reason itself in regard to rational cognitions (on account of its success), e.g., mathematics and physics – but not in metaphysics or pure rational cognition from concepts. – Skepticism: the prejudice of trusting no rational cognition on account of failure.

*(The adequacy of reason with regard to all of its use even without needing a critique of its own capacity. – This has produced skepticism. – Criticism is confidence in oneself restricted to the condition of the self-knowledge of reason.)

2675. 1753–59. *V*, 51, opposite §182.[23]   16:463

Hypotheses are indispensable. 1. They are experiments of the under-standing. One must approach many a truth along the path of probability. 2. They are encountered everywhere. E.g., dividing. 3. They present the truth either by means of manifold agreement, e.g., hypotheses about the movement of the earth, or by showing which grounds one does not have to assume, e.g., gravity. 4. They encourage the understanding thanks to the prize of invention.

---

[a] a consultative vote; the unanimity of votes is the ward of liberty. Free veto.

Hypothesis subsidiaria. If in the application of a hypothesis or showing agreement with the *phaenomenis* yet another presents itself. The weaknesses of probability.

16:465 **2678.** 1764–68? 1769? (1771?) 1773–75??? *V*, 51.

A hypothesis is an opinion about the truth of a ground based on its adequacy for consequences; if the impossibility of all other grounds is proven (this happens when all of the consequences of the assumed ground agree with the appearance), then it becomes a certainty; if that which is explained through its consequences can also be independently proven *a priori*, then the hypothesis is confirmed. (*Later addition*: I.e., if the matter of the ground is independently certain, or even the universal form.

The unity from the unity of the ground)

The **fruitfulness** of a hypothesis: if further true consequences follow from it. Simplicity. That it not be arbitrarily *a priori*.

(*Later addition*: An opinion as the ground of a system is a hypothesis.)

Some *hypotheses* are necessary, such as: there is another world; some are contingent.

16:466 The absolutely necessary *hypothesis* is that of the necessary being. One cannot prove it *a priori*.

Freedom is a necessary *hypothesis*, without which practical propositions would not be possible. There is a God, another world: a moral *hypothesis*.

There are subjectively necessary *hypotheses* of the possibility of cognition by means of reason, e.g., that everything has a beginning.

The possibility of a hypothesis must be certain. Rational *hypotheses* are not allowed.

16:480 **2714.** 1773–76? 1770–71?? 1764–68?? 1776–79?? *V*, 53, at §189.[24]

(*Later addition*: All certainty is either theoretical or practical;* the former is either [*crossed out*: mathematically certain] empirical or rational certainty [*crossed out*: the latter apodictic].)

16:481 Empirical or apodictic, and the latter is intuitive or discursive.**

(*Later addition*: I am morally certain about what it is necessary to assume as true in accordance with my conscience. E.g., the deed of a criminal who admits it.)

An apodictic,[a]

Mathematical proof, which possesses evidence.

Hypotheses cannot be proven mathematically.

---

[a] According to Adickes, this phrase stands under "or apodictic, and the latter" from two paragraphs above.

*(Practical certainty is also based on either empirical or rational laws of the will;[a] the former: of prudence, the latter: of morality and of duty. I am morally certain if I know that assuming something to be true and acting in accordance with it correspond to my duty in its entirety.

(*Later addition*: **Practical certainty is either **pragmatic** in accordance with rules of prudence (in which case it is merely a hypothetically necessary rule, as in games of chance) or moral in accordance with principles of morality (in which case the rules are absolutely necessary, and the **hypothesis of obeying them** *in concreto* is thereby practically certain, an article of faith for reason). Of the presumed moral certainty of the existence of bodies.)

2716. 1780–89. *V*, 53, §189.   16:482

That is morally certain which is taken to be true on the basis of principles that are inseparable from the maxims of duty.

One cannot say of any cognition in relation to an object that it is morally certain, but can only say of one's belief in relation to us that it possesses moral certainty. I find myself obliged to think in this fashion.[25]

Moral certainty is the greatest certainty.

2743. 1780–89? (1776–79?) *V*, 57, at §201.[26]   16:494

I can no doubt be immediately certain of my perception, but not of experience, i.e., of the objective validity of judgments from perception; to experience belongs frequent comparison in order to distinguish what   16:495 the understanding does from what is sensible. And often agreement with the judgment of others as well.

2766. 1780s? (1776–79?) *V*, 58, at §206.[27]   16:501

Matters of faith (*a priori*) are (*later addition*: true propositions which yet do not lie in any experience) those with regard to which one can merely not know anything but also cannot opine anything and with   16:502 regard to which one cannot even assert probability, but only that it is not contradictory to think of an object for them. The rest is a free (logical) affirmation of them as true, which is necessarily only from a practical point of view, given *a priori*.

2770. 1780s? (1776–79?) *V*, 58, at §206.   16:502

He is without moral faith who does not assume that which it is to be sure impossible to know but which it is morally necessary to assume.

Rational faith is the cognition of the necessity of a hypothesis of   16:503 reason, without which the absolutely necessary practical laws would

[a] According to Adickes, Kant wrote *stimmt* and *mit* over *gründet* ("is . . . based on") and *auf* ("with"), respectively. These additions produce the following sentence: "Practical certainty agrees with either empirical or rational laws of the will."

be entirely nugatory. It is therefore a necessary hypothesis of practical reason.

2773. 1780s. *V*, 58, at §206.

Faithful:* he who acts on *a priori* belief;** he is opposed to the slave of the senses.

*(theoretical: he who is capable of a moral rational faith, where no knowledge is possible.)

**(Morality is such that he who is not capable of acting merely from the belief that virtue and good conduct will someday receive their good consequences, but for whom knowledge of that is necessary, does not act from moral principles. In a moral faith mere possibility is sufficient as an objective ground. For theoretical belief more is required, and there one cannot determine the standard.)

2788. 1764–68? (1769?) (1760–64?) *V*, 61, §§214, 215.[28]
Fides est vel asserti,
vel promissi,
vel speculativa; posterior si sit absque promisso, est moralis.[a]

Belief is actually a practical *hypothesis* [*crossed out:* for moving our will with regard to] (*later addition:* which is connected in a necessary fashion with) what is cognized in and for itself as certainly good.

One does not say: I know that the human race has a beginning, but rather: I believe it. Therefore, it is a *hypothesis*, under which alone I can understand its existence by means of reason, although I cannot understand it itself by means of reason. The beginning of the world and its infinite duration are equally unintelligible; the former, however, completes my cognition through reason, the latter does not. (*Later addition:* The former *hypothesis* is a necessary *hypothesis* of reason.)

Thus I believe every necessary *hypothesin*. This means: **assuming** something even if it is an arbitrary affirmation; one does not assume mathematical propositions.

Of propositions of reason, which are believed. Are more than opinions. One cannot do without them.

2789. 1780s? (1776–79?) *V*, 61, §215.[29]

In knowing and believing the subjectively inalterable affirmation of something as true is believing, not having an opinion.

There are properly speaking not 3 but 2 sources of cognition:* experience and reason. 1. The former, either one's own experience or that

---

[a] Belief is either to be asserted, to be promised, or speculative; if it would be the latter without a promise, it is moral.

communicated by others. 2. Reason: either knowing or believing, i.e., either from speculative or practical reason. Rational belief.

(*Later addition*: N.B. Affirming something to be true differs either in   16:512
the sources or in the manner and degree. In the latter case it is knowing or believing. Historical belief is not a special principle of cognition, but belongs to experience. Knowing belongs to the theoretical cognition of reason, believing to the practical.)

*(*Later addition*: Both can be a knowing. If one calls them believing, one acknowledges them to be uncertain, and in this case it is not allowed on the basis of such a belief to venture something that would be wrong if this cognition is in error. E.g., forceful conversion.)

2790. 1790–1804. *V*, 61, §215.   16:512

(*Later addition*: Rational-) belief (as not a source of cognition) is a hypothesis insofar as it is held to be necessary from a practical point of view. There are thus pragmatic and moral beliefs. The latter is pure rational belief – it contributes nothing to cognition.

2793. 1790–1804. *V*, 62.   16:513

Belief is not a particular source of cognition. It is a way of consciously affirming something to be true in an incomplete fashion; and if it is considered as restricted to a particular kind of object (which does not belong to belief alone), it distinguishes itself from opinion not by degree but rather by the relation which it has, as cognition, to acting. Thus, e.g., a merchant, in order to make a deal, needs not merely to be of the opinion that there will be something to be gained thereby, but also to believe it, i.e., his opinion must be sufficient for an undertaking into the unknown. – Now we have theoretical cognitions (of that which is sensible), in which we can reach certainty; and with regard to everything that we can call human cognition, the latter must be possible. We must have the same sort of certain cognition in practical laws, and entirely *a priori*; but these laws are based on a supersensible principle (freedom), indeed **in ourselves**, as a principle of practical reason. This practical reason, however, is a causality with regard to an equally supersensible object: the highest good, which is not possible in the sensible world by means of our resources; nevertheless, nature, as the object of our theoretical reason, must agree with it, for it should be met with in the   16:514
sensible world as the result (effect) of this idea. We should thus act in order to make this end real. In the sensible world also we find traces of an artistic wisdom, and now we believe that the cause of the world works toward the highest good in accordance with moral wisdom; and this is taking something to be true in a way that is sufficient for acting, i.e., a belief. – Now we require this not for acting in accordance with moral laws, for they are given by practical reason alone; but we require

the assumption of a highest wisdom for the object of our moral will, toward which, out of the mere rightfulness of our actions, we cannot avoid directing our purposes. Although this would not be, objectively, a necessary relation to our power of choice, the highest good is still subjectively necessary as the object of a good (even human) will, and the belief in its attainability is necessarily presupposed with it.[30]

There is no middle way between acquiring a cognition by means of experience (*a posteriori*) or by means of reason (*a priori*). There is, however, a middle way between the cognition of an object and the mere presupposition of its possibility, namely, an empirical or rational ground, the latter, namely, an assumption in relation to a necessary extension of the field of possible objects beyond those the cognition of which is possible for us. This necessity exists only where the object is cognized as practical and as practically necessary by means of reason; for assuming something for the purpose of the mere extension of theoretical cognition is always contingent. This practically necessary presupposition of an object is that of the possibility of the highest good as the object of the power of choice, and hence also that of the condition of this possibility (God, freedom, and immortality). This is a subjective necessity of assuming the reality of the object for the sake of the necessary determination of the will. This is the *casus extraordinarius*, without which practical reason cannot sustain itself with regard to its necessary end, and here the *favor necessitatis*[a] comes in useful for reason in its own judgment. It cannot obtain the object logically, but it can only oppose itself to everything that hinders it in the use of this idea, which belongs to it practically.

16:515   This belief is the necessity of assuming the objective reality of a concept of the highest good, i.e., the possibility of its object as the *a priori* necessary object of the power of choice. If we look merely to actions, we do not require this belief. If, however, we wish to extend ourselves through our actions to the possession of the end that is thereby possible, we must assume that this end is thoroughly possible. – Thus I can only say: I see myself necessitated by my end, in accordance with the laws of freedom, to assume as possible a highest good in the world; but I cannot necessitate others by means of these grounds (the belief is free).

16:515   **2794.** 1790–1804. *V*, 62.

Rational belief can never lead to theoretical cognition, for in that case the objectively insufficient affirmation of something as true is mere opinion. It is merely a presupposition of reason from a subjective but absolutely necessary practical point of view. The disposition to the moral laws leads to an object of the power of choice determinable by pure reason. The assumption of the feasibility of this object and thus also of

---

[a] the favor of necessity

the reality of its cause is a moral belief, which is necessarily affirming something to be true freely and in a moral respect, as the fulfillment of one's ends.

2835. 1773–77? (1770–71?) (1769?) *V*, 69, at §249.[31]   16:536

	with consciousness	(*later addition: intuitus*)
repraesentationes	*perceptiones*	*conceptus**
(*later addition:*	of that which is given,	*forma logica*
	[*crossed out*: *perceptio*] *repraesentatio*	
	a posteriori)	

(*later addition: repraesentatio a priori:*   16:537
   vel notio vel idea)
   notiones   *ideae*

                                vel intuitivus
(*later addition: communis   singularis* <
                                 vel [*crossed out: discursivus*]
                                 cogitativus)

  * (*later addition: Cognitio per conceptus est cogitatio, praesertim per conceptus a priori.*)[a]

Idea est conceptus archetypus, contains the ground of the possibility of the object. It is the representation of the whole, through the limitation of which other representations come to be. It is a unique representation (of the object), and everything different is merely the limitation thereof; e.g., the *ens realissimum* is the transcendental idea.[32] It can never be thought *in concreto*, but precedes all judging *in concreto*. E.g., the idea of justice is the model idea in the judging of an Aristides.[33] Order, unity, and completeness are possible only as a result of an idea, thus also the world that is supposed to contain such things. Whether non-contingent things always presuppose an idea as their *principium*, which determines them among all that is possible. God is the inhering subject of all ideas as the *ens realissimum* and also the first cause of everything contingent.

Many sciences are expounded without first laying down the objective idea. Morals, metaphysics.

Drawing the parts on the basis of the whole.

The classification of kinds is, in our case, only nominal and originates in comparison; but it would be real if the idea were known to us. E.g., the classification of a horse and then what is altered in it in accordance with the difference in circumstances. There must be unity in the idea, namely, in that which contains everything in a certain kind of relations or things.

In all sciences, especially of reason, the idea of the science, its universal synopsis, its outline of the extent of all cognitions, and consequently the

---

[a] cognition by means of a concept is cogitation, especially by an *a priori* concept.

whole thereof, is the first thing that must be sought. This is architectonic.

16:538 The idea of humanity, of the republic. The idea of the science of justice. That of a happy life is lacking in most people.

The idea is contrasted to empirical concepts. A perfect republic is a mere idea. Many people have no idea of what they want; therefore, they act according to instinct and impression.

An idea cannot be obtained through composition. The whole is here prior to the part. Thus the idea of the best world, in which things are determined. This idea is a whole, which provides the parts by means of limitation; how that is possible is incomprehensible.

The genius has the idea rather than the component concepts. An imitative mind never attains to ideas. In philosophy everything depends on the idea.

16:538 **2836.** 1775–77? 1776–78? (1773–75?) (1772?) *V*, 69.

1. *Repraesentatio.*

2. *Perceptio* (with consciousness).

3. *Cognitio** (relation with consciousness to the object) (later addition: *perceptio obiective spectata*[a]).

*(*Later addition*: A perception that is merely related to the subject as its state is called sensation; that which is related to the object: cognition.)

4. *Cognitio est vel intuitus vel conceptus* (later addition: *repraesentatio discursiva*).[b] In the first case I am passive (receptivity), in the second case, active (spontaneity). *Intuitus* is individual, *conceptus* is *repraesentatio per notam communem.*[c] The understanding is here the formal cause of concepts.

5. *Notio* (*conceptus*** *intellectualis*): if the concept even with respect to its content arises from the understanding.

16:539 6. *Idea*: concept of reason, *cui nullus respondet intuitus,*[d] (later addition: which can have no object in experience,) if the concept of the understanding can have no object of experience *in concreto* and contains the archetype of the use of the understanding, e.g., the world-whole. The idea (later addition: can thus serve only a regulative (theoretical or practical), not a constitutive use) must be subjectively necessary for reason, not for the empirical use of the understanding, but for the *principio* of the thoroughgoing interconnection of our empirical use of the understanding.

An idea is a fundamental concept necessary in order either to complete objectively or to regard as unlimited the understanding's action of subordination.

---

[a] perception considered objectively
[b] cognition is either intuition or concept (discursive representation)
[c] representation by means of a common mark
[d] to which no intuition corresponds

**(*Conceptus est vel empiricus vel intellectualis.*)

(*Later addition: Conceptus* (*intuitus etiam*) *est vel empiricus* (empirical cognition is called experience) *vel purus, hic vel intellectualis* (*notio*) *vel rationalis* (*idea*).[a] [The latter] is a concept of reason, which, for reason in its completion, is subjectively necessary, but only in that which is intellectual. For in that which is sensible there is no completion.

a. Conceptus est cogitatio. b. Exhibitio cogitati est relatio conceptus ad intuitum. c. Exhibitio a priori: constructio (objective reality of the concept through presentation).[b])

2914. 1764–66? 1769? *V*, 74, at §§268–9.[34]   16:574

All empirical concepts, e.g., water, tree, etc., are representations of the understanding and can only be treated synthetically: I cannot analyze what is in them, but learn through experience what belongs to them. Only rational concepts, e.g., virtue, fate, etc., can be treated analytically.

2920. 1769–Ca. 1770–71? (1764–68?) *V*, 74.   16:576

Declaration.

Exposition (analytic*: either of the *a priori* concept or of its use).

Definition.**

Definition is either a precise declaration or an adequate exposition; the former occurs *in conceptibus factitiis*, the latter *datis*.[c] Exposition is either analytic: of what I already think in a universal concept (in the concept of the regular hexagon I do not think the equality of the sides   16:577 with the radii of the circle); [or] it is synthetic if I add what belongs to it; the latter is empirical.

*The given representation's sense which has been made distinct

**The determinate presentation of a——[*illegible*]

2925. Late 1769–1772? (1769?) *V*, 74.   16:578

Through declaration a distinct concept is made.

Through exposition a given concept is made distinct.

Through definition a distinct concept is made complete and precise.

2936. 1771–72? (1773–75?) 1776–78?? *V*, 75.   16:581

The definition of the empirical concept (*later addition:* what I think through the concept of experience) originates *per analysin* and is always nominal; the definition of the object that is to be real must always originate *per synthesin.*

---

[a] The concept (intuition as well) is either empirical . . . or pure; the latter is either intellectual (the notion) or rational (the idea).

[b] a. A concept is a thought. b. The exhibition of a thought is the relation of a concept to an intuition. c. *A priori* exhibition: construction.

[c] constructed concepts, given concepts

The definition of artifacts[a] is also arbitrary.

(*Later addition*: Instead of the definition of empirical concepts their exposition, and indeed empirical exposition, is necessary.)

The use of the definitions of empirical concepts is never to draw the consequences of the marks enumerated therein, but rather is synthetic. But the use of rational or arbitrary definitions is always analytic. – Definitions of empirical concepts are only for the understanding and in order to understand the word that one uses; and because the word contains much or little of the object, it is more an arbitrary determination. By contrast, if the concept is given by means of reason in the company of a word, its meaning is inalterable because no *synthesis* produces or can change it. I will not explicate water but rather describe it for the sake of the word. And then adduce the experiences of it.

16:584   **2947.** 1776–89. *V*, 74.

All definitions originate either from the *analysis* of a given concept or from the *synthesis* of a manufactured one. This synthesis is either one of exposition or construction. The manufactured concept is either made arbitrarily or from the given appearances. The concept is then not given, but rather the matter for it.

All concepts are either given or manufactured. The former are given either *a priori* or *a posteriori* (empirically); the latter are manufactured either *a priori* or empirically. The former *per analysin*, the latter *per synthesin*. In the former the concept is only made distinct; in the latter it is itself produced.

In the case of given concepts everything occurs by means of exposition, which is never complete. In the case of manufactured concepts, by means of aggregation. If the concept is manufactured from what is given *a posteriori* in the object, then it is called a synthetic concept of experience.

16:585   **2950.** 1776–89. *V*, 74.

Making any concept distinct is *explicatio*. Every distinct representation of manufactured* concepts is *declaratio*; of given concepts: *expositio*, of either empirically given concepts or concepts given *a priori*. The former, synthetic; the latter, analytic.

*(Synthetic. In their case declaration must precede the concept.)

16:585   **2951.** 1776–89. *V*, 74.

***Arbitrary** concepts must (*later addition*: become distinct by means of declaration, given concepts by means of exposition) be defined; *a priori* **concepts** may never be defined; **empirical concepts** can never be defined only described. *Definitio. Expositio. Descriptio.*

[a] *Sachen der Kunst*

*The *completudo* of *analysis* is never certain (*later addition*: that of an empirical concept is impossible. Thus only in mathematics and in hypotheses can one begin with definitions.)

Elementary propositions for definitions.

2962. 1776–89. V, 76.   16:587

I need a definition only if I want to predicate the *definitum* of some other certain concept. E.g., if the question is: What is virtue?, then I only need exposition; but if the question is whether holiness is virtue?, then I must know this concept completely. I do not want to know what   16:588 virtue is, but rather which properties belong to the concept of virtue, and in that case I must know everything.

2994. 1770–71? 1773–77? 1769?? V, 77, at §§280–4.[35]   16:606

All definitions are either of concepts (logical) or of things (real). Things are defined if they are only given through experience and the distinct, complete concept is sought from experience through observation.

Definitions of concepts are either [*crossed out*: of arbitrarily manufactured concepts or of given concepts] of concepts that are given *a priori* or *a posteriori*. A complete explication can be given of the former. The logical definition of the latter is only nominal. The real definition cannot be given at all. *A priori* concepts can be defined synthetically if they have   16:607 been given arbitrarily, or analytically if they have been given *a priori* but not arbitrarily. E.g., virtue, substance. *Definitiones* are either diagnostic or genetic.

(*Later addition*: All definitions are either synthetic or analytic propositions. The former, either of empirical or pure intuitions. The latter, arbitrary.)

2995. 1770–71? 1773–77? 1769?? V, 77.   16:607

Concepts that originate from the understanding can all be defined, whether they originate arbitrarily or through the nature of the understanding. Definitions of names are possible for all objects (some *positio arbitraria* often enters into them as well). Real definitions, which contain the possibility of the thing itself, are only to be found for concepts that are given through the understanding. [*Crossed out*: They are *per anal[ysis]* and are arbitrary] And here nominal and real definitions coincide; however, in the case of arbitrary concepts they are synthetically produced, in the case of the natural concepts of the understanding they are analytically produced; empirical concepts can only be nominally explicated. Fundamental concepts of the senses not at all. (It is lexicographical if I make distinct a word of a language in another language not through a synonymous one but through many.) Various concepts seem to be empirical but have originated through the under-standing. E.g., earth: one says of that no pure earth is to be found. Or it is to be only the abstraction of a concept. There are real definitions of that which is given or already thought (but not under the suitable names).

E.g., metaphysics.

Pedantry in explication: if one determines the signification of a word when it would not be mistaken for another in any event, or also if one forces the other to include all the marks when some suffice for the purpose.

16:610 **3004.** 1776–79? 1780–89?? *V*, 76.³⁶

Given things in nature, if they are brought under a common mark, stand, by means of this mark, under a determinate concept, which is their nominal definition. For names should be distinguishing marks, serve to form classes, indicate sameness in certain parts. But not properties and that which is internal, consequently not grounds of explication but rather grounds of classification.

16:610 **3005.** 1776–89. *V*, 77.

Nominal explication: that which designates the object (also if need be by means of description).

16:611 Real explication: which explains the possibility of the object by means of inner marks. Objects of experience permit merely nominal explications.

The definition of right as coercive law is nominal.

16:629 **3042.** 1773–75? (1775–77?) *V*, 81, at §292.³⁷

Judgment is a cognition of the unity of given concepts: namely, that *B* belongs with various other things *x*, *y*, *z* under the same con-cept *A*, or also: that the manifold which is under *B* also belongs under *A*, likewise that the concepts *A* and *B* can be represented through a concept *B*.

16:629 **3043.** 1773–77. *V*, 81.³⁸

All judgments are analytic or synthetic. The affirmative ones among the former rest on identity, since the predicate is contained in the subject; the negative ones: since the predicate contradicts the subject.

The synthetic judgments: there the subject is contained **under** the predicate or not.

16:629 **3044.** 1773–77? (1772?) 1775–78? *V*, 81.

A judgment is the relation of the subordination of concepts under one another.

A judgment is the representation of the unity in the relation of cognitions.*

If several cognitions are considered as one, then through one of them the others are also posited.

*(Later addition: The [crossed out: subordination] connection of a cog-   16:630
nition [crossed out: under] with its general condition in accordance with concepts. The connection of different cognition[s] [crossed out: in accordance with] through concepts.)

3045. 1776–79. V, 81.   16:630

A concept, by means of its universal validity, has the function of a judgment. It is related to other concepts *potentialiter*. The actual relation of one concept to others as a means for their cognition is the judgment.

Our cognition thereby becomes distinct.

The matter of judgments.

The form of judgments.

Quantity.

All relation of concepts is either of comparison

            or of association,

            or of inclusion or connection.

A judgment is the unity of a concept out of the relation (connection) of different concepts.

(Later addition: A judgment is the representation of the unity of the relation of the ground of cognition to the possible cognition of an object. Thus it is the clear representation of the unity of the consciousness of   16:631
different representations.

N.B. To judge is to represent one concept as contained in another or as excluded from it: 1. a subject under a predicate. 2. a consequence under its ground. 3. parts of a sphere under the whole.)

3046. 1776–1780s. V, 81.[39]   16:631

The categorical judgment constitutes the material of the others.

The **matter** of all judgments: either concepts or another judgment.

All distinct cognition is cognition made clear through a judgment.

Understanding.

What is made distinct by means of an inference of reason is an intensively distinct cognition (adequate).

3047. 1776–1780s. V, 81.   16:631

A judgment is the mediate cognition of one representation through other representations. The relation of mediate [crossed out: cognition] representation to the immediate one is (the relation in the judgment or) the form; the subject is the immediate representation, the predicate the mediate one.

16:633   **3051.** 1776–1780s. *V*, 81.[40]
The representation of the way in which different concepts (as such)
*belong to one consciousness** (in general (not merely mine)) is the
judgment. They belong to one consciousness partly in accordance with
laws of the imagination, thus subjectively, or of the understanding, i.e.,
objectively valid for every being that has understanding. The subjective connection pertains to the particular situation of the subject in
experience.
     *(universally necessary (empirical or *a priori*))
     (*Later addition*: **Concepts belong to one consciousness only insofar
as they are conceived under one another, not next to one another (like
sensations).)

16:633   **3053.** 1780–1804? 1776–78?? *V*, 81.
A judgment is the consciousness that one concept is contained under
another. either as its predicate or its ground or as a member of its division.
This is the matter of judgments in general. The form is that of quantity,
quality, relation, modality.

16:633   **3054.** 1780–1804? 1776–78?? *V*, 81.
The categories represent that objective unity of consciousness as
16:634   concepts of things in general, because it is actually by their means
alone that things are conceived as objects corresponding to our
representations.

16:634   **3055.** 1790–1804. *V*, 81.
Judgment: The representation of the way in which different concepts
[*crossed out*: representations] belong to one consciousness objectively*
(for everyone).
     *(i.e., in order to constitute a cognition of the object.)

16:636   **3063.** 1776–79? (1773–75?) 1780–89?? *V*, 82.[41]
Quality of judgments: affirmative or negative.
The relation of concepts. (Exponent):
The subject to predicate
The ground – consequence } form of judgments.
– whole – part
Categorical,
Hypothetical,
Disjunctive.
Quantity. Universal, particular, singular.
16:637   Modality. Problematic, assertoric, apodictic.
     It is of great importance to know which propositions, problematically
expressed, I can employ sufficiently. E.g., there can be a future life. For

problematic propositions are often incontestable, although assertoric ones are open to objections.

Likewise assertoric ones, although they are not apodictic. E.g., empirical propositions.

Problematic propositions as grounds of other truths are called hypotheses.

The proposition: *quidam homines non sunt eruditi*[a] can be expressed by means of fig. 1 (*non omnes*).[b]

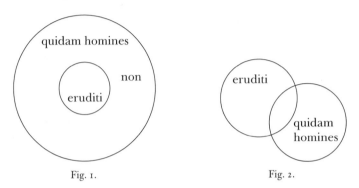

Fig. 1.   Fig. 2.

The infinite proposition: *quidam sunt non-eruditi*[c] by means of fig. 2 (*quidam non*).[d] The concept of men of learning is limited with regard to human beings, i.e., narrower than the latter.

That the learned and not-learned together make up all human beings, consequently human beings are thought through the learned, but with a limitation.

The learned are either considered as if they all stand under the concept of human beings, but only as a part of their sphere (the other part is not learned). Or a part only of human beings is considered as if it, along with the concept of men of learning, makes up a *sphaeram*. The latter limits the concept of human beings.

Through negative predicates I place my understanding outside of a determinate sphere into an infinite space.

The negative proposition indicates that something is not contained   16:638 under the sphere of a given concept; the infinite proposition: that something is contained under the sphere that lies outside of the given concept; consequently, it presupposes that outside of its sphere there is another in which it is contained, and therefore that it belongs to a sphere which limits the former one. Fig. 2. The former occurs in accordance with the

[a] Some men are not learned.
[b] not all
[c] Some men are non-learned.
[d] some not

principio exclusi medii[a] (between *a* and *non a* there is no third thing) etc., etc. The latter in accordance with that of thoroughgoing determination, which is infinite. The former is the principle of determination: of two opposed judgments, one is true. It says only that the proposition "*anima non est mortalis*"[b] is opposed to the proposition "*anima est mortalis*."[c] The latter occurs in accordance with the principle of thoroughgoing determination, which is supposed to occur with regard to a thing in general, [and] determines only with regard to thinghood in general, i.e., to reality, and beyond the sphere of a concept it adds an infinite sphere of the determination of all things, namely, of thinghood, i.e., of reality. Outside of the *sphaera* of a concept there is space for an infinitude of spheres.

The proposition "*anima est non-mortalis*"[d] is a judgment of determination which says that of two opposed predicates *a* and *non a*, the latter applies to the soul. Judgments of determination are all infinite in order to determine a thing thoroughly, not merely to indicate the relation of connection or opposition. Logic does not look at content, i.e., the determination of the concept, but rather only at the form of the relation: agreement or opposition.

16:639

16:640 **3068.** 1776–89. *V*, 82.

In the *iudicio affirmativo* the subject is thought under the *sphaera* of a predicate; in the *iudicio negativo*, the subject is posited outside of the *sphaera* of the latter. In the *iudicio infinito*, the subject is thought in the *sphaeram* of a concept that lies outside of the sphere of another concept.

In the universal judgment the *sphaera* of a concept is entirely enclosed inside of the *sphaera* of another concept; in the particular judgment, a part of the former is enclosed under the sphere of the other concept; in the singular judgment, a concept that has no *sphaeram* at all is consequently enclosed merely as a part under the *sphaeram* of another concept. Thus *iudicia singularia* are to be valued equally with the *universalibus*, and, conversely, a *iudicium universale* is to be considered a singular judgment with regard to the *sphaera*, much as if it were only one by itself.

16:640 **3069.** 1780–89. *V*, 82.

Although [*crossed out:* restriction] exclusion is a negative action, the restriction of a concept is yet a positive action. Therefore, **boundaries** are positive concepts of restricted objects.

All that is possible is *a* or *non A*. Thus if I say: something is *non A*, it is a *judicium indefinitum*. For beyond the *sphaera definita A* it is not

---

[a] principle of excluded middle
[b] The soul is not mortal.
[c] The soul is mortal.
[d] The soul is non-mortal.

determined under which **concept** the object belongs, but rather merely that it belongs in the sphere outside of *A*, which is actually no *sphaera* at all, but only the bordering of a sphere on that which is infinite or the boundary itself. The remainder is infinite when one takes away a determinate part from that which is infinite.

3115. 1769–75? (1764–68?) *V*, 87, at §§311–12.[42]   16:665

Practical judgments are thought either problematically (i.e., practical in a logical sense); or categorically (without any condition): morally; or hypothetically: *imperativi* of skill.

The practical *imperativi* of mathematics are actually possible necessitations for actions: *imperativi possibiles*.

The rules of prudence are *imperativi actuales*, and indeed: in which inclination rules.

The rules of morality are *imperativi actuales*, and indeed: in which reason rules.

3116. 1769–75? (1764–68?) *V*, 87.   16:666

Theoretical propositions are those that relate to the object.

Practical propositions are those* that relate to the action by means of which an object is produced.

*(*Later addition*: which determine (declare) the action through which an object becomes possible, which therefore is the necessary condition of the latter.)

Objectively practical propositions contain the idea of the action through which the object becomes possible;

subjectively practical propositions contain the conditions in the subject through which it becomes possible. If conditions of the opposite are present in the subject, or if the idea is not sufficient for execution, then the *studium* of the subject, hence of the hindrance, must precede.

Subjectively practical propositions are not necessary where the idea at the same time contains the construction.

3118. 1776–1789. *V*, 87.   16:666

Concerning the form of practical propositions: that is treated in logic, and distinguishes them from theoretical propositions.*

Concerning the content of practical propositions: that is treated in morals, and distinguishes them from speculative propositions.

(They are sources of practical propositions.)   16:667

*(These do not say what pertains to the object, but rather, **through which action a certain object is possible**. Thus not the relation of cognitions, but of freedom to an object of cognition which is thereby possible. Practical propositions are either rules (conditioned *imperativi*) or commands (unconditioned *imperativi*).

16:673   **3133.** 1775–79. *V*, 88, at §315.[43]

A postulate is actually a practical immediately [*crossed out*: necessary] certain proposition. But one can also have theoretical postulates for the sake of practical reason, namely, a theoretical hypothesis that is necessary from the point of view of practical reason, such as that of the existence of God, of freedom, and of another world. Practical propositions are objectively certain; subjectively, they can only become practical insofar as that hypothesis serves as their ground.

16:678   **3145.** 1790–1804. *V*, 90, at §323.[44]

A judgment from mere perceptions is not possible except insofar as I assert my representation as a perception. I who perceive a tower, perceive the red color in it. I cannot, however, say: the tower is red; for that would be not merely an empirical judgment, but rather also a judgment of experience, i.e., an empirical judgment whereby I acquire a concept of the object. E.g., "In touching a stone I sense warmth" is the former: but "The stone is warm" is the latter. – In the case of the latter I do not attribute to the object what is merely in my subject; for a judgment

16:679 of experience is the perception out of which a concept arises from the object. E.g., whether luminous points are in motion in the moon, or in the air, or in my eye.

16:679   **3146.** 1790–1804. *V*, 90, at §323.

A judgment of perception* is merely subjective; an **objective judgment from perceptions** is a judgment of experience.

*"I sense warmth in touching the oven" is a **perception**: "The oven is warm" is a **judgment of experience**.

16:709   **3200.** 1780–89. *V*, 98, at §352.[45]

1) Inferences of the understanding (*later addition*: are immediate inferences) infer the particular from the general, or the particular from the particular (*later addition*: but immediately), but never the general from the particular, because they are supposed to provide determining judgments.

2) Inferences of the power of judgment go from the particular to the (*later addition*: empirically-) general (*later addition*: are ways of progressing from the *individuis* to the *generibus*], from some things that belong to a certain kind to all of them, or from some properties in which things of a single kind agree to the remaining ones insofar as they belong to the same principle. They are nothing but ways of coming to general concepts from particular ones, thus kinds of reflecting (*later addition*: not determining) judgment; consequently not ways of determining the object, but rather only the manner of reflection about the object for arriving at acquaintance with it. (*Later addition*: They are inferences for

arriving at provisional, not at determining judgments. – Analogy and induction.)

Are the inferences of the power of judgment immediate inferences? No, they are grounded on a principle of the power of judgment: namely, that many things are not found to be in agreement without a common ground, thus that what pertains to them in this fashion will necessarily exist on the basis of a common ground. (*Later addition*: – Analogy, induction.)

(*Later addition*: 3. Inferences of reason[a] are mediate inferences of the particular from the universal *per iudicium intermedium.[b]*)

3276. 1769–1772? (1764–68?) (1773–77?) *V*, 110, at §401.[46]   16:755

Every inference of reason must yield necessity. Hence induction and analogy are not inferences of reason, but presumptions (*later addition*: inferences of the power of judgment, namely for itself) or empirical inferences.

3277. 1769? 1770–71? 1773–75? (1776–78?) *V*, 110.   16:755

There are inferences from the particular to the general in empirical sciences, in which experiences are to become *principia*; for were there no general propositions they could not be used for making inferences. Thus empirical principles are always true only *per inductionem* and assert that what holds for all the members of a species with which I am acquainted also holds for the rest of them.

There cannot be an inference from part of a whole concept to the rest; or, if everything that I perceive in the things of one species is consistent, then it is also consistent with regard to the rest of what is always perceived to be connected with those determinations. Inference from analogy.

3280. 1773–78? (1778–79?) *V*, 110.   16:756

Induction (*later addition*: extends the empirically given from the particular to the general with regard to many objects; analogy extends the given properties of a thing to several properties of the very same thing) generalizes what one knows about the things of a species and (synthetically) extends it to things of the same species that one does not know.

Analogy also gives [*crossed out*: what one knows about one thing to others, in which one does not know it] to things of a species, about which one knows something consistent, the rest which he knows in one but not in the others. E.g., earth and moon.

---

[a] *Vernunftschlüsse*, i.e., syllogisms
[b] through an intermediate judgment

16:756 **3281.** 1776–78? (1778–89?) *V*, 110.
On the necessity [*crossed out:* of empirical generality] **of general propositions** (*later addition*: through induction), i.e., strictly speaking, particular propositions that in use hold *instar generalium.*[a] They are rules that permit an exception, though rarely, like grammatical rules, because
16:757 they are empirical. But if no exception has been encountered, then it is right to presume that the ground of the truth lies in the constitution of things and not merely in the circumstances of their perception.
We cannot do without such general propositions.

16:757 **3282.** 1776–89. *V*, 110.
Induction infers *a particulari ad universali*[b] (*later addition*: by means of induction one acquires general, not universal propositions[c]) in accordance with the principle of universalization.[d]
Analogy: from partial* similarity of two things to total similarity, in accordance with the principle of specification.[47]
Through analogy: **on the whole**, but not **entirely** similar things.
*(**One in many**, therefore in all: induction.
Many in one (which is also in others), thus also everything else in the same thing: analogy.)

16:759 **3287.** 1776–89. *V*, 110.[48]
The power of judgment is twofold: the determining or reflecting power of judgment. The first goes from the general to the particular, the second from the particular to the general. The latter has only subjective validity. – (Inference from analogy and induction is logical presumption.)
(*Later addition*: They are principles of the [*crossed out:* empirical] procedure in the amplification of our cognition by means of experience.
We can, to be sure, think a being (that is incomprehensible to us) by means of analogy, but we cannot infer from a relation among things that are given to the same relation among things that are unknown to us.)

16:761 **3294.** 1790–1804. *V*, 109.
If what we perceive in things [*crossed out:* as belonging together with their species-concept to the unity of] must be thought as belonging to one and the same species, then the rest of what is required for the very same species, although we do not perceive it in them, can be presumed of them. E.g., sponges agree with plants with regard to growth; thus, in accordance with the analogy to them, they will also agree with them

[a] as if they were a universal
[b] from the particular to the general
[c] *general-, nicht universalsatze*
[d] *Allgemeinmachung*

66

in that they reproduce by means of seeds. I cannot, however, infer that because animals, as far as we know, have circulation of their humors, that plants are also so constituted. For, as regards the species, they differ in what concerns the ground of the given determination, since the former arbitrarily includes nourishment.

Therefore, we can indeed **think** the causality of a cause of the world on analogy with the constitution of a cause in the world, namely, being a cause in the way that human beings (that is, by means of the understanding) are the cause of a clock, but we cannot infer the former causality from the future constitution of the things of the world. For in the first case we only have similar relations; in the second, a similar thing – God and causes in the world, however, are entirely heterogeneous things.

Imagining something in accordance with an analogy – inferring.

3

Notes on Metaphysics

This chapter presents a selection from the notes (*Reflexionen*) that Erich Adickes edited under the title "Metaphysics" in volumes 17 and 18 of the *Akademie* edition, published in 1926 and 1928. This is by far the largest group of Kant's surviving notes, touching upon issues central to his works on theoretical philosophy through and beyond the second edition of the *Critique of Pure Reason* (1787) but also upon the metaphysical foundations of his practical philosophy and his moral theology, and thus this chapter is the largest of those in this volume. It is divided into four main parts, following the dates that Adickes provided for the notes: 1. Notes Prior to 1773; 2. Notes from 1773 to 1780, the crucial period for the composition of the *Critique of Pure Reason*; 3. Notes from the 1780s, including material from the period of the composition of the *Prolegomena to any future metaphysics* (1783) and the preparation of the second edition of the *Critique*; and 4. Notes from the 1790s, revealing Kant's continued thinking on some of the topics of the first *Critique*, especially his continued work on the "Refutation of Idealism" that he had added to the second edition. A small amount of material from volumes 17 and 18 is presented elsewhere in the present volume or the Cambridge edition: the first three reflections in volume 17, **3703** through **3705**, were presented in conjunction with Kant's 1759 essay "On Optimism" in the volume *Theoretical Philosophy, 1755–1770*, translated and edited by David Walford in collaboration with Ralf Meerbote (Cambridge: Cambridge University Press, 1992), pp. 77–83, and several notes found among the notes on metaphysics but directly addressing topics in moral philosophy are included in Chapter 4 below. But the many notes on freedom of the will that Kant included throughout the reflections on metaphysics, although they obviously bear on Kant's moral philosophy, are included in their original sequence here.

The notes in volumes 17 and 18 came from two types of source. As in the case of the reflections on logic (Chapter 2) and moral philosophy (Chapter 4), many of the notes came from Kant's annotations in his interleaved copy of the textbook he used for his lectures, in this case Alexander Gottlieb Baumgarten, *Metaphysica*, fourth edition (Halle: Carl Hermann Hemmerde, 1757), here abbreviated as "*M.*" This volume had come to the university in Dorpat, now Tartu, Estonia, after Kant's death, through his student Benjamin Gottlob Jäsche, who taught there. It was also the basis for an earlier edition of Kant's reflections by Benno Erdmann,

Reflexionen Kants zur kritischen Philosophie, in two volumes, *Reflexionen Kants zur Anthropologie* (Leipzig: Fues's Verlag, 1882) and *Reflexionen Kants zur Kritik der reinen Vernunft* (Leipzig: Fues's Verlag, 1884), reprinted in a single volume with an introduction by Norbert Hinske (Stuttgart-Bad Canstatt: Fromann-Holzboog, 1992). Adickes as well as Erdmann used the original volume for their editions of the notes, but the whereabouts of the volume since World War II is unknown. According to Adickes, Kant began annotating this volume about 1764, or almost a decade after he began lecturing on metaphysics; whatever earlier edition or editions of Baumgarten he had previously used did not survive (see 17:257–8). Baumgarten's text was in Latin, and Kant uses Latin liberally throughout these notes, sometimes writing whole notes in that language. Georg Friedrich Meier, the disciple of Baumgarten who produced the German logic textbook that Kant used in his logic lectures, also produced a German translation of Baumgarten's *Metaphysica* in 1767, but Kant did not adopt this for his lectures. The complete text of the fourth edition of the *Metaphysica* is reprinted on pp. 5–226 of volume 17. For each of Kant's notes from this source, Adickes provides both the page number of its location in Kant's copy as well as, when possible, the number of the section in Baumgarten's book to which the note is connected; unfortunately, the text of the *Metaphysica* included in volume 17 does not include the original page numbers.

A second textbook from which annotations are included in volume 18 is Johann August Eberhard, *Vorbereitung zur natürlichen Theologie* (Preparation for natural theology) (Halle: im Waisenhause, 1781), on which Kant apparently lectured twice, in 1783–84 and 1785–86. These lectures formed the basis for the *Lectures on the Philosophical Doctrine of Religion* edited by Karl Heinrich Ludwig Pölitz in 1817, translated in the Cambridge edition in *Religion and Rational Theology*, edited by Allen W. Wood and George di Giovanni (Cambridge: Cambridge University Press, 1996), pp. 335–51. There are 120 pages of those notes (**6206–6310**, 18:488–606, including Eberhard's text); a small selection of them is included in this chapter.

The other type of material included in volumes 17 and 18 and translated here are various "loose sheets" (*lose Blätter*, abbreviated "*LBl*"), that is, unbound sheets of paper, sometimes dated letters to Kant that he used for scrap paper, that somehow survived Kant's death and made their way into various private and public collections during the course of the nineteenth century. Many of the *lose Blätter* that Adickes published were included in two prior publications: Rudolf Reicke, *Lose Blätter aus Kants Nachlass*, volumes I–III (Königsberg, 1889, 1895, and 1898), originally published in the *Altpreussische Monatsschrift*, volumes 24, 25, 28, 30, 32, and 35; and Theodor Haering, *Der Duisburgsche Nachlaß und Kants Kritizismus um 1775* (Tübingen, 1910). The notes in the latter volume (named not after the city of Duisburg but after a family of that name who originally owned them, and referred to below as "*LBl* Duisburg") are a subset of the notes included in Reicke's volumes that are datable with considerable certitude to 1775 and which offer a remarkable window into a crucial stage in the development of the *Critique of Pure Reason*. Adickes suggests but does not explicitly assert that he had seen and worked from many of the original sheets that Reicke also edited (see 14:xix), but in any case he also provides the location for each note included in Reicke's three volumes in his own headings to the notes (we have not reproduced those citations in our headings). A small number of the *lose Blätter* that Adickes edited were not included in either Reicke or Haering; we simply cite whatever names for them Adickes provided. We also include with the reflections on the "Refutation of Idealism" from 1790 one sketch that has turned up only much more recently, "Leningrad Fragment 1," which was edited and published by Reinhard Brandt and Werner Stark in *Kant–Forschungen, Band 1: Neue Autographen und Dokumente zu Kants Leben, Schriften, und Vorlesungen* (Hamburg: Felix Meiner Verlag, 1987), pp. 18–21.

In his edition of the notes on metaphysics in Kant's copy of Baumgarten, Erdmann correlated the notes with the chapters of the *Critique of Pure Reason* and then ordered the notes within each chapter into four chronological periods, based on their contents and his own conception of Kant's philosophical development. Adickes had followed a somewhat analogous procedure in his editions of Kant's notes on anthropology (volume 15) and logic (volume 16), presenting the notes in the order of Baumgarten's chapters and sections but within each such grouping dividing them into not four but thirty-two chronological groups. As noted in the Introduction to this volume, he based this chronology on a variety of indicia, including ink, handwriting, and location of the notes on the page as well as the occasional dated letter. In volumes 17 and 18, Adickes's primary division of the material is into into twenty-eight of his thirty-two chronological periods (the four earliest periods, covering the years 1753–1763, being missing from the metaphysics notes), and then within each of these chronological periods the notes are sequentially ordered in correspondence to Baumgarten's pages and sections. The *lose Blätter*, meanwhile, are placed at the beginning of each chronological section. This means that Kant's notes on any given topic or section in Baumgarten are scattered in their supposed chronological order throughout volumes 17 and 18. This makes it difficult to find all the notes on a particular topic, even if they are separated by only a few years, until one has become familiar with the contents of Baumgarten's book, and we considered reordering the notes topically instead of chronologically. However, since Adickes's ordering and therefore numbering of the notes has been widely adopted in secondary literature on Kant, in the end we decided to preserve Adickes's sequence for our presentation of the notes within this chapter so that any note we have included may readily be found in its numerical sequence. Our division of the chapter into four main chronological periods is only meant to break up the chapter. We hope that our inclusion of Adickes's references to the page and section numbers of Baumgarten, the cross-references we have provided in our endnotes, and the index to this volume will make it possible for readers to find Kant's reflections on particular topics from different periods without too much difficulty. (Adickes's headings also cite Erdmann's numbers for those notes included in both editions, and Adickes provided a table correlating Erdmann's numbering of the notes to his own at 18:x–xxiii. This table lists Erdmann's numbers in order in its left-hand columns and the corresponding *Akademie* edition numbers, not in their own order, in its right-hand columns; so it is easy to find the *Akademie* edition number for any reflection included in Erdmann but not *vice versa*. We have not reproduced the table here.)

Volumes 17 and 18 present no fewer than 3,066 notes, and the range of topics convered by them is very large. So here we can give only the most general intimation of the contents of our selection from these notes. The very first note included here (**3706**) is an early but detailed statement of Kant's critique of the ontological argument for the existence of God, and the very last notes in the chapter are discussions of moral theology (**6451, 6454**): the failure of traditional rational and natural theology and the need to replace it with moral theology obsessed Kant throughout his career, and he recurs to these issues throughout the notes on metaphysics. For a sampling of notes on the proofs of the existence of God, see **3733, 4253–4, 4259, 4725, 4729, 4733, 4741, 5500–1, 5506–8, 5624, 5633–4, 5758–83, 6962–3, 6027, 6038, 6317, 6317a, 6323,** and **6389**. For a sample of notes on the project of a moral theology, which is alluded to as early as 1764–66, see **3819, 3909, 4253, 5103, 6047, 6091–2, 6096, 6098–6100, 6107, 6109, 6111, 6113, 6132–3, 6142–3, 6173, 6432,** and **6151** and **6154**, already mentioned. In this connection, also see the rare notes on teleology, **6136–7**. From among the notes on Eberhard's *Preparation for Natural Theology*, **6206, 6210, 6225–7, 6235–6, 6244, 6275–6, 6278, 6280, 6287, 6290, 6303,** and **6308** are included.

The critique of traditional theology and its replacement by moral theology remained Kant's project from beginning to end; he was still working on it in the latest stages of the *Opus postumum* after 1800 (see the selection in the Cambridge edition, *Opus postumum*, edited by Eckart Förster, translated by Eckart Förster and Michael Rosen [1993], pp. 200–56). But in between Kant's earliest and latest notes on these issues comes the vast bulk of the notes and fragments on metaphysics, providing our evidence about the evolution of Kant's thought in the years leading up to the publication of his inaugural dissertation *On the Form and Principles of the Sensible and Intelligible World* in 1770; during the "silent decade" of the 1770s in which he published almost nothing while gearing up for the *Critique of Pure Reason*; during the period from 1782 to 1787 in which he publicized and defended the *Critique* in the *Prolegomena to any Future Metaphysics that would come forth as Scientific* (1783) and then revised the *Critique* for its second edition in 1787; and finally during his remaining years, in which he continued to think about the issues of the *Critique* and strive for clarity about them. The selection of notes for this chapter has been guided primarily by the aim of making the most important evidence of Kant's development during those phases of his career readily available.

Kant began to understand the difference between analytic and synthetic judgments as early as 1764; by 1769, he had introduced the idea of synthetic *a priori* judgments as the special concern of metaphysics; and he made important progress on his conception of the basis for synthetic *a priori* judgments by 1775. Some of the notes giving evidence of this development are **3716, 3738, 3747, 3750, 3914, 3923, 3928, 3944, 4477, 4674, 4675, 4676, 4678,** and **4684.** As early as 1769, Kant also realized that only the subjective validity of fundamental metaphysical concepts could explain how we could have synthetic *a priori* cognition by means of them: see, for example, **3930, 3938, 3957–8, 4292,** and **4634.** Kant also began developing his view of space and time as the fundamental forms of human experience as early as 1764, and continued to discuss his view throughout his notes: see **3717, 3941–2, 3950, 4077–8, 4188–91, 4315–16, 4425, 4503, 4507–8, 4511–19, 4529, 4673, 4720, 4756, 5313, 5315, 5317–20, 5323, 5327, 5329, 5650, 5726, 5876, 5879, 5885–6, 5898, 5906, 5958–60, 6346,** and **6357.** Kant was clarifying the distinction between particular intuitions and general concepts by 1769, in preparation for the next year's inaugural dissertation, although once he had clarified this distinction he did not revert to it as often as he did to the substance of his view of space and time; see **3955, 3957, 3961, 3970, 3974, 3976,** and **4073.** It was also at this time (1769) that Kant discovered that the mismatched limits of sensibility and ambitions of reason give rise to the "antinomies" that could only be resolved by his distinction between the sensible appearances of things and the way they might be in themselves, and he frequently returns to the antinomies in later notes as well: **4000, 4210, 4617–18, 4708, 4742, 4756–60, 4780, 4936, 5095, 5263, 5639, 5962, 5972–9,** and **6241.**

By 1769, Kant realized that his discoveries required a radical reconception of the nature of metaphysics itself, as the critique of the forms of human experience rather than an objective science of things in themselves. Especially during the years from 1769 to 1772, he wrote numerous notes in the introductory pages of his copy of Baumgarten concerning the nature of metaphysics and the new conceptions of critique and transcendental philosophy, and he would continue to revert to this issue for years to come. See, for example, **3946, 3949, 3952, 3964, 3970, 3988, 4148, 4152, 4163, 4168, 4284, 4364, 4366, 4369, 4445, 4453–9, 4466, 4468, 4627, 4651, 4789, 4855, 4865, 4889–90, 4892, 4897, 4945, 4957, 4966, 4970, 5062–3, 5070, 5073, 5083, 5100, 5115–16, 5119, 5645, 5649–50, 5665, 5667, 5674**, and **5679**.

Around 1775, Kant took the fundamental step of connecting the categories or "titles of the understanding," which he had begun to systematize around 1772 (see **4476, 4493, 4496, 4672, 5189**, and **6221**) with the "exposition" of experience or the determination of objective relations in time, and introduced the idea of apperception as a form of self-consciousness as well (**4676–7**). Thus he introduced ideas that would become key to the "Transcendental Deduction of the Categories" and the "System of All Principles" of empirical knowledge in the *Critique of Pure Reason*, above all the "Analogies of Experience," although he did not yet express a need to *separate* the transcendental deduction and the system of principles. The key documents here are those fragments at the heart of the *Duisburg Nachlaß*, **4674–84**; on the concept of experience itself, see also **4679, 5596, 5607**, and **6343–4**. About two years after this, Kant was clearly attempting to outline the whole *Critique of Pure Reason*; see especially **4756–70** as well as **4849** and **5536**. Another important sketch of the whole project is the undated *loses Blatt* B 12, which the *Akademie* edition printed in volume 23 (23:18–20), preceding the notes transcribed from Kant's own copy of the first edition of the *Critique* (23:20–50), which have been incorporated into the Cambridge edition of the *Critique of Pure Reason*, edited by Paul Guyer and Allen W. Wood (Cambridge: Cambridge University Press, 1998). *LBl* B 12 has been placed at the start of the section of Notes from the 1780s.

The next major group of notes come from the period from the early 1780s, after the publication of the first edition of the *Critique*. Some of these notes seem to be preparation for Kant's attempt to consolidate and defend the *Critique* in the *Prolegomena to any Future Metaphysics*, published in 1783 and in part a response to the unfavorable review of the *Critique* published in the *Göttingsche Anzeigen von gelehreten Sachen* (see Brigitte Sassen, ed., *Kant's Early Critics: The Empiricist Critique of the Theoretical Philosophy* [Cambridge: Cambridge University Press, 2000], pp. 53–77), while others appear to be preparations for the revised second edition of the *Critique*. Among the latter are a number of sketches of revised versions of the "Transcendental Deduction of the Categories," a topic to which Kant returned in the 1790s as well. Here see especially **5636–7, 5642–3**, and **5923–35**, and from the 1790s, **6350, 6353, 6356**, and **6358**. One of Kant's concerns in the revision of the "Transcendental Deduction" was to clarify his conception of inner sense; in this context see **5646, 5655**, and **6354** (an earlier discussion of inner sense can also be found in **5049**, from 1776–78).

One of the chief innovations of the second edition of the *Critique of Pure Reason* is its "Refutation of Idealism," in which Kant argues that a subject can only be conscious of the temporal order of its own states by correlating them with external objects. This argument transposes into an epistemological key an argument in ontology that Kant had made as early as 1755, namely that a substance cannot undergo any change unless acted upon by another substance (*New Elucidations of the First Principles of Metaphysical Cognition*, Proposition XII, 1:410; in *Theoretical Philosophy, 1755–1770*, p. 37), and a few of the notes here take up that earlier form of the argument (**4094** and **5400**). What is striking, however, is that Kant was clearly dissatisfied with the published version of the new, epistemological argument – indeed, he was already attempting to improve it in the Preface to the second edition of the *Critique* (B xxxix–xli) – and no fewer than a dozen attempts to improve the argument from 1788–1790 have survived. All of these are included here: **5653–4, 5709, 6311–16, 6319, 6323**, and **Leningrad Fragment I**.

Finally, Baumgarten's *Metaphysica* includes three chapters bearing on the freedom of the will, the chapters on *Spontaneitas*, *Arbitrium*, and *Libertas*, and Kant's numerous notes on these chapters from every period of his work demonstrate his lifelong concern with this issue. We have included an extensive selection of these notes here, the first of which may be from as early as 1764 and the last of which from as late as 1795: see especially **3855–60, 3865–72, 3922, 4033, 4219–29, 4333–9, 4441, 4541, 4545, 4548–9, 4551, 4724–5, 4783, 4788, 5104, 5121, 5434–6, 5440–1, 5612–20, 5964, 5972–3, 5975, 5977–8, 5995, 6007, 6077, 6348–9, 6449**, and **6446**.

Because of its length, this chapter originally consisted of four computer files, and therefore there were four sets of endnotes. In order to avoid excessively cumbersome superscripts, that numbering of the endnotes has been retained here.

* *
*

I.

NOTES PRIOR TO 1773

17:240 **3706.** 1760–64? (1753–59?) 1773–77??? (*LBl* Kuffner 1, pp. 1–iv)

If existence could also be counted as one of the various predicates that may be counted as belonging to a thing, then certainly no proof that would be more conclusive and at the same time more intelligible than the Cartesian one could be demanded for demonstrating the existence of God.[1] For among all possible things there is one in which all realities that can be joined together in a being are to be found. To these realities, i.e., truly positive predicates, there also belongs existence; consequently, existence belongs to the most real of all beings on account of its inner possibility. Against this one objects in vain that such a possible thing includes existence within itself only in the understanding, i.e., only as soon as the thing itself is posited in thought, but not outside of thought, for then we would have to say of all predicates that belong to a possible thing that they would not belong to it in fact, but would only be posited in it in thought. The latter indeed occurs when one arbitrarily combines something with a concept that is not necessarily posited thereby; e.g., in this way wings are posited of a horse in thought in order to form a Pegasus, hence wings belong to some horse or other only in thought. On the contrary, where the connection of a predicate with a thing is not 17: 241 arbitrary, but is combined through the essence of the things themselves, the predicate does not belong to it because we think it in the thing, but rather it is necessary to think such a predicate in it because it belongs to the thing in itself. For this reason I cannot say that the equality of the angles with two right angles belongs to a triangle only in thought, but rather it belongs to it in itself.[2] This also does not prevent my only thinking such a possible thing; for it is always something in itself, even though no one thinks it, and the predicate belongs to it in itself, even though no one combines it with the thing. This is how matters also stand with existence, if it could be regarded as a predicate of things. For it would necessarily belong, among all that is possible, to that in which all reality exists, i.e., a most real being will necessarily exist, and its possibility would include reality as well. If without my thought or the thought of any other thing existence did not belong to the most perfect being, then the thought of this being would be completely false. For if the thought is correct, then it can represent no other predicates than those which also occur in the thing without these thoughts.

Here it is not a question of whether more in general is posited through a real thing than through a non-real one, but rather whether more predicates are posited in it; now no more is posited in God's goodness, insofar as it is considered as existing, than in the goodness which lies in His possibility; the difference, however, consists only in the fact that in the first case the thing itself is posited with what is contained in it, but in the 17: 242 second case the relation of [the parts of] this manifold to each other is posited.

The essential difficulty is no doubt that our linguistic usage, insofar as it seems to express our most precise idea, always labels existence a predicate, which gives the appearance that it comes from the immediate constitution of our concept. I say: through an existing thing: existence belongs to a thing, etc.; I consider the existence of things in particular and distinguish it from possibility. This feature of our judgments

very much deserves to be examined. This does not mean to philosophize, if one solely seeks to establish that something is a delusion, a
deception of the understanding, but rather one must also learn to have
insight into how such a deception would be possible. This illusion is
itself a real appearance in the nature of our mind, and either I must be
able to explain it, or I have cause to fear that my judgment, which declares some opinion or other to be a delusion, might itself be one such
illusion.

I now ask: if existence is not a predicate of things, how can I then make
use of the expression "existence" at all; for this differentiates something in
the thing, which can be attributed to it, from the thing itself. E.g., reality
belongs to a certain thing. Because the very same thing can be posited
in various ways, this positing itself seems to be a mark of the difference
which, as a predicate, one could attribute to a thing or separate from it.
It is, however, certain that this difference merely pertains to how this
thing is posited with all that belongs to it, and not to what is posited
in it. In accordance with the difference in the way the thing is posited,
something different is posited thereby: namely, through its predicates
17:243 in relation to the subject only relations and its possibility; through the
thing, insofar as it is posited *absolute*, the thing itself. Thus we do not
differentiate the possible from the real through a predicate that belongs
to the one more than to the other.

The concept of an existing thing can never be altered in a judgment
in which the thing would be the subject and existence the predicate.

On the contrary, something existent must be the subject and everything that belongs to it must be its predicates.

17:243 **3707.** 1760–64. *LBl* Duisburg 5, pp. I–III.

Preparation of the Certainty and Uncertainty of Cognition in General.

Uncertainty is either an uncertainty of things or of insight. Although
the objects of cognition in themselves are certainly that which they are,
one can nevertheless attribute uncertainty to these things, insofar as
from what one cognizes in them and is thus given nothing of the rest
of what one is looking for is established, be these data ever as completely cognized as one wishes. If in an alloy of three different metals
whose specific gravity as well as the weight of the entire lump and its
hydrostatic relation to water are given, then one may cognize these data
however one wishes; nevertheless in this connection it remains uncertain
in which relation they are mixed with one another, and indeed because
17:244 the cognized parts in themselves are such that this relation remains undetermined from them. This kind of uncertainty, which one could call
objective uncertainty, must be encountered in the cognition of every
restricted cognition. To him who does not cognize everything in this

fashion, some things (in accordance with his constitution) must remain unsettled by his partial cognitions, though he may make comparisons with this cognition however he wishes.

Now if one cognizes that from certain data that one knows certain other items are undetermined, then to that extent no error can occur in our cognition, and the same cognition is therefore not objectively uncertain. If the apparent diameter of a star is known but the distance is unknown, then it remains uncertain what the true magnitude of the star is, although no error can arise from this uncertainty alone. Likewise if in the observation of an angle it is known that a mistake of two seconds cannot be noticed, then everything that more or less depends on such a magnitude is undetermined by observation, and if one cognizes this as such a case, then to that extent no error can occur.

Since uncertainty consists in the possibility of erring, i.e., making a judgment that is false, all grounds for this possibility are either negative or positive, namely they consist either in the fact that grounds are lacking for a certain true judgment or in there being positive grounds for judging, which judgments are nevertheless not in conformity with the constitution of things. The first ground in itself is not sufficient for understanding the possibility of error. For because I do not know certain things, it does not yet follow from this that I can make a false judgment. For provided that I cognize that I would have to know these items in order to judge, then if I find that I do not know them, I would not be willing to judge and would be protected from all error. In the case of the astronomer, as long as he indeed knows the apparent diameter of a comet but not the parallax, it is to that extent objectively uncertain how remote and how large it is, but it is impossible for him to err in this, as long as he is aware that he cannot judge. Even this ignorance of certain   17:245 given items is not in itself a ground of the possibility of erring, even if the person is not aware of this indeterminacy; for as long as there is no ground that induces him to pass judgment on a thing about which he does not know enough, then he is protected from all judgment. The common man is therefore protected from many errors; for, since he is untroubled with regard to most things over which men of learning so eagerly exert themselves, even if he hears the questions that are raised, and most questions never enter his mind, there is nothing that would induce him to judge. Consequently, one sees that uncertainty in the subjective sense still presupposes a certain ground for making judgments. If, moreover, uncertainty in the objective sense, of which, however, one is not aware, is added [sic].

Therefore, in the case of any impulse to make a judgment, if the consciousness of objective uncertainty is present, error is impossible, as one can see in geometry. The greater the desire to judge or the habit of judging is [sic]. We have only referred to objective uncertainty, insofar as it is joined with the [*crossed out*: subjective] internal grounds of judging, in order to make intelligible the subjective possibility of judging. But even if this desire is indifferent, nevertheless the grounds for differentiating the true from the false are either hidden and relatively small compared to the agreements that a false cognition has with a true one, or not. (Since we infer by means of analogy, many agreements can be a ground for errors, e.g., reason in animals.) In that case, since one has many but not all the differentiating grounds, error is only possible through ignorance of the indeterminacy of cognition from these grounds and the inclination to judge.

Certainty must be just as possible in philosophical as in mathematical cognition and must be sufficient for conviction in both of them. One cannot say that one certainty is greater than the other; nothing is ever more certain than that which is certain. As regards the type, however, it does not concern certainty but rather clarity.

17: 246

(*Later addition*: All uncertainty is a possibility of erring. To err means to make a false judgment. The possibility of erring exists either under a potential or an actual condition. The former means that one could err if one were willing to judge; the latter that there is also, from real grounds, a conditioned possibility of judging where it is nevertheless possible to err. The potential possibility of erring rests on the constitution of things, namely, that since what one cognizes of them does not determine what pertains to them or not, the actual condition of uncertainty is the ground for judging, in which a potential uncertainty is still hidden. This ground for judging is hidden in the apparent similarity of the procedure in the case of a false cognition with that in the case of a true one. In the first place: Where I do not notice that in the marks of the thing something is forgotten, in that case nothing is forgotten. 2. Things which are similar in certain parts are similar in others. 3. What belongs to many belongs to all.

In the type of designation: since the signs of similar things are regarded as identical.

The uncertainty of that for which various causes are possible. The existence of bodies.

17: 247 Method of mathematics: taking the *medium* from the many.

Provisional judgments.

On philosophical opinions and hypotheses, on noticing the grounds for why an opinion is uncertain.

Uncertainty is of two kinds: either when one does not find in the thing itself sufficient grounds for approval, or when, regardless of all of one's conviction drawn from the expectation of similar cases, one is afraid of erring in calculating.

Uncertainty is either a possibility of erring under the condition that one would be willing to judge of that for which there are no *data*, or a conditioned possibility of judging in that for which one has no *data*.

Immediately certain propositions: before one makes a concept distinct, but through which one begins this.

Immediately certain proposition: many thinking cannot produce a thought.

17:248

Immediately certain proposition. Can exist only if the subject cannot be thought without the predicate, not if it seems that one cannot deny it.)

3709. 1762–63. At *M* LIV, §§1–3.[3]

17:249

Prolegomena Metaphysicorum.

In our entire body of cognition some cognitions must ground others. Many concepts ground other concepts, and many judgments ground other judgments. The concept of time, motion, and measurement grounds the commonest concept of an hour. Whoever mentions the word "friendship" relies on the concepts of love, honesty, etc. It is the same way with judgments. Whoever says that envy is a vice is relying on many concealed judgments: that love of one's neighbor is a duty, that whatever is contrary to duty is a vice, that envy is malicious and opposed to love, etc. One can call fundamental concepts *notiones fundamentales*; one can call fundamental judgments *judicia fundamentalia*. Those fundamental concepts which do not in turn presuppose others are called *notiones primitivae* (first fundamental concepts) and judgments of such a kind are called *judicia primitiva* (first fundamental judgments). But something can be seen as a primitive either in itself or in relation to something else. Something is a *cognitio absolute primitiva* insofar as no other cognition at all grounds it; however, the cognition is *respective primitiva* insofar as it is either not in the power of a subject to cognize its ground or it is not in conformity with a certain rational aim. The concepts of good and evil are grounded in various things that philosophers clearly know, but the common man certainly cannot penetrate too far into his concepts, and for him they are *notiones primitivae*. It is the same with the concepts of space and time in common cognition. Some of these fundamental concepts can be *notiones primitivae* with regard to the entirety of human understanding, although *in sensu absoluto* they may be only *derivativae*, e.g., simultaneity, successiveness, etc. One can call these *notiones primitivas in sensu subjectivo*. Whether they are also such *in sensu objectivo* cannot be decided by human beings. It is the same with *judicia in sensu subjectivo prima* as regards some people, e.g., proverbs; or as regards everyone, e.g., *principium contradictionis*.

17:250

If we now call *principia* all cognitions that ground other cognitions, then there is *respectus* with regard [*breaks off*].

17:252 **3712.** 1762–63? 1764–66? (1766–68? 1769?) 1773–75?? 1776–78?? *M* 31, at §109.[4]

The mark of the absolutely necessary being cannot consist in the contingency in the existence of other things, for then this necessity is only *hypothetica antecedentis,*[a] therefore, not in the fact that it is regarded as a final ground of all that exists, but rather in the fact that it is a ground of everything in general, both of what exists and of what is possible; for since possibility in general is certainly necessary, then so is that which contains the ground as well.

17:255 **3716.** Before 1764–66? 1764–68? *LBl* Berliner Staatsbibliothek 29.

A rational cognition that has no other *principia* than empirical concepts can only be a critique;[5] one can understand the universal (e.g., the pathetic) only through the particular, and general rules can only be abstracted from the particulars of practice. It is the same with the doctrine of the probable.

Truth has objective marks; but the certainty that these objective marks are to be met with in every case can only have subjective ones, i.e., the harmony of cognition with itself.

A general concept is empirical if it cannot be understood unless one cognizes its *concretum.* E.g., one cannot obtain a concept of water through any definition unless one has seen it. Above all, all concepts of beauty, simplicity, and of the ridiculous are comprehensible only in their *concreto.* Therefore, rules cannot here give rise to practice, but rather practice makes the rules.

As regards the judging of something ethical, the question is not whether it is agreeable, but rather whether it is good. We cognize therein
17:256 the possibility of a connection with happiness, but it does not rest on this connection. The principles of moral judging should not be grounds of inclination toward the good, for these belong to feeling. The most vicious human being, however relatively small the moral inclination toward the good may be, takes it all the same for the best. The principles of this judgment should be firmly grounded.

All sciences and arts are either related to the culture of healthy understanding or not. In the latter case a complete lack of taste also prevails. The age of healthy reason and of the arts and sciences is only the age of honor; this is found only in republics and monarchies, thus not in the feudal system of government, where there is far too much inequality.

(*Later addition:* The *principium* of identity and contradiction is for reason what space and time are for the senses. Universal: the *principium* of consensus (whether of identity or difference). The *principium* of the highest reality is parallel to the sum total of all sensations.)

[a] the hypothetical necessity of an antecedent

Perfection is what constitutes the worth of the person; happiness, what constitutes the worth of the condition.

(The principle of sufficient reason is grounded on the fact that one can negate everything in and for itself; thus, in order to posit something, something else, to which this negation is opposed, must be posited. This connection, however, is either in accordance with the laws of reason or of the senses.)

This principle, however, only claims to say that nothing can be cognized in accordance with reason without a ground.

If we wish to posit something by means of reason, then we need a ground. I.e., positing *a priori* is by means of a ground; it would then have to be intuition.

In the proposition: everything that exists has a ground, there lies: 1. some other thing, 2. whereby the consequence is determined; the former, *dependens*, the latter, *contingens*. 17:257

All ideas of metaphysics are analytic, except for space, time, and force.

Analysis rests on the propositions of identity and contradiction. All of these and other propositions, however, are grounded on the proposition that the understanding posits nothing *absolute*, but rather only insofar as it is necessitated to do so, by means of a condition, either analytically or synthetically. 17:258

The idea of the possible. The idea of totality or a whole. 17:259

Metaphysics is not a philosophy about objects, for these can only be given by means of the senses, but rather about the subject, namely, the laws of its reason.

We have laws for the use of our reason *a posteriori*; these cannot be applied to concepts, but rather only to objects of experience.

Metaphysics thus treats only the subject dogmatically, but it treats the object, with regard to synthetic judgments, problematically.

All judgments are either logical, which assert relative existence, or real, which assert absolute existence. All being in itself (positing) is an existence either *respective* (*hypothetice*) or *categorice*.

Universality is understood either synthetically, and then it holds only for cases of experience of *synthesis*, or analytically, and holds, in accordance with reason, for concepts.

To determine the boundaries of reason first takes something positive, namely, showing the extent of rational knowledge, and something negative, namely, the limits, and finally, also the quality of the boundaries, as it were, the figure.

Cognitions are of two kinds: either those that pertain to objects that are given, or those that refer to the concepts of the form in which reason considers every object. The latter are merely subjective and also can alone have a universality of reason as well.

In synthetic judgments I represent to myself an identity for the sake of the predicate, not, however, the predicate for the sake of the identity.

The fundamental concepts of *analysis* are: possibility, impossibility, necessity, contingency, unity, etc.; of *synthesis*: space, time, and force.

Not all *conceptus superiores* are *abstracti*, but only the *a posteriori* ones arise analytically; the *a priori* ones are not *abstracti*. These *abstracti* are empirical or rational.

17:260 **3717.** Before 1764–66? 1764–68?? *LBl* Berliner Staatsbibliothek 27.

The *principium* of the form of all experiences is space and time.

The *principium* of the form of all judgments of pure reason: identity and contradiction.

The *principium* of the form of all *a posteriori* judgments of reason: ground and force.

Comparison, derivation, composition.

The possible is contradistinguished: 1. from that the concept of which contains a contradiction; 2. from that whch is determined or the true; 3. from the real.

In all empirical judgments there is the fundamental formula: in each thing there is that which contains the ground of a sensation; there is also the same subject which contains the ground of the others. The *synthesis* is one of composition or derivation.

All necessity and contingency which we can represent to ourselves is conditioned. The unconditioned is thought problematically.[6] Neither of them can be thought as absolutely contingent (e.g., free action) or as absolutely necessary.

Every relation is either of combination or of comparison or of composition.

All combination (in the real sense): space, time, and force.

All definitions are grounded on the concept of essence: therefore, we can define nothing but concepts of pure reason and arbitrary ones.

All abstract cognitions have first grounds *a posteriori*.

The universal judgment, which does not arise by means of abstraction *a posteriori* and thus not empirically, is not abstract, but rather is a purely rational judgment.

In metaphysics the grounds of cognition must be derived *a priori*, although the objects must be derived *a posteriori*.

17:261 If the grounds for that which must exist are derived from that which occurs, then they are *a posteriori*. The *synthesis* is twofold: of the coordinated and of the subordinated.

The *synthesis* of reason or experience.

Besides the principle of sufficient reason, this one holds also good: all *analysis* includes conversely the possibility of a *synthesis*.[7] Accordingly, in every series of subordinated things there must be a first one, because otherwise no complete *synthesis* and thus also no *analysis* would take place.

The synthetic principle of the understanding is [*breaks off*]

Mathematical *analysis* is always a philosophical *synthesis*, only there I think the whole prior to thinking the parts; if, however, I think the parts prior to thinking the whole, then it is a mathematical *synthesis*. All *synthesis* rests on coordination and takes place through the understanding.[8] But *analysis philosophica* rests on subordination and takes place through reason. The ground is not a part of the consequence, nor conversely.

In all images of things I coordinate nothing but immediate marks and partial representations.

ab represents the action of coordination, but *ac* represents the action of subordination.

The soul has three dimensions. Sense and its clarity, understanding and its form as well as its matter (i.e., extensiveness) of coordination, and reason, which is the height of subordination.

Whether this is not also the case with relation to feeling?

Because all negations only serve to prevent errors and to demonstrate ignorance, metaphysics is a very useful science not insofar as it extends knowledge but rather insofar as it prevents errors. One learns what Socrates knew.[9]

Taste pertains to appearances and not to sensation, consequently, to the constitution of the object insofar as it is an object of the senses, and it is thus, as a cognition, subjected to universally valid rules.

The sensible is a perfection, and confusion is not essential to it, rather distinctness of coordination can take place.[10]

17: 262

Mathematics exhibits the greatest dignity of human reason, metaphysics, however, its limits and its proper vocation.

In everything beautiful I need only the understanding and as little reason as possible for it; for it should be pleasing in appearance. Hence coordination.

Note: that the rules of the beautiful are given through experience, thus that one cannot conceive of the beautiful shape of a rational being without a human figure.[11]

3731. 1764–66? (1762–63?) *M* 330, at §§803ff.[12]

17: 272

The question why something exists presupposes the thought that it is possible that something does not exist as well. This thought, however, pertains either to the existence of substances or to their relations. As to the latter, this kind of composition, which could not be understood from the necessary existence of substances, is a proof of the contingent existence of this composition. But as to the existence of the substance itself, the question of why it exists is grounded on the inner possibility of thinking its non-existence.

17: 273

There are only three kinds of concepts of things: first, an absolute one from internal determinations; second, a respective one from the relation to possibility; third, a relative one from the relation to the reality of other things. No absolute necessity can be proved from the first concept, for anything along with all its internal predicates can be negated without contradiction. Also not from the third, because this is only a *necessitas hypothetica consequentiae.*[a] Thus there remains the second, that possibility itself is in such a relation to reality that it includes such a thing.

The absolute necessity of a thing must be able to be cognized without any determinate condition.

How do we cognize absolute possibility? *Data* for it must always be given to us.

If I say that a certain predicate is impossible for a thing, then I am saying that it does not belong to it, i.e., it contradicts it, though not what I think in it, but rather what belongs to it. (The question is whether I can say that it contradicts the remainder of a thing, besides its opposite.) Thus whatever is impossible contradicts something; whatever is absolutely impossible contradicts everything, namely, the contradiction rests on no particular determinate condition.

17:274   **3733.** Before 1764–66? (1762–63?) *M* 331, at §§803ff.

The thing that contains the ground of the internal possibility of things is absolutely necessary.[13] Conversely, the thing that is absolutely necessary contains the ground of the internal possibility of things; for if things were to be internally necessary without that, there would be no impossibility whatsoever in their not existing. Or because the opposite of a thing cannot contradict itself, it must contradict some other thing.

Whatever contains the ground of an internal possibility contains the ground of all possibility. For if we were to suppose that something else that is possible is left over, this would not agree with any other possible thing; that is, it would contradict something that is possible; but whatever contradicts any other possible thing is impossible. The necessary being thus contains the ground of all possibility.

In every possibility the formal and the material are different. The ground of the former is the *principium contradictionis*; of the latter, any existence that contains the ground of reality.

Accordingly, the most real being contains the ground of all possibility (*later addition*: it is not a particular ground of the internal possibility of [some] things and not of others) and is absolutely necessary.

The necessary being is all-sufficient (*later addition*: the most perfect *transscendentaliter*), i.e., the most real as a ground.

---

[a] hypothetical necessity of the consequences

The necessary being is a unique being.[14] For if we posit several, then any one of them could be negated, while leaving all of the others; be-cause, however, if something necessary is negated, the impossible arises, then it would be possible that something possible would be impossible. Moreover, each of them would be a consequence of the others: *regressus in infinitum curvilineus.*[a]

17:275

The necessary being is a simple being.[15] For if a whole is necessary, then the parts must be so as well; in that case, however, there would be many necessary beings.

The world is thus not a necessary being.

The necessary being is the highest good, for, among all that is possible, goodness is a reality without which the worth of all existence is equal to nothing.[16] Thus it contains the ground of everything good. The good, however, consists in the relation of things to beings that have cognitions and feeling, and to a being which for its sake contains the ground of things.

The necessary being has the most perfect understanding and will.[17]

The necessary being is thus a person, who contains by means of un-derstanding and will the ground of all existence. I.e., it is a god.[18]

3738. 1764–66. *M* 2.

17:278

All analytic judgments teach what is in concepts but confusedly thought; synthetic judgments, what should be thought as combined with the concept.[19] In all judgments the concept of the subject is something *a*, which I think in the object *x*, and the predicate is regarded as a mark of *a* in analytic judgments or of *x* in synthetic ones. $/\frac{}{a}/\frac{}{x}/$

All analytic judgments are rational and vice versa. All synthetic judg-ments are empirical and vice versa.[b] Material first principles of reason are elementary principles; synthetic principles, if they were also rational, would be called axioms; but, since there are no such things, there are said to be only analogues of rational principles in mathematics. In philosophy synthetic principles cannot be given except *a posteriori*, i.e., empirically, and analytical principles *a priori*, i.e., elementary propositions, go beyond the material.

We can compare ideas[c] in their relation to thought either in accor-dance with the rules of the intellect as empirical and synthetic, or to the rules of reason, as rational and analytic, or to the rules of the analogue of reason, i.e., the imagination or genius.[d] Crusius accepted the latter for many of his principles.

---

[a] regress in an infinite circle
[b] The remainder of this note is in Latin.
[c] *notiones*
[d] *ingenii*

Locke saw the distinction between synthetic and analytic judgments in his essay concerning human understanding.[20]

17:280 **3743.** 1764–66? (1769?) *M* 3.
All mathematical concepts are synthetic.[21]

17:280 **3744.** 1764–66. *M* 3.
There are synthetic propositions from experience, thus *principia prima synthetica*; (the definitions of mathematics) the *axiomata* of the mathematics of space are also of this sort.
Principia rationalia cannot be synthetic at all.
All empirical propositions are synthetic and vice versa.
All rational principles are analytic.

17:281 **3747.** 1764–66. *M* 3.
All *principia* of human cognition are *vel formalia vel materialia.*[a] The former contain merely the relation of concepts in judgments: either logical or metaphysical. The latter contain only the relation of things and are synthetic. (*Later addition*: Either [they are principles] of analytic [cognition] and are called logical and hold good for every understanding, and are objective (only not vice versa); or [principles] of synthetic [cognition] and are called real, and because they are asserted universally without the senses, they are either principles of the form of the understanding or of sensibility; in the first case they are merely subjective laws. In the second, they are objective only under the *hypothesi* of sensibility; if, however, the hypothesis already lies in the subject, they are objective.)

17:281 **3749.** 1764–66. *M* 3.
One can connect concepts with one another, in order to form a larger concept from them (synthetic); or one can think of concepts as connected with one another in order to cognize what is contained in them.
The concepts of causes are synthetic and thus empirical.

17:281 **3750.** 1764–66. *M* 3.
All *principia primitiva* are either **elementary propositions** and ana-
17:282 lytic or *axiomata* and are synthetic. Difference of an analytic and synthetic proposition in general. The rational ones are analytic; the empirical ones, synthetic; likewise, the mathematical ones.

---

[a] either formal or material

86

3803. 1764–66. *M* 123, at §392, in *Partes universi simplices.*   17:297

Every Spinozist is an egoist. It is a question whether every egoist is necessarily a Spinozist.[a]

3806. 1764–66? (Before 1764–66?) (1766–68?) *M* 147, at §448, in *Sub-*   17:298
stantiarum mundanarum commercium.[22]

The difference between *influxu ideali* and *reali* does not produce a different system, but is merely a correctly determined concept of *influxus* in general. Because, however, all *influxus* is ideal, it can be inferred from this that it is not possible to think a *harmonia* of substances in their self-activity otherwise than insofar as they depend on one substance.*,[23]

Space and time are the first relations that all things obtain thereby and the first grounds of the possibility of a world-whole.

*(The theory of the *influxus idealis* is not a particular system, but rather a ground for the abolition of *influxus physici*. Then must it be demonstrated how a *harmonia sub conditione influxus realis* is possible. Then the possibility of a *harmoniae praestabilitae*, or rather its necessity, must be shown.)

3809. 1764–68? (1769?) *M* 329, in *Theologia naturalis, Prolegomena.*   17:300

The possibility of a thing is twofold: either 1. that what exists is connected in a certain way, in accordance with laws that are already in it by means of its own properties, e.g., if there is wood, then a house made out of wood is possible, or also that an effect flows from forces, or 2. possibility, where nothing exists; because in that case there is no material for anything, then there cannot arise the concept of any object. Thus *logice* the concept of possibility may well precede actuality in accordance with given concepts, but *realiter* it does not precede everything actual. Thus a being that contains the material for all possibility and yet whose possibility can be distinguished from its actuality is just as absurd as if one would take its space away from an object – one could not then say that it was possible.[24]

3814. 1764–66? 1764–68? *M* 333, opposite §815, in *Existentia Dei.*   17:302

All judgments are logical or real. The latter are of existence and cannot, if they concern absolute necessity, be cognized by means of the principle of contradiction.

3818. 1764–68? (1769?) *M* 337, at §826, in *Existentia Dei.*[25]   17:303

Analogy of those born blind with regard to colors and tones.

With respect to the moral, the cognition of the properties of God is dogmatic and positive, with respect to the theoretical critical and

---

[a] This note is in Latin.

negative. The most important thing is that one does not commit an error. Thus the theoretical cognition that we need is very simple.

17:303 **3819.** 1764–66. *M* 338, at §828.

Moral properties.	⎫	Omnisufficiency of duration, of
The goodness of the creator,	⎪	power, of cognition. Eternity,
The holiness of the lawgiver,	⎬	omnipotence, omniscience.[26]
The justness of the judge.	⎭	

17:310 **3843.** 1764–70? (1773–75?) *M* 100, at §329, in *Causa efficiens.*
The relation of cause to effect is not a relation of identity; consequently there is neither similarity nor equality between cause and effect, but conformity. The cause is known and named from the effect. *Talis est notio qua talis, qualis oritur e notione causati.*[a]
We know each thing in the world only as a cause, but in the cause we know only the causality of the effect, thus only the effects, and thus not the thing itself and its determinations through which it produces the effect.

17:313 **3855.** 1764–68? (1769–70). *M* 252.[27]
Life is the capacity to initiate a state (of oneself or another) from an inner principle.[28] The first is not a complete life, since that whose state is alterable itself always requires something outer as its cause. Bodies may well have an inner *principium* for affecting one another (e.g., interconnection), also for preserving an externally imparted state, but not for initiating anything on their own. Thus is proven all alteration, all origin of a first beginning, and hence freedom. However the beginning can be comparatively first, namely in accordance with mechanical laws, e.g., when a dog ravages some carrion, movement begins in him which is not caused by the odor in accordance with mechanical laws but through the arousal of desire. In animals, however, this is just as much of an external necessitation as it is in machines; thus they are called *automata spiritualia.*
17:314 But in human beings the chain of determining causes is in every case cut off, and thus one also distinguishes what is immaterial as a *principium* of life from what is material. Among human beings the spirit is free and wills the good; the animal is an *automaton*; now if only this spirit would always be efficacious on the animal spirit and not get mixed up with the forces of the latter, we would find more proofs of freedom.
(Later addition: libertas est independentia a necessitate externa. libertas est vel originaria vel derivativa. Arbitrium autem est vel sensitivum, vel intellectuale; illud est vel brutum vel liberum.)[b]

---

[a] The notion of the cause is such as arises from the notion of what is caused.
[b] Liberty is independence from external necessitation. Liberty is either original or derivative. The will however is either sensible or intellectual; it is either animal or free.

3856. 1764–68? (1769?) *M* 252.   17:314

In the case of freedom, to be determined means not to be passive, either through the way in which objects affect or through a highest productive cause. I can say: at this moment I am free (*liber aut devinctus*)[a] and **unconstrained** to do what I prefer; yet it is unavoidably necessary that I act thus. It is a law of self-activity, which makes the opposite impossible. Even with regard to the morally evil one can be determined by just such a free resolve. No! one can be determined to that only passively or not at all, because the free will always remains and thus cannot be constrained at all, but does not always exercise its activity.[29]

3857. 1764–68? (1769?) *M* 252.   17:314

A substance that is not externally determined to produce something that previously did not exist acts freely, and this freedom is opposed to internal or external natural necessity. It acts from the free power of choice insofar as the causality of the action lies in its preference and is not passive. The difficulties concern only the first idea of freedom,   17:315
and it is incomprehensible in the case of the necessary being as well as in the case of contingent beings, but from different grounds, because the **former cannot initiate** but the latter cannot **first** initiate. The first degree of independence is the self-activity of a substance in general; the second degree is independence in acting from all external determining causes; the third degree is independence from one's own nature.

Thus the negative [independence] is genuinely incomprehensible; the positive [independence] of motives is comprehensible.

3858. 1764–68? (1769?) *M* 275.   17:315

In all actions the ground, the causality, lies, as far as its matter is concerned, in nature; but as far as its form is concerned, it lies either merely in nature, e.g., attraction, or in another faculty, which directs the forces of nature internally. The latter is freedom.

3859. 1764–68? (1769–70?) *M* 275, at §708.[30]   17:315

Freedom is a practically necessary fundamental concept.

The first necessary thing is not to be comprehended, since there is no ground for it; the first contingent thing is also not to be comprehended, since there must be a necessary ground for it. The former is not to be comprehended since it is necessary but has no ground, the latter because it is contingent even though it does have a ground.[31]

---

[a] either free or constrained

17:315 **3860.** 1764–68? (1769?) *M* 275, at §708.

For freedom 1. *spontaneitas simpliciter talis (automaton) (independentia a causis subiective necessitantibus (stimulis))*[a] is required, so that determinations can be imputed to the subject as his **actions**. 2. The faculty of

17:316 the *arbitrii intellectualis*,[b] so that it can be imputed to him as a *factum*.[c] Since everything that happens presupposes a satisfaction in accordance with laws of the faculty of desire, the *complacentia*,[d] which is independent from the subjective necessitation, must be intellectual, and the former therefore presupposes this.

The greatest difficulty is here: how a subjectively unconditioned power of choice can be conceived (*est obiective hypotheticum*)[e] in (in accordance with) the *nexu causarum efficientium sive determinantium*,[f] or, if one starts from that, how the imputability of actions is possible.

17:317 **3865.** 1764–1769. *M* 281, at §719.[32]

Freedom is actually a faculty for subordinating all voluntary actions to motives of reason.

17:317 **3866.** 1764–68? 1771?? *M* 283.

Stimuli do not [*crossed out*: move] necessitate our power of choice *objective*, i.e., that which one **should** do is independent of all sensible stimulations.

17:317 **3867.** 1764–68? 1771?? *M* 283.

No one counts as freedom the faculty of being able to desire what is worthy of being abhorred (evil).

We thus have sensible cognitions, sensible pleasure and displeasure, and sensible desires. The faculty in accordance with motives of reason is freedom. The possibility of consciously willing what is disapproved of by reason is the weak will; the aptitude for willing evil is the evil will.[33]

17:318 **3868.** 1764–68? (1762–63?) (1771? 1773–78?) *M* 283.

The faculty for actively willing the known good that is in our power is freedom; but the faculty for willing the known evil the hindrance of which is in our power does not belong equally necessarily to freedom. The latter is also not really a faculty, but a possibility of being acted

---

[a] spontaneity *simpliciter* and as such (automaton); independence from subjectively necessitating causes (stimuli)
[b] intelligent will
[c] deed
[d] pleasure, satisfaction
[e] it is something objectively hypothetical
[f] in the nexus of efficient or determining causes

upon.[a] Evil actions certainly stand under freedom, but do not happen through it.[34]

3870. 1764–68? (1762–63?) (1771? 1773–78?) *M* 283, at §723.[35]   17:318
(*Later addition*: The pathological is what is in conformity with the determination of force in accordance with impressions.)

(*Later addition*: The practical is everything that belongs to action in accordance with rules, or everything that is connected with the determining rules of actions. *Necessitatio est vel pathologica vel practica*:[b] the latter can be objective, the former cannot be.)

Something is considered as practical in general insofar as it is considered in accordance with the laws of the power of free choice. If it occurs in accordance with the rules of the power of choice that is good,[c] then it is moral, hence practically and morally possible or necessary. To practical   17:319
philosophy there belongs only the understanding and a physical feeling, to moral philosophy understanding and a moral feeling. A human race would be possible even without the latter.

3872. 1764–68? 1771?? *M* 284.   17:319
The free will is as it were isolated. Nothing external determines it; it is active, without being passive. The *motiva* are only objects that harmonize with the internal law of its activity.* The good moves only through a good will, i.e., it is only the effect that is possible in accordance with laws of such a will. Whether it be determined by incentives or by *causis efficientibus* (of the divinity), the subject is attached to a foreign cause by means of a chain, and its actions are only derivative, the good as well as the evil.

Freedom consists in the capacity to act **independently of external** determining grounds in accordance with the intellectual power of choice. All sensibility is subordinated to this. Hence we conceive of our power of   17:320
choice as subject to hastiness or a series of obscure representations, which are the causes of error. The actions that happen in accordance with mere laws of sensibility. In the human being we must distinguish between the animal, i.e., what happens in him in accordance with laws of sensibility, and the spirit, in accordance with laws of reason. His power of choice as an animal is really always determined by *stimuli*; yet his will is still free insofar as his reason is capable of altering these determinations of the power of choice. Why reason sometimes fails to do this and the person does not act in accordance with the intellectual will is unknown. But precisely on this account does it happen that the human being considered

[a] *zu leiden*
[b] necessity is either pathological or practical
[c] *der guten Willkühr*

as a spirit blames himself as an animal, is in contradiction and conflict with himself, wishes that he had other inclinations, but often loses himself in sensibility. One use of the spirit is to order the animal sensations and direct means in accordance with animal ends. The other is to consider the ends themselves *intellectualiter*.

How is it **possible that one can blame oneself** if the self is not so to speak twofold? For otherwise one could not indeed make any judgment about himself other than that which is derived from himself and also agrees with himself.

*(Not objective but subjective grounds necessitate *actualiter*.)

17:338   **3909.** 1766–68? (before 1764–66?) (1769?) *M* 335, in *Existentia Dei.*
transcendental concept of God.
God as the highest being. (*Later addition*: defense against *atheismus*.)
metaphysical[;] psychological:*
God as the highest intelligence. (*Later addition*: defense against *Deismus*, which strictly speaking attacks anthropomorphism.)
moral [concept of God]:
17:339   God as the highest good. (*Later addition*: defense against Epicurea-nism.)³⁶
(*Later addition*: He cannot be a just lawgiver for morals if he is not at the same time that of nature, and indeed in its entirety.³⁷ For if he did not have fate entirely in his power, then he could not command absolutely. But for that he must be a creator: this is necessary for speculation, not for religion.)
a. Moralitas contra Epicureos. (*Later addition*: Moral theology, theolog-ical morals.)
*(*Later addition*: We can only cognize God psychologically in accor-dance with the analogy with the forces of nature, which contain the complete causality of perfection. For we have no *data* of God, but only *data* of his relation to the world; hence we cognize him in those only [*breaks off*])

17:341   **3914.** 1769? 1769–1770? 1771? *M* I.
Nothing in metaphysics is empirical except what concerns the general laws of thought in the human soul.
Hence synthetic principles hold good not rationally but rather sub-jectively and universally; and it is not possible that the understanding should begin from concepts and merely compare concepts analytically, if some rules do not ground the *synthesis*.

17:342   **3916.** 1769? 1764–68? *M* II.
The comparison of concepts in accordance with the law of the imag-ination is not to be entirely rejected. Things that are always found to

be combined with one another provide the presumption that they are combined in accordance with the law of the understanding. Hence the inference from induction. In accordance with the law of mother-wit, the inference from analogy.

3917. 1769? (1764–68?) *M* II.   17: 342

(*Later addition*: All cognition has two *terminos,*[a] *a priori et a posteriori;* hence *principia prima a priori* or *a posteriori.* The *principia absolute prima a priori* are all indemonstrable; metaphysics thus contains only *principia comparative prima.*)

(*Later addition*: All ideas of pure reason are ideas of reflection (*discursivae* and not *intuitus,* as Plato maintained).[38] Therefore, objects are not represented thereby, but rather only laws for comparing concepts that have been given to us by the senses.)

All cognition has grounds; and among these, primary grounds. The   17: 343 primary are either those which naturally precede in origination, or those into which they ultimately resolve themselves and out of which they can again be synthesized: *a priori* or *a posteriori.* Grammar: empirical, rational.

(*Later addition*: empirical or intellectual principles.)

The primary grounds behind cognition are experiences.

The science for arriving at the highest grounds *a priori* is metaphysics. This science is analytical.[b] Fundamental concepts, fundamental judgments.

Method of nature.

Conditioned indispensability of this science in the higher[c] judgments of reason.

History. Names.

Order of disciplines.

(*Later addition*: grounds of self-understanding
                            testimony of others
                            proverbs)

3918. 1769? (1764–68?) *M* II.   17: 343

The *territorium* of metaphysics. Parts.

Its function determines its value. It is not the satisfaction of curiosity   17: 344 but rather the determining of boundaries, partly positive, partly negative.

It is a science of the ends of our cognition. Comparison with mathematics.

---

[a] starting points
[b] *auflösend*
[c] According to Adickes, *höheren* could instead be *sicheren,* and thus the phrase would read "in the certain judgments of reason" (*bey sicheren Vernunfturtheilen*).

3920. 1769. *M* III.

In all judgments of the understanding things are like this. (If anything *x* can be cognized by means of a representation *a*, then *a* is a mark of something *x*; but the cognition of *x* by means of *a* is a concept. Thus extension, motion, ignorance, etc., is a mark of something *x*.) If anything *x*, which is cognized by means of a representation *a*, is compared with
another concept *b*, as either including or excluding this concept, then this relation is in the judgment. This judgment is thus either the cognition of agreement or of opposition, so that in the thing *x*, which I know by means of the concept *a*, either *b* is contained as a partial concept and thus *x*, which is cognized by means of *a*, can also be cognized by means of *b*, or *x* negates the concept of *b*.

In all judgments matter and form are to be considered. The former are concepts of the subject $(y + a) = x$ and the predicate *b*. Second, the form, which is called, among logicians, the concept of combination (*copula*). (One can represent any concept in relation with all others; those which it includes stand toward it in the relation of affirmation, those it excludes stand over against it in negation.) The possible concept of a thing is called *x*; the representation by means of which I think it, *a*. Any form of judgment is either affirmation or negation. The former represents the relation in which the concept of the thing $y + a$ contains the mark *b* and thus is partially identical. Negation consists in the fact that the concept of the thing $y + a$ is what is opposed to the mark *b*, and negation consists in the representation of nullification.

3921. 1769. *M* IV.

The predicate is not a partial concept of the subject, but rather a representation of the [*crossed out*: whole] subject by means of a partial concept. The understanding always cognizes something by means of a clear or obscure judgment, in that it resolves something into its predicates. All of our concepts are marks drawn from sensation. Sensation itself is not an object of the understanding, but its marks; hence, e.g., the concept of the human being is nothing other than the representation of something that has the predicates into which we can resolve the concept of a human being. Therefore, in every judgment the subject in general is something = *x* which, cognized under the mark *a*, is compared with another mark. Hence it is also no wonder that we do not
cognize a subject prior to all predicates except the I, which nevertheless is no concept but rather [*crossed out*: a sensation] an intuition. Hence by means of the understanding we cognize in bodies not the actual subjects, but rather the predicates of extension, solidity, rest, motion, etc. The cause is: by means of our senses only the relations of things can be revealed, and we can represent the absolute or the subject only from

our selves. The idea of substance actually comes from the *repraesenta-tione sui ipsius,*[a] insofar as we represent that something is separate from us, and predicates cannot be thought without a subject and without an ultimate subject; the constant predicates together are then called the subject.

By means of a predicate I do not represent a part of the thing or have a concept of the part, but rather I represent the object itself and have a partial concept of it; therefore, designation by means of mathematical signs is impossible. Let $y + s$ be the thing itself, which is represented under the concept s, and let its predicate be p. Then $y + s - p = 0$, hence $y + s = p$.

3922. 1769. *M* III–IV.   17: 346

Material principles seem to be: whatever happens, must have a ground. Every successive series has a beginning.* The former proposition implies the latter: for since the beginning is a coming-to-be or event, there must in turn be a ground for it. The idea of freedom designates a coming-to-be without an antecedent determining ground. The nature of our under-standing entails in accordance with this rule that nothing contingent is conceivable without a connection to grounds, and that a consequence (in time) without a ground and an occurrence of something without a connection to its ground cannot be conceived, because then the under-standing would be entirely unusable.

*(and every series of subordinated things has a first member.[†])   17: 347

[†](*Later addition*: It is difficult to conceive of a beginning in the series of all things, which everything else succeeds, as a **creation**. It is likewise equally difficult to conceive of an infinite series that has passed. It seems to be false to use the idea **all** of an infinite series, and yet the necessity of the *causa prima* is based on that, for otherwise **everything** would be *causatum*.)

Another synthetic principle is: whatever thinks is only a simple subject. Everything must (not *absolute* but *respective* to another) exist sometime, either simultaneously with it or successively to it.

It does not follow that that which must be judged in accordance with the laws of our understanding must be true if it concerns things which our understanding is not determined to judge in accordance with the terms of its use.

We borrow the law of sufficient reason from corporeal appearances; but if we would make it universal and apply it to things that are elevated above the idea of our understanding, then we confuse the idea of absolute incomprehensibility for us with that of intrinsic impossibility.

---

[a] representation of oneself

17:348 **3923.** 1769. *M* IV.

Some principles are analytic and concern the formal aspect of distinctness in our cognition. Some are synthetic and concern the material aspect, in which case they are the arithmetical, geometrical, and chronological principles. Likewise, empirical principles. There are, however, further principles which concern the use of reason in *synthesi* in general. The nature of our reason, however, has this law, that it does not cognize things immediately, but rather mediately; hence it can expect everything that happens only in accordance with a ground, and whatever is not determined by another ground is irrational to it.

That matter is lifeless is a rational and not an empirical judgment, because although one perceives much life in matter, one distinguishes this from material properties. By contrast, that matter has attractive forces is empirical.

17:349 **3927.** 1769? 1771–75?? *M* V.

Fundamental empirical concepts by means of abstraction, which cannot be further resolved into their elements, although one can show the determination in their cause, are innumerable. The fundamental rational concepts, in terms of which alone the sensed properties of things can be explained, are, in the case of external objects, space, time, motion. In the case of internal objects: (A.) 1. immediate representation of the present, of the past, of the future. 2. comparison, differentiation, and identity. 3. relation (logical) of connection and opposition. 4. consciousness, judgments, inferences. (B.) 1. feeling, pleasure, displeasure. 2. in relation to the judgment of the understanding or of the senses. (C.) desire, etc. [*Crossed out*: Fundamental concepts that are common to both sensations] Through the nature of the understanding, not *abstrahendo* but rather *iudicando*,[a] arise the fundamental concepts of *synthesis*. Existence, possibility, unity, substance, *accidens*, relation, *respectus realis*, *logicus*, necessary, contingent. Whole, a part. Simple, composite, ground, consequence, force, cause.[39]

17:350 **3928.** 1769. *M* V.

The *principia* of the form of all analytic judgments (of the existential judgments of things *absolute* or of predicates *relative*) are the principle of identity and of contradiction, and the proofs are conducted by demonstrating identity or opposition with the predicate by means of the *analysin* of the **given** concept.[40] The *principia* of the form of synthetic judgments are: whatever is always combined with a known part of the possible concept of a thing also belongs as a part to this concept, etc. The proposition that every body is impenetrable is analytic, not only because body cannot

---

[a] not in forming concepts but in making judgments

be thought without impenetrability, but because it can be thought solely by means of impenetrability; this mark belongs as a *pars* to the notion of body. But that every body is inert is a synthetic proposition; for inertia is *compars*[a] with the concept of what is thought by means of the expression "body," thus to a whole concept which is combined in a necessary fashion with those partial concepts that belong to the notion of body. If one had the whole concept of which the notions of subject and predicate are *compartes*, synthetic judgments would be transformed into analytic ones.[41] One wonders to what extent there is something arbitrary here.

So much for the *nexu logico*. As for the *nexum realem*, its *principia materialia* are experiences; the formal *principia* are: everything that happens has a determining ground, and second: everything has a first ground. These *principia* are both synthetic, the former for the use of our reason, the latter for the *termino*[b] of this use. For in accordance with the former in the series of causes determining one another we always see into higher grounds, and in accordance with the latter we acknowledge that this series is bounded. It is, however, just as impossible to represent a series of subordinated grounds that has no beginning as it is to conceive how it begins. Nevertheless the proposition that everything that occurs has a determining ground is the proposition that makes an infinite series necessary, the *principium* of the form of all of our rational judgments about real connection. But the proposition that all series of subordinated things and all successive series have a first member is a synthetic proposition, which is abstracted more from the boundaries of our understanding than from the object of cognition. 17:351

The first member in the series of causes is always the power of free choice. That this has no determining ground is an empirical proposition, but to that extent is uncertain; its certainty, however, depends on the fact that otherwise there can be no beginning at all.

Of the possibility of alteration, i.e., of coming into being and cessation in general.

3929. 1769. *M* 432. 17:351

Properly speaking, the representation of all things is the representation of our own condition and the relation of one representation to another in accordance with our inner laws. The impossibility of separating concepts or their combination without any laws of our understanding is merely subjective; equally so the possibility. We cognize the possibility of free actions only empirically; understood rationally, it contradicts the laws for using our understanding. *Analysis sine termino*[c] makes the

[a] in part equated
[b] terminus, i.e., stopping point
[c] an analysis without an end

synthesin impossible. Therefore, in accordance with the laws for the use of our understanding, we posit a ground in everything that occurs; but for this very reason the *synthesis* is impossible (just this is applied to the *analysin* of body *sine termino*, where no synthesis is possible[a]). From the first relations in accordance with the laws of our understanding, no further ground can be provided. The *analysis completa* led from multiplicity to unity, in the *serie succesivorum* to the *principium*, in the *simultaneis* to *monas*.

17:352   The *axiomata* (*synthetica*) of philosophy concern solely the relation that can be cognized only subjectively in accordance with the laws of our understanding.

17:352   **3930. 1769. M 432.**
Some concepts are abstracted from sensations, others merely from the law of the understanding for comparing, combining, or separating abstracted concepts. The origin of the latter is in the understanding; of the former, in the senses. All concepts of the latter sort are called pure concepts of the understanding, *conceptus intellectus puri*. We can of course set these activities of the understanding in motion only when occasioned to do so by sensible impressions[b] and can become aware of certain concepts of the general relations of abstracted ideas in accordance with the laws of the understanding; and thus Locke's rule that no idea becomes clear in us without sensible impression is valid here as well;[42] the *notiones rationales*, however, arise no doubt by means of sensations and can also only be thought in application to the ideas abstracted from them, but they do not lie in them and are not abstracted from them. Just as in geometry we do not derive the idea of space from the sensation of extended beings, although we can clarify this concept only on the occasion of the sensation of corporeal things. Hence the idea of space is a *notio intellectus puri* which can be applied to the abstracted idea of mountains and of kegs.

The philosophy of the concepts of the *intellectus puri* is metaphysics. It is related to the rest of philosophy as *mathesis pura* is to *mathesis applicata*. The concepts of existence (reality), possibility, necessity, ground, unity and multiplicity, whole and part (everything, nothing), of the composite and the simple, space, time, alteration, motion, substance and accident, force and action, and everything that belongs to ontology proper, are related to the rest of metaphysics as general arithmetic is to *mathesi pura*.[43]

---

[a] Kant actually wrote "*wo keine* synthesis *unmöglich ist*," i.e., "where no synthesis is impossible."
[b] *sinnlichen Empfindungen*

98

3932. 1769? (1769–70? 1771?) *M* 432. 17:353

The ideas and rules of reason are also used in the relation of empirical concepts, and this is their natural and proper use; in that case, however, they are grounded on *iudicia empirica primitiva*, which are general only through induction. But these very judgments of reason, insofar as they are pure, are themselves to be universal. *Philosophia pura* is not certain in itself like *mathesis pura*.

3937. 1769 *M* VI. 17:355

One ought to conceive of something absolutely necessary, since everything that exists is necessary, but not everything can be hypothetically necessary. But one cannot conceive of anything absolutely necessary. One must conceive of the world as bounded, but one also cannot conceive of its boundaries.

Those synthetic propositions which in accordance with their nature do not negate the very conditions of comprehensibility that they set hold objectively, as in the case of *commercio substantiarum.*[a]

3938. 1769. *M* VII. 17:355

In addition to those determinations without which the objects cannot exist, there are in our reason further conditions, without which we cannot conceive certain objects through reason, even though these conditions are not determinations of the objects themselves. These *conditiones* are therefore subjective, and their concepts do not signify anything in the object. All synthetic judgments of pure reason are accordingly subjective, and the concepts of them signify actions of reason toward itself.

3941. 1769. *M* VII. 17:356

Metaphysical concepts pertain 1. merely to the relation of coordination: *absolutum et relativum*, whole, part, *continuum, discretum*, one, all (the first, the last, a single one); 2. or to that of subordination in the logical sense: universal or particular; 3. to subordination in the real sense: ground, consequence, cause, effect. Whence arises the concept of the first cause, the final consequence, the cause of everything, of anything. 4. to existence: necessary, contingent, possible; 5. Substance (subject, predicate), simple, composite, *action, passio (vis, receptivitas) spontanea, iners.*[b] A whole of substances. World.[44]

Space and time. Duration, instance, eternity, beginning, end. Alteration, persistence. Location, extension, point. Space and time: motion, rest. Omnipresence. 17:357

---

[a] the community of substances, or interaction among substances
[b] action, passion (force, receptivity), spontaneous, inert

Effect in space: filling, force, mass.
Effect in time: alteration, creation, annihilation.

3942. 1769? 1764–68? *M* LIV.

A cognition is true which is in agreement with the constitution of the object. Since the representation of external objects is only possible by means of the idea of space,[45] all of the axioms of space and what can be derived from them agree with the object, likewise all relations of concepts in accordance with the rule of identity. For the ideas then agree among themselves. But since the metaphysical concepts of ground, substance, etc., are not properly speaking representations of the objects, while even the most perfect sense cannot have a sensation of these in anything and things can be represented on the whole without these relations, although not by means of our reason, thus these concepts are not objective; therefore in the axioms of them everything is subjective. Hence, if they are falsely regarded as objective, neither truth nor falsehood holds for them. In general, if one would find the concept of cause, then outside of the relations of connection in accordance with ideas of time one will find no explanation that does not include a circle, and there seem to be no others.

The surest proof that they are not objective is that they stand in evident self-contradiction.

3944. 1769? 1772?? *M* XXXXIII.

The logical form of our cognition is to be distinguished from the metaphysical: the former is *analysis*, the latter is *synthesis*.

3946. 1769? 1772??? *M* XXXXIII–XXXXIV.

All pure philosophy is either logical or metaphysical. The former contains only the subordination of concepts under the *sphaeram* of the other, either immediately, in judgments, or mediately, in inferences. However, it leaves the concepts themselves that can be subordinated to one another undetermined, and does not decide which predicates belong to things in accordance with the laws of pure reason. Therefore, cognizing the primary predicates of things by means of pure reason, hence finding the primary fundamental concepts and the principles with which we judge by means of pure reason, is a matter for metaphysics.

(*Later addition*: Metaphysics pertains to cognitions solely by means of reason; logic, to all cognitions, even empirical ones. All rational concepts are universal; logic demonstrates only the relation of the universal to the particular in general. Metaphysics, however, demonstrates the origin of the universal concepts to which all cognition must be traced back if appearances are to be transformed into concepts.)

Metaphysics is thus a science of the fundamental concepts and principles of human reason, and not of human cognition in general, in which there is much that is empirical and sensible; logic is a science of the relations of general concepts and propositions in general. Logic derives concepts and propositions from metaphysics or some empirical cognition and teaches how to use them.

Logic contains the concept of the general; metaphysics contains general concepts of reason (*later addition*: the former treats of the relation of general concepts to one another, the latter demonstrates the general concepts under which the rational concepts of things are contained; the   17: 360 former is logical theory, for logical praxis is tautological unless the subject's cognition is presupposed); logic contains propositions that express the relation of the general to the particular without predicate and subject, but metaphysics contains general propositions. It contains the elements out of which all rational cognition is composed.

Logic leaves undetermined the particular nature of human reason and is valid for everyone's reason; metaphysics demonstrates the general concepts that flow from the nature of human reason and their particular laws.

3948. 1769. *M* XXXXIV.   17: 360

If the question were whether further discoveries are still to be hoped for in empirical sciences, there would be no doubt about that, because further experiences yield further and new cognitions. If the question is whether new discoveries are to be expected in the science of pure reason, then it is clear that in mathematics, logic, and pure morality many are possible, because in accordance with the rule of identity all sorts of arbitrarily presented combinations can be inferred from universal concepts. But it is quite otherwise with metaphysics. Here it is not asked what flows from universal to particular in arbitrarily assumed relations   17: 361 in accordance with the rule of identity, but which relations are really the primary grounds of general rules. Now since these relations are given neither through the senses in experience nor through the understanding in an intuitive and individual concept, nothing further can occur than that one analyze one's confused concepts. From this, however, only a science of the subject can arise. Since no object is hereby given, through this slicing and analyzing of our ideas we can also not discover anything beyond them.[46]

3949. 1769. *M* XXXIV.   17: 361

Mathematics and morals (*purae*) stand under logical rules; the pure cognition of that which strikes the outer and inner senses, hence the first rational grounds of outer and inner appearances, stands under metaphysical ones. In both cases one must consider that which is most general in the outer and inner senses in accordance with its first rational grounds.

Thus there is no philosophy of pure reason except logic and *metaphysica*.

The fundamental concept of logic is that of the general, insofar as it contains some things under itself or does not; things are thought in accordance with this relation, but they are not represented in it. The concept of species or genus is not given, but rather is only the relation according to which *conceptus dabiles*[a] can be compared.[47]

Logic provides no fundamental concepts of reason at all, but rather fundamental concepts of the laws in accordance with which we make concepts distinct by means of each other in general. Thus it contains the rules without which we can obtain no distinct cognition of things; metaphysics, however, contains the rules without which objects cannot be cognized by us at all.[48] Logical propositions are rules that we employ at will as means for making cognitions distinct by means of comparison. Metaphysics displays the marks that are given through the nature of reason (logic demonstrates only the use of the marks in general).

17:362   **3950.** 1769. *M* XXXXV.

Space, time, and number are synthetic concepts. [*crossed out*: and are objective.]

If the concepts are also synthetic, but the propositions are analytic, i.e., in accordance with the rule of identity, then they are objective.

If, however, the concepts are subjective, i.e., of no object at all, neither of a given condition of the representation of the objects (space and time), nor arbitrary concepts of quantity, then the judgments are nevertheless objective and universally valid, i.e., either universally true or false, if their form is analytic. If, however, their form is synthetic, then they are subjective; and they are objectively valid only as rules of appearances, consequently as empirical judgments.

17:362   **3951.** 1769. *M* XXXXV.

Dogmatic *philosophica pura* contains two disciplines.

1. The rules of the universally valid use of the understanding;

2. the rules of the universally valid use of the free will.

In both cases judgment is made in accordance with the *nexu logico*[b] [and] not from any *datis* of experience; but in *physiologia transscendentali* the *data* from experience in accordance with the relations of space and time are given in such a way that the most universal concept of the object

---

[a] concepts that can be given
[b] logical connection

of all outer and inner sensations can be taken and the ground thereof can be sought.

3952. 1769. *M* XXXXVI.　　　　　　　　　　　　　　　　　17:362

Metaphysics is a science of the laws of pure human reason and thus subjective. Objective, pure philosophy has either analytic *principia* with-　17:363 out any axioms of experience or synthetic ones. The former rest[a] on universal judgments in accordance with the rule of identity and on the subordination of the particular under the general. Hence the universally valid rules of the understanding and the will, hence *logica et moralis pura*. The latter have[b] for their object the most general rules of the outer and inner senses and thus contain the pure rational grounds to which all of the natural sciences of the outer and inner senses can be brought.

3953. 1769. *M* XXXXVI.　　　　　　　　　　　　　　　　　17:363

The principles of space are objective; whether, however, a thing is in space or not is subjective, because the concept of space is not objective.

3954. 1769. *M* XXXXVI.　　　　　　　　　　　　　　　　　17:363

A major error arises if one confuses the *genus* with all the *individuis* and regards as a consequence in accordance with concepts that which is merely a lawlike appearance of the immediate intuition. Hence the ground is not something objective. What we call a real ground is only a concomitant appearance for the intuitive concept. And in that which we call reason, although all of its pure concepts, by means of which we infer from the general to the particular, especially as regards its fundamental concepts, have their reality, they have it only because they lie in the things and can be abstracted from them. Accordingly our reason only makes good the lack of *intuitus*.

Thus if I say that a principle is subjective, i.e., it contains the *conditiones* under which alone we can judge by means of our reason in accordance with laws of experience, this does not mean that our reason must assume this law in the objects; for it does not apply to them at all; one can thus say neither that it is true or that it is false.

3955. 1769. *M* XXXXVII.　　　　　　　　　　　　　　　　　17:364

All cognitions are either empirical, insofar as they presuppose sensations, or pure cognitions, insofar as they have no sensation as their ground. The latter, namely the pure cognitions, are either [*crossed out*: individual] *conceptus singulares* and are called *intuitus puri* or general [*crossed out*: concepts] and are pure rational concepts. The empirical cognitions

---

[a] Reading *beruhet* as "rest" rather than "rests."
[b] Reading *hat* as "have" rather than "has."

are sensation, appearance, and the empirical concept; from the first the matter of all cognition is to be derived; the second adds the form of intuition; the third brings both under a general concept.

3957. 1769. *M* XXXXVII–XXXXVIII.

All human cognitions can be divided into two main genera: 1. those which arise from the senses and are called empirical; 2. those which are not obtained by means of the senses at all, but rather have their ground in the constant nature of the [*crossed out*: cognitive power] thinking power of the soul, and can be called pure representations. Since all of the materials for thinking must necessarily be given by means of the senses, the matter of our entire body of cognition is empirical. For this very reason all pure concepts must pertain merely to the form of cognitions. Now we have a twofold form for cognitions: the intuitive and the rational form. The former occurs only in the immediate cognition of individual things, the latter in general representations; the former I will call intuitive concepts, the latter concepts of reason. Now in all empirical cognition we can look

first merely to the matter, and this consists of sensation; second, to the form of intuition; third, to the form of reason in concepts. The form of appearances rests solely on space and time, and these concepts do not arise through the senses or sensation, but rather rest on the nature of the mind, in accordance with which the various sensations can be represented under such relations. Hence, if all sensation from the senses is set aside, then the concept of space and time is a pure concept of intuition, and because everything that the understanding can cognize in experiences lies in it, it is a concept of the understanding; and although the appearances are empirical, it is nevertheless intellectual.[49] Likewise, sensations and appearances that have been made general are not pure but rather empirical concepts of reason; if, however, one leaves aside every effect of the senses, then the concepts are pure concepts of reason, such as: possible, substance, *etc.* Hence all pure concepts are intellectual and intuitive, or rational and [*crossed out*: discursive] reflecting concepts. Furthermore, all cognitions are either given or invented. The matter of cognition cannot be invented, hence only the form can be, and in the form only the repetition; thus every invention of reason pertains only to mathematics; in contrast to this the form that is given in geometry is space.

Because one can describe only the form of experience, it belongs to the understanding.

A science of pure reason is possible and also necessary. It is, however, either philosophy or mathematics; the former considers what exists, and solely the reason which *respectus* exists; the latter: how many times the homogeneous exists.[50] Space is an object both for philosophy and mathematics. Judgments about space that are intuitive are not yet mathematical, also not philosophical. Both judge space not *a priori* from the principles of space which reason cognizes, but rather from *a posteriori* principles, i.e., intuitively and individually, although not empirically. The philosophy of pure reason is **either dogmatic**, and in that case its object is given by means of what all the senses have most in common, and as it were by means of the *genus* of the senses: thus, first, the power of representation and the faculty of desire, such as the objects of inner sense; 2. space and time, consequently general mechanics, as the most general element of the outer senses; hence dogmatic pure philosophy is theoretical logic, theoretical morals, and general natural science.[51] **Second**, it is critical, consequently subjective. It is zetetic, skeptical, problematic. 17: 366

3958. 1769. *M* XXXXVIII. 17: 366

All cognitions from experience (empirical) belong either to sensation and contain the matter of empirical cognition, or to appearance and contain at the same time the form, or to the concept and contain what is general in different sensations or appearances. Sensation represents individual objects insofar as they stimulate the senses, e.g., red, black, sweet, hard, warm, etc., consequently only the matter of empirical cognition.[52] The form of objects is thought in accordance with space and time. The form of empirical cognition is that of coordination; the form of rational cognition is that of subordination.[53]

If one removes all matter of cognition, consequently everything that stimulates the senses, then the empirical form of the appearances still remains; if one also removes this, then the rational form remains; and cognitions of the first kind are pure concepts of intuitions, cognitions of the second kind are pure concepts of reason.[54] 17: 367

3961. 1769. *M* IL. 17: 367

All cognitions from experience are called empirical and are either sensations or apearances or concepts. In the first, everything is given by means of sense and is merely the matter for cognition; the second contains the sensations in accordance with the form of space and time; the third contains the sensations or appearances made general through reason.

If one leaves aside both of the latter actions, sensation remains. If one leaves this aside, then there remain pure concepts 1. of the understanding: of coordination, 2. of reason: of subordination.

3963. 1769. *M* L. 17: 368

Rational cognitions are either, as far as their matter is concerned, given by the senses, and have only the form of reason, e.g., general concepts, or they express the form of reason itself; the former are empirical, the latter are *notiones purae*.

17:368   **3964.** 1769. *M* L.

Metaphysics is a critique of pure reason[55] and not a doctrine. Logic is the doctrine 1. of pure reason, 2. of mixed reason. The application of pure reason to objects that are given by means of experience occurs only in the case of empirical concepts, where the particular can be inferred from the general.

The science of a cognition considered *subiective* is critique; the science of cognition considered *obiective* is doctrine.

There are certain general concepts that are given by means of the nature of reason, in accordance with which other concepts and their relation are thought. E.g., subject and predicate. These are metaphysical. There are representations that are given by means of the senses and are made general by means of reason.

17:368   **3965.** 1769. *M* LI.

There are pure concepts of intuitions, arbitrary ones of invention, and universal ones of reason.

A concept that cannot be regarded as an impression of the senses is pure.

Principles:

1. We cognize everything through judgments that we do not cognize through the senses.
2. All judgments of our reason are mediate.[56]

17:369   **3969.** 1769. *M* LII.

Our reason contains nothing but *relationes*. Now if these are not given through relations in accordance with space and time in experience nor through the repetition and composition of the one out of the many in pure mathematics, then they are not *relationes* that apply to objects, but only relations of our concepts in accordance with the laws of our reason.

17:370   **3970.** 1769. *M* LII.

Intuitive concepts of the senses, concepts of the understanding about abstraction, concepts of reason about the relation which general cognitions have.

The relations of the senses are space and time, those of the understanding the general and the particular, consequently also all judgments and the rules of all inferences. Those of reason: the ground and the consequence, namely *obiective:* the ground of things (real ground).

The relation of identity and difference is logical (likewise the relation of the general and the particular), that of repetition is mathematical, the rest are metaphysical – namely, the real relations.

Metaphysics is the critique of human reason, logic is the general doctrine thereof; the former is subjective and problematic, the latter entirely objective and dogmatic.

3972. 1769. M LII.   17:370
The concept of the ground (the consequence) contains not only that something that exists is accompanied with something else, but further that this relation is universal and necessary: for where one such thing *b* exists, such a ground *a* exists, and where a [*crossed out*: ground] *a* exists, the consequence *b* exists. Now all real grounds and even their possibility are cognizable only *a posteriori*; this reveals a constant accompaniment, but no universality of connection, hence the concept of a ground is not objective.   17:371

3974. 1769. M LIII.   17:371
In the use of pure reason a particular confusion arises from the mixing up of 2 concepts. Everything (*singuli*) has a ground; everything taken together, however, cannot have a ground, and thus something is without a ground. The former is a useful rule of reason for the explication of appearances; the latter is a consequence of the *synthesi completa*, which is impossible for our understanding.[57] Likewise: everything that is to be posited by reason is necessary; everything, however, is necessary under its *hypothesi*.
All concepts are either sensible concepts or concepts of reason. The **first** are either of sensation or of appearance; these have as their ground the form of space and time. The **second** cannot be found through any *analysin* of experience, although all experience is coordinated to them, and are pure concepts of reason, if no object of experience is thought through them; in the latter case, however, they are empirical concepts. E.g., a *genus* is a pure concept, but a stone in general or the *genus* of stone is an empirical one.
The rational science of the rules for judging objectively, i.e., of all judgments and inferences, insofar as they arise *per analysin*, is logic. The rational science of synthetic cognitions and judgments is metaphysics.
Space is not a concept of reason, but metaphysics seeks the rational concept of it.   17:372

3975. 1769. M LIII.   17:372
Since through reason, i.e., through that cognition which is not any sensation, there arise only concepts through which it remains **undetermined** whether the thing is posited or not, something additional is required that necessitates us to posit something. Thus the concept of a ground has a subjective origin, and the statement that

something is posited by means of another thing or for the sake of another will signifies *obiective* only that things accompany or follow one another.

The idea of the ground (cause) arises from experiences.

To cognize through reason whether something does not exist or is not possible, or that something exists or that it is necessary, is the same thing. By contrast, everything the existence of which I cognize by means of the senses, but not by means of reason, appears contingent.[58]

The only concepts of pure reason through whose relations truths can be discovered in accordance with the rule of identity are [those of] magnitudes; but these are also arbitrary inventions.

17:372 **3976.** 1769. *M* 1.

It is necessary to assume, in accordance with the subjective law of reason, a first action from which everything else follows; it is, however, just as necessary to assume in general a ground for every action, and thus no first action.[59]

There are pure fundamental concepts of intuition or of reflection; the former are the principles of appearance, the latter of insight; the former display coordination, the latter subordination.[60] Because everything is represented in time, all of our concepts of reason are always at the same time thought under the condition of *phaenomeni*; the conditions of the 17:373 latter do not agree with the former. In time no first moment is possible, yet in the case of the ground there should be one.[61]

If the comprehensibility of a thing is to be complete, then we would have to have a first ground; but we also cannot posit a first ground by means of reason, and thus it follows from this that no absolute positing of comprehensibility is complete by means of human reason.

The simple concepts of reason, indeed all simple concepts, are subjective; the objective ones consist in the agreement of cognition with itself and are thus composite. Hence the concept of the **first thing** is subjective, for it contains the concept of **everything**.

All real relations (space and time excepted) are given by means of experience (in accordance with the relations of space and time) and thus cannot serve as propositions of pure reason.

17:373 **3977.** 1769. *M* 1.

All truth consists in the necessary agreement of a cognition with itself. If the cognition that is to agree with itself constitutes the form of appearance, e.g., space and time, then every judgment is objective and either true or false. But if the cognition concerns solely a law of human reason, by means of which we compare concepts, then it is not objective at all, consequently neither true nor false. Hence ground and consequence is not any property of things that is given by means of reason alone, but rather is given only by means of experience. It is, however, a law of reason to look to this relation; all general rules of reason about cause and effect have no validity whatsoever for objects.

3980. 1769. *M* XXXXII.   17:375

If I will understand something in nature, then I must not go outside of nature with my explanation. But if I will understand nature as a whole, then I must go outside its boundaries.

3984. 1769. *M* XXXIX.   17:376

Everything that occurs, i.e., what one is necessitated to cognize as having occurred for experience, has a ground; but what one wills to occur has no further ground. For everything that is determined by means of the power of choice has no further ground for why it is thought so and not otherwise than this power of choice. Because something first arises through the will, it can just as little be asked in the case of arbitrary ideas which are a ground of actions as it can in the case of arbitrary speculative ideas [*breaks off*]

3986. 1769. *M* XXXXVIIVIII.   17:376

One can assume that the motion of a body is only a successive pres-   17:377
ence of a great efficacy of impenetrability in space, where the substance does not alter its place, but instead this effect of the impenetrability successively occurs in different locations, as happens, in the case of sound, with the airwaves. One can also assume that there are no substances at all in space, rather a greater or lesser efficacy of a single highest cause in different locations in space. From this it would follow that matter is infinitely divisible.

3987. 1769? 1770–71? 1773–75? 1776–78? *M* XXXXVIIVIII.   17:377

The concept of God is the only idea that is thoroughly determined by means of reason and is also given as the highest ground of all determination.

3988. 1769. *M* 2.   17:377

[*Crossed out*: In our judgments we pay attention either only to the idea of a thing alone and to that by means of which we think this very thing, or to the idea's relation to others.]

We have two types of concepts: those that can arise in us because of the presence of the thing; or those by means of which the understanding represents the relation of these concepts to the laws of its own thought. To the latter belongs the concept of ground, possibility, existence. There-   17:378
fore, the principles about the former are objective; those about the latter are subjective.

Metaphysics is a science for insight into the relation of human reason to the primary properties of things.

All fundamental rational concepts are concepts of form; the empirical ones are *principia* of the matter. The former are exclusively subjective, i.e., abstracted from the laws of our thought. The latter are objective, abstracted from the representation itself by means of which the object is represented. The understanding is applied to the experiences only in accordance with the laws of the understanding; but the abstracted idea of the relation of the sensible representation in general, in accordance with the laws of the understanding, makes up the pure rational concept. The understanding proceeds in accordance with a natural law when it thinks one thing and many. This understanding, applied to the sensation of a body, abstracts the idea of a whole not from the body but rather from itself.

The *philosophia pura* concerning rational concepts is only subjective and never synthetic; the *principia* of *philosophiae applicatae domestica*[a] are the first laws of experience in combination with the *principiis rationalibus*, insofar as such *principia* relate to the *empirica*. The proposition that nothing comes from nothing, and the proposition that everything has a ground, make the same mistake, that they are expressed rationally although they are only empirically valid.

The idea of undetermined freedom cannot be thought at all in accordance with the laws of our understanding; it is not, however, for this reason false.

By what does one cognize the multiplicity and unity of substances[?] The representation of the I is really a unity; but is the differentiation of places a proof of multiplicity?

If one only observes [*breaks off*]

17:381 **3999.** 1769. *M* 4, in *Possibile*.

Since we form rational concepts only through judgments, but in these the object[b] is represented by means of predicates, we represent an object of thought to ourselves and its **being** or **not being** as a predicate; if we abstract from this then there still remains an object of thought, which, as long as it does not negate itself, is something possible.

The possibility of judgments is contradistinguished from the truth and the possibility of actual things.

The contradictions of pure reason arise from the fact that it does not, like empirical philosophy, draw general propositions from particular ones, but rather judges universally from pure concepts, although a

---

[a] domestically applied philosophy, i.e., philosophy applied to our actual experience
[b] *Sache*

110

terminum of subordination or coordinations is required, which contradicts universality.

By means of reason we can cognize only the possibility of judgments, but can never entirely cognize the objects, because this involves the presupposition of the possibility of matter, which must be given by means of the senses and therefore *a posteriori*. The falsehood of the form in the *synthesi* cannot be constituted by anything other than the contradiction of the consequences with other certain cognitions.

Possibility is only a form, but the possible also contains matter.

4000. 1769. *M* 4.   17:381

Some things hold *obiective* under an arbitrary condition, others *subiective* under a condition given through the understanding. These given conditions are appearances (space and time are always the basis). Thus,   17:382 although if the concepts of ground and consequence were objective, then one of the two propositions that there is a first cause or that there is not would have to be true, since neither of them is objective, both may be true at the same time as subjective laws.[62]

4005. 1769. *M* 6, at §16, in *Possibile*.   17:382

We can only cognize conditional possibility by means of reason. The absolute possibility that we cognize through reason is in accordance with   17:383 the *principio contradictionis* and concerns propositions in which we analyze the concepts.

All absolute possibility must otherwise be given by means of experience; what exists is intrinsically possible.

4006. 1769? (1770–71? 1773–75? 1776–78?) *M* 6, at §17, in *Possibile*.   17:383

In all elementary representations we can derive possibility only from reality, because the former is given to thought only through the latter.

If under certain conditions something always occurs in the same way and yet has no natural ground in these conditions, then it must have its ground in an intention or in freedom. E.g., if a game always comes out the same way. Thus freedom is a primary ground and is not comprehended along with that which occurs.

4007. 1769? (1769–70?) *M* 7, at §20, in *Connexum*.[63]   17:383

We must cognize a ground for everything that exists if we would cognize its existence* by means of reason; thus we cannot cognize that which is absolutely necessary. In everything that is subordinated we must assume a first element that is intrinsically necessary;** thus there is a conflict of subjective laws.

*(*Later addition*: Thus it is a subjective rule of reason. 2. Everything that is contingently an object of experience (that occurs) has a ground: is an objective rule of experience.)

**(*Later addition*: a principle that we assume only because otherwise we could not have *a priori* insight into anything.)

17:385   **4012.** 1769? (1770–71? 1773–75? 1776–78?) *M* 7, at §20.

The *principium rationis*, likewise the *principium rationati*,[a] is a rule of healthy reason and is thus restricted to the objects of experience.[64] The boundaries of the sensible world are thus also the boundaries of its use. If one goes further and would generalize its validity, then one errs and brings it into science.

17:387   **4017.** 1769. *M* 15, at §§53–4, in *Ens*.[65]

Praedicata logica are concepts by means of which I can cognize or posit certain things. Accordingly all concepts are predicates; they signify either things or the positing of them: the former is a real predicate, the latter only a logical one.

Concepts are undetermined with regard to many predicates, but the things are not. For that reason thoroughgoing determination pertains to actuality, and there is more in existence than in possibility. This also follows from the fact that through possibility I posit merely the concept, through actuality the thing. If God takes existence away from a thing, then he does not take any predicate away from it, but rather the thing itself (*later addition*: but not the possibility or the concept of the thing). Whoever denies existence removes the thing with all of its predicates.

Existence can of course be a logical but never a real predicate of a thing.[66]

17:391   **4033.** 1769. *M* 29, at §§102–4, in *Necessarium et contingens*.[67]

All absolute necessity is either of judgments or of things. The former, as logical, is always a conditional necessity of the predicate. The necessity of things that we can cognize is always conditional, for in itself we can always negate anything since where we affirm nothing we also do not contradict anything by means of its denial. The concept of the necessary is nevertheless in the first instance a concept given through reason, since through it alone is anything determined. Absolute necessity is a boundary concept, since without it there would be no *completudo* in the series of
17:392   the contingent. However, this boundary concept is itself problematic and cannot be cognized by reason *a priori*, because it is a *conceptus terminator*,[b] thus not something into which we can have insight *a posteriori*, for that

---

[a] the principle of reason, the principle of that which has a reason or "is grounded"
[b] a concept that terminates or draws a boundary

is the same as not to have insight, yet it is also not immediate; it is thus problematic.

The highest *principium* of everything contingent is that which is absolutely necessary, and the highest *principium* of the possibility of **origination** is freedom. It is thought that with regard to a freely acting being every state of affairs that is within its power constitutes a *terminum a priori*, which is not connected to what has preceded by means of a natural link. It is not itself a link in a larger chain, at least not as far as the activity is concerned.

4034. 1769? 1770–71? (1773–75?)(1776–78?) *M* 30, at §105, still in *Necessarium et contingens.*   17:392

The reality of the *omnimode contingentis*[a] (free action) can no more be comprehended than that of the *omnimode necesarii*.[b] The latter is the case because if *necessitas* is *mediata*,[c] the first necessity is not to be understood; the second, because [*crossed out*: if the *contingentia* is only *respectiva*][d] the existence of such a thing is not to be comprehended.

4035. 1769? 1770–71? (1766–68?) 1773–75?? 1776–78?? *M* 31, at §109.[68]   17:392

All necessity is a necessity of judgments or of things: in the case of the former, if I would think the opposite, then I preserve the subject and negate its identical predicate; in the case of the latter, if I will think the opposite then I negate the thing with all of its predicates; hence in the former case I can cognize absolute necessity from the principle of contradiction, but in the latter case I cannot cognize it.

4073. 1769. *M* 71, at *M* §239, in *Monas*.[e,69]   17:404

Concepts are either intuitive or [*crossed out*: rational] reflexive.

The former are either sensible intuitions or pure intuitions, depending on whether the matter or merely the form of sensible representations is in them. Reflexive concepts are either empirical or pure; the former are universal concepts containing matter from the senses, the latter containing the form for that. Space and time are concepts of pure intellect. 17:405
Metaphysical notions are concepts of pure reason.

Space is either determining (possible) or determinate (actual).

4077. 1769. *M* 72, at §239.   17:405

Space and time precede things; that is entirely natural. Both, namely, 17:406
are subjective conditions, under which alone objects can be given to

---

[a] that which is in every respect contingent
[b] that which is in every respect necessary
[c] mediated
[d] if the contingency is only relative
[e] This note is in Latin.

the senses. Taken objectively, this would be absurd. Hence the difficulty about the location of the world and time before the world. Yet in absolute time no location is determined without actual things, hence absolute time cannot yield any ground for the explanation of the *phaenomenorum*.

17:406 **4078.** 1769. *M* 72, at §239.

That space is a mere *phaenomenon* and something subjective, not a representation of the things, can be seen from the fact that relations can be represented in it that are **not effects** but rather **merely grounds of the possibility of effects**, and these grounds are not themselves any things.

17:413 **4094.** 1769? (1764–68?) *M* 123, at §392, in *Partes universi simplices.*[70]

The egoist can only be refuted through the fact that no alteration is possible in a single substance by itself.[71]

The idealist regards all his external (actual) representations as *spontaneas*; the egoist everything external, as possible.

17:418 **4108.** 1769? (1769–1770?) *M* 318, at §782, in *Status post mortem.*

[*Crossed out*: Is the soul always in this sensible world or]

The transition either into another world or another [*crossed out*: relation with] region of this one.

The 1st question: is the soul after death a pure spirit or still the soul of an animal[?] The answer is based on deciding the question whether the soul still exists in connection with the world in accordance with the current law of sensibility, thus also in connection with the corporeal world. Some sort of sensibility may well remain.

2nd question. Is the other world another region of the sensible world or is it different in form[?] Answer: ***objective***, there can be **only one** world, for all substances outside of the highest cause make up a whole; but ***subjective***, i.e., as to how the subject represents it, there can be another world. And in that case it is to be surmised that **sensibility diminishes** and thus the transition from the *mundo sensibili* to the *intelligibilem* proceeds *per approximationem. Intuitus* is *comparative* intellectual, the more inner sense grows.

The *mundus vere intelligibilis*[a] is the *mundus moralis.* The principles of its form are valid for everyone, and from it one can infer God as the *causam mere intelligibilem*; but this *mundus intelligibilis* is not an object of intuition, but rather of reflection. God's intuiting would at the same time provide the *intuitum intellectualem* of the world.[72]

[a] truly intelligible world

Those who assume an *intuitum mere intellectualem*, which naturally begins after death, maintain that after death the soul sees itself in the other world and does not pass into it (departing of the soul), that it always belongs to the *mundo immateriali* as the true substance, that the corporeal world is only a certain sensible appearance of the spiritual world, that actions here are *symbola* of the real character in the intelligible world, and that the virtuous person does not proceed to heaven but only sees himself in it.　　17:419

3. If the other world is this very sensible world, although in another relation, then the soul always has a body, either a normal (in accordance with the laws of normal sensation) observable body: *metempsychosis*, or one that is visible only through the power of choice of the departed soul: *apparitiones, spectra*, either by means of external or internal influence. *Prodigia*.

4111. 1769? (1770–71?) (1766–68?) (Prior to 1764–66?) *M* 319, at §782.　　17:420

It is splendid that on this earth the course of the world does not harmonize with moral laws, because otherwise no human being would himself know whether or not he acts from prudence or morality, and purely moral motives could not be felt.

4117. 1769? (1769–70?) *M* 329, in *Theologia naturalis, Prolegomena*.　　17:423

The inference from contingent things to a necessary being says no more than that the existence of alterable things is not completely comprehensible unless a being is assumed at which the question "why?" comes to a stop, i.e., which is necessary in itself. But something without any condition, thus subaltern necessity without a first condition, is just as little comprehensible as a necessary existence. That shows that the inference from alterable things to a necessary being does not prove that such a being necessarily exists, but only that such a concept, if it is possible, is requisite for explanation; and about this being one can say in turn that its necessity cannot be comprehended without a condition under which it is necessary.

4122. 1769? (1773–75?) *M* 346, at §850, in *Existentia Dei*.[73]　　17:425

Coming to be, ceasing to be, and being altered occur only in time. About that which is not in time nothing can be said.

Alteration is not an intellectual predicate at all. Hence it is not the things but their *phaenomena* that are altered; but this alteration is itself a *phaenomenon*.[74] The things in themselves are constant, and the alterations [are] appearances of their limits. We do not know what corresponds to the alterations in the *intellectualibus*.[a]

[a] intelligible beings, i.e., things in themselves

It is certainly a question whether the concept of substance, which indicates the constancy of something through the change of its determinations, is a concept valid only among *phaneomenis*; for taken *intellectualiter* the substance can only be identical to its determinations, and inherence cannot be a special relation of something in the thing to the subject.

Time is also eternal, i.e., the *finita*[a] are, compared with each other through representations, i.e., insofar as one cognizes the other, all in time.

4143. 1769? 1770–71? (1773–75? 1776–78?) *M* 386, at §942, in *Finis creationis.*[75]

The end of creation is always a connection of the world with the divine, highest pleasure, although not as its ground but rather as its consequence. In moral things, humans are partly dependent upon their ends. If they could feel their own moral perfection even without the accomplishment of those ends, then the gratification would not arise from the actions, but the latter from the former.

The highest happiness among creatures under the conditions that they can generally be regarded as good is the final end. Thus the highest happiness that is harmonious with morality.

Thus our actions are never directed at the satisfaction of divine desires. The ends of our actions do not lie in God, but in the creatures; thus the honor of God is not the end but the ground of good actions.

4148. 1770–71? 1773–75? *M* I.

Critique is a science not for producing but for judging certain things in accordance with rules of perfection; thus metaphysics is a science for judging connections from pure reason. Beyond logic, which is a propaedeutic science for all forms of learning, rational learning contains a critical part of experience and reason and two dogmatic parts: the first is metaphysics, the second mathematics and morals in pure reason, and physics and psychology in the empirical science of reason.

4152. 1769–70. *M* 432.

That ontology is nothing other than a transcendental logic (subjective), applied metaphysics, however, is merely negative, and nothing but morality remains, whose *data* are given by the human will, and the *principia formalia* are analytic.[76]

---

[a] finite things

4163. 1769–70. *M* 1, in *Prolegomena metaphysicorum.*　　　　17:440

All sciences of pure reason are either those that consider the rules of universal cognition in general through pure reason or the particular rules of pure reason themselves. *Logica. Phaenomenologia generalis,*[77] *Noologia generali* have as their end merely the rules of universal [*crossed out:* and non-empirical] cognitions that are not given through any experience. Noology applied to that which is given through experience, although not through grounds of experience, is theoretical: metaphysics; or practical: morality.

4168. 1769–70. *M* 2.　　　　17:441

Metaphysics [*crossed out:* is a science] has either merely objects[a] of pure reason for its object[b] or [*crossed out:* also] objects[c] of the senses, the grounds and nature of which it makes known not through the senses but through pure reason; the former is the general part, the latter the special part (*Metaphysica applicata*) and consists of *pneumatologia* and *somatologia pura*; the *phsyiologia* of inner or outer senses must precede both of these parts, but not *metaphysica universali*, namely ontology and *theologia generali*,　　17:442 the first of which considers the supreme *principium* of all cognitions through pure reason, the second the supreme *principia* cognizable through reason of all things. In *ontologia* **everything** is considered *disiunctive*, in *theologia naturali* and *cosmologia* everything is considered *collective*.[78]

4172. 1769–70. *M* 6, opposite §16, in *Possibile.*[79]　　　　17:443

The principles of pure reason are two: 1. those *per analysin* from the confused concepts given through pure reason, e.g., substance, whole, necessity, etc.; 2. those *per synthesin* from the concepts given through reason. Those concepts given through reason prior to all experience although abstracted on the occasion of experience from the laws of reason, e.g., the concept of the ground, are forms impressed on the ordering understanding for the use of experiences.[80]

4174. 1769–70? (1770–75?) *M* 8, at §20, in *Connexum.*[81]　　　　17:444

Everything that occurs is in the series of succession and is represented therein. Nothing, however, can be represented in absolute time, but things are represented in a successive series only insofar as there is conceived a real connection of things by means of which one member draws the next after itself; thus nothing in a series can be cognized as

---

[a] *obiecten*
[b] *zum Gegenstände*
[c] *Gegenstände*

real if the transition from the preceding member to it is not necessary in accordance with a general law. I.e., without a ground, even if one does not cognize it.

The relations of things are in general always represented by means of real connections, and time is only the form of appearance in which these things connected in such a way are intuited. Time produces no representations of connected things.[82]

4180. 1769–70? 1772–75? *M* 32, opposite §§113–14, in *Necesssarium et contingens.*[83]

That which is hypothetically necessary without an absolutely necessary *principium* permits an extensive use of reason if one does not think of the boundary, and is therefore better suited for the understanding than mere approximation; if, however, one denies it (*atheismus assertorius*), this use of reason is again made useless, for the entire chain is contingent, because it requires something outside of itself which is not attached to any further link, and this is denied. The concept of the absolutely necessary is thus an essential condition of the use of our reason, but only a presupposition, not, however, a product of it. For I finally remove every condition, what remains can no longer be cognized *a priori*, i.e., with insight. I reach for a higher standpoint and am in empty space, which is infinite and through itself makes everything possible and bounds it. But *respective* to the things subordinated to it, we can adequately understand what is required for the boundary concept itself to hold for all things. It is the same with freedom, the first beginning of origination. We know well what proceeds from freedom and its presupposition, and it is also necessary for us to presuppose it. But no one can comprehend the origination of a free action, since it is the beginning of all origination. I am a substance; predicates terminate with me; and I am not one myself. This self I know with certainty as the *terminum* of my imputations. But I am contingent in all parts and am not the independent thing of existence, although [I am] with respect to inherence, etc.[84] That without the presupposition of which I cannot employ my reason (necessity) is, *respective* to me, the condition of my reason; but that without the knowledge of which I cannot completely employ my reason is merely a boundary for reason.

4188. 1769–70? 1771? *M* 71, at §239, in *Monas.*[85]

Space is not a concept of experience: 1. experiences are possible only by means of it; 2. it is not an object of the senses; 3. its immediate principles do not have the contingency and particularity of propositions of experience and also are not appeals to experience. It is also not a concept of reason: 1. it is not a general, but rather an individual concept;

hence all spaces are parts of a single one, and its principles are cognized by means of an immediate intuition.[86]

4189. Late 1769–70? (1769?) *M* 72, at §239.　　　　　　17:450

In time there is found the relation of things among one another with regard to existence in general, whether they are simultaneous or successive, and the magnitude of their duration. They all appear as in one whole of existence, although with vanishing magnitude in both coming to be and passing away. In space there is the relation of things with regard to their community: all as in one whole, which makes possible all community.

Because we **intuitively** cognize **not merely the space of the object** that affects our senses, but **the whole of space**, space must not merely arise from the **real affection of the senses**, but rather must precede it. Because, however, it is still represented as something real, it will be the effect of the feeling of omnipresence; and time will be the effect of the dependence of all things on the existence of one, just as space is the consequence of the community of things.

4190. 1769–70? (1769?) *M* 72, at §239.　　　　　　17:450

All existence in time is contingent. For it is an unceasing disappearance and origination; and from the fact that a thing exists it does not follow that it will exist. Necessary existence is the sole complete existence.

Existence in time is to necessary existence as an infinite line is to the motion of a point in space, with regard to extension.

4191. 1769–70? (1769?) *M* 72, at §239.　　　　　　17:451

These are the rules of space: 1. that, since it is only the condition of the appearance of outer things, one must not regard it as the condition of the existence of the things themselves, unless the things themselves must merely be appearances; 2. that the predicates of space must not be regarded as predicates of things, but of their appearances, hence the propositions that express the possibility of things are not valid for space; 3. that space is something entirely true with respect to outer appearances, because it is the condition of them.

4210. 1769–77. *M* 119, at §381, in *Notio mundi negativa*.[87]　　　17:457

In time the world either exists from eternity (*a parte priori*[a] to all time) or not from eternity, yet nonetheless in time (in a part of time *a priori*). Both are false. For the part of time outside of or prior to the world, or rather absolute time, is indeed a condition of actual, but not of

---

[a] from the first part

non-actual things, in which their *positus*[a] would be determined with regard to the preceding part.

It is not possible to represent an infinite world. But the world (*phaenomenon*) and time are only something in representation. If I wanted to say whether an infinite world in itself is not possible, then the sensible world is nothing in itself. The world is finite as far back as I would go; it is impossible to cognize the world back into infinitude; thus the sensible world, as far as I go, is always finite. But is the world therefore to be measured *a parte priori*?

17:462 **4219.** 1769–70. M 275, opposite §708, in *Arbitrium*.[88]

The difficulty in comprehending human freedom lies in the fact that the subject is dependent and yet ought to act independently of other beings.

The necessary being cannot begin to act, the contingent being cannot act in a first beginning.

17:462 **4220.** 1769–70? (1769) (1764–68?) M 276, at §710.

Freedom is really only the self-activity of which one is conscious. When one allows oneself to approve of something, this is an *actus* of self-activity; but one is not conscious here of one's activity, but only of
17:463 the effect. The expression: I think (this object) already indicates that with respect to the representation I am not passive, that it is to be imputed to me, that the opposite depends on me.[89]

17:463 **4221.** 1769–75. M 276, at §710.

Freedom is the capacity to produce and effect something *originarie*. But how *causalitas originaria et facultas originarie efficiendi*[b] obtain in an *ente derivativo* is not to be comprehended at all.

17:463 **4222.** 1769–70. M 276, at §710.

Our *arbitrium* is not sensitive, but the *actus arbitrii* are either sensitive or intellectual. For *arbitrium* is not inclination, but is rather the choice between inclination or reason.

17:464 **4225.** 1769–70? (1772–75?) M 284, opposite §724, in *Libertas*.[90]

Since freedom is a complete self-activity of the will not to be determined by *stimuli* or anything else that affects the subject, in its case it comes down only to the certainty of personality: that it is, namely, conscious that it acts from its own power of choice, that the will is active and not passive, that it acts neither through *stimulos* nor through foreign

---

[a] position
[b] original causality and an original capacity for efficient causation

impressions. Otherwise I must say: I am driven or moved to act in such and such a way, which is the same as to say: I am not acting but being passive. If God rules the determinations of the power of choice, then he acts; if the charms of things necessarily determine it, then they necessitate; in both cases the action does not **arise** from me, rather I am only the means of another cause.

In the sensible world nothing is comprehensible except what is necessitated by preceding grounds. The actions of the free power of choice are *phaenomena*; but their connection with a self-active substance and with the capacity of reason is intellectual; accordingly the determination of the free power of choice cannot be subjected to the *legibus sensitivus.*[a]

The question whether freedom is possible is perhaps identical with the question whether the human being is a true person and whether the I is possible in a being of external determinations.   17:465

The I is an inexplicable representation. It is an intuition that is unchanging.[91]

4226. 1769–70? (1769?) (1764–68?) *M* 285, opposite §§724–5.   17:465

Freedom does not consist in the fact that we might have preferred the opposite, but only in the fact that our preference was not necessitated *passive*.

The *arbitrium sensitivum* without consciousness is *brutum*.

The *arbitrium* is determined to an action either actively or *passive*. In the first case it is still free even though the *motiva* are *obiective necessitantia.*[b] For it does not act necessarily because its subject is affected by a passive quality, of sensibility, of objects. The human power of choice is never determined *passive*. The *arbitrium* that is determined solely *active* is a good will. But since a good will is determined to good actions by itself and freely, even if the substance is *causatum alterius,*[c] the mixture with the *sensitivo* is just as great as if the *rationes ad determinandum* were *incompletae.*[d] For this reason the human will is not determined to any sort of actions by itself. Its power of choice is thus to be sure a free but indeterminate power of choice (the divine power of choice is determinate). The *arbitrium brutum* is determined *secundum rationes sensitivae*, the divine power of choice is determined *secundum intellectuales,*[e] the human power of choice is not determined by any grounds. Its actions **could** all **have** occurred in accordance with **reason**. Hence it is free. But is there

---

[a] laws of the sensible world
[b] objectively necessitating
[c] That is, even if the content of choice is suggested by something external to the will.
[d] as if the reasons for the determination were incomplete
[e] according to sensible grounds; according to intellectual grounds

not a determining ground, not indeed in the human power of choice in general, yet in the circumstances and conditions? and if this is not the case, then from whence do the actions really occur[?] Answer: all *stimuli* of the sensible power of choice cannot make what is **active** in the human being **passive**. The higher power of choice still decides for itself; but why it sometimes decides on the side of sensibility, sometimes on that of reason, for that no law can be given, because there is no constant law of both powers.

17:466

In the case of an active *principio* the circumstance, whether past or present, has no influence in determining the action of the subject. The subject is always itself the source of actions. But why does it act thus and not otherwise[?]

17:466 **4227.** 1769–70? (1769?) (1764–68?) M 285, opposite §§725–6.

If human beings were completely intellectual, then all of their actions would be actively determined but still free, and would be contingent only with regard to alterable opportunities. These actions could also be imputed to them together with the praise, even though they were creations of a higher being. For they would be regarded as self-active principles and as worthy of his goodness. If they were completely sensible, then their actions would be determined only passively; nothing could be imputed to them, and they would not be capable of any praise and punishment. Now they are in part sensible, in part intellectual, yet in such a way that the sensible certainly cannot make the *intellectuale* passive, yet the intellectual also cannot overpower the actions except by a certain measure of preponderance over the sensibility. Thus the human being is not determined either *active* or *passive*; and since the sensibility as well as the strength of reason depend upon the circumstances, his actions depend in part on the circumstances, in part on the use of his reason, and cannot be entirely imputed to him. He is free, if one takes this in the most exact sense: freedom properly consists only in the possibility **of doing something good**. Yet whether the action really arises from this *principio* or from what is sensitive depends on the conditions. Just as in a game each throw can win, regardless of the preceding and accompanying circumstances.

17:467 **4228.** 1769–70? (1769?) (1772–75?) M 285, opposite §726.

Through the consciousness of our personality we see ourselves in the intellectual world and find ourselves free. Through our dependence on impressions we see ourselves in the sensible world and find ourselves determined. Our intuitions of bodies all belong to the sensible world; accordingly experiences agree with the laws of determining grounds of the sensible world. But our intellectual intuitions of the free will do not agree with the laws of the *phaenomenorum*.

4229. 1769–70? (1769?) (1764–68?) *M* 285, opposite §725.   17:467

Freedom cannot be divided. The human being is either entirely free or not free at all, since he can either act from an independent *principio* or is dependent on conditions.

4253. 1769–70? 1771? *M* 327, in *Theologia naturalis, prolegomena.*[92]   17:482

a. The proof 1. that all possibility must be regarded as a determination of the highest reality and presupposes such a being is grounded on the fact that since the *omnimoda determinatio*[a] is only possible through the *omnitudinem metaphysicam,*[b] but in this the negative predicates presuppose the *realia*, and that since every *ens limitatum*[c] is only possible through the presupposition of a *realis*, everything presupposes a *realissimum;*[d] this however is the necessary subordination of the concepts in accordance with the law of human understanding.[93]

2. The absolute necessity of a thing is a boundary concept. We cannot have any insight into it by means of contradiction. That which contains the matter for all possibility is its real ground and is **necessary** *realiter.*

We cannot have any more insight into the necessity of a perfect being in itself than into that of an imperfect being.

b. the proof *a contingentia*[e] infers from concepts, namely that the limited cannot be necessary. Consequently it must presuppose necessity in   17:483
the *realissimo*. The cause is that the general concept of a being that has limits comprehends many things under itself, but that of the unlimited is a *conceptus singularis.*

c. The physico-theological proof infers from the incomplete acquaintance with the perfection of the world to the supreme God and from there back to the greatest perfection of the world.

d. The moral proof infers from the geometrical yet objective necessity of actions under the moral laws, yet also to the necessary assumption of a ruler.

The proof from a *primo motore*[f] that the world does not exist from itself belongs among the negative proofs.

That the *ens realissimum* or *summum* has understanding.

4254. 1769–70? (1771?) (1772–75?) *M* 327.   17:483

The existence of God can **be cognized only by means of the understanding**, because its concept is a highest concept of the understanding

---

[a] that which is determined in every way
[b] the metaphysical totality
[c] limited being
[d] most perfect being
[e] from contingent things
[f] prime mover

that is not limited to objects of experience, but whose *omnisufficientia* is intellectual.

It cannot, however, be cognized from an assumed, arbitrary concept, and thus cannot be cognized in itself (unless by means of immediate intuitions).

Thus [it can be cognized] only in relation to the world, but in relation to what is valid for any world; for this is only intellectual.

The intelligible world is that the concept of that which is valid for any world; consequently, it does not contain physical laws, but rather objective and moral ones.

17:484 The intellectual concept of the world is thus the concept of perfection. The intelligible world is thus the moral world, and the laws thereof are valid for any world as objective laws of perfection.

Thus one can only infer from the necessity of the moral laws in this as well as in any world to the original and universally valid ground of the essential ends of things, hence to the existence of the most perfect being; and its concept is that which makes us perfect, and thus is practically certain. The *mundus intelligibilis* is the world of rational beings considered in accordance with objective laws of freedom.[94]

The supreme principle of morality is the correspondence of free actions with the original and universally valid laws of the power of choice or with what is essentially combined with the ends in the world. Thus the concept of God is [*breaks off*][a]

17:491 **4275. 1770–71. *M* XIII.**

Analysis of reason. *Principium contradictionis, identitatis*; yields objectively valid propositions.

Synthesis of reason: various laws (*axiomata subreptitia*), [yields] subjectively valid propositions.[95]

The conditions of our reason which 1. cognizes objects only mediately and not by means of intuitions, thus the *conditiones* by means of 17:492 which a cognition of them is possible for it, and the necessity of positing something *primitive* and without *conditiones*.

Intuitions of the senses (in accordance with sensible form and matter) yield synthetic propositions that are objective. Crusius explains the real principle of reason on the basis of the *systemate praeformationis* (from subjective *principiis*); *Locke*, on the basis of *influxu physico* like *Aristotele*; *Plato* and *Malebranche*, from *intuitu intellectuali*; we, on the basis of *epigenesis* from the use of the natural laws of reason.[96]

---

[a] Adickes says that it is possible that this sentence actually ends with a period instead of breaking off. If so, then it would read as follows: "Thus there is the concept of God."

The common sense of human beings, *sensus veri et falsi*,[a] is a *qualitas occulta*.

Antithesis: a method of reason for discovering the *oppositionem* of **subjective laws**, which, if it is taken **for objective** *per vitium subreptionis*, is *scepticismus* (*in sensu obiectivo*); if, however, it is only a [*crossed out*: critique of the subject] propaedeutic, then it is a *methodus scepticus* for the determination of the subjective laws of reason. *Antithesis subiectiva*.

4277. 1770–71. *M* XIII. 17:493

In this world I can only become happy in accordance with the laws of sensibility, and therefore I depend on the mechanical laws and the [*crossed out*: animal] sensible power of choice of human beings. (The latter could be in consensus, and then I would also be happy in accordance with my desert.)

4284. 1770–71? 1773–75? 1776–78? *M* XV. 17:495

Metaphysics is not a science, not scholarship, but rather merely understanding acquainted with itself, hence it is merely a correction of the healthy understanding and reason.

Scholarship and learning are means for making their teachings practical through example. Metaphysics serves to decide the boundaries of other sciences and keeps mankind at its vocation, which concerns the use and the limits of its reason; it is logical self-cognition. It is strangely bitter, because it strikes down idle pride and removes imaginary knowledge; it makes our possessions more secure, though at the cost of those that are merely imaginary, and is an obstacle to the flood of books.

It is religion that derives the greatest profit from metaphysics: everything in religion that is moral is secured by metaphysics, protected from enthusiasm and unbelief, and freed from dependence on scholastic subtleties. Metaphysics allows our actions to flow from the sources 17:496 of the healthy understanding, without having to question the uncertain and always changing pedantries of the schools.

4285. 1770–71? 1773–75? 1776–78? *M* XVI. 17:496

Only what has a logical quality is called an object, e.g., *subiectum* not relative to other concepts, but in itself. These objects are distinguished from appearances, which can indeed be brought into logical relations, but to which this logical quality does not absolutely belong. If there runs parallel to an appearance a logical positing that pertains to the *data*[b] of the appearance and not the relation of one representation to another, then this is objective. E.g., ground, cause.

---

[a] sense of truth and falsehood
[b] the fact of beng given

Thereby alone can we conceive of appearances as corresponding to things, so that they are grounds of a possible and universally valid cognition. This they can be, however, if they are in conformity to logical form.

17:498 **4292.** 1770–71? 1773–75? 1776–78? *M* XVII.

The *conditiones* without which objects cannot be given are objective, although in accordance with laws of sensibility. The *conditiones* without which they cannot (even when they are given) be cognized (understood) are objective. Those, without which we cannot have insight into them (cognize them through reason),* are merely subjective; but these subjective *conditiones* are objective with regard to the employment of reason with respect to experiences (*leges convenientiae*).

*(*Later addition*: possibility, necessity)

17:499 **4296.** 1770–71? (1773–75?) 1776–78?? *M* 5, at §14(?), in *Possibile*.

The proposition that everything has a ground is a law of reason; but the law that everything that occurs is constantly accompanied with something else is a law of appearances.[97]

17:499 **4298.** 1770–71? (1776–78?) *M* 6, next to §17.

Possibility: agreement (*non repugnantia*) with a rule; actuality: simply being posited; necessity: being posited in accordance with a rule.

17:500 The first is thought, without being given. The second is given, without being thought. The third is given insofar as it is thought.

17:500 **4299.** 1770–71? (1776–78?) *M* 6, next to §18.

The relation (of an object) to perception (*perceptio*) is existence; to thought, possibility; to thought, insofar as it determines existence: necessity.[98]

17:501 **4303.** 1770–75? (1775–76?) *M* 15, at §54, in *Ens*.

The *principium contradictionis* is the **formal condition**, but not the *principium* of all possibility.

17:503 **4315.** 1770–71? (1769?) *M* 71, at §239, in *Monas*.[99]

One can only conceive of spaces insofar as one carves something out of the universal space. Space precedes things; hence it cannot be a predicate of things, but only a law of sensibility, which as the condition of all possible appearances certainly precedes everything actual.

17:504 **4316.** 1770–71? 1769?? *M* 72, at §239ff.

The predicate of space and of place does not apply to the substance, but to the sensible representation. Corporeal parts are comparative

126

substances in accordance with laws of sensibility and *phaenomena sub-stantiata*. The quantity of substance in a body (not of its space) is to be judged from the magnitude of its effect at the same velocity. Now with regard to this there is nothing simple. Now it is a question whether with regard to space there is anything simple and determinately numerable.

4333. 1770–71? (1769?) (1773–75?) *M* 277, at §710, in *Arbitrium.*[100]   17:508

That the human will is free means the same as that reason has a capacity*a* with respect to the will and the other capacities and inclinations. For reason determines itself, and without this all other capacities would be determinate in accordance with the laws of efficient causes and would be externally necessary. Reason cannot be determined, i.e., affected; for otherwise it would be sensibility and not reason.

4334. 1770–71? (1769?) (1773–75?) *M* 282, at §719ff., in *Libertas.*   17:508

On freedom

We can consider one of our actions either as something that happens,   17:509
i.e., as an appearance, or as something that ought to happen, i.e., as an intuition of self-activity for possible effects. In the first case it is subjected to the laws of determining grounds; in the second case it is something intellectual, in which the subject is not passive; here the *regula rationis determinantis* rules only as a *principium comprehensionis* or *logicum,*b i.e., that one cannot know the actions *a priori* (except in the case of the perfect understanding) otherwise than through determining grounds. The good understanding has determining grounds, but in accordance with laws of the understanding, through intellectual *motiva*; the affected understanding surrenders to sensibility.

Something happens necessarily, i.e., in accordance with the empirical concepts of necessity, which yet admits a contingency with regard to the concepts of reason. The understanding must itself excite the sensibility for the latter to determine the action; thus it happens in accordance with the laws of the sensibility and yet of the understanding. We know only the most proximate determining grounds of sensibility, and it is in accordance with them that the action must always be explained.

4335. 1770–71? (1769?) (1773–75?) *M* 282, at §719ff.   17:509

It is true: all morality must aim at something useful. But it is not the utility but the universality that makes it morally good, namely that it

---

a *Vermögen*
b The rule of determining grounds applies only as a principle for understanding or a logical principle.

is good only as a rule and without it no universal rule would obtain. Even in the case of duties of obligation the action is not to be omitted even if it would be harmful, and it is in precisely this that the obligation consists.

4336. 1770–71? 1769? (1773–75?) *M* 282, at §719ff.

We cannot infer the reality of freedom from experience. Nevertheless we only have a concept of it through our intellectual inner intuition (not the inner sense) of our activity, which can be moved through *motiva* *intellectualia*, and by means of which practical laws and rules of the good will are themselves possible for us. Thus freedom is a necessary practical presupposition. It also does not contradict theoretical reason. For as appearances actions are always in the field of experience, as objective *data* they are in the field of reason and are approved and disapproved of. Sensibility is here under the laws of reason and yields [*breaks off*]

4337. 1770–71? (1769?) (1773–75?) *M* 282, at §719ff.

Contingently preferred actions (the freedom of human beings) are those that are not determined through any rules. Necessarily preferred actions (divine freedom) are those that are determined only in accordance with the rule of the good power of choice.

4338. 1770–71? (1769?) (1773–75?) *M* 288, opposite §730ff.

Freedom from all external necessitation of our power of choice is clear through experience, as is the motivating force of intellectual grounds of good; we could not otherwise impute guilt to other beings. We can ascribe it to ourselves, even the good that God effects in us. Thus morality and religion are *in salvo*.[a]

But how does speculative philosophy stand with regard to the possibility of this freedom? The proposition that everything that happens has a determining ground, i.e., something else by means of which it is necessitated, is the principle of the alterations of all passive substances (of all appearances of that which is given *a posteriori*; but the actions of giving something *a priori* are not included under that), thus of the body and also of the soul insofar as it is modified, i.e., in everything that is distinct from the actions of freedom. To this extent this principle is objective. But as a *principium* of activities it cannot be objective, for then a first beginning would be possible; but in the states of a being as passive there is no first beginning (this lies in that which is active). Freedom should be a capacity to first initiate a state. Passive states are mere consequences and necessarily belong to what precedes. In the present moment I can say that for me the entire antecedent series is as nothing. I commence my state now as I

---

[a] in good order, i.e., consistent with each other

will. The difficulty is not *secundum possibilitatem fiendi*, rather *cognoscendi.*[a] One can have no insight into the possibility of freedom, because one can have no insight into a first beginning, whether the necessity in existence in general or in freedom in the origination of events. For our understanding cognizes existence through experience, but reason has insight into it if it cognizes it *a priori*, i.e., through grounds (that, namely, which is not necessary in accordance with identity, rather which is posited *realiter*); now there are no grounds for that which is first, thus no insight into it is possible through reason. It lies in reason, to be sure, that there must be a first (*natura*) action which is the basis for everything contingent; but a first *tempore*[b] cannot be comprehended at all, because time itself and what is in it do not depend on reason. Further: that that which is determined in its entire existence by another being must terminate the determining grounds of its actions in itself cannot be comprehended, but only because it cannot be comprehended how it is a substance. Now this is not an objection, but a subjective difficulty; for the I proves to be the end point of the grounds of the actions. "I do this" does not mean [*crossed out*: or indicate] that another effects it; and even if I say "I suffer this,"[c] this still signifies the intuition of a subject that exists for itself and suffers.

4339. 1770–71? (1769–70?) (1772–75?) M 292, in *Psychologia rationalis.*[d]   17:511
Applied philosophy is that whose object is represented by an empirical concept; the empirical concept, however, insofar as it is a ground of the cognition of the object by means of analysis, does not have any principles except rational ones.[101]

4344. 1770–71? (1773–78?) 1769?? M 326, in *Theologia naturalis.*   17:513
Following those laws in accordance with which we must infer with healthy reason the existence of certain things, their properties, and their laws in the world, we must also infer the existence of a supreme, wise being, thus practically adequate for responsibility. But as far as the condition of the comprehensibility of this supreme cause is concerned, by means of which we would demonstrate *a priori* the strength of our reason, and thus in accordance with logical rules of synthetic or dogmatic cognition, this use of reason misfires. Now no one can make the excuse that because he cannot have *a priori* insight into something he also does not have to assume it; for one also has no *a priori* insight into gravitational attraction and yet assumes it in one's actions.

---

[a] The difficulty lies not in the possibility of the existence [of freedom] but in knowledge of it.
[b] a temporally first action
[c] *ich leide dieses*, that is, "I am passive with respect to this."
[d] This note is in Latin.

Deismus is that which acknowledges no theology other than the transcendental one. **God as a spiritual being** (intelligence) in distinction from the eternal and necessary nature is called the **living God**.

17:514   **4345.** 1770–71? 1773–75? (1769?) (1766–78?) M 337, at the conclusion of §826, in *Existentia Dei*.[102]

That the human being has a capacity to ascend in his cognitions to the divinity means nothing more than that he has a capacity to complete his concepts and to produce an idea of the *maximi*.

17:515   **4348.** 1770–71? 1773–75? 1776–78? M 352, at §865, in *Intellectus Dei*.[103]

Our understanding cannot cognize anything concretely (it cognizes only the manner of sensibility in accordance with rules for disposing it) except that which is in it itself.* Now the good is that which is necessarily related to it itself or the inner analogical being, thus the understanding has *a priori* cognitions of it. God, however, cognizes objects in themselves *a priori*. Hence they must be given through him, his understanding is therefore that of an *archetypus*.

*(The understanding can cognize *a priori* that of which it is itself the free author; for only the cause through freedom is the cause through understanding.)

17:515   **4349.** 1770–71? 1773–75? (1773–76?) M 354, at §869–70, in *Intellectus Dei*.[104]

Cognition is either sensitive or intellectual; objects are either sen-
17:516   sible or intelligible. No world other than the sensible world can be given to us; thus every *mundus physicus (materialiter)* is *sensibilis*; only the *mundus moralis (formaliter)* is *intelligibilis*. This is because freedom is the only thing that is given *a priori* and consists in thus being given *a priori*; the *a priori* rule of freedom in a world in general constitutes the *formam mundi intelligibilis*. This leads, in accordance with grounds of freedom, to the presumption of the *intelligibilia*, God and a future world, in which everything (nature) will be in accord with the moral laws.[105]

The *mundus intelligibilis* as an object of intuition is a mere undetermined idea; but as an object of the practical relation of our intelligence to the intelligences of the world in general and to God as the practical primordial being of the world it is a true concept and determinate idea: *Civitas dei*.

17:520   **4364.** 1771? (1769–70? 1772? 1773–75?) M I.

Theoretical philosophy is either [*crossed out: pura*] *rationalis* or *empirica*. The latter is *psychologia* and *physica*. That which is *rationalis* has either no object from experience at all and is called *transscendentalis*, or it has its object from experience, to be sure, but *principia* from reason, and is called *metaphysica* (*psychologia rationalis* and *physica rationalis*); finally it has an object of reason insofar as it is cognized *per analogiam* through concepts of experience.

4366. 1771? (1772–75?) *M* II.   17:521

Metaphysics is *philosophia pura*. The form of all cognition is merely rational, and the matter is sensitive; therefore, metaphysics is philosophy about form.

4368. 1771? (1772–73? 1773–75?) *M* II.   17:521

Our material concepts can never apply to anything other than what we have sensed; and thus our material principles can also be regarded only as laws of experience and can never be more universal. But if one extends our manner of judging to the concepts of form, then there results a law of subjective employment.

4369. 1771? (1772–73? 1773–75?) *M* II.   17:521

The question is whether metaphysics deals with objects that can be cognized through pure reason, or with the subject, namely the principles and laws in the use of pure reason. Since we can cognize all objects through our subject, especially those that do not affect us, it is   17:522 subjective.

4370. 1771. *M* 432.   17:522

On what basis do I know that *canones* of reason are not axioms, i.e., that they can be used only *a posteriori* and *descendendo*, but not *a priori* and *ascendendo*[?] For the subjective laws of reason are rules for its use in application, the objective ones, however, for its use in explanation.

All immediately certain propositions are either 1. **Fundamental formulae** or 2. *axiomata* or 3. *canones* or 4. **elementary propositions** of *analysis* or 5. **immediately certain** propositions of *synthesis*. The **first** are the principles of identity and of contradiction. The **second**: objective principles of *synthesis*, space and time. The **third**: objective principles of *synthesis qualitativae*. The 4th and **fifth**: material propositions immediately contained under the principles of form of *synthesis* as well as of *analysis*.

[*Crossed out: Axiomata*] *Formulae primitiva* are valid for every cognition.

The synthetic fundamental concepts of reason as well as the synthetic fundamental concepts of appearance provide occasion for axioms, which however both serve only for the *a posteriori* use of reason.

The use of *a posteriori* principles, if one applies them *a priori*, is a rational cognition of objects *per analogiam*, e.g., of space, of pleasure and displeasure from God.

17:524 **4373.** 1771. *M* 432.

All truth consists in the correspondence of all thoughts with the laws of thinking and thus among one another. That is the object for us, whether and to what extent it is given to us mediately or immediately through experience. There are no objects independent of all experience and also no laws of the understanding. (E.g., substance: that this concept is something must be inferred from the experience of the constancy of a certain subject in all circumstances.) We accordingly have concepts 1. in order to explain *phaenomena*, 2. in order to have insight into the grounds of the morally good and evil. Everything that is through these laws, e.g., cognition of the highest good (God), is practically true. The cognition of the very same object [*breaks off*]

17:524 **4375.** 1771. *M* 432.

Of the objects of the senses we have only representations that are consistent with our *phaenomenis*, and of the things themselves we have representations (by means of reason) only as they are consistent with
17:525 the laws of our understanding. Even the concept of God is possible and necessary for us only insofar as it is necessarily in conformity with the laws of the understanding which we necessarily obey in judging the world. It is thus only an appearance, namely, of the understanding, which derives its certainty from the necessity of confirming our moral principles, from which all oughts must ultimately be derived. In the case of physical appearances, we come, in accordance with the laws of the understanding, to the idea of a necessary cause; in the case of moral appearances, we come, in accordance with those laws, to the idea of a perfect author. One acts absurdly if one does not think a cause for every motion and a common cause for every combination; it is just as absurd to posit moral rules that are even superior to happiness without God. What are the appearances of reason? (Subjectively determined general cognitions.) The contradiction of principles arises, therefore, when one judges in accordance with the rule of reason with regard to its employment in the world and afterwards wants to judge *in abstracto* from any such relation.

17:525 **4377.** 1771? (1769–70?) *M* 432.

The laws of pure reason can only contain the ground of the possibility of objects relative to the mind, insofar as they concern objects the essence of which exists in relation to the soul, i.e., the morally good.

17:528 **4385.** 1771. *M* 2, in *Prolegomena Metaphysicorum*.

The metaphysical concepts are: 1. possible; 2. being (2*b*. necessary); 3. one thing posited to another (whole); 4. one thing posited in another (substance); 5. one thing posited by means of another (ground). The last three are real relations. The unity of the multiplicity: *a.* the unity of the whole; *b.* the unity of the predicates in a subject; or *c.* the unity of the consequences through a ground.

4386. 1771? 1773–78? *M* 3, in *Possibile.*   17:528

The supreme principle of human reason is either that which expresses the condition under which alone we can cognize things by means of our reason, or that under which alone things are possible; subjective, objective. The principles of acquisition, of *genesis,* or of the mere cognition of possibility.

4425. 1771. *M* 73, at §244, in *Monas.*[106]   17:541

Spatium est quantum, sed non compositum.[a] For space does not arise through the positing of its parts, but the parts are only possible through space; likewise with time. The parts may well be considered *abstrahendo a caeteris,* but cannot be conceived *removendo caetera,*[b] they can therefore be distinguished, but not separated, and the *divisio non est realis, sed logica.*[c] Since the divisibility of matter seems to come down to the space that it occupies, and it is as divisible as this space, the question arises whether the divisibility of matter is not as merely logical as that of space.

4439. 1771. *M* 160, at §§471–2, in *Naturale.*[107]   17:547

One cognizes the course of nature through the senses, and the order of nature through reason; the greater is reason, the more order does one discover. In the absence of reason everything seems to be accident (*later addition:* or blind necessity). Nature is always a *principium* of order.

The order of nature is different from the order in accordance with rules of perfection (i.e., of a good will, how things must be if they are to satisfy). The order of nature is completely necessary for the moral order, and the most perfect world will attain this perfection in accordance with the order of nature, since only under this condition is it possible to use understanding.

(*Later addition:* Freedom also stands under the order of nature.)

4440. 1771. *M* 242, in *Voluptas et taedium.*   17:547

There are three sorts of physiological effects of the human soul.

1. the [*crossed out:* sensation] mere representations, 2. connection, 3. comparison.

---

[a] Space is a magnitude, but not a composite.
[b] The parts can be considered in abstraction from each other, but the others cannot be removed.
[c] The division is not real, but logical.

Three kinds of cognition, and they differ objectively:
1. sensation, 2. form of intuition, 3. concept.
Three uses of reason:
1. Inner sense or intuition of oneself and one's thoughts. 2. General representations and the relation of their spheres (logical use). 3. The form of *thesis* and *antithesis*. The use of pure reason contains either absolute or comparative concepts. The former are either intuitive, i.e., concerning the matter (good), or discursive: concerning mere form (existence).

17:548

(*Later addition*: The animals also have a *facultatem diiudicandi (iudicium sensitivum)*, but not *iudicandi (iudicium intellectuale)*.)[a]

17:548 **4441.** 1771 (1773–75?) (1776–78?) *M* 277, at §710, in *Arbitrium.*

One can regard freedom as if it were the influence of a special cause, namely, one of intelligence, which, however, does not determine on its own; and yet again one can regard the influence of sensibility as a special cause. The former provides a ground of explanation for character; the latter, for nature or temperament. Although in each case the person may have done otherwise than what he wants, even now the opposite is possible (as in a game in which one has often scored): yet on the whole this freedom is to be regarded like nature, and actions are sufficiently (practically) determined from character and temperament.

17:552 **4445.** 1772. *M* VIII.

(*Later addition*: Possibility of such a science. With regard to that which is not intuitable.)

Prolegomena. Some sciences contain merely an employment of the understanding with regard to various objects of curiosity and advantage, and logic is the general organon thereof, namely, instruction in its employment.

Other sciences have the determination of the understanding itself as their aim, namely, with regard both to its capacity and to its highest ends, or the objects to which the understanding and the will are restricted by means of the highest laws of nature. Thus all other sciences are organons of skill, at best of prudence, while metaphysics is that of wisdom.

The employment of metaphysics with regard to the theoretical is merely negative; it does not open up the cognition of things and is not **dogmatic**; for where should it get the cognition of things without the senses[?] **Mathematics constructs arbitrary concepts** of magnitudes as hypothetical conditions, from which consequences ought to be able to be drawn, by means of mere repetitions. In the case of the question of

---

[a] a faculty of discrimination (sensitive judgment), but not of judgment (intellectual judgment)

what a thing is, however, we can invent no concepts nor any relations. They must relate to that which is given at least as the grounds of its employment. Metaphysics only prevents the false employment of reason, which steps beyond its limits and regards the *intellectualia* as objects, although they serve only as the *modo cognoscendi* of the *sensitive dabilium*[a] and if need be as the limitation thereof, insofar as it wants to employ the *sensitiva* beyond their limits. Pure reason is dogmatic only with regard to the objects of the will; with regard to speculation, however, it is (merely apparently) cathartic. In metaphysics there are no hypotheses, first because the possibility of a highest ground of reason would be assumed entirely without a rule, and because metaphysics wants to posit limits to reason in its pure employment.

17:553

Aristippus: our judgments of that which is **agreeable** (likewise, all judgments which express mere appearances) are always true, be the objects constituted as they will, because agreeableness signifies something that is in us; however, the judgments that this or that object exists are uncertain, because the obects are distinct from us.[108]

4450. 1772–78. *M* VIII.

17:556

Aristotle erred by including in logic a division of general concepts by means of which one can think objects; this belongs to metaphysics. Logic has to do with concepts whatever they might be, and deals only with their relation.[109]

4452. 1772. *M* VIII.

17:557

The genuine concepts of reason pertain only to the relation of things in general. The objects are sensitive; only the use of reason with respect to them takes place in accordance with merely intellectual laws; if the objects are intellectual, then this is a form of enthusiasm.

4453. 1772–78. *M* VII.

17:557

The *quaestiones* of metaphysics are all raised by means of common reason and our most important ends; it is not an *organon* of science, but of wisdom, and has the negative utility of negating hindrances that are opposed to the most important cognition.

4454. 1772. (1773–75?) *M* IX.

17:557

In the critique of metaphysics one can make use of two kinds of methods. The first is to examine proofs and to search for their *paralogismos* or *petitiones principii.*[b] The second is to oppose one proof to another, indeed a proof equally convincing as the opposite. This latter method is the best.

---

[a] as the way of knowing the things given by the senses
[b] the fallacies of an ambiguous middle term and of begging the question

For since the errors in metaphysical inferences consist chiefly in the fact that what holds only of the conditions of sensible cognition is asserted of the object, a proof can appear so rigorous that one perceives with difficulty an error that one discovers better by means of a *demonstratio oppositi*.[110]

17:557 **4455. 1772. M X.**

It is the discipline of pure reason. Aesthetics: the critique of taste.

17:558 The idea of metaphysics: is it a critique or a doctrine; is its procedure zetetic[a] or dogmatic? The question is: what can one cognize by means of mere reason without any experience (mathematics, morality)? What are the sources, conditions, and boundaries[?] Transcendental philosophy is the critique of pure reason. *Studium* of the subject, mistaking the subjective for the objective, prevention.

17:558 **4457. 1772. M X.**

In *metaphysica applicata* much is dogmatic; in transcendental metaphysics, everything is critical. Can anything be discovered through metaphysics? Yes, with regard to the subject, but not with regard to the object.

As critique it has utility. Even if religion and virtue are not grounded on it, but have other sources, it serves to get rid of hindrances. Critique of science and *organon** of wisdom (which has more to do with forbearing than with acquiring. Socrates.)

It is necessary; the *quaestiones* are given to it through healthy reason and moral issues. It is indispensable.

*(a propaedeutic thereof; morality is an *organon*.)

17:559 **4458. 1772. M XI.**

In metaphysics, like an unknown land of which we intend to take possession, we have first assiduously investigated its situation and access to it. (It lies in the (region) hemisphere of **pure reason**;) we have even drawn the outline of where this island of cognition is connected by bridges to the land of experience, and where it is separated by a deep sea; we have even drawn its outline and are as it were acquainted with its geography (ichnography), but we do not know what might be found in this land, which is maintained to be uninhabitable by some people and to be their real domicile by others. We will take the general history of this land of reason into account in accordance with this general geography.[111]

---

[a] a method that raises questions

4459. 1772. *M* XI–XII.   17:559
Utility.
What is it that provides the ultimate motivation for the deep investigations of metaphysics and in what is the true importance of such a
science to be found[?]

  1. It is not immediate curiosity that it satisfies, thus its utility is not
     that of a science.
  2. It also does not satisfy as an *organon* of other sciences, e.g., of
     natural science.
  3. Thus it satisfies only as a propaedeutic for wisdom. But in that
     case in what do the preeminent questions that it resolves or the
     important cognitions to which it is supposed to be the key consist[?]
     The answer to this question is in turn important insofar as it is a   17:560
     ground for our conduct and confirms the principles of life.

But if the principles of life have other sources, independent of this, if in
order to support them no science but only practically sufficient cognition
is necessary, but if this itself is given from practical sources even without
strict logical perfection, then this science can serve only for the security of
the teachings of wisdom against all inroads of a putative reason: which is
a very great service. The belief in God gives the metaphysical inferences
favorem utilitatis.[a]

(*Later addition*: Attack not against the things, but against the assertions:
speculations.)

4460. 1772. *M* XII.   17:560
[*Crossed out*: Analytical part *Princ*]
Genetic part: Sensibility and reason.
Zetetic part: *a. Analysis, Principium Contradictionis.*
            b. Synthesis.
            c. Antithesis. Skeptical part.

4461. 1772. *M* XII.   17:560
There are 2 supreme practical principles. 1. What we must do in
order to become worthy of happiness. 2. What sort of ground we have
for practically sufficient belief that one should become happy insofar
as one is worthy of this happiness. Thus a practically sufficient ground
for belief in God and another world. (*Later addition*: All other sciences
have only a value as a means to contingent ends (which it would be more
sublime to regard with contempt), but to the extent that they improve
the understanding, which is the universal *organon* of all ends, they have   17:561
a value that is greater than the end.)

---

[a] the benefit of utility

17:561 **4463**. 1772–73. *M* XII.

The universal longing of human beings is to be happy; but a [*crossed out:* restriction and] condition to which reason (not the desires and sensibility) restricts this longing is: being worthy of this happiness.

Now if the worthiness to be happy is the only condition of the hope of also becoming happy, then the precepts of ethics precede those of prudent self-love. But if these laws should acquire their incentives through the hope of becoming happy, then it is necessary that one at least be able to believe that the world stands under a wise government.

17:561 **4464**. 1772. *M* XIII.

If metaphysics is handled in this way, then it is not a hindrance to any experiential science because of intellectual *fictiones*, it defends morality
17:562 against false subtlety and promotes the practical, it is advantageous to the beautiful arts, and promotes the inner knowledge of mankind.

(*Later addition*: It is the demarcation of pure reason and the border guard to ensure that pure reason does not expand past its boundaries, confuse itself, and disturb religion and ethics with its chimera.)

17:562 **4466**. 1772. *M* XVII.

The critique of pure reason [is] preparation for metaphysics in theoretical philosophy.

17:562 **4468**. 1772–73? 1776–78? *M* XVIII.

That reason needs a discipline. That if it is not pruned but spreads its
17:563 shoots wildly it brings forth blossoms without fruits. That therefore a master of discipline (not a disciplinarian), which governs it, is necessary. That without this discipline it does not agree with religion and ethics, that it introduces big words, and, insofar as it does not know itself, it confuses the healthy and experienced understanding.

17:563 **4469**. 1772–75. *M* XVIII.

The skeptical method is the best and only one for beating back objections by means of retorts. Does there then arise from it a universal doubt? No, but the presumptions of pure reason with regard to the conditions of the possibility of all objects are thereby beaten back. All judgments of healthy reason with regard to the world and the practical receive thereby their great reputation. Healthy or practical reason can never be persuaded that there is no God, if only subtle reason does not seek to gain status from it.

17:564 **4473**. 1772. *M* XIX–XX.[112]

The question is, how can we represent things completely *a priori*, i.e., independently of all experience (even *implicite*), and how can we

grasp principles that are not derived from any experience (and consequently are *a priori*); how it happens that objects correspond to that
which is merely a product of our isolated minds and how these objects
are subjected to those laws that we prescribe to them. Pure mathematics and metaphysics teach that there are such *a priori* cognitions; it is,
however, an important investigation to have insight into the ground of
their possibility.[113] That a representation, which itself is an effect of
the object, corresponds to it is readily comprehended. But that something that is merely the offspring of my brain may relate to an object
as a representation is not so clear. Moreover, that one impression in
me stemming from objects in me is combined with another one, consequently that we connect one representation with another one in conformity to experience, is also comprehensible. But that we can, from
within ourselves,* validly connect properties and predicates with the
represented objects, although no experience has shown them to us as so
connected, is difficult to understand. To say that a higher being has already wisely put such concepts and principles in us is to run all philosophy
into the ground. How a relation and connection are possible, where only
one of the *relatis* is given, must be sought in the nature of cognition in
general.

*(*Later addition*: Being able to say something universally of objects
without requiring that they disclose it to us.)

Experiential cognitions are not mere impressions. We must ourselves think something in the case of impressions so that such cognitions arise. Thus there must be cognitive actions that precede experience and by means of which these cognitions are possible. Likewise,
experiences never yield truly universal cognitions, because they lack
necessity. For cognition that is certain, reason requires universal propositions. Thus certain universal judgments must lie in reason prior to
experience.

17:565

4476. 1772. *M* XXVff.   17:565
The categories of *synthesis* can well be called: *substantia, causatum (et
independens), compositum (et simplex).*[a]
The categories of *analysis: Totale (perfectum, completum) et partiale. Fini-   17:566
tum et infinitum (particularitas est infinita). Unum et plura.*[b]
The idea of the *thesis: Realitas* (*later addition: quae, qualis, quanta*)[c]
The idea of the *synthesis: Materia et forma.*

---

[a] substance, the caused (and the independent), the composite (and the simple)
[b] total (perfect, complete) and partial. Finite and infinite (particularity is infinite). One
and many.
[c] Reality (what, quality, quantity)

In *analysi* the whole is prior to the parts, in *synthesi* the part is prior to the whole.

idem et diversum[a] [crossed out: quantitas qualitas]: realitas, negatio	comparison	(later addition at right of bracket:
consentiens et oppositum[b] (forma affirmationis et negationis):	combination	Judgments of relation, 1. of
externum et internum (quantitas, qualitas):	relation	consensus, compatibility)
absolutum et relativum		

17:566 **4477.** 1772–75? 1776–78?? *M* 3, at §7, in *Possibile*.[114]

Analytic propositions can be proved from the *principio contradictionis* or *identitatis*, but not synthetic ones; how do we get to these? 1. Empirically. 2. Through pure intuition. 3. Through subjective conditions of the representation of the understanding.

17:567 **4478.** 1772–75? 1776–78?? *M* 3, at §7.

The *principium* of all synthetic judgments of pure reason (not of pure intuition) is that everything that contains the conditions without which an apprehension would be impossible is true. The *principium contradictionis* is valid for all cognitions, insofar as they are regarded as merely possible. I.e., whatever contradicts the concept that I could have of an object is false.

17:569 **4483.** 1772? (1773–75? 1776–78?) *M* 6, at §18, still in *Possibile*.[115]

Even for possibility there needs to be something that is given. The first *data* are not cognized as possible *a priori*, rather they constitute the condition of all our judgments of possibility, so that only that is possible which is in agreement with the *a priori* conditions of empirical cognition. Logical possibility, the *principium contradictionis*, is not objective, only cognition. We cannot think up any possibility of intuition, of reality, of real relation, of what is necessary, except insofar as the principles thereof are given in experience.[116]

17:571 **4493.** 1772–75. *M* 58, at §191ff., in *Substantia et accidens*.[117]

Only three types of *respectus reales*[c] are possible:
  1. that of consequence to ground, *dependentiae ab una et causalitatis ab altera partes*;[d]
  2. that of part to whole;
  3. that of *accidens* to substance.

---

[a] the same and different
[b] agreement and opposition (the form of affirmation and negation)
[c] real relations
[d] dependence on one part and the causality of another

In all three there arises unity: of subordination,* of coordination, and   17:572
of inherence of many accidents in a substance. The I is the intuition of
a substance.[118]

All three have their boundaries:
1. the *independens* and *absolute necessarium*:**
2. the *totalitas absoluta* (*completa* [or] *infinitum*), i.e., a *synthesis* than
   which none greater is possible;
3. the *substantiale*.

The first concept indicates how things belong because of one another;
the second, to one another; the third, in one another. All three are *ter-
mini.*[a] The first, the *necessarium* and its *oppositum*: the *absolute* or *primum
contingens* (*libertas*); the second, the *universitatem*: everything aggregated
and its *oppositum*: no aggregate, *simplex*; the third, substantiality and its
opposite: mere relation.

We have no insight into any of the three; the first, because the condition of necessity or, on the other hand, all necessity is lacking; the second,
because the *terminus* of the *synthesis* is lacking, and because in the third
the predicates are lacking. All these relations are only the realized logical
[forms] of the relation of subject and predicate, of *antecedente* to *conse-
quente*, and of the universality of the concept of the subject. Subject and
predicate with the appended *est* means *existere*. The *identitas*: necessity.
Or only universality: necessity; particularity: contingency.

*One can also think a subordinated division.

**It is not yet clear that the first ground (e.g., freedom) is something
that is necessary.

4496. 1772–75. *M* 60, at §200, still in *Substantia et accidens*.   17:573

Three *principia*. 1. In everything actual there is the relation of
a substance to an accident (*inhaerentia*); 2. that of the ground to
the consequence (*dependentia*); 3. that of parts and of interconnection
(composition).

There are thus three presuppositions: subject, ground, and parts; and
three real *modi*: insition,[b] [sic] subordination, and composition. Consequently, there are also three *principia*: 1. a subject that is not a predicate;
2. a ground that is not a consequence; 3. a unity that in itself is not
composite.

4503. 1772–75? (1769–70?) (1773–75?) *M* 71, between §236 and §237,   17:576
in *Monas*.[119]

Space and time only permit of boundaries, but not of totality. The
first beginning and the outermost boundary of the world are equally

[a] end-points
[b] inherence

incomprehensible. For the former is at once both a being and a non-being, and both seem to indicate an absolute space and time, i.e., something which acts as a boundary and yet contains nothing.

17:577   **4507.** 1772–75? (1769–70?) (1773–75?) *M* 71, at §239, in *Monas*.
Space is neither a thing in itself nor an actual real relation by means of which one thing posits something in another; consequently, it is not a concept of the understanding; because a concept of the understanding has some object, space therefore does not refer to an object but rather to the subject, and indeed not to sensation, but rather to the form of the senses.[120]

17:577   **4508.** 1772–75? (1769–70?) (1773–75?) *M* 71, at §239.
The *axiomata* of space and time are, with regard to sensibility, certain and intuitable. The principles that everything exists somewhere and at some time and those of shape and place are mere conditions of sensibility.

17:578   **4511.** 1772–75? (1769–70?) *M* 71, at §240, still in *Monas*.
Is space **prior to** things? By all means. For the law of coordination is prior to things and grounds them.
But is space **sensible without things**, or can one observe it only by means of things?[121] Yes, therefore empty space as an **object** of the senses, e.g., between planets, is impossible.

17:578   **4512.** 1772–75? (1769–70?) 1771?? *M* 71, at §240.
Pure space is merely a potential relation and is represented prior to things, but not as something real. Empty space without anything filling it is possible; but absolute space, to which created things stand in a real relation, is impossible. For no substance is present somewhere without having an effect, and indeed externally; in absolute space, however, there are no correlates.

17:578   **4513.** 1772–75. *M* 71, at §239.
Space and time yield nothing real. Only sensation makes something present. Therefore, the real understanding is an activity parallel to sensation.

17:579   **4515.** 1772–75? (1769–70?) *M* 71, at §239.
Space is the ground of the possibility of relations, indeed of their necessity. Possibility and actuality are not different in space and time. In both, the part is possible only by means of the whole. Both are so connected that space exists for all time, i.e., necessarily. Time pertains to being in general, space to external being. Both are the sole given grounds of *synthesis* without any inferences.

142

4516. 1772–75? (1769–70?) *M* 71, at §239.　　　　　　　　　17:579
Space and time are that which is necessary in intuition. Time expresses the entire existence of things.

4518. 1772–75? (1769–70?) *M* 71, at §239.　　　　　　　　　17:579
That time is the form of inner sense can be seen from the fact that one can have it in thought but can never intuit it as something external like extension. Substances are in space; their condition (*accidentia*) is in time. All predicates have for the *copula*: *est, fuit, erit.*[a]

4519. 1772–75? (1769–70??) *M* 72, at §239.　　　　　　　　　17:579
The synthetic propositions of space do not lie in the general concept of space any more than the experiential propositions of chemistry concerning gold lie in its general concept; rather, they are extracted from　　17:580
the intuition of it or found in the intuition of it.

4525. 1772–75? (1772–75? 1776–78?) *M* 111, at §354, in *Notio mundi.*　17:582
The world is the **absolute** whole of possible experience. We may well conceive of an absolute world-whole, but not in space and time. The absolute-whole in appearance is a contradiction.[122]

4529. 1772? (1773–75?) 1776–78? *M* 119, at §§380–1, in *Notio mundi* 17:583
negativa.[123]
The boundaries of appearance cannot appear. Hence no finite world　17:584
can be represented to the senses. If I stick my hand out beyond the world, to that extent the larger world appears; the rest of space does not appear except insofar as I place something in it. Hence appearance without an object (the void) is not possible. However, an infinite time *a parte ante* is certainly necessary in appearance, and in the concepts of reason mathematical magnitude does not occur at all; but the understanding cannot thereby attain to a complete exposition of sensibility.

4534. 1772–78? (1790s?) *M* 124, at §394, in *Partes universi simplices.*[124] 17:585
Simple beings (as such) can never be parts of the sensible world. For in that case they would be parts of the object of outer sense, i.e., of that which is extended; but that which is extended does not consist of simple parts. Hence any principle of life must be counted among the intelligibilia, thus the soul as well. But one knows nothing about the intelligible except its relation to the appearances in the sensible world for which it is the substrate. Thus what it is outside of that (after death) is absolutely unknowable. This is also the ground of our ignorance with regard to

---

[a] is, will be, was

all organized beings and beings that organize matter, the possibility of which, since it rests on a principle of life, cannot be understood. Simple beings have no place in the world.

17:586   **4536**. 1772–76? (1770–71?) *M* 128, at §401 and §402, still in *Partes universi simplices*.

The question whether body is something real outside of me is answered thus: bodies are not bodies outside of my sensibility (*phaenomena*), and thus they exist only in the representational power of sensing beings. Whether something outside of me corresponds to these their appearances is a question about the cause of this appearance and not about the existence of that which appears itself. This existence as an object is the representation of interconnection with all appearances in accordance with laws.[125]

17:587   **4541**. 1772–76? (1769–70?) *M* 275, at §708, in *Arbitrium*.[126]

The universal grounds of the sensible power of choice are inclinations.

The universal grounds of the rational power of choice are principles.

17:588   In accordance with theoretical principles the concept of the hypothetically necessary power of choice is more probable; in accordance with practical principles the absolutely independent power of choice is more probable.

17:588   **4545**. 1772–76? (1769–70?) *M* 275.

The concept of the conditionally necessary power of choice is only a *hypothesis* of theory and must be assumed in order to explain free actions as *phaenomena*. The concept of the unconditionally free power of choice is a *postulatum practicum*, which everyone really assumes, and with regard to which one contradicts oneself when he demands a use of understanding on the part of others.

17:589   **4548**. 1772–75? (1769–70?) *M* 276, at §710.

Freedom is twofold: either the power of choice or power.[a] The form is internal, the latter merely external.

The freedom of the power of choice (*arbitrium liberum*) is *independentia a stimulis*[b] and is called practical freedom. By contrast, the *arbitrium brutum* is *necessitatum a stimulis*.[c] (The *arbitrium liberum* has either *spontaneitatem practicam* or *transscendentalem*.)

The *necessitatio arbitrii bruti* is pathological, that of the *arbitrii liberi* is [*crossed out*: intellectual] practical. The *causae impulsivae*[d] of the former

[a] *Gewalt*
[b] independent of stimuli
[c] necessitated by stimuli
[d] moving or impelling causes

are *stimulia*, those of the latter, *motiva*. The *actus arbitrii liberi* are either *originarii* or *derivativi*; the former is transcendental freedom, the latter merely practical freedom.

4549. 1772–73? (1770–71?) (1773–75?) (1776–78?) M 283, at §723, in   17:590
Libertas.

Freedom consists in the subjective independence of the power of choice from everything that influences our senses internally and externally. Right*a* is the objective independence of our power of choice from others, i.e., the restriction of each power of choice through the condition of reciprocal consensus and the necessity of actions that flow from these conditions. The wisest and best-hearted person, who stakes everything on what is best for us, does not thereby have a right over us.

(*Later addition*: One also may not transform the title of right into that of goodness and religion. The latter should serve only for execution.)

4551. 1772–73. M 288, at §§730–1.   17:590

In the judging of actions **that have happened** [*crossed out*: imputation] we nevertheless presuppose that they all have their determining grounds (although not determined by others), and we impute them, even though they may flow from the inborn character of the person: we only impute them all the more, in part because one still knows that everyone has a   17:591 higher power of choice under which even this character stands, in part because each has still acted in accordance with his own preference and inclination and thus not against his own inclination, whether he does good or evil, and one understands that in accordance with the rule of the higher will the punishments and rewards are appropriate to such a character, and he knows himself to be worthy of them, because he can renounce his self, hence his inclinations as well.

4557. 1772–76? (1769–70?) M 315, at §777, in *Immortalitas animae*   17:593
humanae.

I cannot say: I know there is another life; rather: I believe it. This much I do know, namely, that no one can prove that there is no other life. One also cannot say that one believes that there is no other life; rather: one can only not believe that there is one. This reveals more an enduring lack of insight than an insight into the opposite. The hope of another world is a necessary hypothesis of reason with regard to ends and a necessary hypothesis of the heart with regard to morality. It is thus practically set upon certain grounds, but theoretically obscure and uncertain. Beyond this world one can only know that which obliges us in this world.

---

a *Das Recht*

17:595 **4565.** 1772–75. *M* 329.

It is not more comprehensible that a most real being exists than it is that a limited one does; however, from the presupposition of it it is
17:596 easier to derive limited beings. Accordingly, here there is a necessity of assuming such a being for the sake of the grounds of speculative reason. It is not easier to have insight into the necessity of a completely holy will and its connection with moral perfection than it is to have insight into a will that is limited; however, we require it for morality. In such a way both proofs are valid for the subject, which is also enough for the highest ground of actions.

17:601 **4582.** 1772–75? (1776–78?) *M* 330, in *Existentia Dei.*[127]

The need of reason to cognize a highest being is that of a necessary *hypothesis* of the employment of reason: 1. of pure reason; 2. of empirical reason (both are speculative); of practical reason. (*Later addition*: Hence, 1. transcendental theology; 2. natural theology: cosmotheology, physicotheology; 3. moral theology. All of these are: 1. to determine the concept of the highest being; 2. to demonstrate its existence. All this cognition is a belief, as is always the case when we return to first causes. Transcendental theology alone is deistic; natural theology alone is anthropomorphic; moral theology alone is not adequately secured against objections. Transcendental theology safeguards against them.)

17:602 **4585.** 1772–75? (1776–78?) *M* 330.

1. Pathological origin of theology; 2. speculative origin, sophistical; 3. Moral origin. Thus there are also different religions. [*Crossed out*: The 2nd is deism.] God is in all these cases only a necessary *hypothesis* of the employment of reason with regard to one's own happiness or to speculation or to morality.

17:603 **4589.** 1772–75? (1776–78?) *M* 334, at §816.

We need the concept of God as the concept of a supreme ground of things by means of freedom. 1. In order to explain the origin of contingent beings, and second: to determine the final ends and hopes of rational beings. The former in the series of speculation, the latter in that of *praxis*. The former is of use only as regards the beginning of nature. Natural events themselves must not be explained by means of it.

17:605 **4598.** 1772–78. *M* 335, at §821.

In the doctrine of nature causes are introduced only as necessary
17:606 hypotheses, but not as absolutely necessary, since another cause of the same *phaenomeni* would still be possible.

4599. 1772–78. *M* 335, between §820 and §821.   17:606

Prudence and morality cannot cohere except through the *hypothesis* of a third being, which is powerful and good and at the same time holy and just.

4616. 1772–75. *M* 379, at §926, in *Creatio mundi*.   17:610

The world considered *intellectualiter* has no beginning; not because it has endured for an infinite time, for then it would be considered *sensitive*, but rather because in this respect it is not considered in time at all.

The *sensibilis mundus* has no beginning because a first beginning is impossible. He who considers the world *sensitive* cognizes no boundaries in it.

4617. 1772–76. *M* 379, at §926.   17:610

The world cannot be conceived as having a beginning in accordance with grounds of reason, and in accordance with grounds of sensibility it cannot be conceived as not having a beginning.[128]

4618. 1772? (1775–76?) *M* 380, at §927.   17:610

If we consider the world as the sensible world, we will find no beginning in the *regressu* of appearances. But these appearances are not actual things; thus one does not actually say: the world is in itself without a beginning, but rather: the appearance (in relation to us) has no beginning. In appearances there is no absolute boundary of increase or diminution.

The world has a beginning, not, however, as appearance, but rather as being in itself.

4619. 1772? (1775–76?) *M* 380, at §928.   17:611

The causal relation of the intellectual to the sensitive and the determination of sensibility in accordance with merely intellectual principles or vice versa cannot be understood by us at all. E.g., the first ground of composition, the first action through freedom, the origin and beginning of the world.

4626. 1772–73. *M* X.   17:613

The *analysis* of pure reason yields only distinctness in the representations that we already have.

The synthetic propositions pertain to the conditions of judgments through pure reason and are subjective. Thus pure reason cannot teach us to cognize objects other than in application to the senses.

4627. 1772–73. *M* X.   17:613

Metaphysics has neither the utility in use nor the brilliance of discovery and the strength of rational insight that mathematics has; but its end is a universal human end, and thereby it precedes all theoretical knowledge.

4629. 1772–73. *M* XX.

The fundamental concepts of all of our cognition are [*crossed out*: quality (what exists), quantity (how many times)] 1. being in general (quiddity); second, how something is; third, how many times it is.

That through which things are given is sensation; how they are given, pure intuitions.

Through the understanding either things or only their sensible representations are thought. Number needs space and time for its intuitive representation.[129]

Logical form is for the understanding's representation of a thing what space and time are for the appearances themselves: namely the former contains the positions for ordering them. The representation through which we refer its proper logical position to an object is the real and pure concept of the understanding: e.g., something that I can always use only as a subject; something from which I must infer hypothetically to a *consequens*, etc.[130]

In order for our sensations to acquire a determinate position* in space and time they need a function among appearances; however, position in space and time is determined by proximity to other sensations in space and time; e.g., from the condition of my sensations that has something in common with the preceding ones another one follows; the sensation of a resistance is at the same time combined with weight in the same space.

Through the determination of the logical position the representation acquires a function among the concepts, e.g., *antecedens*, *consequens*. Yet the sensitive function is the ground of the intellectual one.

*(a determinate position is different from an arbitrary one.)

4631. 1772–73. *M* XXI.

Space is a *datum*.

Logical actions are *actus* by means of which we place and order the *data* for representations of things *respective* to each other. Representations thereby obtain logical functions. The real function consists in the way in which we posit a representation in and for itself; thus it is an action (*a priori*) which corresponds to every *dato* (*a posteriori*) and by means of which the latter becomes a concept.[131] These actions are the sources out of which the logical actions are possible. From these arise all cognitions: namely, how we can grasp *data* and form something for ourselves that is called cognition. In nature no *data* can come before us unless, when one perceives the laws therein, they correspond to the universal kinds according to which we posit something, because otherwise no laws would be observed, or any object whatsoever, but only confused internal alterations. Therefore, since we can represent objects only by means of our alterations, insofar as they have in themselves something in conformity with our rules for positing and negating, the real functions are the ground of the possibility of the representation of things, and the logical functions are the ground of the possibility of judgments, and consequently of cognitions. For an object is only called that which [*breaks off*]

4633. 1772–73. *M* XXII.¹³²   17:615

How can cognitions be generated in us the objects of which have not yet been exhibited to us[?] Where the objects must not be guided by our cognitions, but the latter by the objects, it seems that they must, at least as far as their fundamental elements are concerned, be given to   17:616 us before they can be thought. It is therefore the possibility of every *a priori* cognition which is constant for itself without having been created by the objects themselves that constitutes our first and most important question. A question [*crossed out*: even understanding the importance of which] which even to have put forth and understood already has some merit, namely in a part of philosophy which owes nothing to experience and the senses. There are in fact entire sciences of this sort. Pure mathematics, which flows entirely from pure sources *a priori*, without including among its grounds anything from experience, has enjoyed in this way incomparable progress and a rightly admired and until now envied good fortune. But there is no lack of others which, wanting to have equally pure origin, have found themselves in endless contradictions. Hence it is good to investigate the *a priori* sources of cognition in general, without turning our back on this distinction, and only afterwards making them comprehensible.

4634. 1772–73. *M* XXII–XXIV.   17:616

We know any object only through predicates that we can say or think of it. Prior to that, whatever representations are found in us are to be counted only as materials for cognition but not as cognition. Hence an object is only a something in general that we think through certain predicates that constitute its concept. In every judgment, accordingly, there are two predicates that we compare with one another, of which one, which comprises the given cognition of the object, is the logical subject, and the other, which is to be compared with the first, is called the logical predicate. If I say: a body is divisible, this means the same as: Something x, which I cognize under the predicates that together comprise the concept of a body, I also think through the predicate of divisibility. x @ is identical   17:617 with x b. Now a as well as b belongs to x. Only in a different way: either b already lies in that which constitutes the concept a, and thus can be found through the analysis of that, or *b* belongs to *x* without being contained and comprised in *a*. In the first case the judgment is analytic, in the second synthetic.[133] The case that was adduced is an analytic judgment, but the proposition: Every body is heavy, is a *synthesis*; the one predicate is not involved in the subject, but is added to it.[134] Now we can have insight into all analytic judgments *a priori*, and what can only be cognized *a posteriori* is synthetic. Hence properly empirical judgments are synthetic. But there are judgments whose validity seems to be established *a priori*, but which are nevertheless synthetic, e.g., everything that is alterable has a cause; whence does one arrive at these judgments? On what basis do we associate one concept with another of the same object when no observation and experience indicates that[?] Nevertheless all proper axioms are such synthetic propositions, e.g., between two points there can be only one straight line. By contrast, the proposition "every magnitude is equal to itself" is an analytic proposition.[135] The principle or the norm of all analytic propositions is the principle of contradiction and of identity. There is (if I consider both together) no *axioma* but only a formula, i.e., a general model of analytic propositions; for it contains no *medium terminum*.

We have, accordingly, *a posteriori* judgments, which are synthetic, but also *a priori* judgments which are still synthetic and which therefore cannot be derived from any experience, because they contain true universality, hence necessity, and also clearly include concepts which we could not have drawn from experience. These concepts may lie in us where they will: whence do we derive their connection[?] Are they revelations, prejudices, etc.[?]

17:618   If certain concepts in us do not contain anything other than that by means of which all experiences are possible on our part, then they can be asserted *a priori* prior to experience and yet with complete validity for everything that may ever come before us.[136] In that case, to be sure, they are not valid of things in general, but yet of everything that can ever be given to us through experience, because they contain conditions by means of which these experiences are possible. Such propositions would therefore contain the condition of the possibility not of things but of experience. However, things that cannot be given to us through any experience are nothing for us; hence we can very well treat such propositions as universal from a practical point of view, only not as principles of speculation about objects in general.

Now in order to determine what sort of concept that is which must necessarily precede all experience and through which alone experience is possible, which are therefore given *a priori* and also contain the ground for *a priori* judgments, we must analyze an experience in general. In every experience there is something through which an object is given to us and something through which it is thought. If we take the conditions that lie in the activities of the mind by means of which alone it can be given, then we can cognize something of the object *a priori*. If we take that through which alone it can be thought then we can also cognize something *a priori* about all possible objects. For by that means alone does something become an object for us or a cognition of it.

We will investigate the former. That through which an object of experience is given to us is called appearance. The possibility of appearances on the side of the human mind is sensibility. In sensibility there is a matter, which is called sensation, and with respect to that and its diversity we are merely passive, and the multiplicity of impressions determines that we do not find anything in us *a priori* which we could have known from ourselves *a priori* before the impressions. One can never represent in thought any impression of a new kind. But the appearances also have   17:619
a form, a ground lying in our subject by means of which we order either the impressions themselves or that which corresponds to them and assign each part of them its position. This can be nothing other than an activity, which is to be sure naturally aroused by the impressions, but which can still be cognized prior to them.

(If we place something in space and time, we act; if we place it next to or after another, we connect. These actions are only means to bring about each position; but one can take them separately; if we take several at once or posit one action simultaneously with another, this is a kind of action, through which we posit something in accordance with the rule of appearances, where this positing must have its special rules, which are distinct from the condition of the form with regard to which they are to be located in appearance.)

4636. 1772–73. *M* XXV.   17:619

A priori cognitions must not pertain to determinate things (since   17:620
these are not yet given), but to universal representations of things in general, and thus to intuitions (not to sensations, for it is these through which something determinate is given) or to thoughts in general. (One can intuit something without thinking something thereby or thereunder.)

All cognitions come to us through thinking, i.e., through concepts; they are not intuitions.

4638. 1772–73. *M* XXVI.   17:620

All cognition consists in judgments. Now the judgments may be immediate or mediate (rational inferences); [*crossed out*: a determinate] thinking is called judging. Even the concepts are predicates. Accordingly, concepts for which no object is given, but which are nevertheless to express the manner of thinking objects in general, contain that which is thought in the judgments about the relation of two concepts to each other.

Universally valid concepts have a logical [*crossed out*: function] position among the concepts. The position in a judgment is a logical function; it is [*breaks off*]

The determinate logical function of a representation in general is the pure concept of the understanding.

17:622 **4642.** 1772–73. *M* XXVII.

Everything that constitues a law for our representations *a priori*, [*crossed out*: every *actus*] consequently the relation of the representations to a universal law that is established *a priori*, is the object. That which is thought under such a law represents the thing as it is, i.e., as it holds for all appearances. For this reason, however, it must be something determinable *a priori*, because only thereby can we think; for thinking means nothing other than determining representations from that which is universal.

The concepts of the understanding express all the *actus* of the powers of the mind, insofar as representations are possible in accordance with their universal laws, and indeed their possibility *a priori*.

17:622 **4643.** 1772–73. *M* XXVIII.

Every pure cognition *a priori*, in which thus no sensation is given, is transcendental.
1. The transcendental aesthetic.
2. The transcendental logic.
3. The transcendental critique.
4. The transcendental architectonic.[137]

17:624 **4648.** 1772–73 (1773–75? 1776–78?) *M* XXVII.

Motion is something that happens, thus that belongs to the actual appearances and not to the merely sensible form, and also presupposes 17:625 something moveable, i.e., alterable with regard to its position, which cannot be cognized *a priori*, rather it presupposes empirical concepts, which also presuppose concepts of the understanding.

17:625 **4651.** 1772–73? 1773–75? (1776–78?) *M* XXIII.

A learned journal should properly announce the progress of a science. 17:626 This has thus far not been able to happen with metaphysical works. Now it can happen, and indeed as far as completeness, distinctness, and precision are concerned. Yes, the completion of the science can be announced, indeed before very long.

4659. 1772–73. *M* 31, at §109, in *Necessarium et contingens.*   17:628

The common proof of the necessary existence of a most perfect being is that if it did not exist it would lack a perfection, namely existence, thus that it already contains existence in its concept. I reply: if it did not exist, the most perfect being would not be lacking something, rather the most perfect being would be entirely missing. Indeed, there can be no contradiction if the thing itself is negated and nothing is left. The most perfect possible thing that does not exist is the most perfect among all of those things that are merely possible.

4662. 1772–73. *M* 32, at §114, in *Necessarium et contingens.*   17:629

In appearances, substances are only empirically necessary, i.e., they are interconnected with the entirety of appearances as far as time is concerned; but they are not absolutely necessary, since they could be negated together with all other appearances. Empty space and time.

II.
FROM THE *DUISBURG NACHLAß* TO THE *FIRST CRITIQUE*: 1773–1780

4672. 1773–75. Kant's remark on the reverse of a letter from E. T.   17:635
Kortum of 18 November 1773 (10:142f.).[1]

First there must be certain titles of thought, under which appearances can be brought in themselves: e.g., whether they are regarded as magnitude or as subject or as ground or as whole or merely as reality (figure is no reality). On this account I will not regard whatever I want in the appearance as either subject or predicate, rather it is determined as subject or *respective* as ground. Thus what sort of logi-   17:636
cal function is actually valid of one appearance in regard to another, whether that of magnitude or of the subject, thus which function of judgments. For otherwise we could use logical functions arbitrarily, without making out or perceiving that the object is more suitable for one than another. Thus one can think an[a] appearance without bringing it under a title of thinking in general, hence without determining an object for it.

In order for appearances to belong to or be determined in accordance with certain rules, it is necessary that they be represented as belonging under one or another function of them. Thereby do they become determinate objects of thoughts; otherwise there is nothing in their relations

---

[a] Presumably Kant here meant *keine Erscheinung* rather than *eine Erscheinung*, i.e., "one cannot think any appearance . . ." rather than "one can think an appearance."

(for sensations are not thoughts) that makes them thinkable for the understanding.

17:636 **4673.** 1773–75. Kant's remarks on a letter from D. F. Lossow of 28 April 1774 (10:167).

P. I.

[*crossed out*: unitary. I.e., all representations constitute in my inner condition through the unity of intuition] For as intuition of a single subject all objects belong only to one [*breaks off*]

Together with the sense, under which they are offered to our understanding [*breaks off*]

1. Time [is] unitary. Which is to say as much as: I can [*crossed out*: cognize] intuit all objects only in myself and in the representations to be 17:637 found in my own subject [*crossed out*: and thus cognize them immediately only in accordance with the form of inner intuition], and all possible objects of my intuition stand in relation to each other in accordance with the particular form of this intuition.

2. It is infinite, without a first and last. For it is the [*crossed out*: *datum*] condition of coordination through the inner sense, which must not be determined and restricted except through the representations which are given in accordance with it. The receptivity of coordination[a] cannot restrict itself.

3. It is necessary, i.e., it does not depend on anything, but grounds all of them, and is therefore [*crossed out*: the first *datum* of possibility] the condition of inner intuitions and grounds the possibility of all intuitions.

4. All things and all states of things have their determinate position in it. For they must have their determinate relation to all [*crossed out*: possible] other objects of intuition that can be given through the unity of inner sense.

5. It precedes all real things and hence can itself also be cognized *a priori* as the condition of objects.

The inner determinations are not in space.

We cannot get beyond the world with these concepts.

1. Thus if a subject is a thing in general and the predicate is space and 17:638 time or a concept constructed on those as a condition, then the judgment is transcendent. Everything is somewhere and some time. I do not say that it is false; only it is not conclusive, *non liquet*. What [*crossed out*: however] is false is that from this subjective thing something universal and objective should follow.

2. If the subject is given only through predicates of inner sensation and the predicate contains a condition of outer sensibility, it is also transcendent.

---

[a] *Zusammenordnung*

P. II.

Comment.

Space is nothing other than the intuition of mere form even without given matter, thus pure intuition. It is a singular representation because of the unity of the subject and the capacity, in which all representations of outer objects can be placed beside one another. It is infinite, since there are no boundaries in the capacity for sensing. It is necessary, since it is the first condition of the possibility of outer representations; consequently it is the ground of the capacity of outer representations, and we cannot represent the opposite, since we would otherwise have to have an [*crossed out*: another] even higher capacity. It is something real, which does not depend on the existence of things; [*crossed out*: rather] for the capacity to intuit does not depend on the existence of things, and can therefore be cognized *a priori*.

Space is not an object of intuitions (an object or its determination), but the intuition itself, which precedes all objects and [*crossed out*: through which] in which if the latter are posited, the appearance of them is possible. It is a pure intuition *a priori*. But how is such an intuition possible[?] It is nothing other than the consciousness of one's own receptivity for sensing representations (impressions) of things in accordance with certain relations among them.   17:639

***Spatium absolutum*, this riddle of philosophers**, is certainly something correct (but not *reale*, rather *ideale*), otherwise one could not assert anything about it *a priori*, not, to be sure, through general concepts, but rather through properties that can be perceived in it through an immediate grasp. It is, however, nothing external, rather it is the condition of the form of all outer representation subsisting in the mind itself. **It is nothing imagined (*ens imaginarium*)**. For it is the sole real condition of the representation of real outer things. The **order of things that are next to one another** is not space, rather **space is that which** makes **such an order or better coordination** in accordance with determinate conditions possible. If it were a merely general concept of order, then one would attempt to see how much one could derive and how one would arrive *a priori* **at the necessity of such an** order; for to derive it *a posteriori* is, first, contrary to what is self-evident, and then it would have only the consequences of an observation, but not of a fundamental representation.

Space as an outer representation would also have to have something in the object by means of which it is effected in the mind. Then it would not be an *a priori* representation. However, it exists even where there is nothing at all, thus no influence,[a] and the mere form is not imparted to us by influence.

---

[a] *Einfluss*

That there are in general things that correspond to the sensibility must be cognized by the understanding; thus the **ideality of space** is nothing other than **the distinction between sensibility and that which is posited by it** and the understanding and that which is thought by it.

17:640 By ideality the reality of **bodies** (certain beings that correspond to them) and certain properties is not denied, indeed there is not even anything other than a negative thought about them.[2]

The ideality of space does not negate its reality with regard to bodies, i.e., all outer objects of sensibility, and space really pertains to them; rather it only distinguishes objects of the senses as such from things in themselves. No space pertains to a thing in itself (as condition or determination), but every object of the outer senses is conceived through the condition of space.

P. III.

The propositions of the properties of absolute space and time come across as strange; thus one either denies absolute time and makes it into an *abstracto* or *empirico* or one makes time objective and makes it into a most real ideal, i.e., into a chimera.

We have no intuitions except through the senses; thus no concepts can inhabit the understanding other than those that pertain to the disposition and order among these intuitions. These concepts must contain the universal and rules. The faculty of rules *in abstracto*: the learned understanding; *in concreto*: the healthy understanding. The healthy understanding has the edge in all cases where the rule must be abstracted *a posteriori* from the cases; but where the rule has its origin entirely *a priori* there the healthy understanding does not occur at all.

P. IV.

Space is the condition that pertains to our sensibility with regard to

17:641 all outer appearance, for it is the form of this capacity of the mind for perceiving things as external. Hence bodies are representations that are possible only under this condition [*crossed out*: and are themselves nothing], to that extent space is surely something real. [*Crossed out*: Ideality] But by means of a body there is not conceived an object of cognition in general, but rather a thing as an object of outer sense. Space as a predicate thus does not pertain to a thing in itself, but only to the object of the outer sense. It is the condition not of things, but of the phenomenon of things, and indeed of the outer sense. Hereby the sensibility is only distinguished from the understanding, through which something is represented not as it is given to us as an object of the senses, but rather it is conceived independently of them.[3]

The origin of different predicates of space, which were otherwise regarded as objective, can now be explained through this concept. 1. Space is unitary, because it is the form of representations of all possible outer objects in a unitary subject. 2. Space is infinite. For the capacity to receive several impressions of outer objects, or the susceptibility to them, has no limits in itself. 3. Space is necessary, for it is that on which the possibility of the senses is itself grounded.

The representation of space is nothing imaginary that is related merely to the subject (all-embracing), but is rather a condition for representing outer things and a means for ordering them. The order is in accordance with the inner form.

The omnipresence of space and the eternity of time. That space is always present, i.e., it is itself the condition of all presence, for through it is presence cognized.

The former means that we cannot intuit anything as present except insofar as it is somewhere in space.

Reason is the faculty of *a priori* rules.

An *a priori* rule is a rule of reason. A rule from concepts *in abstracto* is a 17:642 law. Reason is the faculty of laws. A rule of the construction of concepts is called a formula. A symbolic formula–

Concepts of reason are unconditionally valid concepts, thus the all, the first, the transcendent. Unconditional necessity, the unconditional *principium* (the independent *principium*), the unconditional (unrestricted) all.

Space and time contain the conditions of the rules of appearance, hence they lie at the basis of all categories with regard to their application.

The question whether space is something ideal (not imaginary) or something real does not interest different sciences at all. It is not considered in mathematics, mechanics, and general physics; although Leibniz as well as Newton (I name them here only at the head of other great names) assume its reality, the latter its subsistent reality and the former its adherent reality, in their application to objects in the world both proceed as if both space and time were self-subsisting containers of things, and even if their ideality is proved by us, that makes no difference with regard to such investigations. But where these answers are to be transcendent, then it is another story.[4]

Different things are in different places, and conversely: the difference of places proves the difference of things (this is a proposition that already pertains to empirical understanding).

Even if we cannot comprehend many propositions from the concepts of space and time, we must note that they are not representations of reason, but of intuition, and [*breaks off*]

R 4674–4684: Loose sheets from the Duisburg Nachlaß[5]

4674. 1773–75. *LBl* Duisburg 7, pp. I, II. 17:643
P. I.

The principles of appearance in general are merely those of form, namely time.

The *principium* of the exposition of appearances is the ground of the exposition in general of that which is given. The exposition of that which is thought depends solely on consciousness, but the exposition of that which is given, if one regards the matter as undetermined, depends on the ground of all relation and of the concatenation of representations (sensations). The concatenation is grounded (like the appearance, not on mere sensation, rather in inner principles of form) not on the mere appearance, rather it is a representation of the inner action of the mind in connecting representations, not merely for placing them next to one another in intuition, but for constituting a whole as regards its matter. Thus there is here a unity not by means of that wherein but rather by means of that through which the manifold is brought into one, hence universal validity. Hence it is not forms but rather functions on which the *relationes* of appearances depend. The exposition of appearances is thus the determination of the ground on which the interconnection of the sensations in them depends.

By a universal concept of a sensible *dati*, in which the reality and at the same time its relation to the sensible condition in general is indicated, we understand the action of sensibly determining an object in accordance with such conditions; e.g., that which happens signifies the action of determining something in accordance with its succession in time. Now x is this determinable, which contains the conditions of determination; a however signifies only the action of determining in general. It is therefore

17:644 no wonder if something beyond the action of determining is contained in x, which is expressed through b (in the concept a yet more is contained, which belongs to what determines it in the mind, i.e., the manner of cognizing how this is generated or specified in the mind, or what flows from its specification or is combined with it as condition). E.g., in space, beyond the general action of constructing a triangle, the magnitude of its angles, and in inner sense, beyond the general designation of that which happens, the conditions under which alone this occurrence (as apprehension) can be determined in the mind. These conditions in x are found in intuition through the construction of a, e.g., the triangle, but in a real concept through the *concretum* of the subject in which the representation a is posited. Thus the relation which is thought through a is to be determined only through the real condition of the subject, which consists in the function of relative positing in general and in regard to the *dati a* in particular; since the subjective condition x should suffice for all these positings,[a] the determination of a, i.e., b, must be a general action, by means of which the appearance of a expounds b, i.e., [*breaks off*][6]

[a] *positionen*

158

Synthetic propositions of appearance are objectively valid only of relation.

In synthetic propositions the relation among the concepts is not properly represented immediately (for this occurs only in analytic propositions), but only in the conditions of their concrete representation in the subject, whether intuition or appearance. This subject contains the conditions of the representation of everything of which we have concepts, and in its sensibility [*crossed out*: must the object] must that which is objective in it be determined. x always signifies the object of the concept a. But there can be no object except that of either pure or empirical intuition. As far as the latter is concerned, the concept can pertain   17:645
either to a given object of the senses x or to conditions of sensibility under which an object, insofar as it merely corresponds to the concept x, must be given, and under which alone it can be cognized as subject to a.

P.II

It is a proof that space is a subjective condition that since propositions about it are synthetic and thereby objects can be known *a priori*, this would be impossible if space were not a subjective condition of the representation of these objects.[7]

By contrast, the synthetic judgments of experience are cognized *a posteriori*, because they are immediately directed to given objects.

But now if anything were to be known *a priori* about things concerning not merely the form of their appearance, but with regard to the rest of their constitution, etc. [*sic*]

The x drops out, because it is to signify the object that is thought through a; but since b is compared merely with the concept a and is thereby already determined, so is the rest of x indifferent; if a is considered *adiective*, then the proposition is not always universal.

b must be a determination of a and not an analytic predicate. Analytic predicates are identical and tautological. Of analytic hypothetical judgments. disjunction, dichotomy. (categorical judgments are the foundation.) The concept substance and *accidens* provides a *synthesin* in itself, likewise cause and effect and a multitude in a real unity. That nature now must stand throughout under one of these *syntheses* in accordance with the different relations to the inner sense.

x is therefore the determinable (object), which I think through the concept a, and b is its determination or the manner of determining it. In mathematics x is the construction of a, in experience it is the *concretum*,   17:646
in regard to an inhering representation or thought in general x is the function of thinking in general in the subject, therefore the real concept a is determined altogether 1. through the subject, 2. with regard to succession, through the ground, 3. with regard to coexistence, through composition.

[*Crossed out*: The condition through which *a* acquires an object *x* is enunciated in *b* but] *x* is the object. This can be given *a priori* in the construction, but in the exposition (which is something completely different from observation, which has not combined anything *a priori* with *a*) the *a priori* conditions in the subject can be cognized under which *a* is in general related to an object, namely something real. This object can only be represented in accordance with its relations and is nothing other than the subjective representation of the subject itself, but made general, for I am the original of all objects. It is therefore conjugation as a function that constitutes the exponent of a rule.

Reality must be given in sensation. Magnitude we can construct in accordance with intuition. The real *synthesis* is not given to us merely in sensation, and also cannot be constructed, but nevertheless lies in the appearance neither as intuition nor as sensation. For experience still gives us cognition of substance, effect and cause, and whole (although we cannot conceive of the latter *a priori*, namely, how among many things one reciprocally determines all the others and is determined by them, and can only comprehend many together in our thoughts). These three-fold concepts pertain to objects as appearances (possibility, etc., only as concepts *a priori*); in the case of magnitude I do not need any sensation, only time, in the case of real synthesis I need sensation in general as well as time. (Threefold dimension of *synthesis*. How can we, then, represent *a priori* the *positiones* of the postulates of *synthesis*[?] There are three functions of apperception, which are met with in [*crossed out*: all] the thought of our state in general and under which all appearance must on that account fit, because in it there would lie no synthesis in itself if the mind did not add it or make it out of the *datis* of appearance. The mind is thus itself the archetype [*crossed out*: of the possibility] of such a *synthesis* through original and not through derivative thinking.)[a]

17:647

Concepts provide only the outline of objects, namely that which is a sign of their representation. *b* is always compared with the object *x* by means of *a*, but *x* is never considered solely in the concept *a*; in the latter case *b* pertains either to the way the object *a* is given *a priori* (*obiective*) in intuition, or *a posteriori* in experience, or *a priori*, but [*crossed out: subiective*] in the subjective perception of apperception. This last pertains only to cases of perception, and indeed to the *synthesin* in such cases, i.e., to the relation. Apperception is the perception of oneself as a thinking subject in general.

Apperception is the consciousness of thinking, i.e., of the representations as they are placed in the mind. Here there are three exponents: 1. the relation to the subject, 2. the relation of succession among one

---

[a] There is no right-hand parenthesis in the text; this location is conjectural.

another, 3. of composition. The determination of *a* in these *momentis* of apperception is subsumption under one of these *actibus* of thinking; one cognizes it as determinable in itself and thus objective, namely the concept *a*, if one brings it under one of these general actions of thinking, by means of which it comes under a rule. Such a proposition is a principle of the rule, thus of the cognition of the appearance through the understanding, by means of which it is considered as something objective, which is [*crossed out*: not] thought in itself independently of the particularity in which it was given.

4675. *LBl* Duisburg 8. Kant's comments on the letter from Bertram (not further identified) of 20 May 1775 (10:182).[8]   17:648
P. I.

The same entity can subsist with opposed predicates one after the other. Something is posited outside us only insofar as its representation constitutes persistence and a particular point of relation.[9]

If my representation succeeds something, its object would not also follow that unless its representation were determined as a consequence of something, which can never happen except in accordance with a universal law. Or there must be a universal law that all succession is determined by something preceding, otherwise I could not posit any succession of objects for the succession of representation. For to posit objects for my representations always requires that the representation be determined in accordance with a universal law, for the object consists precisely in the universally valid point.[10]

Likewise I would not represent anything as outside of me and thus make appearance into experience (objectively) if the representations did not relate to something that is parallel to my I, through which I refer them from myself to another subject. Likewise if manifold representations did not determine one another in accordance with a universal law. The three relations in the mind therefore require three analogies of appearance, in order to transform the **subjective functions** of the mind into objective ones and thereby make them into concepts of the understanding, which give reality to the appearances.

Everything that is simultaneous in reciprocal relations belongs to a whole: *contra vacuum* [*crossed out: separans*] *interrumpens* (*vacuum terminans*);[a] from this follows continuity [*breaks off*]

All of this is grounded on conditions of experience: consequently it is not necessary and is also not understood as such; rather, it is *analoga*   17:649
of axioms that take place *a priori*, but only as anticipations of all laws of experience in general.

---

[a] contrary to an interrupted vacuum (a vacuum with terminations)

Everything that happens is connected *a priori*; everything that is simultaneous is connected *comitative*; everything that exists is connected *inhaesive*.

The axioms have a primitive certainty, the analogies a derivative one, the petitions an adopted one. The derivative certainty from the nature of our thinking in general, not as appearances, but as actions of the subject, which thinking, insofar as it is to yield an object, must be in a substance, determined through a ground, and connected with the whole of the power of representation. It is therefore derived from the subjectively real conditions of thinking in general. Everything that **belongs to an aggregate** objectively is in reciprocal determination to one another, for otherwise it is only a subjective ideal whole.

P. II.

Intuition	Thought	*a priori*
Sensibility	Understanding	Reason

The understanding thus combines the two extremes by connecting the *a posteriori data* with *a priori* conditions, but only *in concreto*, hence only for an empirical cognition.

The ideal or real subject

The ideal or real series

The ideal or real aggregate.

The former are only actions of the mind, the latter is something in the objects in themselves in relation to thinking without distinction of the subject.

Both are distinguished through the necessity of the relations, which flows from the universality; the subject, whatever lies at the ground; the members of the series, from which something determinate always follows; the manifold, each of which is determined by the others and in turn determines them.

17:650   The aggregate considered *obiective* must have a common ground of its unity, by means of which the elements of the manifold depend on one another. The consequence of this is: many things that agree with one another have a common ground.

Continuity in space and time.

On the intellectualization of apprehension.

a and *b* can be in three different sorts of relation by means of *x*: either

$$x$$
$$\wedge$$

$a : b$ or $a : x : b$ or $a + b = x$.

The inner necessity of appearance, namely where it is freed from everything subjective and is regarded as determinable through a universal rule (of appearances), is that which is objective. That which is objective is the ground of the consensus of appearances among one another.

In all three unities necessity obtains. Everything aggregate is contingent; hence there must be something, by means of which its *respectus* becomes necessary. All occurrence is contingent, hence its origin must be necessary. Everything that [*breaks off*]

That which is objective is the ground of the consensus of appearances. Hence threefold consensus: 1. in a common subject, 2. in a common beginning, 3. in a common whole.

P. III.

All of our cognitions are distinguished according to the matter (content, object) or form. As far as the latter is concerned, it is either intuition or concept. The former is of the object, insofar as it is given; the latter, 17:651 insofar as it is thought. The faculty of intuition is sensibility, that of thinking is the understanding (that of thinking *a priori*, without the object being given, is reason). The understanding is thus opposed to both sensibility and reason. The perfection of cognition with regard to sensibility is aesthetic, that with regard to concepts is logical. Intuition is either of the object (*apprehensio*) or of our self; the latter (*apperceptio*) pertains to all cognitions, even those of the understanding and reason.

Transcendental logic deals with cognitions of the understanding with respect to their content, but without determination with regard to the way in which objects are given.

The condition of all apperception is the unity of the thinking subject. From this flows the connection of the manifold in accordance with a rule and in a whole, since the unity of the function must suffice for subordination as well as coordination.

P. IV.

Key. Tub.

Inkwell. Quill and knife. Paper. Writings. Books.

Pants. Boots. Mantle. Cap. Night-stockings.

Napkins. Tablecloth. Handtowel. Plates. Cups. Knife and fork. Salt cellar.

Bottles. Wine and beer glasses. Wine bottles.

Tobacco. Pipes. Tea set. Tea. Sugar.

Brushes.

Of concepts that cannot be determined *a priori*, i.e., constructed.[11]

17:652   If *x*, which is the objective condition of *a*, is at the same time the subjective condition of *b*, there then arises a synthetic proposition, which is only true *restrictive*. E.g., all existence belongs to a substance; everything that happens is a member of a series; everything that is simultaneous is a whole whose parts determine each other reciprocally. *x*, the time wherein it is determined what happens, is the subjective condition of what in the concept of the understanding is thought of only as the consequence of a ground. The subjective condition signifies the condition of the specification of the concept of the understanding corresponding to this relation. Such principles are not axioms. There are no actual anticipations of appearance. One finds them confirmed through experiences, since laws of experience thereby become possible. Other appearances yield no laws. They are not self-evident, since it is not the appearances but the experiences that become possible through them. *Synthesis* of thinking and appearance.

The subjective conditions of appearance, which can be cognized *a priori*, are space and time: intuitions.[a]

The subjective condition of empirical cognition is apprehension in time in general and therefore in accordance with the conditions of the inner sense in general.

The subjective condition of rational cognition is construction [*crossed out*: in time] through the condition of apprehension in general.

[*Crossed out*: Rules of critique

Laws of intuition. Analogies of nature]

The general relation of sensibility to the understanding and to reason is either that through which it is given *a priori*, thus the sensible condition of intuition, second, the sensible condition of the judgment in general concerning that which is given, finally the sensible condition of the *a priori* concept. The *a priori* rules which enunciate these conditions contain in general the relation of the subjective to the objective. Either of the subjective through which the objective is given, or of that through which it is thought as given in general (as object) or determined *a priori*.

17:653   Everything that is given is thought under the universal conditions of apprehension. Hence the subjective universal of apprehension is the condition of the objective universal of intellection. Everything is thought *a priori* under the subjective condition of construction, although the latter is only problematic, i.e., the condition is not given, yet is necessary for the construction. To determine *a priori* is to construct.

---

[a] Here Kant writes *intuitionen* rather than *Anschauungen*.

4676. 1773–75. *LBl* Duisburg 10.   17:653
Pp. I–II.

In all reality there is the relation of substance to *accidens*, in that which
happens, that of ground to consequence, etc.

The principle of identity and contradiction contains the comparison
of two predicates *a* and *b* with *x*, but only in such a way that the concept   17:654
a of *x* is compared with *b* (*substantive*), thus the *x* is idle. It is a principle
of form, not of content, thus merely logical. A principle of analysis, from
which nothing can be cognized *obiective*. It can be cognized in categorical,
hypothetical, and disjunctive form. If I refer both predicates to the *x* and
thereby to one another, then it is synthetic: no *x* who is learned is lacking
in science, for there [*crossed out*: it signifies] it needs the restriction of time,
namely: at the same time.[12] The lack of science contradicts learnedness,
to be sure, but not the person *x* who is learned, except insofar as he is
learned. Thus the contradiction is directed either to the concept *a* that
I have of *x* or to the *x*, to which this concept does not necessarily apply.
The synthetic validity of *b* and *non b* with regard to *x*, which can be
thought through the concept *a* or *non a*, is called alteration.

But if *a* cannot be separated from *b* in *x*, e.g., no *x* which is a body is
indivisible, then it can be seen that the *x* which is thought through *a* can
never be thought through *non a*, that no entity that has the nature of a
body can ever become incorporeal and that the *a* itself is with regard to
x no predicate, but is rather an alternative concept for it and thus valid
substantive.

The distinction between affirmative and negative propositions and
the principles of affirmation and negation, which are the same as far as
their contents are concerned.

But if *a* and *b* are not identical, whether they are used affirmatively
or negatively, and *x* is not thought entirely determinately through the
concept of *a*, then *a* and *b* are not in a logical but in a real relation (something different) of combination, hence not one of involution. Thus their
relation is not determined through their concepts themselves, but rather
by means of the *x*, of which *a* contains the designation. How are such
syntheses possible[?] *x* must be a *datum* of sensibility, in which a *synthesis*,
i.e., a relation of coordination, takes place; for [*crossed out*: a discursive]
this contains more than is thought through its concept *a*, and is the rep-   17:655
resentation of *a in concreto*. Now there are three cases where a transcendental subject is sensible and yields a relation of concepts: either it is the
[*crossed out*: construction] intuition of *a* or it is the appearance of *a* or . . .[a]
the empirical cognition. In the first case the relation of *a* : *b* follows from
the construction of *a* = *x*. In the second [*crossed out*: and third] case it is

---

[a] Here we omit a repetition of "the appearance of *a*."

drawn from the [*crossed out*: the example of the empirical object of *a* in *d*] sensible condition of the intellection of *a*, in the third case from observation. The first two syntheses are *a priori* (all three are objective). For in the second case *a* signifies a universal sensible condition of perception, *x*, however, signifies the condition of the subject in general, in which the relation of all perceptions is determinable (for perceptions are not merely objective, but presuppose sensation, which has only subjective validity). Thus *a* will signify the universal in perception, *x* the sensible condition of the subject (*substratum*) in which this perception is to acquire its position. Consequently the condition of disposition. Finally, *b* [is] the universal function of the mind for determining the position of *a* in *x*, thus the exponent for determining the relation of perceptions [*crossed out*: to one another in the mind], hence their position in accordance with a rule.

P. III.

17:656   If something is apprehended, it is taken up in the function of apperception. I am, I think, thoughts are in me. These are all relations, which to be sure do not provide rules of appearance, but which make it such that all appearance is to be represented as contained under a rule. The I constitutes the substratum for a rule in general, and apprehension relates every appearance to it.

For the origination of a rule three elements are required: 1. *x*, as the *datum* for a rule (object of sensibility or rather sensible real representation). 2. *a*, the *aptitudo* for a rule or the condition, through which it is in general related to a rule. 3. *b*, the exponent of the rule.

Now if a norm for the rule of appearances in general or of experiences is to arise – e.g., everything existent is in substance – then *x* is sensation in general as the *specif* [*ication*] of reality. By being represented as reality it becomes the material of a rule or sensation becomes capable of a rule, and *a* is only a function of the apprehension of appearance as given in general. Now since everything must be given in time, which therefore comprehends everything in itself, thus *b* is [*crossed out*: a function] an *actus* of apperception, namely the consciousness of the subject which apperceives [itself] as that which is given in the whole of time is necessarily connected with it, for otherwise the sensation would not be represented as belonging to me.

Transcendental thetic: on the erection of the principles of pure reason. Antithetic: on the (natural) use of these principles. For general logic also 17:657   deals with [*crossed out*: their] natural use by the common understanding. The fundamental rules of the latter are abstracted from the common understanding, although not borrowed and derived from it. The universal rules, however, or the principles of **thinking in general** without determinate objects or determination of cognition from its relation to the objects is always dialectical.

P. IV.

We think of everything by means of predicates, thus there is always a relation to x. But in judgments it is a relation of $a : b$, which are both related to x. a and b in x, x by means of $a : b$, finally $a + b = x$.

The absolute predicate in general is reality and whence.[a]

Determinate predicates (relational predicates) which are real pertain only to relations. Of these there are three. According to the three relations in judging.

The relational predicates are transcendental, the relation of predicates is logical.

What expresses the relational predicate in the mind for action and on which is grounded its relation on the one side to sensibility, on the other side to the logical, so that it acquires through the former reality, through the latter the form of thinking[?]

Is the x the form of inner sensibility or that which is real in apprehension?

4677. 1773–75. *LBl* Duisburg 11.   17:657

P. I.

Only because the relation that is posited in accordance with the conditions of intuition is assumed to be determinable in accordance with a rule is the appearance related to an object; otherwise it is merely an inner affection of the mind.

Everything that is **thought** as an object of intuition stands under a rule of construction.

Everything that is **thought** as an object of perception stands under a   17:658
rule of apperception, self-perception.

Experience in general. Either intuition or sensation.

Appearance is made objective by being brought as contained under a title of self-perception. And thus the original relations of apprehension are the conditions of the perception of the real relations in appearance, and indeed just insofar as one says that an appearance belongs thereunder is it determined from the universal and represented as objective, i.e., thought. When one does not represent it as belonging under the functions of self-sensation, but rather represents it by means of an isolated perception, then it is called mere sensation. We can determine this just as *a priori* from the functions of perception with regard to the objective, i.e., the conditions which are independent from the individual relations of the senses, as we can with regard to the relations of space and time. The mind must have a faculty for apprehending, and its functions are just as necessary for perception as is the receptivity of appearances.

If we intuited intellectually, then no title of apprehension would be needed to represent an object. In that case the object would not even

---

[a] *wovon*, i.e., that which from all else flows

appear. Now the appearance must be subordinated to a [*crossed out*: ground] function by means of which the mind disposes over it, and indeed to a universal condition of this, for otherwise nothing universal would be found therein.

All synthetic propositions have a condition of sensibility (an expansive one), either for the intuition (pure construction or empirical exposition) or of thinking through the understanding (specification) or of insight through reason.

17:659 The *x* thus always contains the condition.

Either an objective condition of appearance or a subjective one of pure intuitions, both in judgments whether the predicate is sensible,

or an objective one of the understanding with regard to [*crossed out*: perception] intellection or a subjective one of reason with regard to conception, both in the case of intellectual predicates.

In the case of an analytical proposition the subject is thus always taken substantively. The concept of learnedness is contradictory to the concept of the unlearned.

P. II.

All appearances are related to the concept of an object that is valid for all of them, e.g., appearances of a rectangle; thus they stand under rules of judging, by means of which this concept can be determined (optical illusion). The perceptions are not appearances alone, i.e., representations of appearances, but of their existence. E.g., that reality exists, that it is successive, that it is simultaneous with other reality. Perception is position in inner sense in general and pertains to sensation in accordance with the relations of the apperception of self-consciousness, in accordance with which we become conscious of our own existence. All perception thus likewise stands under a rule of judging.

The presumption is not an anticipation, because it does not determine, but only says that something is determinable in accordance with a certain given exponent according to a rule that is yet to be found. It thus serves
17:660 to search for this determination and to expound the appearance, and is the *principium* for judging it. E.g., that which happens has its ground in something preceding.

17:660 **4678.** 1773–75. *LBl* Duisburg 12.
P. I.

That in the soul there lies a *principium* of disposition as well as of affection. That the appearances can have no other order and cannot otherwise belong to the unity of the power of representation except insofar as they are in accord with the common *principio* of disposition. For all appearances with their common determination must still have unity in the mind, consequently must be subject to such conditions by means of

168

which the unity of representations is possible. Only that which is requisite for the unity of representations belongs to the objective conditions. The unity of apprehension is necessarily combined with the unity of the intuition [of] space and time, for without this the latter would yield no real representation.[13]

The principles of exposition must be determined on the one side by the laws of apprehension, on the other by the unity of the faculty of understanding. They are the standard for observation and are not borrowed from perceptions, but from their ground as a whole (originally, and abstracted from that).

Pure thinking (*a priori*), but in relation to experiences, i.e., to objects of the senses, contains principles that contain the origin of all experiences, i.e., of that which is thoroughly determined for the experiences.

We must expound[a] concepts if we cannot construct them. We cannot construct appearances, although we can do so for intuitions. Yet we must have rules for their exposition. These rules are really rules of appearance itself, but insofar as the inner in them is to be discovered in their solution. Thus the rules for the solution of appearances are actually the conditions of apprehension, insofar as it proceeds from one to another of them and conjoins them.

17:661

[*Crossed out*: The perceptions stand under rules of intuitions, the conjoined ones under rules of]

The principle: Everything that is thought stands under a rule, for only through the rule is it an object of thinking.

The *synthesis* (the *principium* of it) contains rules of thinking *a priori* but insofar as it is **determined** to objects. Thus there is therein 1. pure thinking (*a*) and its rules, 2. the condition of the object, i.e., **under** which something is given (or brought) as an object for thinking (*x*), 3. the determination of the thought from this relation (*b*).

The *principium* of *analysis*: a rule of thinking in general. The principles[b] of thinking insofar as it is restricted by the condition of the subject or determined to the subject are not fundamental principles,[c] but restrictions. (1. Of the possibility of empirical *synthesis* in general.) Cognition is determined *a priori* to an object if it 1. pertains to the condition by means of which the object is given (construction), and the cognition only represents it through concepts of appearance. 2. if it pertains to [*crossed out*: conditions of apprehension in general, through which] appearance, insofar as it contains the conditions for forming a concept of it, [P. II.] 3. if it pertains to apprehension in general, insofar as it contains the condition of the unity of perception as well as intellection, i.e., of the

---

[a] *exponieren*, i.e., provide the concepts with an exposition
[b] *principien*
[c] *Grundsätze*

consensus of appearances among one another and with the unity of the mind, consequently of exposition.

The second applies to appearances, insofar as they can be brought under titles of thinking, e.g., whatever exists, is substance; the 1st to appearances among each other *a priori*, e.g., a triangle has three corners; the 3rd to that which constitutes the thoroughgoing determination of appearance.

Beside these there are subjective *principia* of thinking and objective ones of thinking or determining in accordance with rules *a priori*.

17:662 Of the synthetic propositions: all objects of the senses are in space and time.

All objects of experience stand under a rule of sensibility.

Sensation

Intuition   Appearance

Concept

The determinability of the object in accordance with the sensation: *perception positiva*,

The determinability of the object in accordance with the intuition: construction,

The determinability of the object in accordance with the appearance: disposition,

The determinability of the object in accordance with the concept: comprehension.

In an analytical proposition the x drops out completely, because a taken substantively already stands in a determinate identical relation with b.

But in synthetic propositions the x is that in which a is determined and b is determined through the condition of a.

In the (through the) construction x the concept a (triangle) the equality of the three corners of the triangle etc. is determined. Through the specification x of the concept a the relation b is at the same time determined in this a.

If I determine a coming-to-be *specifice* in time, i.e. [as] a reality in the series of time, so is time to be sure the condition in which, but the rule the condition through which.

If x is the sensible condition under which the a is specifically determined, then b is the universal function through which it is determined therein.

17:662 **4679.** 1773–75. *LBl* Duisburg 13.
P. I.

We are conscious of ourselves and of our own actions and of appearances insofar as we become conscious of the apprehension of them, either by coordinating them or by apprehending one sensation through the other.

We would thus not become conscious of the appearances at all unless [*breaks off*]

An object of the senses is only that which has an effect **upon my senses**, hence which acts and is a substance. Hence the category of substance is fundamental. Every beginning of a state of representation is always a transition from a previous one, for otherwise we would not perceive that something has begun. Thus, since the same subject is always valid for one object as well as for the other and also the boundary is common to them, the one that succeeds belongs to the one that precedes as to that which determines it. In the unity of the mind a whole is only possible insofar as the mind determines one partial representation reciprocally from the other and all are collectively comprehended in an action that is valid for all of them. 17:663

$$x : a = m : n$$

If a indicates the condition through which x is given, then the relation of $a : b$ follows in accordance with the principle of contradiction and is valid universally without the restriction of simultaneity. E.g., in every reality (as long as it is given through the action of the subject) there is a relation of substance to *accidens*. Here x signifies the subject. a the apprehension of the object. $x : a$ is therefore the relation of the original action of the [*breaks off*]

The mere apprehension already declares that behind the appearance there must be a substance, a cause of the juxtaposition; only the observation and judging must indicate which is the substance, etc. Where there is an action, there is substance,[14] e.g., in the case of light, warmth; but whether the light is substance does not follow from the apprehension, but from the exposition of the appearance. That something is represented as having occurred is enough to regard it as an effect; for the apprehension of it is in fact an effect that occurs in the mind, etc.

The intellectual functions therefore make a beginning with the apprehension, only the specification gives us the rule of the application of this concept; hence determinate rules of *synthesis* can only be given through experience, their universal norm, however, *a priori*.
P. II.

Empirical intuition is appearance.

Appearance of which one is conscious is perception. 17:664

Every perception must be brought under a title of the understanding, because it otherwise yields no concept and nothing is thought thereby. By means of these concepts we make use of the appearances, or rather the concepts indicate the way in which we use the appearances as the matter for thinking. 1. intuition in general for magnitude, 2. sensation, in order to determine the real relation in appearance. We saw, the stone weighs something, the wood falls, the body moves, i.e., it acts, hence it is substance. The field is prepared, the meadow is dried out, the glass is broken: these are effects, which are related to a cause. The wall is strong, the wax soft, the gold dense: these are connections in that which is composite. Without these sorts of concepts the appearances would all be separated and would not belong to one another. Even if they had the same relations to one another in space or time, these would not be determined from the objects of the appearances, but would merely be placed next to one another.

Experience is perception that is understood. We understand it, however, when we represent it to ourselves under a title of understanding. Experience is a specification of the concepts of the understanding through given appearances. Appearances are the matter or the substrate.

Experiences are therefore possible only by means of the presupposition that all appearances belong under titles of the understanding, i.e., in all mere intuition there is magnitude, in all appearance substance and *accidens*, in their alteration cause and effect, in the whole of them interaction. Thus these propositions are valid of all objects of experience. The very same propositions also hold for the mind with regard to the generation of its own representations and are moments of *genesis*. But all appearances must be brought under the title of apperception, so that they are constructed in accordance with intuition as well as [*breaks off*]

The conditions of subsumption under these concepts, however, are derived from the sensible relations, which stand in analogy with the action of the understanding and belong to the inner sense, of which apperception [*breaks off*]

Why is that which acts regarded as if it were continuous and as if only the actions, effects, and juxtapositions vary[?]

17:665 **4680.** 1773–75. *LBl* Duisburg 14.

Everything that happens is, on account of the determination of its concepts among the appearances, i.e., with respect to the possibility of experience, represented as contained under a rule, the relation to which is expressed through a concept of the understanding. Thus in the appearance x, in which a is a concept, there must be, in addition to what is thought through a, conditions of its specification which make necessary a rule whose function is determined through b. a cannot be specifically determined in the time in which it occurs except by means of a rule. Thus no experience of a can take place without a rule. Thus the principle of sufficient reason is a *principium* of the rule of experience, namely for ordering it.[15]

The proposition that everything that follows something in time follows something else in accordance with a rule or that in respect of its succession there is a rule **does not lie** in the specification of the concept *a* of occurrence or contingency, for by that is intended only the **appearance**. (Only the occurrence is already an existence in accordance with a rule of time.)

The ordering of appearances in accordance with the relation of space and time requires a rule, just as appearance itself requires a form.

4681. 1773–75. *LBl* Duisburg 15.   17:665
P. I.

Something must always precede an occurrence (condition of perception).

Prior to an occurrence all sorts of things can precede it, but there is one thing among them on which it always follows.

A reality is always attached to a point in time and to that which determines it, something accompanying it, by means of which the point in time is determined for it (condition of perception).[16]

There are all sorts of things that accompany it, but among these there is something that always exists.

[*Crossed out*: An aggregate is many things in reciprocal relation, but   17:666
among these there must]

With regard to that which is simultaneous there is always composition (condition of perception).

All sorts of things can be taken together; but [*crossed out*: where the many is reciprocally determined this connection is objectively] where something is to be considered as objectively combined together, there is a reciprocal determination of the manifold among one another.

If there were not something at all times, thus something permanent, *stabile*, then there would be no fixed point or determination of the point in time, thus no perception, i.e., determination of something in time.

If there were not something that invariably preceded an occurrence, then among the many things that precede it there would be nothing according to which that which occurs belongs in a series, it would have no determinate position in the series.

By means of the rules of perception the objects[a] of the senses are determinable in time, in intuition they are merely given as appearances. In accordance with these rules quite a different series is found from that in which the object was given.
P. II.

Nothing synthetic can be objectively valid except that which is the condition through which something is given as an object or through which something that was given is thought as an object. An object is only thought insofar as it stands under a rule of appearance, and the

---

[a] Here Kant crossed out *Sachen* and replaced it with *obiecten*.

17:667 receptivity of the rule is that which makes the appearance objective; thus it is not the appearances that stand under a rule, but the **objects**, which are their ground. They are expounded in accordance with this rule.

Without such rules of perception no experiences could be made, since these are the titles of the appearances, just as the sensible concepts are the titles of intuitions.

Rule of presumptions as judging of appearances provisional to determining judgments.

One can, to be sure, see much but understand nothing that appears unless it is brought under concepts of the understanding and by means of these into relation to a rule; this is the assumption through the understanding.

The *synthesis* contains the relation of appearances not in the perception but in the concept. That all relation in perception nevertheless presupposes a relation in the concept indicates that the mind contains in itself the universal and sufficient source of *synthesis* and all appearances are exponible in it.

principia of perception.

[*Crossed out*: Rules] Principles of observation or of the exposition of appearances in general.

They are presumptions of experience.

Analogies of understanding.

Axioms of intuitions, analogies of understanding, petitions of reason.

17:668 We perceive something only by being conscious of our apprehension, consequently of the existence in our inner sense, hence as belonging to one of the three relations in the mind. All observation requires a rule.

The intellectual element of perception pertains to the power of inner sense. The [*crossed out*: principles] analogies of observation pertain to the thoroughgoing perception or to the thoroughly determinate perception.

All combinations are made through the mind, and the mind does not combine anything *obiective* except what is necessarily determined by its *correlato*; otherwise the representations may well be juxtaposed in perception, but not connected in the concept.

Only that which is capable of fixed principles in the mind do we call an object. Thus judging must precede objective judgments. For everything else which does not assume such principles is nothing for us and also cannot be perceived. For perception requires a conjugation in accordance with a universal ground.

17:668 **4682.** 1773–75. *LBl* Duisburg 16.
P. I.

The concept of what happens is a determination of sensibility, but through the understanding, insofar as something is placed in the temporal succession. Now this cannot happen except in relation to something that precedes. Accordingly the rule that what happens is determined by something preceding it asserts nothing other than (that all of this is determinable in the order of time) that the determination of a position of something existing in time must take place through the understanding, hence in accordance with a rule.

Reality is that through which something is an object of perception. "In every reality there is a relation of the accident to substance"^{a} means 17:669 the same as: The determination of an existence in time in general can only take place through something that exists at all times.

The analogies of appearance say the same as: If I were not able to determine every relation in time through a universal condition of relation in time, I would not be able to assign any appearance to its place.

Thus the concepts of substance, ground, and whole serve only to assign every reality in appearance to its place, insofar [P. II] as each represents a function or [*crossed out*: potential of] dimension of time in which the object that is perceived is to be determined and experience to be made from appearance.

4683. 1773–75. *LBl* Duisburg 17.   17:669
P. I.

1.

A synthetic proposition that holds of everything in general is false, and especially that whose subject is a pure concept. Unless it is not to hold *obiective* (absolutely), but only under the subjective restriction of the use of reason.

Only the conditions of sensibility make synthesis possible. 1. of pure, 2. of empirical intuition (of outer and inner sense).

Further, of the empirical or rational use of my understanding. For only in the sensible condition of *a* does there lie something in which, beyond the concept of *a*, someone can still cognize *b*.
P. II.

2.

All synthetic propositions possess a homogeneity, although it seems that one concept is intellectual, the other empirical. In the exposition they are [*crossed out*: empirically] homogeneous. One merely takes its specification instead of the concept.[17]

Concipere means to make a concept of something *a priori*. The prin- 17:670 ciples of conception [*crossed out*: apply to subjects^b] are either those of thinking in general or of absolute positing or of *a priori* composition. In the first case, the sensible condition is [*crossed out*: receptivity^c] all of

---

^{a} Kant's quotation marks
^{b} conjectural; Kant wrote "*subj*"
^{c} conjectural; Kant wrote "*Empfang*"

sensibility, in the second, all thinking with regard to a *dati* in general, in the third, the whole in itself or totality.

The understanding cannot determine anything in sensibility except through a universal action. E.g., coming-to-be through a universal condition of succession. Existence through a subject of all existence. Simultaneity through a universal existence.

17:670   **4684.** 1773–75. *LBl* Duisburg 18.
P. I.

How can one know what is contained in a thing in general that is not given to the senses other than that which one actually thinks through its concept *a*[?] But since a time in which something happens is not to be distinguished from another, the succession can only be determined through a rule of time, and thus we can represent more to ourselves in the sensible condition than was thought in *a*, namely in this time as a construction (of the triangle) where, if the same member exists, likewise the *correlatum* exists. Thus we represent the object to ourselves through an analogue of construction, namely that it allows of being constructed in inner sense, namely that as something always follows something else, so when something happens it follows something else, or that this representation is one of the universal actions of the determination of appearances, which 17:671   thus yield a rule, just as a triangle is constructed only in accordance with a rule and serves as a rule for all.

In analytical judgments the predicate properly pertains to the concept *a*, in synthetic ones to the [*crossed out*: condition of the] object of the concept, and the predicate is not contained in the concept. But the object that pertains to a concept has certain conditions for the realization of this concept, i.e., of its position *in concreto* (for every concept is a universal action, which presupposes a *substratum* in which the representation of the object can be placed). Now the condition of all concepts is [*crossed out*: properly] sensible; thus, if the concept is also sensible, but universal, it must be considered in its *concreto*, e.g., a triangle in its construction. If the concept does not signify pure but empirical intuition, i.e., experience, then the *x* contains the condition of the relative position (*a*) in space and time, i.e., the condition of determining something universally therein.

Otherwise appearances are determined through time, but in *synthesi* time is determined through an appearance, e.g., of that which exists or happens or is conjoined. These are the most general in appearances, of which [*crossed out*: the real] the reality is the matter.

On the intellectualization of appearance, e.g.: Something exists, something occurs. This is indeed already an *intellectuale*, posited in the form of time. That something is reality (sensation), the occurrence is existence as consequence. Now through what does the appearance become intellectual?

In a synthetic judgment 2 pure concepts of reason can never stand in relation to each other, rather a pure concept of the understanding with a concept under a sensible condition, whether of appearance or of *a priori* representation. The cause of this.

The totality of the laws of free action, which are naturally determined through the collective faculty of choice, is right. By the faculty of choice I understand the determining will accompanied with power.   17:672

Why do the analogies of the understanding have no self-evidence[?] They are nevertheless constitutive, but not directly objective.*a*

4708. 1773–79? 1771? Opposite *M* 76, §§252–25, in *Finitum et in-*   17:682
finitum.[18]

(Later addition: Lex isonomiae.)[b]

A first beginning is impossible. For a beginning can be thought only in accordance with the laws of sensibility, and consequently only in a time occupied by objects of sensibility. Consequently, a first beginning, before which no phenomenon may precede, cannot be thought. Thus all generatings are only alterations. But a first cause can surely be thought, because this is merely something intellectual. This therefore cannot serve for the explication of appearances: the cause of appearances must be *in commercio* with the world. From which it follows that nothing can arise without something's being abolished in exchange, so that the sum of reality remains [the same]. For otherwise time itself (absolute time) would stand in relation to the alterations, and the cause of the alteration would be outside of time. The *universum* itself cannot move, neither in empty space nor much less in a completely full space. For otherwise, in the first case, there would be an appearance, the *correlatum* of which is not an appearance; in the second case, a motion would not be in any space at all. Hence every cause of motion is in interaction with the world, and no motion is possible except one in which just as much is generated on the opposite side. A spirit that simply moved matter would [*crossed out*: determine] produce this motion of the *universi*. That which can move   17:683
only insofar as it remains at rest in the sum, is in union with the matter.

4713. Ca. 1773–76. At *M* 93, §§307ff., in *Causa et causatum.*   17:684

Everything that exists is necessary, either absolutely or conditionally,* hence *ut causatum alterius.*[c]

---

a The second page of this note, written in Latin, concerns arguments for immortality, and presumably represents a note for a lecture in Kant's metaphysics course rather than his work on the emerging *Critique of Pure Reason*. It is omitted here.
b "law of isonomy," i.e., "law of equality before the law"
c as the effect of another thing

*(Later addition: We therefore also cognize a necessity in all relations of the manifold in that which is composite, which must always be derived. Nothing can be originally contingent, rather the opposite: everything *causatum* is contingent in itself. Only the question arises: what is contingent, and on what is the *principium necessitatis*[a] based? On the fact that otherwise there would be no determining grounds *a priori*.)

The *principium rationati* says only: everything that happens is necessary under a condition.

Everything must be objectively determined *a priori*.

Everything that is alterable has a beginning, and thus comes into being, is contingent, and is *causatum alterius*.

17:685 **4716.** 1773–75? (1769–70?) Opposite *M* 118, §377, in *Notio mundi affirmativa*.

The proof by Leibniz, who takes the world *intellectualiter*, of the representative power of the monads, isn't bad, except it proves more than it says: it leads to an idealism.[19]

17:685 **4717.** 1773–75? (1775–77?) At *M* 119, §380, in *Notio mundi negativa*.[20]

That in the series and aggregate of sensibility there is no beginning and no totality, i.e., determinability with regard to the *omnitudinis*,[b] is because the totality must here be sufficient prior to determination in accordance with the conditions of sensibility, consequently prior to addition or progress without boundaries. But this is not a judgment about the world in itself, in the concept of which the all precedes, and from which alone every part is determinable. In this series there are no true things or true causes, but rather only appearances; and appearance in general must be without end, because in it alone can the undetermined action of sensible cognition proceed without end.

17:686 **4720.** 1773–75? (1771?) (1769–70?) *M* 129, opposite section heading ("*Prima corporum genesis*") and *M* §406.

17:687 Space contains something different from the concept of time: first, that the concept of time, hence the whole of sensibility, can be thought in the determinations of space; second, that a force which I posit somewhere in space does not remain, as the *principium* of appearances, merely a force, but rather through the relations of space with everything external it has determinate conditions, and thus provides a determinate concept of the possibility of the object. Third, space is the ground of the possibility of that which is external, hence of the object; by contrast, time concerns only its state and in general pertains to mere existence as the ground of the relations of things in their existence and as the measure of their duration.

---

[a] principle of necessity
[b] with regard to the whole

Hence time is not a ground of the possibility of things, especially not of substances. Hence positive *principia intellectualia* are possible in physics, but not in [*crossed out*: cosmology] psychology; in the latter everything is negative in relation to the doctrine of pure nature.[21] 1. Absence of parts; 2. no such *commercium* as matter has; 3. no such origin and perishing as body has.

4723. 1773–75. At *M* 281, §719, in *Libertas.*[22]   17:688
Appearances are representations insofar as we are affected. The representation of our own free self-activity is one in which we are not affected, consequently it is not appearance, but apperception. Now the principle of sufficient reason holds only as a *principium* of the exposition of appearances, consequently not as a *principium* for the exposition of original intuitions.

4724. 1773–75? (1776–78?) At *M* 281, §719.[23]   17:688
We cannot prove freedom *a posteriori*, because the absence of the perception of determining grounds provides no proof that nothing of that sort exists. We also cannot cognize its possibility *a priori*, because the possibility of the original ground that is not determined by another cannot be comprehended at all. We thus cannot prove it theoretically at all, but only as a necessary practical *hypothesis*.

4725. 1773–75? (1776–78?) Opposite the end of *M* 282, §720.   17:688
The practical concept of freedom is that which suffices to perform actions in accordance with reason, thus that which gives the imperatives of the reason their force; the speculative or sophistical concept of freedom is that which suffices to explain free actions in accordance with reason. The latter is impossible, because it is that which is original in the *derivativo*.

4729. 1773–75, at *M* 326, §803, in *Existentia Dei*.   17:689
Negations in general mean: not some realities. This however presupposes the opposite, namely everything with a restriction. Therefore the concept of all reality as a *substratum* of reason is necessary for us;   17:690
but we cannot on that account regard a highest reality as necessary in itself. Further, in accordance with the *principio exclusi medii*[a] each thing is considered in relation to everything possible, as in a division, hence as in a whole of reality.
The existence of a thing can never be proven from mere concepts, since existence is not one of the predicates and since from concepts nothing but relative affirmation or negation, not the absolute positing

---

[a] principle of excluded middle

of the thing together with its predicates, can be inferred. The concept, which lies at the basis, is a necessary presupposition and on that account seems to be a concept of a necessary being.[24]

17:691   **4733.** 1773–75? (1770–71?) (1776–78?) Opposite *M* 336, §822 ff., in *Existentia Dei*.

The objections with regard to the existence of God and his properties [*crossed out*: must] are all derived from the condition of sensibility, which has been taken to be intellectual, and from the subjective conditions of comprehensibility, which have been held to be objective (that existence has a magnitude we know from time; this magnitude is called duration; but then we separate time from duration, and that is intellectual; from that arises eternity, in the concept of which there is no contradiction except with the sensible conditions). One must not struggle so anxiously with this play of grounds and countergrounds. He who is in a fortress need not fire a battery at every bravo.

Infinite and unique space, the condition of the possibility of all outer presence of things as they appear, is certainly not a proof of the existence of a ground and primordial being, which comprehends everything and in which everything is sustained, from which also all unity and relation derives, since it is as it were possible through its position in the all; yet it is still a proof that the human mind cannot think any connection without a common ground nor any determinations without one thing that contains them all. Likewise with time, in which all existence lies. This serves for the subjectively necessary assumption of such a being, hence also as sufficient for *praxi*.

17:693   **4741.** 1773–75? (1776–78?) 1769? 1770–71?? At *M* 380, §§926–41, *Creatio mundi*.[25]

Physicotheology. Chief rule. One must not appeal to God as an imme-
17:694   diate cause in any particular case, but rather only in general with regard to the final *substrati* in the world (substance) – unless there is a revelation. For our reason is not a faculty the progress of whose use we can arbitrarily cut off. It is a law to itself. It is contrary to reason to cut off further research and wantonly suspend all further effort by presuming to judge what God has done immediately. For reason alone can determine what is appropriate or not. There is for us an indeterminate interval between an occurrence or arrangement of nature and God, where we must apply our powers to explain everything in accordance with laws of nature.

17:694   **4742.** 1773–75. At *M* 380, §§926–41.[26]

Nothing absolutely first is to be encountered among appearances, but it may well be in the *synthesis* of the understanding. Thus there is to be sure no first beginning, but there may be a first cause, part, action, etc. Something first as a *phaenomenon* would appear as the boundary of nothing. The antinomy of reason is therefore nothing other than the difference between principles of reason insofar as the *data* are sensible, i.e., dependent on objects, or intellectual, i.e., given by the mind itself, which is certainly consistent with regard to particular possible experiences but not with regard to the whole of them. Hence all the actions of human beings considered *a posteriori* are empirically determined, but *a priori* are undetermined and free.

4756. 1775–77. *LBl* Duisburg 21.[27]   17:699

P. I.

A. Space   Dialectic of [*crossed out*: Appearances] Sensibility

1. Is space something actual (real)[?] *Substantia, Accidens, relatio. Idealitas spatii. Hobbes: est phantasma rei existentis tanquam externae. Carthesius spatium habet pro abstracto extensionis Materiae. His accedit Leibnitz. Clark vero defendit realitatem spatii. Newton: est sensorium omnipraesantiae divinae.*[a] Epicurus asserted the subsisting, Wolff the inhering reality of space.[28]

2. Is there a *vacuum mundanum et extramundanum*[?][b] It would be an appearance without an object to determine its intuition and its position. In the latter case, motion of the world whole. In the former, outer intuition without objects. If *vacuum* means the same as: what is not filled with (impenetrable extended) matter, then a *vacuum* is possible.

3. All parts of space are in turn parts. The point is not a part, but a boundary. Continuity.

4. All given magnitudes of space are parts of a larger one. *Infinitudo.*   17:700

5. Unity, hence a pure intuition and not a concept of the understanding.

B. Time. Absolute space and time or adhering space and time.

1. Time is nothing real. Clarke holds it to be real as pure time, Leibniz holds it to be an empirical concept of succession.

2. Is there an empty time before the world and in the world, i.e., are two different states separated by a time that is not filled through a continuous series of alterations[?] The instant in time can be filled, but in such a way that no time-series is indicated.

3. All parts of time are in turn times. The instant. Continuity.

4. All given times are parts of a larger time. Infinity.

5. Unity of time. Concept of the totality.[c]

---

[a] Substance, accident, relation. Ideality of space. Hobbes: [space] is the phantasm of things existing as if externally. Descartes abstracted space from the extension of matter. Leibniz agreed with this. Clark defended the reality of space. Newton: it is the sensorium of the omnipresent divinity.

[b] a vacuum inside or outside the world

[c] *Allbegriff*

Dialectic of the Understanding.
Transcendental Doctrine of Magnitude.
Continuity of space and time and of all magnitudes.

Space and time do not consist of simple parts (their parts are themselves magnitudes), i.e., absolute unities: continuity.

The magnitude of a thing in space and time is continuous.

The magnitude of a ground is called degree, *intensive, extensive, protensive*.

Determination of a magnitude by number and given unity (likewise of its magnitude).

The infinite is greater than any number. Allness or totality (the all)[a] is not to be understood in a series, nor to be comprehended in an aggregate.

The infinite of continuation or juxtaposition. The infinitely small of composition or decomposition. Where the former is the condition, the latter does not occur.

Infinite space and infinite past[b] time are incomprehensible.

In the world there is encompassment,[c] process, and division into the infinite.

17:701   Whence is mathematics demonstrative? Because it is [*crossed out*: rational cognition] cognition in *a priori* intuition.

What are the boundaries of mathematical cognition? That which can be represented *a priori* in intuition, thus space and time and alteration in time.

P. II.

The perfection of a thing (*in sensu adiectivo*) is that totality of the manifold which is requisite to constitute a thing. A perfection (*in sensu substantivo, transscendentali*) is reality.

Transcendental Doctrine of Appearance
Reality and Negation
[*Crossed out*: Is there a vacuum]

(The sum total of appearances)

In mundo non datur saltus,
In mundo no datur hiatus,
In mundo non datur abyssus nihil.[d]

All parts of space and time are in turn times. Everything passes over from nothingness into something only in time.

There is nothing simple in appearance, hence no immediate transition from one determinate state (not of its boundary) into another.

[a] *Die Allheit oder totalitaet (das All)*
[b] *verfloßene*, i.e., time that has flowed
[c] *Umfang*
[d] In the world there are no leaps, no gaps, no empty abysses.

There is no empty time between two states. Alteration is only the continuation of the process.

All appearance consists in turn of appearances, no sensation is simple. Appearance, however, does not consist of nothingness and appearance, hence not of the empty and the full.

On the ideality and reality of appearance in general.

All spaces and times are parts of a larger one.

All parts of space and time are themselves spaces.

In the propositions of the infinite of extension and division philosophy makes a sophistry out of mathematics. In those of the empty and the full sophistry [*breaks off*]

Space and time belong only to the appearances, and thus to the world,   17: 702
not outside of the world.

A *hiatus*, a cleft, is a lack of interconnection among appearances, where their transition is missing. Appearances become possible through space; the emptiness of space is not a cleft and belongs together with the determination of sensible intuition.

The proposition that all alteration is continuous precludes the cessation of a substance.

The proposition that if an alteration in the whole of appearance were to cease, it would never begin again; likewise, that every part of appearances is implicated with the others and alters through their alterations, hence that every thing is continuously altered. Beginning belongs to appearance, origin to the ideas of reason.

Transcendental Doctrine of Experience

Antithesis: there is no [*crossed out*: substance, rather everything is appearances]

1. Something as substance, that is, matter, does not arise and does not cease to be, from nothing comes nothing, i.e., matter is eternal (*ex nihilo nihil (in mundo) fit*),[a] although dependent.

2. Every state of the world is a consequence, for in the continuity of alteration everything is arising and ceasing, and both have a cause.

Antithesis. For otherwise there would be no first beginning.

3. All appearances together constitute a world and [*crossed out*: it is not isolated. 1st, it is a world, i.e., a whole as substance] belong to real objects (contrary to idealism). God as cause does not belong to the world. For only through the agreement of representations with objects do they agree among themselves and acquire the unity that perceptions must have in order to be appearances.

To no. 2. Whatever happens has a ground, i.e., is determined through [something] in accordance with a rule. Unity of [*crossed out*: simultaneity]

---

[a] Out of nothing comes nothing (in the world).

17:703 succession. For without this rule no unity of experience would be possible. From this it follows that the sequence of appearances in the world has no beginning at all. But whether the world itself has an **origin**, that belongs to intellectual concepts.

17:703 **4757.** 1775–77. *LBl* C 10.
P. I.

The principles of the possibility of experiences (of distributive unity) are at the same time principles of the objects of experience).[29] 1. Unity of intuition (of appearance), 2. of the givenness or existence of appearances (of experiences).

Immanent principles (space and time are conditions of appearance) or transcendent ones (they are not).

The former are those of the empirical use of [*crossed out:* the understanding] reason, the latter those of its pure use. The agreement of reason with itself as a whole.

The former needs (has) no *a priori* first, rather an *a posteriori* one and from thence *progressus* or *regressus in infinitum*.

Immanent principles of the empirical use of the understanding:[30]
1. There is no boundary to the composition and decomposition of appearances.
2. There is no first ground or first beginning.
3. Everything is mutable and variable, thus empirically contingent, since time in itself is necessary but nothing is necessarily attached to time.

Transcendent principles of the pure use of the understanding:
1. There is a first part, namely the simple as *principium* of composition. And there are limits to all appearance together.
2. There is an absolute spontaneity, transcendental freedom.
3. There is something that is necessary in itself, namely the unity of
17:704 the highest reality, in which all manifoldness of possibilities can be determined through limits, as shapes are determined in space and through which is also determined all states of everything that exists in time.

Since space and time are only conditions of appearance, there must be a *principium* of the unity of pure reason through which cognition is determined without regard to appearance.

Ground of the antithetic or
apparent Antinomy of pure reason

The former are principles of the exposition of appearances, the latter of the spontaneity of **pure** reason. Agreements with itself in a whole, hence also of morality.

P. II.

We must have principles of the original unity or systematic unity of our cognitions, i.e., of their spontaneity, insofar as we act independently and would practically and *originarie* determine the appearances themselves or ourselves among the appearances.

They are principles of the self-determination of reason [*crossed out*: of the unity of actions that]

or of the unity of the whole of the determinations of our reason.

For reason all possible cognitions constitute a whole, thus the synthesis of absolute unity is the condition of reason.

Among the appearances the soul is a substance together with the body, it appears only as the entelechy of the body. It is not in communion with the body, but in union with it, and is no relation of the place to the body. For it is intelligible, but the body is merely *phaenomenon*. But there is no relation of the *noumeni* to the *phaenomeno*.

Dialectic.
Rules.[31]

1. Not to judge by rules of appearance that which does not belong to the appearances at all, e.g., God with space and time.
2. Not to subject to its conditions what does not belong to outer appearance, e.g., spirit.
3. Not to take for impossible that which cannot be comprehended and which cannot be represented in intuition: the totality of the infinite or of infinite division. The infinite of the series, the finitude of the derived without the *substratum originarium*.

17:705

Further, not to confuse the principles of the absolute unity of reason with those of empirical unity.

a. Simplicity of the thinking subject.
b. Freedom as the [*crossed out*: *principium*] condition of rational actions.
c. *Ens* [*crossed out*: *infinitum*] *originarium* as *substratum* of all combination of one's representations into a whole.
   [*Crossed out*: not to confuse its real unrestricted totality with]
d. Not to confuse the restriction of the world as far as its origin and content is concerned with boundedness.

Principles of reason are those of the conditions of the [*crossed out*: determinations] unity of our cognition insofar as they are determinable *a priori*, consequently only those which contain the completeness of speculative cognition *a priori*, which agree with the ideas of the practical *a priori*.

185

4758. 1775–77. *LBl* B 10.
P. I.

The principles of [*crossed out*: the synthetic use] synthesis of pure reason [*crossed out*: *a priori*] in general are all metaphysical.

Those of the synthetic use of reason with regard to the intuitions that
can be given in experience are principles of the empirical or physical use. Those with regard to the intuitions that cannot be given *a posteriori* are principles of the hyperphysical or transcendent use. (The former are mathematical, the second dynamical.)

The principles of the hyperphysical use pertain to the collective universality of synthesis, those of the physical use to the distributive universality.

1. Principle. The principles of the possibility of experiences are also principles of the possibility of the objects of experience. Example.

2. Principle: In everything that transcends the boundaries of experience, we can only assume *a priori* principles of the absolute unity of synthesis, i.e., of the unity of the use of reason *a priori*.

    1. Mathematical principles *a priori* and their possibility. Evidence.

    2. Metaphysical principles of mathematical synthesis in general. Infinitude of the synthesis of intuition with regard to composition (progressive) as well as decomposition.

There is no other synthesis of appearances but with appearances, consequently that which is empirically possible, hence there is no synthesis of empty appearances.

A. Dynamical principles.

Mathematical and dynamical principles of experiences:* the former of intuitions, the latter of the relation to apperception, i.e., to existence.

*(All appearances stand under rules of a dynamical unity, thereby becoming experiences.)

Mathematics deals with nothing except what can be given *a priori* in intuition. Not with reality, etc. Not with existence.

Object and its existence.

The transcendent principles are principles of the subjective unity of cognition through reason, i.e., of the agreement of reason with itself.

Objective principles are principles of a possible empirical use.
P. II.

Everything actual must be able to be cognized *a priori* (possible) and must also be given or determined *a priori* (necessary).[32]

There must be two sorts of principles of unity *a priori*. Unity of the intellection of appearances *a priori*, insofar as we are determined through them, and unity of the spontaneity of the understanding, insofar as the appearances are determined through it.

The unity of the relation to the whole of cognition, hence of principles of the totality of *synthesis* and the *termino a priori*, the first, the outermost (for what is given in intuition is the *terminus a priori*), hence the *synthesis* of composition and not merely of decomposition are principles not of the empirical use of reason with regard to appearances, but of its architectonic and pure use. The simple of substance. The spontaneity of action, the [*crossed out*: original] primordial being, the universal cause are the cardinal concepts, on which the unity of [*crossed out*: the whole in] the use of reason depends.

The understanding itself (a being, that has understanding) is simple. It is substance. It is transcendentally free. It is affected by sensibility (space), it is in communion with others. All of its objects constitute one thing (a composite), which is called the world (unity of space). The totality of appearances is immeasurable, but is restricted and restricting. The whole is contingent or dependent. Everything is grounded on an original understanding, which is the all-sufficient ground of the world.

The necessary unity of time and space is transformed into the necessary unity of a primordial being, the immeasurableness of the former into the all-sufficiency of the latter. The beginning of the world in time into its origin. The divisibility of appearances into the simple. The [*breaks off*]

Unity of reason. Unity of the self-determination of reason with regard to the manifold of the unity of rules or principles. Not of the exposition, i.e., of the analytic unity of appearances, but of the determination (comprehension), i.e., of the synthetic, through which the manifold as given in general (not merely to the senses) necessarily has unity. 17:708

4759. 1775–77. *LBl* B 8. 17:708
P. I.

On the principles of empirical [*crossed out*: exposition] intellection in distinction from principles of comprehension.[33]

How one can deceive both the dogmatic enemy of religion and the dogmatic scribbler on religion through an apparent antithetic and thus a misplaced skeptic[ism].

How one can refute this skepticism itself through the dogmatic principles [*crossed out*: of the positive] with regard to the practical use of reason.

How from the principles of the unity of reason with regard to totality one can derive principles that conflict with the [*crossed out*: conditions] principles of determination among appearances, which must always be partial and conditioned, but which must be regarded as belonging to cognition of the whole.

There is a *synthesis prototypam* and *ectypam*: the former of self-determination *a termino a priori, no empirice dato*, from nothing, the latter *a termino a posteriori* – the former *simpliciter*, the latter *secundum quid.*[a, 34] I am, I act, I together with all the manifold, I insofar as I exclude the manifold. The principles of absolute *synthesis* are rational and conditions of practical cognition *a priori.*

1. Principles of intuition. That conditions of intuition are not conditions of things.
2. Of the understanding, e.g., *principium rationis.*
3. Of reason.

Reason proceeds from the general to the particular, the understanding from the particular to the general. The latter is general only *secundum quid* and belongs to the empirical or physical use of reason. The former is absolute and belongs to its free or metaphysical use. Likewise to the moral use.[35]

P. II.

Exposition and [*crossed out*: comprehension] rationality.

To appearances. Unity of experience and unity of reason.

Principles of the exposition of appearances presuppose that they are all **conditioned**, hence that nothing is posited absolutely.

1. No absolute totality (*totalitas secundum quid*) [*crossed out*: of synthesis] of composition, hence infinite [*crossed out*: regressus] *progressus.*

(Unconditional limitation *in mundo phaenomenon. Inter phaenomena non datur univers[al]itas absoluta.*)[b]

2. No absolute [*crossed out*: division of] totality of decomposition, hence no unconditional simplicity.

(*non simplicitas absoluta.*)

Infinite progress cannot be comprehended and the unconditioned cannot be made intuitive.

3. No absolute totality in the series of generation, no unconditional spontaneity.

(*non causalitas absoluta.*)

4. No unconditional necessity. All things can be taken from time and space.

(*non necessitas absoluta.*)

World in a physical sense
Simple in a physical sense
spontaneitas in a physical sense
necessitas in a physical sense

All of these propositions are objectively certain as principles of empirical use, but are contrary to reason.

---

[a] There is an original synthesis and one that is a copy, the former from *a priori* starting points with no empirical data, the latter from *a posteriori* starting points, the former on its own, the latter dependent on another condition.

[b] Among data no absolute universality is given.

To things in general.[a]

Principles of rationality or comprehension of them. From the general to the particular: absolute synthesis.

1. Unconditional all of the dependent whole. Origin of the world.
   (*in mundo noumeno datur univers[al]itas.*)[b]
2. Unconditionally simple.
   (*monas.*)
3. Unconditional spontaneity of action.
   (*libertas transscendentalis.*)
4. Unconditionally necessary existence.
   (*necessitas absoluta originaria.*)
   (The world in a metaphysical sense
   The simple in a metaphysical sense)

These propositions are subjectively necessary as principles of the use of reason in the whole of cognition: unity of the whole of the manifold of the cognition of understanding. They are practically necessary with regard to . . . [*breaks off*]

The partiality of sensibility and the totality of reason conflict subjectively in the determination of cognition:

the conditions of empirical use in the exposition of appearances,

the conditions of rational use in the comprehension of appearances.

The *canon* of empirical use concerns universality of appearances, that   17:711
of rational use *universita[lita]tem* of things.

That which cannot be determined in appearances is not **on that account** impossible.

There must be principles of the self-determination of reason, which are different from those in which reason is determined by appearances and their conditions. These are principles of the unity of cognition as a whole, hence not of partial but of total unity.

4760. 1775–77. *LBl* B 9.   17:711
P. I.

The ground of the antinomy of reason is the conflict: 1. All empirical *synthesis* is conditioned, the mathematical as well as the dynamical. A. All appearance has parts and is itself a part. B. Everything that happens is a consequence (what is, is conditioned) and is itself a ground. There is thus no first and last. No simple, no boundary of magnitude, no first ground, no necessary being. I.e., we **cannot arrive at these among the appearances** and must not appeal to them. By contrast, the transc.[c]

---

[a] This contrasts with "To appearances" above, although here Kant centers the heading.

[b] Universality is given in the noumenal world.

[c] We have retained this abbreviation here because we have no way of knowing whether Kant intended "transcendent" or "transcendental."

synthesis through pure concepts of reason is unconditioned, but also takes place through purely intellectual concepts; thus there is actually no antinomy. The world is restricted. It consists of simples. There is freedom. There is a necessary being. [*crossed out*: ground of this *synthesis*] The ground of these principles. Unity of the entire use of reason, through which it has collective unity.

1. The infinite of addition (composition) and of division (decomposition). The finite. 2. The infinite of derivation. 3. The infinite of contingency.

The principles of the possibility of experiences pertain . . . [*breaks off*]

17:712   The *synthesis* of the parts and the whole is always conditioned in empirical cognition, thus also those of effects and causes (*substantiale*) and of the contingent. For they pertain to the unity of appearances, where the manifold rather than unity is given. Determinable unity: where the unity depends on the rule of *regressus*. By contrast, the unity of the pure use of reason (simple, free, necessary) is determining and a *progressus* which begins from the *a priori* condition, e.g., from freedom in morality. These conditions do not belong in the field of appearances and make *synthesis a priori* possible in general.

What can never be an object of our senses is absolutely impossible as appearance, consequently there is also no empty space. But that something might be presented in appearance that will be regarded as a consequence of empty space is entirely possible.

P. II.

Only the conditions of empirical *synthesis* are objective.

Skeptical principle of the comprehension of appearances.

There is nothing that is absolutely first in the synthesis of appearances (because everything is conditioned).

(No absolute boundary)

1. Nothing that is first in the aggregate in space and time. (The absolutely first in those is that whose boundary is determined by nothing. The boundaries can only be determined among appearances. The empirical synthesis is always conditioned.) I.e., the whole of appearances is *a priori* unbounded. The **totality** thus cannot be determined through successive addition.

2. No absolute first in composition (no absolute boundary of division) (nothing simple), no **simple** part of the extended or of alteration.

17:713   3. No absolute boundary of subordination [*crossed out*: of consequences and grounds] in the series of actions and effects. No first action. No transcendental freedom.

4. No first cause (no primordial being).

For all appearance is possible only in space and time. But time (and space) is only determinable through appearance. It is however without anything first.

These propositions are contradicted merely by the incomprehensibility of the propositions (which does not, however, contradict the exposition of appearances): There is a *regressus in infinitum* (from the empirical *termino*) of dimension, of division, of generation, and of dependency. With experiences we always remain in the chain of appearances.

But insofar as the things lying at the ground of appearances are considered, which can consequently be thought only through concepts of the understanding, the unity of their synthesis demands something absolutely first of the inner state of reason (i.e., unconditioned) [*crossed out*: of the *synthesi* of totality] of origin, of composition, of action, of existence in general. These are conditions of the (subjective) unity in the use of reason with regard to appearances, just as the latter are principles of the manifold. In the former unity of condition, in these unconditioned unity.

4763–5. 1775–77? (1773–75?) 1770–71?? *LBl* K 10.[36]   17:720

(**4763**) Everything transitory is a contingent thing, but not the transitory itself.

(**4764**) The numerical group[a] that is not a part (infinite). The   17:721
unity, that is not a numerical group (simple). A ground that is not a consequence.

(**4765**) On the principles [*crossed out*: *a pr*[*iori*]] of pure understanding.

All appearances have a determinate magnitude (the relation of which to another is assignable).

The infinite does not appear as such, likewise not the simple.

For the appearances are included between two boundaries (points) and are thus themselves determinate magnitudes.

Sophistical principles (from subjective grounds of reason). [*Crossed out*: All possible magnitudes are] No object of intuition (it should say: no appearance) is infinitely great and infinitely divisible, i.e., all have boundaries of extension and division.

The totality in the case of the infinite and of the parts of the finite (the infinitely divisible) is impossible for the human understanding, but not in itself.

All appearances are real and *negatio*; sophistical: All reality must be sensation.

Everything that exists (insofar as it exists) is substance and *accidentia*; insofar as it happens (follows): a consequence from a ground; insofar as it is simultaneous: composed in a whole and reciprocally determined.

Sophistical: [*crossed out*: All substance is necessary; Everything alterable is contingent] Everything that endures in appearance is substance. (determined in itself.) (*phaenomenon substantiatum*.)

---

[a] *Menge*; the modern translation "set" would be anachronistic.

17:722　　　Everything that happens is determined in the series. There is no absolutely first beginning.

17:723　　**4772.** 1775–79. At *M* 39, §135, in *Reale et negativum*.[37]
　　　First the analytic of the categories. Without synthetic propositions. Distinction of pure concepts of the understanding from those applied to *phaenomena*.

17:725　　**4780.** 1775–79. Opposite *M* 76, §255, in *Finitum et infinitum*.
　　　Infinitude is the absolute impossibility of a complete synthesis (not of the completeness of the object) of the composition or decomposition of a given object. The [*crossed out*: synthesis of] appearance is infinite, and its division proceeds to the infinite. This infinitude concerns the dynamical as well as the mathematical *synthesis*. By contrast, in the intellectual the synthesis is complete, but the condition for cognizing this completeness *in concreto* is sensible (a first or outermost). Reason therefore demands independence from the sensible, but the determination of its concept can only be sensible (antinomy). The omnisufficience of reason regarded as determining is with regard to us an origin of the practical laws of our reason, which necessarily presuppose completeness as a hypothesis.

17:726　　**4783.** 1775–79. At *M* 120, §382ff., in *Notio mundi negativa*.
　　　Free actions happen in accordance with a rule* just like natural ones. But they are not therefore determinable *a priori* like the latter; both are thus in conformity with reason, while blind fate and blind chance are *qualitates occultae* and are contrary to reason.
　　　*(There are rules contrary to which actions cannot happen, although the actions are not to be determined in accordance with these.)

17:728　　**4788.** 1775–79. At *M* 363, §890, in *Voluntas Dei*.
　　　We can very well understand and have insight into divine freedom, but not human freedom. If the human being were merely intellectual, then we could have insight into his power of choice through reason; likewise if he were a *brutum*. But not as a sensible and rational being, since his action is subsequently a *phaenomenon*, but antecedently a *noumenon* under practical laws.
　　　(*Later addition*: The will is a property of a being by means of which it is a cause of objects through its understanding – the faculty of desire only through its representation.)

18:5　　**4849.** 1776–79. *LBl* D 17.
　　P. I.
　　　The purpose of metaphysics: to make out the origin of synthetic *a priori* cognition. 2. to gain insight into the restricting conditions of the

empirical use of our reason. 3. To show the independence of our reason from these conditions, hence the possibility of its absolute use. 4. To thereby extend the use of our reason beyond the boundaries of the world   18:6 of the senses, although only negatively, i.e., to remove the hindrance that reason itself makes (from the principles of its empirical use). 5. To show the condition of the absolute use of reason, so that it can be a complete *principium* of practical unity, i.e., of agreement into a sum of all ends.

These same principles of amplification are in turn negative with regard to empirical use, where nothing counts except nature.

The dogmatic use of our reason beyond the boundaries of possible experiences cannot be objectively determining, and no new synthesis takes place, rather there is only an agreement of theoretical with practical unity, where the practical use is led beyond the boundaries of the pragmatic, hence also beyond the present world, in accordance with the analogy of empirical use, but in relation to the conditions of a complete unity, and thereby the business of our reason is completed *a parte priori* and *posteriori*.

Liberation of the unity of reason from the restrictions of its empirical use makes possible its transcendental use.

Since the amplification of reason is here merely negative, yet the absolute unity of the cognition of objects in general and of all of its ends (free from all restrictions of sensibility) is demanded for the absolute spontaneity of reason, the amplification is practically necessary.

Reason is the faculty of the absolute unity of our cognitions.
P. II.

The principles of the completion of our cognition, i.e., those (of the absolute unity of the use of reason) of the absolute whole thereof are the *synthesis* of reason.

They contains conditions of wisdom, i.e., of the agreement into the sum of all our ends.

We complete only through that which is independent, thus not through sensibility.

The determination of all objects through mere reason is thus the   18:7 completion of our cognition of the understanding in the *progressu* of my existence.

1. With regard to the self-cognition of reason. Completion *in progressu*.

    a. I belong in a world-whole.

    b. I am simple.

    c. [I am] free. Intelligence.

    d. My existence is not externally dependent on the body nor contingent.

(*Later addition*: Among empirical principles belongs this: That the manner of the existence of all things of the world is contingent, only the *ens originarium* necessarily exists in all understanding.)

Here I do not consider myself as soul, but as intelligence. The *synthesis* is here merely negative, namely to abstract the conditions of sensibility from me as intelligence.

And the ground of this synthesis is the freedom of reason from the restricting conditions of sensibility, which is a negative *principium* of morality, thus of wisdom.

2. Completion *in regressu* from the conditioned to the unconditioned. There is an *ens originarium*

    a. which is all-sufficient and unique,

    b. simple,

    c. a free cause (intelligence),

    d. necessary in accordance with its nature.

These are the conditions of the complete unity of all objects and hence cognitions. However, this unity is the condition of the agreement of everything practical.

These cognitions are not dogmatic, but only a liberation of the absolute unity of the use of reason in the theoretical and the practical from the conditions of its empirical use, in order to establish [*crossed out*: in accordance with an analogy with that] the principles of its pure practical use.

Reason is free from the conditions of sensibility and must be so in the practical. The continuation of the function of reason up to complete unity beyond the restricting conditions of sensibility.

(*Later addition*: The concepts of the unity of reason, e.g., of the absolute whole – ground, cannot be represented *in concreto* in accordance with the conditions of empirical cognition. However, they also do not pertain to the world of the senses, for that is no object of pure reason, but to the world of the understanding, which lies at the ground of the former.)

18: 8

18: 8   **4851.** 1776–78. *LBl* Berlin Staatsbibliothek 22.
P. I.

Whether concepts are mere *educta* or *producta*.[38,*]

Preformation and genesis.

*(*Producta* either through physical (empirical) influence or through the consciousness of the formal constitution of our sensibility and understanding on the occasion of experience, hence *producta a priori*, not *a posteriori*.)

The doctrine of *ideis connatis*[a] leads to enthusiasm. *Acquisitae*[b] are *a priori* or *a posteriori acquisitae*, the former are not always intellectual. Thus

---

[a] innate ideas
[b] acquired ideas

the division of cognition into sensitive and intellectual is not the primary one, rather the division into *a priori* or *a posteriori* cognition. The former is either sensible or intellectual.

The study of objects is dogmatic or sensible, thus that of the subject is either physiological or critical. Critique separates 1. the pure from the empirical faculty of cognition, 2. sensibility from the understanding. 18: 9

Plato took all *a priori* cognition to be intellectual. Leibniz too, and thus they did not recognize the sensible in space and time. Leibniz also explains it as intellectual but confused.[39]

Synthetic cognition *a priori* is only possible under the principle that every relation of representations to an object and determination of its concept is nothing other than the representation of their necessary connection in one consciousness. Representations, however, cannot be connected in one consciousness if they are not considered as belonging to a *datum* (as object).

P. II.

Metaphysics of Nature and Morals

Metaphysica

General (*generalis*):
Reason and its concepts
themselves constitute the object.
Transcendental philosophy.

Special (*specialis*):
applied to different objects
by reason.

Critique of pure reason   Ontology

Experience   The world itself and
in the world   ideas outside it.

physiologia rationalis

immanent   transcendent

Physica rationalis   *Psychologia rationalis*   *Cosmologia*   *Theologia*

Methods: dogmatic or critical. (*Later addition*: Physiological: Locke.)

On the latter, either how we attain principles and concepts, or: what they contain and how they are possible.

Cognition is called transcendental with regard to its origin, transcendent with regard to the object that cannot be encountered in any experience. 18: 10

From empirical principles one cannot attain transcendental ones, and yet these are the proper goal of metaphysics.

Why not empirical psychology?

The *conceptus intellectuales* are *acquisiti*, but not from the senses. For we acquire the forms of bodies which we make out of clay, thus bricks, although we take the clay from the earth.

Parts: 1. Ontology, cosmology, and theology *rationalis*; the latter two: 1. *transscendentalis*, 2. *naturalis*. *Cosmologia naturalis* has as its object the objects of the senses, outer or inner. And the principles are empirical or rational.

18:10 **4853.** 1776–78. *M* I.⁴⁰

Philosophy deals not with objects, but with cognitions.

18:11 **4855.** 1776–78. *M* II.

All philosophy is either *rationalis* (not logic) or *empirica*. The former: that whose *principia* do not come from experience. The *rationalis* is either *pura* or *applicata*. The former is *transscendentalis*, the latter *metaphysica*, or the former *metaphysica generalis*, the latter *specialis*. *Metaphysica specialis* has as its ground either sensation or feeling. The former is the ground (*materia*) of appearance, the latter of desires. The former [of] the metaphysics of nature, the latter [of] the metaphysics of morals. The former is either *physiologia rationalis* or *theologia rationalis*, *physica generalis* or *cosmologia specialis*, *psychologia rationalis* or *physica rationalis*.

18:12 **4860.** 1776–78. *M* IX.

The imputation against Epicurus that represents his doctrines as absurd deserves no credit. The useful aim of philosophical history consists in the presentation of good models and the display of instructive mistakes, likewise in the cognition of the natural progress of reason from ignorance (not crude error) to cognition.⁴¹ If someone tells me about the very absurd opinions of someone else whom I have already recognized as very acute through a good test, I do not believe him. Perhaps his expression was careless or not understood, just as I do not believe gossip about someone in whom I have perceived unimpeachable uprightness. What would it help me to know it? It is hateful to give in to an accuser.

18:13 **4862.** 1776–78. *M* IX.

Plato's doctrine of ideas should serve to prevent us from seeking in empirical principles that which can have its source and archetype in reason alone, namely, true perfection.⁴² But to seek the idea of the constitution (not of the ends) of things that have merely served as means is vertiginous and fantastical.

4863. 1776–78. *M* IX. 18:13

Organic or spiritual intuition, the former through the **body**.

That our soul, as spirit, without body, should intuit **other** things, i.e., external things, is a trespass of the limits of the *dati*. For we cognize the soul only as the object of inner sense and the body as the medium of the **outer** sense. Our intuition is physical and not mystical; the physical is not pneumatic,[a] but organic.

4865. 1776–78. *M* IX.[43] 18:14

Metaphysics is not an organon but a canon of reason, a ground not of doctrine but of discipline, not dogmatic but critical cognition, not for increasing cognitions but for preventing errors, not about the object but about the rules of the subject, not the mother of religion but its bulwark, not of objective but of subjective use. The important fundamental truths of morality and religion are grounded on the natural use of reason, which is a use in analogy with its empirical use and extends to the boundaries of the world *a priori* and *a posteriori*, insofar as it is the boundary, and thus to what is adjacent but not beyond it. This natural use is not free from the aberrations of speculation, it produces a belief and not knowledge.

4866. 1776–78. *M* IX–X.[44] 18:14

Locke a physiologist of reason, the origin of concepts.[45] He committed the error of taking the occasion for acquiring these concepts, namely experience, as their source. Nevertheless he also made use of them beyond the bounds of experience.

Wolff was a virtuoso of reason, he used it and did not examine its sources at all. Dogmatic, not critical.[46]

Lambert analyzed reason, but critique was still lacking.[47] Crusius (Everything that I can think is possible) assumed innate principles (although not Platonic ideas); but since there could be only principles of the empir- 18:15 ical use of understanding, he was not sure whether he could also employ them beyond the bounds of experience.[48]

4882. 1776–78. *M* XII. 18:18

The appearance of conjugation is a subsumption of a given representation under the general capacity for arranging sensations. The function of this capacity is the concept of the understanding, and its conditions make the rules for the transition from one representation to another. Thus nothing can be perceived except under the presupposition that it stands under a rule.

[a] that is, spiritual

18:19   The concept of the ground is not an appearance, but a function of the mind, under which everything must be able to be subsumed, consequently under rules. Observation amounts only to a case being given. Cognition is the subsumption [of it] under the function and its rules.

    If space were not something subjective, how then should I attain the cognitions of it *a priori*? How should this cognition also conform to objects[?]

    Likewise, if the ground were not something subjective, how then should I come to it *a priori*?

    Human reason happily steps beyond the sensible world and the moral world in the extension of its cognition, but it gets dizzy on the way up.

18:20   **4889.** 1776–78? (1770–71? 1773–75?) *M* XIV.

    Metaphysics is *a priori* cognition of nature, the object of which is at least given by the senses; transcendental philosophy is pure *a priori* cognition.

18:20   **4890.** 1776–78? (1770–71? 1773–75?) *M* XIII.[49]

    A priori cognition is opposed to empirical cognition: philosophy concerning this is transcendental philosophy. Everything that we can cognize *a priori* with regard to objects of experience lies within it.

18:21   **4892.** 1776–78. *M* XIII.

    The most important thing is that before one ventures a doctrine of pure reason a critique of it must first be undertaken. But critiques require knowledge of sources, and reason must know itself. One is driven to this investigation only after lengthy errors.

18:21   **4893.** 1776–78. *M* XIII.[50]

    Locke an influxionist, at the same time a physiologist of the understanding. Lambert, an analyst and architectonical. Wolff, a mere dogmatist and a mathematical mind. Crusius, a pre-stabilist of reason. He denies the subordination of all principles to the *principium contradictionis* and would still assign them some origin, but he can produce no criterion for which are inborn principles and which are fobbed off. Empiricists of pure reason. Healthy understanding. Misologists. Our end in metaphysics. (*In sensibus nihil esse veri.*)[a] Value.

    1. Distinction between *phaenomenorum* and *noumenorum*.*

    2. Origin of the latter. Innate, mystical; or acquired, logical. Plato, Leibniz; Aristotle, Locke. *Formulae* abstracted from the senses, or not.

    *(Distinction in objects or in the cognition of them.)

---

[a] In the senses nothing is true.

4897. 1776–78. *M* XV.   18:22

There is no transcendental doctrine; hence the *organon* of pure reason is a science that displays the use of pure reason with regard to the empirical in general; thus all philosophy of pure reason is either critique or the *organon* thereof. The former is transcendental philosophy, the latter metaphysics.

4900. 1776–78. *M* XV.   18:23

I concern myself not with the evolution of concepts, like Tetens (all actions by means of which concepts are produced), nor with their analysis, like Lambert, but solely with their objective validity. I am not in competition with these men.[51]

4901. 1776–78. *M* XVI.   18:23

Tetens investigates the concept of pure reason merely subjectively (human nature), I investigate them objectively. The former analysis is empirical, the latter transcendental.

4904. 1776–78. *M* XV.[52]   18:24

Transcendental freedom is the necessary hypothesis of all rules,* hence of all use of the understanding. One should think thus and so, etc. Consequently this action must be free, i.e., not already determined by itself (subjectively), rather it must have only an objective ground of determination.

*(It is the [*crossed out*: condition] property of beings for whom the consciousness of a rule is the ground of their actions.)

4907. 1776–78. *M* XVI.   18:25

There is no science of pure intuition except mathematics, and no use of reason that is apodictic and self-evident except for mathematics in the case of objects and morals in the case of actions. All other inquiry is inquiry into nature.

4933. 1776–78. *M* XX.   18:32

The soul is a unity as the object of inner sense, but I cannot infer from that that it persists as an object of outer intuition.[53]

To infer conversely from the synthetic but apodictic propositions about space that it is not anything objective, consequently that it is an object of observation.

The empirical anticipations are not apodictic, consequently not axioms. The expounding and adjectival predicates.

4936. 1776–78. *M* XXI.   18:33

The contradictions and conflict of systems are the only thing that have in modern times prevented human reason from falling into complete disuse in matters of metaphysics. Although they are all dogmatic to the highest degree, they still represent perfectly the position of skeptics for one who looks on the whole of this game. For this reason we can thank a Crusius[54] as well as a Wolff for the fact that through the new paths that they trod they at least prevented understanding from allowing its rights to become superannuated in stupid idleness and still preserved the seed for a more secure knowledge. Analyst and architectonical philosopher. In such a way the course of nature finally leads its beautiful although mostly mysterious order through obstacles toward perfection. Even a *système de la Nature*[55] is advantageous to philosophy.

18:36

4941. 1776–78. *M XXI.*

He who says there is a God says more than he knows, and likewise he who says the opposite. Nobody knows that there is a God, rather we believe it.

18:36

4943. 1776–78. *M XXII.*

If one speaks through synthetic propositions *a priori*, he speaks only about his own thoughts, e.g., that there is a necessary being, etc.; namely, that without this presupposition he cannot have a complete concept of the existence of things. Or he speaks of the *a priori* conditions of cognition of experience, and then it is objective, e.g., that every *compositum reale* has a force connecting all its parts to the ground. However, these propositions are really analytical.

18:37

4945. 1776–78. *M XXII–XXIII.*

There can be no questions in transcendental philosophy the answer to which would be unknown to us.[56] For if the predicate is not determined through the subject, that signifies that the question itself is nothing, because in this case the predicate has no significance at all, affirming neither [the proposition] nor the *oppositum contrarium.*[a] Just as if I were to ask where to look for east when I am at the pole. Our cosmological concepts have significance only in the world, thus none with regard to the boundary or the totality of the world. The possibility of what is sensible rests on the condition of that which is given; but neither the boundary nor the whole can be given to the senses.

I do not know whether the cosmos is as large as 100 million diameters of the sun, because experience has not taught me this. I do not know whether it is infinite because I cannot know this through any experience whatever.

---

[a] that is, affirming neither an affirmative proposition nor its contrary.

4946. 1776–78. *M* XXII.   18:38

If I assume that an *a priori* concept has an object, then I must also be able to cognize *a priori* everything about that object the condition of which is contained in that concept. There is therefore nothing uncertain and indeterminate there, and likewise reason contains nothing other than conditions of its empirical use, and thus all attempts on its part that are transcendent are impossible and in vain. Transcendent concepts are not concepts of objects. They are ideas, *ideae.*

4953. 1776–78. *M* XXIV.   18:39

The belief that there is no God, that there is no other world, is impossible, but opinion [*later addition*: or doubt and uncertainty] about that is quite possible.

Misology and empiricism are opposed to all philosophy.

The empiricism of pure reason. Healthy understanding.   18:40

The doctrine is either the **realism** or the **formalism** of pure reason. The latter permits only principles of the form of the use of our reason *a priori* with regard to **experiences**. Hence it permits neither dogmatic affirmation nor dogmatic denial about what is beyond the boundaries of experience. If religion and morality have other sources of cognition than merely speculative ones, they reveal the practical principles of reason to be necessarily connected with theoretical *postulatis.*[57] A *postulatum theoreticum,* however, is a necessary *hypothesis* of the agreement of theoretical and practical cognition. In that case metaphysics resists all objections from pure reason and shows that they are dialectical, i.e., the dialectic thereof.

If the *dogmata cardinalia* are secured in *respectu practico* although not *speculativo,*[a] then metaphysics illustrates and defends [them].

4955. 1776–78. *M* XXVI.   18:40

In human beings sensibility is not so distinct from reason that both may not apply to the same objects, at least those that are represented in the same way, in spite of the fact that the former is valid of the objects with regard to all possible attitudes of sensibility, the other not.

4957. 1776–78. *M* XXV.   18:41

The appeal to books is no more necessary in the outline of a system of transcendental philosophy than in a geometry.[58] Consensus with the judgment of others provides a ground of proof only where what is at issue is not the rule but its application, i.e., the power of judgment, and where

---

[a] if the cardinal dogmata of metaphysics are secured from a practical although not a theoretical point of view

everything must not be derived from an idea, but instead the concept must be derived from a group of observations that are to be compared.

18:41 **4959. 1776–78. M XXV–XXVI.**

18:42 Now it is ridiculous to ask what sort of opinion you have about the communion of the soul with the body, the nature of a spirit, or creation in time. I have no opinion at all about these things. But what origin in the human understanding these thoughts have, even though they go beyond its boundaries; why these questions are necessary and why with regard to the object they can be answered only subjectively: that I know, and there I am beyond all opinion.

18:42 **4962. 1776–78. M XXVI.**

It is not at all permissible to have opinions in transcendental judgments, any more than in geometry.

18:42 **4964. 1776–78. M XXVI.**

Through my treatise the value of my earlier metaphysical writings is entirely destroyed. I will only attempt to salvage the correctness of the idea.[59]

18:43 **4966. 1776–78. M XXVI.**

All difficulty in metaphysics concerns only the coherence of empirical principles with ideas. The possibility of the latter is not to be denied, but they cannot become empirically intelligible; the idea is not any *conceptus dabilis*[a] at all, not an empirically possible concept.

18:44 **4970. 1776–78. M XXVII–XXVIII.**

The philosopher treats of that which is self-sufficient in and at the basis of all human cognitions; hence among all doctrines philosophy pleases immediately.

Philosophy is the science of the suitability of all cognitions with the vocation of mankind. To this there belongs, first, philodoxy as the cultivation and instruction of all talents, i.e., the suitability of cognition for all possible ends. Second, its suitability for the extended use of reason. Third, the grounding of the supreme maxims of the speculative as well as practical use of reason; here the great erudition, indeed the art of reason in famous men comes to nothing and is without any philosophy. Metaphysics and morals, both architectonic, are the two hinges of philosophy. The philosopher is not a misologist, but rather an expert in the laws of human reason, and the foremost laws are those that restrict the pretensions of reason to the end of humanity. First extended

---

[a] concept that can be given

historical and rational cognition, just as prior to a legislator there must first be a multiplicity of citizens and arts. In order to prescribe laws for reason, one must know them. But only in the maxims of reason is philosophy invested; the other cognitions are philosophical, i.e., they belong to philosophy.

History and description must first of all be treated in keeping with reason (since they were previously adequate merely for curiosity). Afterwards, their interconnection in accordance with maxims of reason; for their system [is] in accordance with the legislative idea of reason.[60] 18:45

4972. 1776–78. *M* XXVIII. 18:45

In the sensible world we follow the principles of empirical cognition, in the intelligible world the principles of pure cognition of the understanding. The latter, however, have no relation to the exposition of the appearances by means of which we are affected, but only to that which is given through the understanding (pure use of freedom), or morality. Now here is the necessary presupposition that there is a God. A belief.

4992. 1776–78. *M* XXXI–XXXII. 18:53

In judging the writings of others, one must choose the method of participation in the general matters of human reason. In the attempt to discover in them that which pertains to the whole, it is worthwhile to extend a helpful hand to the author or rather to the common good and 18:54
to treat errors as incidentals. To destroy everything is tragic for reason as a whole.

Since it would be vain for me to be confident of such extraordinary luck or exceptional acuity that by that method I could avoid all pitfalls or be the only one to find the correct path in such confused terrain, I have expected a better outcome than all of my predecessors only from the attitude of mind that I have adopted and steadfastly maintained; likewise from the length of time through which I have held my mind open to every new instruction, which I doubt that anyone before me has done. I have never made myself at home in the territory of the philosophy of pure reason, I have written no large books in it nor staked my vanity on defending them and remaining of the same opinion.

I have never even looked back at the little efforts that I have put out in order not to seem entirely idle, in order not to remain attached to the same position, and their critique by others, whose gentleness did not deprive me of the courage [*breaks off*]

4993. 1776–78. *M* XXXII. 18:54

One can very well divide mathematics into **pure** and **applied** mathematics, since the objects of experience do not yield any *principia* *mathematica*, rather the latter must be applied to the former.[61] But philosophy must be divided into pure and empirical, since in the latter there lie certain *principia philosophica* that are undetermined in the former. That which is universal in the experiences of inner and outer sense, through which they are all possible, is the boundary of pure reason *a posteriori* and thus of its application. There are, namely, possibilities that are given *a posteriori* but which serve *a priori* as grounds to which the rest can be reduced.

18:55

The qualities, as far as their relations are concerned, must often be given newly by the senses, but quantity *qua talis*[a] and their relations are always, even in applied mathematics, given *a priori*.

18:55 **4996**. 1776–78. *M* XXXII.

The cognition of God is important only with regard to the practical, which however must be sufficiently certain on its own. For otherwise it would not be obligatory on its own, and it would not become so by means of the cognition of God. Thus belief in God must spring from morality, which thereby supports itself. It is good that we do not know but only believe that there is a God. The method of teaching such a thing. Mere speculation is an opinion that oversteps the limits.

18:56 **4998**. 1776–78. *M* XXXI–XXXII.

In experience there is appearance and a real concept. The experience of our alterations contains time as mere form of appearance and the concept of being. Both together comprise something that yields a correct ground in the field of experiences. The first, however, and hence the concept of existence that is thereby affected, does not extend further and has no inner reality, but only the value of a conditioned form of our representations, i.e., it is not a thing in itself or its affection, but only the sensible representation thereof.

18:57 **5005**. 1776–78. *M* XXXII.

The synthetic propositions constitute the content of our cognition,
18:58 of what we know; the analytic ones only the materials for this cognition. With regard to the former (*in concreto*), I do not know more than everyone else; but I know what the understanding can know about them. I know the rules of the understanding with respect to them.

18:59 **5013**. 1776–78. *M* XXXIII.

At the beginning of transcendental science.

My aim is to investigate how much reason can cognize *a priori* and how far its dependence on instruction from the senses extends. Thus

---

[a] as such

what are the boundaries beyond which, without the assistance of the senses, it cannot go. This object is important and momentous, for it shows human beings their vocation by means of reason. In order to attain this final end, I find it necessary to isolate reason, but also sensibility, and first to consider of everything that can be cognized *a priori* whether it also belongs to the realm of reason. This separate inquiry, this pure philosophy, is of great use.

5015. 1776–78. *M* XXXIV.   18:60

It has taken a long time for the concepts to become so ordered for me that I could see them as comprising a whole and clearly indicating the boundaries of the science that I planned. I already had the idea of the influence of the subjective conditions of cognition on the objective ones prior to the disputation,[62] and afterwards the distinction between the sensitive and the intellectual. But for me the latter was merely negative.

One should not believe that everything before now was written and conceived as a mere loss. The dogmatic attempts can always go on, but a critique of them must follow, and they can only be used to judge about the illusion that human reason experiences if it confuses the subjective   18:61
with the objective and sensibility with reason.

Two *metaphysici*, one of whom proves the thesis, the other the antithesis, occupy in the eyes of a third observer the position of a skeptical examination. One must do both oneself.

I certainly believe that this doctrine will be the only one that will be left once minds have cooled from dogmatic fever and that it must then endure forever; but I very much doubt that I will be the one who produces this alteration. In addition to the grounds that should illuminate it, the human mind also needs time to give them force and endurance. And when prejudices are combatted, it is no wonder that at the outset these efforts are disputed by means of the very same prejudices. For it is necessary first to eliminate the impressions and the old habit. I could adduce various cases where it has not been the originator of an improvement but only those who rediscovered it later after many contradictions who got it on track and under way.[63]

I can imagine the objection that various things have not been explained which still ought to have been said. That is much the same as if one should make the objection to one who wanted to write only a short book that he did not write a big one. What is missing in a book does not constitute an error (failed intention), although gaps in what one has pretended is complete certainly do. It takes moderation and a capacity for judgment not to say everything that one knows and not to burden one's work with all sorts of insights that its primary aim cannot tolerate. In the *analysi* I have said some things that are not indispensable, etc.

18:62   **5019.** 1776–78. *M* XXXIII.

I have not cited anyone from reading whom I have learned something. I have found it good to omit everything foreign and to follow my own ideas. I have not argued against systems, etc. I have not cited myself,

18:63   but reformulated everything. I do not approve of the rule that when in the use of pure reason one has previously proven something, one should subsequently no longer cast doubt upon it, as if it were a firm principle.

18:63   **5021.** 1776–78. *M* XXXIII.

According to Priestley[64] and Locke, all cognitions must be empirical, and nothing synthetic can possess true necessity. However, this contradicts the usage that is universal without exception.

18:66   **5029.** 1776–78. *M* XXXV.

The intellectual element in the objects of the senses (or of experience) is not that they are given in some other way than through the senses, but is rather that through which they are thought *a priori*, and how one must think everything through concepts, however it might be given. The ancients seem to have wanted to withdraw from reflecting cognition and believed that the understanding was capable of its own intuitions.

18:67   **5031.** 1776–78. *M* XXXVI.

I have chosen the scholastic method[65] and preferred it to the free [*crossed out*: swing] motion of the spirit and wit, although, since I want every reflective mind to take part in this inquiry, I found that the dryness of this method would scare away precisely readers of this sort who seek the connection with the practical. Even if I were in the greatest possession of wit and literary charm, I would still have excluded the alternative, since I am very much concerned to leave no suspicion that I would take in and persuade the reader, but rather would either allow him no access at all or expect it only through the strength of the insights.

Even this method has only arisen for me by means of experiments.

18:67   **5032.** 1776–78. *M* XXXVI.

All synthetic propositions that express the condition without which it is in general impossible to cognize an object are objective. Those without which it is impossible to cognize it completely *a priori* are subjective.

All of our cognition *a priori* always has *correlata*; if one of those is missing, we cannot completely cognize the other. All of our cognition of magnitude is determinately possible only through limits, thus we cannot cognize magnitude in general *absolute* complete, since in that case we would posit no boundaries.

5035. 1776–78. *MXXXV–XXXVI.*   18:68

Wolff did great things in philosophy; but he got ahead of himself and extended cognition without securing, altering, and reforming it through a special critique.[66] His works are therefore very useful as a magazine for reason, but not as an architectonic for it. Perhaps it is in the order of nature, although certainly not to be approved of in Wolff, that at least the experiments of the understanding should first multiply without a correct method of knowledge, and be brought under rules only later. Children.

5036. 1776–78. *M XXXV.*   18:68

I have not been able to bring these considerations to this conclusion without at the same time attending to the other influences of the pure philosophy that I have at the same time completed. For I am not of the   18:69 same opinion as an excellent man who recommends that when one has once convinced himself of something one should afterward not doubt it any more. In pure philosophy that will not do. Even the understanding already has a natural resistance to that. One must rather weigh the propositions in all sorts of applications and even borrow a particular proof from these, one must try out the opposite, and posptone decision until the truth is illuminated from all sides.

I have always had it before my eyes that I only need to work up transcendental philosophy, that the boundaries of every science must be precisely observed, and that mixing them together only results in illusions. But precisely through this I have lost much that could have recommended the work.

5037. 1776–78. *M XXXVI.*   18:69

If I only achieve as much as being convincing that one must suspend the treatment of this science until this point has been settled, then this text will achieve its purpose.

Initially I saw this doctrine as if in twilight. I tried quite earnestly to prove propositions and their opposite, not in order to establish a skeptical doctrine, but rather because I suspected I could discover in what an illusion of the understanding was hiding. The year '69 gave me a great light.

5040. 1776–78. *M XXXV.*   18:70

If, like Hume, I had all manner of adornment in my power, I would still have reservations about using them. It is true that some readers will be scared off by dryness.[67] But isn't it necessary to scare off some if in their case the matter would end up in bad hands?

18:70 **5041.** 1776–78. *M* XXXV.
All further explanation by the understanding of space, time, and apperception is impossible.[68]

18:70 **5042.** 1776–78. *M* XXXV–XXXVI.
A concept of reason (God, freedom, necessity) never indicates an object, namely an object of intuition; consequently the question whether the world has a beginning can only amount to the question whether I can
18:71 empirically expound a pure concept of reason. There is really no objective question here. Thus it is also not problematic, rather one can always answer it thus: No, such an object cannot be empirically represented. There is no uncertainty in metaphysics.

18:71 **5045.** 1776–78. *M* XXXVII.
That two *opposita* can be simultaneously false but cannot be simultaneously true, because in one the subject is taken as sensible and the predicate as intellectual, and conversely in the other. E.g., There is a first beginning of the world and there is not. In the first case, "beginning" signifies the supreme ground, which is constant; in the second, the first member of the series. Now if the first is taken sensitively, it is false; the second too.[69]

18:72 **5049.** 1776–78. *M* XXXVIII.
[*Crossed out*: The inner sense] Consciousness is the intuition of oneself. It would not be consciousness if it were sensation. All cognition, whatever it might concern, lies in it. If I abstract from all sensations, I presuppose consciousness. It is [*crossed out*: transcendental] logical, not
18:73 practical personality; the latter is the faculty for freedom by means of which, without being externally determined, one can be a cause on one's own. Moral personality is the capacity for motivating grounds of mere reason, by means of which a being is capable of laws and thus also of imputation.[70]

18:75 **5058.** 1776–78. *M* XXXVII.
In all [*crossed out*: universal] judgments the illusion rests on the confusion of the subjective with the objective. Especially in principles of reason, where *a priori* subjective grounds can also be objective.
In transcendental science everything must be derived from the subject, while only some of that is related to objects; hence the dialectic is something that belongs to the nature of the understanding, and a science of that is possible.

18:75 **5059.** 1776–78. *M* XXXVIII.
The subreptions of the power of judgment.[71] 1. That we cognize everything by means of predicates, and therefore have predicates with

an undetermined subject. That we hold that to be the first subject which is always the condition of the other predicates. 2. That we take the conditions of distinguishing among things to be necessary distinctions. 3. That we predicate conditions of outer presence of a subject that is to be internally conceived (a thinking being), and predicate outer conditions, e.g., those of body, of the inner. Representation.

5062. 1776–78. *M* XXXIX.   18: 76

Other sciences can grow gradually through unified effort and accretion. The philosophy of pure reason must be sketched out in a single go,[72] because here it comes down first to determining the nature of cognition itself and its universal laws and conditions, and not to one's judgment withstanding the test of good luck.

5063. 1776–78. *M* XXXIX.   18: 76

The transcendental dialectic is the critique of illusion, just as the analytic is the doctrine of truth.[73] Among the ancients it was often a   18: 77 technique of illusion or a sophistical art. The critique of illusion comes after philosophy. The critique of taste is not a doctrine; taste gives rules and, to be sure, suffers restrictions, but it does not provide precepts; one must not give it the name of a science, especially not one that is borrowed from an old denomination that has an entirely different sense.[74]

5070. 1776–78. *M* XXXIX.   18: 78

Transcendental philosophy is very necessary, because in an empirical philosophy we could be taught our mistakes by experience.

It is strange that here a critique, hence trials of cognition, must first   18: 79 precede before a *canon* can be erected; for it will still never become a doctrine.

5072. 1776–78. *M* XXXIX.   18: 79

In all systems of reason something always remains, and they have been successively enlarged. Mathematics preserves its inheritance and its storehouse grows by new additions daily. In natural science from Aristotle until now something always remains even from false systems, after [they have] been examined; but metaphysics destroys itself entirely, making place for another. The reason for this has not been investigated. What one took to be its basis was the first stones that were laid and which slowly sank in a swampy ground. This necessitates casting its methods under suspicion and investigating its sources in the subject.

5073. 1776–78. *M* XXXIX.   18: 79

The critique of pure reason is a prophylactic against a sickness of reason that has its germ in our nature. It is the opposite of the inclination

18:80   that chains us to our fatherland (homesickness): a longing to leave our circle and to relate to other worlds.

18:81   **5080.** 1776–78. *M* XXXXII.

Among the maxims of reason this also belongs: that nature always constitutes a system, although our cognition is seldom one.[75]

18:81   **5081.** 1776–78. *M* XXXXII.
18:82   Baumgarten: the man was sharp-sighted (in little things) but not far-sighted (in big ones).* Instead of his "aesthetic" the term "critique of the beautiful" would fit better.[76]

*(A Cyclops among metaphysicians, who was missing one eye, namely critique.)

(A good analyst, but not an architectonical philosopher; his outline of the sciences.)

18:82   **5082.** 1776–78. *M* XXXXII.

The metaphysical obstacle to all morality is the denial of freedom, and to all theology the disavowal of necessity.

18:82   **5083.** 1776–78. *M* XXXXI.

Transcendental philosophy proves that we can never get outside the sensible world with our cognition. If it seems to be more general, it is merely subjective. That mathematics itself is the only science that can determine anything independently of experience, thus entirely *a priori*, but that qualities must be given empirically.

18:83   **5086.** 1776–78. *M* XXXXI.

In the intelligible world the *substratum* is intelligence, the action and cause is freedom, the community is happiness from freedom, the primordial being is an intelligence through idea, the form is morality, the *nexus* is a *nexus* of ends. This intelligible world is now already the basis of the sensible world and is the truly self-sufficient [world].[77]

18:84   **5088.** 1776–78. *M* XXXXI.

The unity of understanding in appearance lies in the analogies of experience. The unity of understanding in the principles of these different causes of appearance: where does this lie? Likewise, how does it lead to the existence of God and another world? likewise, to the unity of ends?

18:84   **5089.** 1776–78. *M* XXXXI–XXXXII.

Discipline: We cannot judge synthetically by means of mere concepts of the understanding. They must always contain the concepts of appearances and serve only for their exposition. Mere concepts of the understanding are related to an object just as little as is an intuition of the understanding. This is always determined through sensibility, for our general concept is only a sign of what is concrete. Intellectual cosmology is just as much an *ens rationis* as is mystical cosmology. The usual scholastic and doctrinal methods of philosophy make one dumb, insofar as they operate with a mechanical thoroughness. They narrow the understanding and make it incapable of accepting instruction. By contrast, critique broadens the concepts and makes reason free. The scholastic philosophers operate like pirates who as soon as they arrive on an unoccupied coast fortify it.

5091. 1776–78. *M* XXXXII.   18:85

The cognition of pure reason (speculative) can never be applied further than the field of experiences and has no significance at all beyond its boundaries. Even mathematics contains nothing that cannot be demonstrated in experience.

Necessity in the empirical sense and freedom signify that which is on the one hand determined in accordance with a rule but is on the other hand not determined through sensibility, but rather subjectively, through the synthesis of the understanding.

Sulzer in his minor writings hopes in vain for demonstration.[78]

One can here have an overview of what and how much can be discovered.

5093. 1776–78. *M* XXXXIII.   18:85

The principles of pure reason are that an absolute completeness of the presuppositions of *synthesis* is to be assumed.[79] Hence the *principium necessitatis, contingentiae, compositionis et decompositionis.*[a] They contain the condition of the absolute collective unity (systematic) of cognition in general. In reason there is a nexus of prosyllogisms and episyllogisms.[b] The completeness of this synthesis rests on the completeness of the principles as well as the application.

5094. 1776–78. *M* XXXXIII.   18:86

The concept of a substance already carries with it the concept of freedom: for if I could not act by myself independently of outer determination, then my action would be only the action of another, hence I would really be the action of another, thus not a substance.[80]

---

[a] principles of necessity, contingency, composition, and decomposition
[b] That is, a chain of syllogisms concluding in the premises of a particular syllogism, and another chain of syllogisms starting with its conclusion.

18:86 **5095.** 1776–78. *M* XXXXIV.

It is impossible that the appearances should yield something un-bounded and absolute, whether in extension or division or in causality or the condition of existence in general. Hence these negative propositions are objective and dogmatic; by contrast, reason demands the absolute and complete in synthesis (*principia a priori*). These are practically objective, just as the former are speculatively objective.

18:87 **5100.** 1776–78. *M* XXXXV.

1. Morality: how I become worthy of being happy, without intending the means for participating in happiness. 2. Worldly prudence: how I become happy without regard to my worthiness to be so. 3. Wisdom: how I become happy through becoming worthy to be so. Philosophy is the *organon* of wisdom and must treat the vocation of my nature, the boundaries and the ends of my capacities. The 1st has purely *a priori principia*, the second purely *a posteriori* ones, the third both.

18:88 **5101.** 1776–78? 1778–1780s? *M* XXXXV.

Locke thought he could get by with saying that our concept of body is no more distinct than that of the mind.[81]

18:88 **5103.** 1776–78. *M* XXXXVI.

The intelligible world has laws in accordance with which I fit into every world, not just this world or the sensible world, in whatever con-dition of my own nature and of outer nature or society I may find myself. It has its own *principium constitutivum*, God, and its *principium regulativum*, moral laws. It is consistent with the rules of prudence, if these are broad; it is not an object of intuition; no physiology of it is possible; it is an object of belief as far as its substance is con-cerned, but of reflecting understanding as far as its general laws are concerned.

We also know God only on the basis of moral grounds and in accor-dance with properties connected with morality.[82] Making out the con-nection between the other world and this one depends on a transition by means of analogical inferences. However, the *principia* of the infer-ence by analogy and the *argumenta practica* κατ᾽ ανθρωπον,[a] to which the former are related, constitute the *transitum* from (*argumentum ad modulum humanitatis*) *secundum assumpta humanae naturae, non hominis singularis*.[b]

---

[a] *ad hominem*

[b] The transition on the basis of an argument in keeping with humanity is an accordance with what is assumed to be human nature, not a single person.

5104. 1776–78. *M* XXXXV.   18:89

The maxims of reason consist in the assumption of constitutive unity in the whole of appearances (if one begins *a priori*) and regulative unity in the parts (if one proceeds analytically from the parts to the whole). Thus that no causes can be assumed except those whose law can be found by means of observation (although the ground of this itself is not evident). Thus that there are no spirits, no blind power of choice, etc. But freedom *a priori* in actions. That nothing can be derived immediately from God, since one cannot observe the rules of his actions, although God is regarded *a priori* as the supreme *principium* of unity in accordance with rules, even in the practical. *In summa*: that the understanding maintains its unity in accordance with totality (constitutive) and the unity of rules. It thus does not restrict itself, but it still demands something first as the *principium* of its *synthesis*.

5109. 1776–78. *M* XXXXVII–XXXXVIII.   18:90

That which is original is unrestricted as a magnitude. As a thing in general, it is simple. Original action (the origin itself) is free. Original existence is absolutely necessary. Everything that is externally derived is unlimited; as something that is given in appearance (*mundus sensibilis*), it is composite; as something that has an origin, it is conditioned and dependent; as something that is existent, it is necessarily conditioned. The soul is not an appearance. In it lies, respectively, the entirety of the reality of all possible appearances. It is with respect to sensations   18:91 simple (the I); with respect to actions, free; in regard to all existence of appearances, a necessary substratum, which is not subordinated to any appearance.

We have two principles (*a priori*) of the empirical use of the understanding: principles of the exposition of appearances, i.e., of the determination of concepts through those same appearances; 2. of the architectonic use of reason in relation to the practical. The latter are merely intellectual.

It is a necessary hypothesis of the theoretical and practical use of reason in the whole of our cognition, consequently in relation to all ends and an intelligible world, to assume that an intelligible world is the basis of the sensible world, of which the soul as intelligence is the subjective archetype, but an original intelligence the cause; i.e., just as in us the *noumenon* is related to the appearances, so does this supreme intelligence relate to the *mundi intelligibilis*; for the soul really contains in itself the condition of all possible appearances, and in it they could all be determined *a priori*, if only the *data* were given at the outset.

(Reason, *mundus intelligibilis*. Not a new *synthesis*, but one completed by means of *a priori* boundaries.)

Among the appearances there is no end. Their boundary and thus the completion of the *synthesis* is in the *mundo intelligibili* in accordance with the analogy with our soul and intelligence.

The principles: Everything in the world consists in that which endures and that which is alterable, which inheres in the former. Everything alterable, every state has a cause. And: Everything that influences is in community. This cognition of the *mundi phaenomeni* is never completed. But in the *mundo intelligibili* everything must be completed; consequently

18:92   it is related to the *ens originarium*, where all of that which is unconditioned obtains. No decomposition is completed.

The [*crossed out*: determinability] unity of the absolute whole of our cognition, determinable through reason, is the cause of the synthesis that is extended beyond the sensible world, i.e., the synthesis of the sensible with the intellectual world. From ideas. The idea of the intelligence, independent of appearances, and of the *mundus intelligibilis*, which remains, and of the transcendental principle of the unity of everything.

18:93   **5112. 1776–78. *M* IL.**

The mathematician, the beautiful spirit, the natural philosopher: what are they doing when they make arrogant jokes about metaphysics[?] In them lies the voice that always calls them to make an attempt in the field of metaphysics. As human beings who do not seek their final end in the satisfaction of the aims of this life, they cannot do otherwise than ask: why am I here, why is it all here[?] The astronomer is even more challenged by these questions. He cannot dispense with searching for something that would satisfy him in this regard. With the first judgment that he makes about this he is in the territory of metaphysics. Now will he here give himself over entirely, without any guidance, to the convictions that may grow upon him, although he has no map of the field through which he is to stride[?] In this darkness the critique of reason lights a torch, although it does not illuminate the regions unknown to us beyond the sensible world, but the dark space of our own understanding.

Metaphysics is as it were the police force of our reason with regard to the public security of morals and religion.

18:94   **5115. 1776–78. *M* L.**

It is a strange fate of the human understanding, whether through a natural tendency or the true interest that drives it, to become entangled in a science, and to see itself as it were as condemned to it, which after centuries of efforts by the concerted power of the sharpest minds cannot be carried forward even a single step.[83] If we would (unwillingly) give up the effort, then [*crossed out*: drawn in part through a special tendency] we are in part pulled back by the natural movement of our spirit, in

214

part we are struck everywhere by questions with regard to our most important concern, regarding which we cannot be satisfied except by means of our own insight in this field. I know of only a single science of this sort for the good fortune of humankind, namely metaphysics, a theoretical philosophy of pure reason, i.e., reason free from all sources in experience; it is the stone of *Sisyphus*, which one ceaselessly rolls without ever moving it from its resting place. When I say that metaphysics has not been carried forward a single step, I do not mean by this the analysis of concepts of reason; for analysis is nothing other than the greater clarification of that which we already know, and here various people have done much in the more precise determination of the significance of words. But that is not what is sought; rather what is sought and is to be created is cognitions of objects about which we cannot be instructed by any sense and which therefore do not reside in us: this is that in relation to which all labor has until now been in vain. One can easily be convinced of this if one only considers that even a single cognition that is a determinate contribution to science must be accepted by everybody,   18:95 e.g., air within bodies, while metaphysics has come into fashion in certain places only through persuasion.

5116. 1776–78. *M* LI–LII.   18:95

I have not always judged this science thus. In the beginning I learned from it what most recommended itself to me. In some parts I believed myself able to add something to the common store, in others I found something to improve, but always with the aim of thereby acquiring dogmatic insights. For the doubt that was so boldly stated seemed to me so much to be ignorance without reason that I gave it no hearing. If one reflects with real earnestness on finding the truth, then one finally no longer spares one's own products, although at the same time it seems that they promise us service in behalf of science. One subjects what one has learned or even thought for oneself entirely to critique. It took a long time before in such a way I found the whole dogmatic theory to be dialectical. Yet I sought something certain, if not with regard to the object, then still with regard to the nature and boundaries of this sort of cognition. I gradually found that many of the propositions that we regard as objective are in fact subjective, i.e., they contain the *conditiones* under which alone we can have insight into or comprehend the object. But while I thereby certainly became careful, I was still not instructed. For that there really are *a priori* cognitions that are not merely analytic but extend our cognition, I was still lacking a critique of pure reason   18:96 that had been brought under rules, above all a *canon* thereof; for I still believed I could find a method for extended dogmatic cognition through pure reason. For this I now required insight into how a cognition *a priori* is possible in general.

18:96 **5119.** 1776–78. *M* IL–L.

Metaphysics, insofar as it would go further than the pure principles of the understanding with regard to experiences, has absolutely none other than a negative use, both with regard to the nature of corporeal 18:97 and thinking things and in relation to that which is beyond or above nature. The latter cognitions must be cognized in analogy with empirical principles continued beyond the boundaries of the world, hence as maxims of the general unity of reason. In that case metaphysical concepts serve polemically against dogmatic doubt, in order to set limits to its objections.

The physical use of metaphysics is also to prevent dogmatic synthesis *a priori*, which can hinder the continuity of cognition in accordance with laws of experience, and to that extent it serves for the extension of those laws. 1. That one does not arrive at ultimate parts; 2. that differing density does not presuppose empty space; 3. that there is no material immediate influence without contact; 4. that the world has boundaries. The first and second of these assertions are principles of reason.

Its use in rational psychology: 1. that not all substances are material; 2. that experience is not the boundary of all cognition and this world is not the world in general.[84]

In theology: 1. that the world does not comprehend all things; 2. that not everything is contingent, etc.

Its use is thus thoroughly negative. 1. To get rid of dogmatic denials, which limit the empirical expansion of cognition. 2. To restrict dogmatic assertions, which would uselessly extend reason beyond its practical use.

18:98 **5121.** 1776–78. *M* LII.

The only unsolvable metaphysical difficulty is that of combining the supreme condition of everything practical with the condition of speculative unity, that is, **freedom** with nature or the causality of the understanding with regard to appearances. For freedom is the possibility of actions from causes in understanding. The spontaneity of the understanding in the series of appearances is the riddle. After this, the second riddle is absolute necessity, which is not proposed by nature, but by pure reason. The latter is the original condition of the possibility of nature. In the former, an appearance is not necessary but contingent under the conditions of appearance. In the latter, something exists necessarily without any condition; thus the first absolutely contingent being and the first necessary being.

18:99 **5124.** 1776–78. *M* 1.

The proposition that synthetic *a priori* propositions obtain only as principles of the possibility and exposition of experiences is independent from the explanation of the categories. For from whence should they otherwise derive?

Analytic judgments are not to be despised because they do not amplify.

5125. 1776–78. *M* 1.   18:99

My author Baumgarten is an excellent man when it comes to judgments of clarification, but when he moves on to judgments of amplification he is without any foundation, even though these are the primary requirement in metaphysics.[85]

5127. 1776–78. *M* 2.   18:99
                                                                18:100

1st part of transcendental philosophy is that of immanent cognition *a priori*: Analytic; – the second part is that of transcendent cognition *a priori*: Dialectic. Both parts of the critique.

5130. 1776–78? 1778–1780s? *M* 2.   18:100

Transcendental philosophy has 2 parts: Critique of pure reason and ontology.

5131. 1776–78? 1778–1780s? *M* 2.   18:100

Ontology is the science of the primary cognitions of pure understanding: 1. of concepts, analytic; 2. of judgments.

5133. 1776–78? 1778–1780s? *M* 2.[86]   18:101

Transcendental philosophy (*later addition*: which presents the elements of our *a priori* cognition) is a science of the possibility of a synthetic *a priori* cognition.

5165. 1776–78. *M* 5, §15, in *Possibile*.[87]   18:107

The synthetic conditions (*principia*) of possibility are objective only if they contain the conditions of the possibility of experience, not of conception.

A possibility is that for which there are *data* for thinking it; there is no possibility in that for which there are no *data* for thinking it.

5166. 1776–78. *M* 5, §15.   18:107

The logical concept of possibility: *principium contradictionis* (*analysis*); or the real concept: *principia* of *synthesis*.[88]

5167. 1776–78. *M* 5, §14.   18:107

Subjectively, representations *A* and *B* can succeed each other in this order or conversely. In order for the succession to be objectively valid, i.e., serve for experience, it must be determined, so that I cannot reverse it.[89]

18:108   Why is the *principium rationis sufficientis* set beside the *principio contradictionis* as the only one?

The *princip* of determination, derivation, and division.

18:109   **5176.** 1776–1780s. *M* 5, §15.

In addition to the *principio identitatis et contradictionis*, there must be other *principia* of *nexus* and opposition. For through the former we can have insight only into the *nexus* and *oppositio logica*, but not *realis*. Now which are these *principia synthetica*?

18:110   **5181.** 1776–78? (1773–75?) At *M* 6, §16.

The possibility of that which is possible **only under a certain** condition (presupposition) is restricted through the condition; the possibility of that which is possible in a certain case is extended until that which is possible in all regards is absolutely possible, i.e., possible without any condition.

Conditional possibility pertains to the *causatis*,[a] absolute possibility to the first cause. Possibility *in abstracto* is merely being non-contradictory; this possibility signifies only the admissibility of the idea. Possibility *in concreto* is alone objective, i.e., something in which *omnimoda determinatione interna*[b] are possible. What is possible *omni respectu*[c] is necessary,
18:111   because in that case it is possible *absque hypothesi*,[d] and is at the same time the ground of everything or the all itself, for it is consistent with everything.

18:111   **5184.** 1776–1780s. At *M* 6, §§15, 16.

The analytic *criterium* of possibility is that there is no contradiction nor any insight into one. We cannot have insight into the synthetic *criterion* of possibility **through concepts.** The synthetic conditions of
18:112   the possibility of experience are at the same time the conditions of the possibility of the objects of experience. But this is not the possibility of things in themselves.

18:112   **5189.** 1776–78. At *M* 7, §20, in *Connexum*.

The *principium rationis* as an anticipation, hence with the conditions of sensibility, is objective, for in time there is always something preceding.*
18:113   The *principium rationis* as a *postulatum* of perspicience is subjective.

The *principium terminationis* as a demand of comprehension is subjective.

---

[a] that which is caused
[b] all internal determinations
[c] in all respects
[d] without any hypothesis, i.e., without any condition or presupposition

If both were made objective, they would conflict; but not subjectively.

*(That which, as contingent (arising, *transitorium*), is given only by means of sensation and not *a priori* from ourselves, has a ground. (*later addition*: But what is called contingent is precisely that which does not exist for itself, but only as *rationatum.*[a]) Free actions are given *a priori*. Occurrences, however or what happens, are given only through experience and *a posteriori*. The former is the beginning (*terminus*), cognized in accordance with a general law; the second cannot be cognized without an *antecedens* in accordance with general laws and requires a ground for that.)

5190. 1776–78? (1773–75?) At *M* 7, §20.   18:113
*Principium rationis in **mundo** est cosmologicum, non transcendentale, est principium cognoscendi, non agendi.*[b]

5194. 1776–78. At *M* 7, §20.   18:114
Everything that happens, i.e., which follows something, must always follow it, i.e., with regard to that which precedes it, it stands under a   18:115
rule. Appearances have a rule. 1. That something always precedes. 2. That through it the consequence is determined (always follows on it).

5199. 1776–78. At *M* 7, §20.   18:115
Synthetic propositions. [1.] Everything is in a substance. 2. Everything contingent has a ground. 3. Everything unified has a common ground.   18:116
These very propositions applied to sensibility, e.g., that which happens has a ground.

5202. 1776–78? 1778–1780s?? At *M* 7, §20.   18:116
The *principium rationis* is the principle of the determination of things in temporal succession; for that cannot be determined through time, rather time must be determined by the rule of the existence of appearances in the understanding. *Principium* of the possibility of experience.[90]

Thus it is not possible to determine the position of things in time without the presupposition of this principle, through which the course of appearances is first made uniform. Succession in the concept of consequence concerns only the positing of consequence.

5203. 1776–78. *M* 9, still in *Connexum*.[91]   18:116
In the case of everything passive or everything that is given, apprehension must not only be encountered, but it must also be necessitated

---

[a] something which has its reason in something else
[b] The principle of (sufficient) reason within the world is worldly, not transcendental, is a principle of cognition, not of action.

18:117 in order for it to be represented as given, i.e., the particular apprehension must be determined by the general. The general is the relation to the others and to the whole of the state. In order for it to be distinguished from what is arbitrary, it is regarded as given and as something only insofar as it is subsumed under the categories. It must therefore be represented in accordance with a rule, so that appearance becomes experience and so that the mind comprehends it as one of its actions of **self-consciousness**, in which, as in space and time, all *data* are encountered. The unity of the mind is the condition of thinking and the subordination of every particular under the general is the condition of the possibility of associating a given representation with others through an action. Even if the rule does not strike the senses, one must still represent the object as in conformity with a rule in order to conceive it as representing something, i.e., having a certain position and function among the other determinations. The beginning cannot be determined in accordance with a subjective rule, consequently it cannot be a free action that has its beginning in every point.

Everything that happens but not as a first beginning (freedom) has its determining ground.

18:118 **5208.** 1776–78? (1773–75?) *M* 8, opposite §24, still in *Connexum*.

The things that are given to us *a priori* must also have a relation to the understanding, i.e., they must be a kind of appearance through which it is possible to aquire a concept, as well as a relation to sensibility, i.e., they must be a kind of impression through which it is possible to acquire an appearance. Hence whatever can become known to us *a posteriori* (through the senses) will stand under the general conditions of a concept, i.e., be in conformity with the rules through which it is possible to acquire concepts of things and connect everything with the concepts of things and subordinate them to these concepts. Accordingly everything will appear in such a way that there must be a possibility of cognizing it *a priori*. Free actions are already given *a priori*, namely our own.

18:119 **5211.** 1776–78? (1770–71?) *M* 8, at §22.

That everything which appears must appear in relation to the whole can be seen from space and time. But that it must stand under a rule must be seen from the fact that it would not otherwise appear in accordance with the unity of its relation to this whole.

In the world something is always a succession in appearance as far as time and circumstances are concerned. It is a question whether it is also a real succession, i.e., connected in accordance with a general rule.

5214. 1776–78. *M* 8, at §22. 18: 120

All determination in time can occur only in accordance with an *a priori* principle, i.e., in such a way that everything succeeds something else in accordance with a rule.

5215. 1776–78? 1790s?? *M* 8. 18: 120

That which is the condition under which we posit something in accordance with a rule is the cause. If I arrange for a stork to fly in wintertime, it does not become warm. Hence this is not the cause.

5216. 1776–78? (1773–75?) *M* 9. 18: 121

The empirical laws *a priori* contain the conditions of apprehension and conception (together with intellection). We cannot connect anything in the appearances and thus give them a real form except by combining them to one another, through one another, and with one another, and the appearances determine the mind to this activity. Thus something is possible as an object of experience only insofar as it appears in conformity with the laws of apprehension; i.e., if its appearance were complete, it would have to be interconnected in accordance with the laws of apprehension. Just as nothing can appear except within the universal totality of space and time, so nothing can become an experience except insofar as it is connected with others in accordance with the universal laws of the activities of the mind. Thus nothing happens contingently, i.e., without being subjected to a general rule concerning something with which it is connected (whether this appears together with it or not). For we can encounter the ground of a particular connection in an object only insofar as it contains that which can be subsumed under a general rule for connection. Ground and consequence are not mere apprehensions, but inferences or general actions of transition.

It must be possible to cognize *a priori* everything that is given to us through experience, i.e., its possibility must be able to be cognized from the laws of sensibility or of the understanding, in relation to which alone experiences occur. That it can be cognized *a priori* means that it has an object and is not merely a subjective modification.[92]

5220. 1776–78? 1790s?? *M* 9. 18: 122

The principle of sufficient reason is the *principium* of the order in the course of nature, that of freedom is the *principium* of the beginning in the series of things. Because there must be a beginning in the series of consequences, there must be freedom, and even in the course [of nature] first beginnings are possible. If there is only mere nature, then the series of connected things is continuous. But if there is freedom, then it is interrupted.

18:122   **5221.** 1776–78? (1773–75?) *M* 10.

Everything that happens, happens in accordance with a rule, is determined in general, can be cognized *a priori*. Thereby do we distinguish the objective from subjective play (fiction), truth from illusion. The appearance has an object if it is a predicate of a subject, i.e., one of the ways of cognizing that which there endures; thus the appearances belong to the representation of something enduring only insofar as they are connected with one another and have unity through something generally valid. To be sure, something can appear to us without its ground appear-

18:123   ing to us; but we cannot cognize it without presuming the cognition of a ground, because it would otherwise not be a cognition, i.e., objective representation.

That is therefore a condition of the cognition of objects, hence of the objects themselves, for mere appearance does not yet yield an object. It is, to be sure, not a condition of apprehension, for this pertains to an appearance immediately, without knowing its ground. But the appearance belongs to a whole of time, and in this it can be connected only if it flows from what is universal. Things are not connected through time, rather they are connected in time through what is universal in their determinations.

We [*crossed out:* can] must form a concept of its generation if we completely apprehend the appearance. But this is only possible if the contingent that occurs is necessary when taken in its entirety or in its complete determination (relation). If I did not represent that the occurrence is necessary with respect to the whole or is one aspect of that which is constant, then I would not take my representation to be a cognition and therefore also would not take it to be something that pertains to an object.[93]

18:130   **5248.** 1776–1780s. *M* 26, under §94, in *Perfectum*.

An idea is the representation of the whole insofar as it necessarily precedes the determination of the parts. It can never be represented empirically, because in experience one proceeds from the parts to the

18:131   whole by means of successive *synthesis*. It is the archetype of things, since certain objects are possible only through an idea. Transcendental ideas are those where the absolute whole in general determines the parts in the aggregate or series.

18:133   **5255.** 1776–78. *M* 31, §108, in *Necessarium et contingens*.

Praedicatum est vel constitutivum vel modale, prius determinatio.[a]

Existence is not a constitutive predicate (*determinatio*), it also cannot be discovered *per analysin*, as belonging to its content, from the concept of a thing. Thus it cannot be proven objectively from concepts, although it

---

[a] A predicate is either constitutive or modal, in the first case it is a determination.

can be regarded as a necessary *substratum* in relation to all other predicates as derived.[94]

5262. 1776–78. *M* 32, at §§111–14, still in *Necessarium et contingens*.　18:134

Something is certainly necessary in every *respectu* (*absolute et sine conditione restrictiva*) if it is necessary in itself (*interne*); but we have no concept of the internal necessity of a thing, since positing and cancelling are in　18:135 themselves equally possible; thus absolute necessity as a **necessity** related to everything in general must be grounded in a **presupposition**.

Either something is necessary (*restrictive*) under a condition or it is necessary *extensive* in some application.[a] Nothing is necessary under all conditions, for if it already has a condition then it is not necessary under the opposite of that.

Absolute necessity is the necessity of a presupposition (*hypothesis originaria*) with regard to everything conceivable, namely the *data* for all determination, the sum-total of reality. This is related to the entirety of sensibility and the senses as regards both form and matter. If we had complete insight into all of our sensitivity and form then we would be able to determine antecedently everything that can be an object for us at all.

The *hypothesis originaria* is not necessity under a *hypothesi*, but necessity as a *hypothesis*.

5263. 1776–78? (1773–75?) *M* 33, still in *Necessarium et contingens*.　18:135
[*Crossed out*: That which contradicts itself is not in conformity with the conditions of understanding.]

How the conflict of the subjective conditions or their presupposition imitates or substitutes for the truth. E.g., a mathematical infinitude is possible, because it does not conflict with the rules of insight; it is impossible, because it conflicts with the rules of comprehension.[b] Everything has its ground, since without this there can be no insight into the existence of the thing; something has no further ground beyond itself, because otherwise it would conflict with the conditions of comprehension.[c] There is no (transcendental) freedom. There is freedom. There is　18:136 an absolutely necessary being, since without this there is no comprehension.[d] There is no such being, because such a thing is in conflict with our insight. If, however, these concepts are taken only in accordance with the conditions of apprehension, then they are restricted to the objects of the senses and also have only a restricted significance. E.g., everything that

---

[a] *in irgend einer Anwendung (application)*
[b] *comprehension*
[c] *Begreifens*
[d] *Begreifung*

happens has in a certain ordering a first ground, or rather the *axiomata* are not transcendent, but are valid only as anticipations. So they are valid only of the *datis* of the senses, insofar as these can be understood. E.g., whatever happens has a ground, because without a rule according to which it is given in accordance with laws of sensibility, one would not think any object by means of the representation.

The *principium contradictionis* contains the *conditiones* of thinking in general. The *anticipationes*, which affirm the *conditiones* of the apprehension of the concepts of the understanding (e.g., in every substance there is *aliquid perdurabile*,[a] or a substance endures forever), contain the conditions (*postulata*) of understanding and are therefore always true with regard to sensible conditions.[95]

(To understand something under its determinations (representations), i.e., to think an object or posit something that corresponds to them).

Apprehension without the *conditiones* under which alone something can be given is a function, but not yet a concept, or rather is potential. Understanding something is to cognize, where it has previously been given; insight, however, is to cognize *a priori*; to cognize something logically is to cognize it distinctly.

18:138   **5270.** 1776–78. M 42, §148, in *Singulare et universale*.[96]

The principle of thoroughgoing determination is: *quodlibet existens est omnimode determinatum, i.e., ens quodlibet per se non nisi ut omnimode determinatum dari potest, sed per conceptum de ipse multimode potest esse indeterminatum.*[b]

That proposition possesses the totality of all possible predicates along with their *oppositis* and, since reality belongs only to existence, the totality of all realities together with their *oppositis* in thoughts; and, since everything that does not contain reality always presupposes something else that does contain it, it also has in view the concept of a thing that contains all reality, as *entis logice originarii*,[c] whose reality or the consequences thereof yield all things through limitation and in relation to which alone each thing can be determined from others.

18:139   If I represent the understanding that thinks reality as light and, insofar as it negates reality, as darkness, then I can think of complete determination either as a bringing of light here and there into the gloom, or I can think of the gloom as the mere restriction of the universal light, and thus I distinguish things only through the shadows, the reality lies at their basis and indeed only a single universal one. In the opposite case

---

[a] something permanent
[b] Everything that exists is determinate in all regards, i.e., an entity in itself cannot be given except as determinate in all regards, but the concept of it can be indeterminate in many regards.
[c] a logically original being

I distinguish all things only through their light, as if they had originally been lifted out of the gloom. I can very well think of a negation if I have a reality, but not if no reality is given. Thus reality is the first *logice*, and from this it is inferred that it is also *metaphysice* and *objective* the first and the gloom out of which the light of experience elaborates shapes. Thus, appearances are originally manifold, and unity arises if one abstracts from the manifold.

5277. 1776–78? (1770–71?) *M* 48, in §§165–90, *Prima matheseos intenso-* 18:141
rum principia.[97]

Mathematics is the science of the construction of concepts; hence it pertains only to intuition as such and has only empirical use.

Philosophy pertains only to concepts of being in general, hence to those which correspond to sensation, and thus cannot make its concepts intuitive. Precisely for that reason it also pertains to objects independently of the conditions of intuition.

5285. 1776–78. *M* 59, at §191, in *Substantia et accidens*. 18:143

Since our understanding cannot think except by means of judgments, we also cannot have any concepts of things except by means of predicates, which are connected with something constant as the sign of the subject. Thus the concept of substance and *accidens* otherwise has no meaning.

5289. 1776–78? (1775–77?) (1773–75?) (1772?) *M* 59, at §197, still in 18:144
Substantia et accidens.

1. *Substratum* (inherence). 2. *Principium caussalitatis* (consequence). *a. ratio realis. sive synthetica. Caussalitas quoad accidentia est Vis. primitiva, derivativa. Actio, passio, Influxus*. 3. *Commercium. Reciproca actio. Triplex Unitas, cuius functiones sunt a priori, sed non nisi a posteriori dari possunt (construi).*

Substantia, Ratio, Compositum. Phaenomena. Time is constant, while [*crossed out*: determinations] appearances change.[a]

5290. 1776–78? (1778–1780s?) *M* 59, at §196, still in *Substantia et accidens*. 18:144

The relation of a substance to the *accidens* is mere *actio*.[98] *Vis*. That of substances to one another can be either *actio* or *passio*; if it is *mutua*, then it is *commercio*.[b]

---

[a] 1. Substratum (inherence). 2. Principle of causality (consequence). a. real or synthetic reason. Causality as an accident (property of a thing) is force. primitive or derivative. Action, passion, influence. 3. Interaction. Reciprocal action. A triplex unity, whose functions are *a priori* but can be given (constructed) only *a posteriori*. Substance, Reason, Composite. Phenomena.

[b] In other words, if each substance is both active and passive with regard to the other, then there is interaction.

Since we can only know a thing through its predicates, we cannot know the subject by itself alone.

5294. 1776–78? (1773–75?) 1769?? *M* 60, opposite §§201, 202, in *Substantia et accidens.*[99]

Bodies are *substantiae comparativae, substrata phaenomenorum.*[a] It is ridiculous to want to think of the soul in corporeal terms; for we have the concept of substance only from the soul, and we form the concept of the substance of body only afterwards. The transcendental concepts must not overstep the boundaries of the *intellectualium* and make the sensitive concepts in the same sense into intellectual ones, e.g., substance as *noumenon* or *phaenomenon*: consequently not the proposition: Bodies are divisible.[b]

Necessity cannot present itself in experience, likewise substance; hence the pure intellectual concept is not valid in its complete purity of that which is sensible.

5297. 1776–78. *M* 61, still in *Substantia et accidens.*

The logical relation between substance and *accidens* is synthetic. The subject is itself a predicate (for one can think of anything only by means of predicates, except the I), but for that reason only that which is not in turn a predicate is called a substance: 1. because no subject is thought for it; 2. because it is the presupposition and *substratum* of the others. This can be inferred only from its endurance, while the other changes. Thus it belongs to the essence of a subject that it is permanent.[100] If one assumes that the substance ceases to be, then this cessation proves that it is not a substance, and thus since no *substratum* is thought for this appearance, there are predicates without subjects, thus no judgments and no thoughts.

5298. 1776–78? 1778–1780s? *M* 61.

All concepts are predicates, and these are either substance or *accidens* or relation. Space and time are neither, and therefore are not predicates of objects in themselves at all. Space and time are *a priori* intuitions. For from their concepts the (synthetic) propositions cannot be derived that we have of them *a priori*. How are *a priori* intuitions possible? In no other way than that the form for intuiting something through the senses can be represented in itself, without matter, i.e., without a given object of the senses. Thus space and time are forms of sensible intuition. Thus we can cognize *a priori* much about space and time and the objects in them,

---

[a] substances relatively speaking, the substrata of phenomena

[b] That is, the sensible predicate of divisibility derived from bodies should not be applied to the soul.

i.e., as objects of the senses, that is on that account not valid of the same objects as things in themselves.[101]

5313. 1776–78? (1773–75?) (1780s?) *M* 70, at §239, in *Monas.*   18:150
That space and time are intuitions without things means that they are not objective representations, but rather must be subjective ones.

5315. 1776–1780s. *M* 70, at §239.   18:151
Space is the form of all relations that precede all intuition of outer things.

5317. 1776–78? (1773–75?) 1771?? *M* 71, §239.   18:151
Time is the form of consciousness, i.e., the condition under which alone we can become conscious of things.

5318. 1776–78? (1773–75?) 1771? *M* 71, at §239.   18:151
Space is a mere possibility, but something actual in actual things.

5319. 1776–78? (1773–75?) 1771?? *M* 72, at §239.   18:151
Since inner sense alone is non-deceptive and alteration is perceived by means of it, time seems to be something absolute; yet it is on that account only the form of inner appearance, and we actually have the representation of time, although what lies behind this appearance remains unknown.[102]

5320. 1776–78? (1773–75?) 1771? *M* 72, at §239.   18:151
Time is actual **as the form** of inner sensibility; it is thereby opposed to the *ficto.*[a] For there actually are alterations in us. Bodies would be things even if they were not in us. But space is always only form.

5323. 1776–78? (1773–75?) *M* 71, at §239.[103]   18:152
Space and time are neither things nor their predicates, thus they are nothing objective.

5327. 1776–1780s. *M* 72, at §241, still in *Monas.*   18:153
If the concept of space were derived from the things, as Leibniz thinks, then as propositions of experience the propositions about them would possess no apodictic certainty.[104]

5329. 1776–78? (1773–75?) 1778–1780s?? *M* 73, at §244, still in *Monas.*   18:153
If space were something objective and necessary, whence would we know that[?] From experience we cannot derive a judgment that is at the

[a] the fictional

227

same time to be cognized as absolutely necessary, and it is not cognized nor cognizable *a priori*. The representation would have to be made, but then it would also not be necessary. It must therefore be intuited in God.

18:155 **5338**. 1776–78? (1770–71?) *M* 75, at §248, in *Finitum et infinitum*.

"Infinite" means more than not finite or bounded, but also great beyond all measure when taken as a whole. Hence I can say that the world is neither finite nor infinite, because it is a *phaenomenon* and not a thing. As a *phaenomenon* it has no determinate boundaries and can never be taken as a whole, rather one can only make progress within it.

18:158 **5348**. 1776–78? (1773–75?) *M* 90, at §297ff., in *Successiva*.[105]

Why do we not also say about things in different times (like those in different spaces) that they are on that account different things[?] Because without the identity of things in different times even these different times as such could not be cognized. The permanence of things is the basis of the temporal succession. But that is always possible only in space. Space endures; but space itself can be perceived only by means of things in it (which therefore also endure and by means of which I can cognize space as enduring).

18:160 **5358**. 1776–78? (1773–75?) 1771?? *M* 118, opposite §377, in *Notio mundi affirmativa*.

We do not have sensations of outer substances (only of their outer effects on us), rather we add them to sensations in thought. But only in relation to the affections of our mind; thus not as what they are in themselves, but as that which is permanent in appearance.

18:161 **5360**. 1776–78? (1772?) *M* 118, at §380, in *Notio mundi negativa*.

Since empty space and empty time are not an object of empirical cognition, neither immediately through experience nor through any sort of inference, but since the infinitude of the world is also beyond experience, just like space and time, the totality (*absoluta*) of appearances, i.e., the idea of the world, is a problematic concept. The intellectual possibility of one of these conditions of appearance does not matter here; for they are synthetic propositions, which obtain only as conditions of possible experience.

18:163 **5368**. 1776–78. *M* 119, at §381, in *Notio mundi negativa*.

This says only: we cannot think any absolute totality in accordance with empirical synthesis, yet we must think one in accordance with purely intellectual synthesis, since everything contingent must have a complete cause, not in itself, yet outside itself. We have no image, yet we have a concept. For no image of the infinite is possible and there is no *substratum* for this image in the finite within infinite time and space.

We cannot determinately think of the location of the beginning of the world in empty space and empty time, nor of how something can simply begin in time, and even less of how time itself can begin.

5369. 1776–78. *M* 119, at §381.   18: 163

Between nature and chance there is a third thing, namely freedom.

All appearances are in nature, but the cause of the appearances is not contained in the appearance, therefore also not [in] nature. Our understanding is such a cause of the actions of the power of choice, which as appearances are certainly natural, but which as a whole of appearances stand under freedom.

5399. 1776–1780s. *M* 128, at §402, in *Partes universi simplices.*[106]   18: 172

The imagination presupposes a sense the form of which it can reproduce. If there were no outer senses, we would also not be able to imagine things outside of us as such, hence not in accordance with the three dimensions of space.

If the cause of the intuition of space were in us, we would be conscious of it as a representation of inner sense, and then we would have to attribute space and figure to our representations of things as well as to the things themselves.

Dreams can represent things to us as external which do not exist just then; but we would not even be able to dream of something as external if these forms were not given to us by means of external things. That one would have to believe in the reality of external things if we could not prove it would not be necessary; for that has no relation to any interest of reason.

5400. 1776–78? (1773–75?) (1771?) *M* 128, at §402.   18: 172

The question of whether something is outside me is the same as if I asked whether I represent a real space. For this is something outside me. But this does not mean that something exists in itself, but rather that objects correspond to such *phaenomena*. For in the case of a *phaenomeno* we are never talking about absolute existence. Dreams are in analogy with wakefulness. Except for waking representations that are consistent with those of other people I have no other marks of the **object** outside me; thus a *phaenomenon* outside me is that which can be cognized in accordance with rules of the understanding. Yet how can one ask whether there are really external *phaenomena*? We are certainly not immediately conscious that they are external, i.e., not mere imaginings and dreams, but we are still conscious that they are the originals for all imaginings, and are thus themselves not imaginings.

18:176 **5413.** 1776–1780s. *M* 140, at §430, in *Natura corporum*.[107]

That in the appearance of a rational being which begins only relatively and with respect to time presupposes something else that determines its existence in accordance with a rule has its ground in this as an intelligence in something that does not begin and is not subordinated to any antecedent state in time. In this consists the freedom of a rational being as a cause through its reason. For that is a capacity to determine itself *a priori*. For if the grounds of determination were given subjectively, empirically and *a posteriori*, then the judgment of reason would not be able to be regarded as *a priori*, hence not as absolutely necessary.

In order to judge in an objectively universal and indeed apodictic manner, reason must be free from subjectively determining grounds; for if they determined it, then like them the judgment would only be contingent, that is, in accordance with its subjective causes. Thus reason is conscious of its freedom in objectively necessary *a priori* judgments, namely that only the relation to the object is their ground.[108]

18:176 **5414.** 1776–1780s. *M* 140, at §432, in *Natura corporum*.

One can very well produce rules empirically, but not laws, as Kepler did in comparison to Newton; for to the latter there belongs necessity, hence that they can be cognized *a priori*. Yet one always assumes of the rules of nature that they are necessary, because it is on this account that it is nature, and that there can be *a priori* insight into them; hence they are called laws *anticipando*.[a] The understanding is the ground of empirical laws, hence of an empirical necessity where there can certainly be insight *a priori* into the ground of the lawfulness, e.g., the law of causality, but not into the ground of the determinate law. All metaphysical principles of nature are only grounds of lawfulness.

18:179 **5429.** 1776–79? (1775–77?) 1780–83?? *M* 149, opposite §§449, 450, in *Substantiarum mundanarum commercium*.

Interaction (*commercium*) (its ground, *communitas*, consists in the fact that what goes on with one alteration has an effect on all of them), is twofold: either [*crossed out:* in accordance with laws of] that of real effects or that of ideal ones, which are merely the *phaenomenon* of the effects. The influences of bodies are merely the *phaenomena* of the effects. For matter produces only relations of space; these, however, are not something real or an *accidens* and are therefore no true relation of one substance to another that would alter them internally. The outer relation without the inner, however, is nothing true, but a mere appearance.[b] The interaction of bodies with each other can be understood in accordance with *legibus*

---

[a] in anticipation or anticipatory
[b] *apparentz*

phaenomenorum, whose application, however, requires experience; there can be no insight at all into that of bodies and minds, because the latter can be cognized only through inner sense, and thus their alterations can be cognized *realiter* while the effects of bodies and their forces pertain only to the relations of *phaenomena* in general and not to their inner determinations.

5434. 1776–1780s. *M* 252f., at §§700–7, in *Spontaneitas.*   18:181
Whether we have an experience that we are free?
No! For we would otherwise have to experience of all human beings that they can withstand the greatest *stimulo*. By contrast, the moral law says: They should withstand it, consequently they must be able to.[109]

5435. 1776–1780s. *M* 252, at §§700–7.   18:181
The will is a capacity to act in accordance with the representation of a rule as a law.[110] Capacity of ends. *Stimuli* are a pleasure that precedes the law. *Independentia a stimulis* obtains where the law precedes the pleasure. (*arbitrium purum*.) (*Later addition*: Freedom is the causality of the pure reason in the determination of the power of choice.)

5436. 1776–1780s. *M* 252f., at §§700–7.   18:181
Freedom is the capacity to be determined only through reason, and not mediately, but immediately, hence not through the matter, rather through the form of the laws. Thus moral.

5438. 1776–78? (1772–76?) *M* 281, at §719, in *Libertas.*   18:182
The capacity to produce the motives of willing entirely of itself is freedom. This *actus* does not itself rest on the willing, but is the spontaneity of the causality of the willing. It is concerning this that we either reproach or approve of ourselves.

5440. 1776–78. *M* 281, at §719.   18:182
Freedom, insofar as it is a concept of reason, is inexplicable (also not objective); insofar as it is a concept of the activity and causality of reason itself, it cannot, to be sure, be explained as a first principle, but it is an *a priori* self-consciousness.

5441. 1776–78. *M* 281, at §719.   18:182
All of our actions and those of other beings are necessitated, the understanding (and the will, insofar as it can be determined by the understanding) alone is free and a pure self-activity, which is not determined by anything other than itself. Without this original and inalterable spon-   18:183
taneity we would not cognize anything *a priori*, and our thoughts themselves would stand under empirical laws. The capacity to think *a priori*

and to act is the unique condition of the possibility of the origin of all other appearances. The ought[a] would also have no significance at all.[111]

Freedom and absolute necessity are the sole pure concepts of reason that are objective although inexplicable. For by reason one understands the self-activity for going from the general to the particular, and for doing this *a priori*, hence with an absolute necessity. The absolute necessity: with regard to the determinable; and freedom: with regard to the determining.

18: 187 **5457.** 1776–78. *M* 294, at §742, in *Natura anima humanae*.[112]

On the possibility of the *commercii* of that which is only an object of inner sense with that which is only one of outer sense. In the case of matter we know only the outer immediately, in the case of the soul only the inner. We do not know the *commercium* among the objects of outer sense originally and *a priori*, and similarly we do not know the *commercium* among the inner powers of the soul. But the first *data* of outer cognition already contain concepts of *commercii*, and likewise those of inner cognition. The *phaenomena* are thereby compared with each other with regard to identity. We can therefore have *a priori* insight into neither the natural possibility nor the impossibility [of interaction between mind and body]; consequently all the *systemata* concerning that are in vain, and it is an empirical proposition that inner determinations are grounds of outer ones and conversely, and this is an original power.[113]

18: 188 On the seat of the soul: whether as material substance it is determined with regard to space [*crossed out*: externally] in the body, or only through the *commercium* with the body with regard to the rest of the world. It has its seat, i.e., the first and immediate connection with the nervous system.[114]

Everything of which a universal rule can be cognized through experience is natural. Accordingly, the *commercium* is natural. Immateriality is a properly problematic concept, which cannot be refuted at all.[115]

18: 189 **5461.** 1776–78? (1790s?) *M* 299, at §750ff., still in *Natura animae humanae*.

I as the *correlatum* of all outer intuition am a human being. The outer intuition to which I relate all others in me is my body. Thus as a subject of outer intuitions I must have a body.[116] The conditions of outer and inner intuition determine each other reciprocally (*commercium* of soul and body). The reality of bodies with regard to myself is the interconnection of outer appearances with one another, and with regard to others the agreement in the relations of the outer appearances of that through which others designate their intuition with the designations of

---

[a] *Das sollen*

my understanding, consequently the agreement of all outer appearances with each other. The reality of bodies is not the reality of things, but of appearances, which are related to *x*, *y*, etc. Something that is represented only as an object of appearance and yet is supposed to be no such thing is nothing for us. Idealism denies more than one knows; realism assumes more than what is at issue.

5493. 1776–78. M 331, in *Existentia Dei.*[117]   18: 198
The proposition of the ancients that nothing comes from nothing or that possibility always presupposes something actual is related to the fact that our understanding can only order *data* but not produce them, rather it must always have them at hand; hence all possibility is conditional.

5500. 1776–78. M 331.[118]   18: 199
*Absolute necessity is not internal (whatever concept of a thing I may assume, its opposite is still internally possible). It is not externally possible   18: 200
except as the *hypothesis* of all existence, consequently as the *hypothesis* of all possibility. Now the *substratum* of all possibility *a priori* is the highest reality. Hence the opposite of that is not among the possibilities. For all negations are limitations; consequently for all possibility something unrestricted is presupposed. This is the ground in all respects, hence it is absolutely necessary: positive concept of necessity. *Cartesii* proof.[119] Wolff.[120]
*(The necessity of space and time cannot be proven, but only as a necessary condition of the possibility of things with regard to their form, hence also of the *entis realissimi* as a condition of its possibility with regard to matter; nevertheless both grounds are merely subjective.)

5501. 1776–78. M 331.   18: 200
Proof from thinking in general, and not from the determinate concept of a thing.
The proof of a being that comprehends everything cannot be cognized *a posteriori* nor can it be cognized *a priori* except through the conditions of our reason for determining the object of cognition in totality.[121]
The concept of absolute necessity also cannot be otherwise acquired. It rests on the fact that everything that should be thought is to be given in experience and that *negationes* are limits.

5505. 1776–78. M 332, §812, still in *Existentia Dei.*   18: 202
That which is perfect precedes in the idea *a priori* that which is imperfect, and the latter is only determinable in the former. (–thoroughgoing determination.)
We would not have a concept of the imperfect if we did not conceive of that which is perfect.[122]

The cosmological proof starts from the existence of the contingent, especially of the *primo motore.*[a] The causality of the cause of the contingent is freedom. But we can have no insight into the absolute necessity of such a being, i.e., necessity in all regards.

Physicotheological proof: Primordial author by analogy.

Moral necessity of assuming a good. Possibility is already enough – atheism.

18:202 **5506.** 1776–78? (1771? 1772–73) *M* 333.

The Cartesian proof[123] is this, that a concept can be so arranged that reality is included among its predicates, although by itself the concept of the thing does not distinguish between its existence or non-existence, and thus that the non-existence contradicts itself. But the cancellation of a thing together with all of its predicates is always possible; consequently this demonstrates the falsity of the presupposition that it is possible to form any concept that cannot be cancelled at all.

18:202 **5507.** 1776–78? (1771? 1772–73?) *M* 333, at §815.

It all comes down to the erroneous concept of **taking existence away from a thing**; it should instead say: taking the thing itself away. Existence does not constitute a *constitutivum* of a concept; no concept contains it
18:203 internally, and thus absolute necessity is not anything internal, but only something relative, but in all relation, namely the universal *substrati* for everything possible.

18:203 **5508.** 1776–78? (1771? 1772–73?) *M* 333.

Even if the existence of God does not follow from the conditions on which we ground the concept of possibility, it nevertheless follows sufficiently from the concession that we can judge *a priori* about this. The subjective conditions of thinking therefore serve very well for convincing *cat anthropon,*[b] but not apodictically.[124]

18:205 **5518.** 1776–78. *M* 336, at §824, still in *Existentia Dei.*

All possibilities presuppose the concept of an *entis realissimi*, and this concept presupposes an existence, because realities that are not given in sensation also cannot be thought, but that which is given in sensation exists.

---

[a] first mover; Kant must mean that the inference from motion to a first mover is an instance of the cosmological argument from contingent motion to necessary motion.

[b] Here Kant writes this Greek expression, meaning "*ad hominem*," in Latin letters.

Absolute necessity rests on the presupposed condition of all possibility, not on the identity of a concept with itself, from which existence does not follow.

5522. 1776–79? 1790s? *M* 336.   18:206

The ground of the transcendental proof lies in this. We can think [*crossed out*: non-first] possibilities only *derivative*, not *originarie*; consequently the totality that is given to us is the *substratum* of possibility, on which, through limitations and altered relations, all our thought rests *a priori*. The subjective ground of all possibility is thus this sum total (subjectively) of reality, which constitutes a unity in us; for in this way alone can the thoroughgoing relation and agreement that is the form of possibility be understood.   18:207

5523. 1776–79. *M* 337, opposite §825.   18:207

Nothing at all is necessary in itself, i.e., in accordance with the laws of our understanding; for there is nothing contradictory in the non-existence of a thing. From the fact that something is not cognized as necessary in itself, however, I cannot infer that it is contingent, i.e., that it could exist or not exist, i.e., that its non-existence is possible as something that follows its existence or its existence as something that follows its non-existence. Although the existence of all things in itself could be cancelled out, that is, the thought of them, the thing is not on that account to be cancelled out. Thus the proof of that which is necessary because if something exists it must be necessary or contingent is not valid. Its existence has no connection at all with the thought of the thing.

5526. 1776–78? (1772? 1775–76?) *M* 337, at §825.   18:208

The first subjective condition of thinking, i.e., of the representation of the possibility of objects, is that all matter of representation be given in sensation and objectively in perception, second, the form of the combination of the manifold. Hence that which contains the matter and the *data* of everything possible is presupposed as an object of perception, i.e., the matter of everything possible exists as a necessary presupposition. The manifold of objects with regard to this totality of reality rests on the form of the restriction of this totality. Hence the basis is the absolute unity of the totality in which everything is possible through restriction. Something must therefore exist as a *substratum* of possibility.

5527. 1776–78? (1772? 1775–76?) *M* 337, at §826.   18:208

An *ens necessarium* is a subjectively necessary *hypothesis* for thinking of any possibility. All possibility of a restricted thing is derived from the idea and presupposes something greater that is restricted. All possibility thus has the *ens realissimum* for its condition.

5528. 1776–78? (1772? 1772–75?) *M* 337, at §826.

Transcendental theology has the advantage that in it alone can the necessity of a highest being be cognized. Hence it alone can thoroughly determine it as unity, etc.

It alone purifies *theologia naturalis* from all influence of empirical predicates, or anthropomorphism. The disadvantage is that the basis of proof is only subjective: for existence cannot be cognized fully *a priori*. But as a presupposition it can still be necessary in the practical use of the understanding.

5543. 1776–78. *M* 379, at §926, in *Creatio mundi*.

Every series has its beginning; but that the entire series has a beginning presupposes that it can be considered in its entirety.

5544. 1776–78. *M* 379, at §926.

A first beginning cannot be thought in accordance with the laws of sensibility. A succession without a first beginning cannot be thought in accordance with laws of reason.[125]

Conceptus hybridus, which constitutes the boundary concept.

5545. 1776–78. *M* 379, at §826.

We must philosophize about nature as if the world has no beginning, and about God as if it has no succession.

To regard God as the highest point of the series is a confusion of kinds.

5548. 1776–78. *M* 379, at §926.

Bounding the world at an empty time and an empty space is impossible. Beyond the world there is no possible appearance. But now the world along with all of its predicates is only the object of appearance.

5552. 1778–79? (1780–83?) *LBl* Duisburg 9.[126]
P. I.

Concepts of Reflexion (their Amphiboly)
[*crossed out*: which lead to paralogisms]

A paralogism is a syllogistic inference[a] that is false as far as its form is concerned, although as far as its matter (the major premise) is concerned it is correct.[127] – It arises when the middle concept[128] is taken in different senses in the two premises – when, namely, the *logical* relation

---

[a] *Vernunftschluß*

(in thinking) in one of the premises is taken as a real one (of the objects of intuition) in the other.[129]

1. Sameness and difference. 2. Consensus and conflict. 3. The inner and the outer. 4. The determinable (matter) and determination (form).[130]

Different relation to the cognitive faculty: to sensibility or to the understanding for difference of things and sameness for the former, likewise for the latter are . . . [*breaks off*]

1. As far as quality and quantity are concerned, identical things are not different (many) things, but are one and the same.   18:219

   For the understanding, to be sure, two drops of water or one egg is the same as another, but not in the intuition in space as *phaenomena*.[131]

2. What is not logically opposed is also not (really) opposed in space and time *a−a*.

3. Outer things (substances) must have inner determinations, but the determinations of matter consist in purely outer relations; hence I cannot make an inference to monads, which have representations, because these are the only thing that is inner.[132]

4. The matter (the constituents of a thing) precede the form – but in intuition the form, which is given by itself alone, precedes the matter.

Something and nothing[133]

1.

Concept without object;
this is nothing. *ens rationis.*
Thought-entity.

2.	3.
Empty object of a concept. *nihil privativum.* Shadows.	Empty intuition without object. *ens imaginarium.* Space.

4.

Empty concept without object.
nihil negativum.

No. 1 and no. 2	The synthetic *a priori* propositions are
A thought-entity is distinguished from a non-entity. axiom, anticipation, analogy, postulate	principles of possible experience, thus they pertain only to objects of the senses. Inference of ontology.

The understanding prescribes the law to nature, but one that does not reach farther than the form of appearances, which grounds the possibility of experience in general. For this must be in conformity with nature as   18:220

object of empirical cognition, for otherwise it would not be nature for us, since it would be impossible for us to find an interconnection in it which would be in conformity with our faculty for bringing the manifold of appearances into an interconnected consciousness, thus it would not be cognizable.

Empirical intuition and concepts constitute experience.

We can have synthetic cognition of objects of experience *a priori*, namely if they contain principles of the possibility of experience in general.

P. II.

That the possibility of synthetic judgment *a priori* depends on the ideality of space and time alone. That if we were to cognize the things in themselves, we would perceive them, thus not cognize them *a priori* as necessary. Because only from the fact that our faculty of intuition has this form can we know *a priori* how things must be intuited by us – these forms are that which is merely subjective in the faculty of representation – and with regard to things as appearances this is objective.

3.^a

That we must underlie all of our pure concepts of understanding with a schema, a [*crossed out*: relation] way of establishing composition in the manifold in space and time.[134] – That this schema is merely in the sensible representation of the subject, thus we 1. cognize only objects of the senses, consequently do not reach beyond them to the supersensible. (Geometry). 2. The concepts, however, can be extended to all objects of thinking in general. But they yield no amplification of theoretical

18: 221 cognition. In a practical respect, however, where freedom is the condition of their use, practical-dogmatic cognition can occur. – God, freedom, and immortality (spiritual nature).

In nature, however, i.e., in space and time, nothing unconditioned can be encountered, and yet reason demands that as the totality of conditions, since it will constitute the object itself.[135] – Hence in cosmology, where nature is considered as the whole of all objects of the senses, antinomies are encountered; – in theology, where we need to consider an object only in a practically dogmatic respect, the relation of a supersensible object lying beyond the world to the things of the world can only be cognized in accordance with the analogy with an intelligence in nature, and also only insofar as it is thought in a moral relationship to human beings.

The unconditioned contains the intellectual (intelligible) (*noumenon*) in three ways, and one can have cognition of freedom and its laws and thereby prove the objective reality of humanity as *noumenon* in the midst of its mechanism as *phaenomenon*. – God as unconditionally

---

^a Kant did not number any of the previous sections of this note.

necessary substance. Freedom as unconditioned causality and immortality as personality (spirit) independent from *commercio* with the body (as
condition).

The categories applied to the intelligible can still ground practically-
dogmatic cognitions, namely if they are directed to freedom and determine the subject thereof only in relation to that; for then we cognize
God only in accordance with the analogy of the subsistence of a thing
through all change of its accidents in time (duration), freedom in accordance with the analogy of causality in the connection of power with its
effects in the temporal series, immortality in accordance with the analogy of the connection of many things at all times, hence the simultaneity
of . . . [*breaks off*]

5553. 1778–79? (1780–83?) *LBl* Reicke Xb 1.   18: 221
P. I.

Just as the senses are related to the understanding, so is the understanding related to reason.[136] The appearances of the first acquire the   18: 222
unity of understanding in the second through concepts, and concepts
aquire the unity of reason in the third faculty through ideas (through
prosyllogisms a higher subject is always found, of which the previous
would be a predicate, until finally a further one cannot be found; likewise
in the case of conditioned inferences, where, however, the prosyllogism
proves the *minorem*).[a]

The *a priori* cognitions that apply to the objects themselves are ex-
hausted in the transcendental analytic and are the categories of the understanding. Thus reason cannot apply to the objects (appearances) themselves, but to the concepts of the understanding of them. And how should
a concept of reason (insofar as there is anything of the sort) be objective, since it does not express the [*crossed out*: condition] unity of possible
experience (as that through which all objects are given to us), but that
of the cognition of the understanding[?] Yet cognitions of reason, which
contain unity that is fully *a priori* and not empirical, must be borrowed
from the logical form of reason, except that they would have to concern a synthetic unity to which the concepts of the understanding are
subjected, and thereby lead mediately to a particular determination of
the unity of appearances. Since reason seeks to bring the cognitions of
the understanding (judgments) under higher (more general) conditions,
as long as such a cognition can still be regarded as conditioned: so one
can say that it is a principle of the use of the understanding for finding the unconditioned [*crossed out*: in the series of the] for that which is
conditioned. [*Crossed out*: Now this unconditioned (which contains the
rule) in all relational concepts of the understanding, for] The concepts

---

[a] minor premise

of relation, however, are nothing other than the unity of the conditioned and its condition, and reason ascends through this relation only to the condition that is itself unconditioned. – Thus all cognitions of reason will be parallel to the three kinds of inferences of reason, and more than those three will not be possible.[137] The principle of pure reason that all conditioned cognition stands not merely under conditions, but finally under one that is itself unconditioned, may be a mere petition or a postulate (we will not yet decide which): yet it is still at least the ground of all application of reason, to which we at least approximate. Every inference of reason is nothing other than [*crossed out*: the cognition] a judgment by means of the subsumption of its condition under a general rule, which is thus the condition of the condition of the conclusion of the inference. The conditioned inference of reason is improperly so called, for there are more conditions of the judgment than merely the ground with respect to the consequence (*conditio consequentiae*). There is also a condition of inherence, etc.

18: 223

The proposition that if the conditioned is given, the whole series of all conditions through which the conditioned is determined is also given is, if I abstract from the objects or take it merely intellectually, correct.

The unconditioned can never be given, but must always exist in thought. Hence ideas. The absolute totality of the conditions is the only unconditioned. Unity of principle for reason. Approximation. Rules of the synthesis of the subordination of empirical concepts.
P. II.

System of transcendental ideas. 1. There are 3 titles in accordance with the three kinds of inferences of reason; there are 4 dialectical inferences in accordance with the 4 categories.[138] In the ideal of pure reason, since there all categories are together in one idea, we do not need to distinguish them; for it is the principle of all possibility, through which the categories themselves are then determined.[139]

On the three sorts of transcendental illusion. There are two ideas and one ideal.* The paralogism of pure reason is properly a transcendental subreption, where our judgment about objects and the unity of consciousness in them is held to be a perception of the unity of the subject.[140]

18: 224

*(The first illusion is that where the unity of apperception, which is subjective, is taken for the unity of the subject as a thing. The second: where the subjective determination of sensibility and its condition is taken for an object. The third: where the universality of thinking through reason is taken for a thought of a totality of the possibilities of things.)[141]

There is no deduction of transcendental ideas except a negative one.

For the conclusion of the dialectic: that all dialectical questions are fully answered.

All concepts of synthesis require a third thing: either possible experience or the idea. With regard to transcendental ideas they cannot have objective validity, but are still deduced as necessary problems or questions.

In the understanding concepts are guided in accordance with possible experience, for reason, however, possible experience is guided by the concepts, just as the exercise of all virtue must be directed by concepts and is possible only through them, even though it never reaches the concept. Possible experience in *regressus* to the conditions is guided by the concepts of reason or transcendental ideas. In that consists the business of reason, namely creating unconditioned unity for the use of reason in the greatest manifold. That concept of reason which combines the greatest particular unity with this universal agrees with possible experience and is to that extent a correct rule. But the concept that does not consist in the relation to possible experience cannot be objectively valid.

The ideal must be completely determined, for the idea is the standard.   18:225
It is the unmutilated existence of a thing in which all possibilities lie as the members of a disjunction.

All three transcendental ideas are connected by an inference of reason. Namely: All objects of the senses are in the end grounded on an existing noumenon.

Reason serves to give necessity to the understanding and scope and unity to the sphere of its use.

The way to regard the particular as a determination of the universal (the truly universal, which is not drawn from the particular as an induction) is an *a priori* unity, which is completely different from the unity of experience.
P. III.

(Lucian's Writings. Part One. Zurich: Geßner, 1769).[142]

The system of dialectical inferences of reason rests on their unity with one another in one inference of reason, in which [there is] 1. subjective unity of all representations, i.e., unity of the subject, second [*crossed out*: collective] synthetic unity of the object or of appearance, [*crossed out*: third] this either of appearances: collectively, or of the thoughts of objects in general: distributively (disjunctively).

Reason first cognizes the universal *in abstracto*, for it seeks to find the universal for the particular, in order in turn to infer from this to the particular.

First section: on the ideas in general.

1. Note. In inferences of reason, if the *major* is a [*crossed out*: concept] proposition of experience (All humans are mortal), it is still a general concept. But since it is only from induction, it is not a cognition from concepts. Yet such a thing is in the end required of reason in order for true universality to arise; for only from this will reason hold something   18:226
to be determined in itself and necessarily.

2. The analytical inferences are certainly from concepts; but the *major* is a universal identical judgment, which does not express a unity of different things, but of unanimous and identical things.

The unconditioned subjective conditions of thinking.

The unconditioned objective condition of appearances.

The unconditioned objective condition of all objects in general.[143]

By an idea I understand a concept that is adequately grounded in reason but for which no object can be given in any possible experience.[144]

To what does the idea apply, then, and why is it grounded in reason in order to be related to objects[?] The idea of the soul is grounded in the fact that the understanding must relate all thoughts and inner perceptions to the self and assume this as the only constant subject, so that complete unity of self-cognition may thereby arise.

The idea of the unconditioned for all conditions of appearance is grounded in reason as a precept to seek the completeness of all cognition of the understanding in subordination.

The idea of the unconditioned unity of all objects of thought in an *ens entium*[a] is necessary in order to seek for the affinity among everything possible and thereby also thoroughgoing connection as unity of principle.

In right only concepts of reason are necessary, but in morality ideas are necessary. An object that is congruent to the former can be given in experience, but not one that is congruent to the latter, since the highest unity of reason contains freedom that is consistent with itself and with all the ends of its determination.

Legislation needs ideas, and these can never be fully realized. But they are not on that account nugatory and superfluous.

18:227 Transcendental philosophy needs ideas just as much as morality does.

Plato's hyperbolic elevation of ideas as archetypes that are in the highest intelligence when it is personified is not to be blamed; they are the standard for things which restrict one another and do not fulfill their end individually, so no experience is congruent with them.[145]

P. IV.

Whether the inference from the human soul through the concept of the world to God and from this back pertains to the intelligible life of the soul?

But whence comes the dialectical illusion in the case of the transcendental ideas[?] [From] that which makes for all illusion: namely the confusion of subjective conditions of our thinking with objective ones. We cannot avoid these, since we unconditionally must think an object and have no other way for thinking of it except that which the particular constitution of our subject brings with it. But we can develop the

---

[a] entity of entities

sophistical inference either *in forma* or *in minore* or *maiore*, since the synthesis goes further than the *data* and the manner of inference allow. The *suppositio* of pure reason obtains when one presupposes what one is supposed to prove and proves it through its consequences. Namely, that which is completely determined *a priori* is presupposed, in order to represent through it the complete determination of everything possible.

If I assume that I am no appearance of inner sense, but something in itself and a *noumenon*, then my inhering *accidentia* must also be *noumena. Atqui:*[a] I represent the series of conditions to myself in appearance; *therefore* they must be given to me in themselves. This conclusion, made into the *minore* in the episyllogism, is: If all appearances are given in one thing in itself, then the idea which determines the things in themselves is given in some intelligence.

One says that something is a mere idea if one cannot even approximate   18: 228
to it.

1. The unconditioned of inherence (or of the aggregate). 2. That of [*crossed out*: consequence] dependence or of the series. 3. That of the concurrence of all possibility in one and of one for all.

Just as the inferences of reason determine a judgment in general through subsumption, so reason determines the objects in the totality of conditions.

In transcendental psychology the sameness, simplicity, and modality of passive existence flow from the one concept of substance.

The absolute is the same as the unconditioned, the latter as that which is complete, which is thought negatively without a restricting condition.

We can think the universal only by means of abstraction from all restricting conditions. Abstraction from the determinations of the self makes the I seem unconditioned.

How can morality rest on ideas, since one still demands that actions should be in accordance with them[?] One can only call them concepts of reason. In their complete purity they are ideas. Rectitude.

We can call reason the faculty of ideas.* There are ideas of sensibility, also those of pure reason. These are either practical or speculative; the latter are transcendental ideas. These are necessary concepts of reason, for which no object can be given in the senses. As pure concepts, however, they must still be derived from the categories; but as concepts of reason they must merely be inferred; as necessary concepts of reason they must contain the necessary conditions of the entire use of understanding, i.e., of its use in its totality, and as transcendental concepts this totality must reach so far that it transcends all sensible intuition; for otherwise they would be immanent. For this the absolute is required, etc. How does the transcendental inference of reason go?

[a] but now; hence

18:229 *(Reason is a faculty for determining the condition of a whole domain. If I say: Caius is mortal, I first consider immortality in the whole
domain of the concept under which Caius is contained, i.e., human beings, and I subsume him under this domain in order to determine him
therein.

1. The unconditioned unity of the synthesis of the subject. 2. The
unconditioned unity of the synthesis of the conditions in appearance.
3. The unconditioned unity of the synthesis of thinking in general. All
through four categories, insofar as they indicate unconditioned unity.[146]

The transcendental idea can have nothing for its object except the
cognitive powers or representations in general in relation to it. Thus 1.
apperception, second, the apprehension of appearance, 3. the concept of
understanding in general. The first is the rational concept of the subject,
the second of the object insofar as it can be given, the third of the object
of thinking in general.

That pure reason has no objective content for its dialectical
inferences.)

18:229 **5554.** 1778–83. *LBl C* 11.
P. I.

Reflecting concepts[147] can be taken logically, hence merely [*crossed
out*: intellectually] analytically, or transcendentally, hence synthetically.
Determined analytically, sameness and difference are analytic, but determined sensibly they are synthetic, and difference in place, regardless
of the identity of the things in themselves, by itself constitutes numerical
difference. Logically, consensus and conflict depend on the principle of
contradiction; in their empirical use, on two realities that together yield
one reality or negation.[148] Logically, the inner and the outer are what
is the predicate of a thing itself or of another one; empirically, what is
in a different place in space. The determinable and the determined: the
substantial and substance.

Hence the most famous proposition of subreption is the *principium
indiscernibilium*.[149]

18:230 Our three higher powers aim at unity, truth, and perfection through
the understanding, the power of judgment, and reason. The last of these,
in a transcendental sense, produces all sorts of confusion.

One can regard the whole monadology as Leibniz's *systema* from the
concepts of reflection. The inner and outer taken intellectually yields
the *monas*, since *compositum* is a *totum relationum*[a] and *representativa* because the *representationes* are internal, place and extension are external.[150]
Space is nothing but the *phaenomenon* of the outer. But then what do
the monads represent if they merely represent each other, thus each

---

[a] totality of relations

represents the representations of the others? (One also cannot derive, with Maupertuis,[151] what is outer in motion from what is inner.) Leibniz. *harmonia praestabilita*. Since the monads do not stand *in commercio* in virtue of their coexistence in space.

P. II.

"Noumenon" properly always means the same thing, namely the transcendental object of sensible intuition (This is, however, no real object or given thing, but a concept, in relation to which appearances have unity.), for this must still correspond to something, even though we are acquainted with nothing other than its appearance. We cannot, however, say that the pure categories have objects; rather they merely determine the transcendental object[152] in relation to our sensibility through the synthesis of the manifold of intuition. Thus no *noumenon* corresponds to them.

The transcendental object that corresponds to the appearances (or also every object) can only be called *noumenon* insofar as it can be represented through the concept of the understanding. Now this is not possible through the category, since the conditions of intuition are lacking, 18:231 thus we have no concepts of *Noumena*.[153]

We can [*crossed out*: think] use these concepts in accordance with an analogy with sensible ones; however, since they have objective validity only in relation to the synthetic unity of apprehension in time, by themselves they are not related to any object at all, and under sensible determination they are related only to *phaenomena*.

5555. 1778–1780s? Kant's note on the reverse of the undated letter from 18:231 Karl George Gottfried Glave (1779?), 10:260.

Just as a pure concept of the understanding arises only from the form of judgments insofar as I make them synthetic (and thereby think an object), so a pure concept of reason arises from the form of an inference of reason. But this is subsumption under the universality of the condition of a judgment; thus the concept is a representation of the totality of the conditions for cognizing an object in accordance with one or another relation. The logical condition of the judgment is the relation to the subject, etc.; the concept of a thing through this logical function is the category. The [*crossed out*: totality] universality of the relation is the logical form of the inference of reason; the concept of a thing through the representation of the totality of the condition of the application of the categories is the concept of reason.

The concept of the totality of synthesis in accordance with the categories of relation is the pure concept of reason.

Without the concept of reason we would, to be sure, have experiences, but the collective unity of experience would be lacking, as that in which all empirical cognition must nevertheless be determinable.

The totality of synthesis in one subject, 2. in one series, third, in one system. *Suppositum* is the presupposition of that which is to be found and 18:232   its conditions in order to find the synthesis of the cognitions through which we can approach it. An idea is such a *suppositum*, which to be sure cannot be given in itself, but which can still introduce formal unity of reason into our cognition.[154]

18:232   **5556.** 1778–83. *M* 15, at §55, in *Ens.*[155]

Analytical possibility rests on the principle of contradiction, and is the possibility of the concept; synthetic possibility, which must be added to this, i.e., it must be added that an object corresponds to the concept, rests on the fact that something is in conformity with the conditions of an object of experience in general. Only in experience can an object be given.

The actual is opposed to the impossible and also to the merely possible.

18:235   **5569.** 1778–83. *M* 28, §101ff., in *Necessarium et contingens.*

Necessity is either logical or real, analytic and synthetic. Synthetic necessity either from concepts or intuitions or the relation of concepts 18:236   to intuitions in general. Necessary existence is either derived or original. *Necessitas originaria vel derivativa.* Necessity as a condition is properly hypothetical, but not conditioned; it is necessity as a presupposition.

The necessity of a thing in itself is that of existence, not that of the relation of a predicate to the subject or of the conditioned to the condition. Existence does not necessarily pertain to a thing that is necessary in itself. For in that case it lies in the concept; rather it is the condition for positing a thing in general.

18:236   **5570.** 1778–83? 1785–88? 1776–78? *M* 29, at §102.[156]

Hypothetical necessity is to be distinguished from the necessity of an hypothesis, which is opposed to the postulated necessity that is there absolute. The former is necessity as a premise, the latter as a principle of cognition. The absolute necessity of a thing is a necessary hypothesis of reason.

Logical necessity: that whose opposite is logically impossible from concepts, i.e., that which contradicts itself. Real necessity: that whose opposite is a non-entity, i.e., whose non-existence cannot subsist together with a concept. The former is the necessity of judgments, the latter of things.

18:237   **5573.** 1778–1780s? (1776–78?) *M* 34, opposite §§117–19, still in *Necessarium et contingens.*

Our concept of possibility is properly derivative; namely, it presupposes something given, which agrees in form with the conditions of understanding. Only a single thing is *originarie* possible, namely the *ens realissimum*, and this is presupposed.

5576. 1778–1780s. *M* 37, at §131, in *Mutabile et immutabile.*[157]   18:238
How is alteration possible in general[?] That cannot be explained, because it is determination **in time** and presupposes forces, but these are *a posteriori*.

[*Crossed out*: All] **Alteration is not a coming-to-be or ceasing-to-be of things** but rather of their **determinations**, while the **thing remains**. E.g., motion is the alteration of the relation of the body, not of the body itself. Inner motion is alteration of the body.

5583. 1778–1780s. *M* 48, in §§165–90, *Prima matheseos intensorum*   18:240
principia.
Mathematics as synthetic *a priori* cognition bases its possibility on the fact that its concepts can be constructed; for they have to do only with space and time, in which objects of intuition can be given *a priori*. These, however, are *quanta*, thus mathematics is a science of *quantis*. But it also considers quantity by means of number, by means of groups[a] which can be constructed in time by counting. Yet this science cannot extend further than the sensible world, for only of this can intuition be given *a priori*.

5585. 1778–1780s. *M* 48.   18:241
Principium of the possibility of mathematics as a synthetic *a priori* cognition. It is synthesis in *a priori* intuition, i.e., space and time. Pure mathematics.
Principium of the mathematical cognition of appearances: All appearance has as intuition its extensive magnitude and as sensation its degree. For (as far as the latter is concerned) every sensation arises from nonbeing, since it is a modification. Thus through alteration. All alteration, however, proceeds from o to *a* through infinitely many small steps.[158]

5589. 1778–1783. *M* 51, still in *Prima matheseos intensorum principia*.   18:241
1. Possibility of pure mathematics.
2. Possibility of applied mathematics. For all things as appearances have a magnitude: extensive and intensive. Through this mathematics acquires objective reality. It does not pertain to *entia rationis*.
3. All things as objects of pure understanding also have a magnitude,   18:242
namely a metaphysical one, but no transcendental magnitude, since there they are compared as things in general with all other things, but here as a concept of the thing with the essence of the thing itself.

---

[a] *Menge*

The possibility of natural science rests on the dynamical principles, which concern the existence of things in combination. The former[a] concern only the empirical intuition and the possibility of empirical concepts of the objects, but not insofar as they belong to a nature.[159]

18:243 **5593.** 1778–1780s. *M* 92, at §307, in *Causa et causatum.*

Mathematics has the peculiarity that it applies only to those objects that can be represented *coram intuitu,*[b] and therefore always has empirical confirmation.

It is possible as synthetic *a priori* cognition because there are two *a priori intuitus,* space and time, in which an *a priori* synthesis of composition is possible. These two objects are *quanta* and indeed *originaria,* and the mere synthesis of them is quantity. All concepts of *quantis* can be constructed in them, i.e., given *a priori* in intuition, likewise all concepts of quantity, i.e., number, which requires time as well as space. The universal is here [*crossed out:* considered] given in the *singulari* in intuition, and in the *singulari* the universal of *synthesis* is considered. In the cases of qualities this is not so. No mathematics can arise through discursive cognitions. Mathematical cognitions as rational cognitions *a priori* are apodictic and as *intuitus* demonstrative, and as both together self-evident.

Mathematics is not distinguished from philosophy by means of the object, but rather through the *modum cognoscendi.* This however deter-
18:244 mines the distinction of the objects. (dynamic principle)

(*Later addition:* Philosophy deals with magnitudes as far as one can get with mere concepts, and mathematics with qualities as far as one can get with mere intuition. E.g., the former with the question of simple parts, the latter with the cause of the gravitation of the moon.)[160]

18:245 **5596.** 1778–79? (1780–83?) *M* 110, §§351–2, *Cosmologia, Prolegomena.*

Principles of the understanding are principles of the exposition of experience.[161] Principles of reason are those in accordance with which experience itself is given *a priori* (through the understanding) (freedom and necessary being). Sophistical principles: where the subjective conditions of reason are held to be objective. Principles of reason are transcendental maxims of speculation. Sophistical principles are transcendental paralogisms.

Transcendental ideas of the *a priori* self-determining reason.

The sophistical *principium* of reason is: what does not stand entirely under the conditions of empirical **determination** is false. Thus all synthesis of magnitudes that is without end is impossible; all dynamical

---

[a] That is, mathematics, presumably including applied mathematics.
[b] in the presence of intuition

synthesis that is not mediately determined (freedom and necessity) is impossible. Yet by contrast there also cannot be any insight into the possibility of ideas of reason.

5599. 1778–1780s? 1776–78?? *M* 110. 18:246
The principles of the possibility of experience are independent of experience. The connection of the *a priori* (necessary) principles with experience is either that they depend on experiences, or that experiences depend on them.

5600. 1778–1780s? 1776–78?? *M* 110, at §350, on the conclusion of the 18:246
Prolegomena to *Ontologia?*
We call nature the object of possible experience. Thus all of our *a* 18:247
priori cognition pertains only to nature.
Principles of understanding are *a priori* rules that contain the conditions of the synthetic unity of possible experience.

5602. 1778–1780s. *M* 110. 18:247
The use of the concepts of the understanding was immanent, that of the ideas as concepts of objects is transcendent; but as regulative principles of the completion and thereby at the same time of the determination of the limits of our cognition they are critically immanent.

5603. 1778–1780s. *M* 110. 18:247
We have spoken in ontology of concepts of the understanding the use of which in experience is possible because they themselves make experience possible.

5607. 1778–1780s. *M* 140, at §430ff., in *Natura corporum.*[162] 18:248
All possible objects of experience have their nature, partly their particular nature, partly that which they have in common with other things. Nature taken substantively means the sum-total of all objects of experience. Nature rests on forces (fundamental forces) and is in general the lawfulness of appearances.

Nature is opposed to: chance
freedom
fate

Things are not in themselves appearances, but are appearances only because there are beings that have senses; in the same way they belong to a nature because we have understanding. For the word "nature" signifies 18:249
nothing in things in themselves, but only the ordering of the appearances of them by means of the unity of the concepts of the understanding or the unity of consciousness, in which they can be connected.

We do not have understanding because there is a nature; for we could never know its rules (laws) from experience; their necessity consists precisely in their being cognized *a priori*.

For just this reason we can have *a priori* cognitions both of appearances and of the nature in which they are connected, since the form of our sensibility is the principle of possibility at the basis of the former and the form of our understanding that at the basis of the latter.

To say "We can determine the constitution of things *a priori*" and yet at the same time "These things have such a constitution independently of our capacity to determine them" is a contradiction; for whence would we derive our cognition in that case?

18:249 **5608.** 1778–1780s. *M* 141, still in *Natura corporum*.

Things are represented as appearances because there are beings who have senses. But these same beings also have understanding, under whose laws appearances stand insofar as their possible consciousness must necessarily agree with a universally valid consciousness, i.e., they have a nature.

Appearances stand to one another in the relation of the manifold in a pure sensible intuition, and their consciousness stands in relation to a common apperception, both *a priori* and necessarily.

1. Nature taken generally and *formaliter*.

Nature of a thing; corporeal and thinking nature.

2. *Materialiter*: as the sum-total of appearances in contrast to the intelligible world.

Nature is opposed to blind chance (accident) and to blind necessity (fate).

18:250 To the latter, if I do not assume an extramundane cause, belong miracles.

(*non datur abyssus, saltus, casus, hiatus.*)[a, 163]

Natural necessity opposed to the supernatural.

Nature is not opposed to freedom but distinguished from it.

Freedom is the independence of causality from the conditions of space and time, thus [*crossed out*: from] the causality of the thing as thing in itself. Natural mechanism and freedom do not conflict with each other since causality is not taken in a single sense.

Casus is absolute contingency. *Fatum* is unconditional necessity in the world.

All laws cognized through experience belong to heteronomy, those, however, through which experience in general is possible belong to autonomy.

---

[a] There is [in nature] no chasm, no leap, no accident, no gap.

The infinitude or finitude of composition or decomposition must in both cases be assumed in the sensible world. Nevertheless these ideas of absolute totality belong to the concept of things in themselves; thus they are both false. By contrast, the concept of natural necessity belongs to the sensible world and that of freedom to the intelligible world, and the idea of totality belongs to the things themselves, which the idea of freedom would contradict if it were ascribed to the sensible world; however, since it belongs to the intelligible world, both can be true.

The causality of a being for thinking of itself, with regard to appearances, as independent from determining grounds of the sensible world is no contradiction, if the being is given only under the concept of thing in itself. Now a rational being as intelligence is given as such; hence freedom can be thought in it. In contrast, no causality of the intelligible in bodies can be thought, because their appearances betray no intelligence; thus also no freedom can be thought in their *substrato intelligibili*, and we   18: 251 do not cognize it by means of any predicate.

We need freedom only for the objectively practical from *a priori* grounds.

The capacity to commence an occurrence absolutely (without the causality itself beginning).

In bodies we indeed have a representation of the intelligible, but we do not know it as a cause. In intelligences that which is intelligible with regard to causality is presupposed; the question here is how something can be a cause.

Antinomy.

5610. 1778–79. M 144, at §440, in *Mundus optimus.*[164]   18: 251

In mundo non datur abyssus,[a] i.e., there is nothing unconditional in the sensible world, because this belongs to the intelligible world; the senses, however, if they assume space and time to be determinations of things, here [extend] into the infinitely empty or full.

In mundo non datur saltus,[b] i.e., all appearances are generated through all degrees of things from 0 to something.

If space and time were conditions of the existence of things in themselves, then in the mathematical antinomies one could not say that both opposites are false, for one would have to be true, nor could one say in the dynamical antinomies that both sides can be true, for one would have to be false. Contradiction is encountered only because as things in themselves space and time would have to contain something unconditioned.

---

[a] There is no chasm in the world.
[b] There are no leaps in nature.

18:252 **5611.** 1778–79? (1776–78?) (1775–77?) *M* 252, at §§700–7, *Spontaneitas.*[165]

Reason is not in the chain of appearances and is with regard to all of that free with regard to its own causality (the actions of reason themselves are also not appearances, only their effects are). If everything were determined by reason, then everything would be necessary but also good. If it were determined by sensibility, then there would be neither evil nor good, in general nothing practical at all. Now the actions are in great part occasioned but not entirely determined by sensibility; for reason must provide a complement of adequacy.[a] Reason gradually draws sensibility into *habitus*, arouses incentives, and hence forms a character, which however is itself to be attributed to freedom and is not sufficiently grounded in the appearances.[166] For that reason all actions cohere with laws of sensibility, but not without the forbearance of the understanding, the opposite of which is always possible in accordance with all grounds of sensibility. Now if one asks whether the understanding itself is not determined in itself as well as with regard to all that it does or forbears, then we must say that no single possible experience can prove this because that would always only be appearance. The understanding itself is not an object of sensible intuition. But determinability through other causes does not hold beyond experience, since beyond this boundary the understanding can only be represented as a cause (the supreme understanding) and the concept of cause serves only as a *principio* of the synthesis of appearances, but not of actions of the understanding.

18:252 **5612.** 1778–79? (1790s?) (1776–78?) *M* 277, at §§708–18, *Arbitrium.*

18:253 We explain free actions that have been committed in accordance with the laws of the nature of the human being, but we do not thereby cognize them as determined; otherwise we would not regard them as contingent and demand that they could and must have happened otherwise. In free actions reason has influence not merely as a comprehending but also as an effecting and driving *principium*. We have no insight into how it does not merely ratiocinate and judge, but fills the place of a natural cause, let alone how it is itself determined to action or omission by means of impulses. How the representation of the good in general, which abstracts from my condition, which yet has an effect on my condition, and how this consideration, which itself contains no affection, can be contained in the series of natural appearance. For the good is a relation of pure reason to an object. We must therefore regard future actions as undetermined through everything that belongs to the *phaenomenis*. Reason makes use of the natural constitution as incentives (honor, peace of mind) in accordance with its laws, but is not thereby determined.

---

[a] *Zulänglichkeit*; one might have expected *Zuläßigkeit*, i.e., "permissibility," here.

The solution is this. The interconnection of reason with the *phaenome-nis* with which it is to stand in *commercio* cannot be understood at all (they are *heterogenea*). The true activity of reason and its effect belong to the *mundo intelligibili*. Hence we also do not know to what degree we should impute. Nevertheless we know that the influencing power of reason is not determined and necessitated by any *phaenomena*, rather that it is free, and (in the case of imputation) we judge the action merely in accordance with rational laws. The actions here in the world are mere *Schemata* of the intelligible [actions]; yet these appearances (this word already signi-fies "schema") are still interconnected in accordance with empirical laws, even if one regards reason itself, in accordance with its expressions, as a *phaenomenon* (of the character). But what the cause of this may be we do not discover *in phaenomenis*. Insofar as one cognizes one's own character only from the *phaenomenis*, one imputes it to oneself, although it is, to be sure, itself determined by external causes. If one knew it in itself, then all good and evil would not be ascribed to external causes but only to the subject alone, together with the good and the disadvantageous consequences. In the intelligible world nothing happens and nothing changes, and there the rule of causal connection disappears.

18:254

5613. 1778–79? (1776–78?) *M* 278, in *Arbitrium*.   18:254

As appearance, every action has its determining ground in another positive or negative action of mine, this in turn in another, and so on *ad infinitum*. There is therefore no complete ground at all among the appearances, thus always only a necessity conditioned under my own preference (to turn my attention toward or away from this or that). This condition, however, since it always remains and is the condition of my own self-activity, is never an externally conditioned necessity. The same action, however, is, as *noumenon* [*crossed out*: determined through my good or evil will], not under the rule of that which happens in me and which must be represented as in a connection determined through another determining ground, except in the case of a good will; in that case the objective necessity (which is a freedom from physical causes) is at the same time a subjective one. In the case of an evil will, by contrast, since it is still a will and not nature, all its actions are objectively impossible and subjectively contingent. For this contingency is the condition under which an objective law can be thought with respect to which an object can be represented as evil. An action that is evil in itself, that one should omit, is evil precisely because we act without an objectively sufficient ground; and the will is evil because it is not subjectively determined through this very rule.[167]

Freedom is the determinability of the power through mere reason. Reason, however, is not a cognition that contains the way in which one is affected by objects; consequently the use of reason itself is freedom.

18:255　**5616**. 1778–79? (1776–78?) *M* 278–9, still in *Arbitrium*.

Everything that happens is sufficiently determined, but not from appearances, rather in accordance with laws of appearance. For there is in freely acting beings a constant influence of intellectual grounds, since the opposite is possible as appearance. However, the action or its opposite is grounded among the appearances in such a way that only the moment of determination is intellectual. But this cannot be used in the empirical explanation, since it is not perceived. For between the intellectual to the determined action there is an infinite intermediate series of incentives, whose interconnection with the given condition can be cognized only in accordance with general laws of possibility. For example: someone charms me into drinking, this charm seduces me, and can therefore be explained in accordance with laws of the senses. The seduction would also be necessary if I were merely animal. Nevertheless it is possible that the intellectual power of choice, which enjoys an exception from dependency on the senses, intervenes; this determines only an alternative course of sensibility. This can also be [*crossed out*: explained and] connected with the first given condition in accordance with laws of reason, but only through an infinite intermediate series of appearances. Thus both vice as well as virtue take place in accordance with natural laws and must be explained in accordance with them. (Honor, health, reward.) Even the morally good actions from elevated incentives, education, and temperament. The explanation also has its ground; only the first direction of these causes, the moment of

18:256　determining them, [*crossed out*: is unknown and] will not to be encountered among the appearances, but also cannot be missed among them, since we cannot observe the appearances back to the moment of their commencement.

The law of cause and effect (*causalitatis*) rests on the condition of the possibility of a unity of experience. In the case of free beings, this unity cannot take place completely except if they are completely intellectual.

The higher power of choice is the capacity to make use of the incentives or sensible stimuli in accordance with their laws yet always in accord with the representation of the understanding (in relation to the ultimate and universal ends of sensibility). *A posteriori*, therefore, we will have cause *a posteriori* to find the ground of the action, **namely the ground of its explanation but not its determination**, in sensibility; but *a priori*, if the action is represented as future (*antecedenter*), we will feel ourselves as undetermined with respect to it and as capable of making a first beginning of the series of appearances. If there is free will, then the appearances of rational beings do not constitute a *continuum* except in the case of firm principles of the understanding. Thus those actions which are ruled partly by understanding but partly by sense cannot be explained in accordance with any rule of one or the other. Prior to the action, we place ourselves solely in the standpoint of the understanding. Now since the understanding is not actually affected, but it can affect the sensibility, one's action is not predetermined, but is instead *sponta-neo*[a] determining; and the **opposite of that which happens without understanding could always have happened**. Thus the action is only conditionally contingent (under conditions of the understanding) insofar as it is irrational.

5618. 1778–79? (1776–78?) *M* 281, at §§719–32, *Libertas.*   18:257

Pure freedom acts in accordance with laws of internally determining grounds, but they do not strike the senses. The animal power of choice proceeds in accordance with sensibly determinable laws. The mixed human power of choice (*libertas hybrida*) also acts in accordance with laws, but their grounds do not appear completely in the appearance; hence in the case of the same appearances the same person can act differently. Here one must first wait for a character, and then one has a law for **explaining but never for determining** the appearances.

5619. 1778–79? (1776–78?) *M* 280, in *Libertas.*   18:257

The difficulty about freedom is how an absolutely first action that is not determined by a preceding one is possible. For the latter is required for the unity of appearances insofar as there is to be a rule of experience. But if we do not reckon the actions of reason among the appearances (principle of reason) and instead reckon the determination to action by means of this to incentives in accordance with laws of sensibility (association, custom): then everything is *quoad sensum*[b] necessary and can be explained in accordance with laws of sensibility. However, it cannot be predetermined, since reason is a *principium* that does not appear and is thus not given among the appearances. Hence the causes and their relation to action in accordance with laws of sensibility can well be cognized *a posteriori*, but their determination to *actu* cannot be. This interconnection of actions in accordance with laws of appearance without determination through them is a necessary presupposition of practical rules of reason, which are in themselves the cause of a regularity of appearances, since they lead to actions only by means of the   18:258 sensibility. There is no *hiatus* for the understanding in the appearances, but these also cannot be determined *a priori*, i.e., from an absolutely first beginning.

The difficulty here does not concern the lack of a sufficient ground in general, but only among the appearances. If the action is determined in the higher powers, in their omissions or perfections, then the question

---

[a] spontaneously
[b] as far as the senses are concerned

is not about the ground of what happens but of what is always there, namely the rational will, by means of which the opposite of evil was always possible.

Reason determines itself with regard to its concepts; sensibility is determined by the objects. Hence the former is also not grounded on conditions of apprehension and apperception, rather it determines the *synthesis a priori*.

One cannot say that the opposite of all our actions must be subjectively possible in order for one to be free (good actions), but only that of those arising from sensibility. But also in this case they are determined under the sensibility, but are still undetermined if taken generally. Sensibility and reason do not determine each other, rather each works according to its laws; but they direct one another (harmony).

The causality of reason is freedom.[168] The determining causality of sensibility: animality.

18:258 **5620.** 1778–79? (1776–78?) (1780s?) *M* 286, still in *Libertas.*

Just as reason does not judge through the senses, but yet in relation to these in accordance with the general conditions of a cognition in general: likewise it does not judge through feeling, but in relation to that in accordance with the conditions of the universal validity of the judgment concerning satisfaction and dissatisfaction. It is appetition made universal, just as the former is apprehension made universal. No feeling distinguishes what is just from what is unjust, rather reason outlines the conditions under which alone a rule for judging about this obtains.

18:259 The satisfaction in the regularity is really a satisfaction in the ground of the constancy and security with regard to everything that is agreeably intended through the use of reason. It is therefore a gratification concerning the use of reason and the happiness ripped away from the blind power of choice.

18:260 **5624.** 1778–79? (1780–83?) *M* 103, opposite §336.[169]

For theology: Every presupposition that cannot be proven either *a priori* or *a posteriori* but is made only for the sake of our rational insight is a hypothesis if the propositions on account of which the presupposition is made are contingent: e.g., contingent perfection in the world; it is a postulate, however, if it is necessary *a priori*: e.g., moral propositions and their motivating force.[a] Thus the presupposition of the existence of God for the sake of morality is a postulate. A hypothesis does not exclude that there may also be other grounds of explanation, e.g., that something other than the supremely perfect being could also be the

---

[a] *bewegende Kraft*

cause of the perfection that we perceive. A postulate determines the ground as the only possible one. So if I were to find order and perfection everywhere in the essence of things, then the existence of God would be a postulate and the primordial being as the all-sufficient ground of the possibility of things would have to be presupposed in all teleological considerations.[170]

5630. 1778–1780s. *M* 364, at §890ff., in *Voluntas Dei.*   18: 262

If we had complete insight into the nature of things, then nature and freedom, the determination of nature and the determination of ends, would be entirely identical. So it is with God; hence all ends in the world follow simultaneously from the essence of things and in an original being would be identical with his nature.

5633. 1778–79? (1775–77?) 1780s?? *M* 401, at §982ff., in *Revelatio.*   18: 265

On the use of the cognition of God that is granted to human reason. 1. Not to puruse and research the concept of him with a theoretical aim, but to regard it merely as a necessary boundary-concept for all natural philosophy and as the *non plus ultra* of human reason. Thus not to want to investigate it. Also not to base explanations of nature on it as a cause and thus to set aside the maxims of the only use of reason that is appropriate for us. 2. To regard it as a concept belonging to morality, although not in order to make morality possible, but to give it the force of an incentive. 3. To use it in conjunction with morality for a religion, in which, however, morality and not theology prescribes the rules, so that we will not, by thinking anthropomorphistically, pervert the moral principles ourselves. With regard to religion, to follow the [*crossed out*: maxims] concepts of reason in accordance with universal laws of nature by regarding them as divinely instituted. To derive the divine punishments and rewards from the universal and at the same time moral interconnection of nature and freedom. To regard the destiny of this life as the progress of nature toward better ends. [To regard] the future life as an effect in accordance with laws of nature, future well-being or misery as something that we naturally expect from ourselves and our conduct, in a word: to seek God in the order of nature and in this way to honor him. For we cannot comprehend how he is in himself; and if we depart from the natural order, we pervert our own vocation.

5634. 1778–79? (1773–75?) 1780s?? *M* 401, at §982ff., in *Revelatio.*   18: 265

The cognition of God should not serve to alter our use of reason in accordance with the order of nature and morality, but to give it com-   18: 266 pleteness, so that we can connect the former with ends and the latter with the physical laws of the course of nature.

III.
NOTES FROM THE 1780s[1]

23:18   *LBl* B 12.

    P. I.

The unity of apperception in relation to the faculty of imagination is the understanding. Rules.

In relation to the reproductive faculty the unity is analytic, in relation to the reproductive, synthetic. The synthetic unity of apperception in relation to the transcendental faculty of imagination is the pure understanding. This transcendental faculty is that which universally determines all appearances in general with regard to time in accordance with rules that are valid *a priori*.

The first three faculties are not to be explained.

The transcendental synthesis of the imagination lies at the basis of all the concepts of our understanding.

The empirical use of the imagination rests on the synthesis of apprehension of empirical intuition which can then also be reproduced or made into another in accordance with the analogy therewith. In the latter case it is the productive imagination.

The productive imagination is either pure or empirical. The pure one.

The imagination is a synthesis, in part productive, in part reproductive. The former makes the latter possible, for if we had not previously brought it[a] together through synthesis then we could not also connect with others in our subsequent state.

The productive imagination is 1. empirical in apprehension, 2. pure but sensible with regard to an object of pure sensible intuition, 3. transcendental with regard to an object in general. The first presupposes the second, and the second presupposes the third.

The pure synthesis of the imagination is the ground of the possibility of the empirical synthesis in apprehension, thus also of perception. It is possible *a priori* and produces nothing but shapes.[b] The transcendental synthesis of the imagination pertains solely to the unity of apperception in the synthesis of the manifold in general through the imagination. Through that a concept of the object in general is conceived in accordance with the different kinds of transcendental synthesis. The synthesis happens in time.

23:19   All appearances concern me not insomuch as they are in the senses but as they can at least be encountered in apperception. In this, however, they can only be encountered by means of the synthesis of apprehension, i.e., of imagination, but this must agree with the absolute unity

---

[a] *es.* It is not clear what this refers to, for there are only feminine antecedents for this neuter pronoun.

[b] *Gestalten*

of apperception, thus all appearances are only elements of a possible cognition insofar as they stand under the transcendental unity of the synthesis of imagination. Now the categories are nothing other than the representations of something (appearance) in general so far as it is represented through transcendental synthesis of imagination, thus all appearances as elements of possible cognition (experience) stand under the categories.

All intuitions are nothing for us if they cannot be taken up into consciousness. Thus their relation to possible cognition is nothing other than the relation to consciousness. But all connection of the manifold of intuition is nothing if it is not taken up into the unity of apperception, thus every cognition that is possible in itself belongs to a possible cognition insofar as it belongs with all other possible cognitions in relation to a single apperception.

P. II.

The manifold, however, cannot thoroughly belong to one apperception except by means of a thoroughgoing synthesis of imagination and its functions in one consciousness. This transcendental unity in the synthesis of imagination is thus an *a priori* unity under which all appearances must stand. Those [*sic*] however are the categories, thus the categories express the necessary unity of apperception under which all appearances belong insofar as they belong to one*ᵃ* cognition *a priori* and necessarily.

It is no wonder that the understanding can prescribe to experience *a priori* laws that contain the conditions of all empirical ones. For through this understanding that unity is alone possible which appearance must primordially have in apperceptions and through which it conjoins into one experience. It [*breaks off*]

The understanding as the ground of all analytical unity in judgments is thus also the ground of rules and the source of them.

The suspension of the restriction seems to be an amplification. Something and nothing. Being and non-entity. Paralogism of the power of judgment.   23:20

Sensibility, imagination, and apperception cannot be further explained.

Summary concept of the faculty of pure understanding with regard to objects.

If the objects that are given to us were things in themselves and not mere appearances then we would have no *a priori* cognition of them at all. For if we took it from the objects, then the cognition would be empirical and not *a priori*, but if we would form concepts of them independently from them then this would have no relation at all to any object, thus it would be concepts without content; from this one sees that there must be

---

ᵃ *einem.* This could also be read simply as the indefinite article "a."

appearances. Now as representations these belong to one and the same apperception as [*breaks off*]

18: 267 **5636.** 1780–83. *LBl* E 67.
P. I.

The *quaestio facti* is in what way one has first come into the possession of a concept;

The *quaestio iuris* is with what right one possesses and uses it.[2]

The universality and necessity in the use of the pure concepts of the understanding betrays their origin and that it is either completely impermissible and false or else must not be empirical.

In pure sensibility, the pure power of imagination, and pure apperception lies the ground of the possibility of all empirical cognition *a priori* and of the synthesis in accordance with concepts, which has objective reality. For they pertain only to appearances (which are in themselves contingent and without unity), so that one properly cognizes only oneself as the thinking subject, but everything else as in this one thing. Heautognosy.[a]

All representations, wherever they might come from, are in the end as representations modifications of the inner sense, and it is from this 18: 268 viewpoint that their unity must be regarded.[3] To their receptivity there corresponds a spontaneity of *synthesis*. Either of apprehension as sensations or of reproduction as images[b] or of recognition as concepts.[4]

Transcendental principles of mathematics (not mathematical principles), namely that all intuitions and sensations are magnitudes and that the mathematical propositions about magnitude have reality, although only as of appearances.[5]
P. II.

No appearance can ever demonstrate an empty space or an empty time. Since appearances are nothing in themselves, that is, not objects subsisting for themselves, empty space is a perception of an extension without matter of appearance.

Every magnitude has a quality, i.e., continuity. Every quality has a magnitude, i.e., intensity (degree). The boundaries of extensive magnitudes are not at the same time the boundaries of intensive ones, but the latter can diminish unnoticed down to nothing.[6] The limits of intensive magnitudes, e.g., weight, are on that account not the boundaries of extensive ones (or if the latter are equal, the former are also equal), rather the latter can grow infinitely. Against atoms and the void.

Since the objects of our senses are not things in themselves, but are only appearances, i.e., representations whose objective reality consists

[a] This coinage, not used in the *Critique of Pure Reason*, would mean "knowledge of oneself."
[b] *Einbildungen*, i.e., products of the imagination

only in the constancy and unity of the interconnection of their manifold, the objects do not yield the concepts, but the concepts make it such that in them we have objects of cognition; since as representations they are also modifications of inner sense, their possibility rests on the synthesis of appearances in time.

It is a very important question, whether the categories are of merely empirical or also trans.*ᵃ* use. To the schematistic.

5637. 1780–83? 1788–89??? *LBl* C 8.⁷   18:268
P. I.   18:271

Key – through the nature of synthetic judgments *a priori.*

If no space were given *a priori* in our subject as the form of its sensible intuition and objects outside us were merely given in this form, then no synthetic propositions that at the same time hold of actual outer objects would be possible *a priori.* For if we were to derive the representations from the objects as they are given in themselves, then everything would depend merely on experience and no synthesis would hold *a priori* together with the necessity of the judgments, at least not objectively. If time were not given subjectively and thus *a priori* as the form of inner sense (and no understanding to compare it), then apperception would not cognize the relation in the existence of the manifold *a priori,* for in itself time is no object of perception; it would to be sure determine the succession and coexistence of representations, but not the position of objects in time, hence it would not constitute experience if it did not have rules for the time that is determinable in the object; but this cannot be derived from the object.⁸

I ask everyone whence he would derive mathematics and the necessary synthetic propositions about things in space if space were not already the condition of the possibility of the empirical representation of objects in   18:272
us *a priori,* through which these can be given to us.⁹ As far as existence is concerned, we determine the manifold of appearance *a priori* through the categories. I ask: whence should this synthesis be derived if time, the condition of the possibility of all perception, did not lie at its ground *a priori* and if the rules of the determination of existence in this time and through this among one another did not therefore flow prior to all perception from the subjective constitution of our [*crossed out*: intuition] sensibility, on which everything objective rests.

From this, however, it follows that our synthetic propositions *a priori* can be valid only of appearances, but not of things in themselves,*ᵇ* that

---

ᵃ Kant's abbreviation is not expanded since there is no way to tell whether he meant to write "transcendent" or "transcendental," although the former would be appropriate here.
ᵇ Here Kant uses a period and starts a new sentence.

the former are given only through the *synthesis* and as far as it reaches, that therefore the concepts do not reach them as things in themselves beyond all possible *synthesis*, through which then the misunderstandings arise that proceed from relative totality, which is all that there is in all empirical synthesis, to absolute totality.

Reason, which will not let this restriction stand, supposes that our experience and also our *a priori* cognition pertain immediately to objects and not first to the subjective conditions of sensibility and apperception and by their means to unknown objects that can be represented only through the former. Hence it strikes off on different paths. 1. The empirical path and universality through induction. 2. The fanatical path of intuition through the understanding. 3. That of predetermination through innate concepts. 4. The *qualitas occulta* of the healthy understanding, which gives no account. [P. III.] If one concedes this, then all critique of pure reason is suspended and the door is opened wide to all sorts of fiction. Hence it belongs to the discipline of pure reason to investigate it and to bar these paths in accordance with its discoveries. P. IV.

To 66.[a] [*Crossed out*: Again this happy man can] To be healthy, active to an advanced age, and useful to the world through insights is a good fortune that is not to be begrudged to anyone. Now if even this brave mathematical man controlled all judgment over this his sphere

18:273 or could say (with that *de gente hircosa centurionum*): *quod sapio, satis est mihi.*[b, 10] But since these tasks of human reason are essential and can never be set aside, at least someone must fast over them to the point of becoming ill, so that after this one everyone can be healthy and still satisfy reason.[11]

Not only does reason overlook the ideality of the objects of the senses, it also bristles against this as it does against everything that restricts its sphere of influence. Hence it is necessary to investigate the paths that it takes. The first is empiricism. But not only does *a priori* mathematical cognition refute the falsehood of this putative origin of our cognition, but also the concepts that are present in experience contain a necessity (cause) that experience cannot teach; thus Locke, who earned almost too much honor after Leibniz had already refuted him, falls by the wayside.[12] There thus remain epigenesis, mystical intuition, and involution. Finally there is also the *qualitas occulta* of common reason.

It is false that our sensibility is nothing other than a confused intellectual representation. Incorrect concept of the sensible.

All of our cognition is grounded on what is subjective insofar as it represents an object through the synthetic unity of the manifold.

---

[a] It is not clear what this number (which might also be "6b" or "bb") refers to.
[b] with that dirty man from among the centurions: what I know is enough for me

No *dogmata*.

For the *Canon*: The end of all of metaphysics is God and the future, and the end of these is our conduct, not whether we ought to make it accord with morality, but whether it is without consequences.[13]

Transcendental propositions are either those that [assert] an object, to   18:274
be sure, but no concept, rather only its problem, or those that to be sure assert a concept, but no object (its reality). In both cases this is because reason reaches further than understanding.

We have no permission to appeal to God. The contingency of mathematics and the possibility of explaining all order from natural laws. God. We also cannot prove necessary generation through understanding synthetically.

The discipline of the opponent. He asserts more synthetically than he can prove.

Whether there are pure hypotheses of reason. Permission for that.

Finally, on the speculative interest of reason. Even if one had realized those ideas of reason, one would still have to explain nature as if there were no beginning, nothing simple, no freedom, no absolute contingency and as if there were no cause to be found outside of the world. For nature is our problem, the text for our interpretations. Who knows what Epicurus would have thought of that, and also what sort of gibberish he would have come up with for explanations of nature.[14]

P. II.

Among all of our thoughts there is not the least trace of the intuition of objects other than those of the senses and no thoughts that pertain to anything other than the exposition of appearances. An intellectual intuition of objects outside of us, that do not exist through us, also seems to be impossible.

If one assumes intellectual intuitions, this yields no cognition of the   18:275
understanding through concepts and thus no thought and also no communicable cognition.

If it were supposed that we had everything *a posteriori* through experience and the immediate perception of objects, thus even space and time, then we would not know anything of them other than contingent truths. We cannot cognize anything of them synthetically *a priori* unless these intuitions are given to us *a priori*, consequently not through objects, but through the subject, although its relation to the objects, since these are given as appearances through those subjective conditions.

Now reason abhors principles that are not its own work. It is its maxim to assume that everything can be explained. Consequently no sensible primitive intuition.

Now the logical system of the cognitions of the understanding is either empirical or transcendental. The former Aristotle and Locke, the latter either the system of epigenesis or that of involution, acquired or inborn.[15] The so-called healthy understanding is an *asylum ignorantiae.*[a]

P. III.

Cognitions do not need to be originally inspired; we see this in the case of the synthetic *a priori* cognitions of mathematics.

That one must not assume a *mundus intelligibilis.*

A sensible world in general is the object of an intelligence. But it would not be that if it were not the work of an intelligence. For without rules of order there is no nature. These, however, are contingent, consequently an arrangement.

Every explanation of something purposive in accordance with general laws of nature would otherwise be deceptive. E.g., the flattening of the earth.[16] It is out of the question to explain *organisatio* mechanically; but if this could work, one could always aim at it. Who then makes the existence of a most perfect being comprehensible[?] The contingency indeed increases with the perfection.

18:276

18:276 **5638.** 1780–82. *LBl M* 21.

Our concept of the world is neither too great nor too small for empirical synthesis, as long as what is understood thereby is the totality of appearances unlimited by any restricting condition, hence a problematic concept which merely serves as a rule.[17]

If one says that the conditions [*crossed out*: for something given] are given along with the conditioned, that means that the rule is given in accordance with which the former can be found; but the totality of the series is not thereby given: the collective all. That the synthesis of *regressus* is unlimited (*indefinita*) seems to be the same as: the series is infinite (*infinita*); that the *synthesis inversa in consequentia*[b] has a beginning seems to be the same as: the series has a beginning. We have an outermost for the senses (relatively) and also a first for the use of our reason: that is where we begin.

18:276 **5639.** 1780–83? (1778–79?) (1785–88?) *LBl* E 65.
P. I.

The proposition that the concept of an absolute totality of the series of conditions must be either too great or too small means that such a concept is not possible at all.[18] For absolute time must be determined in such a way that the synthesis is congruent either with a part of it or with the whole of time. But we have a concept of the magnitude of time only by means of the appearances. Our concepts of the world are transcendent, and by means of such a proposition it would be asserted that they are

[a] refuge for the ignorant
[b] the inverse synthesis from consequences (to their grounds)

all immanent and only thereby can be suitable for the objects. But that there can be no totality in the empirical synthesis of the appearances means that with regard to the empirical, time is given *indefinita*, but not as infinite, for it is only given through the synthesis, which is always finite.

It is a remarkable rule or maxim of reason, which belongs to its discipline, that one must not prove any transcendental proposition of reason apagogically from concepts, since it will thereby often be shown that our concept is mistaken on both sides. E.g., that there can be no absolute freedom of religion, and on the other side that there must be an absolutely complete freedom of religion. One has a mistaken concept either of religion or of freedom. Yet the same sort of antinomy serves for a skeptical method for examining the correctness of our concepts and presuppositions. One indicates the hindrances and contradictions on both sides and is thereby restrained from judging dogmatically for one or the other, and is thus driven merely to criticize one's judgment.[19]

[*Crossed out*: The unrestricted synthesis is not] The infinitude of synthesis in one series is not the infinitude of the manifold of its members considered as given, for this [*crossed out*: member] manifoldness is given only through the synthesis. It is as if merely potential in the *progressus*.

Since the series of conditions cannot be given, although the concept can be, one must say that the series is too large for the concept rather than that the concept is too small for the series, for the series is adjusted to the concept, and not the converse.

P. II.

If I say that the world is too large for our thoughts, does this mean the same as that our thoughts are too small for the world[?] That which is given is the world, and not the thoughts. Thus where does the fault lie: in the world or in the thought[?] The fault lies in the thought, for we think further than what is given empirically; for a world is not given empirically, rather everything that is given and that we can think belongs – in the world.

It should be said: the thought of the world must be neither too great nor too small for it, hence it must fit the world as a sum-total of all [*crossed out*: given] appearances exactly. But the world is a mere synthesis of appearances, in which the ground of the synthesis can always be determined only internally and never outside the appearances. The *synthesis* fits the world in accordance with empirical concepts and as *indefinita*.

Since the concept of appearances is not given prior to the synthesis, but is given only through it, the synthesis in itself is undetermined with regard to the appearances, hence it proceeds infinitely, although the appearance is not on that account given as infinite. It is therefore always finite, and every given world is to be reckoned as finite from its *a priori* point. In contrast, it seems to be potentially infinite [*crossed out*: in the appearances], namely if one considers the synthesis as given through the object. In such a way the thought or the concept in accordance with which we are to think the world is neither too great nor too small for it, rather it is entirely suitable for this problematic concept or the problem that is hidden in the concept, i.e., the **possibility of all empirical cognition in the field of appearances**.

In the senses there is no completed synthesis and nothing complete and unconditioned.

That the world must be neither too great nor too small for our thoughts means the same as that one must conceive of it in such a way that its concept corresponds to the conditions of thoroughgoing empirical synthesis and its rule. Or *vice versa*: the concept of the world must arise from it. Now this is either a synthesis proceeding without end from the conditioned to conditions and a *progressio indefinita*, in which time itself is determined through the *synthesis* of appearances and time neither determines the appearance nor restricts itself with regard to the appearances. For in that case the world is an idea whose object is given only through this synthesis and its rule, but is never given as an absolute whole for itself and all possible synthesis in a collective unity.

18: 279   **5642.** 1780–83. *LBl* D 24.[20]
P. I.

My putative idealism is the restriction of sensible intuition to mere experience and the avoidance of wandering with them beyond the boundaries of appearance to things in themselves.* It is merely the avoidance of the transcendental *vitii subreptionis* in which one makes one's representations into things. I once called this doctrine transcendental idealism, because there was previously no name for it.[21]

*(It would not have paid for the objects of experience to aim their
18: 280   principles so high. One may get *a priori* cognition wherever one will, it is still confirmed by experience and reliable in its use to that extent. Nevertheless it is also agreeable there on account of the scientific will. But where the use goes further than experience, where there is the danger of fiction, where more powerful and apparent conflict takes place, there it is necessary, etc.)
P. II.

For judgments concepts are required, and for concepts [*crossed out*: judgments] intuitions. The concepts, insofar as they pertain to intuitions *a priori*, cannot originate from the individual empirical consciousness of the manifold, otherwise they would not be concepts of the connection of intuition; rather they are possible only through [*crossed out*: the relation of] its combination in one apperception by means of the unity of its synthesis. And therein subsist the *a priori* concepts.

Dialectic. Until now we have only had to deal with appearances, in whose exposition, principles, and use there is only truth, and here there was no idealism. For truth consists merely in the thoroughgoing interconnection of representations in accordance with laws of the understanding. In that consists all difference from dreams. Not in the fact that the images exist for themselves in separation from the mind. But now for the first time there arises an illusion, and indeed a natural and unavoidable illusion, since our judgments assert something of the objects that is not contained in our concepts of them, i.e., in possible experience, and there our theory is the refutation of idealism.

The illusion consists first in the fact that in the field of experience in accordance with mere laws of experience we represent to ourselves a progression that is not an empirical progression, but rather a mere idea, which cannot be an experience. We remain in the world of the senses [*crossed out*: however], and would be led by nothing except the principles of the [*crossed out*: law] understanding that we use in experience, 18:281 but **we make our possible progression into an object in itself**, by regarding the possibility of experience as something real in the objects of experience.

Here the antinomy reveals itself. All ideas that constitute the ground of this dialectic are contained herein: psychological as well as theological ones, but only insofar as they belong in the series of possible experience, which ought to limit itself. Here the ideas should only complete the progression and are cosmological. But another illusion also reveals itself, where they do not belong to the series and would add something to experience, and here the ideas are partly psychological, partly theological. The hypothetical inferences of reason are the guide: for the former the categorical and for the latter the disjunctive. The first take as their ground the subjective connection of all representations in one subject, the latter the objective connection in one idea. There is no concept of the first subject, of the second object there is only an ideal.[22]

If for truth we required something more than the thoroughgoing interconnection of intuitions in accordance with laws of the understanding, in what would we find that if this were not at the same time the representation of a determinate object[?] If in addition to that truth consisted in correspondence with something else that does not lie in our representations, then we would compare it with that. All objects (would be determined only through the representations in me; what they might be in addition in themselves is unknown to me) are at the same time in us; an object outside us is transcendent, i.e., entirely unknown to us and useless as a criterion of truth. Dialectic.

Idealism assumes nothing except thinking beings.[23] We never do that, only we do not regard our representations as their properties. In the senses there is neither truth nor error, for they do not judge at all, hence all appearances are to that extent free of possible error and are no illusion.

The idealist concedes that actual extension and bodies outside us could exist, but are not actual, thus are merely a dream in us. We assert that these are purely representations and can only exist in us, but that their objects may nevertheless exist outside us, although we know nothing of what they may be in themselves.

Synthetic unity of apperception *a priori* is the synthesis of the manifold in accordance with an *a priori* rule. The logical function is the action of unifying the same consciousness with many representations, i.e., of thinking a rule in general. The unity of intuition *a priori* is only possible through the combination of the manifold in one apperception, which must therefore take place *a priori*, consequently also the unity of the *synthesis* of all empirical intuitions, since they are to be encountered in space and time.

Now what do I have to assert in order not to be an idealist?

Idealism is a metaphysical conceit that goes further than is necessary in order to awaken thought. This applies to the philosopher as well as to the theologian. Syncretists. Semipelagians.[24]

5643. 1780–88. *LBl* C 3.
P. I.

In all synthetic *a priori* cognition there is first *a priori* intuition, then, second, a concept of the synthesis of the manifold *a priori* must be thought. On this are grounded the principles of synthetic cognition in general. For these contain nothing except the conditions under which alone certain intuitions are brought under concepts of their synthesis. The latter are called **categories**.[25]

We can have a sensation of something without thinking it, so the question arises whether we cannot also think something without having a sensation of it. (*a priori*) However, we can also intuit without having a sensation. Now if we are to think without having a sensation, then this must relate to that sort of intuition.

Intuition is the immediate relation of the power of representation to an individual object.[26] A concept is its representation through a mark that it has in common with others.[27] Intuition belongs to the senses, a concept is for the understanding.

Concepts of the synthesis of the manifold of possible intuitions are nothing other than the combination that the representations can have in one consciousness insofar as they are necessary with regard to an intuition, only thought synthetically, i.e., that to one (to the concept of the object) something **else** is added in order to produce the representation of **one** object.

In the representation of an object which the manifold of its intuition is to contain, the synthetic unity of the latter is necessary. The representation of this necessary unity, under which everything manifold in intuition must stand, is, if it is to be cognition of an object of intuition, the principle of synthetic unity in general, and must itself take place *a priori*.[28]
P. II.

Something that is **determined** with regard to the functions of [*crossed out*: magnitude] judgments is the object, and this determination is determination of the object, and likewise with the others. The categories are therefore concepts for the determination of the objects of our cognition in general, insofar as intuition is given to it. Thus principles for making out of appearance experience, which is purely objective, i.e., universally valid empirical cognition, where the *synthesis* must thus be determined *a priori*, for otherwise it would not be necessary and universal. For we know an object only as a something in general, for which the given intuitions are only predicates. Now how these can be the predicates of a third thing cannot be cognized through their comparison, but only through the way in which the consciousness of the manifold in general can be regarded as necessarily combined in one consciousness. [*Crossed out*: The concept] In the representation of an object the manifold is united. All intuitions are only representations; the object to which they are related lies in the understanding.

A synthesis can never be cognized as necessary and thus *a priori* from   18:284
the representations that are to be combined synthetically, but only from their relation to a third concept, in which and in relation to which this combination is necessary.[29] This third concept is that of an object in general, which is thought precisely through this synthetic necessary unity and which is determined with regard to the logical functions of such judgment. For thereby does the manifold of representations first become objective, i.e., cognition, and does appearance become empirical cognition.

I cannot cognize *a posteriori* that something is objectively determined, without determining it objectively in accordance with an *a priori* rule; for everything that is objectively determined must be able to be determined *a priori* from the concept of the object, to be sure not as far as its matter is concerned but still as far as the form of connection is. Through the very same representations through which the concept of an object is determined does there arise a concept which, conversely, objectively determines those representations.

5644. 1783–4. *LBl* Berliner Staatsbibliothek 19.   18:284
P. I.

(*Later addition*: Nature does not satisfy us completely, neither with regard to efficient causes nor with regard to ends.)

(*Later addition*: It is something other: science of pure reason, and science of the principles of pure reason in general. The possibility of such a thing is transcendental philosophy.)

(*Later addition*: Metaphysics. Either [*crossed out*: *pura* or] *universalis* – *Ontologia*, or *specialis* and *applicata*: 1. cosmology, which contains objects of experience –, 2. Theology.

Metaphysica pura. Ontologia is the system of pure principles *a priori*. Logic is a science of the principles of reason, pure itself, to be sure, but not dealing with principles.)

A science is not adequately determined just by containing the first principles of human cognition, but rather by the fact that this cognition is of a particular kind, *a priori*. [*Crossed out*: Logic also] Cognition from *a priori* principles is cognition of pure reason and either pure mathematics or pure philosophy. Metaphysics: the system of pure philosophy, of speculative or practical philosophy (of nature or of morals). All cognition from concepts has its metaphysics. Mathematics is rational cognition through the construction of concepts in intuition, and on that account pertains only to objects of the senses. Philosophy, rational cognition from concepts, thus also pertains to things that are not objects of the senses. Even the possibility of mathematics.

18: 285

Things can only be given through the senses, yet we can cognize much about them *a priori*. Things that cannot be given to the senses, if they are to be cognized *a priori* (*later addition*: that we can only become aware of them on the occasion of experience proves nothing) constitute *metaphysicam puram*.

(*Later addition*: Metaphysics proper has 2 parts: the 1st pertains to things as objects of the senses: psychology and general natural science; the second to objects as ideas: World and God, which still belong necessarily to reason. Thus 1. all elements and principles of pure thinking in abstraction from all objects (ontology) – 2. application to objects: a. of the senses, b. of pure reason.)

Thus *metaphysica* is either *pura* or *applicata*.

Rational cognition from concepts is philosophical, pure rational cognition from concepts is metaphysical.

Metaphysics is preceded by transcendental philosophy, which like logic does not deal with objects but with the possibility, the [*crossed out*: domain] sum-total and the boundaries of all cognition of pure reason (also of pure mathematics). It is the logic of pure rational cognition.

Prior to transcendental philosophy, the critique of reason in general. P. II.

As long as I only analyze concepts that have use in experience or propound their principles, things are fine; but when I depart from that and go farther, that's when problems begin. I would first propound everything critically, then particular propositions.

Thus in the first place metaphysics itself is the object, and that which investigates its possibility is critique. 18: 286

(*Later addition*: Ontology is the sum-total of all concepts and principles of pure thinking.)

Second, metaphysics proper is the system of all pure concepts *a priori* that we relate to objects*: transcendental philosophy** (*later addition*: pure reason entirely), ontology (*conceptus dabiles*),[a] cosmology, and theology (*ideales*).[b] (*Later addition*: To explain hyperphysically. hyperphysically.[c] metaphysically. physically.)

*(If concepts are *a priori*, hence not given through objects, they can only be taken from the understanding itself in relation to objects in general. 1. To things in general: ontology; 2. connection in a whole; 3. dependence [*crossed out*: of this] on a ground.)

**(What logic is with regard to cognition, transcendental philosophy is with regard to pure cognition *a priori*.)

Third, these principles applied to objects of outer and inner experience in general. *Physica rationalis, Psychologia rationalis*.

Not *psychologia empirica*.

1. It is partly occupied with things;
2. partly with ideas (in themselves).

All philosophical cognition has its metaphysics, which determines the principles *a priori*.

We have many cognitions *a priori*, which are necessitated for us with regard to experience. E.g., Everything has a cause. But with regard to them we did not need metaphysics.

The objects of experience do not fully satisfy reason itself with regard to these principles. Hence reason goes beyond experience, and with regard to it metaphysics is necessary: God and another world. In the metaphysics there is one part that merely analyzes the use of reason with regard to experience. This is very useful for culture but dispensable for science. Hence there is another part: synthetic, through which concepts are made transcendent. 18: 287

5645. 1785–88? (1760–84?) *LBl* Berliner Staatsbibliothek 36.³⁰ 18: 287
Sheet 1, P. I.

In order to find a way for the need of our age to steer successfully between the two cliffs of dogmatism and skepticism, and at the same

---

[a] the concepts of things that can be given
[b] the concepts of ideal things
[c] Kant repeats this word.

time to determine both of these concepts suitably for this need, we must first of all establish its character with respect to the manner of thinking that makes this caution necessary.

Extensive knowledge and the possession of a large number of sciences do[a] not yet comprise the character of this manner of thinking, for this concerns the quality and specific constitution of the power of judgment and the principles that determine what sort of use is intended for it. Whether our age has advanced very far in knowledge and whether its cognition should be called great can only be judged comparatively; our posterity may well find it still small. But a [crossed out: facility] faculty may well already have ripened so that the later world need add nothing further to it (because it is not the quantity but the quality [crossed out: of the manifold] in the use of our cognitive powers which is at issue), and this is the faculty of the power of judgment (iudicium discretiuum).[b]

18: 288
Our age is the age of critique, i.e., of an acute judging of the foundation of all assertions to which we have been brought by the experiences of many years, perhaps also by the careful investigation of nature through observation and experiment which was set into motion by the famous Bacon of Verulam,[31] not only in the assertions of natural science but also, by analogy, in other areas, of which the ancients knew nothing and where they were therefore accustomed to shaky opinions. It will be difficult for a future age to do better than us in this, unless out of negligence we do not make use of these principles as we should. Certainly no past age has done better than us in this regard, and this can therefore be called the scientific character of our age.

In every science, if we abstract from the amount of knowledge, the essential aim is that it be distinguished from mere opinion, thus certainty. The methods that one uses in them is merely the means to reach this end. Certainty is the inalterability of an assertion of truth. An assertion of truth is inalterable either **objectively**, if we know that no more weighty ground for its opposite is possible in itself, or **subjectively**, if we are convinced that neither we ourselves nor any other person will ever be in possession of greater grounds for the opposite.

The inalterable assertion of truth with consciousness is knowledge, the subjectively inalterable assertion of truth is belief. An assertion of truth accompanied with consciousness of its alterability is opinion.[32]

An example from history. The word "belief" can signify either the source of our cognition or the [crossed out: manner and] degree of the assertion of its truth. In the first sense, no cognition of history can arise except through confidence in the testimony of others, i.e., by our believing others. In the second sense a piece of historical information can

[a] Kant writes "does" (macht).
[b] judgment of distinctions

certainly be knowledge and [P. II] as far as the degree of the assertion of its truth is concerned it does not need to be distinguished from one's own experience, whose right to be called knowledge would not be disputed, by the designation as belief. Thus one knows that a Louis XIV once lived just as surely as if one had seen him oneself, and thus a good part of history is true science; the assertion of truth in it is objectively inalterable. It is impossible that sufficient grounds for the opposite of it would [*crossed out*: ever] have to be conceded. By contrast, I take the history of the first seven kings of Rome to be true on the same sorts of grounds on which all history rests, although in this case they are insufficient, and further in this case I am convinced that no one could ever prove the opposite, since all documents for that are lacking, i.e., I believe in them. But that perhaps before the construction of Rome there was another people and another flourishing city in the very same place, from which perhaps the *Cloaca Maxima* still remains, is an opinion that can be considered; but it is not impossible that one might still find a proof of the opposite, if for instance these subterranean works should be excavated and inscriptions by their builder (say, *Servius Tullius*) should be found; thus I do not recognize inalterability in my assertion of truth in this case.33

18: 289

18: 290

All knowledge is either empirical, i.e., derived from experience, or rational: arising from reason, hence possible *a priori* and self-sufficient. Among the former are counted experience proper and history (i.e., reliable reports, hence knowledge from the experience of others). The second kind of certainty is independent from all experience.

All empirical certainty is bound up with consciousness of the contingency of the truth; for experience very well teaches that something is constituted in one way or another or that something has happened, but never teaches that it could not have been constituted or happened otherwise.

Rational certainty is inseparably bound up with consciousness of the necessity of that which is asserted to be true. All cognition which in its essential constitution is combined with consciousness of its necessity is apodictic. Thus every proposition of reason must be apodictically certain, and in [*crossed out*: propositions] assertions of reason (*assertionibus*) there is neither opinion nor belief.34

All apodictic propositions, however, are of two kinds: they are cognized either from mere concepts or only through the constructions of conceptions. The first are called dogmata, the second mathemata.35 If it could be proved from the mere concept of a body as a composite substance that it consists of simple parts, as Leibniz held,36 then this would be a dogma; but if from the geometrical exhibition of a space that a body occupies and the equally geometrical division of this space its infinite divisibility is proven, then this proposition is a mathema. Thus philosophy

18: 291 alone [P. III] can contain dogmata, because it differs from mathematics, which is just as much rational cognition as philosophy is, in that it judges merely from concepts, while the latter cannot judge otherwise than through the construction of concepts.

Philosophy is thus capable of apodictic certainty, but not of intuitive certainty by means of *a priori* intuition, of the kind that mathematics can provide, but only of discursive certainty from concepts. Hence philosophy certainly contains principles, but only mathematics contains axioms, the former contains proofs (*probationes*), the latter alone demonstrations; the former produces conviction, the latter also self-evidence (*evidentiam*).

Critique. The art of distinguishing opinion from knowledge.

[*Crossed out*: All cognition, even if it is not rational cognition but only historical, nevertheless needs certain principles, which comprise the criteria of truth in it. Thus there are certain principles in accordance with which one judges the probability of a history, not merely those that flow from the nature of the things narrated and thus are taken from reason, but also those that determine the way in which the experience of ancient times can be reliably brought to us.]

Beside rational certainty one can [*crossed out*: oppose] set historical certainty, by which is understood empirical certainty, which does not rest on our own experience (hence it rests on reports of their experience by others). Likewise there is also a rational belief, which is analogical to historical belief, although to be sure it rests on different grounds. In both kinds of certainty the objective inalterability of judgment is intended, while in beliefs of both kinds only subjective inalterability is. That the planets contain rational inhabitants can be believed in accordance with reason, for as many grounds of proof as one can rationally expect of them from our distance yield as great an analogy between them and the earth as is necessary for this conclusion, and one is in addition certain that no one will ever know enough more about them to prove the opposite.[37]

18: 292 Rational belief is called moral certainty if it is sufficient for an obligation to make it the ground [*crossed out*: as principle] of one's actions.[38] For since the moral laws that contain the grounds of obligation also rest on reason and thus are objectively inalterable, to that extent there can be [*crossed out*: rational] certainty [*crossed out*: for rational belief]. But this cannot be called rational certainty (*certitudo logica*), for it must not be assumed from theoretical principles, but must only be assumed as **necessary** [*crossed out*: as true] for the sake of practical maxims, and since these maxims rest on moral laws, which are objectively inalterable, one can call such rational beliefs not moral beliefs but moral certainty. Thus the propositions: There is a God, There is a future life, yield only rational belief for speculative cognition, but nevertheless count as morally

274

certain; for since only through them are all [*crossed out*: well-founded hindrances] objections against obligation in accordance with moral laws cancelled out (namely those that derive from the consideration that the observation or violation of the moral laws may not in accordance with the mere course of nature have any proportionate effect), their [*crossed out*: objective certainty] assumption on account of this necessity [*crossed out*: and objective inalterability] is practically necessary, and it is impossible that there can be grounds for the opposite, because otherwise grounds for the opposite of morality could be possible, and thus this itself would become dubious and uncertain.³⁹

P. IV.

By dogmata one understands apodictic propositions from concepts. Hence mathematics certainly contains apodictic propositions, but no dogmata, because it is not possible from concepts, but only through their construction.⁴⁰ The propositions that between two points only one straight line is possible or that in every triangle the sum of all its angles is equal to two right angles, the first of which is an axiom and the second a demonstrated theorem, are mathemata, i.e., cognitions insight into which and certainty about which are intuitive but thereby still apodictic; but that [*crossed out*: that everything that exists contingently must have a cause is certainly also an apodictic but only a discursive proposition from concepts, hence] every assertion must be truthful and that a lie is contemptible is an apodictic yet discursive proposition from concepts, and can be called a dogma.   18: 293

All apodictic certainty is contained only in two sciences, which comprise the cognition of reason *a priori*: in mathematics or philosophy. Dogmata can be found only in the latter. But philosophy is either theoretical, where reason has to do merely with itself, or practical, where it has to do with the laws of the will. The first part, so far as it contains apodictic, i.e., pure rational cognitions, is called metaphysics, the second, which contains the same sort of practical laws, is called pure morality.

Summary Concept

Between **dogmatism** and **skepticism** the intermediate and only lawful manner of thinking is **criticism**.⁴¹

This is the maxim never to assume anything to be true except after complete **examination of principles**.

All principles are on the one side *a posteriori*, i.e., taken empirically, and this in turn either from one's own experience or on the testimony about the experience of others, hence experience (*in sensu stricto*) or history.

All principles are on the other side *a priori* and taken from reason, but this either from reason insofar as it judges merely in accordance with concepts, hence philosophical princples, or insofar as it judges in accordance merely with the construction of concepts, i.e., their exhibition *a priori* in intuition.

As regards one's own experience and mathematics, the latter does not need critique at all, the former only rarely, in order for illusion not to be taken for perception. But all the more do the history of past times among empirical cognitions and speculative philosophy among rational ones need critique, i.e., examination of principles.

P. V.

Dogmatism is the manner of thinking that is attached to assertions without critique (i.e., examination of principles).[42] The most natural tendency of mankind with regard to cognition is toward dogmatism: 1. on account of laziness, since going back to principles is more difficult than proceeding to the application of principles that have already been assumed and are in circulation. 2. Because through critique cognition is not expanded, but only rendered secure. 3. From fear of revealing the poverty of our knowledge to ourselves and others.

Skepticism is a principle adopted to break with dogmatism, but not [*crossed out*: by means of critique] with the aim of introducing [*crossed out*: the truth] true conviction against it, but rather only in order to topple the persuasions of others. The inclination to this is not natural but artificial and can only arise from displeasure with the usurpation of dogmatism.[43] Occasion for it is provided [*crossed out*: in the historical] 1st in the **empirical cognitions** purporting to know it all, especialy ancient stories and the construction of systems on them, 2nd **in the rational cognitions** of speculative philosophy, namely metaphysics and general morality with their [*crossed out*: questions] assertions of the highest good. It is thus certainly an evil, since it seeks to do nothing but damage, namely to rob human reason of all hope in the most important questions of reason; but it is not stupid malice, for dogmatism, as a usurpatory conceit of approval, can at least not complain about the injustice of the resistance of the misologue. Yet it is to say the least foolishness: for it transforms all assertions of truth into illusion, which it opposes to truth, so it must both concede criteria by which to distinguish that and at the same time it entirely denies these.

Danger is the possibility of a greater evil. There is also a danger in dogmatism as well as in skepticism, in the former that of rousing up a cloud of errors among a small number of truths and of bringing contempt upon the latter themselves because of their relation to the former; in the latter, the denial of our duty of always serving our reason and a laziness in this that is excused by its plausible objections.

This danger can only be averted through the greatest critical diligence, **on the empirical side** in tracking down the sources of history and its derivation from us and **on the rational side** in tracking down the nature and the capacity of human reason in its speculative use in

18:294

18:295

metaphysics as well as its practical use in morality, and in determining their boundaries, likewise their scope and the necessary principles of the latter.

5646. 1785–88? (1776–79?) *LBl* Essen-Königsberg 1.   18:295

The I.

In the appearances of inner as well as outer sense one can never regard oneself as the identical self, even as far as the sensible character is concerned. Only with regard to morality, which is the pure consciousness of our self independent from determination in space and time, does the same subject of free actions under the same laws always exist in everything where we are conscious of our self, and there the whole of our actions is regarded as a unity, and we cannot believe that because we have improved ourselves that we therefore have another personality and cannot **be punished on account of the previous one**, as almost all people believe.[44] Of course this cannot happen with humans as judges. Likewise **one refers evil to one's childhood** (Rousseau: the story about the ribbon)[45] or also what we have done when drunk. Yet improvement is an experience that the character in us is not so entirely evil.

5649. 1785–88? (1788–89) *LBl* D 4.   18:296
P. I.

Tiedemann[46]

Metaphysics can take three paths: 1. That universal cognitions of nature are possible only through experience (also its concepts). 2. That universal cognitions are also possible merely from *a priori* concepts and through reason. 3. That universal cognitions occur, to be sure, *a priori* and prior to all experience, but only so far as they are grounds of the possibility of experience. The first path is empirical, the second dogmatic,   18:297 the third critical, because the critique and analysis of experiences can alone assign them. For the last path it is requisite that pure sensible intuition *a priori* ground empirical intuition and pure concepts *a priori*, which relate only to the unity of the consciousness of these intuitions, ground the empirical concepts.

But that besides sensibility and understanding (both *a priori*) the faculty of reason also contains principles of the use of both, and indeed that the concepts of the understanding be restricted to experience and those of sensibility to the same, so that their conditions not be extended to beings in themselves, God and spirit. At the same time also to give to reason freedom to think of something beyond experience, which is however necessary for the completion of the use of our understanding, but which can never be thought through theoretical concepts except

negatively, and which can be thought positively through moral concepts alone and contains the totality of the conditions for everything.
P. II.

How much does one wish that, if one will rise to extrasensible objects, one will be free of the restricting concepts of space and time, likewise, that if one will come to a complete whole of all conditions of the understanding, one will be free from the progressive conditions that make totality impossible although they belong to experience, in a word, that one will be free of what properly belongs only to the possibility of experience and does not go beyond.

The pure concepts of reason – God (freedom) and another world – are properly of moral origin.

With space and time one can only take two paths: 1. that they are [*crossed out*: mere] concepts, 2. that they are mere intuitions. In the first case they are a. empirical or b. *a priori* concepts. In the second case they are 1. intuitions of things in themselves through observation and yet necessary, 2. formal intuition *a priori*, i.e., consciousness of the way in which objects of the senses are represented to us.

18: 298

18: 298   **5650**. 1785–88. *LBl* D 3.
P. I.

If the concept of space and time were not borrowed from the form of our sensibility, one would have to derive the synthetic propositions about them from the things themselves, thus space and time would have objective reality in themselves either as substances or accidents or relations; but if both were to precede the things, then they would have to be mere concepts, but from concepts no synthetic propositions can be derived.

Metaphysics.

Substance is the ultimate subject of reality. Its relation to the existence of this is called force, and it is this alone through which the existence of substance is indicated and in which its existence even exists.[47] Now since every force has a degree,[48] for many smaller degrees of the same kind there can be many subjects, and a whole can be composed of them, if they stand in community externally, or they can also be so combined that they constitute only one force, in which no external community of different subjects is to be found, i.e., unity of the subject of a high degree of force is the same as the multiplicity of subjects of smaller degrees, indeed the one can be transformed into the other. For if one drop of water were to become one drop of mercury (as far as its weight is concerned), then the number of parts would not be increased, thus not the number of subjects, yet the result would be the same as if 14 drops of water were condensed into one. Thus the simple subject is not divisible, for it is not divisible as if it were composed of many subjects, but rather as a unity of the subject,

18: 299

although of a high degree of force that can be altered into many subjects of a smaller degree of force. "The soul is simple" means that it does not consist of many subjects in space. This cannot be the case, for we do not cognize it through any forces that can appear in space; but from that it does not follow that the absolute unity of the subject could not be transformed into a multiplicity of them without alteration of the degree of reality as a whole.[49]

The constitution of something as an absolute subject that does not inhere in anything else signifies a force that does not consist in a multiplicity of reciprocally determining forces, but rather consists in a degree.

That a being should exist as a unity of substance and nevertheless be able to be dissolved into a multiplicity of them does not involve any contradiction. For it is not necessary that the multiplicity of the subjects must be antecedently given and hence that the substance must already be conceived as composite prior to its dissolution, i.e., as containing that multiplicity of subjects as parts which is possible through the dissolution of it. For if this dissolution is merely the effect of rendering asunder what formerly inhered in one thing, then inherence in a subsistence and the accident are transformed into an absolute subject. That always happens in the dissolution of degree. Here we never have the concept of the multiplicity of the subject, because it is considered internally and not in its external relation (extensively) as far as its magnitude is concerned. Nevertheless, the intensive magnitude can always be regarded as a potential multiplicity of subjects that can be separated; for instead of all degree of force ceasing (through which then the whole subject would also cease   18: 300 to be), these degrees of all forces and with them also the concept of one subject in which they inhere (for in this one this is not at all distinguished from the other) could exist separately from one another. The resisting force in a body could decrease either by the degree of that force being entirely lost or by that which departs from it existing as a separate subject, without any part that is separate from any other being taken away, rather with each remaining although with a diminished degree of force. P. II.

That we could validly infer from immediate perception and indeed universally that all thinking beings must be simple beings would be impossible, for perception cannot yield necessity unless there is a contradiction in the opposite: here the thinking subject is merely considered as the object of its own inner sense, since only the subject of all its own thoughts can be its object, hence, since it must be distinguished from all objects and their manifoldness, it can be represented through nothing other than the unity of apperception, but it is not on that account at all represented as merely a something without further predicates (as a subject). Thus thinking can take place only along with the unity of apperception. I cannot perceive any thoughts outside of myself, hence I also cannot perceive a thinking subject as such. A thinking subject can thus also represent its thought as having originated through the united representation of different separate thinking subjects.

On existence in subjects in general.

We can only think through judgments, since we only have concepts through the necessary unity of consciousness of the manifold of representations. In judgments everything that we think about objects is a predicate and the object that we think is itself a predicate in a further respect. Yet among what exists we must think of subjects in themselves that are not predicates, but our concept of their reality is none other than that of reality and its inherence, hence of force and its particular degrees. Only the subject remains merely a something. But every degree can be represented as composed of smaller ones and each as belonging to a subject, in which case it is a *compositum*, or as all belonging to one subject, in which case it is a simple. Now whether that which has existed as a unity of the subject, i.e., a high degree of force, could also exist as a multiplicity of subjects, and how it comes about that something that has existed as unity of the subject should exist as a multiplicity, can neither be explained nor refuted at all.

On Metaphysics.

I have proven that human reason in its speculative use can reach no other objects than objects of a possible experience, and even in the case of these it can reach nothing more than can be given in a possible experience, hence that since metaphysics does not place its importance in those cognitions that can be found or at least confirmed in the way of experience, but rather in that which goes beyond the bounds of all possible experience, all dogmatic use for it would be lost, indeed even its existence would be lost as useless, if the cognitions that we actually have *a priori* and without help from experience did not allow us to believe that their use, since they are independent of experience, could also reach further than experience, and from this again attacks and difficulties arise through false but deceptive judgments against important cognitions. Now it came down to how *a priori* cognitions, without being derived from experience, could nevertheless apply to all objects of experience and indeed to nothing else. I accomplished this by demonstrating *a priori* intuitions and also *a priori* concepts, the first of which exhibited nothing other than the form of appearances, the latter the form of the concepts of the things in general that appear, whose use, although they are *a priori* representations, extends merely to experience. Here everything that can be accomplished is comprised in one problem: How are synthetic cognitions *a priori* possible?

5653. 1785–89. *LBl* D 11.⁵⁰   18: 306
P. I.

Against material idealism.

It is based on this, that we are **immediately conscious of our own existence**, but are conscious of **outer things only through an inference** from the immediate consciousness of mere representations of things outside us to their existence, which inference, however, is not self-evident in its conclusion, as is proven by the well-known property of our imagination, which is a faculty for intuitively representing objects even without their presence.⁵¹

Against this argument it is sufficient only to adduce that the transcendental consciousness of our self, which accompanies the spontaneity of all the actions of our understanding, but which consists in the mere I without the determination of my existence in time, is certainly immediate, but the empirical consciousness of myself, which constitutes inner sense (as the former constitutes the form of the intellectuality of my subject) by no means occurs immediately, and that the consciousness of other things outside of me (which must also be intellectually presupposed and is to that extent not a representation of them in space, but can be called intellectual intuition, through which we have no cognition of things) and the determination of their existence in space must be simultaneous with the determination of my existence in time, that I am therefore not [conscious] of my own empirically determined existence any more than that of things outside me (which, as to what they are in themselves, I do not know).⁵²

For in space alone do we posit that which persists, in time there is   18: 307
unceasing change. But now the determination of the existence of a thing in time, i.e., in such a change, is impossible without also connecting its intuition to that which persists. This must therefore be [*crossed out*: given] intuited outside of us as an object of outer sense. But since I at the same time determine my existence and thus to that extent am not empirically conscious of myself, I also cannot be empirically conscious of that which persists outside of me, i.e., as given in space, rather I am conscious only of my determination of the representation of it insofar as I am merely affected by it in accordance with the form of space, in that I draw it in space and am thereby simultaneously conscious of my own existence in time.

The intuition of a thing as outside of me presupposes the consciousness of a determinability of my subject, in which I am not determining, which therefore does not belong to spontaneity, since that which is determining is not in me. And in fact I cannot think of any space as in me.* Thus the possibility of representing [*crossed out*: a] thing in space is grounded [*crossed out*: merely] on the consciousness of a determination through other things, which signifies nothing other than my original passivity, in which I am not at all active. That a dream produces [crossed out: the same sort of] illusion of existences outside of me does not prove anything to the contrary; for outer perceptions must always have preceded it. To have originally acquired a representation of something as outside of me without in fact having been passive is impossible. –53

*(Later addition: And through space the representation of an object as outside of me (in intuition) first acquires reality. Conversely, I would also [not] acquire the concept of the existence of something outside of me through space if the concept of a relation that belongs to *commercio* and indeed as given in perception did not lie at its ground. But this concept is that of mere passivity in a state of representations. That this is not inferred, since we do not perceive the cause of the existence of a representation in us, but is an immediate perception, must be proven. – If we were merely affected by our self yet without noticing this spontaneity, then only the form of time would be found in our intuition: and we would not be able to represent any space (existence outside of us). Empirical consicousness as the determination of my existence in time would therefore go around in a circle and presuppose itself – but would be particularly impossible, since even the representation of that which endures would be lacking, in which there is no continuous synthesis as in time.)

18: 308

P. II.

That this is the only possible ground for the proof.

That we ourselves must always simultaneously institute space and the determination of time, but we just as little need to determine thereby our existence in space as the existence of the things of space in time.

Persistence intrinsically pertains to the representation of space, as Newton said. The persistence of the form in our mind is not the same thing (for the form of time is equally persistent), rather [it is] the representation of something [crossed out: persistent] outside us, with which we underlie all determination of time and on that account represent as persistent, and hence cannot regard as spontaneity of self-determination. – The proposition is: the empirical consciousness of our existence in time is necessarily combined with the empirical consciousness of a relation to something outside us, and the one is just as little an illusion from a fallacious inference, indeed just as little an inference at all, as is the other.

The representation of space is the ground of the determination of time on account of persistence (likewise only in it can one acquire a representation of time as a magnitude through a line that I draw, while I am conscious of my synthesis merely in the subject).54 Now that which persists cannot be merely thought in the determination of time and belong

18: 309

to the spontaneity of self-determination, for then it would not be the basis of the determination of time. Consequently it must be represented in relation to the **mere** receptivity of the mind, i.e., in relation to something affecting it, which is different from me, and this representation cannot be inferred, but must be original.

Not everything that is in time is also in space, e.g., my representations: but everything that is in space is in time. In time, namely, I only represent myself both for my self alone as well as in community, and indeed not through inferences, but immediately, i.e., a correlate to my state, although without having cognition of it, and the sensible but real representation of this outer relation is space; this representation itself, however, hence also everything that is represented in space, is in time.

That if I make myself into an object space is not in me, but yet in the formal subjective condition of the empirical consciousness of myself, i.e., in time, proves that something outside of me, i.e., something which I must represent in a different way than myself, is bound up with the empirical consciousness of myself and that this is at the same time a consciousness of an outer relation, without which I could not empirically determine my own existence.

It comes down to this, that I am able to become conscious of myself in an outer relation through a special sense, which is however requisite for the determination of time. Space proves to be a representation that is not related to the subject as object; for otherwise it would be the representation of time. Now that it is not **related** as existing to the subject, but immediately to something distinct from the subject, that is the consciousness of the object as a thing outside me. Thus, that we have an outer **sense** and that even imagination can impress images on us only in relation to this, that is the proof of *dualismus*.

All objects of the senses are in time; but not everything that is in time   18: 310 (i.e., all objects) is in space. But now if all representations of things outside us were only objects of inner sense and representations of ourselves, then the objects of inner sense would at the same time be all objects, and space itself would be time.

The proof of dualism is grounded on the fact that the determination of our existence in time by means of the representation of space would contradict itself if one did not regard the latter as the consciousness of an entirely different relation than that of representations in us to the subject, namely as the perception of the relation of our subject to other things, and space as the mere form of this intuition. For if the [*crossed out*: representation] perception of space were grounded merely on our self without an object outside us, then it would at least be possible to become conscious of these representations as containing merely a relation to the subject. But since in the latter way only the intuition of time ever comes about, the object that we represent as spatial must rest on the representation of something other than our own subject. But that we can be conscious of an outer relation without the object itself, but rather can always cognize only the form of this relation of our self to its presence, is not a difficulty. It is also not an objection that in dreams and vivid fantasies it is possible to [have] the subjective side of these representations without the reality of the object. For without an outer sense, whose representations we merely repeat and combine in a different way (as also happens with inner sense when we fantasize), we would not be able to have any dreams at all.

[*Across the left half of the page*:] On Idealism.

[*At the margin*:]

Preface[55]

18:311   If, in order to explain the purposiveness of the things in the world, we introduce a cause that is the cause in accordance with the analogy of an understanding, that is a tautological explanation, for an end means that which has such a form as if the representation of the thing were at the same time its cause. But if we apply this same causality to the world insofar as it is a moral whole and to the reality of its laws through their outcome, namely the highest good, then it is a different story. For then *idem per idem* is not explained tautologically, but rather an effect is adduced that was not inferred from the world alone.

     Now it is also an issue whether one can say that God is the cause of a substance without at the same time having determined all its actions. To be sure, we do not have the least concept of the possibility of such a causality nor an example of its reality. But if this is assumed, then it would still only apply to the intelligible, with respect to which the concept of freedom is already necessarily intrinsically connected with the concept of a substance, since a substance must be the ultimate subject of its actions and cannot itself be the mode of action of another. We do not know how the substance of the world might be constituted in itself. But in its empirically cognizable character, which pertains merely to appearances, no thing is an object of creation;[56] everything in that is always intrinsically determined in the world of the senses, which does not do any damage to the freedom of the intelligible. Now if one said: in the intelligible character everything is good (because 18:312   time disappears there), only the causality through freedom is not to be comprehended. And the possibility of being the cause of a substance, even less so. Thus the difficulties adduced from this against freedom amount to nothing, because one cannot connect any concepts with the *hypothesi*.

5654. 1788–89 (after 13 October 1788). *LBl* D 7.[57]   18:312
P. I.

Against Idealism.

If there were no outer objects of our senses, hence no sense at all but only imagination, then it at least would be possible to become conscious of this its action as a spontaneity; but in that case this representation would belong only to inner sense and contain nothing persistent that could be the ground for the determination of our existence in empirical consciousness. The mind must therefore be immediately conscious of a representation of outer sense as such, i.e., not through an inference from the representation as an effect to something outside as a cause, which, because it is valid only as an hypothesis, contains no certainty.

But how can the consciousness of a representation of the senses occur as a merely passive determination and yet we be conscious of its object as external, but at the same time also be conscious of it or its appearance as persisting?

Now here it should be noticed that every object signifies something distinct from the representation, but which is only in the understanding, hence even inner sense, which makes ourself into the object of our representations, signifies something distinct from ourself (as transcendental object of apperception). Thus if we did not relate the representations to something distinct from ourselves, they would never yield knowledge of objects; for as far as inner sense is concerned, it consists only in the relation of representations, whether they signify something or nothing, to the subject.

The above proof says the same as this: if there were not an outer sense, i.e., a faculty for being conscious of **something** as outside of us   18:313
immediately (without an inference of reason) and of being conscious of ourself by contrast in relation [to it], then it would not even be possible for the representation of outer things as such to belong to intuition in us, i.e., not even that of space. For inner sense can contain nothing except [*crossed out*: the succession] the temporal relation of our representations.

One can well set time in oneself, but one cannot set oneself in time and determine oneself in it, and yet in that consists empirical self-consciousness. Thus in order to determine one's existence in time, one must intuit something else in an outer relation, which for that very reason must be considered as persisting.

Because time cannot be externally perceived in things, since it is only a determination of the inner sense, we can only [*crossed out*: represent] determine ourselves in time insofar as we stand in relation to things outside us and consider ourselves therein, and that which is outside us introduces an existence insofar as it is not subject to alteration, i.e., that is persistent.

The existence of a thing in time cannot be determined through the relation of its representation in the imagination to other representations of it, but rather through the relation of a representation of sense to that in its object which is persistent.

P. II.

I [*crossed out*: still work my way toward] climb even through difficult subtleties to the peak of principles, not so much as if the healthy understanding would not be able to get there without this detour, but rather in order to entirely rob of power all of the sophistical subtleties that are raised against it.

18:313
18:314

5655. 1788–89. *LBl* B 6.

Trichotomy. Every relation of representations through concepts has a threefold dimension: 1. the relation of a representation to consciousness, 2. of another representation to consciousness, 3. the connection of both together in one consciousness. It is through this that the connection of representations with one another first becomes possible (*connexa uni tertio sunt connexa inter se.*)[a]

I cannot say through inner sense: [*crossed out*: I am in space] Space or spatial relation is in me, but time or temporal relation is in me. On the contrary, time is in me, and I am in time. That [*crossed out*: I as] the thinking thing in the representation of inner sense is mere appearance to itself means nothing more than if I say: I, in whom temporal relation is alone to be found, am in time. The *continens* is at the same time *contentum.*[b]

The proposition that I am conscious of myself as the object of a sense means the same thing as that I cognize myself in the appearance as my existence is given to thought. It also means the same as that I am in time, but the temporal relations are merely in me (it is not possible to represent them as outside me, like those of space, although the representation of the latter is also in me).

It would not be possible for me to represent the temporal relation as intuitable merely in me and yet also to represent myself as an object of intuition in this time if this consciousness concerned myself as a thing in itself.

I intuit myself in time, but not in space; but time is a relation in me, however space is a relation outside of me.

That I am in time, which is however a mere relation in me, consequently that the *continens* is a *contentum* and I am in myself, already

---

[a] What are connected in a third thing are connected among themselves.

[b] That which contains is at the same time the content.

indicates that [*crossed out*: if I place myself in time] I think of myself in a twofold sense.

P. II.

Likewise, if I attend to the representations of inner sense, I dissolve everything into mere temporal relations, and there is nothing absolute for the understanding. – [*Crossed out*: For with the exception of the feeling of pleasure, which is not a cognition[58]] Everything is representation in us, set in temporal relations, and if we ask, what then does it represent, then it is either [*crossed out*: outer things] that which is outside [*crossed out*: in space], which we have just seen relates to mere spatial relations, in which the thing in itself is uncognizable for us, or it is the inner relation of these representations to one another in time, where the pure synthesis that the concepts of the understanding asserts is in turn nothing other than the connection of these representations with regard to the unity of time, where the feeling of pleasure and the faculty of desire connected with it provides those representations with their mere relation to the subject without cognition or to the object through the determination of the causality of the subject, hence also without cognition of the thing in itself, and of this there remains nothing but the idea of something that indicates my self-consciousness [*crossed out*: best determined in accordance with its nature] as an object independent of all these temporal relations, but which yields nothing that would be cognizable in itself and without relation to the causality of my self in the sensible world.

18:315

That which speaks decisively for the empirical consciousness of myself as an appearance, not a thing itself, is the mere manner of determining my existence in this consciousness. **Time exists** as a totality of relations **in me** (not of relations outside me) [*crossed out*: and yet I say I am in time], i.e., I must presuppose my existence (time is the determination of my existence) in order to be able to think of time as the determination of my existence and that of all things outside me. Nevertheless I also still say: **I am in time**, i.e., (I am a determination of time) I must presuppose time in order to be able to [*crossed out*: cognize] determine it (empirically) through my existence. Now if my existence were to be understood here in the same sense, then there would be a contradiction here. Thus my existence which I presuppose must be taken in a different sense than when I consider it merely as the determination of time. But now prior to all determination it is merely the existence of a thing, but a thing which, although it is not determined in time, is yet as an existence (in itself) thoroughly determined, although not cognized by me as such; thus, insofar as time must be presupposed in order to determine me and my existence, it is mere appearance. Nothing is hereby taken away from the experiential cognition of myself, only this does not extend to all possible cognition, and thus the supersensible remains, although at

18:316

the same time any attempt to determine it theoretically is declared to be excessive.

The first means: all things outside me are appearances, for the [*crossed out*: subjective] condition for determining their existence is in me. – The second means: I am myself appearance, and time, which is merely in me, can itself serve me as a condition only insofar as I distinguish my pure I from it.

18:316 **5656**. 1788–89 (after 23 November 1788).[59] Kant's note on a letter from C. F. Heilsberg, 23 November 1788 (10: 554).

That an object corresponds to the categories of magnitude can only be demonstrated in a sensible intuition.[60] If one departs from this in even a single case, then the entire beautiful precision of the system in which one sees the ground from which all **cognition** *a priori* comes is lost.

Numerical concepts are those which first determine the concept of time as that of a *quanti*. They do not presuppose the concept of time, but only its sensible form, and they first determine the concept of time as a *quanti*. However, through that no object in time (likewise no object in space, whose parts all exist at the same time), nor my own existence in

18:317 time, is determined, but only the synthetic unity of the manifold, through which a magnitude is possible, is given, thus the concept of magnitude is given reality without any quality of it (because that can be given only in time) being touched.

Imputation is the judging of an action (of a free agent in accordance with laws) with regard to its origin in freedom. This origin however can only be conceived insofar as it is under moral laws, for that is the causality from freedom.

18:317 **5657**. 1788–89. *LBl M* 20.

N.B. **On transcendent ideas**. I cannot even support the concepts of the primordial being and of the supersensible in general with the categories. But if I call it a cause, I understand thereby only a being from whose concept I can derive my knowledge of the order of the world (the physical and the moral), as I derive these from things in the world which I know through their effects. I do not thereby really attribute anything to this being, but only think of an unknown principle for my theoretical and especially my practical use of reason as a being in the world in which I am to consider and act, and indeed one that is not in accord merely with a sensibly restricted determination. The assertion of my manner of thinking in conformity with this principle, namely that it also agrees with the world in a [*crossed out*: interconnection] domain and duration that is wider than I may understand is the belief in such a being. Its theoretical determination consists of mere words, which apart from the relation of such a concept as a principle of the practical (where it has an absolutely necessary interest) has no significance.

5661. 1788–90. *LBl* Kiesewetter 1.[61]　　　　　　　　　18: 318

Answer to the question: Is it an experience that we think?

An empirical representation of which I am conscious is a **perception**; that which I add in thought to the representation of the imagination by means of the apprehension and comprehension *(comprehensio aesthetica)* of the manifold of perception is **the empirical cognition of the object**, and the judgment which expresses an empirical cognition is **experience**.[62]

If I think of a square *a priori*, I cannot say that this **thought** is an 　18: 319 experience; but this may well be said if I apprehend an **already drawn figure** in perception and think of the comprehension of its manifold by means of the imagination under the concept of a square. In experience and through it I am **instructed** by means of the senses; but if I merely arbitrarily think of an object of the senses, I am not instructed by it and my representation depends on nothing in the object, rather I am entirely the author of it.

But also the consciousness of having such a thought is not an experience, for the very reason that since the thought is not an experience, consciousness itself is nothing empirical. Nevertheless, this thought brings forth an object of experience or a determination of the mind that can be observed, insofar, namely, as it is affected through the faculty of thinking; I can thus say that I have experienced what belongs to grasping a figure with four equal sides and right angles in thought in such a way that I can demonstrate its properties. This is the empirical consciousness of the determination of my condition in time through thought: the thought itself, although it also occurs in time, takes no regard of time when the properties of a figure are to be thought. But experience is impossible without a connection to the determination of time, because I am thereby passive and feel myself to be affected in accordance with the formal condition of inner sense.

The consciousness when I **institute an experience** is the representation of my existence insofar as it is empirically determined, i.e., in time. Now if this consciousness were itself in turn empirical, then this temporal determination, as contained under the conditions of the temporal determination of my state, would in turn have to be represented. Yet another time would therefore have to be given, **under** which (not **in** which) the time that constitutes the formal condition of my inner experience would be contained. Thus there would be a time in which and with which at the same time a given time flows, which is absurd.[63] However, the consciousness of instituting an experience or also of thinking in general is a **transcendental consciousness, not experience**.

18:320

Comments on this Essay.

The action of the imagination in giving an intuition for a concept is *exhibitio*. The action of the imagination in making a concept out of an empirical intuition is *comprehensio*.

The apprehension of the imagination, *apprehensio aesthetica*. The composition of it, *comprehensio aesthetica* (aesthetic comprehension): I grasp the manifold together in a whole representation and thus it acquires a certain form.

18:320 **5662.** 1788–90. *LBl* Kiesewetter 2.

On Miracles.[64]

No motion can be produced in the world either through a miracle or through a spiritual being without causing an equal motion in the opposite direction, thus in accordance with laws of effect and counter-effect in matter, for otherwise a motion of the universe in empty space could arise.

Further, no alteration in the world (thus no beginning of that motion) can arise without being determined by causes in the world in accordance with laws of nature in general, thus not through freedom or a miracle proper; for since time does not determine the order of events, but rather the events, conversely, determine time in accordance with the law of nature (of causality), an event that would occur or be determined in time independently of those laws would presuppose an alteration in empty time, consequently the condition of the world itself would be determined in absolute time.

Comments.

1. One can divide miracles into **outer** and **inner**, i.e., into alterations of appearance for the outer and those for the inner sense. The former happen in space, the latter in time. If miracles in space were possible, then it would be possible for appearances to occur in which effect and counter-effect are not equally large. All alterations in space are, namely, motions. But the cause of a motion that would be produced by a miracle

18:321 should not be sought among the appearances. The law of effect and counter-effect, however, rests on the fact that cause and effect belong to the world of the senses (to the appearances), i.e., are represented in relative space; now since this does not hold of the causes in the case of miracles in space, they also would not stand under the law of effect and counter-effect. Now if a motion were effected by a miracle, then, since it would not stand under the law of effect and counter-effect, the *centrum gravitatis* of the world would be altered by it, i.e., in other words, the world would move in empty space; however, a motion in empty space is a contradiction, namely, it would be the relation of a thing to a nothing, for empty space is a mere idea.

In a similar way it is proven that there can be no miracles with regard to appearances in time. An appearance in time is, namely, a miracle if its cause cannot be given in time, if it does not stand under the conditions of time. But since it is only through the fact that both cause and effect belong among appearances that the latter can be determined in relative time, this could not happen in the case of an effect that was produced by a miracle, since its cause would not belong among the appearances. A supernatural occurrence would therefore not be determined in relative, but in absolute (empty) time. But a determination in empty time is a contradiction, because for each relation two correlates must be given.

2. A miracle is an event whose ground is not to be found in nature. It is either a *miraculum rigorosum*, which has its ground in a thing outside the world (thus not in nature); or a *miraculum comparativum*, which to be sure has its ground in a nature, but in one whose laws we do not know; of the latter sort are the things that we ascribe to spirits. A *miraculum rigorosum* is either *materiale*, where the power that produces the miracle is external to the world, or *formale*, where the power is in the world, but its determination takes place outside the world, e.g., if one holds the drying of the Red Sea for the passage of the children of Israel to be a miracle, it is a *miraculum materiale* if one takes it to be an immediate effect of the divinity, but a *miraculum formale* if one lets it be dried out 18: 322 by a wind, but a wind that was sent by the divinity.

Further, the *miraculum* is either *occasionale* or *praestabilitum*. In the first case, one assumes that the divinity has been the immediate means; in the second, however, one lets the event be produced through a series of causes and effects, which however all exist for the sake of this single event. –

5663. 1788–90. *LBl* Kiesewetter 7.   18: 322

On the formal and material sense of some words.

There are several words that have a different sense if used in the singular than if used in the plural; in that case they are to be taken in a formal sense in the singular, in a material sense in the plural: these are unity, perfection, truth, possibility.* Unity used in the singular is qualitative, used in the plural quantitative. Qualitative unity is to be considered as the ground of the whole, quantitative unity as a part of the whole. Thus, e.g., one cannot say that warmth consists of warmnesses, one thus does not determine its magnitude in accordance with the parts that it contains, but rather in accordance with the effects that it produces, e.g., that it causes a body to expand, and thus one cannot ascribe it a genuine magnitude, but rather a degree, thus the unity that is found in it is a qualitative unity. – The unities out of which discrete magnitudes (numbers) consist are quantitative unities.

Perfection (taken formally) of a thing is the correspondence of its realities with one ideal; **perfections** (used materially) are these realities.**

Truth in the singular (used formally and qualitatively) is the correspondence of our cognition of an object with it; **truths** in the plural (used materially and quantitatively) are true propositions.

Possibility of an object (used formally and qualitatively); **possibilities** (used materially and quantitatively), objects, insofar as they are possible.

18: 323   *(One sees that this is grounded on the titles of the categories: Quantity, Quality, Relation, and Modality.)

**(Thus we speak of the perfection of a clock insofar as we find in it what we can expect of a good clock. The perfections of a clock are those properties of it that correspond to the concept of a good clock. – But we must also distinguish quantitative and qualitative perfection from perfection.)

18: 323   **5665**. 1780s. *M* I.[65]

Logic deals with thought without an object. Physics, with the cognition of things from experience. Metaphysics, with their cognition prior to all experience. The origin is twofold: 1. how we have come to that: psychology; 2. how the *a priori* cognitions are possible: transcendental philosophy.

18: 323   **5667**. 1780s. *M* I.

Metaphysics is the system [*crossed out*: of the principles] of all *a priori* cognition from concepts in general.

18: 324   The science of the possibility, scope, etc., of *a priori* cognition is **transcendental philosophy**. The sum-total of metaphysics. To extract transcendental philosophy and boundaries from what is present to pure reason: the critique of pure reason.

18: 324   **5668**. 1780s. *M* I–II.

Some cognitions are *a priori secundum quid*,[a] others *simpliciter*, where there is nothing empirical.

The criterion of *a priori* cognition is necessity.

18: 324   **5670**. 1780s. *M* II.

Every cognition that is *respective a priori*[b] is called a principle.

[a] *a priori* relative to something
[b] relatively *a priori*

5672. 1780s? (1778–79?) *M* II. 18:324
All cognition has its origin either *a posteriori*, from experience, or *a priori*. Metaphysics is a science of the *a priori* cognitions.
The *principia* of philosophy are either *a posteriori*: [*crossed out*: physiological] physical, or *a priori*: metaphysical.

5674. 1780s. *M* II. 18:325
Metaphysics is the science of the principles of all *a priori* cognition and of all cognition that follows from these principles. Mathematics contains such principles, but is not the science of the possibility of these principles.

5675. 1780s. *M* IV. 18:325
Metaphysics cannot be the foundation of religion, but can well be its shield, and indeed as such it is indispensable. For the opponent possesses a dialectical metaphysics, to which we must oppose the critical metaphysics; and this opponent lies in every natural human reason.[66]

5679. 1780s? (1776–78?) *M* X. 18:325
Metaphysics deals either with objects of pure reason or with objects of experience through pure reason, not in accordance with empirical but in accordance with rational principles.

5680. 1780s? (1776–78?) *M* X. 18:326
1. On principles of pure reason: transcendental philosophy. 2. *Metaphysica applicata* to objects: nature and freedom.

5686. 1780s? (1778–79?) 1776–78? At *M* 4, §11, to *M* §7, in *Possibile*. 18:327
Principium Contradictionis is the principle of all logical possibility, i.e., of concepts, insofar as they can be cognized *a priori*, but not of things.

5687. 1780s? (1778–79?) 1776–78?? *M* 4. 18:327
The possibility of analytic connection can be understood *a priori*, but not that of synthetic connection.

5688. 1780s? (1778–79?) 1776–78?? *M* 4. 18:327
The possibility of a concept rests on the fact that it does not contradict itself; the possibility of a thing rests on the fact that the concept has objective reality, that an example of it can be given, i.e., that an object corresponds to it, e.g., *ens absolute necessarium*.[67]

5699. 1780–84. *M* 10, opposite §29f., in *Connexum*. 18:329
The *principium rationis* is valid only of experience;[68] for we cannot have any concept of a real ground except through experience,

namely where if something is posited something else follows in accordance with a rule (hence is determined). Thus we cannot say anything about the relation of things to real grounds on the basis of mere concepts.

18:331   **5708.** 1780s. *M* 14, in *Ens*.

On the rule in general.

It is the objective unity of the consciousness of the manifold of representations (consequently that which holds universally). The rule is either empirical, if the condition of unity lies in mere perceptions. It can thus not be objective except in relation to possible experience as cognition of the objects of perception. The possibility of experience is thus the

18:332   ground of the [*crossed out*: necessity] objective validity of the rules of perception, and this possibility of experiences is grounded on the necessary unity of the consciousness of representations insofar as cognition (of objects) is to be had therefrom. All representations must be represented in relation to one consciousness and thus as universally subjected to the unity of consciousness (we are not always conscious of this relationship to consciousness, and then this representation is obscure, but nevertheless always compared with this consciousness).

18:332   **5709.** 1785–89. *M* 14, at §55, in *Ens*.[69]

On the existence of outer things.

Idealism is the opinion that we immediately experience only our own existence, but can only infer that of outer things (which inference from effect to cause is in fact uncertain). But we can only experience our own existence insofar as we determine it in time, for which that which persists is required, which representation has no object within us. This representation also cannot be grounded on the mere imagination of something that endures outside us, for it is impossible to imagine something for which no corresponding object can be given. It is that which gives the object in intuition, and insofar as our representation belongs merely to the consciousness of our self it has no such object.

18:332   **5710.** 1780s? (1778–79?) *M* 15, at §55, still in *Ens*.
Everything that exists is thoroughly determined; but it is not this thoroughgoing determination that constitutes the concept of existence, rather that a thing is posited absolutely and not merely in relation to its concept.[70]

I cognize existence through experience, but not the thoroughgoing determination; this is done through reason.[71]

5722. 1780s? 1776–79?? *M* 16, opposite §60, still in *Ens*.[72] 18:335

We cannot assume any object to be possible except that which we exhibit in intuition, thus whose reality can be exhibited; for otherwise, if the representation does not contradict itself, the thought but not the thing is possible.

Logical inner possibility (in accordance with the principle of contradiction) without real possibility (to which no intuition corresponds): empty concept.[73]

We can cognize impossibility only in accordance with the principle of contradiction, but if the issue is objects, then we can cognize impossibility in those for which no intuition can be given.

5723. 1785–89. *M* 16, at §55. 18:335

We place the difference between possibility and reality in the connection with space and time, which we regard as necessary in themselves, hence as the foundations of all reality. Now if we consider things merely in accordance with the form of space and time, but not as connected with it, then they are merely possible. This distinction must disappear if the issue is that of the thing in itself. The second distinction involving both concepts is merely logical: namely what is indeterminate is merely possible; the actual is possible only in that which is thoroughly determined. For the former contains a mere relation of the object to the understanding, the latter with my existence. What is possible in its thoroughgoing determination is necessary if it is possible as a ground in every respect (hence as *independens*). If it is possible only as a consequence then, if the possibility is thorough, there must be a ground for it. The concept of thoroughgoing determination is a relation to omniscience.

5726. 1785–89. *M* 17, at §61ff., §69ff., still in *Ens*. 18:336

Space and time.

From the beginning in accordance with the distinction between analytic and synthetic cognition and the principle of contradiction. Every object of thought is either something or nothing.[74] Either insofar as no thought corresponds to the object, i.e., the thought itself is nothing, i.e., contradicts itself, or no object (nothing in intuition) corresponds to the thought (which does not contradict itself). Thinking, considered subjectively as representation, before it is analyzed, always has an object; but if thinking contradicts itself, then the thought and therefore the object as well are nothing, and both are stricken out. Where the thought remains, then the object, in terms of the *analysi*, is problematic.

Now something can be posited either simply or repeatedly (*iterative*) 18:337 in order to bring about the representation of the object; in the latter case it is multiplicity, in the former unity. All multiplicity is thus homogeneous, and the repeated positing is addition. The object whose representation arises through the multiplicity of the given is a *Quantum*; and the representation of it as an object that contains multiplicity is that of magnitude. That from which something composite is constituted is called a unity and is comparatively not composite (i.e., not composed out of **the same unit**), hence it is simple. Thus units are relatively simple, but in themselves they could again be composite, i.e., magnitudes.

An object of a certain kind is uniform in the same way, e.g., space. As multiplicity, however, the unity can still be unhomogeneous with the *Quanto*, and the unity can be a *Quantum* that is in turn composed out of units of some entirely different kind. Accordingly, not every multiplicity is a magnitude, but only that which is homogeneous with the object in which the magnitude is considered. What is a group, what is counting, what is number, what is infinite magnitude: a given (but this is contradictory) or only infinite progress, through which the magnitude is only negatively determined. Space and time are *quanta a priori*. Measure. The measure of magnitude in itself is totality, of the comparatively given, unity (in intuition). We know only comparative magnitudes. Boundaries: space and time alone have them; magnitudes of pure thinking: limits. In thinking there are limits, in intuition, boundaries.

If the succeeding category is at an end, it must be considered in connection with the previous one. Immediately after the categories the concepts of comparison. Identity and diversity; similarity, equality, congruence. *Oppositum et contrarium.* And subsequently even the categories are compared. On the division in general.[75]

18:338

18:345   **5755.** 1783–84. *M* 28, at §102, in *Necessarium et contingens.*[76]

That existence which can be cognized entirely *a priori* is absolutely necessary; that which can be cognized only under a condition, consequently *a priori secundum quid*, is hypothetically necessary. The concept of an *absolute necessarii* is problematic, i.e., the possibility of such an object cannot be comprehended. The human understanding cannot cognize any existence *a priori* from the mere concept of a thing. It completes hypothetical necessity.

18:345   **5757.** 1785–88? (1780–83?) 1778–79? *M* 28, at §101.[77]

Correspondence with the conditions of an experience in general: possibility.

Connection of a thing with experience in general: actuality.

This connection insofar as it can be cognized *a priori*, i.e., independently from experience, is necessity.

5758. 1785–88? (1780–83?) 1778–79? *M* 28, at §101.   18: 345

From mere concepts the existence of a thing cannot be cognized, 18: 346
hence it cannot be cognized *simpliciter a priori*. But also not under the
presupposition of pure intuitions. Since other than concepts and intuitions *a priori* there is nothing but experience, for necessity there must be
experience which precedes that which is necessary, i.e., which precedes
the condition of actuality.

5759. 1785–88. *M* 28.   18: 346

Everything that exists is thoroughly determined. The absolutely necessary thing is to be regarded as existing, thus as thoroughly determined,
through its concept. *Deus est conceptus singularis*; that every predicate necessarily pertains to him and he is *unico modo* determinable does not prove
the necessity of his existence.[78]

5767. 1785–88. *M* 29, opposite §102.   18: 348

A judgment about the existence of an object is always synthetic. Necessary judgments do not on this account represent the object as necessary.

5772. 1785–89? (1780–83?) 1788–89?? *M* 30, opposite §108.   18: 349

The possibility of things is distinguished from the possibility, actuality, or necessity of their existence. The former consists merely in their
concept containing nothing internally contradictory; it is so to speak the
correspondence of their archetype with the understanding that thinks it.
The possibility of existence, by contrast, signifies the positing of such 18: 350
an object outside of the understanding. Now if thinking itself is not the
cause of this, then the matter and the ground of its combination must
lie outside of it. Existence does not belong at all to the idea of a thing,
and its possibility, if it is complete, cannot be distinguished from that of
its actuality and necessity.

5776. 1785–88. *M* 44, §114, Proposition 1, *Necessaria sunt unico tantum* 18: 351
modo ac ratione determinabilia.[a]

The *autor*[b] calls a thing *unico modo determinabile*[c] which is thoroughly
determined through its own concept; the only such thing is the *ens
realissimum*; for the *mere negativum*[d] is not a thing, and the *partim reale
partim negativum*[e] is not thoroughly determined by its concept. Now
Leibniz, in accordance with the precedent of *Cartesius*, attempted to

---

[a] Necessities are determinable in a unique way and reason.
[b] that is, Baumgarten
[c] determinable in a unique way
[d] that which is merely negative
[e] that which is partly real, partly negative

prove that a thing that is thoroughly determined through its concept also necessarily exists; but the inference was found to be invalid.[79] Therefore he or Wolff attempted to reverse the proposition and to say that every necessary thing is thoroughly determined through its concept, consequently whatever is not thoroughly determined through its concept is not a necessary being.[80] Now since there must somewhere be a necessary being, there must also be a being thoroughly determined through its concept, i.e., such must exist as an *ens realissimum*, hence there must be an *ens realissimum*. But in that case the [*crossed out*: opposed] inverse proposition (*per accidens*)[a] must also be true, but that because only a single thing can be an *ens realissimum*; and indeed because the concept of it is a *conceptus non communis* but *singularis*[b] and the connection of convertibility must on that account be a *conversionem simpliciter talem* and must be constituted from mere concepts, necessity must follow from the concept of the *realissimi* as this follows from the other concept – and that is false.

18:352

18:353 **5780.** 1780s? (1776–79?) *M* 33, at §114.
Even if the concept of a thing can only be determined in a single way, certainly these predicates pertain to it necessarily, but not existence; and an existence could be necessary, although not from the concept that we have or from any other; for existence cannot be inferred from the concept of any thing.

18:353 **5782.** 1783–84. *M* 33, at §114.
That which is necessary must be determined in a unique way, for its existence is to be cognized *a priori*. Now the *ens realissimum* is thoroughly determined by its concept, therefore only this can be an *ens necessarium*. If we want to assume such a thing, we must conceive of it thus; but its existence cannot be cognized *a priori* from the concept of the supreme reality, and everything is relative to the human understanding.

18:353 **5783.** 1783–84. *M* 34, at §114.
The *ens necessarium* is that the opposite of which is absolutely impossible. However, the human understanding cannot have any insight into 18:354 this impossibility except if its non-being contradicts its concept. Now the non-being of a thing never contradicts the concept of the thing in itself; thus the concept of the *entis necessarii* is unattainable for human reason, even though it is necessary to assume it, for otherwise the series of that which is conditionally necessary would never come to an end.
That it is only determinable in a single way follows from the fact that its existence is supposed to follow from the mere concept. Now

---

[a] That is, the proposition "At least one *ens realissimum* must exist."
[b] not a general but a singular concept

everything that exists is thoroughly determined, and existence can therefore only be inferred from a concept that is thoroughly determined; otherwise it does not follow from the concept at all, but only from the assumption of some other existence.

There is **a difference** between **assuming the necessary being for the sake of some other being** and **cognizing** a being **as necessary through its concept**.[81]

We cannot say that a being exists contingently because it is altered, but rather that in that case we cannot cognize its existence from its mere concept; for then it would have to be determinable only in a single way. But we cannot cognize the existence of anything at all from its mere concept, although if we could cognize it then thoroughgoing determination would be contained in its concept.

The concept of the *realissimi* alone fits the concept of the *entis necessarii*.[82]

5805. 1783–84. *M* 37, at §128, in *Mutabile et immutabile*.[83]   18:358

Alteration is the connection of contradictorily opposed determinations in the existence of a thing (which, however, do not contradict the concept of the thing, but are only *praedicatum praedicato*, not *subjecto*   18:359
oppositum).[a]

What makes that possible which is impossible in accordance with the mere concept of a thing? Time. (*Determinationes oppositae* can merely succeed one another.) Thus time does not belong to the concepts of things in themselves, but to the way in which we intuit them.[84]

5811. 1783–84. *M* 38, still in *Mutabile et immutabile*.   18:360

In themselves things cannot be determined *ad oppositum* either by themselves alone nor in community; for *nulli subiecto competit praedicatum ipsi oppositum*, and the *ratio <8 A est etiam ratio >8 Non A*.[b] Thus the time in which alone alteration can be thought is not a [*crossed out*: representation of the] determination of things in themselves; hence all alterations are merely determinations of appearances, and time itself, in which existence is determined as alterable, is not something that attaches to the existence of things in themselves, but merely to our manner of sensible representation (not the representation of the understanding). Thus it is not merely the being that is necessary in itself that is inalterable, but also everything intelligible. However, among objects of the senses every determination that constitutes alteration is necessary, but always only hypothetically *ad infinitum*. The principle of contradiction, insofar

---

[a] one predicate is opposed to the other, but not to the subject
[b] No subject contains a predicate opposed to itself; the ratio "less than 8 A" is actually the ratio "greater than 8 Non-A."

as it is restricted to that which is in time, does not pertain to concepts of things, but to mere appearances; and it is not self-contradictory if each of two predicates that are *opposita* occur in appearance in succession (*later addition*: not at the same time) and neither of them occur as things in themselves.[85]

As an object of sensible intuition I am alterable and cannot bring transcendental predicates of things in themselves, e.g., of the simple or composite, etc., to the concept of myself, but can only speak of my intuition. But as the subject of thinking and merely as an object of reason I cannot in turn cognize myself through any predicates that would give such an object *in concreto*, not through extension or persistence in time but also not through their opposites. Thus all psychology as a doctrine pertains only to the human being as a thinking being, not to the mere I in general; however, psychology as critique avoids taking that which holds of me insofar as I am a human being as holding of me as a thinking being in general.[86]

18:369   **5854.** 1783–84. *M* 57, at §§191–204, *Substantia et accidens.*

The threefold way in which things determine existence. Thus, first, the real relation of the subject, 2nd, to the cause, 3. of the unification in a whole of substances.

The category of relation (of the unity of consciousness) is preeminent among them all. For unity properly concerns only the relation; thus the latter comprises the content of judgments in general and can alone be thought as **determined** *a priori*.

On the section on *substantia* (the relation of realities). A category
18:370   is the concept by means of which an object in general is regarded as determined with regard to a logical function of judgments in general (i.e., of the objective unity on the consciousness of the manifold), i.e., that I **must** think the manifold of its intuition by means of one of these moments of the understanding.[87]

For this reason there are three logical functions under a certain title, hence also three categories: because two of them demonstrate the unity of consciousness in two *oppositis*, while the third in turn combines the consciousness of the two. Further kinds of unity of consciousness cannot be conceived. For if *a* is a consciousness that connects a manifold, and *b* is another which connects in the opposite way, then *c* is the connection of *a* and *b*.

Judicia infinita.[a] "*Anima est non mortalis*"[b] does not signify merely that *A* belongs under the *sphaerum non B*, but rather under the sphere *C*

---

[a] infinite judgments
[b] The soul is non-mortal.

outside of *B*, which restricts and bounds *B*; thus it signifies the limitation of the proposition "*a est b*."[88]

5864. 1785–89. *M* 65, at §216, in *Status*.   18:371

Logic, which propounds objective rules for the use of the faculty of cognition, and ethics, which does this with regard to the faculty of desire (the ought), both presuppose only **faculties**[a] of the mind. Psychology, which explains what happens, and does not prescribe what ought to happen, concerns itself with **mental powers**.[b]

5871. 1780–83? (1785–88?) (1776–79?) *M* 68, at §227, in *Simplex et*   18:373
compositum.

We can only notice change in that which persists. If everything flowed, then the flow itself could not be perceived. Thus the experience of coming and ceasing to be is only possible by means of that which persists. There is therefore something in nature that remains (neither comes nor ceases to be), and this is substance. Only the *accidentia* change. *Principium* of the possibility of experiences. The location designates the substance. In different locations there are different substances; what attaches to what persists in a location and is distinguished from that which persists is *accidens*.[89]

5875. 1780s? (1776–79?) *M* 69, at §231, in *Monas*.   18:374

The only thing that is cognized *a posteriori* in the appearances is the matter or what is real in it, namely that which corresponds to sensation. What is formal in appearances, space and time, is cognized *a priori* and is pure intuition. To experience there belongs in addition to [*crossed out*: appearance] intuition the real in general and unity of the manifold of intuition.

5876. 1783–84. *M* 69, at §239, in *Monas*.   18:374

On space and time.

It is so far from being the case that the sensible intuitions of space and time could be confused representations that they rather afford the most distinct cognitions of all, namely mathematical cognitions. And that they are the forms of sensible intuition makes it comprehensible how mathematical cognitions of [*crossed out*: appearances *a priori*] things *a priori* are possible; which 1. would not occur if the objects of the senses were things in themselves, 2. also not if appearances were nothing other than indistinct representations of things; for in that case

[a] *Vermögen*
[b] *Gemüthskräften*

our cognition of appearances would always be derived merely *a pos-teriori*, since their form would not be in our senses but rather in the things.

The mathematical properties of matter, e.g., infinite divisibility, prove that space and time do not belong to the properties of things, but to the properties of the representations of things in sensible intuition; for since what is essential in these representations is composition, if I cancel that out nothing remains (thus not even anything simple).

18:375 Space is not an *a priori* concept, but an intuition that precedes the concept. For whence should synthetic judgments *a priori* arise? and what sort of an object should be represented by them, since space does not yet contain any object?

Space itself is an *a priori* synthesis.

18:375 **5879**. 1785–88. *M* 69, at §239.

The (concept of) space is itself only a form of composition; thus, if this is cancelled out, everything is cancelled out and nothing remains.[90]

18:376 **5885**. 1780s? 1776–79? *M* 71, at §§238–9.

Space and time are *composita idealia* not of substances or accidents, but of relations that precede things.

18:376 **5886**. 1780s? 1776–79?? *M* 71, at §240.

Space contains the form of all coordination in intuition, time the form of all subordination.

18:377 **5893**. 1780s? 1776–79? *M* 74, at §§247–8, in *Finitum et infinitum*.

The **greatest** and **most unrestricted** is unique (*later addition*: not: it contains everything in itself). Absolute totality is that which is unrestricted in a certain respect.

The progress in the construction of a magnitude is either finite or infinite. Both concern not the magnitude of the thing, but that of the measurement, and hold only of appearances. The **infinite** is never given, but only the condition of the possibility of the *progressus in infinitum* or *indefinitum*.

(*Later addition*: *Infinitudo* is not the idea of the *omnitudo*, also not of the *maximi*, nor of totality.)

The infinitude of possible or actual addition.

18:378 **5896**. 1780s? 1776–79?? *M* 75, at §248, still in *Finitum et infinitum*.

The totality of that which can be thought only by means of a *progressus* to the infinite is impossible. That which can be thought as a *quantum* merely through a concept of the understanding can also be represented as given as infinite, for it is given prior to the *progressus*.

5897. 1780s? 1776–79?? *M* 75, at §248.   18: 378

What is only given through composition is [*crossed out*: on that account] always finite, although the composition extends to infinity.

5898. 1780s? 1776–79?? *M* 75, at §248.   18: 378

Space and time both are nothing other than compositions of sensible impressions. This composition proceeds to infinity, but is never infinite. The magnitude of space presupposes the magnitude of time.

Infinitude of division. In infinite time, infinitely small.

5902. 1785–89. *M* 76, still in *Finitum et infinitum*.   18: 379

A thing in itself does not depend on our representations, and can thus be much greater than our representations reach. But appearances are themselves only representations, and their magnitude, i.e., the idea of their generation through *progressus*, cannot be greater than this *progressus*; and since this is never given as infinite, but rather as only possible to infinity, the magnitude of the world as appearance is also not infinite, but the *progressus* in it proceeds to infinity.

5903. 1780s? 1776–79? *M* 77, still in *Finitum et infinitum*.   18: 379

If space and time were properties of things in themselves, then it would not follow from the fact that they are mathematically infinite, i.e., that the *progressus* in them, insofar as they are given as entirely infinite, is greater than any number, that they are impossible, but only that they are incomprehensible for us. But now space and time are not things in themselves, and their magnitude is not given in itself, but only through the *progressus*. Now since a *progressus in infinitum* that has been given in its entirety is a contradiction, an *infinitum mathematicum datum* is impos-   18: 380
sible, but a *quantum in infinitum dabile* is possible.*[a]* From this, however, it does not follow that space and time in themselves have boundaries, for this is also impossible, but only that they are not things in themselves at all, but always have only those boundaries where our thoughts and representations have come to an end.[91]

5906. 1783–84. *M* 79, at §265, in *Idem et diversum*.   18: 380

Argumentum on the objective reality of time.

It may be objected that the unknown something *x* which at one time   18: 381
produces the appearance of the egg, at another time produces that of the chick in me, so that something must have altered in the object, since it could not have contained the ground of two opposed determinations

---

[a] A mathematical infinite that is given is impossible, but a quantity that can be given *ad infinitum* is possible.

at the same time. I reply: It is the same object, which produces the ground of the appearance of two opposed states as existing successively, and thus the appearance of an alteration. This is not more difficult to explain than how [*crossed out*: appearance] alteration is possible, i.e., where a thing or a group of things should contain the ground of two opposites.[92]

18: 381   **5907.** 1785–88? 1776–79? *M* 80, at §269, still in *Idem et diversum.*

Leibniz's proposition is that *numerica diversitas* must also be *specifica diversitas* and conversely that *specifica identitas totalis* must also be *numerica*.[a,93] This last proposition is valid for an object of pure reason, e.g., an *ens realissimum* is *specifice totaliter idem* with another *realissmo*.[b] If it were in space and time, *numerica identitas*, namely that it is a single being, would not follow from that.

Appearances are different things merely through difference in locations, for the difference of the locations precedes them *a priori* and produces numerical diversity regardless of the quality of the things.[94]

In contrast, the specific difference of things among things in themselves or the difference of quality always constitutes different things. But in the case of *phaenomenis* it can and also must be one and the same thing that is differently determined at different times; thus here it is said: *numero idem potest esse specifice diversum*[c] if by that one understands each determination through a different quality.

18: 383   **5914.** 1780s? (1776–79?) *M* 93, at §308ff., in *Causa et causatum.*

The *Principium contingentiae* signifies that properly speaking nothing exists except what is absolutely contingent, i.e., that its existence must be cognized objectively as determined if it is subjectively determined in perception. – Everything is necessary, either absolutely or hypothetically; yet even so nothing is absolutely necessary, but only in relation to the possibility of objects of experience.

Contingens is, in a logical sense, either that whose non-existence cannot be thought or that whose non-existence is possible; the latter we cannot cognize. It requires cognition of that which is necessary.

18: 384   **5919.** 1780s? (1776–79??) *M* 93, at §307, still in *Causa et causatum.*

The existence of a thing can never be cognized as absolutely contingent or absolutely necessary relative to a concept that I have of it.

---

[a] Numerical diversity must also be diversity of species, and total identity of species must also be numerical identity.

[b] One *ens realissimum* is totally identical in species with another.

[c] That which is numerically the same can be specifically different.

5920. 1780s. (1776–79?) *M* 93, at §307.   18:384

Everything that exists is necessary either in itself or through a cause.

5923. 1783–84. *M* 94–5, at §307ff.[95]   18:385

Deduction of pure cognitions *a priori*.

In experience alone can our concepts be given fully *in concreto*, hence there alone can their objective reality be fully exhibited. Concepts to whose nature it is contrary to be exhibited in experience are mere ideas. Hence the objective reality of all concepts, i.e., their significance, is to be sought in the relation to possible experience. Others, which are, namely, mere ideas, can certainly be assumed as hypotheses, but cannot count as demonstrable.

Now when it is a matter of the possibility of pure cognition *a priori*, we can transform the question into this: whether experience contains merely cognition that is given only *a posteriori*, or whether something is also encountered in it which is not empirical and yet contains the ground of the possibility of experience.

There first belongs to all experience the [*crossed out*: immediate] representation of the senses. Second, consciousness; this, if it is immediately combined with the former, is called empirical consciousness, and the representation of the senses combined with empirical consciousness is called perception. If experience were nothing more than an agglomeration of perceptions, then nothing would be found in it which is not of empirical origin.

But the consciousness of perceptions relates all representation only to   18:386
our self as modifications of our condition; they are in this case separated among themselves, and are especially not cognitions of any things and are related to no object. They are thus not yet experience, which must, to be sure, contain empirical representation, but at the same time must contain cognition of the objects of the senses.

If we ask logic what can be called cognition in general, a concept (or sum of them) is a representation that is related to an object and that designates it; and insofar as we connect (separate) one concept with another in a judgment, then we think something about the object that is deisgnated through a given concept, i.e., we cognize it by judging it. All cognition, hence also that of experience, accordingly consists of judgments; and even concepts are representations that are prepared for possible judgments, for they represent something that is given in general as cognizable through a predicate.[96]

Thus experience is possible only through judgments, in which to be sure perceptions comprise the empirical materials, but the relation of which to an object and the cognition of which through perceptions cannot depend on empirical consciousness alone.

The form of every judgment, however, consists in the objective unity of the consciousness of the given concepts, i.e., in the consciousness that these **must** belong to one another, and thereby designate an object in whose (complete) representation they are always to be found together.[97]

18: 387   But this necessity of connection is not a representation of empirical origin, [*crossed out*: and nevertheless] rather it presupposes a rule that must be given *a priori*, i.e., unity of consciousness, which takes place *a priori*. This unity of consciousness is contained in the moments of the understanding in judging, and only that is an object in relation to which unity of consciousness of the manifold representations is thought *a priori*.

18: 387   **5924.** 1783–84. *M* 94.

The general proposition is: Synthetic cognitions *a priori* from mere concepts are impossible, but they are quite possible 1. through the construction of concepts, 2. from rules that contain the possibility of experience and through which perceptions become objective cognitions. For in experience alone do pure cognitions *a priori* acquire their significance and use.

18: 387   **5925.** 1783–84. *M* 94.

N.B. Synthetic pure cognitions from concepts, which cannot serve for the determination of the objects of experience in general, as is the case with transcendental ideas, have the significance that they determine the boundary of all experiential cognition, i.e., they indicate that this is never adequate and complete by itself; consequently in all respects something that lies at the ground of experience must be assumed; but we can only cognize this to the extent that it lies at the ground of experience, and we are justified in thinking it hypothetically only to the extent that practical propositions that go beyond grounds of experience demand it.

The ground on the basis of which we can cognize something *a priori* is that objects of [*crossed out*: experience] perception are appearances; the reason why we cannot cognize them completely is that we would then
18: 388   take them not as objects of experience, since these are never complete, and if we did take them [as such], then we would contradict ourselves.

18: 388   **5926.** 1783–84. *M* 96, at §307ff.

Space and time are themselves nothing other than forms of the composition of objects of sensation; hence if one were to cancel out all composition, nothing would remain of them.[98] Now the unity of consciousness in this composition, insofar as it is considered as universal, is the concept of the understanding, and this unity belongs to experience as objective cognition, thus *a priori* concepts of the understanding are requisite for the possibility of experience. There must therefore be something that itself precedes experience,* through which it becomes possible; but in it alone must all *a priori* cognition have its reality.[99]

*(For the logical form of the understanding in judgment must precede, and the appearances (as mere appearances) must be regarded as determined with regard to each of these forms, otherwise no experience can arise from them. We can also use the word "experience" in place of the words **"object of the senses."** For we do not cognize the things in themselves; we can know nothing of them except all of our possible experience of them, and only insofar as this is determined *a priori* by the form of sensibility and that of the understanding.)

5927. 1783–84. *M* 96, at §307.   18: 388

It is absolutely impossible to cognize anything synthetic *a priori* about things in themselves, but only about appearances, since synthetic judgments require intuitions, either pure or empirical, but synthetic *a priori* judgments require pure intuitions. This, however, is possible only as a form of our sensibility and is valid only of appearances, not of things in themselves.

A category is the representation of the relation of the manifold of intuition to a universal consciousness (to the universality of consciousness, which is properly objective). The relation of representations to the universality of consciousness, consequently the transformation of the empirical and particular unity of consciousness, which is merely subjective, into a consciousness that is universal and objective, belongs to   18: 389 logic. This unity of consciousness, insofar as it is universal and can be represented *a priori*, is the pure concept of the understanding. This can thus be nothing other than the universal of the unity of consciousness, which constitutes the objective validity of a judgment.

The manifold, insofar as it is represented as necessarily belonging to one consciousness (or also to the unity of consciousness in general) is thought [*crossed out*: as belonging] through the concept of an object: the object is always a something in general. The determination of it rests merely on the unity of the manifold of its intuition, and indeed on the universally valid unity of the consciousness of it.[100]

Two elements of cognition occur *a priori*. 1. Intuitions, 2. Unity of the consciousness of the manifold of intuitions (even of empirical ones). This unity of consciousness constitutes the form of experience as objective empirical cognition.

5928. 1783–84. *M* 97, at §307.   18: 389

Synthetic propositions through concepts are always *a priori* and impossible; but through the construction of concepts (in sensible formal intuition in general) or the combination of universality with empirical synthesis in general they are not only possible, but also necessary. For experience is nothing other than synthetic [*crossed out*: cognition] connection of perceptions in one consciousness (as contained in it necessarily, hence universally).

18:389 **5929. 1783–84. M 97, at §307ff.**

If I think of something through the understanding as contingent in itself, then I cannot think of it through the understanding as existing without a cause. (But why must I think of it as existing through the understanding, why not rather through experience?) (What does contingency signify?)

If I would think of a thing through the understanding, then something must be thought of as the ultimate subject, to which everything
18:390 else pertains as predicate (but what does the ultimate subject signify for me?). If I represent a thing as a [*crossed out*: multiplicity] sum of many homogeneous parts, then I must also think of it as a magnitude; but what is given to me as a magnitude prior to the multiplicity that is thought in it? Every thing has reality; but how is it possible to think of its difference from o[?]

All of this indicates that our understanding certainly has its own rules for thinking of something, but that we cannot give these thoughts any application and significance except through sensible intuition, which we bring under the condition of the unity of consciousness of the manifold, and that in the end the reality of experiential concepts lies only in experience, and indeed in experience in general as such, which without those concepts would be merely a sum of perceptions, while on the contrary the former without the latter would be a merely manifold mode of the thoroughgoing consciousness of oneself in the manifold consciousness of representations.

18:390 **5930. 1783–84. M 98, at §307ff.**

The objective unity of the consciousness of the manifold of representations is their connection either with one and the same concept, e.g., All men (in a word: a universally valid combination of concepts in one consciousness), and then the unity is called logical; or this logical unity of consciousness is regarded as determined in the concept of a thing and constitutes its concept: that is the synthetic or transcendental unity of consciousness.[101] In the former case the unity that concerns merely the relation of the [*crossed out*: representations] concepts is represented [*crossed out*: distributively]; in the latter, that which itself constitutes a concept of the thing through the unification of its manifold in one consciousness, e.g., Many [*crossed out*: human beings] things are outside of one another, and, on the other side: Space is one thing, which comprehends many things outside of one another. The former is the quantity of the concept of a judgment, the latter the concept of a thing as *Quanti.*

5931. 1783–84. *M* 98, at §307ff.   18: 390

A category is the necessary unity of consciousness in the composition of the manifold of representations (intuition), insofar as it makes possi-   18: 391
ble the concept of an object in general (in distinction from the merely subjective unity of the consciousness of the perceptions). This unity in the category must be necessary. E.g., logically, a concept can be either a subject or a predicate. An object, however, considered transcendentally, presupposes something that is necessarily only a subject, and the other is merely a predicate.[102] – Ground – Logically, something can be *reciproce* ground and consequence; but *realiter* everything, if it stands in the community of time, must stand in community. In a magnitude there is the necessary unity of the many.

To experience belongs: 1. intuition (the manifold); 2. connection of the manifold in one empirical consciousness; 3. unity of the connection of the manifold, which is universally valid.[103] Intuition is given *a priori* (*progressus* in it is also finite, also the unity of connection).

5932. 1783–84. *M* 99, at §307ff.   18: 391

Through the category I represent to myself an object in general as determined with regard to the logical functions of judgments: of the subject (not predicate), of the consequence as ground, of the multiplicity in its representation. But why must I always represent every object as **determined** with regard **not only to one, but rather to all the logical functions** of judgment? Because only thereby is objective unity of consciousness possible, i.e., a universally valid connection of perceptions, hence experience as the only reality of cognition.

This unity of consciousness of the connection of our representations is given *a priori* **in us** as the foundation of all concepts, just as the form of appearances is given as the foundation of intuitions. But both are valid only of human cognition and also have objective significance only with respect to it, indeed the category can have no significance *a priori* if there   18: 392
are no *a priori* intuitions.

Thus a category is the **concept of an object in general, insofar as it is determined** in itself **with regard to a logical function of judgment** *a priori* (that one must think the combination of the manifold in its representation [*crossed out*: through nothing else] through this function).[104]

All objects that we are to think must be determined with regard to all the logical functions of the understanding; for **thereby alone can we think**, and through the fact that something [*crossed out*: is represented as determined with regard to these functions] determines thinking in general (as it ought to be thought) is it an object, i.e., something to which a particular thought that is distinct from others corresponds.

All **principles of the pure understanding pertain to sensibility** and indicate the **conditions, under which the representation of sensibility belongs under a category.**[105] They thus determine the **rule of judgments** in general with **regard to the appearances** and are principles of possible experience; for without the categories our representations could not be related to objects, for they alone determine thinking in general in relation to something in general.

18:392   **5933.** 1783–84. *M* 99, at §307ff.

The **unity of the consciousness** of [*crossed out*: the representations in] the manifold in the representation **of an object** in general is the judgment. **The representation of an object in general**, insofar as it is determined with regard to this objective unity of consciousness (logical unity), is a category.

The unity of consciousness is either empirical: in the perception of the manifold, combined through the imagination. Or it is logical: the unity in the representation of the object. The former is contingent and merely subjective, the latter necessary and objective. The former is requisite for concepts, the latter for judgments and their possibility in general.

18:393   The schematism displays the conditions under which an appearance is determined with regard to the logical function and thus stands under a category; the transcendental principles display the categories under which the schemata of sensibility stand.

18:393   **5934.** 1783–84. *M* 100, at §307ff.

Experience is cognition *a posteriori*, i.e., of that which is in the object of sensation *a posteriori*. Sensations yield no cognition at all; thus something must be added to them *a priori* if experience is to be possible. Beyond the *a posteriori* representation only the *a priori* representation from concepts can be added, and this can only be the connection (*synthesis*) insofar as it is determined *a priori* (for the mere comparison of sensations gives nothing except sensation, and no object).

The universal formal principle of possible experience is thus: *all perceptions are with regard to to their connection in one consciousness determined *a priori* (for consciousness is a unity in which alone the connection of all perceptions is possible, and if it is to be cognition of the object, it must be determined *a priori*). The objective unity in the consciousness of different representations is the form of the judgment. Thus all perceptions, insofar as they are to constitute experience, stand under the formal conditions of judgments in general, and their determination through this function is the concept of the understanding. All experiences as possible perceptions stand *a priori* under concepts of the understanding, through which alone they can become empirical cognition, i.e., representation of objects (*a posteriori*).

*(All appearances are *a priori* determinable with regard to their connection in conformity with the unity of consciousness in all judgments in general, i.e., they stand under categories.

Space and time are the forms of combination in intuition and serve to apply the categories *in concreto*.)

5935. 1783–84. *M* 101, at §307ff.   18: 394

All synthetic cognitions from mere concepts pertain only to things as appearances, never to things in themselves, and to the former only insofar as they are intuitions (mathematics) or as belonging to a possible experience.

We cannot represent anything to ourselves *a priori* except that whose grounds we contain in our power of representation, either in sensibility or in the understanding: in the latter either where the understanding merely determines the unity of consciousness *a priori* (theoretically), or where reason merely in conformity with the understanding directs the actions toward objects (practically).

5936. 1780–84? (1788–89?) *M* 109, at §307.   18: 394

Ontology is the science of things in general, i.e., of the possibility of our cognition of things *a priori*, i.e., independently from experience. It can teach us nothing of things in themselves, but only of the *a priori* conditions under which we can cognize things in experience in general, i.e., principles of the possibility of experience.[106]

5937. 1783–84. *M* 99, in *Cosmologia, Prolegomena*.[107]   18: 394

In addition to ontology, the cosmological antinomies (under mere ideas of pure reason), the psychological paralogisms, and the theological idea also belong to metaphysics. The latter two are transcendent, but without any contradiction. The cosmological ideas, however, contradict one another. The psychological ideas take the intelligible to be given empirically, the theological ideas take it to be given *a priori*. Existence from mere concepts.

5938. 1783–84. *M* 100.   18: 395

The transcendental ideas serve to restrict the principles of experience, so that they are not extended to things in themselves, and to show that what is not an object of possible experience at all is not on that account a non-entity and that experience itself and reason are not sufficient, but always turn ever farther and thus away from themselves.

5939. 1783–84. *M* 100.

Ideas. Through the cosmological ideas we would cognize the absolute whole of the series of conditions in the appearances. Through the psychological ideas we would cognize the absolute constitution of an object of experience (not in relation to senses) as that of a thing in itself. Through the theological ideas we would cognize the existence of things from mere concepts (without any experience), i.e., we would make an idea for ourselves that at the same time carries experience with it inseparably and *a priori*.

To want to cognize what the soul is in itself from inner sense is in vain.

5943. 1785–88? 1778–83? *M* 113, at §357, in *Notio mundi*.

Mundus noumenon (*intelligibilis*) is the idea of a whole of substances that is not in turn a part. *Mundus phaenomenon* is the application of this idea to appearances.

In the case of a *mundus noumenon* one can conceive of **several worlds** outside of one another; in the case of the *mundus phaenomenon* there is only a **single** world through space and time. The *commercium* of the substances of the former is possible **only through** *harmoniam praestabilitam*, 1. since **many** substances can be in community **only through a common cause**; 2. since this harmony would not be **any nature** if it were not already laid in the creation of things and therefore preestablished.[108]

Influxus physicus holds in the *mundo sensibili*. In the *mundo noumenon* all substances are intelligible, at least we cannot conceive of them through any predicates other than representations. In the *mundo sensibili* they are extended. The influence between the former and the latter is actually nothing, for the alterations of the latter are only *phaenomena*. Bodies are not substances and motion is not their *accidens*, but only *phaenomena* of the intelligible.

5949. 1780s? (1776–79?) *M* 118, at §380, in *Notio mundi negativa*.[109]

The 4th Antinomy. We need an absolute necessity, but we cannot reach one in the *regressus* in the world. For causality must always begin, and such a cause is contingent. This antinomy is unavoidable if we regard time as a determination of things in themselves and appearances as things. If this is not the case, then there is nothing necessary in the temporal series; but that which contains the ground of appearances is not in the temporal series and can therefore have causality without a beginning and be necessary.[110]

5959. 1780s? (1776–79?) *M* 123, at §§382–6, still in *Notio mundi negativa.*   18: 399

Abyssus, saltus, casus, fatum (Later addition: *Hiatus: vacuum intermedium; circumfusum*)[a] are all concepts of the unconditioned, which can be conceived in a *mundo noumeno* or at least in connection with it, but which do not fit in the *mundus phaenomenon.*[111]

The absolute totality of composition must be thought in the *mundo noumeno*; in the *mundo phaenomeno* the world-whole as given in space and time [would be] an *abysys*, and such a thing cannot be **given**. In the *mundo noumeno* the absolute totality of division would be given, in the case of the *mundo phaenomeno* that would be a *saltus*. In the former, where temporal determination is not attached to existence and there is no **alteration** that requires a cause, **freedom** can be thought; in the latter that would be a *casus*. In the noumenon a **being** that is **necessary** in itself can be thought   18: 400
as cause of the world. In the latter I cannot in accordance with its laws conceive of any relation of the cause of the world to the world except in time, and there causality is always contingent, hence the *causa* itself.

In the sensible world all (*synthesis*) unity is only that of the regress. Without boundaries nothing is given in it. Thus in space and time, which are unbounded, nothing is given with an absolute totality of synthesis, nothing unconditioned is given.

5960. 1780s? 1776–79? *M* 123, at §§382–6.   18: 400

The totality of composition in the sensible world[b] and of division are both false and must be so, because they are taken in space and time.

But the totality of cause and effect,* likewise that of necessity, can both be true, since the one can be considered in the intelligible[c] world and the other entirely outside of every world in the intelligible, hence outside of all dependency, i.e., contingency.[112]

*(For these concepts do not necessarily belong to objects of the senses, namely if one does not want to cognize anything through them, but would only have the possibility of a thought thereof.)

5961. 1780s? 1776–79? *M* 123, at §§382–6.   18: 400

The entire dialectic amounts to this. One would know the sensible world as a thing in itself, although it can only be thought in space and time. Now as a thing in itself there must certainly be an absolute totality   18: 401
of conditions in it. But this is not possible in space and time, neither as regards composition and decomposition nor origination. – But if everything is merely *phaenomena*, i.e., representations, which can always posit something only under temporal conditions, then neither the world nor

---

[a] Gap, leap, accident, fate (hiatus: an internal or surrounding vacuum)
[b] Here Kant first wrote "*Welt*" and then inserted "*Sinnenwelt.*"
[c] Presumably Kant should have written "sensible" rather than "intelligible" here.

313

anything in the world is given, but everything is given only so far as the *progressus* extends, and one contradicts onself if one thinks of a *totum* that would be given in itself and yet places it in space and time.

5962. 1785–89. M 131–3, at §§382–6.[1]

If space and time were considered as conditions of the existence of the world in itself and if the *mundus noumenon* were not distinguished from the *mundo phaenomeno*, then the causality of God with respect to the world would also be determined in time, hence God would belong to the world and his causality would belong, by means of time, in a series of causes and effects. Thus God, like everything that belongs along with the world in a single whole, would be contingent.

The possibility of counting the very same subject that belongs to the sensible world, with regard to its [*crossed out*: connection through] categories (of cause and of existence in general), as an intelligible being, thus of counting it as either in the intelligible world or as outside of all worlds, is really the possibility of using the categories not merely with regard to objects of the senses but also for things in general, but only for something which we do not cognize except as not being appearance; which is quite possible, because it signifies only the possibility of thinking and not determining what is thought by means of predicates of the sensible world.

1. The same being which as a member of the sensible world has a causality that is always conditioned under rules of time-determination can, as unconditioned with regard to time, be the free cause of that same *caussatum*[a] in the sensible world, i.e., it does not stand under the condition of time-determination and yet belongs to a world with the intelligible substrate of the *mundi noumenon*.

2. Everything that belongs in time belongs to one and the same world, even though it is assumed as the cause of the things in it, and it exists contingently, since time does not necessarily require the existence of things and in general necessary substances would not belong to any whole and to any world. It is however possible to think its existence outside of time, thus without counting it as part of a world, hence without robbing it of necessity; and the category of existence is at least a concept that always remains regardless of the fact that it cannot be cognized determinately, e.g., as duration without time. – In a word: if space and time are regarded as properties of things, then it is not possible to escape the contradictions.

The reason why the first two antinomies are both false is that I **had to** ground them both on a contradictory concept, namely, that of a whole in space and time that is also supposed to be an absolute whole,

---

[a] thing that is caused

consequently a thing in itself. For the conflict concerns the composition and division of an intuition, which must [*crossed out*: always] necessarily occur in space and time, since these themselves make possible the concept of it as a magnitude. In contrast, causality and modality of existence – or better – the former antinomies[a] concern the inner possibility of appearances themselves (as *quanta*), while the latter[b] concern their possibility through something else, thus the dependence or independence of their state or their existence itself (i.e., the conditional or unconditional possibility of their existence). In order to answer the first questions I had to seek the conditions among the appearances alone, which here, however, are never complete; in order to answer the second, I **could** seek the unconditioned (since it can exist as something other than a correlatum) outside of appearance in the non-sensible, and there both propositions could be true. – The ideality of space and time is thereby indirectly proved, since self-contradictions follow from the opposite. But I have also proven them directly, and indeed from the fact that there are synthetic *a priori* cognitions, that these, however, are impossible without *a priori* (pure) intuition, and that, finally, pure intuition is impossible where its form is not given in the subject prior to the object, consequently that we can only anticipate appearances, hence that all objects of the senses are mere appearances.

18: 403

Yet the cognition of God remains entrusted to the same grounds of healthy understanding as before; only the enthusiastic recklessness of deciding it by means of speculation in ignorance of the capacity of pure reason or even out of a presumption of inferring up to such a height in analogy with principles of experience is taken away, and the determination is entrusted entirely to morality.

The opposite of the proposition "The world is infinite as regards space and time" is "It is not (given as) infinite"; and in this case the latter of these two propositions is true. But if one asks "What is it, then, if it is not infinite in space or time?", then one can answer in two ways: either "It is finite in space and time," and then one runs into sheer absurdities; or "It is as a given whole not in space and time at all," because an absolute whole cannot be given in these two, because it[c] is a whole of phenomena, i.e., of representations of sense, which are given only in [*crossed out*: experience] perception, not in themselves (although the ground for the possible perceptions, the thing in itself, is given without perception), and these, since

---

[a] After "*oder besser*" Kant writes "*Jene Antinomien*" with a capital rather than lowercase letter, thus essentially restarting the sentence and referring back to the first two antinomies mentioned at the beginning of the paragraph.

[b] That is, the third and fourth antinomies.

[c] *sie*. This cannot refer back to "a given whole" (*ein gegebenes Ganze*), because that is a singular neuter substantive, not feminine or plural; so it would seem to refer to space and time severally rather than collectively.

the progression of perceptions never has a possible boundary in perception, permit a progression to infinity, which thus never constitutes an absolute whole. The same thing goes for division. These two propositions can both be false, since the one contains more than is required for a contradiction. That is the logical solution of the antinomy. However, they are also both false because they contain an impossible condition, namely, that the world is entirely given in space and time (entirely given precisely as a *compositum*, i.e., as a world) and is nevertheless given in space and time. For the first proposition is grounded on the presupposition that a whole of appearances is given in itself and outside of the representations, which is contradictory. And that is the transcendental solution of the antinomy.

Second. The opposite of the proposition "All occurrences (things) in the sensible world stand under the mechanism of natural causality" is "They do not stand under it." Here the two propositions cannot both be false; but they could both be true, since the second contains less in it than is required for contradictory opposition. For in this case it would have to be added that they do not stand under the intended mechanism **as things in the sensible world**. But since it could still be the case that the things of the sensible world that are the causes of occurrences in it could also be causes considered as intelligible beings (for that can also be thought without contradiction and without the concept of cause being cognition), they could to this extent be exempted from the mechanism of natural necessity without contradicting the fact that they belonged to it as things in the sensible world.

The other proposition, that all things are contingent because in space and time they are determined dependently on one another and their existence is alterable, can be conceded, and the opposite, that there may somewhere be a necessary being, does not conflict with it; for the latter is in this case to be posited outside of space and time, hence apart from all dependence on the world, rather everything is to be posited as dependent on it.

Leibniz's preestablished harmony[2] is perhaps only the idea of an intelligible world without space and time, in which the divine universal presence is the principle of the real *nexus* as an intelligent cause, through which the relations in which finite beings intuit themselves (as the form of appearance) are already preestablished in the creation in unison with the rules for a thoroughgoing harmony with the intelligible world, in which alone there is immediate truth.

5963. 1783–84. *M* 125, at §§382–6.

God is either at rest or in motion or both at once (like bodies on the earth) or neither. Now it is the last of these that is true; thus all the rest, hence the first disjunctive proposition, are false. The truth of the last is actually the explanation of the falsehood of the first, for God is not in space at all.

Matter in itself consists either of infinitely many parts or of a determinate number of parts. Neither of these is true, for they both presuppose the totality of the division of space and the absolute reality thereof.

5964. 1783–84. *M* 125, at §§382–6.   18:405

We can evaluate a disjunctive proposition as such as problematic in advance, namely as if its disjunction were not yet settled; and then it says: everything is either *A* or *B*, or *A* as well as *B*, or neither *A* nor *B*. [*Crossed out*: Everything] Something in the world is either nature or chance, or nature as well as chance, or neither nor chance. If both can be true, then   18:406 the opposition is not correct; if both can be false, then the division is not complete.* The world either has a beginning (in time) or exists from eternity. [*Crossed out*: Both cannot be true together, thus the opposition is correct; but the division is incomplete, because the condition of a] Since here the world depends on a condition, namely time, which contradicts completeness, the division is not complete, and it is neither eternal nor begun in time, because it is not total; for as appearance no totality obtains. But if I say: The human soul is either subject to the mechanism of nature in its actions (if I add **merely** then this is an exponible*a* proposition) or free or both together or neither, then the soul is taken in different *respectu*, partly as *phaenomenon*, partly as *noumenon*, since I am conscious *a priori* of its absolute self not merely as appearance. (**I am**: a proposition that is not empirical.) And then both propositions can be true, the opposition is not correct, and the totality occurs in it not as *phaenomenon* but as *noumenon* with regard to the *phaenomeni*. The flower is red or blue or neither of them, yellowish, or both of them, violet.

*(The opposition is correct, but the division is not complete. Human actions are not **merely** nature, but by no means on that account accident; rather they are free, i.e., also to be regarded as if they do not stand at all in the series of the determining grounds of appearance but are determined *a priori*.

Freedom is a capacity to determine oneself to action *a priori*, not through empirical causes. Nature and accident both posit the action under *a posteriori* conditions, namely the members or world-alterations that determine the *positus* of every occurrence in time.)

5968. 1783–84. *M* 114, at §§382–6.   18:407

That in every kind of connection in the sensible world there is never an absolutely first thing, thus that no infinity can be represented as entirely   18:408 given, consequently that there is no absolute totality, proves that the

---

a criticizable or revisable

absolute must be thought of as outside of it it, and that the world itself exists only in relation to our senses.

If **the first thing** can be taken in accordance with mere conditions of sensibility, which is what happens in the case of the composition and division of appearances in space and time, then the completeness of the *regressus* is impossible and there is always a conflict between the assertion of completeness by means of an infinite series and by means of a bounded series.

But if the first thing is not necessarily a determination in space and time (dynamical idea), but can also belong to the intelligible world that as *substratum* is the ground of the sensible world, then a first thing, hence totality is possible in the same world as *noumenon* and, in contrast, infinitude without totality is possible at the same time as *phaenomenon*.

18:408   **5970.** 1783–84. *M* 115, at §§382–6.[3]

In mundo non datur abyssus, saltus, casus, fatum.[a] For the totality of the connection of the conditioned with the condition, i.e., the absolute whole of the series of connection, is either that of mathematical connection, the composition of the appearance, or of dynamical connection, the derivation of existence. Both 1. the way in which the series is totally given; 2. how an entirely given series is resolved: mathematically, the composition or decomposition; dynamically, the first origination or unconditioned existence in general.

Non datur abyssus: namely, totality as given through* an infinite filled space and time, or through a finite series, the absolute-whole given in an infinitely empty space and time.

18:409   *(The world is given neither as infinite nor as finite in an infinite space and time.)

Non datur saltus. The leap in a metaphysical sense is the transition from a *quanto* in appearance to the simple = o, as a part in the concept of appearance and its possibility as well as in its coming or ceasing to be, i.e., alteration. Everything in appearance is *quantum* insofar as it contains time or space (*extensive tale*[b]) or fills it, i.e., is contained in time or space (*intensive tale:*[c] reality in sensation).

Non datur casus. An occurrence without a determining cause (in the world). Totality through determining causes in the series of appearances and in time in general is impossible. **Origination from itself** (*casus*) is also impossible; but the **action of these same efficacious subjects** as **things in themselves**, insofar as they determine the appearances but are not determined through them (since they do not themselves belong to the

---

[a] There is no gap, leap, accident, or fate in the world.
[b] as an extensive quantity
[c] as an intensive quantity

series of *phaenomena*), is freedom. Thus the connection of occurrences in accordance with laws of nature is possible by means of freedom, i.e., actions from intellectual principles, not sensible impulses.

Non datur fatum, i.e., absolute necessity in appearance and its origination, but from an intellectual cause, which is no part of the sensible world nor a substrate.

*Saltus** is the immediate connection of *oppositorum* in the same subject one after another. All appearances are *quanta*, and therefore also all parts of them; for if something existing were simple, then it could be generated or pass away only *per saltum*. But the possibility of generation in time constitutes the possibility of appearances.

**(est progressus immediatus a determinatione aliqua ad eius oppositum, ergo a mera negatione ad quantum vel viceversa.)*[a]

5972. 1780s? 1778–79? *M* 116, at §§382–6. 18:410

Freedom is causality without an external condition. It does not obtain in the *mundo phaenomeno*. But it is possible that there be natural necessity in this world and yet freedom in the *mundo noumeno*. Similarly with absolute necessity in existence: not in *phaenomenis*, which exist in particular places in space and time that are always contingent.

5973. 1783–84. *M* 116, at §§382–6. 18:410

Non datur saltus. Every difference (in appearance) is a *quantum*. However, the *quantum* must be possible by means of *repetitam positionem euisdem;*[b] thus *O* must be regarded as homogeneous with *A*, only as vanishingly or infinitely small; thus there is no *progressus* in the determination of a thing to another state except by means of an increase of the same quality from the infinitely small.

All appearance is *quantum*, and indeed *continuum*. Likewise also the appearance of opposed determinations of the same thing, i.e., alteration is a *continuum*.

Non datur casus. No occurrence happens by itself, rather it is always determined through natural causes. In this way, however, no absolute totality is to be expected. But if I say: a being is *a priori* and thus by itself the cause of an occurrence in accordance with the order of nature, i.e., the way in which it is connected with other occurrences happens in accordance with a natural order, then it is freedom in one relation, namely to the subject as thing in itself, and natural necessity in another, as to a subject as a part in the series of appearances. – *Non datur hiatus*.

---

[a] There is an immediate progression from some determination to its opposite, therefore from a mere negation to a quantity or vice versa.
[b] repeated positing of the same thing

Non datur fatum. All necessity is natural necessity of occurrences, i.e., always determined through grounds in the same series. In this way, however, there is no totality in the series. But if I relate the series entirely **to something outside of it*** that is not a *phaenomenon*, then there can be an absolute necessity of the entire series, but not in it, when I go from the parts to the whole, but rather insofar as everything in the series depends on what is thought of as [*crossed out*: given] outside of it.

(*Later addition: Lex continui.*)

*(*Later addition*: The connection of the conditioned with the condition is always a series; in the dynamic field, however, totality is possible through something outside the series, i.e., something that is not *phaenomenon*.

Non datur hiatus: There is no empty space or empty time in the world; for neither is an object of possible experience. To infer the possibility of closed empty space through an inference from the difference in specific gravity, or even from the figure of a cavity, presupposes that space by itself is an object of perception. If, however, space divides the world into two parts, a *saltus* from one to the other would be necessary in order to connect them, which could be inferred from nothing.)

5975. 1783–84. M 117, at §§382–6.

Non datur casus. In the world everything happens in accordance with the mechanism of nature, namely as a consequence of that which itself occurs insofar as the world is a *phaenomenon*, except insofar as the cause of this mechanism is in the subject itself, i.e., insofar as it can be considered as *noumenon* that determines by itself, independently of *phaenomenis*, i.e., a reason as a principle of spontaneity. In this case, to be sure, everything happens in accordance with the mechanism of nature in the sensible world; but this connection itself is grounded on the ground of appearances in general.

The necessity of the occurrences in nature is not the necessity of things themselves, i.e., of the existence of nature. If the latter is ascribed to the appearances, it is *fatum*. Consequently there is no inner necessity in the existence of nature itself, because it is not an absolute whole, hence such necessity is entirely outside of it.

The capacity to represent things in themselves and to be the cause of appearances through this representation is a capacity to act in accordance with the mechanism of nature and yet on one's own, i.e., to produce occurrences without oneself being dependent on and determined by an occurrence, i.e., freedom.

The capacity to give oneself laws originally is freedom. The capacity to determine the mechanism of nature itself *independenter* from this mechanism is freedom.

The things of the sensible world can be considered in a twofold way: 1. as appearances, and then everything occurs in accordance with the mechanism in general, but they are the subjects in which something occurs; 2. as subjects which represent appearances, and then they certainly represent what happens, but it does not happen in them, rather there is in them the ground of the representation that something occurs.

If among the things of the world we encounter things that are active in accordance with reason, then these are themselves to that extent not appearances; for reason as a cause is not an object of appearance, and is not determined by it, thus it is to that extent free from the mechanism of nature; however, that which concerns the appearance of their effects is efficacious in accordance with the mechanism of nature.

5977. 1783–84. *M* 117, at §§382–6.   18:412
I cannot explain freedom: this it has in common with other fundamental powers. But I also cannot prove it empirically; for it is a mere   18:413
idea of something that does not belong in experience at all.

5978. 1783–84. *M* 117, at §§382–6.   18:413
The sensible is grounded in the intellectual, but not in the same way in which it is grounded in other conditions of sensibility, thus not in accordance with the mechanism of nature. I.e., freedom from mechanism can subsist with conformity with that in one subject in a different sense.

I speak of the mechanism of nature where the causality of the cause of an occurrence is itself an occurrence; and this is how it is with everything that occurs insofar as the cause is an appearance; but insofar as the cause is a thing in itself, then the causality is not itself an occurrence, for it does not arise in time. The objective grounds of reason and of this capacity to determine by means of reason remains, and herein nothing happens and nothing is altered.

In mundo non datur nec casus nec fatum. For it is a connection of the sensible with the intelligible: either as *substrato* of the sensible world or as the cause of appearances that is different from the *substrato*.

In the first [*crossed out*: sense] case it is reason itself as a being in the world insofar as it can act from objective grounds; in the second it is a being that can be cognized only through reason that contains the ground of the *substratorum* of the sensible world. In neither case does the cause constitute a part of the series and thus it is not subject to the mechanism of nature, rather it determines the mechanism itself.

5979. 1785–88. *M* 114, at §§382–6.   18:413
The world is 1. not an absolute totality with regard to space and time, neither infinite nor finite (but only a *progressus*, nothing further,

18:414 since we can only speak of possible experience). *Non datur abyssus.*
Mundus intelligibilis is totality without relation to time and number and
progressus.

2. As regards division, it does not consist either of infinitely many nor
of a finite number of parts (because in decomposition too we speak only
of possible experience). Hence no monads. But the *mundus intelligibilis*
does not consist of *substantiis phaenomenis,* thus it consists of monads.
The latter have nothing of space in their outer relations, thus only inner
forces, i.e., *vires representativas.*[a]

non datur saltus. There is nothing simple in time and space, no simple
alterations.

3. In the world as sensible world everything is nature and thus there is
an infinite *regressus* in the series of causes without a *causa simpliciter tali;*[b]
for nothing can begin absolutely and precede empty time that determines
nothing.

But at the same time, as an intelligible world (because here I do not
think of the connection of space and time, but rather of causes and
effects, which are mere categories), freedom can be thought to determine *phaenomenis* without being determined by them. But freedom only
where there is *Causalitas intellectualis,* i.e., in intelligences that are causes
through freedom.

4. In the sensible world everything is contingent, because everything
is *rationatum.*[c]

18:415 **5984.** 1780s. M 146–7, at §448, in *Substantiarum mundanarum
commercium.*

How is alteration and consequently causality possible? How is *commercium* possible? Very well among *phaenomena.*

18:416 The *commercium* of the soul with matter as *phaenomenon* cannot be
conceived at all; for this would have to be in space. But the soul is not
an object of outer intuition, and thus it must think of both itself and of
matter as *noumenon.* Consequently, also not its existence in time. But if it
is to [*crossed out:* think] determine the latter, then it must have something
outside of itself and in community with it, yet not given in space, but
rather whose intelligible representation it must determine in space in
order to determine its own existence in time.[4]

We must determine something in space in order to determine our
own existence in time. That thing outside of us is also represented prior
to this determination as *noumenon.*[5]

[a] representational forces or forces of representation
[b] a cause simply as such
[c] has a ground (outside itself)

5988. 1783–84. *M* 149, opposite §451, still in *Substantiarum mundanarum*   18:416
commercium.

There are not three *systemata* for explaining *commercium*, but rather
the harmony of the *substantiarum* either *per commercium* or *absque com-*
mercio.[a],[6] In the sensible world there already exists, by means of space, a
condition of *commercii*, and the outer causality (of influx) is not more difficult to comprehend than the inner causality of *actionum immanentium.*
Causality cannot be comprehended at all. But if we assume substances as
noumena (without space and time) then they are all isolated; consequently   18:417
instead of space a third substance must be thought, in which they can all
stand *in commercio* with one another *per influxum physicum.*[b]

5989. 1780s? (1776–79?) *M* 157, at §466, in *Naturale.*   18:417
The existence of things in appearance is determined in accordance
with universal laws. The sum of all appearances is called nature in general.

5990. 1780s? (1776–79?) *M* 157, at §466.   18:417
"World" means the same thing as "nature" taken substantively. Without an inner principle of its alterations in accordance with laws it would
not be a world as a being distinct from God.

5993. 1783–84. *M* 158, at §469, in *Naturale.*   18:417
All philosophical derivation of that which is given or can be given in
our cognition is either physical or metaphysical or hyperphysical. The
first from empirical principles of nature cognized through experience;
the second from the [*crossed out*: capacity] principles of the possibility   18:418
of our *a priori* cognition in general, independent from the empirically
cognized nature of things; the third from the representation of objects
beyond nature. The latter takes our cognition entirely outside the conditions of the use of our reason *in concreto.* The metaphysical manner
of explanation is objective if it rests on the universal conditions under
which alone we cognize objects as given to us. It does not exclude the
supernatural, but restricts our reason merely to the natural.

5994. 1783–84. *M* 158, at §469, still in *Naturale.*[7]   18:418
The order of nature, i.e., its form in accordance with rules, not merely
as regards events, but rather as regards the original predispositions, is
neither automatic nor organic with regard to its origin. The former is
grounded on the inner constitution of the original, from which interconnection in general arises; the latter is grounded on an idea which

[a] either through interaction or without it
[b] through physical influx

uses the individual as an instrument for an arrangement that would not have arisen from the individual things of nature in accordance with universal laws. The former order occurs through inner forces by means of physical influx; the latter through a force that is different from nature in accordance with a predetermined harmony. The order of natural things in accordance with a predetermined harmony is not an order of original nature, but of supernatural art. E.g., the figure of heavenly bodies, the proportion of their magnitudes and distances, plants. Even if we grant an origin of nature, indeed in a being in which the idea contains the ground of causality, but also at the same time of the essence of things, the order is still physical and not arbitrary.

18:418   **5995.** 1783–84. *M* 159, at §469ff.

18:419   If I think of life in nature beyond material (not merely formal) mechanism, i.e., an activity of natural things in accordance with laws of the faculty of desire, there arises the concept of needs and of an organism, whether it be grounded automatically or on a predetermined harmony. Since things other than living beings do not act on their own, but must nevertheless necessarily be originally instituted for the need of the preservation of living natures, the natural order can hardly be grounded on anything other than the idea of an author, hence it must be an organism.

The causality of this living being, i.e., the determination of its faculty of desire, is either autonomy or heteronomy; in the latter case grounded through instinct as an *organon* of ends in the idea of another being; in the other case[a] grounded through freedom in the being's own idea. In the first case there is always only a formal mechanism of nature in accordance with physical laws, in the second case[b] there is a spontaneity in accordance with practical laws, and its nature is not determinable merely organically and physically, but also morally. To this extent these beings do not direct themselves merely in accordance with their natural needs, i.e., in accordance with a foreign and imprinted idea, but in accordance with their own idea, which can originate from themselves *a priori*, and their causality is freedom.

Thus all causality is either [*crossed out*: mere] material mechanism or instinct or freedom.

18:419   **5997.** 1785–88. *M* 160, at §469ff.

No motion can be produced in the world through a miracle or through a spiritual being without an equal motion in the opposite direction, consequently in accordance with laws of the action and counteraction of

---

[a] Kant writes "*im Zweyten*" but obviously means "in the first case."

[b] That is, in the case of causality through autonomy.

matter. For otherwise a motion of the *universi* could originate in empty space.

But further, no alteration in the world (thus no beginning of that motion) can originate without being determined through causes in the world in accordance with natural laws in general, thus not through freedom or an occasional miracle. For since time does not determine the order of occurrences, but conversely the occurrences, i.e., the appearances, determine time in accordance with the laws of nature (of causality), an occurrence that would occur or be determined in time independently from such laws would presuppose a change in empty time, consequently the state of the world itself would be determined in absolute time.

18:420

Motions thus cannot begin by themselves nor through anything that is not itself antecedently moved; and freedom is not to be found in the phenomena, nor is any miracle that would be occasional to be found there, but only *miracula praestabilita*[a] in a world that itself has no beginning.

6007. 1785–88. *M* 308, in §§761–9, *Systemata psychologica.*

18:422

It is not necessary for us to prove the reality of freedom, for as something psychological it lies in the moral law.

Also not its possibility, but only to show that there is no contradiction in it.

6020. 1785–89. *M* 394, at §§800–2, in *Theologia naturalis, Prolegomena.*[8]

18:425

The reason why we cannot conceive of any absolute necessity of a thing is that we cannot represent any thing without thinking it, and cannot cognize through mere intuition. Hence we make a distinction between possibility and actuality,[b] since the latter is to be something that is posited beyond the thought itself. If we could cognize through intuition, we would not find any distinction between possibility and actuality (if the former were not thought through concepts). Now what is actual is possible.

18:426

6027. 1780s? (1776–79?) *M* 332, in *Existentia Dei.*

18:427

The ontological proof must say: A supreme perfection must exist in relation to possibility in general, but not: A being, which we think of as supremely perfect, must exist **on that account**. For the latter does not follow.

The proposition that a being (whatever concept I might think it under) exists is a synthetic proposition and cannot be proven *per analysin.*

---

[a] preestablished miracles
[b] Kant starts a new sentence here.

18:430 **6038.** 1785–89. *M* 351, still in *Existentia Dei.*

It is a necessary *hypothesis* of reason as of a *principii* of the unity of all our cognition to assume a single universal primordial being as the *principium* of everything and to assume that this being is intelligent, because only insofar as it is the cause of everything through understanding is the world ordered in accordance with rules by means of which it becomes an object of our understanding, finally it is necessary to assume it to be a cause through an intelligent faculty of choice so that it should be a *principium* of a rational will for us and of the universal unity of all our free actions. Theism is thus not a dogmatic assertion, but a necessary hypothesis of the thoroughly concordant use of reason, especially of its self-sufficiency.[9]

18:433 **6046.** 1780s? (1778–79?) *M* 353, in *Intellectus Dei.*[10]

A theological morality is not becoming, since then morality makes the existence and will of God into a *principio* of morals; but a moral theology is good, since the morality is made into a *principio* of belief in a God.

In the first case morality is derived from the existence and will of God, in the second, however, the belief in the existence of God and his will is derived from morality.

18:434 **6050.** 1780s? (1776–79?) *M* 355, at §869ff., in *Intellectus Dei.*

On philosophical enthusiasm.*,[11]

Plato rightly noticed that through experience we do not know things as they are in themselves, but only learn to connect their appearances lawfully.[12] (He further understood that to cognize things for what they are in themselves also requires an intuition of the things in themselves, i.e., pure intellectual intuition, of which we are not capable.) He noticed that in order for our representation to agree with the object, it must either be derived from the object or thought of as producing the object.[13] The latter would be the original representation (*idea archetypa*), of which, if it is to be original in all points, we human beings are not capable. Thus the ideas can be encountered only in the original being. The ideas of this original understanding, however, cannot be concepts, but only intuitions, although intellectual ones. Now he believed that all *a priori* cognitions are cognitions of things in themselves,** and because we participate in the former, we also participate in the latter, and among those he included mathematics. But we could not participate in those on our own, consequently only through the communication of divine ideas. But since we are not conscious of them as having been imparted and transmitted merely historically, but rather as being immediately under-
18:435 stood, they cannot be inborn concepts that are believed, but immediate intuitions that we have of the archetypes in the divine understanding.

But we can unfold these only with difficulty. Thus they are mere recollections of old ideas from communion with God. Now this would still not be enthusiasm, but a mere way of explaining the possibility of *a priori* cognitions. But now there comes the suspicion of participating in this communion with God and the immediate intuition of these ideas (mystical intuition) even now, and even of finding in them the immediate object of all of our inclinations, which have previously been applied to appearances as their types only through a misunderstanding (mystical love of God). But since it is probable that between us and God there is a great scale of beings that extends from us to Him – *genii*, astral spirits, eons – one could first attain communion with these and with the prelude to intellectual original intuitions. But since the original ideas are the cause of the reality of their objects, one could still hope by means of them to exercise dominion over nature. And so it was with the neo-Platonic school, which called itself eclectic, since it professed to find its wisdom in the ancients, since it ascribed its fantasies to them, with all the raving enthusiasm with which it infected the world. Finally, with Spinozism. (Theosophy by means of intuition.) The Aristotelian philosophy suppressed this delusion. One began from concepts that we arrived at through experience (*nihil est in intellectu–*).*ᵃ* But now one arrived at *a priori* cognitions without investigating how this is possible in accordance with the foregoing principle. These cognitions extended themselves, and because everything that remains within the sensible world is always conditioned, reason drove the principles that are valid there ever higher and beyond the sensible world, in the confidence that they will there provide an acquisition just as secure as the explanation they had previously given of what is present to us. Now the subjective conditions of reason with regard to comprehensibility began to be held to 18:436 be objective conditions of things in themselves, and since reason is not satisfied until it has grasped the whole, conquests in the supersensible world began to be made. Now since no boundaries are to be found where one can come to a stop in this, one finally also had to take away from all things their individual and separate possibility of existing, even their separate existence, and leave to them all merely inherence in one subject. Spinozism is the true conclusion of dogmatic metaphysics.[14] Critique of the propositions accomplishes nothing here; for the difference of the subjective from the objective with regard to their validity cannot be re-called, since those subjective things that are at the same time objective have not previously been distinguished. The necessity of assuming them is on one at once, and one does not notice that they are merely subjective. That experience is possible only through *a priori* principles does

---

ᵃ The first part of the traditional Aristotelian sentiment that "Nothing is in the intellect that was not first in the senses."

not occur to anyone. Only the critique of reason itself can accomplish anything here. Nevertheless, men of lucid reason, surveying the great extent of the use and misuse of opinions, still hold off this descent into enthusiasm for a whole. – If one will not tread the path of critique, then one must let enthusiasm run its course and laugh at it along with Shaftesbury.[15]

*(The great difference of intellectual from empirical cognition led the ancients to it.)

Sects in China: I am the supreme being.

Sects in Tibet: God is the collection of all holy beings.[16]

18:437   **(And it is precisely the opposite. For only of things as appearances can there be synthetic *a priori* cognitions. For the form of sensibility with regard to intuition can be cognized prior to all objects, for it is given in the subject. Space and time. In this intuition, however, many *a priori* propositions can be given synthetically that are then valid of all objects of possible experience, but also not of any further objects, although the concepts of them as objects in general are merely intellectual, but are only monograms, which do not give anything for cognition *in concreto*, but only cognition *in abstracto*.)

To be sure, one has analytic cognitions *a priori*, if the concept of object is given, whether it be an empirical or a rational concept. But synthetic *a priori* cognitions would not be possible without intellectual cognitions, which are to be found only in God. Whatever human beings are supposed to cognize synthetically and indeed *a priori* must have an object of sensible intuition for its object.

18:437   **6051.** 1780s? (1776–79?) *M* 354, at §869, in *Intellectus Dei*.

*The origin of all philosophical enthusiasm lies in Plato's origi-nal divine intuitions of all possible objects, i.e., in the ideas, since we only intuit them by means of their appearances, and thus only passively.[17] Now on this is grounded, first, Plato's opinion that all of our *a priori* cognition (mathematics), especially that of perfections, stems from the recollection of these prior intuitions and that we must now only seek to unfold them ever more; from this, however, arises the second stage of mysticism, that of even now intuiting everything in God,[18] which then makes all research into synthetic *a priori* cogni-tion unnecessary, insofar as we read it in God; third, since other be-

18:438   ings may be closer to God, we so to speak must perhaps first come to learn those ideas by means of reflection, hence consort with spiritual natures, etc.

*(*Later addition*: Even before Plato one distinguished intellectual cog-nitions from empirical ones and understood the latter when one called them sensible, and thus certainly made a distrinction between intelligible and sensible things. One held all *a priori* cognition to be intellectual, thus

328

even mathematics; and since various sensitive things, and actually only these, can be cognized *a priori*, one had examples of a supposedly intellectual cognition. But to find this distinction important a need of reason to go beyond the empirical was important, since the latter is always conditioned and hence cannot be a thing in itself, which must always have its complete conditions.

The necessity of the hypothesis of such a thing was held to be insight into the necessity of these things.)

The highest degree of enthusiasm[19] is that we are ourselves in God and feel or intuit our existence in Him. The second: that we intuit all things in accordance with their true nature only in God as their cause and in his ideas as archetypes. The third: that we do not intuit them at all, but rather derive them from the concept of God and thus infer from our own existence and our rational concepts of things directly to the existence of God, in which alone they can have objective reality. Now back from the lowest degree to the highest: Spinoza.

6056. 1780s? (1778–79?) *M* 356, in *Intellectus Dei.*　　18:439

Anthropomorphismus regulatively conceived (is the **relation** of an unknown cause in accordance with laws of sensibility) is nothing other than the conditions of sensibility applied to divine actions as a schema for the application of them in empirical use. *Anthropomorphismus* constitutively conceived is the absolute representation of divine properties in accordance with laws of sensibility. The latter offers a target to the opponents; without the former we are deists.[20]

6057. 1780s? (1778–79?) *M* 356, at §874ff., in *Intellectus Dei.*　　18:439

God has not given human beings independence from himself (God), but from the incentives of sensibility, i.e., [*crossed out*: moral] practical freedom. Their actions are appearances and to that extent subject to the merely inner conditions of humanity. Punishments and rewards also　18:440 belong among these. Whatever God did is good, but it does not lie in the sensible world as a mere schema of the intelligible world. Thus space is nothing in itself and is not a thing as a divine work, but rather lies in us and can only obtain in us. Likewise with the agreeable and its distinction from the good.[21] The appearances are not actually creations, thus neither is the human being; rather he is merely the appearance of a divine creation. His condition of acting and being acted upon is an appearance and depends on him as bodies depend on space. The human being is the *principium originarium* of appearances.

6076. 1785–88. *M* 366, opposite §897, in *Voluntas Dei.*　　18:443

The negative concept of freedom is independence,
The positive concept: autonomy through reason.[22]

18:443   **6077.** 1783–84. *M* 366, opposite §897.

    Transcendental freedom (of substance in general) is absolute spontaneity in acting (in distinction from *spontaneitas secundum quid*, where the subject is still determined *aliunde* through *causas physice influentes*).[a] **Practical freedom** is the capacity to act from mere reason.[23]

    In the case of freedom, the causality is *originaria*, although the *caussa* is an *ens derivatum*.[b]

18:443   **6078.** 1783–84. *M* 366, at §898, in *Voluntas Dei*.

    The freedom of the divine will does not consist in its having been able to choose something other than the best; for not even human freedom consists in that, but in being necessarily determined by the idea of the best, which is lacking in the human being and thereby also restricts his freedom.

18:444   **6082.** 1783–84. *M* 368, at §900, in *Voluntas Dei*.

    In the use of means with regard to a presupposed end, the will is certainly often obvious, but hidden with regard to the end itself; e.g., why a human being is formed in this way or that is obvious, but to what end the human species as a whole exists is hidden.

    If a human being is to exist at all, then it is obvious that he must be upright, wise, etc. But that and why a human being should exist is hidden. Whatever always remains hidden is inscrutable.

18:445   **6087.** 1783–84. *M* 370, in *Voluntas Dei*.

    The reader feels a certain nervous [*crossed out*: fear] concern about entering into the considerations and objections of *Hume*, and sees in them the expression of audacity.[24] Yet there is also something noble, upright, and sincere in submitting onself to judgment, like Job, without slavish

18:446   anxiety, not in order to condemn God's ways, but rather in order candidly to confess one's own scruples without allowing oneself, like Job's friends, to be seduced into suppressing them and making flattering protestations of praise out of a worry that one would otherwise be irreverent. God's regime is not despotic, but paternal. It does not say: Do not reason, just obey, but rather: Reason diligently so that you can demonstrate your reverence for God from your own conviction, freely and unafraid, a reverence that would be of no value at all if it were forced out of you. With him who believes slavishly and for that very reason also tyrannically compels others to the same belief, there is nothing to be done. He who

---

[a] spontaneity relative to something else, where the subject is still determined, from another quarter, through causes acting by physical influx

[b] The causality is original, although the cause is a derivative being.

330

has a love of peace does not get anywhere with the other sort through rational grounds.

6091. 1783–84. M 370, §903ff., in *Voluntas Dei.*   18:447

We are not in a position to cognize the wisdom and goodness of God in this world *in concreto* and at the same time in its entire context, because we know rational beings as [*crossed out:* objects] subjects of all ends only on this earth. The new astronomy has in this way done a great benefit to theology. For if we had to regard our earth as the entire stage for divine wisdom, then great scruples would arise.[25]

On our earth we meet with the situation that we should bring forth out of ourselves everything that is good, both in ourselves and in our external circumstances, even the knowledge of the good and the pleasure and satisfaction in it. In that case it would then be impossible for us to be led by agreeableness; for in that case we would have to be able to foresee the good as well as take pleasure in it (we should, however, bring ourselves to our vocation[a] by means of culture). Thus activity would have to be the course to our vocation, but the spur to activity would have to be pain. But it could not also hereby come to pass that every individual would attain the vocation of his existence; thus there always remain deficiencies. Only the species should attain it.[26] It may be different elsewhere, also in the future: faith.

The disproportion between our natural disposition and its development in every *individuo* provides a ground for faith in the future. We do not need to assume antecedently that God is good, instead we infer it, even without God, only in analogy with nature; here is thus found a guide to the highest wisdom and a theology that flows from a firm resolution for progress to perfection.

Human beings should indeed bring forth out of themselves a system of public good; from a universal inclination to relate everything to private inclination there arises nothing but sheer strife and violence. From their own species they should need a lord or at least a sovereignty, and many outside one another. They should create universal peace.   18:448

The role of a human being is perhaps among all those in this planetary system the most artificial and difficult, but also in its outcome the most magnificent. Here we also have happiness, but of course, in accordance with our own conception of it, not *in abstracto* but *in concreto*; for we cannot conceive of any happiness except in the effort to work through obstacles and hazards in the attempt at it: in a word, in the reward for our vigor in bringing happiness forth out of adversity.[27]

---

[a] *Bestimmung*

18:448   **6092.** 1783–84. *M* 371, at §904ff., in *Voluntas Dei.*

We speak of happiness as contentment, but as an idea that we have *in abstracto*, the reality of which we cannot lay out in any determination *in concreto*, not even in fiction.[28] Should it be a complete satisfaction of all desires: why then desire, i.e., lack something, in order to attain it? For this still means that one was not happy previously. (Moreover, the satisfaction of desire increases the longing for more and thereby makes contentment completely impossible.) If, on the contrary, we should be in the possession of well-being without desiring something, then this condition seems to make the being entirely useless, because it involves no activity; moreover, persistence in the same condition and yet with complete contentment is impossible that drags its existence through time, because a part of his existence always stands before him, with regard to which he expects something different from the previous condition.

Religion can only be moral insofar as we revere God in a threefold person. As a lawgiver he cannot be kind, i.e., his law cannot be subordinated to or mixed with an aim at the welfare of creatures. It is aimed at freedom and not at happiness; that the creatures become worthy of
18:449   happiness, not that they become happy; otherwise we represent his law as indulgent, as suited to and compliant with our weaknesses, but not as holy. He wills the existence of creatures as kindly and for no other reason; but as holy he wills that if they exist then they must conduct themselves so as to become worthy of happiness. As just, he indeed presupposes kindness, but restricted by the holiness of the law; justice, however, is not kind, it is also not merely holy, rather kindness in conformity with the holiness of the law is distributive justice. As kind he would not punish, as holy he would not reward (for everything is indebtedness), for he demands the deed regardless of the happiness of one's condition. Thus justice is the third personality.[29]

In human beings, the three personalities are divided into three individuals; in God there is a threefold personality. But this is only in the concept of God from a practical, not a speculative point of view: an idea of the relation to human morality and freedom.

18:449   **6094.** 1783–84. *M* 371, at §904ff.

Theology is not a theosophy for cognizing the intrinsic nature of God, but is only for cognizing him in relation to us and the morality of our will. Likewise religion is not a theurgy for having an [*crossed out:* immediate] influence on God and his will through formulas, spiritual exercises, purifications, and expiations, but is aimed at the improvement
18:450   of our self [through] cognition of it.[30] The question is only: what makes us into better human beings? The moral concept of God and of the threefold personality relative to our practical maxims, not with regard to his own nature. Through a good course of life ones does not attempt

to have an effect on God, but only to make oneself receptive to divine kindness.

6096. 1783–84. *M* 372, at §904ff.   18:450

The 3fold personality that I think in the highest good. 1. Out of inclination I desire to be happy and I relate this wish to an author of happiness. 2. I recognize myself as subjected to the moral law through reason and relate this obligation to the will of a highest being, who can oblige me because he has my fate entirely in his power. 3. The reason in me approves of happiness only insofar as I act in accordance with my duty.[31] And this I relate to a third person, whose position is represented by conscience. Thus a kind person represents my inclination, the second represents my reason, the third my conscience.[32]

6097. 1783–84. *M* 372, at §904ff.   18:450

Subjectively considered, my own person comes first. I would gladly like my happiness not to be restricted by any conditions at all. But objectively I must represent my happiness through another person, and reason is the first person that prescribes the conditions of happiness.   18:451 Subjectively, out of inclination, I would gladly have the application of the moral law to me to happen in accordance with kindness; but reason teaches that happiness does not occur solely in accordance with the holy law, also not solely in accordance with kindness, but in accordance with goodness combined with holiness, i.e., in accordance with justice.[33]

6098. 1783–84. *M* 372, still in *Voluntas Dei*.   18:451

The question is whether the concept of God is necessary from a physiological or from a moral point of view.[34] Since nature must be regarded as contingent from the former point of view, inner necessity cannot be inferred from it, but is only a necessary hypothesis (namely among the properties that are to make up the concept of a divinity) in order to give to phenomena the highest ground that is sufficient for them (not for all other questions of reason). For the perfection and magnitude of the world do not require the presupposition of an omnisufficient being. Thus as a physiological fundamental concept he is not determined and his existence is only a hypothesis.

If morality were grounded on physiological conditions, this is precisely what would follow. We would have to presuppose the existence of God only with regard to our need for happiness and our aim at it. But all morality is necessary from the essence of things, and that without which it would have no objective reality is necessary *a priori* although only in a practical relation. Further, with regard to morals God must first be represented as the highest good, and in order that he can be that he must also be represented as the highest being.

18:451 **6099.** 1783–84. *M* 372–3, still in *Voluntas Dei.*

If it were possible to **know** that there is a God morality would still remain in human beings.

In moral theology

God is represented as the head in a necessary system of ends, not of a contingent system which we hypothetically assume and believe to be
18:452 universal, but one which we know, not through choice among contingencies and a will that arbitrarily establishes ends, whose will is identical with that which is absolutely necessary in the order of ends among rational beings, consequently not as a despot, but as the highest good itself through the nature of things in general. God as the *summum bonum originarium.* The moral properties are not his supreme dominion over beings in accordance with laws of morality, but the self-sufficiency of these laws themselves. Here we lay down as ground what we know with certainty, namely the necessary system of all ends, to which all others must be subordinated as their *conditio sine qua non.* Hence the errors of moral theology are actually destructive, especially anthropomorphism, which however can easily be avoided by regarding God not as the author of the laws but of the obligation in accordance with these laws.[35]

Moral theology is thereby at the same time ontotheology. It is nevertheless a merely practical and subjective certainty, which is grounded on an interest, but on an objectively necessary interest and one which is inseparable from the essence of reason, not subordinate in any respect. If morality were only a pragmatic system of prudence, the belief in God would be a mere hypothesis; instead, it is a postulate.[36]

The highest wisdom in ontotheology is merely relative, and concerns its adequacy with regard to the system of all ends; but in moral theology it is the self-sufficient source of the possibility of things themselves. We are thereby led to derive everything from the order of things as necessary in itself and yet at the same time from God as the self-sufficient principle of all order, and not to turn to God as the being who gives laws that are in themselves contingent and which can be dispensed with, but rather to expect that what is necessary in the nature of things in accordance with laws of morality is also necessary in nature in accordance with physiological laws.

All of the moral properties of God are here to be determined only objectively in accordance with our concepts, not subjectively – for in the latter case we have two *correlata* whose connection we could represent
18:453 in anthropomorphic terms: the moral order and the God who wills it. Rather, his will is this moral order itself. He is kind and indeed infinite, since all possible goodness flows from him, but also holy, since it flows only in accordance with the moral order, and just, since this goodness

does not establish the moral order, but is rather determined in accordance with it.

6100. 1783–84. *M* 373, at §904ff.   18:453

Justice is the restriction of kindness through holiness. Thus it is **actually not rewarding** (*later addition*: for if the reward were merely in conformity to justice, we could expect little), rather only kindness rewards. For where justice does not restrict goodness in accordance with principles of holiness, there kindness is at work.

Actually we ourselves limit the divine goodness through our own guilt, and punishments may not be regarded as positive.

6101. 1783–84. *M* 374, still in *Voluntas Dei*.   18:453

How evil is possible under a good God depends on the question how freedom is possible in beings who are entirely dependent as regards their being, hence on how morality in general is possible in them; for if everything were nature, then everything would also be good, although only physically, and there would be no morality at all.[37] We cannot comprehend the possibility of freedom; but we must nevertheless presuppose it, for rational beings can act only in accordance with the idea of it. Thus it is practically certain. The question of how freedom is possible in created beings is identical with the question of how substance, which nevertheless exists only derivatively, is possible.

With regard to God, where progress to the infinite, which is never completed for a creature, is only an *intuitus*, there is no evil. This exists in the parts only because they are not the whole. Evil seems to belong merely to the appearances; in itself it is only a manifold in the good by degree. Yet for us appearances are the things themselves. We also do not really depend on appearances in acting in ourselves, and are thus free.   18:454 Nevertheless we necessarily represent ourselves as dependent upon them with regard to happiness in the sensible world; thus we are dependent on the latter with regard to the object of the will.

What holiness, kindness, and justice are.

6103. 1783–84. *M* 375, §§914–15, still in *Voluntas Dei*.   18:455

The good in the sensible world is progress toward perfection, not the possession of it; thus happiness is progress toward contentment, not possession of it.

6107. 1785–89. *M* 376, still in *Voluntas Dei*.   18:455

1. Morality exists for itself (in accordance with its principle) without the presupposition of a deity.
2. The highest good is not the determining ground but rather the object of a will determined through the moral law,[38] and

its* possibility, consequently also that of God, is practically necessary.

3. To assume the existence of God is the consequence of the moral law and the **disposition** toward it; for only through this does the highest good become the object of the will.**

*(Nature cannot correspond to morality by itself, without a supreme author with a moral will; for that would have to be a nature in which the good will of the creature would also be a sufficiently efficacious cause of happiness in accord with such a will; this however is not entirely in its power, although the disposition certainly is.)

(The subjective ground of the assertion is here grounded on an **objectively practical law, thus it is **objectively sufficient**, although not **from a logical** but rather **from a practical point of view**.)

6109. 1783–84. M 377, still in *Voluntas Dei*.

If we were to say that it is highly probable that a God exists, this would be a judgment that was not in conformity with the constitution of cognition at all and which would also, were one to allow it, say far too little. For probability can only be thought in a kind of con-
nection the possibility of which is otherwise certain, e.g., that other planets are occupied.[39] But the possibility of a causal connection can only be valid through experience, hence can only be valid of causes in the world; but we have no ground for inferring to a cause outside the world, not one in nature but of nature itself, in accordance with the analogy of nature.[40] Probability is only a judgment awaiting more detailed knowledge.

However, it can be necessary to assume something, and indeed from subjective causes of the use of the understanding in general, although we do not know the object, e.g., that storms and other occurrences, e.g., entire states, occur in accordance with natural laws and from natural causes, since otherwise we could not make use of our understanding. That is a postulate of the universal human reason. Here lies a practical postulate: we should think of occurrences in such a way that we can use our understanding on them.[41] But this practical postulate always has only conditional necessity, namely if we want our understanding to be in unison with itself in accordance with principles. There are however absolute practical postulates of the will, and these are the moral postulates. We should be true and honest without any conditions of an arbitrary end. Whatever must necessarily be assumed regarding certain objects in conformity with this postulate is also a practical postulate. I must think of it in this way, and it is not a mere hypothesis.

Here the ground is objective and fully *a priori*, but not theoretically, rather practically; but the conviction is also only with respect to the practical, not probability but firm belief.[42]

6111. 1783–84. *M* 378, still in *Voluntas Dei.* 18:458

Pragmatic interest from the principle of happiness as a subjectively universal end makes belief in God a mere hypothesis; moral interest from the principle of the system of all ends as the objectively necessary final end of rational beings makes it into a postulate, i.e., an absolutely necessary presupposition of pure reason. God as the highest self-sufficient good, in which alone morality as the highest formal good can have reality, i.e., can become a ground of the existence of an intelligible world, i.e., of a realm of ends.[43]

Happiness as a consequence of morality belongs to it [*crossed out*: as a *corollarium*] and its transcendental truth; but as a ground for morality, happiness[a] abolishes it.[44]

If the cognition of God were knowledge and not a mere belief, moral- 18:459
ity would still very well remain. To believe in God is already moral and has a value. Whether one can say that devils also believe? They fear that a God exists; they do not need him, they do not want him to exist.

6113. 1783–84? (1778–83?) *M* 378, still in *Voluntas Dei.* 18:459

On the world as the object of the most perfect will, as the object of the *summi boni originarii.*[b]

The divine purpose is not the mere happiness of the creatures outside of him, not the satisfaction of an inclination toward honor in him, but rather that which is the necessary consequence of the highest original good, namely, the highest derived good.[45] The best world – i.e., happiness under the conditions under which each is worthy of happiness. The former as the kindly will is in itself unlimited and therefore infinite; the latter as the holy will connects it to conditions. Thus the product of the most kind and holy will is the highest good. Justice is its consequence. In this, however, consists the practical perfection of the highest being. The world as the *ectypon*, i.e., the effect that is evidence of the cause, thus has its greatest perfection in being evidence of a practically perfect and not merely kindly author, and its perfection is thus the honor of God, not that the creature honors him through praise, but through action and deed, and thus is happy in the highest degree.

6114. 1783–88. *M* 378. 18:460

Under a good principle, evil must always be disappearing, and this diminution of evil and progress in goodness is the perfection of the sensible world. Evil is not something substantial, it cancels itself out.

---

[a] Kant actually uses the masculine pronoun *er* rather than the feminine *sie* required by *Glückseligkeit* (happiness); but there is no masculine noun in the sentence, and *Glückseligkeit* is the obvious antecedent.
[b] original highest good

18:460 **6116.** 1783–88. *M* 378, at §§923–4, still in *Voluntas Dei.*
Pleasure in one's condition is welfare.
Pleasure in oneself is self-contentment.[46]

18:460 **6117.** 1783–88. At *M* §§923, 924.
Contentment with our entire existence is happiness;[47] among human beings, this also requires physical causes, i.e., welfare. That happiness which is independent from physical causes is blessedness. Thus only from self-contentment. God is therefore the uniquely blessed.[a]

18:464 **6132.** 1783–89? (1778–83?) *M* 382, in *Creatio mundi.*
Moral theology has as its object God as the highest self-sufficient good, as author of the world, which is thereby the highest created good.[48]
The principle of moral theology is that the positive idea of freedom as the ground of all morality is derived from the idea of the highest good, which is constituted only by the system of all ends, of which we conceive ourselves to be members and from the standpoint of which we should act, since it is to be possible through us and our freedom.[49] Now this system of all ends and freedom is nothing other than a world in which the highest happiness is proportionate to the worthiness to be happy. Thus morality includes this idea as a principle. Such a world, however, is not possible merely through our freedom, but nature must correspond to this law. But nature can so correspond only if there is a God.

18:464 **6133.** 1785–89? 1788–83? *M* 382.
18:465 In accordance with his holiness, God willed the moral worth of rational beings to be the condition of happiness. This consists in the ability of the rational being[b] to ascribe all that is good to himself. Thus the less God gave a predisposition to the good, so that the human being could become the author of the good through freedom, the greater the moral worth. Great predispositions to the good would have diminished the imputation of the good. Now evil sprang from the very conditions under which alone the greatest moral worth could spring: namely, a moral character acquired through one's own effort. Adversity serves to test and train the strength of morality through resistance.
The non-prompt execution of divine justice in this world is also the best means for exhibiting morality in its purity. Thus all apparent objections are rather consequences of the necessary spontaneity, energy, and

---

[a] *das Allein-seelige.*

[b] Kant's pronoun here is the masculine singular *er*, which would naturally seem to refer to God rather than to the (plural) rational beings in the previous sentence. However, the following sentence makes it clear that in the present one he is talking about particular rational beings.

purity of moral character, which can be preserved by that means alone and at which God has directed the highest aim in this life, as the highest condition of the good.

6136. 1780s. *M* 384, §934ff., still in *Creatio mundi.*   18:466
Teleology. The principle that everything has its end and is good either in itself or for something is the supreme natural *principium* of natural science, which is not derived from the hypothesis of a rational author, but because otherwise we would have no standard for our idea of the good, that is, for what would be the means to it if not nature.[50] Anatomy, all things that are interconnected in a system. From this need there springs the hypothesis of a rational cause – for the things in nature cannot be represented as acting on each other purposively on their own. *Hume.*[51]

6137. 1780s. *M* 384, at §934ff.   18:466
It cannot be proved through experience that this world is the best, thus the highest perfection of its author also cannot be inferred from experience. One must make the latter the basis for an inference to the former; but then this proposition can very well be confirmed through experience, especially teleology. For the ancients, who held the world to be the only end, it was more difficult. Hume's objection, derived from the evils of human beings; they are guilty.[52] The guilt is itself an effect of our freedom and limits, and the limits are a particular provision of the progress to perfection.

6140. 1780s? (1776–79?) *M* 386, at §942ff., in *Finis creationis.*   18:467
The objective end of God is (*later addition*: the absolute (uncondi-tioned) good of the world together with that which is its consequence) that the world be the greatest created good in itself by itself, not that it be good **for something**.
However, it is the greatest good in itself insofar as **rational beings** are **happy** and **worthy of this happiness** in it.[53]
As a system of ends through freedom, and in this case also through nature. (*Later addition*: **Honor: not a subjective end.**)

6142. 1780s? (1776–79?) *M* 386, at §942ff.   18:467
The concept of God is not a speculative but a moral concept, not in relation to nature, but to the interest and indeed the moral interest of human beings: it is hereby also determined as a perfect being.

6143. 1780s? (1776–79?) *M* 386, at §942ff.   18:467
Mundus optimus, since otherwise a better will would be possible; the   18:468
highest happiness is not the supreme end, for it is only conditionally

good; morality is also not the supreme end, since it is not the complete end.[54]

Summum bonum (finitum) derivativum. That rational beings be happy in the world, insofar as they are not unworthy of this happiness.

Belief in God through morality. This provides the interest. The moral disposition is impossible without this, although judging [is].

How is it possible that God have an end outside of himself? Not as an incentive, rather it is in him and in the consciousness (of his highest fruitfulness) as *summi boni*.

18:473   **6165.** 1780s? 1776–79? M 391, at §95off., in *Providentia.*

That the evils in the world (on our earth) do not refute the divine wisdom and goodness, rather that it remains possible to regard their admission as not unworthy of a deity: this way of judging is very much justified by the astronomical discovery of so many worlds.[55] There are so many infinite steps (so that every rational creature may very well arrive at the higher ones).

Yet this same discovery in turn strikes down every pretension of the human being to a special provision and eternity and so annihilates him in his own eyes that he does not ascribe to himself enough importance to be an end of creation.

18:473   **6167.** 1780s? (1778–79?) M 392, at §958ff., still in *Providentia.*
18:474   The *nexus* of a *caussae remotae* with the *causa proxima* of a *caussato* is not the *concursus*, but the *causarum immediatarum*,[a] since one constitutes the *complementum* to the insufficiency of the other. Now one cannot think that God concurs with natural effects as such (for he is not *concausa* of nature, but *causa solitaria*),[b] i.e., one cannot conceive of the insufficiency of his own causality in the creation. Thus God cannot concur in the causality of freely acting beings toward his moral ends in the world, for he must not be regarded as *causa* of their free actions. That which gives free actions the *complementum ad sufficientam* toward divine moral ends (holiness) is the spirit of God. This, however, if the actions are still to remain imputable, must also not be *causata*[c] of the holy spirit, but only the removal of obstacles to freedom. The spirit of God is that which gives the moral law motivating force; thus an inner moral life, which is certainly not possible in accord with natural laws, is at work in us. Everything that is morally good in us is an effect of the spirit of God and what is imputed to us is that we make room for this.

----

[a] the connection of a remote cause to the proximate cause of something caused is not concourse but immediate causation
[b] he is not a co-cause, but a sole cause
[c] things caused by

6173. 1780s. *M* 394, at §950ff., still in *Providentia.*[56]   18:476

The actuation of the beginning (of the world itself in creation) of   18:477
substance is **creation**. Continuation is **conservation**. With regard to
the state of things in the world, the actuation of their purposiveness
in the continuation of the world is: 1. in the beginning, providence;
2. in the continuation, either **governance**, insofar as the powers themselves are not found in the world, or **direction**, insofar as they are indeed
in the world but are not the **determining ground** for the purposiveness.

Both, governance and direction together, are *concursus.*

(*Later addition*: *Creatio, conservation, gubernatio.*)

Every extraordinary providence is a miracle. Direction is a formal
miracle, *concursus* a material one.

God is either the author of the perfection of the world through the
order of nature or against it. The former is ordinary providence, the
latter, as *miraculum praestabilitum,*[a] is extraordinary providence.

Through the order of nature, in accordance with our concepts of it,
the final end is not attained.

Matter as an aggregate of substances cannot exist [as] a being that is
necessary in itself. For necessary beings cannot be *in commercio*, hence
cannot form anything composite.

Moral proof. We find **ends** in the world. They give to our insight
an indication of a being that exists in accordance with **the analogy** of a
rational cause of the world. By this means, however, its **concept** is **not
determined** either for theoretical or practical principles of our use of
the understanding: since with regard to the former it **explains nothing**,
with regard to the latter it **determines nothing**.

Only reason, through the **moral law**, gives us a **final end**. This cannot   18:478
be attained through our own powers, and yet we are still to have it as our
aim. It can **only** be brought about **in the world**, consequently insofar
as **nature corresponds to it.**[57] A nature, however, that agrees with the
morally final end would be a **morally efficacious** cause. Thus we must
assume a being **outside** of nature as its cause, which as a **moral being**,
endowed with understanding and will, is the cause of the world. Now
this is **theism**.

What we must merely **assume** from **subjective rational grounds**
(with respect to the determination of our will), but **cannot prove**, is an
article of faith. Thus the existence of God is an article of faith for reason,
and through this proof **alone** is a **determinate concept of the primordial being** given. – The **concepts of nature, omniscience**, etc., are
then connected with this concept. The difference between creation and
conservation does not pertain to God, but merely to the determination

---

[a] preestablished miracle

of the world. Assuming creations in the continuation of the world is contrary to the principle of the possibility of experience.)

6174. 1780s. *M* 394, still in *Providentia*.

For God the universal means the totality that contains everything in itself.

For human beings the universal means the little that is contained in everything else.

Divine providence, if it is general, must also be special; but this is not so in the case of human foresight. For in the case of God the general is the cognition of the whole; for human beings, the cognition of the genus. Now that which is contained in the individual is not contained in the concept of the genus, but is surely contained in the cognition of the whole, which is however impossible for us human beings to grasp.[58] God's cognition determines every part in the whole, that of humans determines the whole through the parts.

Thus for God the particular providence is derived from the universal. It is thereby also possible that, since genera and species can only subsist through the preservation of *individua*, for God both this as well as all other ends can be preserved in accordance with an order of nature which finds in him the ground of possibility itself.[59]

Particular [*crossed out*: concern] dispensation (direction) is that in which an individual occurrence is regarded as the end and the causes as means. It is thus not considered possible in accordance with the order of nature, since it proceeds from the universal to the particular, while the latter allows the universal to follow from the particular.

The cause for assuming such a dispensation is that one otherwise cannot represent how all the particular occurrences in the world could turn out to be purposive, since we cannot form any concept of how among ends God proceeds from the whole and its end to the parts.

The *concursus* of God with freedom (insofar as freedom is morally determined), in order to make nature concordant with freedom and the moral law, can also be considered as lying in the order of nature and must be so considered.

The audacity of judgments with regard to the determination of occurrences as ends and of causes as means and the particular direction of the divine will on the plans of human wisdom.

6175. 1780s. *M* 394, still in *Providentia*.

The correspondence of divine providence with the perfection of the world in accordance with laws of nature is called a *concursus* with freedom and morality. He imparts capacity, opportunities, and incentives for the good. That which is extraordinary with regard to individual good or evil actions is possible; but we can never make it out. The *concursus* of God

18:478

18:479

18:479

342

with the *progressus* of the good in the world is what is essential here. God is not on that account the *auctor mali*,[a] because the human being is free and God gives no incentives toward what is evil; but he can be regarded as the *auctor* of the moral [*crossed out*: law] good, because he is the *auctor* of obligation in accordance with this law.

6206. 1783–84. *Th* II–III, introduction.[60]   18:489

Human reason has the peculiar property that in addition to what is necessary to make a concept of a thing for a certain aim, it further not only **completes** this concept by means of **everything** that constitutes it but also **completes** the object of the concept in the species of thing to which it belongs. We are not satisfied with what would be sufficient for the ordinary use of words in knowing the concept of a body, a human being, a plant: we try to become aware of it in all of its marks, and from that, if the law of economy is applied, there arises the **definition**. But if we have assigned the object to a certain species of things, then we also seek to think it completely with regard to this species. Body belongs to   18:490 matter, and that which is extended but not matter is empty space; hence we form the concept of a completely dense body. It has interconnection; we conceive of a completely hard body without concerning ourselves with whether such a thing is actual or even merely possible. Thus the completeness of a thing of a certain species serves us only as a measure for all other concepts [*crossed out*: things] which we can form of them insofar as they differ from one another merely in magnitude. These magnitudes are alterable; one must compare them with one that is inalterable, i.e., with a thing that contains everything that can be contained in its concept in relation to its species.[61]

We can determine some of these concepts of completion insofar as we have [*crossed out*: a concept, which can be given at least negatively,] determinately and in experience, of that which belongs to its completion (e.g., of the diameter among all the chords of a circle); others are so constituted that we can only think of the completion but can never complete the concept itself. The concept of well-being is empirical, yet much can be lacking in one's contentment with one's condition. Now here there is necessary a concept from the content of which nothing is missing, i.e., the greatest and ever-lasting well-being, i.e., happiness (which we can still never conceive determinately).[62] If this further does not depend on contingent outer causes, but arises from ourselves: blessedness. Now we can still further extend this concept of the satisfaction of a rational being by adding to what such a being enjoys what it does, i.e., contentment with its person and the morally good. The complete moral good is the highest virtue. If that is free from all inclination toward evil: holiness.[63]

---

[a] the author of evils

Thus holiness of will and blessedness of condition together comprise the **idea of heaven**. On the other side, since that the concept of which consists in the relation of cause and effect has two kinds of opposite: a negative $= O$ and a privative $= -$, one can conceive of a condition which leaves no contentment at all: misfortune, and insofar as the being itself contains the cause of that: misery, likewise one can also conceive of a will that intentionally acts contrary to all moral laws, and thus there arises the **idea of hell**. Hence heavenly joys and hellish tortures, heavenly virtue and hellish sin are ideas.

18:491

18:492   These ideas are entirely necessary even if no object corresponds to them. It is not a matter of whether such objects exist, but only of how

18:493   we can better compare our concepts of what exists to each other by comparing them to a third thing, as a common standard, even if it is a mere idea. (The Julian period precedes the beginning of the world by 532 years.)[64]

Now if we conceive of an individual in accordance with these ideas, it is the good or evil **primordial being**; for in both cases this is considered not with regard to what it contains in itself but with regard to what it causes. (Whether in the world there is as much evil on one side as there is good on the other, and whether, just as motion in one direction cannot be imparted without producing precisely as much in the opposite direction (*lex isonomiae*), the principle may be good but its work necessarily contain as much evil as good). Both will always contains everything that is required for activity, but the one will always contain the ground of the reaction against the [*crossed out*: activity] effect of the other. If the existence of the evil being is derived as the, to be sure, limited cause of all evil, then **what is evil** or the devil is not a precise idea, since one does not know how far its influence and effect reach.

Now if we conceive of a complete being not in accordance with determinate concepts of good and evil, but as a thing in general, then this is the transcendental idea of a highest being, which is also necessary in order to think of the difference of all possible things in thoroughgoing determination with regard to **something** and **nothing** in general. Everything is first thought of as in a single thing in order subsequently to be thought more in one thing and less in another through the mere limitation of the archetype. I always maintain the same subject, a thing in general, and through different restrictions of the being that contains everything positive I arrive at all things insofar as they are something, and the differences among them rest as it were on the combination of something with nothing in infinite space. The evil primordial being is also thought as an infinite reality, but as in its effect the contrary of all causality of the former, since then the world does not contain any contradictions, but the intentions still conflict with each other.[65]

In addition to [*crossed out*: counting] judging the idea of a most perfect being to be necessary for the concepts of all other beings, reason [*crossed out*: also] judges it to be necessary for the existence of things. Considered merely as things, these can be distinguished only through negations, thus through limitations of a highest reality. Now the existence of limited things seems to be just as derivative as their concept, and in contrast the existence of a being that possesses all reality alone seems to be able to be original. Shadows are all that is left over from the infinite nothingness, namely night, which without the all-illuminating sun would fill space. It therefore seems natural that light did not first exist mixed with shadows, but arose only through greater or lesser limitation of the light of the sun, which had to precede. The highest reality can limit its own effect, through which it externally reveals its existence; but limited reality contains in itself no sufficient principle of its possibility; consequently its actuality is also to be regarded as dependent. There further arises from the principle of thoroughgoing determination a thorough community of descent, hence kinship with everything possible, because it is only possible in a concept, since all negations are possible only through boundaries placed on the highest reality.

18:494

6210. 1782–84. *Th* I, introduction.

18:496

Theology. We can exhaust this object of cognition, for it is not given to us in itself.

Human reason needs a **threefold** completeness:[66] 1. Completeness of the determination of a subject with regard to all possible predicates. 2. Completeness of the derivation of its existence from the existence of others. 3. Completeness of the existence of all things from one existence, i.e., the community of all in a single cause. Three ideas.

1. Completeness of the determination of a thing relative to a certain concept, e.g., the concept of figure as regular but straight-lined (like the equilateral triangle or square) or curved (the circle). Determination from the principle of the end with regard to all ends: morality, or of an end that contradicts all others. Completeness of friendship.

2. Completeness of derivation. The independent existence, the first beginning, the cause that is not in turn a *causatum*. The idea of freedom as a species of causality that is not externally conditioned. The first human being. The beginning of the world or of chaos (the beginning of order), finally the first existence in general.

3. Completeness of community, i.e., thoroughgoing determination of the many among each other through the dependence of their existence on one, e.g., a commonwealth under a lawgiver. Unity of churches under a primate. The causality of many causes insofar

as it is thoroughly determined through their dependence on one. The world and God.

We have 1. only one concept of a thing in general through which this is thoroughly determined: *ens realissimum*; 2. [*crossed out*: only one concept which] Insofar as this concept is the **only one** that needs no other for its determination, also an existence that is not a consequence of another existence, thus a primordial being; 3. insofar as all other existence is derived and none of them is original, all things [have] community of origin, consequently a complete concept of their connection with each other. The best world. – The all-sufficient being: 1. as the highest being as subject; 2. the primordial being as cause; 3. the being of all beings as the cause of all. Theology.

18:497

18:515 **6225**. 1783–88. *Th* 4, at §2, "The difference between theology and religion."

Theology, insofar as it has influence on ethics, is (moral) religion; insofar as it contains a special object of ethics, it is a cult. The latter would presuppose religion.

For religion it is enough to believe; for a cult one must know, otherwise it is hypocrisy.

18:515 **6226**. 1783–88. *Th* 4, at §2.

Moral religion is that which makes better human beings.

A cult is a religion which, if it is to be genuine, presupposes human beings who are already good, since they should take to heart duty toward God himself.

The mere possibility of divine existence is already sufficient for moral religion, even though it does not amount to belief.

Belief is absolutely necessary for a cult, but is hardly sufficient.

For the proper service of God knowledge is required; otherwise one prays merely to be assured in all cases, not from conviction.

18:516 **6227**. 1783–84. *Th* 4, at the conclusion of §2.

Religion is the **moral disposition** (not the pragmatic disposition) insofar as its grounded on the **cognition of God**. There is to be sure **no religion without cognition of God**; but this certainly does not need to be knowledge; it can merely be a pure idea of God that is morally correct (although as speculation full of error), and, second, it need only contain the conviction that **it is at least possible that there is a God**, or beyond that a **firm belief**. For the former morality is not required; but if it is there, then in combination with that problematic judgment it can yield religion. For the latter a morally good disposition is already required.

What is the *minimum* by way of theology that is requisite and sufficient for religion? (*Later addition*: I. With regard to existence: the possibility of assuming one. 2. With regard to the concept: the moral theology and the metaphysics that is connected with it. (The ancients had a cult without moral religion, consequently also without a theology from reason, rather one from tradition.) Philosophical theology cannot extend that *minimum* with regard to the positive [idea] of God, yet it can bring it to a science through the negative by means of which the errors that are unavoidable in the common theology are averted. – Philosophical (rational) theology is not learned theology;[a] the theology *revelata*, which is founded on ancient sources and ancient languages, is alone a learned theology.)

6235. 1783–84. *Th* 6, at §5, "Difficulties concerning the truth of the cognition of God."   18:519

Moral theology has as its principle: If the laws of duty are established *a priori*, consequently flow necessarily from practical reason, but yet would have no force to move the will without the presupposition of a rational, morally perfect being as the author of all of nature, then this presupposition is inseparable from practical reason, and the idea of God must be instituted not for the observation of nature but in conformity with the need of morality: and I am thereby freed from all further ado with speculation. I can declare speculation entirely incompetent for this end and only demand that it not be able to prove that there is no God, and then I have enough for belief. There is no difficulty in the proposition but only in arriving at it by speculation.[67]

6236. 1783–84. *Th* 6, at §5.   18:519

In moral theology it is enough to presuppose that it is still possible that there is a God, and that no one can ever prove the non-being thereof; hence we are then authorized to ground a practical and indeed for its sake necessary law on this existence through a hypothesis. For these laws are absolutely necessary but cannot become subjectively practical without that presupposition.

The practical indifferentism of theology makes speculative theology   18:520
the only one possible, and if the critique of reason is not favorable to it, then it leads to skeptical atheism. Moral theology, however, permits a theism that can at the same time be critical with regard to speculative theology.

Theology as a principle of virtue serves only to remove hindrances to morality that could be derived from the objections of an empty ideality.

---

[a] *Gottesgelahrtheit*

As a principle of religion it is, through duty toward a higher being, itself a motivating ground for virtue. As a principle of service to God it is the ground of actions the effects of which are directed immediately at God. – A subjectively necessary hypothesis exists when I see no other ground of explanation; an objectively necessary one exists when I have insight that no other ground is possible for human reason.

18:523   **6244.** 1785–88. *Th* 6, at §5.

The **minimum** in rational theology in behalf of morality, where it makes better human beings.

That it is possible that there is a God is sufficient for religion, but not for a cult; for that presupposes not merely belief, but knowledge.[68] The proposition that one should believe presupposes that the one that pronounces it knows what he would have be believed.

The minimum of rational theology is a concept of God that agrees with itself and with the need of reason in regard to principles, especially practical ones, and the possibility of his existence, consequently the authorization to assume it (**to have an opinion**). The maximum is **knowing**, i.e., complete assertion insofar as it is grounded on proofs. The intermediate form, that which is suited to the least ability and the best will, is **belief**, which is the acknowledgment of the necessity of such a hypothesis either for theoretical or practical use (theoretical and practical belief).

The *minimum* of theology is sufficient for virtue, namely mere opinion; for the fear of God (religion) the *majus*,[a] namely belief; for a cult (service of God) the *maximum* in cognition, namely knowledge.[69]

18:541   **6275.** 1785–88. *Th* 19, at §14, "With regard to particular realities."

The atheist allows no existence [of God]: the dogmatic atheist (the denier of God) denies his possibility, the skeptical atheist (agnostic) denies all proof of his actuality. The former denies the concept, the latter the ground of proof.

18:542   The atheist must still concede the **analytic** predicates of God, for one cannot dispute the possibility of such a being.

The deist also concedes the synthetic but merely **transcendental** [predicates of God], but not the **physiological** ones, out of fear of anthropomorphism. He therefore also has no moral use of the cognition of God.

Spinoza was not an atheist in the transcendental sense, nor a deist, for he denied only cosmotheology.

---

[a] that which is more than the minimum but less than the maximum

His error arose, however, from a false ontology, since he conceived of the concept of a substance in such a way that there was only a single one.

One could plausibly say about Spinozism that if all powers and capacities of a substance created and preserved by God are merely divine actions, if we cannot conceive of any other than these, then one cannot understand at all how the subject of them is supposed to be posited outside of God. By contrast, however, if we perceive an effect in ourselves and a countereffect in other things, it is in turn not to be understood how we should be *accidentia*, which can never be subjects of action and passion.

The deist is often such from modesty, the theist often from arrogance.

The relative existence of God as the creator of the world, not as the world-soul.

The synthetic predicate of absolute existence, of relative existence.

Unity. *conceptus singularis*.

Multiple Gods would not, as necessary beings, stand *in commercio*. Manicheans.

Cosmological argument.[70] We cannot infer from alteration to contingency, but rather, if an infinite series is not allowed, we can infer to the necessity of a first member, but also not make comprehensible its first action. 18: 543

Ontological argument. To infer the necessity of existence from the concept of the *realissimi*;

Cosmological argument. To infer its quality as highest reality from the concept of a necessary being.

In the cosmological proof I either infer from the concept of the dependence of everything that is an alteration to something **first**, which is without alteration (*primus motor*),[a] or I infer from contingency to something necessary, and then I ask: what properties does a necessary being have[?] However, the necessity of existence does not allow us to derive any properties at all and is absolutely incomprehensible.

6276. 1785–88. *Th* 19, at §14. 18: 543

By means of the predicate of existence I do not add anything to the thing, rather I add the thing itself to the concept. In an existential proposition I therefore go beyond the concept, not to a predicate other than what was thought in the concept, but to the thing itself with precisely those predicates that were thought in the concept, neither more nor less, only in this case absolute position is thought in addition to relative position (*complementum possibilitas*). The basis of the illusion lies in the fact that the concept of the *entis realissimi* contains the *omnimodam*

---

[a] first mover

determinationem,[a] while all other concepts leave the object undetermined in numerous ways.[71]

18:544 **6278.** 1785–88. *Th* 20, at §14.

According to Mendelssohn,[72] God cognizes the contingency of all things outside himself even in relation to his nature, thus the thoroughly natural or theoretical [*crossed out*: necessity] contingency. But at the same time he recognizes the practical necessity of the same things through his will as the best, and thus the contingency of existing things is a proof of the existence of an intelligent cause, without which they could not exist. He cognizes his own necessity absolutely (without our being able to comprehend it). But since we can have no other concept of the way in which possible things can become actual if not through nature than through a will, we ascribe this concept, which is derived from experience and has only subjective validity, to the things in themselves. If we substitute for the concept of contingency the concept that we can think the opposite, not the conditioned but the unconditioned, then the argument goes thus: what we cannot think as being otherwise, not on account of a contradiction but because otherwise no rule for thinking is given, is necessary; thus we see that everything is merely subjective presuppositions.

In the cosmological *argumento* (*a contingentia mundi**) one must not infer the contingency of the things in the world from their alterations but from their limitations; but in that case one would have had to presuppose that which was to be proven, namely that the *ens realissimum* alone exists necessarily.[73]

18:545 But if someone assumes that time together with all alteration is not a determination of things, but only a particular form of their sensible intuition, the world could still be necessary.

*(This argument, if it is made on the basis of the alterations in the world, can only serve to show that the world cannot be the *ens necessarium*. Otherwise it could go thus: If something exists, then a necessary being exists. *Atqui.*[b] *E.*[c] However, no limited being can be necessary (since it is not thoroughly determined through its general concept, consequently it is contingent, although it is limited only thus far and no less or more); thus the necessary being is unlimited.

The alterations in the world in the end lead only to contingency and to something first as a necessary being. Thus it comes down merely to this: what sort of properties are required to infer from the concept of such

---

[a] that which is determined in all ways

[b] and now

[c] *ergo.* Adickes suggests filling this out thus: "And now something exists, ergo a necessary being exists."

a being its necessary existence[?] Or is the possibility of an absolutely necessary being to be derived from some other concept? (It is a synthetic proposition and thus cannot be derived from mere concepts.) Absolute necessity is a boundary-concept, by means of which we must always necessarily arrive at some first thing, which can only be assumed for the sake of its consequences, but which itself cannot be understood or comprehended.

To infer from effects to the existence of the *entis realissimi* as cause proves this only as *realissimum tanquam causa*;[a] but the possibilities of things, which can only be regarded as determinations of a single universal possibility, namely of the highest being, prove the existence of the *realissimi* as a sum-total [of realities], consequently, if understanding is a reality, they prove that it is intelligent.

All error consists in our taking our way of determining concepts or   18: 546 deriving them or dividing them to be conditions of things in themselves. – One can use Spinozism in order to overthrow dogmatism. The critical and practical philosopher fears nothing from such enthusiasms.

6280. 1785–88. *Th* 21–2, at §15, "Purification of its concepts."   18: 546

The inference *per metabasin* εις αλλο γενος,[b] where I use what is valid for one kind of thing or cognition as a principle for another kind of   18: 547 things or cognitions, is not allowed in logic; but the transition from one kind of inference to another can still be allowed, indeed be necessary, namely that from objective principles of reason to subjective ones: 1. for the sake of the completion of rational grounds in their derivation; 2. for the sake of the abstraction of rational grounds from all determining grounds of sensibility and their self-sufficiency for a procedure that should determine concepts fully *a priori*, as in the case of moral concepts. In such a metabasis[c] there is no probability, but also no knowledge, rather instead of the former there is the necessity of the idea, instead of the latter, a hypothesis, which certainly bears some analogy to theoretical presuppositions, where I must necessarily presuppose something, even though I neither know nor can determinately represent **it** or **anything** similar, for the sake of completeness in my use of reason or even for security of empirical use. I do not really make a transition to another thing, but to another way of using reason, and the necessity of that, insofar as it is to be practical, justifies the theoretical. Without morality the hypothesis would always be unfounded and the purposiveness in the universe would at best lead to Spinozism or an emanation.[74]

---

[a] It proves the *realissimum* as a cause, i.e., the conclusion contains nothing more than the premise.
[b] an inference that jumps from one set of concepts to another
[c] Here Kant writes this Greek word, previously in roman characters, in ordinary German script.

But without such a presupposition morality has no prospect of connecting the objective principle of the (good) will with the subjective principle (of happiness). No system of nature corresponds to the system of reason and freedom, and thus the moral concept would concern a mere *ens rationis* which comes to nothing.

The existence of a merely happy being without morality may well have its own value for this being, but not for a mere observer.[75] The existence of a merely ethical being without happiness certainly has the greatest value for an observer, but not for the subject himself. The value of existence, however, must be determined and certain objectively as well

18:548 as subjectively. For I may well say: I must be truthful, even if fortune should show me no favor; but this holds only insofar as I exist and live, insofar as I exist as a good being. But I do not know why I should exist merely in order to act. Why has the very will (in the idea) that commands me to act ordered my existence[?] I cannot agree with that. Thus morality is conditionally necessary, but the condition (my existence) is in that case not merely contingent, but as far as my wish is concerned impossible. The will with regard to matter does not correspond to the will with regard to form. – A necessary hypothesis of reason, which however in transcendental theology is itself only hypothetically necessary, namely under the subjective condition which I would **explain**. Morality provides an objective condition.

18:555   **6287**. 1783–84. *Th* 28, at §20, "Proofs of the outer reality or actuality of God."

18:556   1. The possibility of the *entis realissimi*, against dogmatic atheism: that all reality can be contained in a common ground, i.e., we do not have insight into real possibility, but only into logical possibility.*

This is not aimed against skeptical atheism, because it doubts only the proofs of actuality.

*(Whether all perfections can be propagated from a single stem and arise from an inner principle of the very same thing is not something into which we have insight (nor do we have insight into its opposite), yet various perfections are only united with difficulty in human beings, e.g., great activity, eagerness with careful examination and investigation, etc.

Against dogmatic atheism it is sufficient that we show that the impossibility of a highest being cannot be proved, since that could only come from the contradiction of this concept with itself; but we do not on that account have insight into its possibility.

Against skeptical atheism it is enough to show that on that account

18:557 every way to arrive at conviction is not cut off just because that which goes through speculation is (for that is what the skeptical atheist (the agnostic) infers). For even if speculative conviction does not occur, moral conviction is still possible.

The speculative doubter is he who asserts that a thing may not be assumed because its existence cannot be proved. This certainly holds in all speculative cognition. Such a one is a skeptical atheist if he is a doubter from every point of view with respect to the existence of God; but he is not justified in that unless he must hold all ethical laws to be empty imaginings, for in that case he would not even need to assume a God from a practical point of view. He who asserts that virtue is its own reward has no need to assume a God.)

6290. 1783–84. *Th* 30, at §21, "Proof itself."   18: 558

That something is actual because it is possible in accordance with a general concept does not follow. But that something is actual because it is thoroughly determined by its concept among all that is possible and distinguished as one from all that is possible means the same as that it is not merely a general concept, but the representation of a particular thing through concepts thoroughly determined in relation to everything possible. This relation to everything possible in accordance with the principle of thoroughgoing determination is the same with respect to concepts of reason as the somewhere or sometime with respect to sensible intuition.* For space and time do not merely determine the intuition of a thing, but at the same time they determine its individuality by means of the relation of its place and point in time, since in the case of space and   18: 559
time possibility cannot be distinguished from actuality, since they both together contain all possibility in appearance in themselves as substrata that must be antecedently given.[76]

From this it follows only that the *ens realissimum* must be given antecedently to the real concept of all possibility, thus that just like space it cannot be antecedently conceived as possible, but as given; but not as [space is not given as] an object that is actual in itself, but rather a merely sensible form in which alone objects can be intuited, so the *ens realissimum* is also not given as an object but as the mere form of reason for thinking the difference in everything possible in its thoroughgoing determination, consequently as an idea that is (subjectively) actual before something can be conceived as possible; from which however it does not follow at all that the object of this idea is actual in itself.[77]

Nevertheless, one sees that in relation to the nature of human understanding and its concepts a highest being is just as necessary as space and time are in relation to the nature of our sensibility and its intuition.

*(Something whose relation to everything possible is determined in absolute space and time is actual. Similarly, that whose relation to everything possible is determined in the absolute representation of a thing in general is actual. Both belong to the thoroughgoing outer determination with regard to possibility in general and thereby also constitute the thoroughgoing inner determination of an *individui*.)

18:579 **6303.** 1783–84. *Th* 61, a comment on the whole of Part I of *Th*.

On moral theology. Here morality is made the basis for all theology.

Conscience is 1. the capacity to become conscious of the rightfulness or wrongfulness of all of one's own actions. 2. The inner standing of this capacity for judging,[a] as a judge,[b] to give an account of the authorization of our actions.

The supreme principle of conscience is that nothing is permitted to be done about which the agent is not entirely certain that it is allowed for him to do it (in general). We cannot undertake anything at the risk of acting wrongly.

A hypothesis disputing which carries the risk of doing wrong but through the assumption of which we can never do wrong is morally certain, and the presupposition of it with respect to the strengthening of morality is moral belief. Moral belief is thus not derived from the correspondence of our judgment with the object, but with our conscience.[78]

18:580 Matters of belief are those in which the morality of the assertion is what is essential. The existence of God and of the future world are matters of belief for mere reason. With regard to speculation they are not of any great importance, and also cannot be proven apodictically. But if morality is their basis, then they are indispensable hypotheses for putting it into effect.

The guideline for conscience in the case of a morally good intention is not to pretend to more conviction than we are capable of having in order to be certain of doing nothing wrong by means of this cognition.

18:601 **6308.** *Th* 105, at §73, in Part II, "On the Communication of Religious Cognition," First Section, "On the sensible manner of communication."

In religion what is required objectively is soundness of belief (orthodoxy), but what is required subjectively is conscientiousness, i.e., [*crossed out*: pure] well-tested uprightness in the confession of that which is taught as orthodox.

If someone chooses what now seems to him sound to believe in accordance with his best capacity, then he can have religion in full conscientiousness, and in fact there is religion only where there is pure conscientiousness. Where there is no freedom of [*crossed out*: choice] public investigation, where either the presence of impressed prejudices or coercion hinders the investigation, there is unconscientious religion, i.e., popery, slavish or hypocritical subjection under the pressure of pious observances.[79] One should not call that religion; it is popery. For

---

[a] *beurtheilenden Vermögens*
[b] *Richters*

religion must be conscientious, and to conscience there belongs free-   18:602
dom. One cannot say that he who assumes even a true religion due to
coercion proceeds conscientiously; for he must know and himself have
insight into something's being his duty, and cannot rely on the assurance
of others. What he does in this regard in accordance with moral laws of
reason, the effort to establish righteousness in himself, etc., that alone
can be counted toward his goodness; the rest is wasted effort and even
further a risky effort, hence impure and mere currying of favor. Popery
is everywhere the same; Catholicism and Protestantism are essentially
distinct. Thus there are arch-catholic protestants and also protestant
catholics. If one assumes [*crossed out*: in the least] that there is anything
we can do to please God other than a good course in life, then there are
no boundaries.[80]

If the character of the people is besmirched in one respect, that extends to the others. Certain observances seem to be necessary for religious education,[*a*] and in these there must be a mechanism that is not
easily altered; but they must be so constituted that even if they were
unnecessary or founded on false stories or merely purported revelation,
they are [*crossed out*: would be] at least ethically indifferent. But confessions of faith in their truth are a burden for the conscience. What I
merely believe I cannot swear to as true, and to swear that I believe it
is certainly an accomplishment for now, but I cannot swear that I will
always believe it, consequently I cannot undertake to do so; and a proprietor who takes his office away from his servant (unless it is that of   18:603
a teacher) because he will not act against his conscience always does
wrong.

IV.
NOTES FROM THE 1790S.[81]

6311. 1790. *LBl* Kiesewetter 3.   18:607

Refutation of problematic idealism.   18:610

Idealism is divided into **problematic** (that of **Cartesius**) and **dogmatic** (that of **Berkeley**).[82] The latter denies the existence of all things
outside of the one who makes the assertion, while the former, by contrast,
merely says that one cannot prove that. We will here restrict ourselves
solely to problematic idealism.

The problematic idealist concedes that we perceive alterations
through our inner sense, but he denies that we can infer from that to the
existence of outer objects in space, because the inference from an effect
to a **determinate** cause is not valid.[83] – Alteration of the inner sense or

---

[*a*] *Religions-Bildung*

inner experience is thus conceded by the idealist, and hence if one would refute him, this cannot be done otherwise than by showing him that this inner experience, or, what is the same, the empirical consciousness of my existence, presupposes outer perception.[84]

One must here distinguish carefully between transcendental and empirical consciousness:[85] the former is the consciousness "I think" and precedes all experience, first making it possible. But this transcendental consciousness affords us no cognition of our self: for cognition of our self is the determination of our existence in time, and for this to happen I must affect my inner sense. I think, e.g., about divinity, and with these thoughts I combine transcendental consciousness (for otherwise I would not be able to think), yet without thereby representing myself in time, which would have to happen if I were conscious of this representation through my inner sense. If impressions on my inner sense occur, this presupposes that I affect myself[86] (although it is inexplicable to us how this happens), and thus empirical consciousness presupposes transcendental consciousness.

In our inner sense our existence is determined in time and thus presupposes the representation of time itself; in time, however, the representation of change is contained; change presupposes something that persists, in which it changes and which makes it possible for the change to be perceived.[87] To be sure, time itself persists, but time alone cannot be perceived;[88] consequently something that persists must exist in which one can perceive the change in time. This thing that persists cannot be our self, for as object of inner sense we are likewise determined through time;[89] that which persists can therefore be placed only in that which is given through outer sense. Thus all possibility of inner experience presupposes the reality of outer sense. For suppose that one were to say that even the representation of the persisting thing that is given by outer sense is also merely a perception given by inner sense, which is only represented as being given through outer sense by the imagination, then it would still have to be possible in general (even if not for us) to become conscious of it as belonging to inner sense; but then the representation of space would be transformed into a representation of time, i.e., it would be possible to represent space itself as a time (with one dimension), which is self-contradictory.[90] Thus outer sense possesses reality, for without it inner sense would not be possible. – From this it seems to follow that we always cognize our existence in time only in *commercio*.

18:611

18:612

18:612 **6312.** 1790. *LBl* Kiesewetter 8, p. II.

On what basis do we cognize the simultaneity of things, since in apprehension our representations succeed one another? From the fact that in this case we can apprehend the manifold both forwards and backwards.[91] Now since in inner sense everything is successive, hence nothing can be taken backwards, the ground of the possibility of the latter must lie in the relation of representations to something outside us, and indeed to something that is not itself in turn mere inner representation, i.e., form of appearance, hence which is something in itself.[a] The possibility of this cannot be explained. – Further, the representation of that which persists must pertain to that which contains the ground of time-determination, but not with regard to succession, for in that there is no persistence; consequently that which is persistent must lie only in that which is simultaneous, or in the intelligible, which contains the ground of appearances.

That even the empirical determination of one's own existence in time is not possible without the consciousness of one's relation to things outside us constitutes the ground why this is the only possible refutation of idealism.[92]

Whether the objects outside us or their representations affect us (the first of which would be called the reality of [*crossed out*: the matter of] outer sense, the second the mere –)[b] can be decided in this way. We need space in order to construct time, and thus determine the latter by means of the former.[93] Space, which represents the outer, thus precedes the possibility of time determination. Now since with regard to time we are affected only by representations, not by outer things, so there is no   18:613 alternative but that in the representation of space we must be conscious of ourselves as being affected by outer things. We do not cognize this by means of an inference, rather it lies in the way in which we affect ourselves in order to construct time as the mere form of the representation of our inner state, for which something other, not belonging to this inner state, must still always be given (i.e., something outer, the construction of which at the same time contains the intuition of time and lies at its ground).

In order for something to seem to be outside us, there must really be something outside us, although not constituted in the way in which we represent it, since other kinds of sense could afford other kinds of representation of the same thing. For the representation of something outside us could otherwise never come into our thoughts, since we are only conscious of our representations as inner determinations and for their object we have inner sense, which, however, we carefully distinguish from outer sense.

---

[a] *sache an sich*
[b] The dash is Kant's.

18:613 **6313.** 1790–91. *LBl* D 8.
       P. I.

Against Idealism.

It can 1st. be refuted by showing that the representation of outer things must not lie in the imagination, but in an outer sense,[94] since the **form** of representation in time, without the addition of that in space, would not make possible any empirical consciousness of one's own existence in time, hence would not make possible any inner experience.

2nd, through the fact that the **matter** of representations in space would not possibly occur in the mind without an outer sense. For the imagination can only create a representation of the outer by affecting the outer sense (in what is internal to its organ), and there would be no material for outer representations in the imagination if there were not an outer sense. However, it is not also required that we can provide a secure universal criterion of every object of the outer senses and of its

18:614 reality, but it is sufficient to have shown that there is an outer sense.[95]

3. Since the imagination and its product is itself only an object of inner sense, the empirical consciousness (*apprehensio*) of this state can contain only succession [*crossed out*: of temporal conditions]. But this itself cannot be [*crossed out*: determined] represented except through that which persists, with which that which is successive is simultaneous. This persisting thing, with which the successive is simultaneous, i.e., space, cannot in turn be a representation of the mere imagination, but must be a representation of sense, for otherwise that enduring thing would not be in sensibility at all.

N.B. I. The simultaneity [*crossed out*: of the representation] of *A* and *B* cannot even be represented without something that persists. For all apprehension is, properly, successive. But insofar as the succession can occur not only forward from *A* to *B*, but also, as often as I want, backwards from *B* to *A*, it is necessary that *A* endure.[96] The representations of sense *A* and *B* must therefore have some ground other than that in inner sense, but yet in some sense, hence in outer sense; consequently there must be objects of outer sense (and as far as dreams are concerned, this object, which produces the illusion of the presence of several outer objects, is the body itself).

N.B. II. Since we would thus not even perceive succession in ourselves, hence could not order any inner experience, if we could not [*crossed out*: at the same time] also be empirically conscious of simultaneity, [*crossed out*: but this is possible only through that which persists in the object of representations] but the latter is possible only through an apprehension that is ordered both forwards and backwards, which does not take place with regard to the objects of inner sense, thus even inner experience can be conceived only through the relation of our sense to objects outside

358

us. Inner sense would otherwise have to represent ourselves as outside ourselves, etc.

If our cognition of outer objects had to be a cognition of them and of space as things in themselves, then we would never be able to prove their reality from our sensory representation of them as outside us. For only representations are given to us, their cause can be (either) inside us or outside us, and sense can never decide anything about this.[97] But if the representations of inner sense as well as those of outer sense are merely representations of things in appearance and if even the determination of our consciousness for inner sense is possible only through representations outside us in space [*breaks off*]
P. II.

18:615

verte. But if the soul itself is only appearance, hence if its empirical intuition is only the sensible form of the way in which its own subject is affected by the apprehension of the manifold of a given intuition, then this latter must be something other than an inner intuition, i.e., an outer one, so that this alone is immediate.

In the distinction between idealism and dualism, the transcendental consciousness of my existence in general is to be distinguished from 2. my existence in time, consequently only in relation to my own representations, insofar as I determine myself through them. This is the empirical consciousness of my self.[98] 3. The cognition of my self as a being determined in time. This is empirical cognition. – That the latter can only be cognition of myself as a being existing in a world and indeed on account of empirical consciousness and its possibility, insofar as I am to cognize myself as an object, can be proven in the following way. – I cannot cognize time as antecedently determined in order to determine my existence therein (thus only insofar as I simultaneously connect my alterations in accordance with the law of causality). Now in order to determine the latter empirically, something that persists must be given, in the apprehension of which I can cognize the succession of my representations and through which the simultaneity of a series in which every part passes away when another arises can alone be a whole. In which I posit my existence.

6314. 1790–91. *LBl* D 2.
P. I.

18:616

On idealism.

We cannot represent any number except through successive enumeration in time and then grasping this multiplicity together in the unity of a number.[99] This latter, however, cannot happen except by my placing them beside one another in space: for they must be conceived as given **simultaneously**, i.e., as taken together in one representation, otherwise this multitude does not constitute a magnitude (number); but it is not possible to cognize simultaneity except insofar as, beyond my action of grasping it together, I can **apprehend** (not merely think) the multiplicity as given both forwards and backwards.[100] There must thus be given in perception an intuition in which the manifold is represented outside of and beside each other, i.e., the intuition which makes possible the representation of space, in order to determine my own existence in time, i.e., an existence outside me lies at the ground of the determination of my own existence, i.e., the empirical consciousness of myself. Thus I must be conscious of the existence of outer things just as much as I am conscious of my own existence in time, although only as appearances, yet as actual things. No one can have inner sense alone, and indeed in behalf of cognition of his inner state, yet that is what idealism asserts.[101]

In the representation of the composite the composition is always our own work.[102] Now we can say that the object corresponds with that. Yet this correspondence cannot consist in the fact that the quality of the composition is similar to the composite, rather one must be the ground or the consequence of the other (the latter is the case if the object is mere appearance). That in the representation which [*crossed out:* belongs] is related to the object of the senses in itself is sensation; but there the representation is related merely to the subject, in accordance with its quality, and the object is a mere something in general.[103] If I omit this something (sensation) and likewise the composition, then there remains the form of intuition and the object as appearance.[104] The sensations, related to the object, constitute the appearance.[a]

18: 617

P. II.

The critical philosophy has the result that we need not ask what the properties of God are in order to know what we have to do in the world, rather we need only ask the voice of reason in ourselves, which teaches us immediately what we have to do and assumes in the highest cause of our existence such a will, whose commands those laws of reason are, and with which are also [connected] all the promises for our wishes, which this same reason in us represents as corresponding with such conduct.

We will not first learn his will from his revelation either in his works or in his text; for these can be interpreted in many ways, and only that sense which we find by means of our **ethical vocation** is indubitably the morally correct one, since those revelations serve to strengthen this in us.[105]

It is not necessary for us to engage in battle with the theoretical doubts against those theoretical dogmas about the divine nature and its intentions or about the doctrine of immortality. For since we can convince the opponent who denies them that he understands just as little

[a] *Schein*

360

about these objects as do others who assert them, we can stand firm in our place without wavering; for the law of our conduct, the hope of being able to accomplish it because we should, the disinterested presentiment of a state of things that is as a whole in harmony with morality, which is for reason the [*crossed out*: most important] highest condition of the possibility of a world in accordance with the rules of wisdom will elevate us to the idea of a wise divinity ruling the world and simultaneously equip this deity with the properties that will strengthen our morality and hold it upright.

6315. 1790–91. *LBl* B 7.   18:618
P. I.

On Idealism.

Experience is cognition of objects that are present to the senses. An imagining is an intuition even without the presence of the object, and the object is then called a phantasm, which can be a production (invention) or reproduction (recollection) of an intuition that was previously had.[106] – The assertion that we can never be certain whether all of our putative outer experience is not mere imagining is idealism. It is thus not an assertion that they are, but rather only that we cannot produce a proof that they are [not], consequently that the reality of an experience held to be outer can always still be doubted.[107]

The idealist thus assumes that it is possible that we have no **outer** sense but with regard to outer intuitions only imagination. – Now, however, the critique proves that this is impossible. For the form of the intuition of inner sense is time, which contains only one dimension of sensible intuition. [*crossed out*: All outer objects must therefore thereby] Thus for my intuition to have three dimensions, as space contains, we would have to think of this our **inner representations as** able to be found **outside us**, which is self-contradictory.[108] – It is certainly possible to take the imagining of outer objects for perception, but only under the presupposition of an outer sense, i.e., that our outer intuition is related to objects actually to be found outside us, for otherwise all of these intuitions would at bottom intrinsically have only the form and dimension of time and not that of space; and this form would not be thought, but intuited, i.e., immediately related to an object, **even if we do not know what this is in itself**, rather only how it appears to us. If this were not the case, then   18:619
we would also have no imaginings, for these are only **sensible intuitions** of outer objects **reproduced as far as their form is concerned**, which can certainly be **inventions**, but **not to the extent that they do not have outer objects at all**.[109] We are first **object of outer sense for ourselves**, for otherwise we would not be able to perceive our **place** in the world and to intuit ourselves in relation to other things. – Hence

the **soul** as the object of inner sense **cannot perceive its place in the body**, rather it is in the place where the person is. – **Leibniz's** *harmonia praestabilita*[110] **necessarily** brings **idealism** with it: since according to it each of two subjects exists in its play of alterations without the influence of the other, each of them is entirely unnecessary for the determination of the existence and condition of the other. – But also the possibility of inner alterations cannot be comprehended without something outer, which contains its ground.[111]

P. II.

Nevertheless this doubt, which, when it is advanced dogmatically, is called idealism, besides being a stimulus for metaphysics, from which, since it promises us so many as yet unopened prospects, one expects that it could have an objection against a matter that is so dear to us, can also, if everything sensible is placed merely in us, yield a hindrance to that which constitutes the final end of metaphysics, that is, advancing to the supersensible.

We have two sorts of intuition: sensible intuition, for which the object must be represented as present, and an imagining as intuition without the presence of the object. The imagining, if one is conscious of it as such, can also be considered as inner sensible intuition.

Now the problem is whether [*crossed out*: and how] a sensible intuition can be distinguished from the imagining of outer objects; the idealist denies [*crossed out*: the first and so judged that] this without doubt on the ground that we immediately perceive our representations as inner determinations of the mind only through inner sense, but not their cause, to which we merely infer, yet the inference from an effect to a determinate cause is never certain, since there can be more than one cause for the same effect, as in this case either the outer object or the subject itself can be the cause, and in this case the latter intuition would be an imagining. The example of the latter is a dream or a hallucination, from which the outer sensible representation as such cannot be distinguished.[112]

Now I say that the outer sensible intuition is distinguished with complete certainty from the inner through the mere form of the former, space, in which we place outer objects, in distinction from the other, whose object we [place] only in time [*breaks off*]

If we could not immediately distinguish them, we could also not do so mediately through inferences to their cause, for [*breaks off*]. I am myself an object of my outer intuition in space and without this could not know my place in the world. Hence the soul cannot know its location in the body, because it would then have to perceive itself through outer sense, thus as outside of itself.

My representations cannot be outside me and an outer object of representations cannot be in me, for that would be a contradiction.[113] But it may well be the case that although the representation is in me, either its object is without contradiction outside me or both the representation and the object are in me. Idealism asserts that it is not possible to distinguish whether along with the representations its object is at the same time in me, even though this is represented in the intuition as existing outside me. – By contrast, the realist of outer intuition asserts that this is possible, and indeed does so rightfully, on the basis of the following ground. [*Crossed out*: That my representation cannot exist outside me (the subject)] What I represent to myself as spatial cannot be counted as a representation of inner sense, for the form of this is time, which has only one dimension. Likewise, I cannot make mere representation into the object of outer sense, for the form of this is space. – Now the question arises, whether that intuition which has the form of outer sense, like an imagining (in dreams or in a fever), is so identical to that which also has an object of outer sense that the two cannot be distinguished from each other. The answer is that in this condition of imagining it certainly cannot be distinguished, for this is a deception of the power of judgment; but the question is properly whether it cannot be distinguished in general, i.e., whether one cannot be conscious that the one is an intuition of the senses, the other to be sure a sensible intuition, but only in an imagining, for which no object outside the representation is present. The answer is that consciousness can accompany all representations, hence even that of an imagining, which, together with its play, is itself an object of inner sense, and of which it must be possible to become conscious as such, since we really distinguish such things as inner representations, hence existing in time, from the intuition of the senses.

18:621

6316. 1790–91. *LBl* D 10.   18:621

Against Idealism.

1) That the ideality of space and time, whch is merely formal, does not contain real idealism, which maintains that no object at all outside of the representation is given in the perception of things in space, rather merely that to this object or these outer objects (which of these is the case remains undetermined) this form of space in itself, under which we intuit it or them, does not pertain, because it belongs merely to the subjective manner of our faculty of representation in perception, which can be inferred from the fact that space contains in itself nothing that could be the representation of a thing or of the relation of different things to one another in themselves, and, if it is considered as such a determination, as an *ens imaginarium* it is a *non ens*.[114]

18:622

2) That the representation of the object outside of us in space is not illusion, i.e., something that merely seems to be outside us, but is

outer, not merely inner intuition, but that it merely seems to us to contain this form of space in itself, because we cannot know that it is mere appearance other than through inferences.

3) That this form of things in appearance is sufficiently distinguished from every other which contains that which pertains not to the objects outside us but merely to our own manner of representation, that we can thereby determine appearances *a priori*, which we cannot say in the case of one tone in distinction from others, in the case of warmth about the perception of a fluid penetrating and extending to all other matter,[115] hence that the form of appearance applies to outer sense in general and not to certain particular ways of sensing and immediately perceiving.

4) That therefore with regard to this universal, sense can and also must be distinguished from imagination through a correct inference, if the objection derived from the possibility of confusion in particular representations of the imagination in a hallucination or a dream is not counted as a proof that we might confuse these faculties (of sense and imagination) while lacking any means for escaping from this ambiguity: that in the realism of outer sense nothing is asserted other than that no imagining of things in general as objects of the senses outside of us could be representable for us if there were not actually such a sense, hence that we do not distinguish this as a faculty distinct from imagination merely through sensation alone, but through a certain inference, and that something outside us must lie at the basis even of an imagining (even if it is not now contained in the putative perception given to us).[116]

18: 623

In the margin, beside 4):

If we cognize a law *a priori*, we ascribe this law to the object: to nature, if it is a law of nature, to freedom, i.e., to ourselves, if it is a moral law, but not arbitrarily, rather as necessary.

Leningrad Fragment 1.[117]

On inner sense.

P. I.

Time is what is merely subjective in the form of inner intuition so far as we are affected by ourselves and hence contains only the way in which we appear to ourselves, not the way we are.[118] We can, namely, represent time only insofar as we affect ourselves through the description of space and the apprehension of the manifold of its representation. Through the intellectual consciousness we represent ourselves but we do not cognize ourselves either as we appear nor as we are, and the proposition "I am" is not an experiential proposition, rather I lay it at the ground of every perception in order to constitute experience.[119] (It is also not a cognitive proposition.) In the case of inner experience, however, which I order, I affect myself insofar as I bring the representations of outer sense into an empirical consciousness of my condition. Thereby I cognize myself but only insofar as I am affected by myself, whereby I am not so much appearance as I affect myself through representations of outer sense (these are representations of appearances), for that is spontaneity, rather insofar as I am affected by myself, for that is receptivity. Space is namely the representation of outer objects in appearance. Only the synthetic apprehension of these representations in one consciousness of the condition of my representations is bound to time, the representation of which is merely the subjective form of my sensibility as I appear to myself in inner sense. – From this it is to be seen that we would have no inner sense and could not determine our existence in time if we had no outer (actual) sense and did not represent objects in space as distinct from ourselves.

One must distinguish pure (transcendental) apperception from empirical *apperception percipientis*, from *apperceptiva percepti*.[120] The first merely asserts **I am**. The second that I was, I am, and I will be, i.e., I am a thing of past, present, and future time, where this consciousness that I am is common to all things as a determination of my existence as a magnitude. The latter is cosmological, the former purely psychological. The cosmological apperception which considers my existence as a magnitude in time sets me into relation with other things that are, that were, and that will be, for simultaneity is not a determination of the actual in regard to the *percipientis* but rather with regard to the *percepti*,[a] since simultaneity can be represented only in that which can be *perceived* backwards [*crossed out*: with regard to past time] as well as forwards, which cannot be the case with the existence of the *percipientis*, which can occur only *succesiv*, i.e., forwards.[121] – What must be given before it is thought is given only as appearance. Hence a cosmological existence is only the existence of a thing in appearance. I am not an object for myself immediately, but only insofar as I perceive an object. Only insofar as I *apprehendire* objects in time and indeed objects in space do I determine my existence in time – that I can become conscious of myself *a priori* as in *relation* to other things even before the *perception* of them, consequently it is necessary that my intuition [of myself] as something outer belongs to the consciousness of my impression as part of the same consciousness,

P. II.

for space is the consciousness of this real relation. Although I am affected here, no inference is required in order to infer the existence of

---

[a] not with regard to the perceiver but with regard to what is perceived

an outer object, because it is requisite for the consciousness of my own existence in time, thus for empirical self-consciousness (of simultaneity), and I therefore cognize myself as well. I am immediately and originally conscious of myself as a being in the world and only thereby is my own existence determinable as a magnitude in time.

In order for me to become conscious of the existence of a particular there is required an inference from a few representations determined in space, but that in general something outside me exists is proved by the intuition of space itself, which cannot arise from the form of outer sense nor from imagination, and the possibility of which is consequently grounded on an actual outer sense. To be affected necessarily presupposes something outer, and thus rests completely on a sense. That we can affect ourselves (which if a sense is to exist at all must at least be assumed) is possible only through our apprehending the representations of things that affect us, i.e., of outer things, for thereby do we affect ourselves, and time **is properly the form of the apprehension** of representations which are related to something outside us.

The difficulty really lies in the fact that it cannot be comprehended how an outer sense is possible (the idealist must deny it), for the outer must be represented before an object can be set in it. But if we had no outer sense we would also have no concept of it. But that something outside corresponds to my representation and contains the ground of the existence of it cannot be a perception, and must therefore lie merely in the representation of space as a form of intuition that cannot be derived from the inner sense in which the connection or the relation of things that are different from one another is thought. The ground for not holding this to be a merely inner determination and representation of one's condition is that the latter lacks that which persists in the change of representations.

The consciousness of our receptivity with regard to the inner **or** outer grounds of the determination of our representation and with the form of sensible intuition that is connected with them must occur in us *a priori*, without needing to infer the latter from actual perceptions, for otherwise space would not be represented *a priori*, which cannot be derived from any inner determining grounds of the power of representation, since in it everything is represented as outside us, and it is impossible to think of representations as existing in space, consequently the inner sense could never yield representations of space, which nevertheless must occur, because it is at least possible to become conscious of such representations as belonging to inner sense. – It is thus impossible that there exists no outer sense but merely inner sense and inferences from its actual perceptions to something outside us, for otherwise objects of inner sense (representations) must also be thought of as in space.

6317. 1790–91. *LBl* G 6.   18:623
P. I.

On the critique with regard to theology.

In order to prove that it is unavoidable for reason to assume an existence of God, and indeed in accordance with a concept that is adequate for both the theoretical as well as the practical use of our reason, insofar as it extends to ultimate principles *a priori*, I must prove that speculative reason can neither give such a concept in concordance with itself nor prove the reality of this concept. – For if I had conceded the latter, then I would either have had to arrive at the use of reason with regard to objects of experience and, since I would then have had to take these for things in themselves, I would first have stumbled into antinomies, on which all speculative reason shatters, and finally I would have sensified[a] and anthropomorphized the divine being; or I would have taken everything to be appearances and only sought the deity among the things in themselves, through pure ontological concepts, in which case no cognition at all would have remained for me. I therefore had to demonstrate the incapacity of the merely theoret-   18:624
ical use of reason, which left it open that this did not contradict the concept of God and his existence, instead of leading to entirely false concepts of God and, in the end, the impossibility of thinking of such a being.

On the possibility of *a priori* cognition.

The question arises whether, if the causal connection were not given in experience, I would need to have insight into it *a priori*? If a manifold existence is successive, the time in which it succeeds must also be perceived. But this cannot happen unless something exists with which all of the successive manifold is simultaneous.

On the manner of proof in relation to possible experience.

If the forms of things with respect to their universal properties are given *a priori* as the condition of the possibility of these things, then I can immediately cognize what these things are themselves with regard to the categories, e.g., of magnitude. But if I would cognize things in general, not merely their form, through categories, I cannot cognize this *a priori* except in relation to possible experience. E.g., that all things have a magnitude can only be proven insofar as it is shown that they can become objects of experience only insofar as they are given in space and time, but that under this condition their apprehension is always a magnitude, thus the object is as well.[122]

---

[a] *sensificirt*

Law of continuity

Between a and $-a$ (attraction and repulsion, e.g., in magnetized particles) there is a point where the predicate of the thing disappears, becomes $= 0$. Thus an acute as well as an obtuse angle can be held to be a right angle that is infinitely smaller or larger; but an acute angle cannot be held to be an obtuse one. Usefulness can be seen as an indifferent matter if it is very small, but not as anything harmful. Hence it is impossible that virtue be the medium between two vices (opposed in their degree).[123] For the vice that has disappeared is innocence.

18:625

On the occasion for the critique.

We have *a priori* cognitions, which we extend without experience: the question arises whether we can also extend them beyond experience and its objects. If we attempt the latter, then we cannot discover our errors through experience, and possibilities that can be thought always remain without reality. Further, even in the case of apparently necessary propositions we cannot distinguish the objective necessity of the propositions from the subjective necessity of thinking of the objects in accordance with the particular nature of our cognitive powers and not otherwise with regard to given sequences without a critique of reason. – But in all of this nothing is wagered; for if we are mistaken, that is merely the failure in an aim of speculative cognition, by means of which we would extend ourselves beyond the bounds of possible experience. We may always err when we say that the objects are real, e.g., the supreme primordial ground of things is an intelligent being, since in accordance with the constitution of our cognitive faculties we cannot make the phenomena comprehensible to ourselves in any other way; but that has no disadvantageous consequences. – But there is in us a property, or reason attributes it to us as practical beings, which is entirely distinct from the properties of nature and whose laws are entirely distinct from the laws of nature, which are indeed contradicted by the latter: namely freedom and under this concept the law of morality for our independence from nature. Now here we have two *a priori* certain laws that contradict each other in the same subject if I represent the subject in the same sense, according to theoretical principles. Hence I am compelled to think of my own subject as object of the senses and at the same time as object of reason as existing in two different ways: 1. as object of the senses, 2. as a being insofar as it is not object of the senses at all. This compels me to the critique of sensibility. But that would also not amount to anything if empiricism and predeterminism were not contrary to all morality. Thus in the absence of critique morality runs into danger from speculative reason. But even here the power of the moral disposition can still outweigh speculation. Yet this same practical reason compels us to assume

18:626

those laws as divine commands, for otherwise they would be without the lawful effect and the course of nature as the principle of practical laws, so far as it aims at one's own happiness, would not correspond at all to the course of nature in relation to moral laws. Thus I must think of a God and assume him, but I cannot prove his existence and comprehend him.[124]

P. II.

Now it becomes interesting not to make the conditions of the cognition of things that is possible for us into conditions of the things;[125] for if we do this, then freedom is abnegated as well as immortality, and we cannot acquire any concepts of God other than contradictory ones. Now this compels us to determine precisely the possibility, the scope, and the boundaries of our speculative faculty of cognition, so that Epicurean philosophy will not take over the entire field of reason and drive morality and religion into the ground, or at least make them inconsequential for human beings.

Further, space and time are such necessary *a priori* determinations of the existence of things that they together with all the consequences dependent upon them would not only have to be [*crossed out*: the restrictedness] conditions of [*crossed out*: God] the existence of the deity, but would also, on account of their infinity and absolute necessity,[a] have to be made into divine properties were they determinations of things in themselves.[126] For if one were once to make them into such determinations then there would be no reason why they should be limited merely to finite beings. Theology, in order not to contradict itself, sees itself compelled to make both only forms of our sensibility, and to place beneath all things that can be experienced by us, as phenomena, *noumena* that we do not know, but with respect to which alone the unconditioned can obtain. Now since the conflict between the principles of the unconditioned in synthesis and the principles of that which is conditioned in space in time, hence the antinomy of reason, simply cannot be set aside without making this distinction between objects and their representations, theology leads to the aesthetic critique.[127]

18: 627

Yet with regard to the theoretical cognition of objects of possible experience the critique has the utility of dissolving the antinomy between the principle of the unconditioned in accordance with mere concepts and the principle of that which is conditioned in accordance with the conditions of intuition, by showing that the latter, no matter how pure it is, is always only sensible and represents the object not as thing in itself but merely in appearance, e.g., the antinomy of the origin of the cosmos, of the whole of the cosmos with regard to space, of absolute and

---

[a] Kant actually writes "*nothwendigkeit und Nothwendigkeit*."

unconditioned causality, and of the unconditional necessity [*crossed out*: or contingency]*a* of things. At the same time it is also necessary against skepticism, which aims precisely at robbing the clearest convictions of reason of confidence in themselves through contradictions – idealism is not so dangerous, but it very much restricts our field of experience and creates belief in a claim even against our empirical cognitions. – But if it is shown that the determination of our own existence in time presupposes the representation of a space, in order to be able to represent the relation of the determinations of inner intuition to an enduring object, and that space, which is merely a form of intuition, still cannot be the form of inner intuition, because that is not space but time, then outer objects can have their reality (as things in themselves)*b* secured precisely by the fact that one does not treat their intuition as that of a thing in itself; for if it were this and if the form of space were the form of a thing that pertains to it in itself even without the particular constitution of our subject, then it would be possible that we should have the representation of such a thing even without it existing. But it is a particular kind of intuition in us that cannot represent that which is in us, hence existing in temporal change, because then, as mere representation, it could be thought only in temporal relations; thus such an intuition must consist in a real relation to an object outside us and space really signifies something which, represented in this form of intuition, is possible only in a relation to a real thing outside of us. – Thus the refutation of skepticism, idealism, Spinozism, likewise of materialism, predeterminism.

18:628

Some judge that it is difficult to make the content of the critique and by its means metaphysics together with its final aim comprehensible from a single point of view, even for those who are good enough not to misjudge its good aim, and hold it to be entirely useless chicanery with [*crossed out*: previous] merely speculative rational proofs [*crossed out*: of God] of the most sublime [*crossed out*: belief] ideas, on which the contentment of mankind depends, since in the end the critique extends even to these, although only as matters of belief for pure reason, what one apostle said to the other, namely that therein things are encountered which are too elevated for many and which confuse the simple. [*Crossed out*: To the end] As far as the first is concerned, the very facility with which the whole plan can be overseen is a strong recommendation for this system and a confirmation of the unity of its principle, and, as far as confusion is concerned, such a critique is not composed to be delivered to the simple, but to the most subtle reasoners, who think of no subject as

---

a Kant did not actually complete the word "*Zufälligkeit*," but wrote only "*Zuf*" before crossing it out.
b *Sachen an sich*

too elevated for themselves. And there this critique is to prove precisely that these matters are far too elevated for speculative insight for these thinkers and for everyone, and it is to confuse them in the illusion of such insight (persisting in which is their own fault), in order to bring them down to the lower level of which all humans are capable, where every matter of belief must be just as accessible as it is to the most subtle researcher.   18:629

There are three supersensible objects with which human reason has been and will remain unremittingly occupied at all times: God, immortality, and freedom. Of the latter alone do we have an immediate conviction of its reality, yet without having insight into it. It is natural to begin with it in order to then judge about our possible cognition of the others.

6317a. 1790–91. Kant's comments on the reverse of a letter from Ludwig   18:629
Ernst Borowski of 22 March 1790 (11:142).
P. I.

On the highest reality of the categories as principles of possible experience.

We would have no experiential concept without empirical intuition, i.e., without something corresponding to sensation that is placed in space and time, the properties of which are cognized *a priori*, although they are not in themselves any constitution of things, but only of our manner of representation.

     a. We acquire concepts of magnitude only in space and time, but only insofar as we generate them and compose them from homogeneous elements as mere intuition without sensation.[128]

     b. Of quality: since we move from mere intuition to sensation in a certain degree, which is all the quality of things*a* that they have as things in general,*b* not mere forms.[129]

     c. [*breaks off*]

On the distinction between the logical and transcendental validity of principles.

This distinction concerns only that between the principles of the form   18:630
and matter of judgments. Where the judgment asserts the formal condition of the mere possibility [*crossed out*: of the judgment] of a concept (like the principle of contradiction), the principle also holds of things

a *Dinge*
b *Sachen*

negatively, i.e., everything is impossible the thought of which is self-contradictory, and all objects stand under the principle to the extent that the concepts of them must not be opposed to it. By contrast, the proposition that everything has its ground, related to things, has no validity (it is rather false); but it is valid of judgments as propositions. Likewise the principle of division. – Thus all merely logical principles hold as constitutive principles (not merely *conditio sine qua non*) merely of analytical judgments, namely where judgment is to be made merely from concepts. With regard to synthetic judgments, nothing can be determined through them. This does not mean that they do not hold of them to the extent that they can even be contrary to them, but rather only that they do not [*crossed out*: determine] provide such cognition. One could say: synthetic [*crossed out*: cognitions] judgments determine an object in regard to that which was undetermined by the concept, while analytical judgments are merely explicative. For the former as *a priori* judgments no transcendental investigation of the possibility of such cognitions is required, but it is required for the second, since [*crossed out*: there] intuition must still be added to the concept.[130]

Theology.

Here the issue is not theoretical doubt about belief in God, but rather that we can form no objectively determinate concept of such a being at all, and, if we would represent it to ourselves in accordance with the subjective conditions of our rational explanation, we can still get nowhere with the concept in expanding our theoretical cognition. Only the concept of it as a being which is the cause of the possibility of the accomplishment and attainment of all moral ends set forth for us by reason is in conformity with the subjective conditions of the theoretical and especially the practical use of reason, and inseparable from that.

P. II.

N. II. of the critique with regard to theology.[131]

18:631

1. God is eternal. Eternity is infinite duration: duration, however, an existence [*crossed out*: without] represented as a magnitude. Now we cannot conceive of this without time. However, the existence of God cannot be an existence in time. Thus in the word for his eternity we do not have a concept of it that is the least usable for cognition.

2. God is omnipresent. Things, however, are outside of him and also outside of each other. (Now we can only conceive of such a presence in the case of the existence of a thing in space.) But things are not in him, for that would be Spinozism or pantheism. However, he is also not in them. For in that case, as an extended being he would either be partly in one and partly in another, or as a simple being

he would be entirely in each, and since these things are outside of each other, he would be outside of himself.

3. God is intelligence: but [*crossed out*: not to be thought so that] his understanding is not a thinking, yet we have no concept of any other understanding.[132]

4. God is the cause of things through a will in conformity with his understanding, but his will is not of the kind that takes an interest in its object. But we cannot conceive of a will whose satisfaction does not depend in part upon the existence of its object.[133]

5. God is blessed. But when we omit from our concept of happiness precisely everything that carries with it limits of the dependence of satisfaction on contingent causes, we cannot conceive of any rational pleasure except in the agreement of all objects of the will inside us and outside us with our ends. However, we cannot even posit what we call ends in God, for we would otherwise abnegate blessedness as self-satisfaction.

6. God is merciful, kind-hearted, patient: these are likewise anthropomorphisms, and if we were to take these away, then nothing would remain to lend these words a sense by means of which we could cognize an object.

Everything thus comes down to this, that we conceive of God merely in accordance with his relation [*crossed out*: with regard] to a world under natural and moral laws, and indeed as the highest member in the series of conditions, but as himself unconditioned, through which, however, all inner determinations of this primordial ground by means of which   18:632 his essence might be cognized fall away, and nothing is left except the relation of being a primordial ground of the world in accordance with such laws, in the representation of which, to be sure, we can always make use of our subjectively conditioned manner of representing such relations, but only in order to form for the sake of the practical use of reason an analogical conception of a being that is objectively entirely hidden from us.

Belief in God.

Reason cannot reveal to us the supreme condition of our ends in the moral law without at the same time determining the final end of our existence as one that can at the same time be our end. Now this is always happiness; but morality commands that it can be our final end and in general that of the rational beings in the world only under the condition of the worthiness to be happy. Now just as the morally disposed reason cannot conceive of happiness without good conduct, it also cannot conceive of good conduct without happiness if it considers itself as legislative for nature.[134] Thus, if it seeks the necessity of the moral laws in the supersensible substratum of the rational cosmic being, it must also conceive of the principle of happiness in the same thing, hence it must conceive of a deity combining both of these elements of the final end.

18:633   **6319**. 1790–95. *LBl* E 74.
        P. I.

Idealism.

A specifically distinguished imagination must be grounded in another sense, for the imagination is only an inner determination of sense to the same intuition that it had as sense.[135]

On the critique of pure reason.

The two difficulties in it consist in the fact that it is shown that it is not self-contradictory that: I. The soul cognizes itself theoretically only as *phaenomenon*, hence it cognizes itself, but only as appearance. – The solution is this: it does not cognize itself through concepts, which are merely the simple actions of synthesis that belong to cognition in general, namely not through the consciousness of these concepts, for that would be a contradiction, since it should cognize itself as an object, but only by means of the application of these concepts to inner intuition. But time cannot be determined in it without the representation of space and the product in it through the imagination. Space, however, lies in its outer sense, which must affect the imagination in a certain way, and thereby also the inner sense with regard to the inherence of this representation, even the feeling of pleasure, etc. But even the empirical consciousness of the representations of reason as well as of the categories and of thinking in general always belong only to appearance, since it is an occurrence, and nothing intellectual remains as cognition except the I – practically, however, freedom, together with its laws.

    II. How we can speak of the intelligible, e.g., God, through categories, regardless of the fact that these validly **yield cognition** only for *phaenomena*, hence how we can speak of a being that cannot be represented as *phaenomenon* at all.

18:634   P. II.

On the soul in the birth, the life, and the death of the human being. We can have no experience of this, thus we must either make inferences from experience or give proofs *a priori* from the mere capacity for thinking in life or from freedom as the presupposition for the practical use of reason. But since the former must always be inferred from what is sensible and the latter merely from the supersensible, which is given to us [*breaks off*?]

    The identity of the person concerns the intelligble subject in all the difference of empirical consciousness. The latter can be very much altered. But to the extent that it remains coherent, it is the cognition of itself as the same person and is required for imputation.

6323. 1792–94. (April–August 1793). *LBl* F 7. 18:641
P. I.

Cosmological proof of the existence of God.[136]

The proposition goes thus: if the necessity of the existence of a being consists in its being thoroughly determined by a single concept, then it has all reality. –

idem aliter.[a] If the necessity of the existence of a being can be cognized from concepts, then it must be cognized as the most real being. – But the necessity of a being can never be cognized through concepts of it.

Or conversely: If the most real being is to be cognized as a necessary being, then its existence must be cognized from concepts. Now the latter is false, therefore the former as well. – For if in the antecedent [*breaks off*]

Or if a necessary being [*crossed out:* is to be cognized as such] exists, then its thoroughgoing determination must follow from a concept of it (but not to infer the converse). Here it must be remarked that this thoroughgoing determination follows from the concept of a necessary being and not from other concepts, which is false.

– Or if a being is absolutely necessary, then it must be thoroughly determined through its concept. – [*Crossed out:* The consequence is not obvious. But if one wants to say that it must be thoroughly determined (although not through its concept), then it would not have to be the most real thing.] It should say: if it is to be **cognized** as such a thing. For if it is also necessary but this absolute necessity does not provide any cognition of the being as such a thing, then one can have no concept of it that determines it problematically.

If one concedes that it cannot be inferred from the concept of the being of a highest reality that it on that account (from concepts) exists, but if it can nevertheless be inferred that the highest reality exists if a necessary being is assumed (which is already a sort of contradiction), then the concept of a *realissimi* must be a **further** concept, which does not contain merely the concept of the *necessarii* but yet further things. But then the constitution of the being (as far as its reality is concerned) 18:642 is not thoroughly determined through the concept of necessity, which is nevertheless what is supposed to happen in the concept of reality.[138]

The concept of a necessary (modality) being is completely indifferent with regard to all possible, merely non-self-contradictory determination.

A necessary being must possess all reality; for if it did not have all reality, then it would not be thoroughly determined through its concept, hence it would not be a being that is constituted necessarily, as it is.

---

[a] the same thing put another way

Now since we cannot discover any concept from which the necessity of its object can be cognized, the *omnitudo realitatis* is only the *conditio sine qua non* of the concept of a necessary being, without which, to be sure, a thing cannot be, but through which it does not become everything that is, i.e., through which we cannot cognize its existence although we thereby think everything that it is.

P. II.

The real is opposed to the negative,

as well as to the ideal,

and to the formal.

The merely formal ideality of the objects of the senses is proven in the transcendental aesthetic.

The material ideality of the objects of outer sense, namely that no outer object corresponding to them exists at all, is refuted through the fact that otherwise we would not even have any inner sense and our empirical consciousness in time, since time as a magnitude can be cognized only in outer [*crossed out*: alterations] objects.

Only space and time have a formality the properties of which can be given synthetically *a priori* (not so with colors).

On the putative necessity of giving something real (for the underlying pleasure or displeasure) for the incentive of the will in moral laws.

Idealism.

The impossibility of determining our existence in the succession of time through the succession of the representations in us and yet the reality of this determination of our existence is an immediate consciousness of something outside of myself that corresponds to these representations,* and this intuition cannot be an illusion. – The possibility of this consciousness of an object as outside us lies in the simultaneity of the manifold of intuition, since I can arrange its successive apprehension[a] forwards or backwards, which cannot happen in the case of the representation of the manifold in time without the limits of space.[139]

*(And which does not exist merely in my representation but rather as thing in itself, for otherwise from this representation itself no time-determination of my existence would be possible.

The thought of, e.g., a relation of things outside us in accordance with more than three dimensions is certainly possible, but it is not on that account clear that such an object must also be possible, at least it would not be space. Here one says: such a thought lacks proof of its objective reality, although considered logically it is possible.)

On God as the greatest aggregate of reality: *ens maximum*; or the highest ground: *ens summum, ens entium*.

[a] *Zusammennehmung*

376

Complaints about the trouble that metaphysics causes in matters of state and religion. In both anarchy is supposed to be introduced. To restrict the supreme power so much that it finally does not count at all, or to alter things in religion so long and so often that none is left. The importance that one thereby gives to metaphysics.   18:645

1. The reality of the empirical manner of thought in contrast to the ideality of the rational. Palliation of the former through the latter.
2. Reality as regards matter in distinction from mere form, as with filled space and space not as a property of things but merely of the manner of representation.

6338. 1794–95? 1796–98 (first half of 1796)? (1796–98?) *LBl* Kuffner   18:658
4.[140]

It is a proof of the ideality of space that it is a magnitude that can always be represented only as a part of a yet larger one (i.e., it is infinite).[141] – A   18:659
second is that, no matter how small we may represent a space as being, I can think of all given things as in an even smaller space without the things in the one space being the least different, considered internally, from those in the other. – It is thus not the sum of things in themselves. – Likewise with time.

6338a. 1794–95. *LBl Opus postumum* IV. Convolute, N. 39/40.[142]   18:659
P. I.

Magnitude is the determination of an object in accordance with which the apprehension of its intuition is represented as possible only through the repeated positing of something identical. – Elucidation through space and time as magnitudes.[143]

Thus magnitude is for us only a predicate of things as objects of outer sense (for intuition is possible for us only through sense).[144] The concept of the magnitude of a thing in general, if the restriction to sensible intuition were omitted, would go thus: It is the determination through which many homogeneous elements taken together constitute one. But one can have no insight at all into the possibility of a thing in accordance with this concept; consequently one does not know whether the definition has declared a thing or a non-thing. – This general concept of magnitude is not a piece of cognition.

The above concept of magnitude is not an experiential concept; for it contains the conditions of apprehension in general and of the unity of the concept in accordance with its rule, from which all experiential concepts first become possible. Hence it also has intuition *a priori* and the concept of the understanding of synthetic unity of the manifold of intuition in apperception. A definition that has no [*crossed out*: de-   18:660
termination] relation to application *in concreto* is transcendent (without significance).

Theorem: All objects of the senses [*crossed out*: are] have extensive magnitude. For space and time, as that in which alone their manifold can be intuited, are only cognizable as magnitudes. This proposition is a principle of the possibility of experience, in accordance with which perceptions are to be arranged and connected into the unity of cognition of the object.

Categories of magnitude (*Quantitas*). 1. Unity (mathematical, not qualitative, measure – this itself considered as a magnitude and a part of it used for the measure of other magnitudes). 2. Multiplicity. Multitude. Number. – Largeness and smallness. Nothing is absolutely large. Indeterminate multitude. The largest and smallest. Infinite multitude of progress. 3. Totality. Number – aesthetic comprehension, comprehension of the multitude. Infinite magnitude of comprehension (the absolute all* is the absolutely greatest). Regress into the infinite. Continuity. The infinitely small, $1/\infty$.

*(If one calls God infinite, one treats him as homogeneous with creatures, only as great beyond measure (the aesthetic value of the designation).[145] Totality of reality is better, and identical with unlimited.)

Since things, space and time included, cannot be cognized in experience otherwise than through the conditions of the apprehension of the manifold thereof and of the unity of their combination, which is in conformity with the *a priori* concept of them, laws of all possible experience (objects) must hold for them, since experiential cognitions are possible only in accordance with this principle. – *Quanta* are all *continua*. Multitudes are not *quanta*. Where the unit is specifically determined, e.g., sheep, that is not a *quantum*, but a multitude.

Quality.[146]

18:661 Here sensation is combined or not combined with intuition for empirical apperception, i.e., the intuition is empty or partly empty, partly perceptible. Each sensation can be thought of as gradually disappearing, i.e., as decreasing from stronger to weaker, thus as [*crossed out*: disappearing] decreasing to nothing or to a part, and in the same way it can also be increased, hence sensation and the reality of the object that corresponds to it has a degree.

It is subjectively represented as a unity, namely with regard to empirical apperception, but one that passes out of existence as a magnitude, not through division.

P. II.

The concept of magnitude is not a concept derived from experience.

It lies strictly *a priori* in the understanding, although we develop it only in experience.

For that which cannot be **perceived** in the object also cannot [*crossed out*: arise] be derived from experience. Now the concept of magnitude [*crossed out*: is] contains only that which the understanding does for itself, namely producing a whole representation through the synthesis of repeated addition; there is thus nothing contained in this that demands a perception; thus it presupposes no experience, although it is contained in every experience. – Hence it can also be applied *a priori* to intuitions, space and time. But it is also not derived from these, rather only applied to them, and by means of them it acquires objective reality in things in space and time. It contains nothing more than the synthetic unity of consciousness that is required for a concept of the object in general, and it is to that extent an element of cognition, but not yet cognition except in application to pure or empirical intuition.

1. **Concept**. 2. The origin thereof (synthetic division) (*a priori*). 3. Domain (only to objects of the senses). 4. Principle (under these concepts) – **Predicables** (possibility of pure *mathesis*).

A.
Concept of Magnitude

18:662

1. Definition and synthetic division. 2. Origin of the concept. 3. Domain, 4. Principle – in that case predicables.

B.
Concept of Quality

1. Definition and synthetic division. – Definition: The quality of a thing is the determination that represents it as a something or as mere absence, i.e., whose concept contains a being or non-being.

Division. Reality, negation and limitation. (Possibility [*crossed out*: of *mathesis intensorum*[a] or] of **dynamics**.)

C.
Concept of Relation

Definitio: It is the real relation of a thing to something else (which is either its own predicate or in other things). The former is the inner, the latter the outer relation. A real relation is opposed to the merely formal relation, since the former is a relation of reality to another reality. (Possibility of physics) Everything as demonstrable science from *a priori* principles.

N.B. One can give no proof of these propositions that hold of all things in general. For if one uses the pure categories, one cannot know whether anything like them can pertain to anything. If one takes the conditions of intuition in space and time, then one does not know whether these can

---

[a] the mathematics of intensive quantities

be presupposed in all things; for one has no insight into their necessity in the case of all concepts, rather they are only conditions under which we must represent things to ourselves.

Quality is the determination of a thing which is not increased although the thing itself is enlarged, e.g., figure. Understanding in contrast to the senses. Mass in contrast to weight. Divisibility into the infinite in contrast to extension. Reality in contrast to negation.

P. III.

18:663   The object in general. 1. As regards the form of intuition without a something contained by this form. (Space and time). 2. The object as something, *aliquid sive obiectum qualificatum,*[a] is the occupation of space and time, without which both are empty intuitions. This something is set in space and time in the second class of the categories. 3. This real thing in space and time, determined in acordance with relations thereof or conceived *a priori* for relations in them. 4. Something as object of an empirical intuition (of the immediate) of a thing outside me. Against idealism. Thus something as object of the senses, not merely of the imagination.

The (metaphysical) physiology of objects of experience follows from transcendental philosophy or the doctrine of essence in accordance with *a priori* principles: the doctrine of body and the doctrine of soul. From them, cosmology and theology.

Quality

It is that inner determination of a thing through which it can be distinguished from another as a unity. It is opposed to magnitude, which is the inner determination of a thing in accordance with which it can be distinguished from others as a multiplicity. Multiplicity, however, is the determination of a thing, which can be explained just as little as unity can be. The quality of a thing that distinguishes it as a something from mere form is reality, and to it corresponds sensation.[147]

Quality is that inner determination of a thing that can become greater or smaller without enlargement or diminution of the thing. (E.g., weight (in the case of the same mass) is not a quality, for it can only be increased through enlargement of the thing; but mass is a quality, for it can grow, without the body growing in measure.) Continuity is quality, velocity, finally sensation (reality) between *a* and o.

The relation of things to empty space is not an object of possible perception. Likewise in the case of empty time.

18:664   The combination of reality with the concept of magnitude (is intensive), namely absolute unity of reality can have magnitude. But what does not have reality and is absolute unity (the point) has no magnitude.

---

[a] something or the qualified object

Of limits of reality in contrast to boundaries in space, on unlimited – on infinite reality. – That all manifoldness of things as things in general consists only in the limitations of the totality of reality, which presupposes a single being. – That negations are mere limits: transcendental theology. Those are mere ideas, which concern the constitution of our thinking, without one regarding them as cognition of things.

On the possibility of things in accordance with all of the preceding categories,

insofar as the concepts of them are to have objective reality, e.g., magnitude (transcendental definition, 2. metaphysical).

On the respective predicates (concepts of reflection): either logical or real; respectively, of identity with regard to the concept of magnitude, of agreement and conflict with respect to the concept of quality, etc. *Lex continui.*

P. IV.[a]

1) The **geometrical** law of continuity: space and time, therefore spatial and temporal quantities are continuous, i.e., each of their parts in a homogeneous whole are themselves quantities. Any part of them is a sum of homogeneous parts: discrete quantities in them are contradictory, except in the sense that any space is a sum of homogeneous parts. E.g., a vessel full of fruit is not a quantity of fruit, except in abstraction from the intervals between the materials of the fruit which fill the space. – A discrete quantity is a **multitude**.

2) The **dynamical** law of continuity. The momentum of accelerative forces is a continuous quantity, e.g., it is always possible to assign a smaller one which will not be uniform with the given acceleration.

3) The **mechanical** law of continuity: No change in the state of rest or motion of a body or in its speed or direction is possible except in an interval of time, through infinitely smaller differences from the initial state, which gradually lead to the latter, e.g., in any change no degree is the smallest, there is always another which precedes or succeeds it.[148]

4) The **cosmological** law of continuity. The continuum of forms. There are no diverse species in nature between which there are not some intermediate species. – Mistake. This is true of possibilities, not actualities.[149]

18:665

Leibniz's **logical** principle of continuity: a geometrical supposition. Whatever impinges on anything in motion has some speed, even if it is assumed to be at rest. For this is infinite motion. The author argued for this rule in the question of living forces.[150]

---

[a] Kant wrote this page in Latin.

The transcendental principle of continuity. No progress from one reality to its opposite is possible except through intermediate determinations, which are equivalent to a cipher or a nullity, e.g., in oscillations – in the magnet – (in the transition from vice to virtue) – in the transition from pleasure to boredom.

18:665   **6339.** 1794–98. *LBl* G 22.

A great reason for also assuming the difference between objects as *noumena* and as *phaenomena* to be a necessary hypothesis is that without this freedom cannot be defended at all, but without this presupposition, there is no morality.

18:667   **6342.** 1796–98. *LBl* E 2.

We could not cognize things *a priori* if the subjective in our power of representation and hence the way they appear to us did not lie in us *a priori* as the condition under which alone they can come before us thus and not otherwise.

We can cognize how things are in themselves only through perception. But in that case [*breaks off*]. If space and time were the forms of things in themselves, then we could cognize them only through perception, thus not as necessary.

We can only cognize things in accordance with what they are in themselves (*noumena*) and in general *a priori* insofar as we make them ourselves.

18:667   **6343.** 1796–98 (around May 1797). *LBl* D 12.
         P. I.

The final aim of all metaphysics is to ascend from the cognition of the sensible to that of the supersensible. Now the Critique of Pure Reason proves that this can never be accomplished in a theoretical respect, but

18:668   it can very well be done in a morally-practical respect by means of the transcendental concept of **freedom**, which in respect to the **theoretical** faculty of cognition is [*crossed out:* fully] transcendent and absolutely inexplicable and indemonstrable,[151] but which with respect to the pure **practical** faculty (determinable through pure reason alone) has indubitable **reality** through the categorical imperative.[152] – The reality of the concept of freedom, however, inevitably brings with it the doctrine of the **ideality** of objects[a] as objects[b] of intuition in space and time. For if these intuitions were not merely subjective forms of sensibility, but rather of objects in themselves, then their practical use, i.e., actions, would

---

[a] *Gegenstände*
[b] *Objecte*

depend entirely on the mechanism of nature, and freedom together with its consequence, morality, would be annihilated.[a]

6344. 1796–98 (around May 1797). *LBl* E 53.   18:668

All objects are: 1. the *sensibile*, 2. the *aspectabile*, 3. the *intelligibile*.[b]

There are 2 cardinal principles of metaphysics as a whole: the ideality   18:669
of space and time and the reality of the concept of freedom. If one does
not concede the first, then there are no synthetic *a priori* propositions
for theoretical cognition; if the second is not true, then there are no
unconditional practical synthetic *a priori* propositions, i.e., no laws of
duty. If, however, there are none of the latter, then there is no ground
for thinking the concepts of God, freedom, and immortality as [*crossed
out*: concepts] ideas of the supersensible. – **Mathematical** and **dynamical** potencies. – Between the two, the power of judgment concerning
purposiveness in objects, which is a [*crossed out*: merely] subjective and
thereby objective principle.

A *quantum* in contrast to which every other that can be given (*dabile*)
can be thought only as a part of a still greater *quanti* is infinite. That *quantum*, however, which in comparison with every other assignable *quanto*
can only be considered as a part is infinitely small. That all of the extended parts of the world could be put into a drop of water or into an
even infinitely smaller space demonstrates the ideality of space, when
everything is always considered as relatively, never as absolutely large or
small.[c, 153]

6345. 1796–98 (around May 1797). *LBl* F 22.   18:670
P. I.

Nature and freedom. *A priori* cognition in both cases. The mathematical and dynamical faculty of reason in the sensible and the supersensible.

(Against idealism). Whether we could think of things as existing simultaneously if they represented merely that which is in us and in our
mind. The thoughts within me are never simultaneous.

(Schlettwein and Hufeland).[154]

---

[a] Several disconnected phrases at the end of this note are omitted: "In accordance with
the letters, not the intended spirit"; "what the same man says in [this?] connection"; "An
insurrection of dogmatists in measure."

[b] At the margin, the following words are written: "On the manner of writing: no one;
once; muse; concludes."

[c] Here Kant wrote in the margin, "For the sake of others who have combined with the same
aim, I set forth the news, that he who regards himself as the one who best understands
me, etc." According to Adickes, this was an attempt to formulate part of a polemical
response to Johann August Schlettwein that Kant was attempting to compose at this
time. For the relevant documents, see 12:362–70. See also **6346**, note 155.

How are synthetic propositions* about the supersensible possible? As regulative principles of practical reason. Those concerning the sensible are possible as constitutive principles of theoretical reason,

*(possible *a priori*, the [latter] as theoretical, objectively determining propositions concerning objects as appearances, the [former] as practical, merely subjectively determining propositions about objects as things in themselves.)

18:670   **6346.** 1796–98. *LBL* E 39.

Two times are not simultaneous and two spaces are not successive. But since there are nevertheless two different series of existence in one time and likewise different sums in one space, one cannot consider either of them as properties inhering in objects of the senses, but rather only as forms for the composition of the manifold in a sensible intuition.

18:671   Since the conditions of space and time, which lie at the basis of all representations of experience, carry necessity with them, hence lie *a priori* in the representational faculty of the senses, this cannot happen except insofar as they lie in the subject and its sensible form of intuition; for it alone is given prior to all experience.[155]

Suppose that we cognized the objects of the senses as they are in themselves when we are immediately conscious of them; then this would not be any *a priori* cognition, but mere perception, which carries no necessity with it, but rather only the content that things are thus but not that they necessarily must be so.

This ideality of *a priori* intuitions in the representation of the senses, the form of the composition of the manifold of intuition in **one** apperception through the understanding together with the schematism of the power of judgment, – finally that through reason in the practical.

The infinity of actual space proves that it is merely the form of intuition. For that which is given but which can never exist except as part of a whole is infinite. Now that quantum which can only exist as part of another *quanti* is not a thing that is given objectively.

Further, however large the given world may be, it can still be contained in the space of a drop of water, the head of a pin, etc.; on account of infinite divisibility. Thus they cannot be composed out of things in themselves.[156]

18:671   **6348.** 1796–98 (Summer 1797). *LBl* E 21.

18:672   That the form of intuition (not the form of thinking) of objects in space and time is represented *a priori* and as necessary demonstrates its subjectivity, namely that it does not belong to the constitution of objects, but must rather lie *a priori* in the sensibility of the subject, by means of which one can certainly know *a priori* in which form they will be intuited by us and thus how they will appear to us: yet at the same time that it is a kind of representations, namely of how things **are** or at least must be conceived.

Second, freedom is a property of which we are not immediately conscious through inner sense, but which is demonstrated apodictically (namely, negatively) through the concept of duty. This property represents a being like the human being not as it appears, but as it is. – However, this *a priori* principle of cognition is merely practical.[157]

Both together are the *cardines* of the critical philosophy, and all metaphysics has them as its aim.[158] These together with the doctrine of taste constitute the entirety of the principles of [*breaks off*]

The forms that we cognize through experience cannot be cognized *a priori*, for otherwise they would lose the character of necessity.

Transcendental concepts can be called **sense-free**.[a] Transcendental philosophy is also sense-free. Everything, in which there is nothing empirical but yet everything is universally valid. E.g., the **categories**. Transcendent: what is not an element of cognition at all.

6349. 1796–98 (around June–July 1797). *LBl* M 13. 18:672
P. I.

If the appearances of the senses were the things in themselves, then they would all possess necessity in the chain of effects and causes and there would be no freedom, thus also no categorical imperative, which nevertheless commands unconditionally through reason.

If the object of inner sense, the soul, were not a mere appearance of itself, but a pure consciousness of its thinking, then we could not have in us the juxtaposition of representations in time, consequently in a form that is thought synthetically *a priori*, and would thus have no experiential   18:673
cognition of ourself.[159] For what contains representations combined in relations of space and time is mere appearance.

On *Aenesidemus*[160] and the diallel. – To answer Tieftrunk.[161] – How can a subject intuited by itself cognize itself merely as appearance?

One cannot have any cognition of an object at all through the mere category: 1. that many together constitute one; 2. that reality has a degree; 3. that something is so constituted that something else is the necessary consequence of it; 4. that the existence of a thing is absolutely necessary for itself.

Likewise, one can also have no cognition through intuitions alone, and, if they are empirical, no *a priori* cognition, unless the rule precedes.

The ideality of space and time (consequently the concept of all objects of experience as appearances) and the practical reality of the rational concept of freedom are the two cardinal points of metaphysics.[162]

---

[a] *sinnenfreye*

On the **spectacle** that one makes with the proposition that in inner intuition one is only appearance, not the thing in itself. It means only the same as: "inner experience is nothing more than empirical cognition of oneself in accordance with what is subjective in the manner of our intuition of ourself in time (of the apprehension of inner representations), as we represent ourselves internally, not as the subject is in itself; as it is given to us internally, not as it is thought by us." The difficulty concerns only how the subject can order experience in itself. It must not merely

18:674   perceive sensations in itself, but it must arouse them and connect them synthetically, hence affect itself. Thus it is not a thinking but an intuiting of itself.

To Herr Councillor and Director Euler at the Russian Imperial Academy of Sciences at St. Petersburg.[163]

That space and time yield synthetic *a priori* propositions. That this is not possible otherwise than if both are merely subjective forms of sensibility; for otherwise they would be synthetic empirical propositions about the object.

P. II.

Mathematics proves that synthetic *a priori* propositions are real and consequently also possible. But that these are not possible through perception of objects of intuition as things in themselves can be seen from the fact that they would otherwise be empirical and contain no necessity, which is intrinsic only to *a priori* cognitions. That they therefore indicate only the subjective constitution of our sensibility, which yields the form of intuition prior to everything empirical, thus *a priori*, hence that cognition can contain objects of the senses merely as appearances, follows inevitably from this. But that this must be so also follows when we start from the practical-supersensible of freedom. [*Crossed out*: For the categorical imperative could not be valid if actions were determined through natural causes, and no freedom would be possible if the determining nature represented things in themselves. The human being as object in itself would conceive of itself as determinable merely in conformity with natural laws. Insofar as he is to be effective, he must think of himself as a phenomenon considered only under natural laws, for thus can he think of himself as determinant as a noumenon independent from temporal condition.] Conversely, if our actions are free, inner sense can give us only appearances, not cognition of our substance as a thing in

18:675   itself. For if the latter were the case, then all our inner determinations of the soul would become* physically necessary, like everything that happens in accordance with the law of cause and effect, and there would be no freedom.

*(The consciousness of all determinations of the soul (of inner sense) [would] be empirical, thus no practical principle of them *a priori*, as

that on which all unconditioned necessity, thus that of actions of duty, depends, would be possible.)

That the concept of freedom and its reality are a sufficient ground for assuming the existence of God and a future life. – The moral imperative contains an ought and for that very reason a capacity for overcoming all of nature on account of its causality (for resisting it). This capacity is necessary for the capacity of a being to make these decrees of practical reason harmonious with nature, or *vice versa*. Such a capacity, however, is in God.

6350. 1796–98 (July–August 1797). *LBl* Reicke Xb9.   18:675
P. I.

Synthetic *a priori* propositions are possible only under the presup-position of the **subjective form** of inner and outer intuition, for the objects must always be in conformity with these. This is the principle of the ideality of space and of time.

If the subject affects itself in representations of inner sense, these are only ways in which the subject appears to itself, and experience is only the composition of representations of inner sense ordered in accordance with the categories.

Myinda, the blind cow game, is more fun than blindfolded fighting *andabaratum.*[a]

Things considered as they are in themselves, not as appearances, are not qualified for any theoretical cognition, for they are mere ideas. But to conduct oneself in conformity with these ideas is a real concept of   18:676
practical reason. *Myinda metaphysica* or anti-critique of pure reason.[b]

One can never have an experience of a supersensible nature: God, freedom, spiritual being; for between the two there must be an action and a reaction.

What is an object? That whose representation is a sum of several predicates belonging to it. The plate is round, warm, made of tin, etc. Warm, round, being made of tin, etc., are not objects, although the warmth, the tin, etc., [are].

An object is that in the representation of which various others can be thought as synthetically combined.[164]

In every judgment there is a subject and predicate [*crossed out:* and an object which]. The subject of the judgment, insofar as it contains

---

[a] This appears to mean something like "Pin the tail on the donkey is more fun than a fight between blindfolded gladiators"; whether this was intended to have any philosophical significance is not obvious.

[b] In light of the previous paragraph, perhaps this means that to reject the critique of pure reason is to allow speculative metaphysics to continue unguided, like a game of pin the tail on the donkey.

various possible predicates, is the object. The predicates all depend on the subject, as warm depends on the warmth.

Warm, four-cornered, deep are predicates. – The warmth, the rectangle, the depths are objects. – Likewise with rational and reason. The determinable in a judgment, the logical subject, is at the same time the real object.

I can analytically explain what it is to be virtuous; but virtue itself is subsequently composed synthetically from that.

Note. Principle of synthetic universality, insofar as it flows from the analytical. – 2 parallel lines, intersected by a third [*breaks off*])
P. II.

The subject of a judgment, the representation of which contains the ground of the synthetic unity of a manfiold of predicates, is an **object**.

That which contains the synthetic (real) universality of a concept is the object. – What merely contains the analytic (logical) unity is the logical (subject). **Reinhold**.[165]

18:677   The concept that contains the synthetic unity of the apperception of the manifold (what might pertain to it) is the concept of an object. It is also the subject of a judgment that has many predicates.

That which is [*crossed out*: represented] thought in a judgment is the object (matter); the thought of it through the predicate is the form in which I think it. Thus the concept [*crossed out*: of virtuous good fortune] wise is the predicate in a judgment, e.g., The virtuous person is wise.[a]

18:677   **6351**. 1796–98 (at the earliest October 1797). *LBl* Berliner Staatsbibliothek, No. 21.
P. I.

Berlin News, 30 September 1797.

"The Royal Academy of Sciences is not of the opinion of those who regard it as mathematically proven that there are pure subjective representations; it is rather **convinced** that there are essential grounds to the contrary, which have to this date not been satisfactorily answered, and that there is no lack of strong grounds **for the universal empirical origin of all of our cognition**, which have perhaps not been put in their best light up to now."

N.B. The prize question is posed by the Philosophical Class of the Academy of Sciences until 1 June 1799. The director is Herr Selle.[166]

18:678   Such a ground of proof is an internal contradiction. For if it is to be universally valid, then it must contain unconditional necessity, consequently be proven *a priori* and hence independently from

---

[a] At the bottom of the page the following was written: "To the Society of Artists for the mechanical reproduction of paintings in Duisburg. On the words once, never, always."

everything empirical. For only through necessity does one cognize *stricte* universality.

P. II.

There would not be any reservation if, when a medical doctor accepted the commission of the academy to respond to this formulation of their problem, he was able to introduce not only strong but indisputable grounds for the universal empirical origin of all of **his** (medical) cognition. – But how such a problem could migrate into the philosophical rather than the medical faculty is not to be comprehended.

Of synthetic *a priori* practical cognition it can also be said that it is merely subjective; the freedom (of the will) is the first – and the transcendental concepts of God and immortality apply only to the principles of my action. I should act as if there are a God and a future life.

How are synthetic propositions about the supersensible possible? As regulative principles of practical cognition, not as constitutive principles of theoretical cognition.

The supersensible that is given is the concept of freedom; consequently no synthetic-theoretical proposition that would be objectively transcendent is possible.

On objects as things in themselves. That there must be such things in our reason can be seen from the counterpart of the sensible in general.

6353. 1796–98 (second half of 1797). *LBl* Reicke Xb12.   18:679

What if Herr Beck begins with the categories, which have no significance for themselves, then progresses to *a priori* intuitions that correspond to them, and thus arrives at space, time, and reality [?][167]

The system of the *Critique of Pure Reason* revolves around 2 cardinal points: as system of nature and of freedom, each of which leads to the necessity of the other. – The ideality of space and time and the reality of the concept of freedom, from each of which one is unavoidably led to the other analytically. In accordance with one to synthetic-theoretical *a priori* cognition, in accordance with the other to synthetic practical but equally *a priori* cognition. The nature of the human being in itself cannot be determined *a priori* without this determination (to actions) presupposing freedom; for otherwise this determination would not be *a priori*. Something supersensible must therefore be assumed under which the sensible can be regarded as determinable, and conversely something sensible *a priori* in accordance with which the supersensible determines sensibility [*crossed out*: empir . . . to activity] to deeds. The 1st principle: all objects of our cognition, if they are to [*crossed out*: become] yield experience, can only be considered as appearances. The 2nd principle is the categorical imperative: All actions from freedom can only be conceived in accordance with the principle of the correspondence of the universal   18:680
validity of their maxims for universal legislation.

18:680   **6354.** 1796–98 (second half of 1797). *LBl* Reicke Xb6.

Inner sense is not yet [*crossed out*: the consciousness through which] the cognition of myself, rather [*crossed out*: only representation of inner appearances] we must first have appearances by means of it, and then subsequently form a concept of ourself through reflection on this, which then has as its consequence empirical cognition of myself, i.e., inner experience.[168] – But that even this experience in another relation in turn allows us to judge ourselves only as appearance, not as we are absolutely in ourselves, follows from the fact that the form of inner sensory intuition may rest entirely on the specific constitution of the subject, since we must be affected by something, but in every case through attention to ourselves, and thus all inner intuition is **passive**.[169] We also encounter such a form in our sensory intuition (of the inner), namely time, which can never be conceived (as it however really is) *a priori* and thus can be [*crossed out*: represented] conceived as **necessarily** belonging to the subject. This representation of time also cannot be derived from concepts, but only from the appearance of the subject in regard to myself. Now this constitutes a doubled I, but not of consciousness (I appear to myself, in this empirical consciousness I am to myself both that which is observed and the observer, who [*breaks off*])

18:680   **6355.** 1796–98 (second half of 1797). *LBl* Reicke Xb6.

That synthetic *a priori* propositions are only possible through the
18:681   subjective form of sensibility, consequently that their objects can only be represented as appearances, can be seen from the fact that they bring necessity with them, but not from concepts through *analysis*. – For suppose that we could perceive things **in themselves**, then such propositions would lack necessity and universal validity. But if they are merely appearances, then we can know *a priori* how they must appear to ourselves; for they could have no other intuitions than what the subjective constitution of our sense allows. – But this has no relation to the fact that in what concerns colors each of us may have his own sensibility. For this is sensation, consequently not objective, but rather merely subjective, and it has in itself no universality and necessity.[170]

18:681   **6356.** 1796–98 (second half of 1797). *LBl* Reicke Xb7.

1. How are synthetic *a priori* propositions concerning things that may be an object of experience possible [?] 2. How are synthetic *a priori* propositions concerning things that cannot be objects of experience, i.e., concerning objects of pure reason, possible? – The former only insofar as objects (outer objects as well as the inner object of inner sense) can be cognized merely as appearances in theoretical cognition; the latter merely as objects that [*crossed out*: determine] correspond to the final end of reason for pure practical cognition of ourselves.

6357, 1796–98? 1799–1804? After Michaelmas (end of September) 1797.   18:681
LBl E 77.
P. III.

Since only the subjectivity of the form of sensible intuition can make possible synthetic *a priori* propositions (as pertaining merely to objects in appearance), it can also be comprehended why they are contradic-   18:682 tory to the principles of pure reason and concepts formed in accordance with that, e.g., that space consists neither of infinitely many parts nor of a finite number of them. Why the space that is given and the time that has passed is neither finite nor infinite; namely, because here the concept is not underlain by or subjected to the object in itself, but only to the constitution of it through the composition of the manifold in appearance.

It is the same whether we say that space is infinitely divisible or that it consists of infinitely many parts. Likewise as concerns the infinitude of the space and time that are represented as given.

Only through and for the moral law do the theoretical ideas of God and immortality acquire their (practical) reality.
P. IV.

How are synthetic *a priori* propositions objectively possible with regard to the cognitive faculty, the feeling of pleasure and displeasure, and the faculty of desire, and subjectively possible with regard to the supersensible? – from the centering*a* of the power of representations, through which the object is conceived on the one hand as appearance, on the other as in itself.

6358. 1796–98 (November–December 1797). *LBl* G 3.   18:682
P. II.

The whole of the critical philosophy.

First, the division according to the categories.

a. Mathematical and dynamical potencies. Constitutive and regulative principles: the former of the faculty of cognition, the latter of the faculty of desire. – A. All representations given in intuition as appearances,   18:683 B. as things in themselves. (Appearances not empirical representations of intuition, e.g., colors, rather representations of intuition given *a priori*). – The sensible as such, considered universally, indicates a supersensible.

Principle: Synthetic *a priori* propositions (theoretical ones) represent all objects to me only as **appearances**. – The things in themselves thought *a priori* are related to the **supersensible**.

b. Dynamical potencies. 1. **Freedom**: basis of the constitutive principles of the supersensible. 2. **Necessity**: basis of the regulative.

---

a *Centriren*

Theoretically transcendent – practically immanent. α. God. β Immortality of the soul. – Freedom: ideality as concerns the subject and reality with regard to its causality. Concepts of reason and ideas. – Putative antinomies of reason with regard to the totality of conditions, which are all contingent and conditioned in comparison to the unconditioned, which exists only in pure reason, i.e., in the idea. The practical ideas as a regulative principle to act as if there were a God and another world. – The scholastic is systematic (*simplex et unum*), the popular fragmentary.*

P. III.

*I do not see why one should not begin, with Herr Beck,[171] with the categories, although at the same time conceding that these pure concepts of the understanding can produce no cognition at all without subordinating sensibility to them as *materia circa quam.*[a] E.g., **quantity** (as one in many), **quality** (as many in one) are thought as contained; **Relation**: as when if something is given in perception something that is really different is also given *a priori* as a consequence; **modality**: as the form of the connection of all perceptions (in one experience) makes the reality of this manifold cognizable in one experience *a priori*. – Here Herr Beck would only remark that these categories lack objective reality, namely one does not see whether something is possible or not. Now he would apply the latter to appearances in general in space and time as intuitions and thus follow the synthetic method, which approach would yet have in itself another standpoint.

18:684

P. IV.

To the empirical cognition (of experience) there belongs: 1. Intuition, i.e., representation through which an object is given, 2. a concept, through which this is thought, 3. composition of the manifold of intuition, 4. unity in the consciousness of it.

The empirical element in the consciousness of an intuition is called perception (*animadversio*) and has a degree, i.e., intensive magnitude; pure intuition has merely extensive magnitude (space and time). Space and time in which nothing is perceived (no empirical representation of the object encountered) are empty.

To the composition of the manifold of intuition in conformity with the rule that is contained in the concept of it there belongs the synthesis of the manifold of intuition into one concept (category) and then that of the perceptions into the possibility of an experience.

To ascend from the morally practical to ideas and indeed to theoretical ones of God and immortality and then in turn to descend to the sensibly practical: religion, the state, and private happiness. Here the subjective in practical reason is also the determining ground of the objective in

---

[a] as it were as their material

appearance, for which synthetic-practical *a priori* propositions supply the grounds.

On the Cognition of the Sensible and Supersensible.

Synthetic *a priori* propositions can give us cognition of objects only as appearances, not as what they are in themselves. – For since by means of such a synthetic proposition I say more about the object than what is contained in my representation of it, I assert about it something that does not pertain to it, i.e., it is without truth. (The spontaneity of an empty judgment.) – It is not possible to go beyond my given concept *a priori* except through a judgment which contains the relation of the object to the constitution of the subject and its faculty of representation or rather first to its receptivity to be affected by the object in a certain way, which thus only says how it appears to me, not how it is. With this restriction I can say *a priori* how the object does and must appear to me.

18:685

P. III.

One cannot think of a kind of representation as **restricted** with regard to a certain principle without opposing it to another one that is general with respect to it. I.e., if I designate a cognition as being restricted to the sensibility of the subject then I must conceive of a cognition of the supersensible in opposition to this, and can subsequently investigate whether and how (in theoretical or practical use) reality can be provided for this.

To investigate the supersensible, which must be assumed as necessarily existing either outside me or inside me, if not in a theoretical then in a morally practical respect, is thus an inescapable task of reason. God and immortality, through the law of freedom (morality). All philosophy aims at these three points, striving namely to ascend from the sensible to the supersensible (metaphysics).

6359. 1796–98 (between 5 November and 11 December 1797). 18:685
LBl C 2.

P. I.

1. A note (to the essay on the false subtlety of the four syllogistic figures)[172] which would present in all briefness the essential difference between the procedure of the understanding in its logical function and that in its transcendental function; 2. a note (to the essay on the use of teleological principles in philosophy – at the end)[173] which would present the difference between the exposition and the deduction of the categories, whereby at the same time it could be noted how the proposition on p. 177 of the *Critique of Pure Reason* that the application of the categories to the appearances is to be mediated and made possible through the transcendental determination of time (because it is

18:686

homogeneous with both the appearances and the categories) is to be understood.[174] The difficulty seems to arise because the transcendental time-determination itself is already a product of apperception in relation to the form of intuition and thus itself raises the question how the application of the categories to the form of intuition is possible, since the categories and the form of intuition are heterogeneous. In general, the schematism is one of the most difficult points. – Even Herr Beck cannot find his way about in it.[175] – I hold this chapter to be one of the most important.

N.B. The intuition of time is not homogeneous with the categories, rather the determination of time, the unity of the representations in the synthesis (composition) of the given intuition [*breaks off*].[a]

N.B. 1) That the categories in themselves and for themselves alone do not have any object or sense (since they are mere forms of thought) and the possibility, e.g., of something composite (which makes one out of many) cannot be explained.

N.B. 2) If it comes down to metaphysics with the philosophical principles of *a priori* cognition, then there can be no fragmentary judgment, rather judgment must be systematic;[176] a critical dogmatic philosophy is a non-entity.

P. II.

The categories as functions (subjective possibility) of the composition of the manifold, insofar as the many constitute a one in the representation of something (*entia*). *a*) **Magnitude** in pure intuition, *b*) in sensation, quality of the empirical intuition or perception of the homogeneous, *c*) of the real ground and the consequence in sensations, i.e., of causality, *d*) of experience, empirical cognition, consciousness of the existence of an object of given perception.

The composite as such cannot be cognized as composite as given in intuition, but only through the composition of the manifold, thus through the concept of synthesis.[177]

The merely subjective element in intuition as the representation of an object is **appearance**. The form of appearance insofar as it is an *a priori* representation, not an empirical one, is called pure intuition. Thus representations of colored objects are not pure intuitions.[178]

The rediscovery of something thought is selective memory. Holding together both what has been thought and what has yet to be seen is the power of comprehension. The power of judgment (namely, the negative power) is what lasts longest in the process of aging. If this disappears then age makes one childish.

18:687

---

[a] Here Kant inserts the unrelated remark that "The desire to dominate is the rule in the faculty of jurisprudence."

N.B. That time is expressed by a line (which is however space)[179] and space through a time (the distance travelled in an hour) is a schematism of the concept of the understanding. *Compositio.*

6360. 1797. *LBl* Essen-Königsberg 11.   18:687

P. I.   18:688

1. The doctrine of the objects of the senses, both outer and inner, as appearances. 2. The doctrine of the supersensible (unconditioned) as a regulative principle, not a constitutive one, and so as practical things in themselves, namely, not to proceed from the concepts of God and immortality to morality, but rather from morality to those concepts.

A quantum, for which any magnitude given to it can always be conceived only as part of another homogeneous one, is infinite. – However, that an object can always exist only as a part proves that it is not a true entity but a thought-entity.[180] That we do not intuit it as composite, rather that we are always conscious of the act of our composition in accordance with a certain form of intuition. What is infinitely small. – Through categories alone, since they contain merely thought, we do not cognize any object (matter). One cannot even have insight into the possibility of an object in accordance with them, e.g., how many homogeneous things constitute one, or how something positive can nevertheless also be determined negatively with regard to the same predicate, or how, if something actual is given, another actual thing must necessarily follow from it, or finally how the existence of a thing can be absolutely necessary. The intuition of space and time connected to the real (that which is sensed) alone gives us cognitions that in the end (even pure mathematics) can prove the reality of their concepts merely through their correspondence with the possibility of experience, in which case, however, the intuitions can provide *a priori* cognitions only if they are not assumed to be things in themselves, but only appearances, i.e., the subjective form of our sensibility, because one can only know the constitution of these *a priori* for themselves alone, let the objects be what they might, hence only these   18:689 are given *a priori*.

That a person can also represent himself from one side as appearance is not more difficult to understand than that this can be the case with outer objects, once one has assumed the possibility of representing oneself as an object, which cannot be further proved. For he is then in part the object of his sense, in part of his faculty of thinking. In the first case he is conscious of how he affects himself empirically, and he represents these impressions in the form of time. In the second he is conscious how he affects the subject and is to that extent in the act of spontaneity.

One cannot be immediately conscious of the intuition of something composite as such, but only of the composition (*synthesis*), i.e., the self-activity of composition. Hence the categories.[181]

Of pressure, attraction, and both together in the origin of reciprocity: Impact.

P. III.

Philosophy (as the doctrine of wisdom) is the doctrine of the determination of the human being with regard to the final end given by his own reason.

A. To this, as theoretical science of the object in general, belongs the determination to discover the highest condition for the conditioned in general (the totality of conditions) through reason, and since, if the representation of the object is sensible, this is always in contradiction with itself (antinomy), yet nevertheless something unconditioned must be assumed in order to reach the conclusion of the inference: that the cognition of things through sense never gives more than mere appearance: never the things in themselves.

B. That the practical cognition from reason can never be given un-

18: 690   conditionally (consequently it can be given only through the concept of duty), which grounds the concept of freedom, which can be cognized only through this imperative.[182] – Now with this the doctrine of right (and the doctrine of right for states and peoples that is to be found therein) – both as pure rational cognition through concepts – are grounded.

C. That from this non-sensible a step to the supersensible is still open, namely to the concepts of God and immortality, which, dogmatically expounded, contain only transcendent attempts, but which, critically expounded, in accordance with the preceding critique of one's own faculty of reason, do not give cognition of objects (which are unattainable by us), but the ideas of which provide a regulative (not constitutive) principle to act as if those ideas also had objective reality.

Now the doctrine of taste as belonging to the power of judgment in accordance with principles. —

18: 700   **6389**. 1790–95. M 25–6, in *Necessarium et contingens*, §§101–23.[183]

Assume a necessary being.[184] Then you represent a being whose non-existence is impossible. But you have no concept at all of such a thing; for you can cognize impossibility only through a contradiction; however, the non-existence of a thing never contradicts itself, since that a thing exists is not an analytic proposition following from its concept but a synthetic proposition. – Now you could well say that since everything that exists must be thoroughly determined, if you are to provide some concept of the necessary being which thoroughly determines it *a priori*, it could only be the concept of the *realissimi*. – But I cannot say that if I did not think the *necessarium* under the concept of the *realissimi* (we never represent the existence of substances as necessary, but only their *accidentia*) that a contradiction with the concept of the *necessarii* would arise, since even if I assume a *realissimum* the non-existence of this thing contains no contradiction (such a relation of concepts is only possible if the concept of the *realissimi* contains only a partial concept of the *necessarii*; for in that case I can very well infer from the *necessario* to the *realissimum*, but not also from this to that necessity; but the concept of the *realissimi* itself comprises in accordance with the presupposition the entire concept of the *necessarii*, since it is assumed just in order to represent the *necessarium* in its thorough determination); for the necessity can just as little be deduced from the concept of a being that is determinable in two ways (the contingency thereof) as it can from that which is determinable only in a single way, since the existential proposition is always synthetic and whether it exists or not cannot be inferred from concepts, whether one that contains a thoroughgoing determination or one that leaves it undetermined in many respects, hence its objective reality can neither be affirmed nor denied. 18: 701

It is not that the necessary being is determinable only in a single way, for it could exist even if *non-A* as well as *A* were contained among its determinations; rather, if the existence of a thing is to be cognized from its concept, then this concept must already contain the thoroughgoing determination in itself; e.g., this could happen only from the concept of the *realissimi* if in general the existence of a thing could be cognized from its concept; for this is the only concept which represents an *ens singulare*.

But the absolutely necessary [*crossed out*: being] existence cannot be derived from the concept of any thing; thus even if it is conceived by us as a necessary being, which is the modality of its positing, it is still entirely undetermined what predicates this concept contains.

There is no reason why the *partim negativum*[a] should not exist just as necessarily.

The concept of a necessary being is 1. the concept of a thing that is not undetermined with respect to any possible predicate *A* or *non A*, i.e., of an *individui*; but through this concept it is 2. undetermined; consequently it is logically contingent whether I ascribe *a* or *non A*[b] to it. 3. from the necessity of its existence it does not follow that it is thoroughly determined by its concept, i.e., is an *ens realissimum*. 18: 702

The proof of the **necessary existence** of a *realissimi* is this: if it did not exist, it would not possess all perfection, for it would be lacking existence (as a perfection of a thing). – the proof of the **highest reality** as a predicate of the necessary being is: If this did not possess every perfection, then it would in itself be undetermined through its concept

---

[a] That is, a being defined by the totality of negative rather than positive predicates.
[b] Kant switches from a lowercase to an uppercase letter here.

whether it possesses a certain perfection or not, consequently, however it may exist, it would still be possible that it does not exist, hence [*crossed out*: a contingent being] its existence (the thoroughgoing determination) would be contingent.

One thinks here that the first proposition must be synthetic and *a priori* while the second is merely analytic: for in the former I go from possibility (though is even this given?) to actuality – but in the latter from the actuality, that is here at the same time determined as necessary, to the concept that alone contains thoroughgoing determination (which must always be thought in existence) and which seems to be identical with the previous concept, hence through an analytic proposition, not beyond the concept, but to that which is contained in it. – Yet the proposition is still synthetic; for I go beyond any concept that I might have of a necessary being as such a thing if I infer from the concept that it is the only one for me which contains thoroughgoing determination to the condition of the possibility of the thoroughgoing determination of the object itself (in intuition), or make the former concept into the latter; for in intuition it can, regardless of its necessity, contain many negative predicates in its thoroughgoing determination, only I cannot derive them from a single concept or comprehend them together in it.

18: 706 **6403.** 1790–95. *M* 57, in *Substantia et accidens,* §§191–204.

In every alteration the substance persists, since the alteration is the succession of the determinations of one and the same thing. This is a merely logical proposition in accordance with the rule of identity. But it does not say that in general substance does not arise or cease to be, but only that it remains during the alteration.[185]

This proposition also holds only of corporeal substances in space. For there arising or ceasing to be is always an alteration of that which is not substantial, namely of space, which remains,[186] but which is not an object of experience at all, hence that alteration is also not an object of experience, hence there would be no alteration. The persistence of matter in all change of relations is proven from the fact that matter itself is a mere sum of relations, which cannot disappear without all other relations, hence everything possible in outer experience, also disappearing.

18: 708 **6413.** 1790–95. *M* 94–5, at §§307–11, in *Causa et causatum.*

Every synthetic predicate, i.e., determination, has its ground, namely something else through which it is connected *a priori* with the concept of a thing. For otherwise the determination would not be objective. However, the reality of an *entis realissimi* is not a determination. But the existence of a thing is a synthetic predicate of our representation of things, and one cannot say: it has a ground (*rationem existendi*), but only: *rationem cognoscendi,* and this not merely *a posteriori,* but also *a priori.*

The concept of cause is valid only of objects of experience;[187] for that something exists can only be cognized by means of experience; and of that which is not an object of experience it is valid only insofar as it can be thought in accordance with the analogy of experience. But that something in such objects is contingent cannot be cognized from concepts and the possibility of the opposite, i.e., the consistency of the opposite with concepts; for the contingency here concerns existence as the predicate of a synthetic judgment. Thus the opposite of what belongs to existence is possible only if it is not determined in accordance with any law of experience and any analogy with that. Hence nothing is contingent except that which occurs but without a cause or respectively without an external cause. Motion inheres in a body *accidentaliter*. It arises 18: 709 *accidentaliter*. It is a contingency, i.e., an occurrence, but not in accordance with concepts, i.e., absolute possibility of the opposite. For everything that is deteminable through experience is necessary, for otherwise the connection of perceptions would not be objective. Logical contingency is still physical necessity.

Omne contingens, h.e. quodcunque contingit, est rationatum alterius,[a] every occurrence is an effect of a cause: this can be understood in two ways, it being understood to mean either merely the determination of a thing or its existence as a substance. In the first meaning, it is a possible concept of experience, and the proposition is a principle of nature; in the second it is a problematic concept that is entirely empty, where namely the existence of the subject is itself supposed to be an occurrence and to follow its non-existence – empty. – This contingency of the thing can be understood just as little as its necessity. *Contingentia absoluta* is just as uncognizable as *necessitas absoluta*.

6420. 1790–95. M 118, in *Notio mundi negativa*, §§380–91.   18: 711

If space and time were something given in themselves, then they would have to be considered as infinite magnitudes. Now they are nothing but forms for infinite increase or diminution.

6421. 1790–95. M 118.   18: 711

In the mathematical antinomies both propositions are false, because the unconditioned is supposed to be a part of the appearances and yet as such can never be unconditioned. In the dynamical antinomies both propositions can be true, because the unconditioned is the ground of the appearances but not a part of them, and one proposition holds of things in appearance, the other of their relation to the intelligible ground.

---

[a] Everything contingent, i.e., whatever occurs contingently, is grounded in something else.

The first two antinomies are grounded on the unconditioned totality of the conditions – the second two on the unconditioned ground of the existence of the conditioned. Hence the first 2 are false; the others can be true.[188]

18:711   **6422.** 1790–95. *M* 119, §382, still in *Notio mundi negativa*.

Freedom is a sensibly unconditioned capacity of a substance to determine itself to action.

18:711   **6424.** 1790–95. *M* 123, still in *Notio mundi negativa*.

Idea. A pure concept of reason must be a subjectively necessary concept of reason, and this is that of the unconditioned, consequently of the absolute totality of conditions (for reason is a faculty for deriving the particular from the universal).[189] Now as quantum the world is composite, and the possibility of a *quanti* which is itself still a part is always still
18:712   conditioned; thus only the concept of the absolute totality of the whole of substances is in conformity with reason's concept of the world. Now however contradictions arise, one may say either that the sensible world as an absolute whole of things is infinite (infinitely given) but also that it is given as finite. This is because it is a contradiction that a world should be given in itself in space and time, because it is not a thing in itself. That the sensible world is infinite does not mean that it is as such actual. For since it exists only in the representation, not in itself as one thinks it, it is only given as far as progress reaches, hence it is never completely given, i.e., the last member goes off into the infinite.

18:712   **6425.** 1790s? (1778–79?) *M* 138, at §424ff., in *Prima corporum genesis*.

One can say that matter is infinitely divisible, but not that it consists of infinitely many parts; it is somewhat similar to Euclid: that two parallel lines infinitely extended can never intersect is not identical with the proposition that they intersect at an infinite distance. For the latter would yield a triangle whose angles equal more than 2 right angles. It is the same with the proposition[s] that the world-space can be infinitely extended and that it is infinite (we can say the latter of pure space, but only as an idea). One can also give a proof of this from the fact that if a given space consisted of infinitely many parts the world-space would be infinite.

18:714   **6432.** 1790–95. 1778–79?? *M* 340, in *Existentia Dei*.

On God and immortality.

If in order to obligate us the moral law needed God and a future life, then it would be absurd to ground the belief in the reality of that which can satisfy that need on the need itself.

However, the moral law is firmly established by itself, independent of any theoretical presupposition; indeed instead of this supersensible, which surpasses all our insight, it also has as its ground freedom (which itself lies beyond nature in another field). This law as a principle of wisdom leads our reason in its practical use to the final end of a highest wisdom: the greatest happiness combined with virtue as the final end of all things, which, however, so far as we can see makes necessary an eternity of our existence and a moral author of the world for realizing the constitution of the world that is requisite for that.

Even if one could [*crossed out*: assume] believe in neither immortality nor the existence of God, the moral law and the end of a will in conformity with it (the highest good) would still have their powerful influence on the will; yet we would not admit such a scandal from a practical point of view into our principles, but would rather promote the satisfaction with our existence and the world that we have in view as a permissible hypothesis.

The *argumentum a tuto*[a] is good for actions, but very evil for the [*crossed out*: determining ground] inner confession of belief.   18:715

6434. 1790–95? 1776–79?? M 342, in *Existentia Dei*.   18:715

Irrational concepts (*conceptus surdi*) are to be distinguished from ideas; they are, namely, concepts of the understanding from which one has withdrawn everything that is requisite for an example and application *in concreto*, which therefore can have no significance although they are, to be sure, free of contradiction. E.g., 1. God is eternal, i.e., his existence has a magnitude, but not that of time. However, we cannot think any magnitude of existence, i.e., a duration, except as in time.[190] 2. His presence has a magnitude in regard to the totality of things outside one another (in space). Yet it is not to be taken as in space, for then God would be outside of himself. 3. He is the cause of substance. But the way in which he is a cause must be different from that which we know; for there nothing can be the cause of a substance.   18:716

6437. 1790–95? 1773–78?? M 346, in *Existentia Dei*.   18:716

That no [*crossed out*: theoretical] cognition of God in a speculative respect is possible for humans, since we must abstract from our concepts of things everything that makes things cognizable by means of them, hence nothing remains to give them reality. The categories are concepts of things, the objective reality of which is problematic. Through them we can think a thing but not cognize it.   18:717

---

[a] literally, an argument from security, i.e., an argument to the conditions that secure the consequences of acting in accord with the moral law

6442. 1790–95. *M* 357, in *Intellectus Dei.*

One has cause to represent God in accordance with the analogy with an understanding, i.e., that just as a clock, a ship, etc., is related to its cause (an intelligent being), so is the world related to the unknown cause, which we call an infinite understanding, although it certainly has in itself nothing similar to that. – But from the causality of things through understanding we cannot infer to a cause of the world of the same sort, i.e., that has understanding, just as we cannot infer from the artworks of bees that they have understanding, since just as in the latter case the causality is of a far lesser *species* so in the former case it is of a far higher kind than we signify through "understanding."[191]

It is also not, as it were, probable that such a cause exists. For all probability must lie on the path to certainty, to the extent that the latter can be reached through progress in the mere amplification of what is missing.[192] But here the *data* are such that they never lead there at all.

6443. 1790–95. *M* 357, in *Intellectus Dei.*

That our idea of a highest being as an intelligent being has objective reality can only be inferred from the objective reality of the concept of freedom, which makes it necessary for us to direct our actions toward the highest good in the world that is possible through our cooperation, because we thereby assume its possibility, or at least must so conduct ourselves as if we assume it (in that we must not only act as is requisite for a best world, but must also make it into our incentive), from which it then follows that, since our capacity alone does not suffice for it, we must assume a highest original good, consequently the concept of the latter has objectively practical reality, although in a theoretical relation it is transcendent, hence only an object of belief.[193]

The mere categories (of substance, cause, community) provide mere ways of forming concepts of things in general for ourselves, i.e., concepts of the synthetic unity of a manifold that may be given to us in one consciousness, which for that reason must be in us *a priori*, since a *compositum* is not perceived by us as such, but must always be made, and the action of making such a thing, i.e., of giving to the manifold the unity of consciousness in one representation, must reside in us *a priori*.[194] These categories, however, have no objective reality by themselves, since they do not contain the way in which a manifold may be given to us. Since this cannot be given to them by the theoretical faculty of cognition, i.e., as belonging to a cognition of the nature of objects, only their practical reality with regard to the concept of freedom (which presupposes merely the form of unity, not the intuition itself) is left as immanent to our reason, in order to think the highest being by analogy with those which we cognize in nature in accordance with their spontaneity.

6446. 1790–95? 1776–79? *M* 369, opposite §902, in *Voluntas Dei*.   18:720

Human actions cannot be considered merely as *phaenomena* and hence as determined in accordance with empirical laws; they are at the same time *noumena* and have a relation to the causality of the pure understanding and the pure reason. What arises from this as a cause is good.[195] The possibility of acting from reason, i.e., from the motivating ground of that which is good in itself, is freedom. This possibility is to be found in all agents, because the incentives of sensibility never determine, not even evil actions, and no action is empirically certain in accordance with laws of *phaenomenorum*. The higher will is therefore always free (*a stimulis*),[a] and between its motivating grounds and the empirically determined faculty of choice there is a connection which can only be represented in accordance with the analogy of the connection of appearances and which does not constitute a series [with the latter]. Thus it remains incomprehensible how the very same reason that produces certain actions could have produced other ones in their place. With regard to these actions as *phaenomenorum* the transition from the intellectual to the sensible and the **first ground of origination** is not comprehensible for the human understanding, and freedom is a **necessary hypothesis**. Among the *noumenis*, however, the *effectus* of freedom are not in accordance with what happens in time, but in themselves; in the soul things are to be judged otherwise, and that which was evil there can here be on the whole good.

6451. 1790–95. *M* 382, in *Creatio mundi*.   18:723

On Moral Theology,

One can know the final end of all things because it is moral, namely the highest contingent good. This yields the concept of a highest original good, i.e., a moral author of the world, and this concept determines that author as the most perfect being, since the physico-theologian could demonstrate only a being of great perfection. Objectively, morality actually yields no proof, rather only a subjectively morally necessary assumption of the conditions under which the object of morality, the highest good, as regards that side of it which it is not in our power (namely, the side of happiness), is alone possible.

First, the representation of the world as a system of the *nexus finalis physici* (*causarum finalium physicarum*,[b] among which the human being must also be). Thus a rational primordial being, but not yet God, since the concept of the perfection of the world drawn from experience does not suffice for that. Now, the representation of the world as a *systematis*

---

[a] from (sensory) stimuli
[b] a nexus of physical ends (of physical final causes)

18:724 *caussarum finalium moralium*[a] for the highest good. For the human being, who is a member of the *nexu finalis physico*, but who finds in himself a principle of a higher *nexus finalis*, will also relate his existence with respect to that higher *nexus* to that same rational author; but the concept of that author is of a being as the author of the highest good, for this alone is in conformity with the orientation toward ends of the moral human being. Thereby is the assumption of a living God as a moral being and thus also as an all-sufficient being accepted.

This is not an objectively sufficient theoretical proof, but a subjectively-practical sufficient moral proof. The assumption of God is not necessary to fulfill a duty in individual actions, but in order to work toward the object of the extended moral disposition, the highest good, without which the moral disposition certainly has incentives for action (from the form of morality), but no final end (with regard to the matter, i.e., the object of the rational faculty of choice). Artistic wisdom we see in corporeal things, moral wisdom we find in ourselves as a rule.

18:724 **6454.** 1790–95. *M* 388, at §942ff., in *Finis creationis*.

Moral Theology.

The moral need to assume a highest moral good is not a pathologically conditioned need to have incentives of self-love toward the good actions 18:725 that the moral law commands; for it is a moral need to assume even a just judge, thus not a being from whose goodness we hope but whose holiness we must fear. In face of the uncertainty of the purity of one's actions, even the thought of such a judge is more fearsome than attractive. – But for our law-giving reason, even if we do not represent ourselves as standing under laws, but project the highest good for the world in accordance with moral laws, everyone would will that virtue be happy and vice be punished. This wish is alone purely moral, not in the least self-serving, and is unavoidable for rational human beings, and this makes it into a necessity to assume a living God as the moral author and ruler of the world, to the extent that we relate our idea of the world not to theory but to our practical vocation. Hence the oscillation if one weighs this matter theoretically and then in turn looks back to the satisfaction of our practical incentives.

It is not a passive interest, but an active interest in the idea of merely rational being which considers itself as morally law-giving.

1. On the end of creation,
2. of the best world,
3. of the end of God in this object.

[a] a system of moral final causes

4

Notes on Moral Philosophy

This chapter presents a selection of Kant's notes on moral philosophy. The material is drawn primarily from the *Reflexionen zur Moralphilosophie*, pp. 7–317 of volume 19 of the *Akademie* edition, which was published in 1934 and completed by Friedrich Berger after the death of Erich Adickes in 1928. These *Reflexionen* are for the most part Kant's notes in his copy of the textbook for his lectures on ethics, namely Alexander Gottlieb Baumgarten, *Initia philosophiae practicae primae* (Introduction to the first [principles] of practical philosophy) (Halle: C. H. Hemmerde, 1760) (abbreviated "*Pr*"), although, as with the material on metaphysics, the volume also includes loose notes (*Lose Blätter*) from other sources. Also as in the case of metaphysics, the material is divided into chronological strata, each of which first presents the *Lose Blätter* assigned to that period and then the notes to Baumgarten in the order in which they are found in the book. The material from Volume 19 is, however, preceded by several selections from volume 15 (Anthropology), volume 16 (Logic), and volumes 17 and 18 (Metaphysics), which bear directly on Kant's moral philosophy. As noted earlier, notes on freedom from volumes 17 and 18, which bear on Kant's moral philosophy as well as his metaphysics, have been left in their original places and translated in Chapter 3. Volume 19 also includes extensive notes on Kant's political philosophy (pp. 445–613). A selection of these will be presented in a later volume in the Cambridge Edition, *Lectures and Drafts on Political Philosophy*, along with other important materials on Kant's political philosophy, notably the *Naturrecht Feyerabend* lectures of 1784, the introductory pages of which also give an illuminating account of Kant's general moral philosophy delivered in the very months in which he was composing the *Groundwork for the Metaphysics of Morals*.

The materials to be presented in this chapter touch on a wide range of issues and offer indispensable evidence for the development of Kant's views in moral philosophy. The very first note from Kant's anthropology lectures (**679**) gives early evidence of Kant's view of the unique unconditional value of the good will. The subsequent notes from the anthropology material (**1113, 1117, 1158–9**, and **1179**), bear on Kant's view of moral character. From the materials on logic, **3345** presents Kant's view that no special learning is required for knowledge of the moral law and our duties under it. A number of selections from Kant's notes on metaphysics (**5444–50**) concern the nature of moral law and moral motives.

In the notes on moral philosophy proper, we see above all that while Kant developed his view of the formal as well as universal character of the fundamental principle early on, so that his view of it as a categorical imperative was well developed by the end of the 1760s (e.g., **6601, 6639, 6725, 6734, 6754, 6765, 6801–2, 6850, 6853, 6854**) and even earlier than that was clearly connecting the fundamental principle of morality with the unparalleled value of human freedom (e.g., **6598, 6605, 6850, 6854, 6856, 6859, 6867**) and stressing the purity of morally estimable motivation even earlier (**6753, 6754, 6864, 6866**), he struggled for years to give a proper account of the relationship between virtue and happiness (**1171, 1187, 6589, 6621, 6629, 6838, 6856, 6857, 6876, 6881, 6883, 6907–11, 6958, 6965, 6971, 6977, 6989, 7197, 7199**, and especially the extensive *Lose Blätter* **7200–2**). His views on moral feeling also underwent a long process of development (e.g., **6581, 6598, 6757, 6760, 6796**). Perhaps the single most important thing we can learn from Kant's notes on ethics is that the doctrine of the highest good, in which he attempts to explain and indeed guarantee the necessary connection between virtue and happiness, which is briefly mentioned in the "Canon of Pure Reason" of the *Critique of Pure Reason*, not mentioned at all in the *Groundwork for the Metaphysics of Morals*, then reintroduced in the *Critique of Practical Reason* and stressed in the *Critique of the Power of Judgment*, the Preface to *Religion within the Boundaries of Mere Reason*, and the contemporaneous essay "On the Common Saying: That may be right in theory, but it is of no use in practice," is hardly an afterthought in Kant's moral philosophy, but a central issue throughout its development. From an early date, Kant held that the fundamental principle of morality could not make any reference to the happiness of the individual agent and that the pure motivation to morality must likewise make no such reference, but at the same time that a moral principle that would not at least under ideal circumstances eventuate in a system of "unselfish happiness," as he called it in "Theory and Practice" (8:279–80n), would not be credible. Kant's constant return to this issue, especially in numerous notes from 1776–78 (**6816–7029**), demonstrate the centrality of this issue for his moral philosophy.

* *
*

I.

NOTES FROM ANTHROPOLOGY, LOGIC,
AND METAPHYSICS

15:301   **679.** 1769–70. *M* 252.

That which gratifies is not for that reason absolutely good, but it is good for a human being when it is durable, or rather, since good is an objective predicate, it is not good but is agreeable to him (for in general nothing is necessarily agreeable).

Therefore nothing other than [*crossed out*: that which necessarily] the will is good. What does not have a will is only conditionally good, even if it has understanding. A very clever person can be very good if his will corresponds with his entire person, i.e., with the essential relations of all of his organs and powers. One can assume that the human being aims his ends at the wants at which his whole nature aims, and that this aim is not the end of something alien, with which his will corresponds, but his own end; then if his [*crossed out*: actions] will is in agreement with these ends, then he properly agrees with himself. It is, however, objectively necessary to want that which one wills; consequently the correspondence of his will with his essential ends is good.

Dedication proceeds from that which belongs to our condition to the worth of our person. He who is well dressed, well served, etc., holds himself to be a human being of much worth and has little esteem for the poor. Hence the disfavor of the poor.

Necessity is twofold: the subjective necessity of [*crossed out*: things] causes and the objective necessity of worth. We do not ask merely by what means a thing necessarily exists, but rather why it is necessary, i.e., good that it exists. This is called necessary ends, not of the author, but of that will which wills its own individual existence. This fundamental good or the supreme primitive good is not to be made out.

15: 302

1020. 1773–75? 1775–77? 1776–78? 1778–79? M 251.   15:456

Everything that is desired or abhorred must be represented (*ignoti nulla cupido*);[a] but not every representation is the cause of a desire. That in the object which pleases practically as belonging to one's condition or person is desired, either practically or [as] wished. The *placens* or *displicens* is the *causa impulsiva*.[b] People can desire the same thing, but from different motivating causes: honorableness pleases one person because it causes a good reputation, etc. The *causa impulsiva* is either an impression or a concept, a representation of satisfaction or dissatisfaction through the senses or the understanding, of the agreeable or the good. The first impel *per stimulos*, the second *per motiva*. The *arbitrium immediate determinatum per stimulos* is *brutum*.[c] *Motiva* are either sensitive *quoad materiam* and *immediate* and intellectual only *quoad formam aut media*,[d] but then they are still *stimuli*, because an action derives its name from its cause and not its manner. The *motiva intellectualia pura*

---

[a] I desire nothing of which I am ignorant.

[b] That which pleases or displeases is the moving or impelling cause.

[c] The power of choice determined immediately by stimuli is brutish (or animal).

[d] Motives are either immediately sensible as regards their matter or only mediately intellectual, on account of their form.

are what please immediately in the concept; now this is nothing other than a good will, since everything else can only please conditionally as a means (e.g., the works of creation, the talents of human beings) and has the condition that there is a will to make good use of all this. Thus moral goodness alone is absolute goodness, and the *motiva moralia* are *pura*. But that which is the universal necessary means for distinguishing motives, namely the enlightenment of practical reason, is also a *motivum purum*. Hence practical truth.

1021. 1773–79. *M* 252.

The causality of the representation with regard to (*later addition*: oneself is pleasure) the actuality of the object (*later addition*: objects in general) is desire (*later addition*: life; the *consensus* with life: pleasure). The representation must hereby, however, have a relation to the subject of determining it to action. This relation is pleasure, and indeed in the reality of the object, i.e., an interest (interest does not belong to judging). The interest rests on the satisfaction with our condition, which depends on the reality of the object. (That which carries an interest with it is called the *causa impulsiva*). An *elater*[a] is the subjective receptivity to be moved to desire.

(*Later addition*: Pleasure in the object is satisfaction, in the existence, gratification.)

All desire is either **practical**, which can contain the ground of the existence of the object, or **idle**; the first is the **power of choice**: the capacity to desire that which is in our power. The power of choice is either sensible or intellectual. The first is affected by *stimuli*; the second is a capacity to act independently of *stimuli* and in accordance with motives. The *arbitrium intellectuale* is always *liberum*; but the *arbitrium sensitivum* can be either *liberum* or *brutum*, the latter if it is necessitated by *stimuli*. The *arbitrium intellectuale* is either also necessitated *subiective* through *motiva*, and then the subject is pure intelligence – the idea of an *arbitrii puri* is not affected by *stimuli* – or it is moved but not necessitated through *motiva* and is likewise affected but not necessitated by *stimuli*. That is the *arbitrium humanum* as *liberum*.[b] If our power of choice were also to feel the objective necessitation subjectively as its own, that would not be opposed to freedom, and the capacity to act in opposition to objective necessitation does not demonstrate freedom. This is spontaneity, and indeed pure spontaneity, of the power of choice.

The faculty of ends (*later addition*: of the unity of aims), i.e., the power of choice which is directed toward the sum of all incentives, is the will.

---

[a] a spring or elastic force; see also **1056** (15:470–1): "The possibility of a representation being a *causa impulsiva* is *elater animi*."

[b] That is the kind of liberty that the human power of choice has.

(*Later addition*: aim – end – intention – maxim – disposition – law.)

An *elater* is the capacity of a *causa impulsiva* to determine the desire to a deed, insofar as it rests on the constitution of the subject. Hence many *motiva* are not sufficient *elateres* for human beings. Either we take special interest in nothing or no interest in anything intellectual or only as much interest as suffices for wishing.

We cannot prove that we are free (*physice*); but we can only act under the idea of freedom (*practice*).

The *arbitrium humanum* is not necessitated by *stimuli*, thus is not *brutum*, it is rather *liberum*, but as subjectively *liberum* it is also not necessitated by *motiva*, thus it is not *purum*, but sensitive,[a] *affectum stimulis*.[b] Nothing is **more** opposed to freedom in all respects than that the human being have a foreign author.

1113. 1769? 1770–71? 1773–75? 1776–78?? *M* 287, at §§730–2, in 15:496 *Libertas*.[1]

Character is the general ruling *principium* in the human being for the use of his talents and qualities. Thus it is the constitution of his will and good or evil. A human being who has no constant *principium* of his actions, hence no uniformity, has no character. The characters of the English are all different, thus the nation has no character; those of the French, by contrast, are similar. The human being can have a good heart, but still have no character, since he is dependent on changing circumstances and does not act in accordance with maxims. Firmness and unity of *principii* belong to character. There are many people who can be called neither good nor evil; he does not have a manly understanding, he is like a child. Character is not formed through instruction, but through habituation to constant laws. We must judge a person from his character, not from his actions. He who is without character is contemptible. What is unique and distinctive in character (that in the character from which I know the person alone, without comparing him to others). The question whether the person is good or evil is difficult to answer. The second question: what is unique in his character? and in that what is natural? what is merely acquired, perhaps indeed a habit? The distorted (*later addition*: affected) character in the choleric person. To be fashionable is to lack character.[2]

1117. 1769–70? 1771–72? *M* 287.   15:499

The will in accordance with instinct is temperament, that in accordance with principles is character.

---

[a] *sensitiv*
[b] affected (but not determined) by stimuli

Temperament is grounded on sensitivity (natural) and consciousness of one's capacity (talent). The person of choleric temperament is **sensitive** to insults and feels **courageous** to respond to them; the person of sanguine temperament is also sensitive, but weak; the former is therefore unruly, the latter peaceful. The melancholic is made ill.

15:512 **1158.** 1772–73. M 300.

A determinate character: from which one can judge in advance everything that can be determined through rules. Good-heartedness does not belong to character. Character is good in itself, but through *principia* it becomes evil.

15:513 (In order to appear to have genius, one abandons all rules.)

In order to seem to have a character or to be satisfied with oneself in the absence of one, one often holds to rules and makes ones for oneself that are often opposed to one's heart, because one does not trust his power of judgment to be able to determine without rules. An internally assumed (artificial) character. A submissive, an honest character.

15:513 **1159.** 1772–73. M 302.

The personal worth that we attribute to a human being rests on talents and dispositions. The former belongs to his capacities, the latter to his will.[a] The former are means to good ends, the latter a will to make use of those. (Through talents a person is good for something, through dispositions he is good in himself.) The first comprise the conditional worth of the person, the second the unconditional worth.

The source of dispositions is threefold: the mind, the heart, and the character. They stand on the side of the natural, the temperament and_____.[b] What is natural is considered more as passive, the temperament as active. The natural and character. The former contains the mind and the heart.

(To take mind of a *reproche* and to take it to heart. He who takes nothing to mind also takes nothing to heart.)

(On a naturally evil mind, heart, character. Parents must be mild.)

15:518 **1171.** 1772–75. M 309.

The moral feeling can only be set into motion by the image of a world full of order, if we place ourselves in this world in thought.* This is the intellectual world, whose bond is God.

We are in part really in this world, insofar as human beings really judge in accordance with moral principles.

---

[a] *Wollen*
[b] Kant's blank space.

*(Happiness would be the **natural** consequence of that, which is something entirely different from the merely arbitrary happiness through divine providence, in that we would create our good fortune for ourselves and could really bring it to such a moral world-order.)[3]

1173. 1773–75? (1772–73?) *M* 303.　　　　　　　　　　　　　15:519
Morality[a] from principles is virtue, morality from taste is correctness (*politesse*).

1175. 1773–75? (1772–73?) *M* 303.　　　　　　　　　　　　　15:519
The good that can be imputed to someone, i.e., that stems from his good will, is his merit; that which can certainly be ascribed to him, but which is not from his good will, is his talent. The latter determines outer worth (in the market of Algiers),[4] the latter determines his inner worth before conscience. The former: what he is good for; the latter, how good he is.

1179. 1773–75? (1772–73?) *M* 304.　　　　　　　　　　　　　15:521
What is essential in a good character is the **worth** that one places **in himself** (in humanity), with regard to actions related to himself as well as in relation to others. For character signifies that the person has derived the rule of his actions from himself and from the **dignity of humanity.** Self-selected and firm resolves demonstrate a character, although only if they are similar to one another. He who binds himself to arbitrary rules makes an artificial character; for those are not maxims.

Morality consists by no means in the goodness of the heart, but in the good character, and that is what one is to form.

The recommendations of the good heart are a true nourishment for self-love and are apt to give a person worth in his own eyes out of mere wishes, but to make him hard-hearted toward others. Those who praise 　15:522
the good heart must not take uprightness to be something so common.

1187. 1773–75? (1772–73?) *M* 309.　　　　　　　　　　　　　15:524
Morality brings happiness from fate and chance under a rule of our own reason and makes ourselves into its author. One is worthy of what one deserves in accordance with a rule that is valid for all; consequently 　15:525
the worthiness to be happy is bound up with morality. Morality is the supreme condition of all use of freedom and also of all our desire, because it determines each particular action before the whole of happiness.

That human beings do not want to be virtuous comes from the fact that they do not want to make sacrifices without being certain of reward.

---

[a] *Sittlichkeit*

The moral law necessarily contains a promise because otherwise it would not be binding. He who cannot protect cannot command.

16:789 **3344.** 1773–78? (1790s?) *V* 115, at the end of §422.[5]

Empirical natural science: analytic; rational natural science: synthetic. Morality, that there is one: analytic.

To begin with chronology in history is synthetic. – In morality, [to begin with] freedom and natural necessity. – In the explanation of an adage.

16:789 **3345.** 1772? (1773–77?) 1776–78?? *V* 115, at §§422–6.

It is still always a question whether much learning is necessary in order to know how human beings should live in a manner well-pleasing 16:790 to God, so that if all Greek were lost, no one would know how he should become blessed, or whether human beings have assigned and defended their rights among each other. In both cases no rules need to be given other than those that his natural understanding teaches everyone when he acts or claims a right against others on the basis of his actions. Deep, hidden grounds of right, which no one could come up with in his civic actions, could not count for him even if they really lie therein. If the valid[a] rules of reason cannot determine what is to be done, then one could have injustice just because one is not learned or has not asked someone who is learned. The positive laws would constitute an entirely disjoint collection. In a trial the parties must not be considered as scholars, thus the advocate (who only brings order to their claims) must not represent himself as learned, i.e., engage in subtle argument[b] about them. One party must adduce the basis in right on which he has grounded his claim, while the other must justify his entitlement. Neither should engage in subtle argument about right in general, but rather should speak only of his disposition in the action at issue and his opinion about right, while the judge should deliver the basis in right for the decision. Philosophy must determine what is of no utility in all of this. Here everything comes down to the fact that actions must be brought under rules and indeed universal practical rules. There is always a difference to be made out between universal civil right and an arbitrary constitution. There is also a difference between the use of learning in sharpening the judgment of the judge and the basis in right on which the parties can lean.

16:791 Since no one can complain that his right has not been administered if he has received satisfaction without delay and partiality in regard to the concepts that he has formed of his right (and likewise its opposite), while the *publicum* needs no learning in order to feign its concepts of rights and

---

[a] *currente*
[b] *vernünfteln*

those who would feign a right that does not lie in the common concepts need intrigues in order to do so, legislation requires no learning, and even less so does the administration of *justice.*[a] Where a particular constitution or the local* positive law (of which there should be few) requires it, there the principles must serve as precepts. Otherwise unlearned peoples would not be able to administer any rights.

*(or where guile and uncertainty in the proofs of *pactorum*[b] is to be prevented.)

There are two concepts of right, the first of which requires learning and reflection, and the second of which does not, but only an understanding that is practiced in dealings. The latter concept is inferred from the unity of the wills of the participants; the former from the conditions for the distribution of right or the determination of the distinction among the manifold that stands under a rule. (When someone demands something on the basis of his right, he must name it and also be able to suppose that his counterpart must have been able to think the same thing. Consequently he does not demand that something be given to him on the basis of concepts unknown to him, but only that his basis in right be compared to that of the other. The law must therefore be related to the concrete but universal concepts of right.)

Justitia distributiva presupposes that all rights in the possession of which one does not commit an injury to others must be demonstrated. *Justitia commutativa*, however, etc., e.g., when someone borrows something and injuries result from that. Whether the advocate is a middleman who can give up his part [in] the matter in order to seek a right therein, and how the law gives preference to this investigation on the part of the advocate. In the case of commutative justice it comes down to what sort of right follows from the relation of the parties alone. In the case of distributive justice: what follows from the relation to the whole.[6]

4611. 1772–73. *M* 363, between §891 and §892, in *Voluntas Dei.*   17:609

Morality is the correspondence of the free power of choice with the end of humanity and of human beings in general, namely with necessary conditions of the universal ends of humanity and of human beings.

4612. 1772–73? (1776–78?) *M* 363, at §890, in *Voluntas Dei.*   17:609

We should have as much of a share in universal good fortune as we contribute to it. Morality itself is comprehensible only from the idea of such a will.

16: 792

---

[a] Here Kant has written *iustice* in Latin rather than *Recht* in German.
[b] compacts or contracts

17:635 **4671.** 1773–75. Kant's note on a letter from his brother J. H. Kant of 3 July 1773 (10:140f.).

All morality consists in the derivation of actions from the idea of the subject, not from sentiment.[a] The idea is universally valid with regard both to ends (*abstrahendo*) and the relation to all (*combinando*).

The sources of all experiential cognition are transcendental. They are inner anticipations.

18:159 **5350.** 1776–89. M 103, at §337, in *Utilitas*.

A value:[b] for which something else can be given as an equivalence. Virtue has no price. Dignity is the inner value, which therefore has no price.[7]

18:159 **5351.** 1776–89. M 105, at §341, in *Reliqua causarum genera*.

Objective causes are only in the free will.

How these can at the same time be subjective, i.e., *causae efficientes*, is not to be explained. *Hypothesis* of freedom.

18:159 **5352.** 1776–89. M 105, at §342.

An action that has its inner worth has no *causam impulsivam*.

18:183 **5444.** 1776–78. M 283, at §723, in *Libertas*.[8]

Nothing is absolutely good (unconditional in every respect) except the existence of freely acting beings, and in these, not understanding, happiness, etc., but the disposition to make good use of everything that
18:184 is mediately good. Thus the practical disposition of good aims. This is therefore the goodness of the will.

18:184 **5445.** 1776–78. M 284, at §723f.

The moral laws do not arise from reason, but rather contain the conditions through which alone it is possible for free actions to be determined and cognized in accordance with the rules of reason. This happens, however, when we make the universally valid end the basis of actions. Thereby do particular ends agree with those which one can regard as if all things were possible through them.

The morally good demands complete unity of the ground of the action before reason, consequently that it be derived from the *idea archetypa*, which is the end of the entire world.

What is in conformity to the conditions under which everything happens in accordance with *a priori* rules necessarily pleases. For it produces

---

[a] *Empfindung*
[b] *Werth*, elsewhere translated as "worth." It could easily be so translated in the last sentence of this paragraph, but not here.

concordance with all of nature, and thus a consciousness of the concordance of actions with oneself and everyone else. Only from the whole and the supreme ground can that be derived which in accordance with universal laws [*breaks off*]⁹

5446. 1776–78. M 284, at §723f. 18:184

Moral laws are those which contain [*crossed out*: the necessity of actions from the] the conditions through which free actions become concordant with the universally valid end, thus the private will with the original and supreme will. Either with the universal ends of nature or of freely acting beings. The will is thus considered in accordance with the unity of the ground, namely insofar as all wills lie in a single will: that which is the cause of nature and every other [will].

5447. 1776–78. M 284, at §723f. 18:185

The constitution of the morally good will is good conduct (of human beings), it is virtue if it happens from inclination, and fear of God if it happens from obedience toward God.

5448. 1776–78. M 284, at §723f. 18:185

Moral motives should not have merely *vim objective necessitantem*ᵃ for the [*crossed out*: practical] conviction of the understanding, but *vim subjective necessitantem*,ᵇ i.e., they should be *elateres*.ᶜ The subjective condition, under which they can be such, is called **feeling**. If it were a real feeling (*proprie*), then the necessitation would be pathological; the *causae impulsivae* would not be *motiva*, but *stimuli*; not goodness but *iucundum*ᵈ would move us. Thus the *sensus moralis* is only called so *per analogiam* and should not be called sense but disposition,ᵉ in accordance with which the moral motives necessitate within the subject just like *stimuli*. It is thus *in sensu propria* a non-entity, a merely *analogon sensus*, and serves only to express a faculty (not a receptivity) for which we have no name.¹⁰

5450. 1776–78? 1772? M 415.¹¹ 18:185

Nature and freedom are two principles of the determination of our concepts. For explanation we can use freedom only *secundum quid*;ᶠ for only nature provides the final determining grounds. For this alone contains principles of real conduct. If I would provide a ground why

---

ᵃ objectively necessitating force
ᵇ subjectively necessitating force
ᶜ springs of action, a word Kant often uses as the equivalent of *Beweggrund*
ᵈ pleasure
ᵉ *nicht Sinn, sondern Gesinnung*
ᶠ in relation to something else

someone behaves in this way or that, the appeal to his free choice is a circle.

18:193   **5477.** 1776–78? (1773–75?) *M* 318. Opposite §782, in *Status post mortem.*
     The moral *postulata* are evident, their opposite can be brought *ad absurdum morale.* Their ground is that good conduct is the only condition under which one is worthy to be happy. The ground of their necessitation does not lie in their offering means for the desire for happiness, but in prescribing the *conditionem sine qua non* through which they are restricted. But our longing to be happy is equally necessary and at the same time appropriate. Now mere worthiness cannot move without hope that it will also allow us to partake of the end; thus it is a necessary moral *hypothesis* to assume another world. He who does not assume this falls into an *absurdum practicam.*[12]

18:194   The *dilemma practicum* shows that prudence and honesty can coexist in the hope for another world.
     It is a fundamental principle of reason that we should not demand to be happy if we are not worthy of that. It is also another such principle that we should not be required to conduct ourselves as so worthy if we cannot hope to become happy.

18:203   **5510.** 1776–78? (1773–75?) *M* 335, in *Conceptus Dei.*
     The *summum bonum reale*[a] is the universally valid cause.
     The *summum bonum formale (finale) (ideale)*[b] is the free power of choice, that which is universally valid for every power of choice; hence this is also the form of the causality of the former.

18:203   **5511.** 1776–78? (1773–77?) *M* 335.
     It is part of moral theology that in the most perfect world moral evil must be possible, for in such a world there must be both freedom and a stimulus to evil. Whether it is possible that God does not hinder it can be understood only by he who cognizes the relation of the parts to the whole.

18:212   **5541.** 1776–78? (1773–75?) 1769?? 1770–71?? *M* 374, at §914, in *Voluntas Dei.*
     There is nothing evil[c] in nature, but only ills[d] in its parts. In freedom alone is there evil. Nature in its entirety is good, and evil concerns only a part, as every part can be involved in a collision.

---

[a] real highest good
[b] formal (final) (ideal) highest good
[c] *Böses*
[d] *Übel*

416

Imperfection is to be distinguished from an ill (which is positive), and this from evil, which is an absolute ill and not merely relative. All ills 18:213
derive from the absence of unity in the world-whole. From this arises conflicts. In the case of perfect unity not only with regard to substance but also with regard to its forces everything would necessarily correspond to the nature of the being and thus be good. In human beings, evil rests on what is animal, what rests on impressions and inclinations, and the opposition of this to what is rational, which is aimed at universally valid ends.[13] If we were to consider the human being prior to the development of his reason as a *species* of animal, then we would find the origin of evil.[14]

II.
NOTES ON MORAL PHILOSOPHY FROM
1764 TO 1770

6560. 1762–63? 1769? *Pr* 112, at §168. 19:77

The weakness of human nature consists in the weakness of the moral feeling relative to other inclinations. Hence providence has strengthened it with supporting drives as *analogis instinctorum moralium,[a]* e.g., honor, *storge,[b]* pity, sympathy, or also with rewards and punishments. When these are among the motives, then morality is not pure. The morality that excludes all these *motiva auxiliaria* is chimerical.

6581. 1764–68. *Pr* I. 19:93

Of the *sensu morali.[c]* The rules of prudence presuppose no special inclination and feeling, but only a special relation of the understanding to them. The rules of morality proceed from a special, eponymous feeling, upon which the understanding is guided as in the former case.

According to the Stoics, active love has its maximum when it is equal to one's powers. There is no internal measure in space, but only arbitrary ones; but a circle is an absolute measure.

The doctrine of the mean is really that a greatest good [*breaks off*][15] 19:94

6586. 1764–68? 1762–63? *Pr* III. 19:96

There are different grades of the determination of our power of choice:

1. In accordance with universal laws of the power of choice in general, right.

---

[a] analogues of moral instincts
[b] parental love
[c] moral sense

2. In accordance with universal rules of the good in general, goodness.

3. In accordance with universal rules of private good, rational self-love.

4. In accordance with particular rules of a private inclination, sensuous drive.

19:97   The *motiva moralia* are of different grades:

1. The right of another.

2. My own right.

3. The need of another.

4. My own need.

Utility to myself is not the ground of a right.

Utility for many does not give them a right against one.

Right is not grounded on motives of goodness.

In moral matters, we see very sharply but not clearly through *sentiment*; e.g., a braggart is held in contempt for a *criminis publici*, since one will not entirely sacrifice private duties for public ones. One takes pity on a miscreant.

19:97   **6589.** 1764–68? 1769? *Pr* XV.

Something is good insofar as it is in agreement with the will; agreeable, insofar as it agrees with sensation; now I can think of a will while abstracting from the charm*a* of the person who wills or of the subject to whom this charm is a response; thus I can think of something good without regard to charm. Yet without all charm nothing is good; but goodness consists in the relation to the will, until finally absolute goodness consists in the correspondence of happiness with the will.

18:98   Beauty always concerns what is accidental in goodness, namely the relation to taste.

19:98   **6590.** 1764–68? 1769? *Pr* XVI.

Whatever contributes to the happiness of human beings does not thereby belong to their perfection. If the righteous man is unhappy and the vicious man is happy, then not human beings but the order of nature is imperfect.

In duties toward oneself the worth of a person and not of the condition must comprise the motive. Soul and body and their perfection belong to one's person. Perfection does not consist in accidental goods, e.g. knowledge, elegance, etc., but in the essential. The perfection of one's body must be given preference over all pleasures. Only in view of great obligation to comply with the right of another, e.g., to preserve one's virginity, is the body no longer attributed to the person; accordingly death itself, although not voluntary death, is bound up with the worth of one's person.

a Anmuth

6593. 1764–68. *Pr* XVII.   19:98

The order of reflection on human beings is as follows:

1. The natural indeterminacy in the type and proportion of his ca-   19:99
pacities and inclinations and his nature, which is capable of all sorts of
configurations.

2. The determination of the human being. The actual state*ᵃ* of human
beings; whether it consists in simplicity or in the highest cultivation*ᵇ* of
his capacities and the greatest enjoyment of his desires. Whether a natural final end is illuminated by the degree of ability would be very worthwhile to investigate. Whether the sciences belong to this
necessarily.

(4. The wild or the raw human being [*crossed out*: of nature]. Whether
this condition would be a state of right and of satisfaction. Difference
between the personal perfection of the raw human being and that which
he has in the view of another. Whether the human being can remain in
this condition.)

3. The human being of nature should be considered merely according to his personal properties without looking at his condition. Here the
question is merely: what is natural and what is from external and contingent causes? The state of nature is an ideal of outer relationships of
the merely natural, that is, of the raw human being. The social condition
can also consist of persons of merely natural properties.

4. Émile[16] or the ethical human being. Art or cultivation of powers
and inclinations which harmonize the most with nature. Through this
the natural perfection is improved.

5. In the outer condition.* The social contract (civil union) or the
ideal of the right of a state (according to the rule of equality) considered
in abstracto, without looking at the special nature of human beings.

6. Leviathan:[17] the condition of society, which is in accordance with
the nature of human beings. According to the rules of security. I can be
either in a state of equality and have freedom to be unjust myself and
suffer, or in a state of subjection without this freedom.

7. The union of nations: the ideal of the right of nations as the completion of society in view of outer relationships.

The social contract, or public right as a ground of the [*crossed out*:
public] supreme power. Leviathan or the supreme power as a ground of
public right.

*(The state of nature: Hobbes's ideal. Here the right in the state of   19:100
nature and not the *factum* is considered. It is to be proved that it would not
be arbitrary to leave the state of nature, but instead necessary according
to the rules of right.[18]

ᵃ *Stand.* Throughout **6593**, *Stand* is rendered as "state" and *Zustand* as "condition."
ᵇ *cultur*

With the right of war individual persons would lose all matter of right; however, in the case of nations, because they can be seen as at peace with each other, one only has a right to attack the whole and the goods which belong to it.)

6596. 1764–68. *Pr* XVIII.

All right action is a *maximum* of the free power of choice when it is taken reciprocally.

The human being is disposed to see the extreme in every quantity, the *maximum* and *minimum*, in part because he does not stop in addition and subtraction without this *terminum*, in part because he needs a measure: The greatest is thought either [as] undetermined, insofar as one thinks the mere extending, as (number) space, time (everything); or [as] determined: if the greatest depends on determined relations. The greatest of all beings can be thought to be determined in many ways according to relations which the many realities of things can have toward one another, in order to diminish or increase the quantity.

This greatest is itself given either through certain determinations of a thing, which are in changing relations toward one another, or it consists merely in arbitrary increase. The latter is an ideal of fiction, the first is an ideal of reason, which is differentiated into the merely mathematical and the philosophical ideal. The smallest (of what is moveable) can be called a moment.

There is no real *maximum* and *minimum* in an absolute sense in quantitative *continuis*, but there are in *discretis*.

6598. 1769–70? (1764–68?) *Pr* IV.

The means are only the form of intention, or the method of execution, the end is the matter. Actions are rational with regard to the means or to the end; in the first case reason determines the form, in the second case reason also determines the matter of the intention.[19]

The understanding is only mediately good, as a means to another good or to happiness. The immediate good can be found only in freedom. For, because freedom is a capacity for action, even if it does not please us, freedom is not dependent upon the condition of a private feeling; however, it always refers only to that which pleases, so it has a relation to feeling and can have a universally valid relation to feeling in general. Hence nothing has an absolute worth but persons, and this consists in the goodness of their free power of choice.[20] Just as freedom contains the first ground of everything that begins, so is it also that which alone contains self-sufficient goodness.

The moral feeling is not an original feeling. It rests on a necessary inner law to consider and to sense oneself from an external standpoint.[21] Likewise in the personality of reason: there one feels oneself in the universal and considers one's *individuum* as a contingent subject like an *accidens* of the universal.

6601. 1769–70? (1764–68?) *Pr* V.   19: 104

Of the ethical ideal of the ancients, the highest good. It is either negative or positive, that is, the absence of vice and pain, innocence and modesty, or virtue and happiness. These last are either so subordinated that happiness is a necessary consequence of virtue or virtue is a necessary form of the means to happiness. The first is Stoicism, the second is Epicureanism. Finally, the ground of the highest good is either in nature or in community with the highest being. The former *principium* is natural, the second mystic. This latter is the Platonic theory.[22]

We highly respect everything that is good in itself; we love that which is good *respective* to us. Both are sentiments. The former is preeminent in the idea of approval, the latter is more a ground of inclination. Whatever we find worthy of the highest respect we really respect highly; whatever we find worthy of love we do not always love, namely if it is not especially connected to us.

Both sentiments are somewhat opposed to one another. Partiality toward us makes us love, but not highly respect, the one who is partial to us.

We have a greater drive to be respected than to be loved – but a greater drive to love others than to respect them. Because in love toward another one senses his own superiority, in respect for another he limits this superiority.

All real moving causes of action are either pathological (or subjective) and are called impulses or they are . . .[a] (objective) and are called *motiva*. The latter are pragmatic or moral. The universal pragmatic *imperativi*   19: 105 are also categorical; however, they are more like such sentences which say what everyone wills rather than what he should will.

6603. 1769–70? (1764–68?) *Pr* V, VI.   19: 105

Whatever pleases only under the condition of a certain inclination or feeling is agreeable; whatever pleases under the condition of a certain nature of the power of cognition, through which all objects of feeling must be known, is beautiful; whatever has a universal and necessary relation to happiness in general without relation to a special feeling or a special cognitive ability, is good.[23] E.g., nonexistence necessarily displeases, although this displeasure is outweighed by special aversions; illness, mutilation of a person require no special feeling in order to displease. Everything right has a general relation to happiness, insofar as each produces happiness through himself, but in such a way that the

---

[a] Kant's ellipses.

rules of private intention do not contradict one another according to universal laws. All duties of love consist in the desire to further universal happiness (not merely one's own) through one's own actions.[24]

An arbitrarily fabricated intention without motivating grounds [*breaks off?*]

6605. 1769–70? (1764–68?) *Pr* VI.

There is a free power of choice which does not have its own happiness as an aim but rather presupposes it. The essential perfection of a freely acting being depends on whether this freedom [*crossed out*: of the power of choice] is not subject to inclination or in general would not be subject to any foreign cause at all. The chief rule of externally good actions is not that they conform with the happiness of others, but with their power of choice, and in the same way the **perfection** of a subject does not depend on whether he is happy but on whether his **condition** is **subordinated to freedom**: so also the universally valid perfection, that the actions must stand under universal laws of freedom.

6607. 1769? 1770? 1772–73? *Pr* VI.

The ancients did not coordinate happiness and morality but subordinated them; because both amount to two different things whose means are distinct, they are often in conflict. The Stoic doctrine is the most genuine doctrine of true morals but the least suited to human nature. It is also the easiest to examine. The Epicurean is less true but [*crossed out*: more] perfectly suited to the inclinations of humans. The Cynic is most in accord with human nature in idea but least natural in execution and is the ideal of the most artificial education as well as of civil society.

The Stoic ideal is the most correct pure ideal of morals, however incorrect [applied] *in concreto* to human nature; it is correct that one
should so act but false that one will ever so act.[25] The ideal of Epicurus is false according to the pure rule of morals and thus false in the theory of moral *principii*, although correct in moral doctrine; only it conforms most often with human volition. The Cynic ideal concerns **only the mean** and is correct in theory but very difficult in *praxi*, although the *norma*. The former ideals were merely theories of moral philosophy, the Cynic ideal merely a doctrine of the mean.[26]

6610. 1769–70? 1764–68?? *Pr* VII.

Morality is an objective [*crossed out*: dependence] subordination of the will under the motivating grounds of reason. Sensibility (*practice*) is a *subordinatio* of the will under inclination.

Inclinations, united through reason, agree with happiness, i.e., with well-being from the enduring satisfaction of all our inclinations. Single inclinations, if they hinder attention to the satisfaction of the remaining ones, contradict happiness. [*Crossed out*: Affects] Passions thus naturally contradict not just morality but also happiness.[27] Happiness, however, only contingently agrees with morality (*actualiter sive subjective*[a]); but *objective* it agrees with morality necessarily, i.e., the worthiness to be happy.

6611. 1769–70? 1764–68?? *Pr* VII–VIII, 139.   19: 108

(*Later addition*:[28] Concept, idea, ideal. The concept is a universal ground of differentiation (mark). Only the *a priori* concept has true universality and is the *principium* of rules. Concerning virtue, only a judging in accordance with concepts, hence *a priori*, is possible. Empirical judging, in accordance with representations in pictures or in accordance with experience, gives no laws but only examples, which an *a priori* concept requires for judging. Many are not capable of deriving their principles from concepts.[29]

An idea is the *a priori* cognition of the [*crossed out*: pure] understanding, through which the object becomes possible. It refers to the objectively practical as a *principium*. It contains the greatest perfection for a certain purpose. A plant is possible only in accordance with an idea. That exists only in the understanding and, for humans, in concepts.[30] The sensible is only the image, e.g., in the case of a house the idea contains all the ends.[31] The sketch is only the sensible in conformity with the idea. All morality rests on ideas, and its image in the human being is always imperfect. In the divine understanding there are intuitions of itself, hence archetypes.

An ideal is the representation of an object of sense in conformity with an idea and the intellectual perfection in it.[32] Ideals pertain only to objects of the understanding and occur only in human beings and are *fictiones* to them. It is a fiction used to posit an idea in intuition *in concreto*.

The three ideals of morality from concepts. The mystical ideal of Plato's intellectual intuition.[33] Holiness is an ideal of supersensible influence.

Concept of plants, but not idea.)

The ideal of innocence. Of prudence. Of [*crossed out*: wisdom. virtue]   19: 109
Of wisdom and of holiness. (*Later addition*: ideals, etc. etc. The Cynic ideal was negative.)

In the 1st, simplicity in morals and moderation in well-being.

2. Morality is seen as the necessary consequence of the prudent aim at happiness, therefore well-being in amusements and virtue in the active cognition of the means.

---

[a] actually or subjectively

3. Wisdom has as its sole end the good, perfection; and well-being depends not on things and sensations, but instead the wise person is happy in his virtue. To the Epicureans special laws of morality were dispensable, to the Stoics special laws of prudence were dispensable.

4. Holiness sees well-being as blessedness. Results from community with God.

(*Later addition*: Platonism: with God through nature; Christianity: through supernatural means. Philosophy or fantasy. Enthusiastic, fantastic, mystical.)

The Epicurean ideal consisted in the **satisfaction** of the whole union of inclinations,[34] the Stoic ideal in power and dominion over all inclinations.[35] That of holiness, in moral peace with all inclinations, i.e., their harmony, or also release from them, the Cynic ideal in the extermination[a] of all inclinations.[36]

(*Later addition*: The Cyrenaic[37] philosophy. De la Mettrie[38] makes morality into mere adroitness in satisfying our desires. Helvetius.[39])

19:110   (*Later addition*: 1. The natural human being (not the raw and animal but the wise human being who is regulated according to the intentions of nature). 2. The man of the world. 3. The wise man. 4. The Christian and Platonist.)

(*Later addition*: The highest good. The grounds of the highest good lie either in nature, and the precepts are only negative, like moderation and innocence, namely not to corrupt nature, or in art, applied to happiness (prudence), or in morality (virtue, wisdom), or in a being above nature: holiness and blessedness.)

(*Later addition*: Morality, worthiness to be happy, lies in conduct. All worthiness lies in the use of freedom.)

19:112   **6619.** 1769–70? (1764–68?) *Pr* IX.

Epicurus takes the subjective ground of execution, which moves us to action, for the objective ground of **adjudication.** Zeno reverses this.[40] That Epicurus reduces it all to bodily stimuli appears to be more an opinion, used to explain the decisions of human beings, than a prescription. The **greatest spiritual** joys find the ground of their own approbation in the intellectual concept, to be sure, but their *elateres* in the sensible.

It is noteworthy that the representations of utility and of honor are not able to produce any strong resolution to emulate virtue, unlike the
19:113   pure picture of virtue in itself; and even if one is driven in secret by a view to honor, one does it not for the sake of this honor alone but only insofar as we can imagine that the principles of virtue have produced it through

---

[a] *Vertilgung.* A variant reading is *Verneinung*, "denial."

a hidden conviction. We must hide the mechanism of our self-interested impulses from our own eyes.

The most powerful means to impel human beings toward the morally good is thus the representation of pure virtue, in order to esteem it highly and to see clearly that one can esteem oneself only insofar as one is in conformity with virtue, but also to show that this is the only means to become valued and loved by others, followed by the greatest security and ease; one does not do the good for the sake of these, but they accompany the good. One must excite the inclinations that most closely agree with morality: love of honor, sociability, freedom.[41]

The *praxis* of morality thus consists in that formation of the inclinations and of taste which makes us capable of uniting the actions that lead to our gratification with moral principles. This is the virtuous person, consequently the one who knows to conform his inclinations to moral principles.

(*Later addition*: The presently anticipated uses can also impel us, even without any morality, to the same action that ethics would command. Only no one would ever undertake such actions universally and in accordance with a universal rule from mere motives of self-love, without any moral motive or conviction thereof.)

6621. 1769–70? (1764–68?) *Pr* X.   19:114

The doctrine of virtue does not so much restrict the gratifications of sensibility as teach how to choose among the various types of them those that have greatest agreement with the rules of universal approbation, which in turn is always the best universal rule of prudence. Because to rely upon one's directing oneself in every case not with a rule but according to the greatest gain is too anxiety-producing and always leaves the mind uneasy. (Moreover the conduct that one universally prescribes must also be assumed as if its intention were known and approved universally.) There are, however, various sources of satisfaction from which we can choose. If by following universally approved means I cannot acquire riches, still I will have the confidence of my friends; I will be restricted, but can live without worry over responsibility, or freely. (*Later addition*: Science, skill, prudence, wisdom, knowledge, skill, etc., etc. Because knowledge can exist without skill.)

In general, nature seems to us to have in the end subordinated sensible needs for the sake of all our actions. Only it was necessary that our understanding at the same time projected universal rules, in accordance with which we had to order, restrict, and make coherent the efforts at our happiness, so that our blind impulses will not push us now here, now there, just by chance. Since the latter commonly conflict with one another, a judgment was necessary, which with regard to all of these impulses projects rules impartially, and thus in abstraction from all inclination, through the pure will alone, which rules, valid for all actions and for all human beings, would produce the greatest harmony of a human being with himself and with others. One must place in these rules the essential conditions under which one can give one's drives a hearing, and posit these rules as if their observation in itself could be an object of our volitions, and we must prosecute even with the sacrifice of our happiness, although to be sure they are only the constant and reliable form [thereof].[42]

Epicurus placed the ends of all virtuous as well as vicious actions merely in the relationship of the objects to sensibility, i.e., to the satisfaction of inclinations, and he distinguished virtue only through the form of reason with regard to the means.

Zeno posited all ends of virtuous actions merely in the intellectual and the conquest of the whole of sensibility.

According to him, self-approval was the whole of true happiness. Yet the contingencies of conditions were not a person's own. The merely inner worth of the person.[43]

6624. 1769–70? (1764–68?) *Pr* XI.

The theories of the ancients appear to be aimed at bringing together the two elements or essential conditions of the highest good, happiness and morality.[44] Diogenes brought happiness down to something negative, namely simplicity of nature.[45] Epicurus brought morality down to self-produced happiness. Zeno brought happiness down to self-sufficient morality. The systems of the moderns try to find the *principium* of moral judgment. Besides those who derive it from empirical sources (custom or authority), they divide themselves into the moral theorists of pure reason and those of moral sentiment. Among the former, ___[a,46] takes the rule of truth to be the guiding rule of morality, Wolff assumes it to be the concept of perfection.[47] But the general concept of perfection is not comprehensible through itself, and from it no practical judgments can be supplied; rather it is itself more a derived concept in which that which occurs in particular cases is given the general name "perfect." From this concept (from which one would certainly not judge what pain or pleasure is) all practical precepts are derived (although only tautological rules, namely that one should do the good), with regard to morality as well as to happiness, and this difference is not shown.[48]

6625. 1769–70? (1764–68?) *Pr* XI.

All systems derive morality either from reason or from feeling (from the coercion of authorities and from custom).

[a] Kant's gap

Those from reason: either from truth or from perfection (the middle road of inclination: Aristotle). Wolff turns the general name of "perfection" into a ground for determining morality and does not name the conditions under which actions and ends are good and deserve the name "perfection."[49]

6626. 1769–70? (1764–68?) *Pr* XI.   19:116

The doctrine of moral feeling is more a hypothesis to explain the *phaenomenon* of approbation that we give to certain actions than any-   19:117
thing that should firmly establish maxims and first principles that are objectively valid concerning how one should approve or reject something, act or refrain from acting.

6627. 1769–60? (1764–68?) *Pr* 1.   19:117

The conditions without which the **approval*** of an action cannot be **universal** (not stand under a universal principle of reason) are **moral**. The moral conditions of actions make the actions that agree with them permitted and restrict the pathological actions. The approbation of an action cannot be universal if it does not contain grounds of approbation that are without relation to the sensible impulses of the agent. Universal approbation accordingly pertains to the objective end of the matter or of a capacity, e.g., of the freedom of speech, and this restricts all subjective ends. Hence the ends that the human being has from inclination are to be distinguished from the end for which the human being has this or that quality, limb, or inclination. The latter[a] is the primordial or original end, the former the properly subordinate end.

*(Either the negative approval of the permissive will or the positive approval of the desirous will.)

6628. 1769–70? (1764–68?) *Pr* 1.   19:117

The first investigation is: Which are the *principia prima dijudicationis moralis*[b] (*later addition*: theoretical rules of adjudication), i.e., which are the highest maxims of morality and which is its highest law.

2. Which is the rule of application (*later addition*: for practical application of adjudicative rules) to an object of adjudication (sympathy for others and an impartial spectator). 3. Through what do the moral conditions become *motiva*, i.e., on what rests their *vis movens*[c] and thus their application to the subject? The latter are first the *motivum* essentially bound up with morality, namely the worthiness to be happy.[50]

---

[a] Following Berger in substituting *dieser* for *jener* here; if this is not done, then both clauses of this sentence refer to ends from inclination, which makes no sense.
[b] first principles of moral adjudication
[c] moving force

19:117   **6629.** 1769–70? (1764–68?) (1771–72?) *Pr* 1.

19:118   If it were certain that all good actions met with no advantage and that good fortune were merely a prize for cunning or a gift of blind accident, then a well-thinking person would still follow the moral rule from sentiment, as long as it did not bring about his own greatest injury, on account of its greater beauty. If happiness could thereby be immediately attained, then the moral beauty would be entirely entwined with self-interest and would never earn the honor of merit. Now being virtuous brings a natural advantage in accordance with universal laws, although in exceptional cases vice can also be a means to gratification; but now since virtue does not carry with it any certain advantage, one must therefore unite the motivating grounds with the utility that they produce.

19:120   **6633.** 1769–70? (1771–72?) *Pr* 1.

The supreme principles *diiudicationis moralis* are to be sure rational, but only *prinicipia formalia*. They do not determine any end, but only the moral form of every end; hence *in concreto* the *principia prima materialia*[a] are presented in accordance with this form.

19:120   **6634.** 1769–70? (1764–68?) *Pr* 2.

Hutcheson's principle is unphilosophical, because it introduces a new feeling as a ground of explanation, and second because it sees objective grounds in the laws of sensibility.[51]

Wolff's principle is unphilosophical, because it makes empty propositions into principles and offers the *abstractum* in all *quaesitis* as if it were the ground of cognition for the *quaesitii*,[b] just as if one were to seek the ground of hunger in the desire for happiness.[52]

The ideal of the Christians has the peculiarity that it makes the idea of moral purity not only into the [*crossed out*: ground] *principio* of adjudication, but also into the unremitting guideline by which he should be **judged.** The incapacity that we would like to plead is not clear, and hence the greatest anxiety arises from the ideal of holiness. The Christian lifts this anxiety by saying that God would make good this lack of holiness, thereby doing away with the inner incapacity for following rules. Whoever believes that one must make himself worthy and capable of this supplementation through all natural efforts is the practical Christian. But whoever believes that one must merely be passive in regard to all

---

[a] first-order, material principles of actions; concrete maxims falling under the general formal principle of moral judgment (the *principia formalia* of *diiudicationis moralis*)

[b] That is, Wolff offers what is just an abstract restatement of a question as if it were an answer to the question.

those actions in order to produce them through the labor of his heart
and to produce his dispositions, and that in place of these certain religious efforts can move the divinity to pour holiness into them [*breaks
off*]53

19:121

6639. 1769–70? (1764–68?) *Pr* 4.

19:122

The categorical (objective) *necessitas* of free actions is necessity in
accordance with laws of the pure will, the [*crossed out*: hypotheti-
cal] conditional: in accordance with laws of the will affected (through
inclinations).

6648. 1769–1775. *Pr* 15, at §36, in *Obligatio in genere.*

19:124

An action that is good in and of itself must necessarily be good for
everyone, thus not related to feeling.

6659. 1769? 1770–71? (1773–75? 1776–78?) *Pr* 20, still in *Obligatio in
genere.*

19:126

Lex moralis est vel absoluta (unconditional) *vel hypothetica.* (*Later
addition*: The former obligates without any condition, the latter is restricted through conditions of its necessity.)

6674. 1769? 1764–68? 1776–78?? *Pr* 36, at §72, in *Lex.*

19:130

The moral laws are grounds of the divine will. The latter is a ground
of our will by means of its goodness and justice, in accordance with which
God connects happiness with good behavior.

If there were no God, then all our duties would vanish, because there
would be an absurdity in the whole in which well-being would not agree
with good behavior, and this absurdity would excuse the other.54

I should be just toward others; but who protects my right for me?

III.
NOTES FROM 1770–1775

6688. 1770–71? (1773–75?) 1769?? 1764–68?? *Pr* 4–5.

19:133

(*Later addition*: The correspondence of the will with the form of reason
can be determined *a priori*, it is universally valid satisfaction.)

If the primary grounds of morality rest on reason, then it is a question
whether departure from the teachings of ethics are to be attributed to
error or to evilness of the will.

(*Later addition: Responsio*: False moral judgment is to be attributed to
the weakness of reason (against prejudices of self-love); action contrary
to these judgments is to be attributed to the powerlessness of reason over
the inclinations. Reason moves only pure spirits, and the means to move

human beings is that they appropriate the universal through the love of honor, empathy with the inclinations of others, or ease with regard to their responsibility. Weakness in the representation of these alien judges leaves the judgment of reason ineffective. All of these supplementary sentiments pertain to that which is connected with the judgment of reason and not to what is connected with actions by chance or physical

19:134 necessity. It is the consequence of an action if it were universally known, consequently correspondence with the universally valid rule.)

19:134 **6689.** 1770–75. *Pr* 4.
An action is morally good insofar as it is possible in relation to every will and to every inclination.

19:135 **6698.** 1770–71? (1772–73? 1773–75?) (1769?) *Pr* 5, in *Obligatio in genere*.
The moral precepts are valid for every rational and free being, let their inclinations be what they will.

The obligation is also the same for all degrees of inclination to the contrary; only the imputation is different, for the latter concerns to what extent the action can be attributed to the subject himself, i.e., to his freedom.[55]

19:138 **6709.** 1772–75? (1771?) *Pr* III.
Since there are three kinds of *respectus:*[a] 1. of the substance to the *accidens*, 2. of the parts in a whole, 3. of effect and cause, so there are also three chief parts in morality: 1. Duties toward oneself, 2. toward other human beings (*a.* that they do not contradict themselves, *b.* that they unite themselves through a common ground. Right and love). In the same way, moral possibility, existence, necessity. In the nature of the human being there is something that cannot vary. Those are the fundamental properties of the soul. To these even the human being as an animal is subjected.

19:138 **6713.** 1772–75? (1771?) *Pr* VI.
Everything that necessarily pleases without relation to the subject
19:139 pleases objectively. What pleases from grounds of reason pleases necessarily, thus objectively; such a thing is therefore objectively necessary; hence good actions are objectively necessary.

Personality is the independence of the will from inclinations.[56] Hence morality is correspondence with personality.

The will to be happy is necessary, but in accordance with determinate inclinations it is contingent.

---

[a] relations

6714. 1772? (1771?) *Pr* 3, in *Obligatio in genere*.　　　　　19:139
　　Morality is in agreement with universal and general utility and hence meets with necessary approval. This also seems to be the true cause of its preeminent goodness.

6718. 1772? (1773–78?) *Pr* 6, in *Obligatio in genere*.　　　　　19:140
　　The *motiva moralia* must be expounded as pure and unmixed with *stimulis* and *motivis* of prudence.
　　The universal validity of the will is possible either if the private will of each would be the ground for the will of all, or if the will of all would be the ground for every private will.
　　The first is only possible if each private will is good; but from the correspondence with each private will no correspondence[a] is possible, thus no rule, except insofar as the former is restricted by the latter. Thus the first is the law, the second is love.

6723. 1772–73? (1773–78?) *Pr* 7, in *Obligatio in genere*.　　　　19:141
　　The freedom of a perfect being is objectively unrestricted, that of an imperfect being is restricted, bounded. Unboundedness is lawlessness.

6725. 1772. *Pr* 9, in *Obligatio in genere*.　　　　　　　　19:141
　　The whole difficulty in the dispute over the *principium* of morality is: how is it possible to have a categorical *imperativus*, which is not conditional, under neither *sub conditione problematica* nor *apodictica*[b] (of skill, prudence)[?] Such an *imperativus* expresses what is originally and *primitive* good.[57] It is admirable that the primitive[c] good, the condition of all that pleases, pertains only to a will. This is because all perfection of an idea as well as its reality presupposes a will, and because every- 　19:142 thing contingent and all origins are grounded on freedom. All necessity of judgment is grounded on universality, or else the latter is grounded on the former. Hence the ground of the necessity that moral propositions enunciate is to be placed in the universal validity of the grounds of volition (completely necessary, *absolute*, denotes not inner necessity but overall necessity).

6734. 1772–73? 1773–75? 1776–78? *Pr* 26–27, in *Coactio moralis*.　19:144
　　An action is unjust insofar as it is impossible if others presuppose this principle to be in us. E.g., a lie. It is impossible to deceive someone who knows that he is being deceived, or unfaithfulness in a contract. It

---

[a] Berger suggests that this occurrence of "correspondence" (*Übereinstimmung*) should be preceded by "universal."
[b] under neither problematic nor apodictic conditions
[c] Here *primitive* is in German script; in the previous sentence *primitive* was in roman script.

is also impossible to will and to approve of such actions as a universal authorization. An unsocial person is one who has maxims that are such that if another person holds the same maxim he cannot deal with that other person. Money belongs to this. The pleasant human being wishes that all human beings would be like him; the unsocial the opposite. The just person demands it. Justice is a ground of the possibility of society, although without wish. Goodness is an impulse to society. Demand of others what you will that others should demand of you.

19:145 **6737.** 1772? 1776–78?? *Pr* 30, at §63, in *Lex.*

The supreme *principium formale* of morality must be truthfulness. For we can be liberated from all other obligations by others taking them over for us, but we can never be liberated from this one.

19:145 **6738.** 1772? 1776–78?? *Pr* 30, at §63.

An action is right in general insofar as one is free with respect to it. But a right is the freedom through which the freedom of another is restricted: *jus quaesitum. A natura* all are free, and only actions that restrict the freedom of no one are right.

19:148 **6753.** 1772? *Pr* 34, at §70, still in *Lex.*

It is necessary to place morality before religion in order for us to present a virtuous soul to God; if religion precedes morality then religion without *sentiment* is a cold ingratiation and morals an observance based on need without a disposition. Everything must be absorbed pure and unmixed and then be united so as to accompany one another rather than to be mixed together.[58]

19:149 **6754.** 1772? *Pr* 34, at §§69–70.

I. The *principium* of morality is not sensual, neither *directe* or pathological, lying neither in the physical (doctrine of skill) nor the moral sense (the latter is impossible,* because no sense intrudes on the intellectual); nor *indirecte* sensual or pragmatic (doctrine of prudence): considered according to your true happiness (*epicurism*). There reason serves only as the means to determine how the greatest sum of inclinations can be satisfied, and the means for this. The *principium* of morality is thus intellectual (*pure*),** but not tautological (*perfice te, medium tene*[a]). II. The *principium* is not external, outside the nature of action, lying in the will of another.

*(If such a moral sense were possible, then necessary, categorical, and universal laws could not be grounded on it.)

** (They contain the correspondence of actions with their previously given ends and the form of this correspondence in general: 1. correctness

---

[a] convince you to hold what is obvious

(truth), 2. perfection, 3. not more, not fewer; they are thus tautological rules and proceed from the relation of actions to ends, not the ends themselves.)

6757. 1772? *Pr* 35, at §71, still in *Lex.*   19:150
Moral feeling succeeds the moral concept, but does not produce it; all the less can it replace it, rather it presupposes it.[59]

6759. 1772? *Pr* 35, at §71, still in *Lex.*   19:150
Religion is not a ground of morality,[a] but *vice versa.*
  1. If morality[b] were grounded on cognition of the divine existence, then the consciousness of morality[c] would be bound up with that of the divine existence.
  2. We would not be able to cognize the goodness of the divine will.
  3. The *vis obligatoria*[d] is in the moral relation of the divine will to ours, not in its power.

6760. 1772. *Pr* 35, above §71.   19:151
The *principium* of moral adjudication is not the divine will.
————(5. nor the middle way. *Aristotle.*)
————4. not the general concept of perfection.
————2. not the general concept of happiness.
————1. not private happiness. (*Later addition*: that would be empirical.)
————3. not the moral feeling* and taste.**
         (*Later addition*: Taste is relativistic in relation to the subject.)
————3. but is rather reason.
Judicia moralia sunt rationalia.[e]
The *sentiment* pertains only to the understanding and is really the healthy reason in moral matters.
*(The consciousness of the worthiness of happiness is regarded as a possession thereof, hence as moral gratification. Moral taste, however, or discrimination, rests on a subordination of lower cognition under higher cognition, since one represents every action only from a universal point of view.)
**(Virtue also has propriety; it has a certainty purity and order in   19:152
appearance.)
The moral judgment of approbation and disapprobation is made through the understanding, the moral sentiment of gratification and

[a] *der Moral*
[b] *die Moralität*
[c] *der Sittlichkeit*
[d] obligatory force
[e] Moral judgments are rational.

aversion through the moral feeling, but in such a way that the moral judgment does not arise from the feeling but rather the latter from the former. All moral feeling presupposes a moral judgment by means of the understanding.[60]

We can even approve or disapprove of actions and find them worthy of aversion without a noticeable feeling. The aversion itself will finally be generated through practice. *sentiment*. Moral instinct.

In execution, ethical duties have their origin more in feeling than in moral concepts, duties of right more in concepts than in feeling; hence only the latter have determinate rules, in the former it is more a matter of comparison with my feeling. Nonetheless a good action may be done merely from moral concepts or principles without any feeling: charity without compassion, marital faithfulness without love. And often out of feeling without principles: instinct. All love as well as esteem is a kind of feeling. One cannot give such a thing to oneself, and with regard to God only the latter is possible. We always value goodness from feeling higher than that from principles (yet the former must be guided by the latter), because it is otherwise inconstant and often false. The principles are too weak and can be overcome through sophistry. One always believes [himself] to be more secure if sensibility is alongside of reason and gives it its blessing in order to enchain the capricious person. The good cast of mind[a] is really this good feeling and, since it is by itself without principles, it is weak and more good-hearted than noble. The evil cast of mind can even be equally correct in its judgment, but the evil heart really consists [*crossed out*: either] in the fact that it is not even capable of good principles [*crossed out*: or only]. For the man who always has good principles but cannot coerce his desires has a good heart but an evil temperament. The moral feeling is good, but the desires are not coercible. – But there is also an evil heart, which one could distinguish from the evil cast of mind, where the principles are good but the inclinations are not merely too strong but also have immediately evil ends. Envy. Misanthropy. Revenge. (*Later addition*: Quarrelsomeness. Conceit. Crudeness. Falseness.) Likewise, those whose natural inclinations already tend toward something good, toward the happiness and love of others, have a good heart and, although they are not formed thus, can yet have a good cast of mind. Education can contribute much to a good **understanding**, less to a good **cast of mind**, and nothing at all to a good **heart**.[61]

19:153

19:153   **6762.** 1772. *Pr* 36, still in *Lex*.

What cannot stand under a universal rule of the pure will is morally incorrect. The correspondence of the free [*crossed out*: power of choice] action with the universality of the pure will is morality.

---

[a] *Gemüth*

434

6765. 1772? 1776–78? *Pr* 37, at §74, still in *Lex.*   19:154

That action whose intention considered as a universal rule would necessarily contradict itself and those of others is morally impossible.

The disposition to conduct one's actions in accordance with the universal *principio* of rules is moral: if the will is subjected to the form of the understanding in general.

The driving force of the understanding rests on its being opposed to   19:155
all *principiis* of actions that make the use of rules impossible.

6794. 1773–75? 1772? *Pr* IV.   19:163

It is indisputable that virtue would make [one] **happy** if **everyone** practiced it; but Epicurus asserted that it would make one happy even if one practices it **alone.**[62]

Although we do not, as Chrysippus says, commit evil solely from **ignorance** (*later addition*: hence the moral system of truth). Thus only **one virtue**, namely the science (and proficiency of the good).[63] (Aristotle.) The *adiaphora*[a] rich or poor: concerning them one can decide as one wants, but not concerning the *honestum* and *turpe*.[b] Health is to be wished for, but is not an object of approbation, illness is to be abhorred (fled), but it is not to be blamed.

6795. 1773–75? 1772? *Pr* V.   19:163

The essential laws are those without which freedom would be a dangerous monster;[64] namely, freedom must not be used in such a way that it is contradictory to [1.] the humanity in oneself, 2. the freedom of others. There are thus rights of humanity and rights of human beings: Rights of humanity on one's own person and the very same rights with regard to others.

6796. 1773–75? 1772? *Pr* V.   19:163

Morality consists in the rule of actions from the standpoint (station) of the universal participant or representative:

  1. of the participant in nature with regard to himself;

  2. of the participant in freedom with regard to others. In the latter   19:164
case, from the standpoint either of the representative of the power of choice of others or of their welfare.

The universality is either of the property or of the things that have a certain property. *Universalitas interna* or *externa*. Moral feeling is that through which the universal objective *principia* of judging become subjective ones of resolution, thus that through which absolute rules become maxims.

---

[a] things that are morally indifferent
[b] the virtuous and the vicious

Freedom is independence from incentives, hence also from feelings.[65] Hence there can never be a feeling that is necessary through reason insofar as reason necessarily determines the power of choice through the universality of rules. Logically, reason is the ground of the rule. What is valid universally is also valid in the particular case that is contained thereunder. And in the practical domain in general: only that which pleases in its universality (in the totality) can please in the particular case which is contained under the former. What restricts freedom is only universality for the power of choice with regard to all actions. The pleasure in that rests on the agreement of all actions of the power of choice among one another through consensus with that which is the universally valid in them.

6801. 1773–75? 1772? *Pr* VI.

It is of the greatest necessity for reason to assume certain practical rules as principles that necessitate absolutely (categorically), without resting on the conditions of utility, e.g., to have no intention against one's own life or not to sacrifice one's own person to another's intentions. Since in the determination of utility everything is contingent (the universal condition, however, of all [*crossed out*: intentions must be that the person [is?] not the essential] free actions and of the preeminence of freedom itself, which makes human beings capable of a moral and inner worth, is namely this, that he is never to be overwhelmed through animal incentives into willing something that reveals a *principium* of action against itself, etc. etc.), so must [*crossed out*: the same action which without regard to its utility and damages] that, which is an antecedent [*crossed out*: action] condition for making use of his freedom necessarily restrict freedom, hence the essential determinations of his own person and of life itself. No intention opposed to these can obtain, although to be sure they themselves cannot simply be the intention itself. Essential determinations are those without which one would either not be a human being or would not be a free being at all.[66]

One should not have the intention of speaking an untruth because, as one who can indicate his meaning, one must not destroy that significance.[67] One should not kill himself because, when he does with himself as he pleases, he **considers** himself **as a thing** and loses the dignity of a human being.[68] One offends another when he treats as belonging to himself what is **not his** thing. The suicide also displays freedom in the greatest opposition to itself, hence in the greatest breakdown of his delusion. Humanity is **holy** and invulnerable, as much as in one's own person as in that of another.[69] One's own consent is here unimportant, because one does not have a volition to cease to be anything at all. All duties, namely those that are necessary, consist in our giving preference to and honoring not the welfare of human beings but rather humanity and dignity. Thus the right of humanity is that which limits all freedom through necessary conditions. A human being can pursue great actions even in misfortune and indeed, where he sacrifices his life but not because he hates it, there he truly is worthy of life. One who values his life less than the comfort of happiness is not worthy of life.

All such duties must be weighed independently of duties toward God, because we can judge the latter only from the dutifulness of actions in themselves, and this life is entrusted to our own recommendation.

Suicide is perhaps not so pernicious on the assumption that there is no other world; however, without this assumption it is indeed heinous. How would you regard a friend about whom you were never certain whether he would not contemplate suicide? (*Later addition*: Against suicide. As long as a human being lives, he has the opportunity to practice good and even heroic virtue. He must regard his life even in the greatest wretchedness as the challenge of fate to his steadfastness.)

6802. 1773–75? 1772? *Pr* VII.   19: 166
The universal and supreme practical law of reason is that reason must determine free actions. We can only have a satisfaction in actions if we see these actions agreeing with reason. It is necessary for a rational being first to bring freedom under the universal law of reason. This consists in the disposition of action taken universally agreeing with the free power of choice (with itself) and with freedom first ceasing to be unconstrained and lawless.[70] Appetites do not provide universally agreed-upon laws; either nature or the power of choice yields the general point of reference in relation to which there must be a universal correspondence of actions. On what, then, does the satisfaction in the correspondence of actions with that which would necessarily please when taken universally rest? and   19: 167
why does this universal validity please us? Whence are we determined to derive the particular from the universal? Because we see reason as the necessary condition of judgment as much in practical judgment as in theoretical.

Actions are not correct, freedom is without a rule, if freedom does not stand under such restriction from the idea of the whole. We ourselves disapprove of it. This is the necessary condition of practical form, as space is of intuition.

IV.
NOTES FROM 1776–1778

6820. 1776–78? (1778–89?) *Pr* I.   19: 172
Moral philosophy is the science of ends insofar as they are determined through pure reason. Or of the unity of all ends (that they do not conflict with themselves) of rational beings. The matter of the good is

empirical, the form is given *a priori*. Morality is the good from principles of spontaneity. Hence the universality of the good.

19:172 **6822.** 1776–78. *Pr* IV.

In the metaphysics of morals we must abstract from all human qualities, from application, and from their obstacles *in concreto*, and seek only the canon, which is a pure and universally valid idea.[71]

19:176 **6837.** 1776–78. *Pr* IX.

Epicurus was concerned only with the value of the condition, he knew nothing of the inner worth of the person. Zeno did not concede the value of the condition, but recognized as the true good only the worth of the person.[72]

The latter philosopher ascended above the nature of the human being, the former fell beneath it.

19:176 **6838.** 1776–78. *Pr* X.

Epicurus wanted to give virtue an incentive and took from it its inner worth.

Zeno wanted to give virtue an inner worth and took from it its incentive. Only Christ gave it inner worth and also an incentive.[73] The concept of virtue is not mystical but natural. The incentive is freed from all obstacles of nature. The incentive based on the other world is also in itself the same as a renunciation of all advantages. These incentives alone are not contingent or uncertain and serve as a rule. The other (intellectual) world is actually that in which happiness harmonizes precisely with morality: heaven and hell, the former designed for the greatest happiness, the latter for misery. The other world is a necessary moral ideal. Without this ideal, moral legislation is without governance. It alone concerns the inner worth of actions. Through the hoped-for reward of another world, virtue becomes unselfish and yet has support or a refuge. The incentive is to be withdrawn from sense as far as possible.[74]

19:177 **6843.** 1776–78. *Pr* 2.

The *principium* of the necessary unity of our actions. From self-inclination arise actions that do not necessarily have unity among themselves and others.

The principle of self-love is to be sure the universal subjective principle of incentives, but not of the judging of actions and their objective worth.

19:177 **6845.** 1776–78. *Pr* 3.

What corresponds with the private will is agreeable; a universally valid will is good. What contains the conditions through which it becomes possible that one will can achieve concord with others is right; that through which it actually agrees [with them] is good.

6847. 1776–78. *Pr* 131.   19:178

Rules belong so necessarily to the nature of our understanding, they depend so inseparably upon freedom under the name of the ought, above all when freedom is used with regard to free beings, that we turn away from the ground of all our judgments and the consciousness of our nature if we deprive freedom of a rule restricting itself in practice. Also, the representation of the highest being is necessary because this representation is a *principium* of rules.

The necessary conditions of universal agreement belong just as much to the valid rule of practical as of speculative reason.

6849. 1776–78. *Pr* 132.   19:178

The **primary ought**[a] (original = *absolute* or the universal idea of duty) cannot be comprehended. All happiness should be a product of freedom, or freedom must limit itself *a priori* to the universal consensus about happiness. The ground is: because otherwise one will find oneself blameworthy. This is the necessary condition of the *principii* of happiness from reason, and thus of a *principii* that is necessary in itself and not contingent like that of chance.

6850. 1776–78. *Pr* 132, above **6861**.   19:178

The primary ought is a condition under which alone freedom becomes a capacity in accordance with constant rules that determine *a priori*. This rule-governedness is, however, a necessary requirement of reason with regard to a capacity that dynamically determines *a priori*.

The will that is limited by no object and hence is pure must first not contradict itself, and freedom as the dynamical condition of the intellectual world and its *commercii* must have unity.

The independence of freedom from sensibility presupposes a dependence of freedom on the universal condition of consensus with itself.[75]

6851. 1776–78. *Pr* 133.   19:179

If your will ought to agree with all your inclinations through universally valid conditions, then your will must agree with that to which inclinations themselves are all related, namely yourself, i.e., your personality. Duties toward oneself.

Your actions ought to agree with your freedom and with what is universal in your inclinations, with the freedom of others and with what is universal in their inclinations.

---

[a] *das erste Sollen*

With your inclination and with the inclination of others, with your freedom and the freedom of others.

The universally valid will is a pure will that is not affected through impulse and inclination, and its object is the good.

6853. 1776–78? 1778–79? *Pr* 134, above **6862.**

The subjection of freedom under the legislation of pure reason. To go from the universal conditions of ends in general to the particular. Pure reason, i.e., reason separated from all sensible **incentives**, has **legislative force** with regard to freedom in general, which every rational being must acknowledge, since without conditions for universal consensus with regard to itself and others **no use of reason** with regard to itself would take place at all. Now that through which the supreme power **contradicts itself** is a natural and necessary **object of aversion**, just as in the case of logical contradiction.

6854. 1776–78? 1780–89?? *Pr* 128.

Metaphysical concept of morality. A. Inner power of choice. Form of the inner moral sense.

1. We do not abstract the concept of freedom from experience. When we want to act, we consider the prospective action as completely problematic with regard to the present moment, and the ought is a condition of the consensus of the prospective action with reason, which is thus not at all in a predetermined interconnection with appearances, i.e., with nature.
2. The free power of choice is particular. The question is always what I want in general given certain conditions; the universal, however, is not given through experience.
3. The power of choice is particular. I have only one power of choice in relation to all of my ends.
4. *A priori* rules for the unity of the inner power of choice can be given without regard to the matter of volition. These rules contain a categorical necessity. *(analogon* of nature)[76]

Power of Choice in Community

1. Freedom in community has conditions that also cannot be drawn from experience.
2. It is unity of the outer power of choice for reason. Any other concept of freedom is in itself contrary to reason.
3. Categorical rules can be given for this *a priori*.

Summa: freedom in accordance with laws, insofar as freedom itself is a law, constitutes the form of the moral sense. The matter is the moral feeling, which has no object except consensus with the end of humanity and of human beings in general.

1. Categories of morality. – Functions of freedom are in everything that is practical.[77]
2. Principles: in part *constitutiva*, moral; in part *regulativa*, juridical.

6856. 1776–78? 1780–89?? *Pr* 129.   19: 181

The dignity of human nature lies solely in freedom; through it we alone can become worthy[a] of any good. But the dignity of a human being (worthiness) rests on the use of freedom, whereby he makes himself worthy of everything good. He makes himself worthy of this good, however, when he also works toward participating in it as much as lies in his natural talents and is allowed by outer agreement with the freedom of others.

6857. 1776–78? 1780–89? *Pr* 129.   19: 181

The worthiness to be happy consists in the service that actions do for happiness, that is, if these actions were universal, then, at least insofar as it is up to freedom, they would actually make oneself as well as others happy. One says: A person deserves to eat who makes his own bread or who provides bread for others.

6858. 1776–78? *Pr* 130.   19: 181

It is true: without religion morality would have no incentives, all of which must be derived from happiness. The moral commands must carry with them a promise or a threat. Happiness is not encouragement for the moral command in this life; rather, it is the pure disposition of the heart that constitutes genuine moral worth; this, however, is never truly known by others, and is often completely misjudged.[78] Certainly there has never been a human being who kept watch over the purity of his morals with complete conscientiousness but who did not at the same time hope that at some time this care would be of a greater importance and who did not expect from a world-ruling higher wisdom that it would not be in vain to have dedicated himself to this painstaking observation. Only the judgment regarding the worth of actions, so far as they are worthy of approval and happiness, must still be independent of all cognition of God.

6859. 1776–78? 1780–89? *Pr* 130–1.   19: 182

In morality we require no other concept of freedom than that our actions do not follow the thread of instinct in accordance with experience, but intermix reflections of the understanding with the incentives. Through instinct there arises a lack of coherence, because instinct, when it alone governs, has rules, just as does the understanding when it alone governs; the understanding, however, which does not prescribe rules

---

[a] Here Kant uses the word *würdig*, which plays on the words *Würde* (dignity) at the outset of this sentence and *Würdigkeit* (worthiness) in the next.

for itself, makes everything unruly when it fills in for the lack of instinct. Freedom from instinct thus requires rule-governedness in the practical use of the understanding. Thus we represent to ourselves rule-governedness and unity in the use of our power of choice as possible only through our understanding, tying our power of choice to conditions that bring it into consensus with itself. Where, however, this use of the understanding is really from, whether it itself has its causes in the predetermined series of appearances or not, is not a practical question.* It suffices that the laws of the consensus of the power of choice with itself, which is not to be expected from impulses but can come only from reason, alone have this effect and are thus in accord with our supreme will (with regard to the sum of all ends) and are good.[79]

*(There can be no dispute whether we should follow these laws of consensus or not, and whether actions are in accord with them or against them, good or evil. An important dispute, however, may admittedly arise about whether these laws or their opposite would with certainty always be determining causes of human behavior, or whether for human beings everything does not rather run its course according to these laws or against them, allowing no possibility of the opposite, like the movement of machines. That the understanding should have the influence of an efficient cause on appearances through objective laws is the *paradoxon* that makes nature (the sum of appearances) different from freedom, insofar as our actions are not determined through natural causes (as mere appearances). The self-activity of the understanding is another genus of

19: 183 cause. Otherwise the understanding produces nothing but ideas. How the understanding becomes a cause of appearances is a *paradox*. It could just as well be instinct.

The necessity of actions from the understanding, insofar as one makes use of it, is certain, and also that one must make use of it.)

19: 183 **6860.** 1776–78? 1780–89? *Pr* 131.

We cannot have any concept of how a mere form of actions could have the power of an incentive. Yet this must be if morality is to obtain, and experience confirms it. This formal causality, as efficient, is not determined among appearances. It is thus always new, without regard to everything that may occur. What determines the action is only our self and not any foreign predisposition, no chain of appearances that is empirically determined. Freedom is the apperception of oneself as an intellectual being that is active.

19: 183 **6861.** 1776–78? 1780–89? *Pr* 132, under **6850.**

The apperception of sensation is substance, that of self-activity is the person. The value of the person rests on the freedom that agrees with itself according to original rules.

6862. 1776–78? 1780–89? *Pr* 134, under **6853**.   19:183

Everything finally comes down to life; that which animates, or the feeling of the promotion of life, is agreeable. Life is unity; hence all taste has as its *principio* the unity of animating sensation.[80]

Freedom is the original life and, in its coherence, the condition of the correspondence of all life; hence that which [*crossed out*: increases] promotes the feeling of universal life, or the feeling of the promotion of universal life, produces a pleasure. Do we, however, ourselves feel good in the universal life? Universality makes all our feelings agree, although there is no special type of sensation of this universality. It is the form of *consensus*.

6864. 1776–78. *Pr* 136.   19:184

1. The ***principium*** of **moral judgment** (the *principium* of the conformity of freedom with reason in general, i.e., lawfulness in accordance with universal conditions of consensus) is the rule for the subordination of freedom under the *principium** of the universal consensus of freedom with itself (with regard to oneself as well as other persons).[81]

2. The **ground** of **moral feeling**,** on which the **satisfaction** in this consensus in accordance with principles rests, is the necessity of satisfaction in the form of actions by means of which we agree with ourselves in the use of our power of choice.*** The absence of **moral feeling** (we necessarily take satisfaction in rules) rests on **not** taking **as much interest** in the **form** as in the **matter**, and not considering an object from the perspective of **universality** or connecting it to one's feeling. This is not any special feeling but rather in general a way to consider something from the universal perspective.[82]

3. The **incentive****** of moral **conduct** is in turn to be distinguished from the above and rests on the resolve to act according to a previously adopted resolution (of a universal **maxim**). Thus on the power of reason with regard to freedom.

*(*Later addition*: The *Principium* of universal practical legislation of pure reason with regard to freedom in general.

The system of morality from *principiis (legibus) arbitrii puri.*[a] I.e., the *systema* of [*breaks off*]

Only in the practical does pure reason give objective principles.)   19:185

**(*Later addition*: How can morality, which indeed is an object of reason, be felt? It relates to all our actions according to our pleasure or displeasure and contains the condition of their consensus in the universal; through this it relates to the feeling of pleasure in accordance with form.)

---

[a] principles (laws) of the pure power of choice

***(*Later addition*: The epigenesis of happiness (self-creation) out of freedom, which is restricted by the conditions of universal validity, is the ground of the moral feeling.

In Smith's[83] system: why does the impartial judge (who is not one of the participants) adopt that which is universally good? and why does he have any satisfaction in this?)

****(*Later addition*: How can reason provide an incentive, since it is otherwise always only a guideline and it is inclination that drives, the understanding prescribing only the means? Agreement with oneself. Self-approbation and trust. The incentive that can be **united with duty** but must **never** be put **in its place** is either inclination or coercion. The first because inclination (even benevolent inclination) must be ruled by duty. The second because the need for coercion is in itself already a weakening of the power of duty.)

19:185 **6866.** 1776–78. *Pr* 136.

19:186 The motivating force comes from the feeling of satisfaction insofar as it is applied to oneself and to self-esteem, and especially in accordance with its universally valid price, i.e., inner worth. Elevation of humanity.

19:186 **6867.** 1776–78. *Pr* 137.

The *principium* of morals is autocracy of freedom with regard to all happiness or the epigenesis of happiness in accordance with universal laws of freedom.[84] Happiness has no self-sufficient worth insofar as it is a gift of nature or of luck. Its origin from freedom is what constitutes its self-sufficiency and harmony. Thus good conduct, i.e., the use of freedom in accordance with those laws in which happiness is the self-creation of the good or rule-governed power of choice, has an absolute constancy, and worthiness to be happy is the correspondence with the highest good through nothing other than the completion of the capacity of the free faculty of choice, insofar as it agrees with happiness in its entirety in accordance with universal rules. The moral feeling proceeds here from the unity of the ground as well as from the self-possession of the sources of happiness in rational creatures, as that to which all judgment of worth must be related. The good use of freedom has more worth than contingent happiness. It has a necessary inner worth. Thus the virtuous person contains happiness (*in receptivitate*) in himself, no matter how bad the circumstances may be. He has in himself, as much as is possible, the *principium* of the *epigenesis* of happiness. Hereby it must be assumed that originally a free will that is universally valid is the cause of the order of nature and of all fate. Only then is the ordering of actions in accordance with universal laws of the consensus of freedom at the same time a *principium* of the form of all happiness.[85]

6871. 1776–78? *Pr* 137.

We have **no special feelings** at all, although we have various senses and capacit[ies] for sentiment.*a* There is only a principle of life and thus only a *principium* of the feeling of pleasure and displeasure;* this can also be stimulated through reason (through the rule-governedness or unruliness of freedom).[86] And whether this moves us just a little, or is indeed even resisted! still it excites the feeling with regard to our entire existence and all of our powers into consensus and opposition, since the free use of those powers and freedom in general is the most important and noblest thing, which, if it were without a rule and inconsistent with itself, must displease every rational being, since their reason requires *a priori* rules by means of which to order all of the manifold under principles for their secure use.

*(Thus we certainly do not consider the objects of feeling, sensations, as all the same, but we compare the feelings of pleasure and displeasure and are able to prefer a gratification of the senses to a moral good.)

6875. 1776–78? 1769? *Pr* 139.

The end that is necessarily universal is that all of one's ends be attained, i.e., happiness.

6876. 1776–78. *Pr* 138–9, at §203, in *Conscientia*.[87]

The **mistake of the philosophical sects** was that they wanted to **make morals independent of religion** (*later addition*: that they expected happiness to be connected to morals by nature and insisted upon only as much morality as was necessary to make themselves worthy of this natural happiness); the **nature** of things, however, **contains no necessary connection** between good conduct and well-being, and thus the **highest good** is **a mere thought-entity**.[88]

But even without religion one must have a concept of this, in spite of the fact that religion alone can prove the reality of this *summi boni* with regard to human beings. If the course of the world determines all consequences of good and evil actions, then worldly prudence is the good conduct that leads to the highest good. For this, however, it would be required that one consider morality to be the rule, but with the proviso for all exceptions that conditions make advisable to our advantage. For the painstaking following of rules would be pedantry, since rules do not command absolutely whose end is not a necessary consequence of them.

Happiness is only a conditioned good.

The highest good contains a pathological (immediately agreeable, but not always good) and practical good. Good conduct and faring well.

---

a *Empfindungsfähigkeit*

The good will, in order to avail itself of all **gifts of nature** and **gifts of fortune** (inner and outer good), makes us completely worthy of those gifts.[89] Because worthiness is correspondence with the universal end.

Happiness is not a genuine good; worthiness is indeed a genuine and the **supreme good**, but not the **complete good**.[90]

(Nature, art, above nature.)

6881. 1776–78? *Pr* 139.

One must never say that one places one's end in gratification, rather that whatever immediately gratifies us is our end, because gratification is only the relation of an end to our feeling. The satisfaction in the rule-governedness of freedom is intellectual. Hence the end is not always self-seeking, if the end is not the altered condition of our own senses.

My gratification is thus either selfish or universal and spiritual. When something pleases me but not by affecting my senses, then the gratification is intellectual and a free gratification.

6883. 1776–78? (1769?) *Pr* I.

We understand nothing of a purely moral happiness or of blessedness. If all materials that our senses afford us were eliminated, then what would be left of uprightness, goodness, and self-control, which are only forms for ordering these materials in themselves? Since we can understand all happiness and the true good only in this world, we overstep the boundaries of our reason if it would paint for us a new and also higher perfection.[91]

Earnest delight and the mind that is, as it were, moved with majesty and gravity is entirely different in sentiment from jocular joyfulness. The question is: which is fitting for the human being? The former comes close to pain and draws from it a certain agreeable extract, the bitterness of which prevents facile joy from going stale.

6890. 1776–78. *Pr* III.

Nothing at all can be [*crossed out*: in its self] absolutely good except a good will. Everything else is either mediately good or good only under a restricting condition. Universal happiness is very good or agreeable for those who enjoy it, but it is not absolutely good, i.e., in the eyes of everyone, i.e., in the universal judgment of reason, if those who enjoy it do not have any worthiness for it in their conduct. Talents are very good as means; but this ultimately comes down to what will the subject has for the use of these talents. Every type of perfection in the highest being: eternity, omnipotence, omnipresence, is in itself sublime and terrifying as long as a good will to use these perfections well is lacking. The free will and its constitution is alone capable of an inner goodness. Hence not happiness but the worthiness to be happy is that which constitutes the supreme condition of everything good.[92]

6892. 1776–78. *Pr* VIII.   19: 195

The concept of morality consists of the worthiness to be happy (the satisfaction of one's will in general). This worthiness rests on correspondence with the laws under which, were they universally observed, everyone would partake of happiness to the highest degree, as can occur only through freedom. But why must one behave so as to be worthy of happiness?

1. – This correspondence with universally valid laws of choice is in   19: 196
accordance with reason a necessary ground of our self-approbation and satisfaction with ourselves, also of what others may do.

If we could be happy without many gratifications of the senses or satisfaction of their needs, then that inner approbation would be a sufficient motivating ground for necessitating us.

But since self-satisfaction elevates the soul and compensates it for the many sensible amusements which it sees as having little legitimacy, because one can overcome them through strength, it is a greater and the greatest motivating ground of reason to make happiness a product of spontaneity independent of sense.*,[a] Thus only in light of the inadequacy for becoming happy without the concurrence of fate does the idea of the possibility of a holy and good being, and indeed only of its possibility, provide the complement.

6893. 1776–78. *Pr* VII.   19: 196

*,[b](Whoever can be content with this satisfaction is the most commendable in his own eyes and those of others, and thus the rule of reason is: one should behave this way, and one always disapproves of the contrary although one apologizes for it.

One approves only of that in which one can have a universally valid satisfaction. Namely, the action of freedom is then considered through reason, i.e., as having arisen from a power of choice, in agreement with itself, which is valid for nature and freedom in general.

Of synthetic principles of the power of choice or the principles of the pure power of choice.)

6898. 1776–78. *Pr* X.   19: 200

The motivating force of the moral concept lies in its purity and its difference from all other impulses. The original *intellectuale* concept is striking only insofar as it is compared to other analogical motivating

---

[a] Kant's footnote is the content of **6893**, which follows.
[b] **6893** is, in its entirety, a footnote to **6892** above.

grounds of honor, happiness, mutual love, and peace of mind and elevated above all others in the comparison. Encomia of virtue and admonitions can be of no value, rather only the development of its concept is. Examples that illuminate the purity of the concept of virtue and an immediate moral aversion are better for education.[93]

6902. 1776–78. *Pr* XI.

19:201

One must not only not cite moral feeling as a *principium*, but must also not, as it were, leave any moral grounds to the decision of feeling, e.g., suicide, nor even any motivating grounds to grounds of feeling, e.g., compassion, aversion. For feeling has no rule, it is also changeable and fickle.

6903. 1776–78. *Pr* XI.

19:201

Of all deviations from the natural judging and motivating force of morals, the most harmful is when one transforms the doctrine of morals into a doctrine of religion or grounds the doctrine of morality on religion. Because then a human abandons the genuine moral disposition, seeks to win the divine favor, to serve it, or to obtain it by fraud, and allows every germ of the good to die under the maxim of fear.

6906. 1776–78? 1769? *Pr* XII.

19:202

That humans are by nature evil is clear from* the fact that they never agree with their idea of the good by themselves and that they must be coerced, as well as that they reciprocally allow themselves to be coerced by each other. Likewise the human being must be disciplined and the wildness taken away. The good conduct of human beings is thus something coerced, and it is not in accord with their nature. It is a principle of civil as well as state prudence that everyone is by nature evil and is only good insofar as he stands under a power that necessitates him to be good. He has, however, the capacity gradually to become good without coercion, if the incentives for good that lie in him are gradually developed. The child grows up evil without discipline. That means: the animal in him proceeds purely from his inclinations and duty from the idea of the good. Even if he is morally evil, he is still physically good.[94]

*(also from the fact that, when united in a political body, they are always violent, selfish, and quarrelsome.)

6907. 1776–78. *Pr* XIII.

19:202

Happiness is twofold: either it is an effect of the free power of choice of a rational being in itself, or it is only a contingent effect externally dependent on nature. Rational beings can create true happiness, which is independent of everything in nature, through actions that are directed to themselves and reciprocally to one another, and without these nature cannot provide genuine happiness. This is the happiness of the world of understanding. Hence the representation of moral perfection also makes one soft-hearted. Namely one sees so much happiness in something which rests merely on the will. I cannot say I want to be so good if others also want to be so; for then it is not possible to attain the end. I must try for my part to attain the model of perfection in a possible good world.

19: 203

Whatever does not depend on merely contingent conditions but on my power of choice is good in itself.

6908. 1776–78. *Pr* XIII.

19: 203

The world has no worth where there are no rational beings by whom it can be used (not merely be intuited); the purely optional use of the world proceeds from the gratification of life. Therefore this, as the natural end for all rational created beings, was also the sole purpose for which a world is good, not merely for enjoyment but also for use. Only the supreme condition for this aim is the good use which they make of themselves and the things of the world.

6909. 1776–78. *Pr* XIII.

19: 203

Everything in nature is good only insofar as it is purposive and nevertheless everything is subordinated to the power of choice. Nature agrees with freedom if the ends of the former encompass the latter.

6910. 1776–78. *Pr* XIII.

19: 203

The necessary laws (which are established *a priori*) of universal happiness are moral laws. They are laws of the free power of choice in general, and its rules necessitate *intellectualiter*; hence, because only these laws and these alone bring happiness into the cause of freedom and thus bring with them the worthiness to be happy, all sensible *stimuli* and *motiva felicitatis*ᵃ *a posteriori* are under them.

The greatest natural ends of a rational being pertain only to rational beings, and hence the enjoyment of sense is far from a genuine part of happiness.

6911. 1776–78. *Pr* XIII.

19: 203

Happiness *a priori* can be placed in no other ground than in the rule of the consensus of the free power of choice. This is a ground of happiness prior to all knowledge of means through experience and a condition of their possibility in all cases. Through it the world pleases the understanding; they are creators of happiness and not its *usurpateurs*.⁹⁵

19: 204

ᵃ stimuli and motives for happiness

19:204 **6913.** 1776–78? 1769? *Pr* XIV.

A human being is worthy not of as much good as he has received but as he has done. Good with regard to himself, good of mere consensus (in accordance with form) or of supplementation (according to matter). Why do actions alone provide worthiness? Why is only freedom and its quality the supreme ground of the good? I believe that actions are themselves also called good because they alone contain reason's condition for happiness in accordance with universal laws. For nature provides no other distribution than one that is determined for particular cases and is thus artificial, namely that of nature modified by the highest being. Blind nature, however, does not have any secure correspondence. Moreover, nature is subordinated to freedom in accordance with its essence, and freedom is, as self-active, lord over everything.

19:209 **6931.** 1776–78. *Pr* 4, in *Obligatio in genere*.

Freedom is 1. independence from external causes. 2. From inclinations: thus the capacity of the rational power of choice [for] either conditioned or unconditioned representations of reason.

What is possible through freedom is practically possible, i.e., moral. (*Later addition*: or pathological. The former is either pragmatic or moral.) Actions from inclinations in cases in which it was possible to act through freedom are also free.

19:209 **6935.** 1776–78. *Pr* 5, in *Obligatio in genere*.

Happiness is itself only conditionally good. Thus actions that occur[a]

19:210 on account of happiness are only mediately good. But the condition is valid for everyone, and the necessity is objective; yet what is agreeable in particular is subjective and has only private validity.

19:211 **6944.** 1776–78? (1772?) *Pr* 6, in *Obligatio in genere*.

Only understanding is necessary for moral judging; for moral willing it is necessary that one actually love the good more than the agreeable; for moral execution it is necessary that one possess strength of the higher will over sensibility.

19:211 **6946.** 1776–78. *Pr* 6–7, in §14, in *Obligatio in genere*.

The law pronounces the obligation to actions but must also determine an effect of them in conformity with obligation, thus also be pragmatic. The obligation is pragmatic; but the pragmatic element does not serve as a motivating ground, but for equilibrium against sensible motivating causes; the pragmatic flows here from the moral.[96]

---

[a] Reading *geschehen* instead of *gesehen*.

6948. 1776–78. *Pr* 7, at §17, in *Obligatio in genere.*   19:211

The pure power of choice is the condition for all others (*conditio sine qua non*), for it is the condition of the possibility of actions from universally valid principles, consequently of the use of reason with regard to freedom and of the determination of this faculty, which is lawless in itself, in accordance with rules.

With regard to ends, nothing can give universal rules of the use of freedom except pure reason.

Categories of the pure power of choice.

6949. 1776–78. *Pr* 7, in §18, in *Obligatio in genere.*   19:212

Since freedom without morality is an isolation of the human being and separation from divine guidance and a determination through natural causes, the ground of the high worth lies [in] the principles through which this freedom is restricted to conditions of fit with oneself and with nature. Whoever does not have this is not worthy of anything good and is the most dangerous and least dignified creature.

6950. 1776–78. *Pr* 8, still in *Obligatio in genere.*   19:212

Morality consists in the relation of free actions with the laws (conditions) of the general will, either of humanity or of human beings. The general will of humanity pertains to the preservation of that which belongs to the essential ends of human nature. The general will of human beings consists in the object or the form of actions through which it becomes independent from every particular inclination. It signifies the will of each and every part, the will that can be directed to each and every one.

6955. 1776–78? (1770–71? 1773–75?) *Pr* 11, at the beginning of §28,   19:213 still in *Obligatio in genere.*

All moral laws must be certain. The *subsumtiones* can be probable.

Probabilism with regard to what is permitted is evil.

6958. 1776–78? (1770–71? 1773–75?) *Pr* 14, still in *Obligatio in genere.*   19:213

Our actions must not be subjected to the incentives and attractions or aversions of sensibility, because these always have a private relation to the useful. The rule of actions through which, if everyone were to act in accordance with it, nature and the human power of choice would universally concur for happiness, is a law of reason and as such signifies morality.

If reason is merely in the service of sense, namely to execute its demands, then we are placed by reason in a greater contradiction with ourselves and with others than are the animals, who are ruled by instinct, which is concordant with their needs, except that reason chooses

19:214 certain objects not according to the totality of sensations but according to delusions raised up by unfounded fantasy. Now since morality is grounded on the idea of universal happiness stemming from free conduct, we are required to bear in mind the cause and government of the world in accordance with an idea, namely the idea that makes everything concordant or procures happiness through a concordant effort directed toward it; because otherwise no reality could be expected from the moral idea and it would be a merely sophistical concept.

Nature must be regarded as an idea that is an archetype in the Creator but in our case is the norm. There can be nothing more enduring or more fundamental as a precept of our actions than to make the idea into the ground in accordance with which we exist, so that we are not otherwise determined through nature and we make our power of choice free, so that with this power of choice we can act in accordance with this idea, because we are, as it were, constituted this way on account of our own preference.

19:214 **6960.** 1776–78? (1770–71? 1773–75?) *Pr* 15, at §34, still in *Obligatio in genere.*

Freedom is a subjective lawlessness. One does not know in accordance with which rule one should judge his own actions or those of other people. Inspirations, curious taste, evil or empty whims can bring forth effects for which one was not prepared. Thus freedom confuses. The whole of nature would be brought into confusion were it not subjected to objective rules, which, however, can be none other than the universal conditions of consensus with nature in general. Hence without moral laws the human being would himself become more contemptible than the animal and more worthy of hatred than it. Whoever does not conduct himself in accordance with objective laws must be compelled in accordance with physical laws.

19:215 **6961.** 1776–78? (1770–71? 1773–75?) *Pr* 15, at §34.

Beyond agreement with nature, the free will must agree with itself with regard to inner and outer independence from impulses. Without morality, folly and contingency rule over the fate of human beings.

19:215 **6962.** 1776–78? (1770–71? 1773–75?) *Pr* 15, at the conclusion of §34 and §35.

The practical condition of reason is that all actions stand under universally valid rules. Freedom in accordance with nature is a lawlessness, thus like a physiological condition, and as such a mere play of inclinations; if, however, it is to be objective, that is, in accordance with reason, then it must have universally valid rules.

6963. 1776–78? (1773–77?) *Pr* 15, at §35, still in *Obligatio in genere.*   19:215
That which is the necessary condition of the consensus of our desires (immanent and transient) among themselves pleases necessarily and is the *principium formale* of all our actions.

6965. 1776–78? (1770–71? 1773–75?) *Pr* 16, still in *Obligatio in genere.*   19:215
The satisfaction in the happiness of the whole is really a longing in accordance with the conditions of reason for one's own happiness. For I cannot hope to be happy if I were to have something special and fate were to have a special relation to me.

6969. 1776–78? (1770–71? 1773–75?) *Pr* 17, still in *Obligatio in genere.*   19:216
The first question is: why does a certain rule-governedness of actions make [one] worthy of happiness?
The second question is: why **ought** we to act so that we become worthy of this happiness if no being is presupposed who distributes happiness in accordance with worthiness?
Since our happiness is only possible through the consensus of the whole with our natural universal will and we could not rule the whole, we would regard the whole as subjected to a universally valid will, which comprehends everything under itself, and the consensus of our will with [*breaks off*]

6971. 1776–78? (1770–71? 1773–75?) *Pr* 17, still in *Obligatio in genere.*   19:216
The happiness that is only possible from the relation of everything in the world to the private will of the person is also possible only (in a whole) in accordance with an idea. In that, however, the private will of everyone must be contained, consequently only a universally valid   19:217 will can provide the ground for the assurance of happiness; hence we either cannot hope to be happy at all, or we must bring our actions into concordance with the universally valid will. For in that case are we alone capable of happiness in accordance with the idea, i.e., the representation of the whole, and since this capability is a consequence of our free will, worthy of it. The extent of our happiness depends on the whole, and our will must be substituted for the *originario*.

6973. 1776–78? (1770–71? 1773–75?) *Pr* 18, still in *Obligatio in genere.*   19:217
Why is the natural universal desire (for happiness) in accordance with its idea under the supreme original will of nature as well as freedom and bound to it as its condition? We represent to ourselves, namely, that that must occur which we would demand in accordance with our impartial power of choice, if others were subject to our will. Their wills would have to agree with each other and with our supreme will. We would

demand that they conduct themselves in conformity with the idea of their existence, that all wills would have unity.

Happiness can only be found in intelligent beings. Freedom is the first *principium* of the contingent. The manner of being happy depends upon the free choice.

19:218 **6975.** 1776–78? (1770–71? 1773–75?) *Pr* 18.

The human being as a being that has understanding must be very dissatisfying in his own eyes if his [*crossed out*: ends] understanding is subject to the inclinations and does not stand under a rule with regard to his end. This rule must be a rule of reason, i.e., *a priori*, and subject the human being to the universally valid end, for only under this condition can his happiness have a rule.

19:218 **6977.** 1776–78? (1770–71? 1773–75?) *Pr* 19, still in *Obligatio in genere*.

The moral ground is the motivating ground of actions from the original ends of rational beings, i.e., those ends through which alone their existence is possible. Everything that contradicts that existence, contradicts those ends[^a] themselves because it is opposed to their *principio essendi*.[^b] If happiness can be only a product of rational beings in regard to one another, then it is their duty or proper function to provide that. They exist in order to take care of the good fortune of others along with their own. The self-active ends constitute an even greater motive. This is because the consensus of wills is a necessary condition of the unity of wills, which is the essential form of the intelligible world.

19:219 **6979.** 1776–78? (1770–71? 1773–75?) *Pr* 19, between §§41 and 42, still in *Obligatio in genere*.

Morality does not say that I should preserve [my] life, but rather that I should preserve that whereby I am alone worthy of living. But I would also not be worthy of life if I threw it away and placed the worth of life beneath the agreeableness of living.

(Not to preserve life, but to preserve that by means of which one is worthy of life, even at the cost of the sacrifice of life. E.g., to confess a scandalous crime under torture.)[^c]

One has only a negative right over life, namely, to allow **unpermitted** means to one's preservation, but not a positive right to use the loss of such a means to preservation as a means.[97]

[^a]: Kant's pronoun *ihnen* could refer either to "rational beings" or "ends" in the previous sentence, but "ends" is closer.
[^b]: principle of existence
[^c]: Presumably Kant means that if one were to confess to a crime one did not commit one would not be worthy of life.

6987. 1776–78? (1769? 1770–71? 1773–75?) *Pr* 22. At the conclusion of   19:220
§48, "*Ama optimum, quantum potes.*"[a]

This is a universal rule of *philosophiae practicae applicatae.*[b] The moral
rule is a rule of the pure will; it pertains to actions for which one may
or may not have an inclination; indeed, it pertains even to a desire to
produce an inclination; thus here it says: seek to produce an inclination for the good. (*Later addition*: Only grounds of adjudication, not of
execution.)

6988. 1776–78? (1769–75?) *Pr* 22, at §49, still in *Obligatio in genere.*   19:220
From moral philosophers one demands:

1. Doctrines of moral judgment, in order to know what is good and
   what is evil, what deserves aversion, and thus grounds for approbation and disapprobation.
2. Grounds of execution, *caussas subjective moventes,*[c] in order that one
   can really love that which one approves and really avert that which
   one finds worthy of aversion.
3. Precepts for how inclination can be made concordant with principles or be subjected to them.

(*Later addition*: In moral instruction, private utility must never be
mentioned in connection with the moral rule; for the mind is thereby
degraded instead of being elevated, inspired, and ennobled, as it would   19:221
be if it followed its duties from the supreme grounds of the essential and
universal good. The mere expression of aversion before a lie makes a
much stronger impression than all the represented disadvantages or the
contempt of others, from whom one can hide, but one cannot escape
from one's own eyes.)[98]

6989. 1776–78. *Pr* 22, at the conclusion of §48.   19:221

Do the good gladly. Seek your happiness [*crossed out*: through freedom]
under the universal conditions [*crossed out*: of freedom] thereof, i.e.,*
those that tend toward [*crossed out*: are valid for] the happiness and the
freedom of everyone, and that are also valid for the essential ends of
nature.

*(The action agrees with yourself and your essential ends.)

Seek your happiness under the condition of a universally valid will
(for yourself as well as for others, and this for the inclination of others
as well as for their power of choice). This rule does not show the way to
happiness, but restricts the effort at it to conditions for being worthy of it,
in that it makes such happiness concordant with the universal system.

---

[a] Love the best as much as you can.
[b] applied practical philosophy
[c] subjectively motivating causes

19:222 **6998.** 1776–78. *Pr* 24–5, in *Coactio moralis.*[99]

One must coerce oneself to prudent and morally good actions. Hence *imperativi*. The reason is that one's power of choice is also sensible, and the first movement stems from the sensible. The more one can coerce oneself through pragmatic coercion, the freer one is. This coercion nevertheless occurs *per stimulos*, but *indirecte*, namely one proceeds in ac-

19:223 cordance with reflection. Moral coercion is external through the power of choice of another; and if we are free from this, inner coercion still remains; that which is not a matter of debt can still be obligatory; whoever does nothing good is not worthy of voluntary goods from others. Whoever does evil is not worthy of being indulged or spared.

19:228 **7021.** 1776–78? 1770–75? *Pr* 30, in *Lex.*[100]

In general, all inclinations provide merely rules of skill at satisfying them. If it is the inclinations that give the ground, then there are no laws at all. Our freedom must stand under laws, consequently not be subjected

19:229 to an inclination for any sort of gratification, for without law no harmony and unity in our actions is possible at all through mere inclination.

19:230 **7027.** 1776–78? 1770–71? 1773–75? *Pr* 31, still in *Lex.*

The empirical grounds of our choice have no certainty because they have no universal guideline and thus contradictions can occur among them. The rule of their agreement: unity in a whole is supreme. The most extreme dissatisfaction is if everything is left merely to the senses and one does not find any rule of reason.

19:230 **7029.** 1776–78? 1770–71? 1773–75? *Pr* 31, still in *Lex.*

Reason alone can provide no end, also no incentives; it is reason, however, which limits all ends without distinction, so that they stand under a single common rule. Reason alone determines the conditions under which the free power of choice stands under a self-sufficient rule. For drives, taste, and inclinations have no consensus and require a rule.

Reason here creates a satisfaction *a priori*, i.e., one that occurs even when the object is not compared with my inclination or the satisfaction of my drives, because in this case my inclinations in general are included under the universal. That this consideration of satisfaction *a priori* or in the universal has primacy rests upon the following: because the *principium* of order and form is essentially necessary and comes first, without this there is no interconnection among my private gratifications, nor between them and those of others. The regulative comes first, and nothing must contradict it; otherwise there is no interconnection in the manifold, no security. Everything is tumultuous. Satisfaction *a priori* subsists with that

19:231 which brings an order to everything that may please, in order to make it thereby into a whole.

7038. 1776–78? 1780–89? *Pr* 31, at §65 and the first half of §66, still in   19:232
Lex.[101]

Division. All duties are either **external**: toward other human beings, or **internal**: namely not toward other human beings (which thus cannot be demanded or required of other human beings). Both are either passive or active. Passive [*crossed out*: external] duties are those through the power of choice of another. Active: without regarding them as determined through the power of choice of another. Active external duties are free duties, passive ones are coercible duties toward humans. Active internal duty is duty toward oneself. Passive internal duty is duty toward the universal legislator. All our duties regarding God are passive. If I abstract from these, then duties of indebtedness, of merit, and of decency still remain. Moral decency is what is in accord with the dignity of a rational being. Toward God we have none but passive duties, not just moral but also physical (we cannot have an effect on God).[102] Our active obligations toward other humans are meritorious, toward ourselves, however, owed but not coercible duties. Thus the latter are duties owed toward others.

7040. 1776–78? (1772?) *Pr* 33, at §69, still in *Lex.*   19:233
*The universal will provides the law, since without it freedom taken as a whole is lawlessness and thus without a rule, hence reason can determine nothing with regard to action.

We need a universal and supreme will even with regard to ourselves, since otherwise the manifold of inclinations would have no *a priori* rule The will, however, is [*breaks off*]
*(But this universal rule is the universal *Hypothesis* under which the will of the human being can only be good.)

7042. 1776–78. *Pr* 37, at §74, still in *Lex.*   19:233
There must be no talk of moral feeling in the case of judgment (it is not a matter of sense, but of choice), but only in the case of actions or participation.

Intuition, sense, and feeling comprise the entirety of sensibility.

7049. 1776–78. *Pr* 39, in *Iuris peritia.*   19:235
There are two grounds of satisfaction in actions: 1. Correspondence with the object of desire; 2. The correspondence of free actions with a rule for satisfaction in general, i.e., with a universally valid ground, consequently also correspondence of all free actions with each other. The latter is the *principium regulativum*, the former the *constitutivum* of all uses of freedom.[103] The *principia* of the first are empirical, and the use of freedom does not agree with other uses of it. The satisfaction in the conformity of all our actions to rules is the greatest.

The worthiness to be happy is the possibility of being granted happiness in conformity with universal law.

19:235 **7050. 1776–78. *Pr* 40, in *Iuris peritia*.**[104]

Of the duties of human beings with regard to actions: *Jus.*[a] With regard to dispositions, i.e., the motivating grounds for accomplishing those duties: *Ethica*. The motivating ground in the latter is internal, in the former, coercion. *Officia actionum secundum literam vel secundum animam* (dispositions), *haec in Ethica.*[b] The duty of dispositions is moral. All morality rests on dispositions. If I also perform an obligatory action, though not from the impulse of coercion but instead from dispositions, thus *actionem spontaneam,*[c] then it is ethically good.[105]

Dispositions rest on the inner goodness (necessity) of action, duties of coercion on outer necessity. The former: that one deserves to be coerced to that action; the latter: that a coercion to that action can be provided and is rightful.

19:235 **7052. 1776–78. *Pr* 41, in *Iuris peritia*.**

Everything is permitted which taken generally does not contradict the power of choice, consequently is not opposed to the universality of the power of choice.

19:236 What is necessary in accordance with the idea of the common power of choice is necessary *a priori* and thus also permitted. Now coercion of that which is necessary through the universal will is not opposed to any power of choice and is thus permitted. The particular authorization to coerce is granted through the common power of choice. For a particular will yields no authorization, since it can conflict with the wills of others.[106]

19:236 **7054. 1776–78. *Pr* 42, still in *Iuris peritia*.**

The practical laws from the mere idea of freedom are moral.

Those from the idea of inner freedom pertain to all actions and are ethical; those merely from the idea of outer freedom are [*crossed out*: moral] juridical and pertain merely to outer actions.

19:237 **7058. 1776–78. *Pr* 41.**[107]

There is no determinate rule of ends other than the universal validity of the ends of nature and of the ends of human beings, i.e., from the whole of nature and from the ends of human beings. The relation to happiness

---

[a] justice or right; the Latin equivalent of *Recht*

[b] Duties for actions in accordance with the letter or in accordance with the spirit (dispositions), the latter in ethics.

[c] as a spontaneous action

from the personal actions of human beings with regard to nature as well as to each other is thereby brought under determinate principles. He is worthy of happiness whose free actions are directed toward consensus with the universal grounds of free actions, who is thus capable of this from his own action. From the idea of the whole, the happiness of each member is determined.

The universal end of human beings is happiness; that which prepares them in practice for happiness is skill; that which directs skill is prudence; and that, finally, which restricts and directs prudence is morality.

7063. 1776–78. *Pr* 49, in §87, in *Principia iuris.*   19:240

In pragmatic doctrines freedom is, to be sure, under [*crossed out*: doctrines] rules, but not laws. For the rule prescribes the conditions under which a desired end can be attained. The law, however, determines freedom unconditionally.

Laws of **freedom in general** are those that contain the conditions under which alone it is possible for them to agree with themselves: conditions of unity in the use of freedom in general. They are thus laws of reason and not empirical or arbitrary, but contain absolute practical necessity. Rules of freedom in general are laws for contingent commands. The free will that agrees with itself in accordance with universal laws of freedom is an absolutely good will.

7064. 1776–78? 1772? *Pr* 49, at §88, in *Principia iuris.*   19:240

The *principium* of morality is internal, and [if] the [*crossed out*: lawfulness] incentives of actions is this very same *principium*, then the actions are ethically good; or the incentive is not internal to the *principio*, and then the action is juridically good. One can therefore act lawfully from principles or from coercion: because one wants[a] to or because one must.

7065. 1776–78. *Pr* 49, in §88, in *Principia iuris.*   19:240

Lawfulness from principles.
Lawfulness with coercion in the case of a lack of principles.
Lawfulness of subjection under universal coercion.
1. Inner freedom under inner laws.
2. Outer freedom under inner laws.
3. Outer freedom under outer laws.
Freedom under natural laws is impossible. For freedom and nature are opposed to one another, hence the laws are not physical but practical, not what happens but what ought to happen. Second: not conditioned freedom but freedom in general without condition, merely as   19:241
freedom in contrast to problematically or pragmatically conditioned free actions.

[a] *will*

19:241 **7067.** 1776–78? 1769? *Pr* 54, at §93, still in *Principia iuris*.

One can act unjustly toward another merely *materialiter* (*damnum*)[a] or merely *formaliter* (e.g., a non-damaging lie) or both together: *laesio*.[b]

"You should keep your promise" is a rule of the matter of right. "You should not make a promise with the intention of breaking it" is a rule of form. The latter is much greater.

Hence the use of poison in warfare is injustice *formaliter*, even though it does not contradict the right of the enemy.

19:246 **7089.** 1776–78? 1769? *Pr* 61, in *Legislator*.

God does **not make** (he gives) the moral laws or obligation, but only says that they are the conditions of his goodly will. To this extent the latter is holy and in execution just.

19:247 **7092.** 1776–78? 1772? *Pr* 62, in *Legislator*.

God is not the author of the moral law through his will, rather the divine will is the moral law, namely the archetype of the most perfect will and also the *principium* of all conditions for determining our wills [*crossed out*: in accordance with these laws, namely of happiness] in unison with his will, consequently all conditions of a necessary consensus; consequently there is a necessary unity of the subordination of our will under the divine will, but among creatures there is only a contingent unity of two wills.[108]

He also has *potestatum exsecutivam*.[c]

A *legislator, cujus tantum vis executoria obligat*, is *despotes*.[d]

19:247 **7093.** 1776–78? 1769? *Pr* 62.

A human being cannot hope to become happy where he does not become a better human being. The wish for happiness and for forgiveness is selfish, the wish for improvement is a moral wish. Only the moral wish is worthy of a hearing. It is impertinent to pray for happiness or even for release from punishment if one is not a better human being. This treats the divine will not as holy but as a self-centered and despotic will, which does not respect laws of inner decency and listens only to ingratiation. We can, however, expect benevolent assistance with regard to the improvement of our will if we, insofar as it lies within our power, act and conduct ourselves with humility toward the holy law from which we nonetheless stand so far away. Whoever utters supplications in this

---

[a] a loss

[b] an injury or harm

[c] executive power

[d] A legislator who obligates through such executive power is a despot.

manner is not thereby a better human being. A murderer who out of pity   19:248
spares a human being who had fainted was good in that moment.[109]

7170. 1776–78. *Pr* 112, at §168, in *Gradus Imputabilitatis*.   19:262

Moral incapacity. We are incapable of becoming good by ourselves;*   19:263
because for that end we must already be good. But we are capable of
doing each single good thing; because for that it is not necessary that
one be good, but rather one [can] do it from coercion. It is possible for me
to take each particular step in the straight line from the point where I am
to the goal (for I always have new vantage points). But it is not possible
for me to take all the steps in such a way. It is possible in each throw of
the dice that I roll a six, and just as possible as every other result; but it
is not possible for me always to roll a six, because that would require a
ground of necessity. Thus in order to be good a ground of necessity and
not just of possibility is required. The mere possibility combined with
the possibility of the opposite makes it impossible that it always happens
(that would not be contingency).[110]

*(The goodness of the will has its measure in nature like the perfection
of talent.)

V.

NOTES FROM THE 1780S

7196. 1780–89? 1773–78? *LBl* M8.   19:270

Virtue would produce happinesss if it were universally practiced; but
this happiness is not worth as much as virtue, and the latter has its inner
worth without the former.

Freedom is a creative capacity. The good resulting from freedom is
thus original.

The lawfulness of freedom, however, is the highest condition of the
good, and its lawlessness the true and absolute evil, the creation of evil.
The latter must thus already displease reason absolutely and without
restriction, and this displeasure must be greater than displeasure at ills
or mishaps.

Legality consists in correspondence with the universally valid power
of choice, insofar as we are determining or determinable.

7197. 1780–89? 1773–77? 1776–79? (1790–1804??) *LBl* E 62.   19:270
P. I

Morality is the inner lawfulness of freedom, namely insofar as it is a
law to itself. If we abstract from all inclination, then the conditions under
which alone freedom can agree with itself remain [:] 1. that the use of
freedom harmonize under a universally valid law with the determination
of one's own nature, 2. with the ends of others insofar as they harmonize

19:271

into a whole, 3. with [*crossed out*: the power of choice] the freedom of others in general. This perfection of freedom is the condition under which the [*crossed out*: good] perfection of all others and the happiness of a rational being must be universally satisfying (worthiness), and is all that remains if the objects of our current inclination have all become indifferent to us.[111]

The conditions of the sensible world as appearance are not at the same time conditions of the world of the understanding;[a] although the world of sense is without limits and thus its totality is not determinable, it is nonetheless not the world of the understanding, etc. Although all change of appearances in others is determined, nonetheless actions of the understanding are not determined through appearances and do not belong in the chain.

Duty toward human beings: 1. as members of nature, 2. as proprietor (*proprietarius*) *dominus potentialis*,[b] 3. as citizen. The happiness of others is important and valuable to us, but their property is holy. Propriety with regard to everything that belongs to substance is *dominium*. Thus the human being is *dominus a natura designatus*.[c]

19:272

7199. 1780–89? 1776–79?? *LBl* E 61.
P. I

Toward practical philosophy.

The first and most important observation that a human being makes about himself is that, determined through nature, he is to be the author of his happiness and even of his own inclinations and aptitudes, which make this happiness possible.[112] He concludes from this that he has to order his actions not in accordance with instinct but in accordance with concepts of his happiness which he himself makes, [and] that the greatest concern which he has for himself here would be either that he forms his concept falsely or allows himself to deviate from it through animal sensibility, above all from a propensity to act habitually in opposition to his concepts. As a freely acting being, indeed in accordance with this independence and self-rule, he will thus have as his foremost object that his desires agree with one another and with his concept of happiness, and not with instincts; and the conduct befitting the freedom of a rational being consists in this form. First, his action will have to be arranged in accordance with the universal end of humanity in his own person and thus in acccordance with concepts and not instincts, so that the latter will

---

[a] Kant apparently began to write *intelligibel Welt* but altered it to *Verstandeswelt*.
[b] potential proprietor of a dominion
[c] designated as a lord or proprietor by nature. The remainder of this note deals with passion and affect, and is here omitted.

agree with one another because they agree with the universal, namely with nature. Thus the motivating ground of a rational being should not be empirical self-love, because this proceeds from the individuals to all, but rational self-love, which obtains the rule for the individual from and through the universal. In this way he becomes aware that his happiness depends on the freedom of other rational beings, [P. II] and that it would not agree with self-love for each and everyone to have just himself as his object, thus his own happiness [must come] from concepts and be restricted through the conditions that he be the author of universal happiness or at least not contradict others being the authors of their own happiness.[113]   19: 273

[*crossed out*: True] Morality consists in the laws of the production of true happiness from freedom in general. Thus, in the beginning, when the will is directed only toward satisfaction of instincts and well-being, everything evil develops precisely from freedom, when the human being is not to be ruled by instinct, which nonetheless has a wise author. Freedom can only be determined in accordance with rules of a universally valid will, because otherwise it would be without any rule.

(Causality. The property of (pure) freedom through which it is itself the cause of happiness; it is however the cause of happiness through the agreement of a general power of choice.[a] The inner good nature of the will. The will that agrees with the general will is good in itself.)[b]

7200. 1780–89? *LBl* E 64.   19: 274

Worthiness to be happy.

Principles of morals through the concordance of freedom with the necessary conditions of happiness in general, i.e., through the universal self-active *principio* of happiness.

If freedom, without regard to the state in which the free being is found, hence independent of empirical conditions (impulses), is to be a necessary cause of happiness, then freedom must 1. determine the power of choice through principles. 2. through principles of unity not only with one's own person but also with regard to community with others, because freedom that does not agree externally in accordance with universal laws hinders itself in happiness, but freedom that is in agreement thoroughly promotes happiness.

Principles of the unity of all ends in general (prior to any empirical conditions of ends). Hence principles of pure reason.

The *imperativi* of morality contain the restricting conditions for all imperatives of prudence. One is permitted to seek happiness only under

---

[a] *allgemeiner Willkür.* Kant usually writes *allgemeine Wille* to indicate the general will.
[b] The remainder of this note, concerning the political and domestic value of religious observance, is omitted here.

the conditions under which alone one can be worthy of it, i.e., necessarily would partake of it, since happiness is something universal in the satisfaction of ends. Otherwise it is mere gratification. Hence pathologically or practically necessary.

7201. 1780–89. *LBl* G 9.

[*Crossed out*: It is indeed an undertaking worthy of effort: whether that which one professes to know, especially to know *a priori*, could be the object of a science at all; because it would be absurd to want to talk in such cases of probabilities and even further of some probabilities as being as good as certain, where one abandons the law of experience and ventures with ideas into an endless field of mere possibilities, which have nothing in common with objects of experience, and from which judgment thus cannot more or less approach the laws of experience.][114]

The faculty of desire, insofar as it is determinable under the representation of a rule, is called the will. If the rule is considered as the immediate determining ground of the will, then the determination of the will through this rule is objective obligation, i.e., considered through reason; when it includes only the universal in the connection of another determining ground with the will, then the determination of the will in accordance with this rule (objectively) through reason is pragmatic necessitation. Both are imperatives. If the determining ground, differentiated from the rule, is seen merely as a possible object of the faculty of desire, then this determining ground is not a determining ground of the will through reason at all but merely a determining ground of action as means, and the desire determines the will. This is the formal practical necessitation.

The critique of practical reason has as its basis the differentiation of empirically conditioned practical reason from the pure and yet practical reason and asks whether there is such a thing as the latter. The critique cannot have insight into this possibility *a priori* because it concerns the relation of a real ground to a consequence, thus something must be given which can arise from it alone; and from reality possibility can be inferred. The moral laws are of this sort, and this must be proven in the same way we proved the representations of space and time as *a priori* representations, only with the difference that the latter concern intuitions but the former mere concepts of reason. The only difference is that in theoretical knowledge the concepts have no meaning and the principles no use except with regard to objects of experience, while in the practical, by contrast, they have much wider use, namely they apply to all rational beings in general and are independent of all empirical deter-

mining grounds, indeed, even if no object of experience corresponds to them, the mere manner of thinking and the disposition in accordance with principles already suffice.

7202. 1780–89. *LBl* Duisburg 6.   19:276
P. I

We take satisfaction in things that stir our senses because they affect our subject harmoniously and allow us to feel our unhindered life or animation. We see, however, that the cause of this satisfaction lies not in the object but in the individual or also specific constitution of our subject, hence it is not necessarily and universally valid: on the contrary, the laws that bring the freedom of choice regarding everything that pleases into consensus with itself contain the ground of a necessary satisfaction for every rational being that has a faculty of desire; for this reason the good in accordance with these laws cannot be indifferent to us, like, say, beauty; we must also have a satisfaction in the existence of the good because it agrees universally with happiness, hence also with my interest.

The matter of happiness is sensible, but its form of happiness is intellectual:[115] now the latter is not possible except as freedom under *a priori* laws of its consensus with itself, and this is indeed not to make happiness actual but only for its possibility and its idea. For happiness consists in well-being insofar as it is not externally contingent, also not empirically dependent, but rests on our own choice. This choice must determine and not depend on determination by nature. That, however, is nothing other than well-ordered freedom.

Only he is capable of being happy whose use of his power of choice is not contrary to the *datis* of happiness that nature gives him. This property of the free power of choice is the *conditio sine qua non* of happiness. Happiness is really not the greatest sum of gratifications but the pleasure of being satisfied by the consciousness of one's own power, at least this is the essential formal condition of happiness, although still other material   19:277
conditions (as with experience) are required.

The function of the *a priori* unity of all the elements of happiness is the necessary condition of its possibility and its essence. *A priori* unity, however, is freedom under universal laws of the power of choice, i.e., morality. This makes happiness as such possible and does not depend on happiness as the end, and is itself the original form of happiness, in which one can very well do without comforts and on the contrary can even accept many of life's troubles without reduction of satisfaction, indeed even with an elevation of it.

Finding one's state agreeable depends on luck, but rejoicing over what is agreeable in this state, as happiness, is not befitting its value; on the contrary, happiness must originate in an *a priori* ground of which reason approves. To be miserable is not the necessary consequence of life's troubles.

No complete satisfaction can be found for the senses, it cannot even be determined with certainty and universality what the requirements for this would be; the senses always increase their demands and are dissatisfied, without being able to say what would be enough for them.[116] Even less is the possession of these pleasures certain, due to the variability of luck and the contingency of favorable circumstances and the brevity of life. But the disposition educated by reason to make good and concordant use of all the material for well-being, [is] certain *a priori*, allows itself to be fully known, and belongs to us, so that even death itself, as a passive state, does not diminish its worth.

P. II

It is true that virtue has the advantage that it would bring forth the greatest [*crossed out*: happiness] welfare from that which nature offers. But virtue's higher worth does not consist in serving as it were as a means. That we are ourselves the ones who as its authors produce virtue regardless of the empirical conditions (which can provide only particular rules of life), that virtue brings **self-satisfaction** with itself, that is, its inner worth.[117]

19:278 A certain basis (capital, property) of satisfaction is necessary, which no one must lack and without which no happiness is possible, the rest is accidental (*reditus fortuiti* [a]). This basis is self-satisfaction (as it were *apperceptio iucunda primitiva* [b]). Consequently it must depend neither on a gift of nature nor on luck and accident, for by themselves these do not have to agree with our essential and highest ends. Since satisfaction must necessarily and universally cohere with these ends – hence *a priori* and not merely according to empirical laws which are never apodictically certain – then satisfaction must 1. depend on the free power of choice, so that we can ourselves make it in accordance with the idea of the highest good. 2. This freedom must indeed be independence from sensible necessitation, but yet not without any law. Thus since no still higher motivating ground and higher good is to be given, then it must consist in freedom in accordance with laws, in a thoroughgoing agreement with itself, which will then constitute the worth and the value of the person.

In consciousness the human being has cause to be satisfied with himself. He has the receptivity for all happiness, the capacity to be satisfied even without the comforts of life and to make himself happy. This is the intellectual aspect of happiness.

In this basis there is nothing real, no gratification other than the matter of happiness, but nevertheless there is the formal condition of unity, which is essential to it, and without which our self-contempt would take away what is essential for the value of life, namely the value of the person. The person exists as a spontaneity of well-being.

The good of life or happiness: either as it appears or as it is. The latter is represented through moral categories which, however, do not refer to

[a] a product of luck
[b] an original agreeable perception

special objects, but to those of life and the world, in order to determine their unity in a unique possible empirical happiness. In themselves they do not represent anything good but merely the form of freedom, the empirical *data* to be used for the true and independent good.

(Happiness is not something felt but thought. It is also not a thought that can be taken from experience but one which first of all makes experience possible. But not as if one could in this way know happiness in all of its elements, rather the *a priori* condition under which alone one can be capable of happiness.

19:279

All of our actions that are aimed at empirical happiness must be in accord with this rule, otherwise there will be no unity in them, which [*breaks off*])

P. III

A human being of such moral dispositions is worthy of being happy, i.e., to come into possession of all the means by which he can bring about his own happiness and that of others.

In order, however, for morality to please above all else and absolutely, it is necessary that it please not from the viewpoint of individual and private suitability, but from a universal *a priori* point of view, i.e., for pure reason, precisely because pure reason is universally necessary for happiness and also worthy of it. Nevertheless pure reason does not gratify, since it does not promise the empirical aspect of happiness; it thus contains in itself no incentives; for that empirical conditions, namely satisfaction of needs, are always required.

Morality is the idea of freedom as a principle of happiness (regulative principle of [*crossed out*: freedom] happiness *a priori*). Hence the laws of freedom must contain the formal condition of happiness *a priori* independent from the aim of one's own happiness.

I hear a prohibition: you should not lie! and why not? because it is harmful for you yourself, that is, it contradicts your own happiness (Epicurus). But I am prudent enough to stick with the truth in all cases where it brings me advantage, yet also to make exceptions to the rule where the lie can be useful to me. But your lie is opposed to the universal happiness! What does it concern me, I answer, let each care for his own. – But this happiness lies near to your own heart, or else you find in yourself an aversion to this lie (Stoics).[118] About that, I answer, I alone can judge. Perhaps others are of such a tender taste that to utter a lie upsets their inmost being, but it is otherwise with me; I laugh when I am able to outwit someone, especially with such deliberateness that it will not be discovered. Your feeling may decide for you, but you cannot make it into a law for me. But, says a third, you may now shun or embrace the lie neither as harmful to you nor as despicable in itself, yet you are not free to do what you wish. – See above you the highest good, which in its idea, which your reason can intuit, rejects the lie along with the person

19:280

who produced it, and disqualifies that person from happiness. Platonist. Whence do you know the idea of this highest being? I do not recall ever having been acquainted with such an idea. Are these ideas not perhaps contingent products of education into established customs? And whence do you know that such a highest being, which you are acquainted with through reason, would abhor the lie because the lie is in itself worthy of abhorrence – but that is just what I doubt and regarding which you have not been able to take away my doubt.

(The doctrinal concept of morality from the principle of the pure power of choice.

This is the principle of self-satisfaction *a priori* as the formal condition of all happiness (parallel with apperception).

The first thing that a human must do is to bring freedom under laws of unity; for without this his actions and omissions are nothing but confusion.*a*

Give a human of great understanding all the means for happiness ready to hand, the impulses will still carry on their game with him and pull the understanding into their neighborhood –)

P. IV

After I have turned away in this manner from all alien attempts at persuasion, I turn back to myself and, notwithstanding that I remain free to conceal it from others and that no one could give me convincing proofs about it, find in myself a principle of disapprobation and of inextinguishable inner aversion, which may occasionally be outweighed by opposing inducements but can never be exterminated. On what does this disapprobation rest? Is it immediate feeling of shamefulness, is it hidden reflection on harmfulness, is it fear of an invisible judge? for it cannot be habit, since habit would not be universal and unconquerable.

19:281

Since the question is whether my freedom in this point is restricted by nothing, I suspect a ground for the solution to this question that would apply not merely to this case but to freedom in general. Freedom is in itself an ability to act and to refrain from action independently of empirical grounds.[119] Thus there can be no grounds that would have weight to determine us empirically in all such cases. The question is thus: how may I utilize my freedom in general? I am free, however, only from the coercion of sensibility, but I cannot at the same time be free from restricting laws of reason; for precisely because I am free from the former I must be subject to the latter, since otherwise I could not speak of my own will. Now this same unrestraint through which I can will what is itself contrary to my will, and because of which I have no secure basis to rely on myself, must be displeasing to me to the highest degree, and a law will have to become known as necessary *a priori*, in

---

a *Verwirrung* (confusion) could also be *Verirrung* (aberration, error).

accordance with which freedom is restricted by conditions under which the will agrees with itself. I cannot renounce this law without contradicting my reason, which alone can establish practical unity of the will in accordance with principles. These laws determine a will that one can call the pure will, which precedes everything empirical, and they determine a pure practical good, which is the highest although only formal good, since this good is created by us ourselves, hence is in our power, and also makes possible everything empirical, insofar as it lies in our power, in accordance with unity with regard to the complete good, namely one of pure happiness. No action must contradict this rule; for then it would conflict with the principle of self-satisfaction, which is the condition of all happiness, whether it arises *a posteriori* or lies *a priori* in our way of thinking, whether it concerns others or ourselves. This constitution of the free power of choice determines the personal and absolute worth of a human being. The remainder of what is internal to him determines only his conditional worth, insofar as he makes good use of his own talents.[120] And he is worthy of the means for happiness only to that extent (for happiness is a product of the individual human reason), 19: 282 because he can agree with rational concepts of happiness only according to these laws.

But in what does this moral law consist? [1.] In the correspondence of natural desires with one's own nature.

2. in the correspondence of discretionary and contingent desires with nature and with one another; consequently in the idea of a universal will and in the conditions under which such a will, which contains and restricts every particular will under itself, is possible.

Without this unity, freedom must be in our own eyes the greatest ill, and we would have cause to be instinctive and hence irrational animals.[121] With this unity, freedom is the greatest and actually the absolute good in all relations.

The idea of the general will hypostatized is the highest self-sufficient good, which is at the same time the sufficient source of all happiness: the ideal of God.

Practical laws either from concepts or from experience. The former are either pure concepts or empirical. Pure practical laws are either analytic or synthetic. How are the latter possible?

7203. 1780–89. *Pr* VII–VIII.   19: 282
Philosophy: 1. theoretical: theory of knowledge[a] and theory of taste; 2. practical: *a posteriori* theory of happiness; *a priori* moral theory.[b]

---

[a] *Erkenntnislehre*
[b] *Sittenlehre*

Logic, aesthetics, and practical philosophy (insofar as they [have] *principia a priori*).[122] Of objects: metaphysics and morality.

Cognition, feeling, desire. Understanding, taste, and will have *a priori* cognitions. Logic, aesthetics, morality.

19:283   Nature and freedom. Morality teaches the objective conditions of conduct, anthropology the subjective ones.

Moral theory of the highest good.

19:283   **7204.** 1780–89? 1776–78? *Pr* 126–7.

The foremost problem of morals is this: Reason shows that the [*crossed out*: universal] thoroughgoing unity of all ends of a rational being with regard both to himself as well as to others, hence formal unity in the use of our freedom, i.e., morality, would, if it were practiced by everyone, produce happiness through freedom and would derive the particular from the universal, and, conversely, that should the universal power of choice determine every particular one, it could act in accordance with none but moral principles. At the same time it is clear, however, that if only one were to subject himself to this rule without being certain that others would also do likewise, his happiness would not be obtained in this way.[123] Now the question arises, what is left to determine the will of every (right-thinking) person to subject himself to this rule as inviolable:* happiness in accordance with the order of eternal Providence, or the mere worthiness to be happy (in accordance with the judgment of all that he did as much as he could to contribute to the happiness of all), or the mere idea of the unity of reason in the use of freedom[?] This last ground is not to be valued lightly. For self-determination from principles alone gives a ground of unity to the precognition of all actions, and, since reason as a determining cause independent of all time and condition of sensibility is aimed at the entire existence of the rational being, so this is a *principium* of free actions in relation to eternal duration. If, however, humans were to live eternally, then this good conduct would also create happiness.[124] The self-contentment of reason also recompenses the losses of the senses.[125]

19:284   Just as the identity of apperception is a *principium* of *a priori synthesis* for all possible experience, so is the identity of my volition in accordance with form a *principium* of happiness from myself, by means of which all self-contentment is determined *a priori*.

Only when I act in accordance with *a priori* principles can I always be constant in the manner of my ends, inner and outer. Empirical conditions create differences.

(Transcendental unity in the use of freedom.)

*(How can this *a priori principium* of the universal agreement of freedom with itself interest me?[126] Freedom in accordance with principles of empirical ends has no thoroughgoing consensus with itself;

from this I cannot represent anything reliable with regard to myself. It is not a unity of my will. Hence restricting conditions on the use of the will are absolutely necessary. Morality from the *principio* of unity. From the principle of truth. That one complies with one's *principium* that one can publicly avow, which is thus valid for everyone. Perfection in regard to form: the [*crossed out*: universal] agreement of freedom with the essential conditions of all ends, i.e., *a priori* purposiveness.)

7205. 1780–89? 1776–78? *Pr* 133.　　　　　　　　　　　19:284

　　Morality is the science that contains the principles of the unity of all possible ends of rational beings *a priori*. 1. Conditions of this unity. 2. Practical necessity of this unity. The unity is pragmatically (empirically) determined from the concepts of happiness. It is determined rationally from this happiness insofar as it is merely an effect of freedom.

7209. 1780–89? 1776–78? *Pr* IV.[127]　　　　　　　　　　19:285

Principles of obligation

Besides the subjective laws through which actions occur, there are objective laws of freedom and reason that contain conditions of possible good actions and thus say what ought to happen. These are imperatives. Imperatives necessitate freedom through grounds of rational preference, thus through itself. An action, however, is necessary in two ways: either because I will something else as a means for my own volition, or from the nature of the power of choice itself. The first either as a means to a merely possible and contingent end, the second as a means to a subjectively necessary end. The first imperatives are problematic, the second pragmatic (the former: skill in relation to problems; the second: prudence, which relates to each one's own happiness). There are also, however, objective laws, which freedom determines or restricts from itself, consequently immediately. These necessitations are called obligations. They can rest on nothing other than freedom insofar as it agrees with itself in regard to all ends in general. 1. Freedom as a *principio* with regard to one's 　19:286 own person, which is restricted through the conditions of personality, so that freedom does not contradict the humanity in one's own person. (duties toward oneself.) 2. Freedom as a *principio* of universal happiness, i.e., agreement with all private inclinations in accordance with a rule. (goodness toward others.)

7210. 1780–89? 1776–78? 1790–1804? *Pr* IV.　　　　　　　19:286

　　The greatest perfection is the free power of choice, and the greatest good can also arise from it, and from rulelessness the greatest evil. Thus the essential condition is the subjection of the free power of choice under rules of its **reciprocal** use, namely how it relates back to freedom. (Second, the restriction of freedom through nature, third, its efficacy for the ends of both.)*a*

I leave the ends of others undetermined. Only I do not hinder anyone from trying to make himself as happy as he can in accordance with his own will, just as long as he does not contradict my power of choice. A negative (restricting) law of freedom is the essential *conditio sine qua non* with regard to others. Negative conditions are essential.

19:286 **7211.** 1780–89? 1776–78? 1790–1804? *Pr* IV.

Morality is the practical universal condition of happiness, and it is a system of happiness from the freedom to make oneself worthy of happiness; threefold unity of the power of choice from threefold universality:

1. Unconditional universality toward everyone and all times.
2. Conditioned universality in accordance with the measure of one's capacity and of one's own happiness with respect to one or another.
3. Collective universality toward the *universalitatem* (this is something individual).

19:287 **7212.** 1780–89? 1776–78? *Pr* VI.

There must be rules for the use of freedom in general, which precede sensory impulses. These rules point toward a freedom in conformity with rules, which is therefore in conformity with the conditions under which alone freedom can be a good. Injury to this cannot be compensated by any good; the dominion of reason ceases and its use in accordance with sensory inducements is unreliable. That is not true freedom where the *principium* alone, independent of the senses, does not give a law.

19:288 **7217.** 1780–89? 1776–78? *Pr* VII–VIII.

The *empiricism*[b] of morality proves only that no one approves of a lie; *rationalism*, however, that no one can approve it,* and indeed for itself alone; hence only in the latter case are moral imperatives apodictic. The cause is: because a freedom without rule taken as universal authorization contradicts itself. The system is thus a rational system of freedom in universal consensus with itself.[128]

Since the good will contains the worthiness to be happy, it cannot be good because it aims at its own good nor simply at the happiness of others, since their happiness is not always good.

---

a This addition is in the margin near the beginning of the note, and it is not clear where it should go.
b Kant writes *empirism* in Latin rather than German script.

Freedom is the greatest good and the greatest ill.[129] The rules of freedom must therefore be the most important. This is confirmed in the following way: that only a good will is good in itself. Even in the case of the highest being the good will is itself the condition on account of which we will the remaining properties.[130]

*(This disapprobation is not unrest but censure, and occurs by means of judgment from the universal power of choice. It occurs without relation to a private final end, thus merely through reason. Here reason is thus the *principium* of constitutive or objective principles. And whatever does not agree with the rational principles of freedom is objectively (practically) impossible. Otherwise rational principles have only subjective validity. The cause: since freedom is an ability to act *a priori*.

7220. 1780–89? (1776–79?) *Pr* 11, with reference to the chapter title   19:289
"*Obligatio*" on *Pr* 4.

One represents freedom, i.e., a power of choice that is independent of instincts or in general of direction by nature. So freedom is in itself a rulelessness and the source of all ill and all disorder where it is not itself a rule. Freedom must accordingly stand under the condition of universal conformity to rules and must be an intelligent freedom, otherwise it is blind or wild.[131]

Whatever the *principium* of the rules for the use of freedom in general is, is moral.

Taste is the *principium* of the rules of sensation, be it for sense or for apperception, or even more satisfaction in the rule-governedness of the sensation of objects or apperception. The rule can concern the concordance of representations with one another or merely with the subject; in the latter case it is feeling.[132]

7229. 1780–89. *Pr* 12, in *Obligatio*.   19:290

All obligation rests on the form of maxims; its matter cannot be made into a universal rule, for it is arbitrary. Even the concept of perfection, if this is to signify a reality or even merely the *consensus* of the many in one, presupposes a feeling of satisfaction.[133] The will as free, however, must be determined, consequently only insofar as it can serve as a rule for all willing.

7242. 1780–89. *Pr* 21, at §48, in *Obligatio*.   19:293

All principles of morality are either those of the will that obeys natural influences and administers law or of the will that is self-legislating. The former is the principle of happiness, the latter of worthiness to be happy. The former is the principle of self-love (benevolence toward oneself), the latter of self-esteem (i.e., satisfaction with oneself). The former is the principle of the worth of [one's] state in the eyes of the person, the latter of the worth of the person herself and even of her existence in the judgment of practical reason in general. The former in accordance with the judgment of one who strives for happiness, the latter in the judgment of a reason that distributes happiness universally. The former places the supreme condition of the highest good in that which is dependent upon contingencies, the latter in that which is always in our control. The former requires much experience and prudence for its application; the latter nothing more than to make one's will universal and to see whether it agrees with itself.

19:294 **7248.** 1780–89. *Pr* 25, at the conclusion of §55, in *Coactio moralis.*
Freedom has dignity on account of its independence; it also has a high price, for through it we are able to become authors of the good in accordance with our own concepts, which we can extend and multiply far beyond the natural instincts of animals.

19:294 **7249.** 1780–89. *Pr* 25, at §56, in *Coactio moralis.*
Obligation is the restriction of freedom, either negative, in order to hinder conflict, or positive, in order to promote the love of humankind by the restriction of self-love.[134]

19:294 **7250.** 1780–89. *Pr* 26, at §58, in *Coactio moralis.*
All obligation is the restriction of freedom to the conditions of its universal agreement with itself. Hence everything that hinders the universality of freedom is subject to rightful coercion; for what is in conformity with the universality of freedom is allowed.[135]

19:294 **7251.** 1780–89. *Pr* 27, still in *Coactio moralis.*
The regulative principle of freedom: that it only not contradict itself; the constitutive principle: that it mutually promote, namely the end: happiness.

19:295 **7253.** 1780–89. *Pr* 33, at §68, in *Lex.*
We should provide only an objective ground for our judgment that something should happen, and this is its agreement with a principle of reason. The subjective ground of moral feeling, when it is conceived of as being stronger than any other, would explain why something happens.[136] Only reason can prescribe what ought to happen. The restriction of the particular will through the conditions of universal validity is a principle of reason in the practical sphere. For otherwise there would be no unconditional unity among actions.

Reason has rules for a conditional use of our powers and principles for the unconditioned use of freedom in general. The latter are necessary and give *a priori* determination to the contingent.

7255. 1780–89. *Pr* 34, at §69, in *Lex*. 19: 295

We have a pure and unconditional gratification which we derive from the universal. For this is necessarily valid in every respect; thus the moral sense is properly sensible pleasure made universal, which is free of restriction.

7258. 1780–89. *Pr* 37, at §74, still in *Lex*. 19: 296

The ground of obligation is still in the divine will, because only that which agrees with our happiness can be obligatory, but only God can do this. Thus morality as a rule is from nature, as a law, from the divine will. An idea, which is realized in theology.

7260. 1780–89? 1776–78? *Pr* 39, in *Iuris peritia*. 19: 296

The principle of the unity of freedom under laws establishes an *analogon* with that principle that we call nature, and also an inner source of happiness, which nature cannot give and of which we ourselves must be the author. We then find ourselves united in a world of understanding according to special laws, which are moral, and in that we are pleased.

The unity of the intelligible world in accordance with practical principles, like that of the world of sense in accordance with physical laws. 19: 297

7261. 1780–89. *Pr* 47, in *Iuris peritia*. 19: 297

The outer rectitude of actions pertains only to the deed and is called legality; the internal rectitude pertains to the disposition from which they arise and to the principle, and is called morality. The *ius naturae* considers actions only as far as their legality is concerned, consequently as they would be if they all had to be enforced through coercion. Ethics considers how **they would have to be** if they were to arise merely from moral dispositions **without any coercion**.

7264. 1780–89? 1776–78? *Pr* 51, in *Principia iuris*. 19: 297

Perfect duty is that which is not restricted to the condition not to violate another duty. It is thus the same as unconditional duty toward oneself and toward others. It is the right of humanity or of human beings. Imperfect duties proceed from the ends of humanity in our person and the ends of human beings.

The first presuppose respect for human beings, the second love. Benevolence without satisfaction, and conversely right requires satisfaction in the law without benevolence.[137]

The right of humanity in our own person cannot have the right of human beings as a restricting condition. But also not the reverse. For 19: 298 another cannot have any right to me insofar as I am a person; thus the possibility of the first is grounded in personality and does not have personality as a restricting condition, including the rights of humanity flowing from personality.

The end of humanity in my own person is the promotion of the natural predisposition, that is, perfection. I cannot have this perfection in another as an end; for everyone judges his culture with approbation according to his special situation and convenience.

19:307 **7305.** 1780–89. *Pr* 110, at §165, in *Gradus imputabilitatis.*

The dignity of humanity in one's own person is personality itself, that is, freedom; for one is only an end in oneself insofar as one is a being that can set ends oneself. The irrational, who cannot do that, have worth only as means.

19:308 **7308.** 1780–89. *Pr* 119, at §177, in *Imputatio legis.*

Nothing in the world is holy but the right of humanity in our person and the right of human beings. The holiness consists in our never using them merely as means, and the prohibition against such a use lies in freedom and personality.

Wherever these two duties conflict, the first has the upper hand.

These duties are *officia necessitatis.*[a]

The *officia humanitatis*[b] are those where both objects are valid for us (not merely not as means) but also as ends, and there the end is our own perfection and the happiness of others.[138]

The last two: the interest of humanity in our person and the interest of human beings.

21:416 *Opus postumum*, Fascicle IV, Sheet 26/32, p. 1.[139]

A law of causality that is not restricted to temporal relation as is natural law thus demands a law of the causality of a freely acting cause (opposed to natural necessity), thus a distinct representation of freedom as a property that one would not be able to salvage if one assumed that time was something that belongs to things in themselves. Hence I have sought to place this in a greater light (creation). In the new edition of the *Critique* I have resolved the difficulty of time as a form of inner sense in accordance with which we do not cognize ourselves as we are but as we appear to ourselves,[140] and insofar as I likewise believe that in the second chapter of the Analytic[141] I have given the reason why in the consideration of a pure **practical** reason the concept of the good can by no means constitute the starting-point but this instead must lie in the principles as practical imperatives, I hope to have satisfied the reviewer in the *Allgemeine Deutsche Bibliothek*, a reviewer who is acute but whom I esteem because of his careful and knowledgeable judgment (although he calls himself merely a lover of metaphysics); since a genuine love of truth

---

[a] duties of necessity
[b] duties of humanity

and also of thoroughness illuminates even his liveliest criticism, a quality that I have not often encountered in polemical writings against me.[142]

VI.
NOTES FROM THE 1790S.

7313. 1790–94. *LBl* Scheffners Nachlaß.   19: 310
Of the highest good in the world of sense.

The absolute-good can and must be thought as a principle for that which can be done through freedom, but because it is itself unconditioned, it is yet not the whole which is required for the highest good.[143] Second: the presentation of this good in the world of sense is not possible in itself, for there that absolute good consists in the lawfulness of our conduct insofar as we are in conflict with the subjective principle of absolute evil: for that is virtue (not holiness). Sins must here be represented as if they do not rest on mere limitations but instead themselves have an effective principle as their ground, which could only be an external inducement.

7316. 1796–98. *LBl* G 10.   19: 313
P. II.   19: 314

[*In the right-hand margin*: Faculty of cognition (theoretical) and faculty of desire (practical) both *a priori*.]

We have *a priori* cognitions of objects. They are concepts (or intuitions): the *a priori* concepts, which are subordinate to no intuitions, are the categories, which by themselves have absolutely no sense and no object but are only forms of thought. E.g., that many together constitute one; one cannot have insight into how that would be possible without examples in intuition.

However, we can cognize nothing intuitively *a priori* except insofar as we perceive the object merely in appearance. For we can still become aware prior to experience of how the object will appear to us if we are conscious of the subjective form of our sensibility, and these forms are space and time. This is cognition (of ourselves and of things outside of us (*a priori*)).

[A] We also have, however, an *a priori* ought (the absolute) in us by means of the idea of freedom, which would not be possible without a categorical imperative available in our will. – Without the ideality of space and time, hence the ideality of objects as appearances, as its basis we would not be able to conceive of the reality of freedom practically at all, because otherwise the ought would always be empirically conditioned.

Synthetic *a priori* propositions belonging to theoretical cognition are possible only through intuition in space and time as natural objects, hence of things as appearances. Synthetic *a priori* propositions belonging to practical cognition are possible only through the idea of freedom. P. I.

We can have no imperatives of duty (category, dynamic, of causality) except under the presupposition of freedom, i.e., of a capacity that is independent of natural conditions in its acting and omitting, thus only insofar as we assume an essence or a property (of causality) of this capacity.

19:315   B. In the practical we can attain cognition of the highest end *a priori*, i.e., without looking for it in the experience of happiness, through the categorical imperative, which discloses freedom to us, while also, however, the categorical imperative unshakeably grounds the concept of duty for that final end which is at the same time a duty, which sufficiently justifies the ideas of God and immortality in practical consideration.

– We can attain cognition of things in themselves (the supersensible), God, and immortality only through the reality of the concept of freedom and thus from a practical point of view, and the categorical imperative is a synthetic *a priori* principle without which we would be able to cognize nothing *a priori* for our ends in general. For we must also set before ourselves such ends which we cognize *a priori* (not empirically), because they concern the supersensible, and those concepts must precede *a priori* all revelation of the supersensible and lie at its ground.

19:316   **7320.** 1800. *LBl* G 20. Page I.
If in the determination of the power of choice the pleasure precedes, then the pleasure is **pathological** –. If however the law precedes the [*crossed out*: freedom] pleasure in this determination and is a determining ground of the latter, then the pleasure is **moral.** Thus they are objectively determining incentives.

19:316   **7321.** 1800. *LBl* L 20.
The concept of freedom and its reality cannot be proven in any way except through the categorical imperative. The concept of God also cannot be proven theoretically and unconditionally, but only conditionally, from a practical point of view, namely the moral-practical point of view. It would be contradictory to seek to acquire favor and happiness from God in the technical-practical point of view, because the will of God to impart these is not consistent with this end.

Belief seeking a reward: the Bible.

5

Aesthetics

Kant lectured on topics in the field of aesthetics, which had been so named by Alexander Gottlieb Baumgarten, the author of the textbooks for Kant's courses in metaphysics and ethics, in his 1735 dissertation *Meditationes philosophicae de nonnullis ad poema pertinentibus* (Philosophical meditations on some matters pertaining to poetry),[1] in his courses on anthropology, which began in 1772–73, and logic, which began much earlier. The courses on anthropology, which used as their text the chapter on *Psychologia empirica* (§§504–699) from Baumgarten's 1739 *Metaphysica* ("*M*"),[2] began with a detailed discussion of the human faculties of cognition, feeling, and desire – this can be seen in the seven transcriptions of Kant's lectures, from between 1772–73 and 1788–89, that were published in 1997 as volume 25 of the *Akademie* edition,[3] and in the textbook on anthropology, *Anthropology from a Pragmatic Point of View*,[4] which Kant published only in 1798, the year after he ceased lecturing – and so it was entirely natural for Kant to touch upon the feeling of beauty and taste in these lectures. He did that from the outset, gradually adding discussions of other topics in aesthetics such as the feeling of the sublime and the nature of artistic genius as well.[5] The inclusion of extensive discussion of topics in aesthetics in Kant's lectures on logic may seem more surprising, but the author of the textbook that Kant used in this course, Georg Friedrich Meier,[6] was a disciple and colleague of Baumgarten, and the discussion of the difference between "logical cognition" and "aesthetic cognition" was a central topic for both Baumgarten and Meier, and Kant therefore took it up in his lectures. Virtually all of the reflections on aesthetics presented in this chapter are from Kant's notes in his copies of Baumgarten's chapter on *Psychologia empirica* and Meier's *Auszug aus der Vernunftlehre*, presented in Volumes 15 and 16 of the *Akademie* edition, respectively (both of these volumes were edited by Erich Adickes).[7] There are, however, several *Lose Blätter* among the notes Adickes presented; the most important of these, included below in section 2, "Anthropology Notes from the 1780s," are **992** and **993**, which are clearly sketches for the outline of the "Critique of the Aesthetic Power of Judgment," the first half of the *Critique of the Power of Judgment*, that Kant produced in the second half of the 1780s, presumably at some point between the second half of 1787, when, having completed the *Critique of Practical Reason*, he began working on what he then still conceived of merely as a "Critique of Taste," and 1789, when he was writing the final version of the book.[8] (**806** is also a long note, which Adickes thought could have come from anytime between 1775 and the late 1780s; it might have been a sketch for a "critique of taste" from an early time, when Kant still thought such a critique could be included in the *Critique of Pure Reason*, or it could be a later sketch for the eventual *Critique of the Power of Judgment*. Much in its language suggests an earlier rather than later date, but it contains also the first use in these notes of Kant's distinction between reflecting and determining judgment, which could suggest a late date for it too.) Baumgarten also touched upon some issues in aesthetics, such as the relation between the feeling of pleasure and objective perfection, elsewhere in *Metaphysica*, and so Kant also touches briefly upon these issues in his own lectures on metaphysics; but there are very few notes on these topics in Kant's reflections on metaphysics (Chapter 3 above).[9]

Along with the lectures on logic and anthropology, but especially the latter, the reflections presented in this chapter provide our chief evidence for the development of Kant's views in aesthetics during the three decades preceding the publication of the *Critique of the Power of Judgment* in 1790. Certain aspects of Kant's mature theory seem to have been in place from the outset. The very first note translated here (**618**), from no later than 1769, already employs Kant's central idea that our pleasure in a beautiful object is due to the free play of our cognitive faculties that it triggers, and Kant discussed this idea in many other notes (**630, 639, 655, 683, 698, 988, 1810, 1931**). The thesis that the pleasure in beauty is distinct from that in either the agreeable or the good is also present from this early date (**672–3, 711–12, 715, 806, 878, 1820a**), as well as the thesis that judgments of taste, in spite of their differences from both ordinary cognitive judgments and moral judgments, are intended to be universally valid (**627, 640, 653, 710, 764, 856, 1512, 1791, 1793, 1796, 1872**). However, in his earlier years Kant maintained that the principles of taste and thus judgments about the universality of pleasure in beautiful objects is empirical or *a posteriori* (**622–3, 625–6**). This is the position that Kant would maintain (in passing) in both editions of the *Critique of Pure Reason* (see the famous note at A 21/B 35–6), so the idea that would become central in the *Critique of the Power of Judgment*, that judgments of taste rest on an *a priori* principle even though they are not derivable from determinate concepts of their objects, was clearly a very late idea for Kant, presumably the spark that suddenly allowed him to begin writing the long-deferred "Critique of Taste" in the second half of 1787.[10] We also see that Kant took up the topic of genius as the source of art as early as 1769 (**621**) and continued to return to it in the early 1770s (**754, 767**), but the topic came in for more detailed consideration beginning in 1776 (**812, 817, 829, 831, 874, 899, 922, 933–4, 949**).

This date coincides with the publication of the German translation of Alexander Gerard's 1774 *Essay on Genius*,[11] which Kant is clearly still disputing in his notorious argument in the *Critique of the Power of Judgment* (§47) that genius is manifest in artistic creation but not scientific discovery. Several notes also provide evidence of Kant's long-standing interest in characterizing what is distinctive about the fine arts (**959, 962, 1855**). Striking by their absence, however, are notes touching upon the ways in which judgments of taste, although disinterested (**745, 827**) and distinct from judgments about the morally good, can nevertheless support or even promote our moral development – among the notes translated here, only **1928**, from sometime in the 1780s, even touches upon this theme. This theme, so central to the *Critique of the Power of Judgment*, is also noticeably missing from Kant's lectures on anthropology before 1788–89. This absence suggests that Kant's late recognition that precisely because of its disinterestedness taste is not irrelevant to but can actually promote morality was, along with his idea that judgments of taste could rest on an *a priori* principle without becoming determinate, one of the insights that suddenly allowed him to write a third *Critique*. The idea that taste could promote morality without losing what is distinctive to it was surely also one of the key ideas that suddenly allowed Kant to link a "Critique of the Aesthetic Power of Judgment" with a "Critique of the Teleological Power of Judgment" into a combined *Critique of the Power of Judgment*. Unfortunately, we find none among Kant's notes on anthropology and logic that can reveal anything about the development of this linkage, unprecedented in any of Kant's previous publications.

I.

ANTHROPOLOGY NOTES FROM 1769–1778.

618. 1769? (1764–68?) *M* 210, at §589–92.[12]　　　　　　　　　　15:265

The strikingly natural or naïve (*later addition*: in the use of the understanding, if nature appears as art, is called naïvety.), the unexpectedly natural.　　　15:266

Poetic art is an artificial play of thoughts.[13]

We play with thoughts if we do not labor with them, that is, are [not] necessitated by an end. One merely seeks to entertain oneself with thoughts.[14]

For this it is necessary that all the powers of mind are set into an harmonious play. Thus they must not be a hindrance to themselves and to reason, although they must also not promote it.[15] The play of images, of ideas, of affects and inclinations, finally of mere impressions in the division of time, of rhythm (versification) and unison (rhyme). The play of the senses is for verse [*breaks off*]

(*Later addition:* Composition.[a] 1. Poetry. 2. Oratory: harmony of thoughts and of the imagination. B. 1. Painting and music: harmony of intuitions and sentiments, both through relation to thoughts.[16]

It is no labor, thus also no servitude, yet is still the knowledge of poesy. It must be counted as a merit of the poet that one learns nothing through him; he must not himself make labor out of play.[17] Poesy is the most beautiful of all play, for it involves all of our powers of mind. It has rhythm from music. Without the measure of syllables and rhymes it is no regular play, no dance.

The sensible play[b] of thoughts consists in the play of speech (versification) and of words (rhyme). It goes well with music. It awakens the mind.

Poets are not liars, except in panegryics. But they have abolished the doctrine of the gods through their fables.

15:267   The play of impressions is music.

The play of sentiments:[c] the novel, theater.

The play of thoughts, sensations (images or forms (theater)) and impressions: poesy. The impressions are only through the language, since they are to accompany the thoughts.

Poesy has neither sensations nor intuitions nor insights as its end, but rather setting all the powers and springs in the mind into play; its images should not contribute more to the comprehensibility of the object, but should give lively motion to the imagination. It must have a content, because without understanding there is no order and its play arouses the greatest satisfaction.

Every action is either business (which has an end) or play that (*later addition*: serves for entertainment) certainly has a point, but not an end. In the latter the action has no end, but is itself the motivating ground.

In all products of nature there is something that is related merely to the end, and something that concerns merely the correspondence of the appearance with the state of mind, i.e., the manner, the vestment. The latter, even if one does not understand any end, often counts for everything. E.g., figure and color in flowers, tone and harmony in music. Symmetry in buildings.[18]

(*Addition: Suaviter in modo, fortiter in re.*)[d]

---

[a] *Dichten*

[b] *Sinnenspiel*

[c] *Empfindungen*. The word *Empfindung* can mean either "sentiment" or "sensation," and it would be misleading to use only one of these translations in all contexts. We will not use either of these English words to translate any other German word, so the reader may assume that whenever either is used it is to translate *Empfindung*.

[d] Agreeable in manner, strong in substance.

619. 1769. *M* 219, at the beginning of *M* §606, in *Iudicium*.[19]   15:268

The primary elements of our cognitions are sensations. This is what one calls those representations in which the mind is regarded as merely passive, acted upon by the presence of an object. They comprise the matter, as it were, of all our cognition.[20] For the form is given subsequently by the soul's own activity. This sensation, insofar as it signifies merely the state of the subject, is called feeling; but if it pertains (is in relation to) an outer object, then it is called appearance.[21] From this we see that all of our representations are accompanied with a feeling, for they are affections of the state of the soul.

620. 1769. *M* 219, at the beginning of *M* §606.   15:268

The first faculty of the human soul and the condition of the rest is sensibility, by means of which the soul receives representations as effects of the presence of the object and does not produce them itself.[22] As something belonging to the state of the subject, the representation of sensibility is called sensation; but as something that is related to an object, appearance. There are sensations without noticeable appearance, and appearances without noticeable sensation; yet both are always present.

621. 1769? (1764–68?) *M* 220.   15:268

All art is either that of instruction and precept or of genius; the former has its *a priori* rules and can be taught. Fine art[a] is not grounded on any   15:269
science and is an art of genius.[23]

(*Later addition*: Even an inference contains beauty: as a cognition it is related to the object, as a modification of the mind that is sensed, to the subject.)

622. 1769? (1764–68?) *M* 220.

The rational cognition of the beautiful is only criticism[b] and not sci-   15:269
ence; it explains the *phaenomenon*, but its proof is *a posteriori*.[24]

(*Later addition*: Science and art; the latter, of imitation or of genius.)[25]

(*Later addition*: All appearance is of succession or simultaneity; the former is ———,[c] the latter the image.)

---

[a] *Die schöne Kunst*. Usually this phrase means "fine art," especially when it is plural and means "the fine arts." Sometimes it means "beautiful art."

[b] *Critik*. This is of course the word that Kant uses in the title of his three main works, where it is translated "critique"; but here he is not referring to his special philosophical project of establishing the bases of our knowledge and practice, but to the ordinary practices of art criticism, literary criticism, and so on. Unless he is using the term in his special philosophical sense, it will be translated in this chapter as "criticism."

[c] Kant's blank.

Good taste occurs only in the period of healthy but not merely subtle reason.

(*Later addition*: Taste for a thing (inclination) is not always taste for the same thing, e.g., music.)

(*Later addition*: The judgment of the amateur, of the connoisseur (the latter must know the rules), of the master.)

In the case of sensation I always judge only subjectively, hence my judgment is not also valid for others; in the case of experience, objectively.

Whether beauty and perfection, hence their causes as well as the rules for judging of them, do not stand in a secret connection. E.g., a beautiful person often has a good soul.

Tender sensitivity[a] belongs to a judgment concerning that which can be agreeable etc. to everyone; receptivity[b] to one's own state; the former pertains to the man, the latter to the woman. The power of choice[c] must rule over this, and a limitation of it to the minimum is moderation, *apathia*.

15:270   (*Later addition*: Beauty in and for itself, if it is not accompanied, say, with vanity, arouses no desire, except only through charm.)[26]

15:270   **623.** 1769? (1764–68?) M 220.

One has no *a priori* grounds for justifying a taste, but only the general consensus in an age of rational judging.[27]

(*Later addition*: One's own or personal sentiments must be distinguished from substituted ones; the latter can be a disagreeable imitation, but still be personally agreeable. (The good is always agreeable in substituted sentiment.))

15:270   **624.** 1769? (1764–68?) M 220.

(*Later addition*: Sensible cognition is the most perfect among all those who intuit; confusion is only contingently attached to it.)

In the case of taste the representation must be sensible, i.e., synthetic and not through reason; second: intuitive; third: concerning the proportions of the sensations, immediate.[28] Thus the judgment of taste is not objective, but subjective; not through reason, but *a posteriori* through pleasure and displeasure; further, it is not a mere sensation, but rather that which arises from sensations that are compared. It does not judge of the useful and the good, but of the contingently agreeable, bagatelles (*later addition*: so far as their appearance is consonant with the laws of the faculty of sensation.)

---

[a] *Empfindsamkeit*; this could often be translated as "sensibility," but we reserve that for Kant's technical term *Sinnlichkeit*.
[b] *Empfindlichkeit*
[c] *Willkühr*

625. 1769? (1764–68?) *M* 220.   15:271

In everything that is to be approved in accordance with taste there must be something that facilitates the differentiation of the manifold (singling out); something that promotes comprehensibility (relations, proportions); something that makes grasping it together possible (unity); and finally, something that promotes its distinction from everything that is possible (precision).[29]

Beauty has a subjective *principium*, namely the conformity with the laws of intuitive cognition;[30] but this is not an obstacle to the universal validity of their judgments for human beings, if the cognitions are identical.

(*Later addition*: In objects of love one readily confuses charm with beauty.)

One cannot very well convince someone who has a false taste; one can convince others that he has a false taste, but can only bring him to abandon his opinion by examples.[31]

626. 1769? (1765–68?) 1771?? 1775–77?? *M* 227.   15:271

(*Later addition*: An idea is the basis of the intuition. Beautiful things, cognitions.)

What pleases in appearance, but without charm, is pretty, seemly, proper (harmonious, symmetrical). If the charm springs from the immediate sensation, then the beauty is sensible; but if it has sprung from associated thoughts,[a] then it is called ideal. Almost all of the charm of beauty rests on associated thoughts.[32]

That the grounds of the distinction of beauty are merely subjective can be seen from the fact that one cannot possibly conceive of a more beautiful shape for a rational being than the human shape.[33]

All cognition of a product is either criticism (judging) or discipline (*later addition*: doctrine) (instruction) or science.[34] If the relations that constitute the form of the beautiful are mathematical, i.e., those where   15:272 the same unit is always the basis, then the first principle of the cognition of the beautiful is experience and its criticism; second, a discipline is necessary that yields rules that are sufficiently determinate for practice (as in the case of the mathematics of probability), and this comes down to a science the principles of which are, however, empirical.

If the relations that constitute the ground of beauty are relations of quality (e.g., identity and difference, contrast, liveliness, etc.): then no discipline is possible, and even less science, but merely criticism. Architecture (in the general sense) (the art of horticulture, etc.) is a discipline, likewise music. For in the former it is a matter of pleasing relations in the division of space, in the latter with regard to time. Hence the

---

[a] *Nebengedanken*

scholastic term "aesthetics" must be avoided, because the object permits no scholastic instruction; one could just as well demonstrate amorous charms by a term of art.[35]

There are immediate sentiments of the senses or hypothetical (and substituted) sentiments. The former arise from everything that pertains to our state and when we ourselves are the object of our consideration. The latter: when we as it were transform ourselves into an alien person and invent for ourselves a sensitivity that we approve or desire. The sensitivity always concerns our own state and its charm[a] or disagreeableness. One can have such substituted sentiments with regard to such states or actions toward which one has no personal sentiment of one's own. E.g., an imagined normal life after an illness; magnanimity were one to win the big jackpot. Voltaire has the most excellent sentiments in the name of the Romans and of everyone in the tragedy.[36] Such substituted sentiments make [us] neither happy nor unhappy except when they are connected *indirecte* with our state. They are only *fictiones aestheticae* and are always agreeable.

15:273

15:273 **627.** 1769? 1769–70? 1770–71? 1772? 1773–75? M 227.

Taste is the selection of that which is universally pleasing in accordance with rules of sensibility. It pertains preeminently to sensible form; for with respect to this there are rules that are valid for all.[37]

15:273 **628.** 1769. M 228.

The inner pefection of a thing has a natural relation to beauty. For the subordination of the manifold under an end requires a coordination of it in accordance with common laws. Hence the same property through 15:274 which an edifice is beautiful is also compatible with its goodness, and a face would have to have no other shape for its end than for its beauty. Of many things in nature we cognize beauty, but not ends; it is to be believed that the satisfaction in their appearance is not the aim but the consequence of their aim.

15:274 **630.** 1769. M 228.

In everything beautiful, that the form of the object facilitates the actions of the understanding belongs to the gratification and is subjective; but it is objective that this form is universally valid.[38]

15:276 **638.** 1769. M 229.

The question is whether the play of sensations or the form and shape of intuitions is immediately agreeable or pleases only through providing

---

[a] Here *Anmuth* rather than *Reiz*.

the understanding with comprehensibility and facility in grasping a large manifold and at the same time with distinctness in the entire representation.[39]

To shape[a] there belongs not merely the form of the object in accordance with spatial relations in appearance, but also the matter, i.e., sensation (color).

639. 1769. *M* 229.   15:276

The sensible form (or the form of sensibility) of a cognition pleases either as a play of sensation or as a form of intuition (immediately) or as a means to the concept of the good. The former is charm, the second the sensibly beautiful, the third self-sufficient beauty.[40] The charm is either immediate, as Rameau believes that it is in music,[41] or mediate, as in   15:277
laughing and crying; the latter is ideal charm.[42] Through neither of these does the object please in the intuition. The object pleases immediately in   15:279
the intuition if its form fits with the law of coordination among appearances and facilitates sensible clarity and magnitude.[43] Like symmetry in buildings and harmony in music. The object pleases in the intuitive concept if its relation to the good can be expressed through a concept that pleases in sensible form.

(conventional or natural taste.)

640. 1769. *M* 229.   15:280

Through feeling I do not judge about the object at all and hence do not judge objectively. Hence I do not believe myself to have erred if I choose other objects of sentiment and also not if I have a dispute with others. A poor building, a ridiculous book gratifies, but it does not please on that account, and the most beautiful building gives him who regards it a poor substitute for a missed meal unless through novelty and rarity, etc. By means of taste I judge of the object, whether my state is much or little affected by it. If I call it beautiful, I do not thereby declare merely my own satisfaction, but also that it should please others.[44] We are ashamed when our taste does not correspond to that of others. In matters of taste one must distinguish charm from beauty; the former is often lost in this or that, but the beauty remains. The decorated room always remains beautiful, but it has lost its charm with the death of the beloved, and the lover chooses other objects. This concept of beauty, says Winckelmann, is sensual, i.e., one does not distinguish the charm from the beauty; for in fact they were just as much connected (though not   15:281
confused) among the ancients as among the moderns, although perhaps

---

[a] *Gestalt*

they were distinguished in the concepts of the artist who wanted to express them.[45]

The beautiful person pleases through her figure and charms through her sex. If you whisper into someone's ear that this admired beauty is a *castrato*, then the charm disappears in an instant, but the beauty remains.

15:282 It is difficult to separate this charm from the beauty; but we need only to leave aside all our particular needs and private relations, in which we distinguish ourselves from others, and then the cool-headed judgment of taste remains. In the judgment of the connoisseur, who cannot view it without abhorrence, the debtor's prison nevertheless remains a beautiful building; but this judgment is without any charm; it pleases in taste, but displeases in sentiment.[46]

15:282 **641.** 1769. *M* 230.

Just as judgments of taste are mixed up with sentiments, judgings of good and evil are likewise never completely pure, but have a strong addition of other representations of beauty or charm mixed in. Benevolence receives strong recommendations from honor, from the love of others, through the flattering reckoning of the happiness of others to one's own account. If generosity is directed toward a woman who is young and beautiful then all these charms are elevated by the interest in sex.

15:284 **646.** 1769–1770. *M* 230.

A representation is sensible if the form of space and time is in it; it is even more sensible if sensation is connected with it (color). It is maximally sensible if it is ascribed to the observer, and indeed as observed by others. Beautiful objects are those whose internal order[a] pleases in accordance with the laws of *intuitus*.[47] Beautiful appearances of objects, e.g., pictures.

15:284 **647.** 1769–70. *M* 230.

Taste is really [*crossed out:* the capacity[b]] the faculty[c] for choosing that which sensibly pleases in unison with others.[48] Now since unanimity is not so necessary in sensations as in appearance, taste pertains more to appearance than to sensation. If we blame someone for a lack of taste, we do not say that it does not have taste[d] for him but that it does not have taste for others. A perverted taste, moreover, is that which applies to what is evil or injurious.

---

[a] *Zusammenordnung*
[b] *Fähigkeit*
[c] *Vermögen*
[d] *schmeke*

648. 1769–70. *M* 231.   15:284
Taste in appearance is grounded on the relations of space and time that are comprehensible to everyone, and on the rules of reflection.

Just because in taste it comes down to whether something also pleases others, it takes place only in society, that is, only in society does it have a charm.[49]

650. 1769–70. *M* 231.[50]   15:287
All of our representations, when they are considered with regard to that which they represent, belong to two main species: sensibility and reason. The former consist in the relation of objects to the capacity of our nature to be stimulated or in a certain way altered by them.[51] The latter, however, applies to all objects as such, insofar as they are considered apart from all relation to the sensitivity of the subject.[52]

Sensible representations are sensations and require sense or appearances and are grounded on the faculty of intuition; the former [*crossed out*: consist] are represented alterations of the state of the subject through the presence of the object; the latter are representations of the object itself insofar as it is exposed to the senses.

There are two sorts of cognitions of reason: through reflection[a] (rational) and through concepts of reason. Geometry contains rational reflection on objects, but only through sensible concepts. Rational reflection[b] is common to all cognition.[53]

653. 1769–70. *M* 232.   15:289
That which pleases in taste is not actually the facilitation of one's own intuitions, but rather the universally valid in the appearance, thus that the universal intuition or the universal rules of feeling are accommodated by the merely private feeling.[54] For in the relation of sensations there is also something that is universally valid, although each sensation may have only a private validity of agreeableness.

The facility of sensations makes for gratification, but not the facility of cognition, except insofar as that which we cognize has a relation to our state. Hence in solitude the proportions of sensibility cannot provide any gratification, but those of what belongs to us can do so in society, for others thereby have something to thank us for.[55]

654. 1769–70. *M* 232.   15:289
In the beautiful there is something that relates merely to others, namely the symmetry, and something that relates to the possessor,

---

[a] *Überlegung*
[b] *Die vernünftige Überlegung (reflexion)*

namely the comfortableness and usefulness; the latter is still to be distinguished from the immediate charm.[56]

15:289 **655.** 1769–70. *M* 232.

The play of shapes and sensations is also present in fireworks.[57] For in the appearance there is either an object, which is always placed in space, or merely a sensation, but in accordance with relations of time; the former is called the shape, the latter the play, both are often found together.[58] One is sensitive either to one's state in action or in passivity, insofar as one feels oneself to be dependent or to be a ground of one's state. Hence sensation is either active or passive. The sensation is active in the case of the form of appearances on account of the comparison that

15:290 one makes. The active sensation is in itself always agreeable as well as all passive ones that promote the active one.[59] But it is not a sensation of the object, but is immanent. All sensation of personality, namely of onself as an active principle, is active; but the sensation of oneself as an object of other forces is passive; and the more it is merely passive, the more disagreeable it is. The passive gratifications seem to be forceful only by means of the active springs that they set into motion.

15:296 **669.** 1769–1771. *M* 236.

Pleasure: A; indifference: *non A*; displeasure: $-A$. There is no indifference of sensation, except only relative to this or that sense; for with regard to all the senses together, i.e., one's state, something is always either agreeable or disagreeable. Likewise in the case of the beautiful or the good. But there is a counterbalance: $A - A = 0$. One says: Satisfaction, indifference, dissatisfaction. Gratification, indifference, abhorrence. Beautiful, ordinary, ugly. Good, worthless, evil. Respect, disdain,

15:297 contempt. Hatred, coldness, love. For just as all simple sensations are agreeable and become disagreeable only through conflict, so all simple relations of sensibility or reason that are positive are good and become evil only through conflict.[60]

15:297 **670.** 1769–1771. *M* 236.

With regard to the beautiful or to taste there is in addition to art the criticism, observation, and comparison of objects with taste through analysis.[a] The science of the beautiful, however, is an attempt to explain the *phaenomena* of taste.[61]

15:297 **671.** 1769–70. *M* 237.

Taste is the basis of [*crossed out*: criticism and] judging, genius however of execution. Criticism is judging in accordance with universal rules.

[a] *Zergliederung*

490

But since these rules must be grounded on taste, a man of taste is better than a learned critic. But there is also a doctrine of judgings that rests on universal principles of reason, such as logic, metaphysics, and mathematics.

He can always be well satisfied with himself whose judging does not demand for perfection more than he is capable of doing. Taste without genius brings dissatisfaction with oneself; sharp criticism of oneself (it is peculiar that this is so difficult) with inadequate capacities makes one write not at all or with much anxiety; in contrast, much genius and little taste brings forth crude yet valuable[a] products.[62]

672. 1769–70. M 237.   15:298

We have dealt with that which pleases insofar as it belongs to our state or affects that and concerns our well-being. Now we speak of that which pleases in itself, whether our state is altered by it or not, thus with what pleases insofar as it is cognized rather than sensed. Since every object of sensibility has a relation to our state, even that which belongs to cognition and not to sensation, namely in the comparison of the manifold and the form (for this comparison itself affects our state, costing us effort or being easy, enlivening our entire cognitive activity or hemming it in): thus there is something in every cognition that belongs to agreeableness; but thus far the approval does not concern the object, and beauty is not something that can be cognized, but only sensed. That which pleases in the object and which we regard as a property of it must consist in that which is valid for everyone. Now the relations of space and time are valid for everyone, whatever sensations they may have. Thus in all appearances the form is universally valid; this form is also cognized in accordance with common rules of coordination; thus what fits the rules of coordination in space and time necessarily pleases everyone and is beautiful. That which is agreeable in the intuition of the beautiful comes down to the comprehensibility of a whole, but the beauty comes down to the universal validity of this fitting relation.[63]

The good must please without relation to the condition of appearance.

673. 1769–70. M 252c.   15:298

A clock is agreeable insofar as it measures time for someone; it is   15:299
beautiful insofar as it pleases everyone in intuition; insofar as it may be connected with a possible willing in general, whether it is connected with agreeableness or not, and thus can serve everyone for the measurement of time, it is good, and thus without relation to the state of the person who is thereby to be affected with charm.[b]

---

[a] und schatzbare
[b] Anmuth

Freedom is necessarily agreeable to everyone, therefore good; likewise understanding.

To love one's own freedom comes from agreeableness; but to love freedom in general is because it is good. But this love itself is good; for whoever loves freedom in general, whoever loves well-being in general, demands it for everyone, thus his will also pleases everyone.[64]

15: 299   **676.** 1769–70. M 252c.

15: 300   The perfection of a cognition with regard to the object is logical, with regard to the subject aesthetic. The latter, since it magnifies the consciousness of one's state through the relation in which one's senses are placed toward the object and through appropriation, magnifies the consciousness of life and is therefore called lively. Abstract representation practically cancels the consciousness of life.

15: 304   **683.** 1769–70. M 242c.

In order for sensibility to have a determinate form in our representation it is necessary that it have an order and not just be grasped together. This order is a connection of coordination, and not subordination of the sort that reason institutes. The basis of all coordination, hence the form of sensibility, is space and time. The representation of an object in accordance with the relations of space is shape, and the imitation of this is the image. The form of appearance without representation of an object consists merely in the order of sensations in accordance with temporal relation, and the appearance is called a sequence (or series or play). All objects can be sensibly or intuitively cognized only under a shape. Other appearances do not represent objects at all, but only alterations. Pantomime is an intuitive form of a series of human shapes, while dance is one of a succession of movements in accordance with time; both together are **mimetic dance**. Dance is to the eye what music is to the ear, only in the case of the latter there are finer divisions of time in more exact proportion. The arts are either formative or imitative.[a] The latter are painting and sculpture. The former concern either merely the form or also the material. That which concerns merely form is landscape design;[b] that which also concerns the material is architecture (even the art of furnishing); even tactics and maneuvers are a kind of beautiful arrangement. To the formative arts there belongs

15: 305   in general the art of producing any beautiful form, such as the art of beautiful vessels, of the goldsmith, the jeweler, the furnisher, even the finery of a woman, just as much as architecture. Likewise all work of gallantry.[65]

[a] *Bildend oder Nachbildend*
[b] *Gartenbau*

Dance loses its charm if one will no longer please the other sex. For that reason the inclination to the dance does not last long among married men; but among women it lasts until they are old because they continue to want to please.

Appearance is a representation of the senses so far as it pertains to an object; sensation, if it pertains merely to the subject. The reflected appearance is the shape, the reflected sensation [*breaks off*]

685. 1769–70. M 242c.   15:305

The play of shapes and sensations requires, first, equal divisions of time (uniformity in the measure of time) or beat, 2. a comprehensible proportion that can be drawn from the relation of the alterations of the parts.[66]

The charm in dance is either corporeal and rests on the seemly motion of the limbs, that in music on the proportionate movement of the vessels of the body through harmonious tones. Ideal charm rests on the relation that the alterable shapes have on the affects or that which the tones that accompany one another have on the human voice and the expression of sentiment.

686. 1769–70. M 242d, with reference to the beginning of *M* §651?[67]   15:306

The contemplation of the beautiful is a judging and not an enjoyment.[a] This appearance makes for some gratification,[b] but nowhere near as much as in relation to the judgment of satisfaction in beauty; rather this consists solely in the judgment concerning the universality of the satisfaction in the object. From this it can be seen that, since this universal validity is useless as soon as society is lacking, then all the charm of beauty must also be lost; just as little would even any inclination to beauty arise *in statu solitario*.[68]

696. 1769–70. M 242.   15:309

All perfection seems to consist in the agreement of a thing with freedom, hence in purposiveness, general usefulness, etc. Since all things in an empirical sense are properly only that which they are taken to be in relation to the law of sensibility, the perfection of objects of experience is a correspondence with the law of the senses, and this, as appearance, is called beauty; it is so to speak the outer side of perfection, and the object pleases merely in being contemplated. Satisfaction through taste and through *sentiment*[c] have in common that the object is approved without regard to the influence that it may have on the feeling of the subject through intuition or use. Only taste approves of something so far as

[a] *Genuss*
[b] *Vergnügen*
[c] Here Kant writes "sentiment" in a Latin hand rather than *Empfindung*.

493

it merely affects the senses; *sentiment* insofar as it is judged by reason. What is most fit for the entire play of the senses thereby indicates correspondence with the sensibility of the human being and through that perfection, since in the end this comes down to consensus with happiness.

15:310 **697.** 1769–70. *M* 242.

There are three sorts of pleasure in an object through feeling: 1. Immediate pleasure through sensation. 2. Pleasure in our state concerning the possession of this object. 3. Pleasure in our person. If the first pleasure obtains without the second then it serves for judging.

15:310 **698.** 1769–70. *M* 242.

In the beautiful it is not so much the thing as its appearance that pleases. Insofar as we compose its representation from parts that are seen in themselves the human body yields a concept that contains nothing beautiful.

There is a beauty in the cognitions of reason. Even usefulness can be a sum of appearances.

15:311 **702.** 1771? (1769–70?) 1773–75? *M* 178.

Since space and time are the universal *conditiones* of the possibility of objects in accordance with rules of sensibility, the concordance of appearance or sensation in the relations of space and time together with the universal law of the subject for producing such a representation of form belong to that which necessarily corresponds to every sensibility, thus to taste.[69] In contrast, the correspondence with sensation is merely contingent. Taste is sociable. Music.

15:312 **704.** 1771? (1769–71?) *M* 178.

One approves of a beautiful edifice just as much whether one has seen it innumerable times or only once. It also arouses no noticeable desire to possess it.

15:314 **708.** 1771? (1770–71?) 1773–75?? *M* 179.

Approval and approbation certainly arise from the understanding, but not gratification. All feeling is always related to me as a human being, and is only felt[a] through the mediation of the body, although the concepts, which effect this appropriation, arise from the understanding.[70]

15:314 **710.** 1771? (1769–70?) 1773–75?? *M* 179.

Taste concerns that which is universally agreeable, either in sensation or in appearance. In neither is the gratification as great as the approval on

---

[a] *empfunden*

494

account of universality.[71] *Sentiment* pertains to that which is universally 15:315
approved without relation to private sensation.

It is good for every human being that his taste not also become an
inclination, but rather serves him only to judge that which pleases everyone and to be sociable in society. It is best for him who is alone that
he have a good and easily satisfied appetite without any special choice.

711. 1771? (1769–70?) 1773–75?? *M* 179 and 246. 15:315

What agrees with the laws of the understanding is true or logically
good. What agrees with the laws of sensibility in general (necessarily
and therefore universally) is beautiful (for all sensibility is connected
with either charm[a] or disagreeableness, and whatever enlivens activity
is agreeable; if this happens universally, then it pleases).[72] What corresponds with the private law of sensibility (of sensation) is agreeable or
gratifies. Since self-sensation is the final ground of relation of all our
activities everything is related to feeling (which is either pleasure or displeasure). What necessarily agrees with the laws of the will in general is
good. But since the will is really an activity in accordance with a certain
cognition, and indeed one that considers the subject either in a private
relation or in a universally valid relation, that is good which universally 15:316
agrees with the activities of the subject in accordance with laws of the
understanding.

712. 1771? (1769–70?) (1773–75?) *M* 246. 15:316

What agrees with me insofar as I consider myself as an *individuum* of
the sensible world is agreeable; what harmonizes with me as determined
through the whole of the sensible world is beautiful; what agrees with
me as a member of the intellectual world is good: first with me as an
individuo and second as a member of the whole.

715. 1771? (1769–70? 1773–75?) *M* 246. 15:317

What fits with the subjective private laws pleases in sensation (agreeable).

What universally agrees with the subjective laws of human beings in
general pleases in appearance: beautiful.

What agrees with the subject in general (whether it is a human one or
another kind) is good. The value of things always comes down to their
concordance with subjects.

721. 1771? (1770–71? 1773–75?) *M* 247. 15:319

Taste does not consist in the capacity to be gratified ourselves by means
of what we enjoy, for that is appetite, but in the [*crossed out*: agreeableness]

[a] *Anmuth*

consensus of our [*crossed out*: feeling] sensitivity with that of others. One appetite has not the least preference over another except insofar as it is the easiest to satisfy and does not conflict with other appetites. But taste, which pertains to what is agreeable to everyone, is to be preferred to appetite. It is not advisable to refine one's appetite, but it is advisable to refine one's taste while minimizing appetite, since taste comes about through a sociable *principio*. People without taste are unsociable and have a strong temptation to indifference toward people unless a dependency on the judgment of others, namely the love of honor, holds them back.

15:321 **726.** 1771? (1769–70? 1773–75?) *M* 247.

One asks whether correspondence and uniformity rule in taste. There must be a misunderstanding of the significance of the word "taste" here. For if one investigates the sense that this has in most cases, then one finds that taste consists precisely in this uniformity and harmony of one's judgment concerning the agreeable and pleasing, and one should rather ask: whether such a thing as taste exists at all, or rather whether in that which pleases there is always to be found a private judgment that agrees with that of others only contingently.

This very question can also be subsumed under this one: whether we find an immediate gratification in that which pleases others and have the means to judge such a thing immediately, without learning it through observation.

It does not seem as if human nature contains a special disposition toward trust, heartfelt benevolence, and friendship. Honor and courtesy constitute almost all of the perfection in its social character. For that 15:322 reason a taste that is not vain is the best that we can strive for in our social relations.

15:323 **733.** 1771? (1769–70? 1773–75?) *M* 248.

The objects of sight are alone capable of beauty because they come closest to pure intuition, in that they represent the object through an appearance which contains the least sensation. Hence even colors, as prominent sensations, belong more to charm than to beauty.[73]

15:327 **743.** 1771? (1769–70? 1773–75?) *M* 249.

The judgment of taste is a social judgment and serves sociability, but also serves for the socialization of that which is agreeable. Good taste concerns that which pleases for a long time. The essentially beautiful is that which harmonizes with the concept of the thing in accordance with sensible laws; for the concept of what the thing should be is presupposed.

745. 1771–72? 1773–77? (1776–78?) *M* 248, at the beginning of §662.[74]   15:327

The [*crossed out*: satisfaction] pleasure in an object is not to be confused with the pleasure in the existence of this object.[75] The former is the pleasure in the judging, the latter in the sensation. The latter concerns that which gratifies, the former, what pleases. The judging is either as of an obj[*breaks off*]

747. 1772. *M* 219.[76]   15:328

One chooses in accordance with taste if the appetite is satisfied and need is stilled. Hence the savage does not choose in accordance with taste.

(Yet appetite and need are not the same.)

753. 1772–73. *M* 219.   15:329

Not the imitation of nature but rather the original fruitfulness of nature is the ground of beautiful art.

754. 1772. *M* 219.   15:330

Genius is like a forest in which free and fruitful nature spreads out its riches. Art is like a garden, in which everything happens according to a method and one is subjected to rules, which precede; in contrast, nature provides material for genius and example for rules.

755. 1772–75. *M* 219.   15:330

Since sensations cannot be communicated (either in understanding or in participation) they occupy the lowest rank of aesthetic perfection. This is foremost an effect of the inclination to communicate. Intuition can be described and preserved in the imagination. Sensation allows for no touchstone, with regard to it everybody is right, and it does not serve the understanding at all.

757. 1772. *M* 220.   15:330

Simple sensations cannot be invented. The ideal of sensation consists only in the enlargement or other combination of sensations, e.g., adventures for a happy age. The ideal of the beautiful always presupposes a *dessin* that has been sketched out by nature, e.g., the human body.[77]

Likewise the ideal of misery, of ugliness: harpies – of evil. Milton has   15:331
imparted to it a fearsome majesty.

762. 1772–73. *M* 297.   15:332

In order to seem like a genius one departs from rules. It is certainly good to go beyond the rules where they arise from the restriction of the spirit; but where they concern merely what is customary and contingent the modesty to become comfortable with them is needed, for otherwise, if everyone else allows himself the same freedom, in the end everything is without any rule.

15:332   **763.** 1772–73. *M* 298.

    Everything that we sense in company touches us all the more. We feel so to speak also for the others. A good speech pleases us more in company than alone. Piety is more instructive and moving in a group. We are ashamed and afraid of one who speaks publicly. All of these emotions also reflect back onto the speaker, who is thereby both more enlivened and made more careful through the judgment of so many others. There are

15:333   really many lights, these images in the mind, which increase the clarity of one another. They are reflexes. A witty insight has more effect on one in company than alone. Everything tastes and pleases better in good company. All of life is amplified in such company. It is indispensable for thinking people.

15:333   **764.** 1772–73. *M* 298.

    Taste is the power of judgment with regard to that which pleases universally in accordance with sensibility. It has a rule, but not through discursive cognition, rather through *intuitum*.

15:334   **767.** 1772–73. *M* 298–9.

    Taste is a social, sensible judgment about that which satisfies, but not immediately through sense and also not through general concepts of reason. Taste concerns the **agreeable**, the **beautiful** (noble), and the **touching**.[78] The latter is not really sublime, although it is often the effect of the sublime. It is the beginning of pain without impression or appropriation and thus a pain in a fictional condition, thus not in our own person, hence a pain that is only assumed.[79] Charm corresponds to that which is touching. Charm is not the agreeableness of the object through its impression, but rather an occasion to transport ourselves into agreeable fictions, like a beautiful prospect, a charming face [or] figure: not through itself, but through the invitation to sexual enjoyment. Hence the same face is pretty on a lad, but without charm. Green plazas and flower beds have a charm because they give us occasion to involve ourselves in fantastical representations of carefreeness and leisure. Taste enables the enjoyment to be communicated; it is therefore a means and an effect of the unification of people. [It is] an accommodation and is entirely necessary so that mere thoroughness, which is only for him whom the object interests, is a rudeness with regard to others. The thorough person who sees or reads something of the sort still has no complete satisfaction in it, because he does not consider it from his own point of view, but only from a common point of view (the impartial observer).[80] The pedant commits this rudeness out of clumsiness and is laughed at. The lack of taste or even the disinclination and indifference toward it always indicates a narrow heart, which restricts its satisfaction to itself. Charms and emotions move against the will, are therefore always too presumptuous, because they disturb the peace of others.* Taste pertains to the judgment, not to the feeling; hence the latter must be transient. Genius, however, pertains to feeling. Taste is therefore the refinement of the power of judgment. We must there as it were forego pleasing 15:335 others. Modesty and agreeableness are the character which lies at the basis of taste. There are to be sure no principles here, but rather that which creates access for them. Obstinacy holds many people back and is therefore opposed to dissemination; hence virtue itself must borrow a recommendation from taste.

*(To storm about my sentiments is mischievous. My sentiment may well be affected, but in such a way that I always keep it in my power. If this degree is exceeded, then the other has not played a game with me, but driven me into his game.

Something must be opposed to the inclinations of enjoyment that is directed at others having to be the judge, thus something in which much is necessary for us to provide for our needs, not in that which concerns the crude needs, but rather in that which cultivates the industry and skill of others. It is an incentive for industry and skill.)

769. 1772–73? 1773–75? 1772?? M 306.   15:335
Moral taste is the capacity to find satisfaction in that in the good which belongs to **universality**. Aesthetic taste: the capacity to find satisfaction in that in sensible satisfaction which belongs to its universality.

Moral taste concerns intentions, aesthetic taste the means to carry 15:336 them out.

Moral feeling is the capacity*a* to be moved by the moral as an incentive.

779. 1772–73. M 323.   15:341
For the theory of taste:
1. The movement (and occupation) of the mind through sensation (sense),
2. Order through concepts (the power of judgment),
3. The movement (and occupation) of the mind through concepts (spirit),
4. Order through sensation (taste).

Sensation as well as concept can have something that is unique and something that is universally valid. The movement and occupation of the mind rests on the unique constitution of the mind, because it pertains to life and the proportion of the forces. By contrast, order pertains to that which is the cognition for everyone, whether it is conceptual or sensible for everyone, and thus pertains to what is universally valid.

---

a [crossed out: *Vermögen*] *Fähigkeit*

15:344 **787.** 1772–77. *M* 324.

When good taste ceases, then the products of the spirit also cease, since taste brings the understanding into good harmony with sensibility and encourages and enlivens the crude efforts of the latter by providing it with a beloved application.[81]

15:350 **803.** 1773–78? 1772? *M* 312.

Nature gives us examples of taste, not for imitation (*later addition*: models. They are the school of culture) but for culture. Yet by means of taste we can perceive the beauties of nature. Taste is generated in society through the relation of sociable intuition. Nature itself reveals luxury. What is gratifying in mere intuition, insofar as it is communicable, is beautiful. The play of shapes as well as of sensations.

15:351 **806.** 1773? 1776–78? (1773–75?) (1780–83?) 1788–89?? *LBl* Ha 41. P. 1.

Something pleases:

In sensation–	Intuition–	Concepts
Gratification–	pleases–	are approved
Comforts, charms,	Facility, constitution,	mediately,
touches–	magnitude–	immediately
Feeling	Taste	Understanding
The agreeable	Beautiful. Sublime.	Good
direct – indirect	Noble	Beauty pleases
Sense – imagination		immediately.
Enjoyment – possession		It is not utility.
with foresight		It is not judged
		in accordance with
For one For the		gratification.
sense entire		Taste is distinguished
feeling		from feeling.
of one's state		Much appetite:
		little taste.
		Taste does not
		belong under sense
		(rather under
		the power of
		judgment).

15:352 (row "The agreeable" marked at this margin)

What is to be in accordance with taste must please universally.
He to whom [what is on] his table tastes good to himself: appetite.
He to whom [what is on] his table tastes good to others: taste.
Thus the universal validity of the satisfaction.
Taste is sociable.

Unsociable people have no taste, but not the converse.

[*crossed out*: Taste is capable of rules, but not *a priori in abstracto*.]

The judgment of taste does not have merely private validity.

It is not an arbitrary convention.

However, taste is based on subjective laws.

What pleases universally in accordance with subjective laws.

Subjective laws, in accordance with which something pleases in sensation or intuition or concepts. Of these, the first cannot be **necessarily** universal, thus it is grounded in experience. But the others are cognitions. Thus what promotes sensible representation or the actions of the understanding in the subject is in accordance with taste.

To confuse charm with beauty indicates little taste. [*crossed out*: The ideal feeling belongs to the sublime.]

Youth has much feeling, little taste.

The English have more feeling than taste.   15:353

A tender, not a coarse feeling must be connected with beauty.

Sensations are related to impressions,

feelings to drives.

The former with regard to representations,

the latter with regard to desires.

The former to distinguishing and perceiving,

the latter to acting.

With regard to the disagreeable what is necessary is sensitivity to distinguishing (in any case, in order to save something else), but little feeling, in order to be driven by that.

The moral sense for distinguishing, the moral feeling for a drive.*

*(One demands that impressions should not be incentives, for one is passive with respect to them. By contrast, insights should contain motives, or in the case of *sens commun* concepts should be combined with feeling, because here one drives sensibility itself through the understanding. If sensibility does not have this receptivity, then the person is without moral feeling. A moral sense is a contradiction; moral feeling, however, consists not in the power of distinguishing, but in the sensible power of desire that is capable of such modification.)[82]

P. II.

What pleases in accordance with feeling (sensation) does not on that account please others; but what pleases in intuition, of that it is demanded that it please others.

Uses of taste: it refines people in order to make the judgment of sensibility shared.[83] Affects and emotions are not shared. Hence taste   15:354
is really an understanding that compares something with the sensibility with regard to satisfaction or dissatisfaction.

(Honor, fashion, vanity.

Boasting and ostentation.)

Beautiful objects and beautiful representations of objects make one unaccustomed to the mere gratification of enjoyment and selfishness and bring the mind closer to morality, in that the satisfaction from intuition is still objective.[84]

It accustoms the understanding to providing sensibility and making it healthy and practical. Likewise: to making the idea intuitive and thereby helping morality in order to unite it with sensible satisfaction.

The essentially beautiful consists in the correspondence of sensible intuition with the idea or also in the correspondence of that which pleases subjectively with the objective.

Summa: Taste liberates from the mere senses and provides a recommendation for the understanding.

Thus everything that promotes the life of our cognition pleases in taste.[85] The animal life through sensation. Emotions and charms must go alongside of the idea of the good, but not replace it.

Taste affords no doctrine, but rather criticism.[86] It requires practical understanding and, in order to preserve it, exemplars.

Everything that facilitates our intuitions, through which one gently brings the concepts of the understanding close or provides sensibility for the intellectual, everything that yields a free play of our faculties, pleases subjectively. The appearance insofar as it is in agreement with the idea 15:355 constitutes the essentially beautiful. Charm is touching through the consensus with our passions by means of novelty and what is extraordinary.

The representations please even if the thing itself displeases. *In summa*: the ground is merely subjective.

Sensation, power of judgment, spirit, and taste. The power of judgment is either sensible or reflecting, and consists in transforming representations into an image or into a concept.[87] The arrangement is related precisely to the *dessein*, the outline, or the theme.[88] Music is so to speak a beautiful sensible cognition.

The formative[a] power of judgment pertains only to the means of harmonious order[b] and its advancement, hence unity, multiplicity, demarcation. It does not pertain to utility or to the mediately pleasing, that which is thorough and enduring in buildings, in the human body, in dress.

No effort must show through, no rumination. The object must be given only in a gentle, clear, and pleasing way.[89]

15:358   **807.** 1776–78? (1773–75? 1775–77?) (1769?) M 213.

The play of nature (art) and of accident. The former agrees with an idea. Idea and play.

---

[a] *bildende*
[b] *Zusammenordnung*

502

Business is different from play. The former is on account of the idea and has a purpose; the latter is an occupation without a purpose.

The play of impressions (music). Of concepts (style). Of images (poesy). Of sensations, feelings. Of passions (game of chance[a] or of blind luck: hazard[b] [*breaks off*])

The play of skill and genius.

Play has its rules, purpose has laws.

Free play. (A forced play is a contradiction.)

A free play in wilderness,

an artificial play in the garden.

(*Later addition*: Joyfulness is a matter of practice. One departs from the jocular, cheerful mood. One can also bring it back if the mind is at peace.)

Play must not become serious or intention[al], e.g., tragedy[c] that de-   15:359
presses.

The play of intuitions is either with regard to shape or to attitude (gesture).

The play of intuitions is [found] in edifices, furnishings, dress, garden.

The play of appearance.[d] Optics.

The play of illustrations or [*crossed out*: pictures] similarities.

In all order there is either intention or play.

A play of impressions, of intuition,* of imaginings, of reflection, of sensations, of thoughts, of passions.

*(After-image;[e] for we picture everything in the mind; the senses picture nothing. Hence what is fleeting in the figure: wavy line.)

Play demands genius, purpose rules.

Play entertains the sociable sentiments of the mind or at least what is social, e.g., emulation.

812. 1776–78? (1773–75? 1775–77?) 1769?? M 216.   15:361

Industry and genius. The former requires capacity (to learn), the latter spirit (an inner life).

Genius is the faculty for producing that which cannot be learned.[90] There are sciences and arts of genius. A production without genius is labor. Genius requires inspiration, labor disposition. Genius derives its product from the sources.

The arts of industry require (natural) capacity,[f] those of genius talent or spirit, namely to produce something out of oneself. The form of

---

[a] *Glükspiel*
[b] *Hazardspiel*
[c] *Trauerspiel*
[d] *Apparentz*
[e] *Nachbildung*
[f] Kant writes "*capacitaet (Fähigkeit)*."

genius is freedom, that of industry constancy, moderation. There are geniuses of idea or execution (often imitation). A genius of execution is a genius in manner and is called a virtuoso. Music, the art of painting, architecture allow and require a genius, even the landscape designer. The arts of industry recognize an example and need it; those of genius are creative, i.e., they proceed in accordance with an idea. The power of judgment and taste determine the limits for genius, hence without these genius borders on madness. In the art of poetry[a] genius has its true field, because to poetize[b] is to create; hence, let the vestment be what it may, mere description does not make a poem. For that reason a poesy without genius is also unbearable, and poets may not be mediocre. The genius reveals himself in the invention or the plot, the virtuoso in the style or manner, the artist in the industrious execution, i.e., in regularity. The genius places himself above rules and gives laws. In poesy genius demonstrates more spirit and sentiment, in oratory more judgment[c] and taste. There is a difference between "this one has genius" and "he is a

15:362   genius." The genius depends on the mood. The spirit fades with age, the power of judgment grows. In mathematics genius actually reveals itself in the invention of methods.

Sensation (intuition) is that which is most prominent in relation to the empirical understanding, the power of judgment in relation to reason, spirit in relation to the practical in general (animation), taste in relation to the moral.

Invention is either from spirit or from industry.

The original belongs to genius.

The Germans are held back from the free movements of their genius by their methodical nature, the ceremony of their language, the pedantry of their instruction in style. They are always constrained in intercourse, comedy. The English are not sufficiently polished, but they are free, and their education is certainly free and unconstrained by the compulsion of propriety, and for that reason advantageous for genius and individuality, although to be sure without taste. The Frenchman is not coerced by custom, but by the law of fashion; hence he is free enough for genius, although constrained by propriety. One can assess a spirit in accordance with its own worth or as a useful product of the age. In the latter sense it can often be approved although it is not approved in the former. E.g., poets of dalliance first make our manners gentle.[91]

Genius consists in the originality of the idea in the production of a product.

[a] *Dichtkunst*
[b] *dichten*
[c] *Urtheilskraft*

813. 1776–78. *M* 216.   15:362

The power of judgment is the activity of the mind in relating the manifold in an [*crossed out*: thing] object to its purpose.

814. 1776–78? (1773–75? 1775–77?) 1769?? *M* 217.   15:362

Feeling is that which in all judgments of sensibility leaves the greatest impression but does not have the greatest value. The relation to the   15:363 facilitation of the use of the understanding and reason is what is most important with regard to sensibility. On the illusion of feeling through the outer signs of emotion, high-sounding words, exaggerations (as when one displays a face set in astonishment, calls out a lot, speaks of something marvelous, but does not recount anything). The sentiments often come from collateral things, are grounded on moods, are fleeting, do not instruct, cannot rightfully demand any sympathy and must follow the understanding.

The power of judgment is the capacity to relate actions to an idea as their purpose. The product displays the power of judgment if it leads to the idea and is harmonious with it. The former are mere materials, the latter the form. Without an idea no order is comprehensible, consequently the appearance is lacking a focal point. The power of judgment goes beyond the understanding (tasteless people have understanding). The power of judgment in the dress of a woman at home. The power of judgment with regard to the dignity of a building, with regard to its ornaments, which must not conflict with its purpose. The power of judgment chooses, genius provides.

817. 1776–78? (1773–75? 1775–77?) 1769?? *M* 217.   15:364

Spirit is that which animates the mind, i.e., sets its activities into a free play, such as curiosity, a broad outlook, etc. The power of judgment determines the idea of what a thing properly should be. The shape, how it appears, must not contradict the idea. The power of judgment therefore binds and limits the play of sensibility, but it gives it true unity and thereby strengthens the impression. The mind is interested through emotions, set into motion and action by spirit, runs through the manifold, reaches the idea, goes back again from there and is proportionate in its choice and relations in accordance with and among all these. The latter is taste, which is nothing other than the judgment concerning the measure of the impressions insofar as this serves to touch the whole sensitivity of the soul proportionately, i.e., without upsetting it anywhere through a contradiction. The utility of taste is therefore primarily negative; what is positive is   15:365 genius, which consists of sentiment, the power of judgment, and spirit.[92]

15:365　**818.** 1776–78? (1773–75? 1775–77?) 1769?? M 217.

Taste is that which is similar to reason[a] in the sensible power of judgment,[93] namely that one can judge as it were *a priori* what will please all others. Sociability demands that we be able to judge what might please our friends, and indeed judge *a priori* what might please the more extended society. When one has been much among people who strive to please without vanity, then one finally internalizes the rule in accordance with which something pleases universally.

15:366　**822.** 1776–78? (1772–75? 1775–77?) M 218.

Feeling arises from the interest[b] that we take in something. If this interest arises from sensation, then it has no universal validity; but if it is immediately connected with intuition, then it is the judgment of all, and
15:367　the satisfaction from this ground makes it into beauty. Hence something is agreeable either on account of the feeling of the senses or on account of intuition.

15:367　**823.** 1776–78? (1770–71? 1773–75? 1775–77?) M 219.

Things have many properties in themselves that remain even if they are not cognized by any rational being, but they never have any value (whether in sensation or appearance or concepts) except in relation to beings by which they can be cognized and for which they can be objects of choice. Intellectual beings are therefore *foci*[c] and never mere means. The value of satisfaction and dissatisfaction is related to possible choice, i.e., to the power of choice,[d] and thus to the *principium* of life. What can be an object of our choice? That which produces our welfare, and thus enlarges the *actus* of life. Thus the feeling of the promotion or hindrance of life is satisfaction and dissatisfaction.[94] (It is not necessary that we also find the capacity to produce life in us, as long as we find in ourselves the grounds to set such acts as are there into play.) We have, however, an animal, a spiritual, and a human life. By means of the first we are capable of gratification and pain (feeling), by means of the third we are capable of satisfaction through the sensible power of judgment (taste), through the second we are capable of satisfaction by means of reason. Epicurus says: all gratification comes only through the cooperation of the body, although to be sure it has its primary cause in the spirit.[95]

(*Later addition*: Nature and art. [*crossed out*: Art and contingency]. The contingent is opposed to that which is sought. *Gout baroc*.[e] The

---

[a] *das Vernunftähnliche*

[b] *Antheil*, not *Interesse*

[c] Plural of *focus*, in classical Latin literally a hearth and figuratively the center of a home; here figuratively as a center of value.

[d] *Willkühr*

[e] baroque taste

contingent and intention. Natural play. Nature combines art and the contingent. Art: nature and the contingent. The contingent in free motion and in the action of the powers of the mind. There is nevertheless method therein; in the conflict or change of representation: that something is art and yet only contingent, that it is nature and yet seems to be art, etc.: that is where the gratification actually lies.)[96]

15:368

824. 1776–78? (1770–71? 1773–75? 1775–77?) *M* 219.

15:368

The feeling of the life of spirit pertains to understanding and freedom, where one has the grounds of cognition and choice in oneself. Everything that is in agreement with that is called good. This judgment is independent of the private constitution of the subject. It pertains to the possibility of the object through us and consists in universal validity for every power of choice; for otherwise another, contradictory power of choice is the greatest hindrance to life. Everything that pleases us in such a way that we are dependent on it is to that extent not in our power and proves to be a hindrance to the supreme life, namely to the strength of the power of choice to have its state and itself under its own freedom.[97] It is more gratifying, but it does not please.

All taste consists in finding that which is satisfying, the source of the sensuously touching, in our actions, comparisons, imaginings, etc.; thereby is it one's own. For humanity consists in subjecting animality to the spiritual.

(*Later addition*: The feeling of life is greater in sensation, but I feel a greater life in voluntary animation, and I feel the greatest *principium* of life in morality.

The social manner in accordance with taste is *conduite*.[a] Sensitivity. Taste in the selection of one's company. It takes understanding to bring guests together.)

827. 1776–78. *M* 213.

15:369

The beautiful must betray no alien interest,[b] but must please unselfishly.[c] No affectation about art, no pomposity about wealth, no charm in application to art, no neediness to betray economy. Like virtue, it must please on its own.[98]

829. 1776–78. *M* 214.

15:370

In all arts and sciences one can distinguish mechanism from genius; for the former, only skill is required, for the second, spirit.[99] Mechanism requires precepts and a rule or method. The German is much inclined to

---

[a] (good) conduct or behavior
[b] *fremdes Interesse*
[c] *uneigennützig*

mechanism and cannot get away from rules. Genius consists precisely in having an idea and not a rule for its basis.[100] Everything that introduces mechanism (e.g., Latin style, *examinatoria*[a]) knocks genius down. The rule, by contrast, is not the doctrine but the discipline of genius. Genius without discipline is crude.[101] One must there seek to bring everything down to mechanical rules.

Sentiment, the power of judgment, spirit, and taste belong to genius and cannot be brought down to rules; hence they are not counted as part of sensibility, because they cannot be reasoned out.[b,102]

15:370 **830. 1776–78. M 215.**

One can very well bring the moments of taste to concepts, but one cannot derive taste from concepts and base it on them, i.e., produce it by means of them.

(*Later addition*: The judgment of taste really concerns the universal validity and the satisfaction in the object on account of this universal validity. For that reason it is also possible to have a dispute about taste.)

15:371 The beautiful is the externally pleasing (as it strikes the senses) and is, to be sure, universal. In our conduct mores[c] and propriety are important, not merely virtue. The external is the vestment for the concepts of the understanding; for this vestment, the images and all means of intuition: language (first, style); the external of language itself: pronunciation or orthography. It is not what is outside; what is inside a room, if I leave aside the competence of the building, is also something external. The external side of friendship is courtesy. The external side of the love of honor is honorableness, breeding, propriety.

15:371 **831. 1776–78? (1773–75). M 215, at §597.[103]**

Spirit is the secret source of life. It is not subjected to the power of choice, rather all its movements come from nature. Reflection rests on planning and diligence. What arises from the spirit is original. When spirit so to speak outruns reflection, errors of judgment[d] may occur, which however will not be noticed in view of the life that they bring with them.

15:373 **837. 1776–78. M 215.**

That which agrees with the subjective laws of cognition with universal validity pleases the sensible power of judgment.

[a] examinations
[b] *ausvernünftelt*
[c] *Sitten*
[d] *Urtheilskraft*

839. 1776–78. *M* 215.   15:374

There is unity of subordination (logical) or coordination (real). The latter belongs to the intuition for going from the particular, i.e., the parts, to the universal, i.e., the whole and the purpose. The faculty is called the power of judgment and does not ratiocinate. It is the sensible advance work of the understanding.

842. 1776–78. *M* 215.   15:375

Just as reason moves from the universal to the particular, so conversely the sensible power of judgment moves from the particular to the totality of comprehension,*a* from the manifold to the unity either of composition or of the idea and aim that sets this action into a lively play.[104]

851. 1776–78. *M* 216.   15:376

In everything beautiful the object must please through reflection in itself, not [*crossed out*: through sensation] through impression, for that is agreeable. It must please universally in accordance with the laws of sensible judging, namely in the appearance. The taste that grasps the latter extends further than the beautiful: it also pertains to the agreeable.   15:377 The agreeable is considered as an object of choice because it affects us. If the beautiful contains a ground of choice that is because of charm. Mere beauty however is a mere object of the impartial satisfaction in sensible intuition.

856. 1776–78. *M* 217.   15:378

Taste is the faculty for distinguishing the universally pleasing in accordance with laws of sensibility. Here the restrictive conditions of private feeling must therefore be able to be set aside and the object be considered only in relation to all types of feeling in general, in order to have that proportion which has the greatest consensus with all.[105] Now since all types of sentiment together are common to every human being, by means of taste something can be judged *a priori* and with universal validity, but only for something well-practiced, namely the ability to perceive that which is touching for all sorts of sensitivities by means of frequent practice. But the proportion is not always the same. Hence something empirical is also involved here, namely the relation of the average among the different degrees of the sensitivity of others. In the judgment of taste the mind is at rest and inspires rest, as spirit inspires motion. I weigh the object, so to speak, against my entire feeling, in that I notice its harmoniousness*b* with regard to the occupation of all the cognitive powers or also the light or gentle play of one of them. Since the

---

a *Zusammenfassung*
b *wohlgereimtheit*

understanding must also run through the other representations even in immediate intuition in order to grasp the object from a universal point of view, taste requires understanding, thus demonstrates it and is advantageous to it. Genuine taste facilitates thinking and agrees subjectively with the concept.[106]

15:379 **859. 1776–78. M 217.**

Reason can only serve to explain the *phaenomena* of taste but not to prescribe [*crossed out:* certain laws and marks of the beautiful] laws to it, for the true ground does not consist in the objective but in the form of inner affection.

15:383 **871. 1776–78? 1772–75?? 1773–77?? M 220.**

Ars aspectabilis est pulchritudo.[a] What the art of intuition presents clearly and readily is beautiful. Hence the art must not be cognized through reason, thus insofar as the object is considered as a means, but in the thing itself. Regularity, proportion, measured division. A regular polygon. A pure color; the distribution of colors for charm (tulips, pheasants). Proportionate tone. The agreement (relation) of *phaenomeni* with an idea in general; to beauty there belongs understanding. The agreement of the *phaenomeni* with the essential end is the superior beauty. The art in appearance. All pure colors are beautiful, because art is already indicated in their being unmixed.[107]

15:383 **873. 1776–78. M 220.**

Taste is choice (not mediate, but immediate), but universally valid choice. Sentiment, the power of judgment, spirit, and taste together all belong among the subjective grounds of satisfaction.

[It is] sympathetic and shareable,[b] hence sociable.

15:384 Feeling does not judge, it teaches nothing, it is not communicable.[c]

15:384 **874. 1776–78. M 219.**

Finally to taste. There are 4 elements that one cannot teach: sentiment, the power of judgment, spirit, and taste. These comprise genius. To be sure, there is still more required for the capacity for genius, but these properly comprise the matter of genius.[108]

15:385 **878. 1776–78. M 242.**

Something (a garden, an elixir) pleases in sensation insofar as it affects our well-being and gratifies.

---

[a] Art that is worthy of being seen is beautiful.
[b] *mittheilend und theilnehmend*
[c] *communicabel*

Something pleases in the representation either through agreement with subjective laws (of the power of representation) and is beautiful, or with objective conditions of satisfaction, where either the ground is universally valid because it can be understood by means of reason (the useful) or the satisfaction is universally valid because it flows from a universal ground (the good).[109]

What agrees with the universal subjective* laws of cognition (not of sensation) of human beings pleases in reflection, merely because it is in harmony with the conditions of reflection. The beautiful gratifies only in society, but it pleases even when alone.[110]

*(The subjective laws cannot, to be sure, be cognized *a priori*, but we can have insight into their universality from our self-consideration, without collecting external appearances. There are also universally valid feelings, such as of sexuality, or of a temperature, or even of a compatibility of a feeling with others, which we can cognize for ourselves. This belongs to taste, but not to the power of the judgment of the beautiful.)

879. 1776–78. *M* 242.   15:385

That appearance which awakes the consciousness of the promotion of life in the intuition is beautiful;* that which does so in sensation is agreeable.

*(either immediately through the object (appearance) or through re-   15:386
flection (beautiful cognition).)

880. 1776–78. *M* 242.   15:386

Taste is sociable sensation.

In the case of the beautiful, the object or the cognition is accommodated to the subjective laws of reflection, in the case of taste, to the universal subjective laws of sensation.

881. 1776–78. *M* 242.   15:386

In feeling, taste, and the pleasure of the understanding the pleasure is considered to be immediate. For mediate pleasure has no special name. In feeling it arises from sensation; in taste from the correspondence with a rule, although an empirical rule (of humanity); in the pleasure of the understanding from an *a priori* rule. The first pleasure has the greatest subjectively motivating force, the third the greatest objectively motivating force. Feeling: subjective magnitude; taste, objective magnitude. The good is cognized without experience, solely through the understanding.

886. 1776–78. *M* 291.   15:387

Everything that indicates an intention, idea, or *dessein*, if it is as it were playing and occurs without the compulsion of a need, is beautiful. Hence pure colors on flowers, because otherwise dirty ones would instead occur.

15:388 A certain carelessness, e.g., with flowers, pleases. Much understanding and understanding everywhere is incommodious. The nature that seems similar to art and the art that in manners seems like nature are called naïve.[111]

15:390 **892.** 1776–78? (1772–75?) *M* 321.

An ideal is the idea in the image, i.e., in an invented representation *in concreto*. The ideal never expresses the entire idea on account of the hindrances *in concreto*, and yet the idea is that in accordance with which the ideal should be judged.

15:393 **899.** 1776–78. *M* 324.

Genius is not some sort of demon that gives out inspirations and revelations. If genius is to have matter, then one must have learned much or formally and methodically studied. Genius is also not a special kind and source of insight; it must be able to be communicated and made understandable to everyone.[112] Genius only comes in where talent and industry do not reach; but if the illuminations that are presented *amant obscurum*[a] and do not want to be seen and examined in the light at all, when they do not yield any graspable idea: then the imagination is raving, and, since its product is nothing, it has not arisen from genius at all, but is only an illusion.

15:393 **900.** 1776–78. *M* 324.

It seems that we must carry an ideal of a beautiful figure with us *a priori* just as we do an ideal of morality, because we could hardly have abstracted physiognomic judgments from experience. Lavater's latest words are appropriate here. They give indistinct concepts that are usable only *in concreto* without rules.[113]

15:409 **922.** 1776–78? (1775–77?) *M* 407, at §649.[114]

The freedom of talent from direction and coercion by rules* [*crossed out*: of which it has no need] is necessary in some beautiful arts. The most in *poesi*, where the occupation is merely a play and entertainment, where rules do not make execution possible. Nevertheless, rules must always lie at the basis and serve for direction, not in order to produce the product but to make the actions harmonious. It requires first of all a mechanism of talent and a genius beyond the finite.[115] Oratory re-
15:410 quires the coercion or direction of a rule more than poesy. Mechanism (*routine*) in accordance with rules in all sorts of sciences, e.g., history, calculation, mathematics. Genius is developed (*later addition*: awakened and formed and practiced) through the presentation of the products thereof;

[a] love obscurity

512

through criticism, whereby it takes rules to heart but does not learn them; through the freedom that one allows it to act in conformity with these rules.

Mechanical talent with diligence and effort is more useful. Genius, which plays, is more entertaining. All initial invention requires genius; but in the long haul the practical, teachable talent is far more useful.

1. Where rules cannot precede the cases of execution.

2. Where, if they do precede, they cannot bring forth such cases.

Freedom of talent from examples.

1. Natural diligence with little talent. 2. Talent with little genius. 3. Genius with little insight or science.

*(The freedom of talent is not an absence of rules.[a] (*Later addition*: The freedom of coercion from rules pertains to thinking, but not to speaking. That must be in conformity to rules, though not explicitly.) It corresponds with rules or itself contains rules, without having needed them in advance. Freedom from coercion is boldness, that from precept and its guidance is naturalness. (*Later addition*: The capacity[b] to learn is naturalness.) The talent in which nature replaces the help of art (makes it dispensable) is genius. To be teachable is to be willing, and teachableness is to be capable of learning. Mathematics is in itself a clear rule.

The rules from which imitation and custom are derived are those which are the most opposed to talent and thus to genius. Poetic freedom is the greatest. Genius with regard to taste and feeling depends on moods, especially the latter. (*Later addition*: sentiment, the power of judgment, spirit, and taste.)[116]   15:411

The play of sensations: music. Sensations through thoughts: poesy. The play of thoughts and sensations connected with a purposive business: Oratory. The play of shapes: dance.)[117]

924. 1776–78. *M* 407.   15:411

A procedure in accordance with a rule, which requires no power of judgment, is mechanical. And proficiency in proceeding mechanically in accordance with rules is mechanism. A habit achieved through practice produces a mechanism. In the case of a mechanism someone else has thought it out before us; we merely imitate. Yet imitation is more than mechanism: for in the latter, we do not have only an example,[c] but also guidance through someone else, e.g., a model.[d] Free imitation.[118]

[a] *Regellosigkeit*
[b] *Capacitaet, Fähigkeit*
[c] *Muster*
[d] *Modell*

15:413 **932. 1776–78. M 407.**

Talent. A property of the mind. It is *genius.*[a] Naturalness in learning, genius in inventing. Imagination. The power of judgment. Spirit. Taste.

Capacity. Gift. Genius. Insight, learnedness, and genius.

In the case of the mechanism of military coercion, nobody (an officer) of genius lasts long. He takes a discharge.

By genius proper we do not understand the soul itself, rather the spirit which as it were gives support to our powers and by means of whose inspiration we can do something to which diligence and imitation would not have helped us. It is the *principium* of the animation of our mental powers. One has no cognition of this spirit properly speaking and does not have its movement in one's power.

I first go behind the designation in my investigation. For a new word does not find immediate acceptance if it is not very suitable. There is in us something which is stimulating and driving but also an animating cause of the mental powers; this *principium* has its entirely special nature and laws. Nothing animates the spirit except for a certain universal which the mind grasps prior to all particulars, and from which it forms its outlook or products. Hence genius consists in this capacity to create the universal and the ideal.[119]

15:414 **933. 1776–78? (1772?) M 408.**

The breeding ground of ideas is the spirit. Thus spirit is encountered only in those inventions of which an original idea is the ground. Since the fruitfulness of the idea in accordance with which products are produced extends infinitely further than the individual execution of them, the latter moves the mind only through the former. The moving power lies in the products that acquire unity through relation to their idea.

The ground of unity among manifold rules is often an idea, and this demonstrates spirit. The expression of the idea through a manifold but united sensibility demonstrates spirit. The more aggregation, the less system; thus all the less spirit as far as form is concerned.

Brainstorm without idea. A shadow of the idea.

The animation of sensibility by means of the idea is spirit.

Genius is not impulse. To chase after genius is to be an enthusiast.

The idea must animate first the understanding, then the sensibility. If it happens the other way around, then it is not inspiration, but feverish inflammation.

One can also use the word "spirit" alone instead of "genius." But then it is not used with the article. The man has not only skill, but also genius. Spirit is not a particular talent, but an animating *principium* of all talents.

---

[a] Kant actually writes *genus.*

One cannot add any adjective to the word "spirit," e.g., his spirit, rather these hold of brains and talents; the spirit is that which animates all of that. Capability. Talent. Spirit.[120]

934. 1776–78? 1772?? *M* 408.   15:415

Spirit is the inner (animating) principle of the **animation** of the (powers of the mind) thoughts. Soul is that which is animated. Consequently spirit animates all talents. It commences a new series of thoughts out of itself. Hence ideas.

Spirit is the original animation, namely that which comes from ourself and is not derived. (Naturalness is the receptivity of the powers of the mind, talent the spontaneity.)

One does not say "the spirit," but simply "spirit."

Rich in spirit (not rich in genius), writing is either rich in sense or rich in images or even rich in words.

Spirit in architecture or music is different from the scholastic and mechanical.

941. 1776–78? 1772?? *M* 410–11.   15:417

Arts of genius are those whose sensible works can be animated* [*crossed out*: and guided] through ideas. Arts of diligence: those where the purpose makes the product possible in accordance with rules. Handicrafts are products in accordance with a model and guideline.[121]

*(or [where] the idea is represented in intuition.)

942. 1776–78? 1772?? *M* 410.   15:418

Spirit is the *principium* of the animation of talents and the powers of the soul through ideas (thus of a purposively animated imagination). An idea animates when it advantageously sets the imagination into a manifold efficacy.[a] Spirit is like this even in society. There can be much sentiment in a writing, much reflection. The prospect of a use from manifold points of view [*breaks off*]

943. 1776–78. *M* 410–11.   15:418

One can be animated without knowing the idea, but by suspecting one.

Since animation is sensible, genius always pertains to the perfect sensibility. But since it depends on an idea, etc. Something can give us occasion for animation without being an animating *principium*, e.g., mere images which set the imagination in train. The perception of genius alone animates internally through sympathy. Arts of genius presuppose ideas.

[a] *Wirksamkeit*

An original spirit is that whose ideas are animating simultaneously through novelty and appropriateness.

One only perceives genius if one goes back to the idea, and not merely through instruction. A *bon mot* can have wit or spirit. Spirit is serious, but wit jokes. **Mathematics is not the land of ideas**, but of concepts made intuitable; it does not go from the whole to the parts, but from universals to particulars.

Yet an entirely new method presupposes an idea.

15:419 Philosophy is the true motherland of ideas, but not of their animation. But nature (knowledge of humanity) and the art that is in competition with it (a second creation),[a] which seeks to go beyond nature as far as intuition is concerned, is the field of ideas that are at the same time animating. Hence arts of genius certainly have nature for their archetype, but have as their condition laws of animation for human beings and in conformity with these they make a new creation, which also has its laws.[122]

15:419 **945.** 1776–78. *M* 410.

The idea is (archetype, to which a cognition is related, unity of generation) the unity of the concept as a *principium* of the determination of the* manifold in the intuition that corresponds to it. All parts are there for the sake of the others, and all for the sake of each, as in an animal.[123]

*(They are not associated and sought together, but generated thereby. The spirit is entire in the whole and entire in every part.)

15:420 **947.** 1776–78. *M* 410.

The power of judgment is the *Censor* of the sensations, in order to distinguish whether they belong to the idea and are connected with it or whether they even hinder and obscure it.

Sensations are either those which accompany the intuition and follow from it, or only emotions from an intuition which one does not communicate. The latter contribute nothing to the idea, are those worth nothing more than for mere amusement, which does not leave anything behind, and only the idea is self-sufficient and can preserve the sensations.[124]

15:420 **949.** 1776–78. *M* 411.
15:421 Genius is not, as Gerard will have it,[125] a special power of the soul (otherwise it would have a determinate object), but a *principium* of the animation of all other powers through whatever ideas of objects one wants.

Invention presupposes an animation of the cognitive powers, not merely the sharpening of the capacity for learning. But this animation

[a] *Nachschöpfung*

516

must be aimed at an end through the generation of an idea; otherwise it is not invention, but accidental discovery.

950. 1776–78. *M* 411.   15:421

The idea animates the imagination, and this in turn gives life to the idea, namely material for its animation, i.e., sensibility as an animal life.[126]

958. 1776–78. *M* 411.   15:422

Spirit is that which affords much to think about. Sensation: what gives much to sense. The power of judgment seeks to make sensations harmonious among themselves in accordance with the object. Taste. To transform private thinking into something universally valid (forced expressions, which one understands only oneself).

There are arts capable of spirit such as horticulture, and spiritless arts such as handicraft.

What is capable of spirit can nevertheless be empty of spirit.

959. 1776–78. *M* 411.   15:423

The formative power that competes* with nature (in the appearance) is called (fine) art; it must have its rule, which however has subjective principles, hence the compatibility of a free exercise of our powers with our laws. It is a creation in accordance with our own sense.[127]

*(not imitative; for art has its own law, just like nature, and its particular world, namely that of appearances.)

961. 1776–78. *M* 411.   15:423

The idea is the *principium* of the rules. Archetype. An idea is a creature of the understanding and not an abstraction by the understanding from the materials of the imagination. Ideas can only pertain to the unity of the whole.

Rules are of the distributive or the collective unity of the whole; the latter are architectonic.

962. 1776–78. *M* 412.   15:423

All beautiful art rests on the combination of intuition with concepts, i.e., of sensibility with the understanding and reason. The more concept shines forth in the intuition, the more a concept is expressed in the intuition: all the greater is the art. But the concepts must not be empirical, i.e., borrowed from the intuition; for otherwise it is mere skill, but not art. If the intuition appears to be expressed merely in accordance with the laws of sensibility and the concept merely in accordance with the laws of the understanding, but both are in perfect agreement with each   15:424 other, then the beautiful art consists precisely in this agreement, since the purposiveness is really artful,[a] but the combination of purposiveness with a mere play of the senses is beautiful.

Beautiful nature is that which seems to be art and yet is nature. Hence also art which appears like nature (as if it flowed from the sensibility in accord with its own laws alone) is beautiful art.[128]

15:424 **964.** 1776–78. *M* 412.

What is essential to beauty consists in correspondence with concepts or at least with the relation to common concepts. Harmony of sensations; hence consensus with understanding. For this is the *principium* of the unity of all our representations.

15:428 **981.** 1776–78. *M* 415.

15:429 The majesty of the creation in a starry sky includes our emotion through the extension of our mind and a bold flight.[129] The admiration of the art in the creation yields an entirely different sentiment, namely that of satisfaction in providence and the good, in order to treasure the value of the creation and to love it. The textbook of divine majesty.

15:429 **983.** 1776–89. *M* 417.

Taste does not concern the useful, but it must harmonize with that. It is a consistent play of understanding and sensibility. It is sociable, hence sociable senses.

There is no private taste. (Public judgment. A banquet.) Taste has universal but not *a priori* rules; it concerns merely the form of the entertainment of the senses without satiety. It loves alteration. Not art, not wealth and utility. Nature, which costs nothing. Facility. Taste in colors and in the colorless. In conversation: not solemnity. Music. Gardens. Buildings. Plays.

15:429 **984.** 1776–89. *M* 417.

The beautiful art lies in the agreeableness of the manner; it is in this that taste consists.

Gustus (objective) est suavitas in modo. Subiective est diiudicatio suavitatis in modo.[b] Courtliness and *politesse*.

Taste is delicate. – Good appetite, good cook.

15:430 Taste is something original, which cannot be learned and belongs to genius.

---

[a] *künstlich*

[b] (Objective) taste is pleasantness in manner. Subjective taste is the judgment of pleasantness in manner.

When everything is equally tasteful, one can still judge better about one part of taste than another. Taste is the greatest culture. The polish of the beautiful. One can only judge of taste through taste.

The writings of the ancients are enduring originals of taste. Without these there would be no durable standard. Dead languages.[130]

986. 1776–89. *Pr* II.   15:430

Whether Hume was right that greater beauties are rare because only rare beauty (or beauty in itself) is called great, thus through a tautology.[131] 15:431 Whether beauty is called great only through comparison or whether it has its ideal in itself.*

The climate in which nature strikes the mean between permitting and refusing charms is the happiest. Garden.

Charms in sandy wastes. Meadows in Norway.

*(One would not know what is beautiful or great beauty if there were no basis in an ideal.)

II.

ANTHROPOLOGY NOTES FROM THE 1780S

987. 1780–83? (1783–84?) *LBl* D 23.   15:431

For anthropology. The human being does not play for himself alone. He would neither seek to hit billiard balls artfully nor toss bowling balls not play *bilboquet* or *solitair*. If he does any of this he does it only in order subsequently to show his skill to others. For himself he is serious. Likewise he would not expend the least effort on the beautiful unless he expects to be seen and admired by others sometime. This is also true of play. Like Selkirk,[132] he might play with cats and goats, but then he compares them with persons by analogy, rules over them, wins their trust, their inclination and respect. Play without human spectators is held to be madness. Thus all of this has an essential relation to so- 15:432 ciability, and what we feel immediately therein is quite inconsiderable. The communication and what is reflected on us is the only thing that attracts us.[133]

988. 1783–84. *LBl* B 11.   15:432

How is an objectively valid judgment possible which is yet not determined through any concept of the object?

(For a rule that is valid for everyone must be valid of the object, and thus the concept of the object must determine the judgment for everyone, and thus be valid for me.)

If the judgment expresses the relation of all the cognitive faculties in agreement for the cognition of an object in general, hence only the reciprocal promotion of the cognitive powers among each other, as it is

519

felt. For in that case no concept of any object can produce such a feeling but only concepts.[134]

If the judgment is related to the object (and only by means of the concept of it to the subject), although no determinate concept of any object nor any relation of the concept to the subject in accordance with rules makes the judgment about it necessary, then it must be related to the object in general through the mental powers of cognition in general.[135] For then the ground of the judgment is contained not in any determinate concept but only in the feeling of a movement of all the cognitive powers, which is capable of being communicated, through concepts in general.

The pleasure is in this judgment, not in the object itself.

The cognitive powers are wit and imagination, insofar as they are in correspondence with understanding. The power of judgment is only the faculty that makes possible the agreement of the two in a case *in concreto*. Acuity is the faculty of noticing even a little agreement or conflict between the two, and is therefore a property of the power of judgment.

15:433 Pleasure is in general the feeling of the promotion of life; that of the promotion of the life of the senses by means of sensation is called gratification and its opposite pain. That in the promotion of life in the play of the cognitive powers in general is called taste. That in the promotion of the life of the cognitive powers in particular is approval.[136]

Whether a judgment or in general a representation will be accompanied with pleasure cannot ever be seen from the concept of the object; but it is analytically certain that if freedom exists as a property of the will such a pleasure will be presupposed. Likewise, that certain kinds of cognition produce pleasure cannot be understood *a priori*, but it follows of itself that if cognition has incentives in itself, a pleasure in the movement of the cognitive powers, whether the sensations are agreeable or disagreeable, will arouse pleasure.[137]

15:433 **989.** 1785–89? (1780–84?) 1776–79? *LBl* Puttlich.
P. I.

The foremost means by which to find gratification in life somewhere is through society. Hence the social inclination and need, but also after long experience the longing for a *retraite*, to live separated from society, thus misanthropy or even anthropophobia, and the final refuge of retreating to one's family in order to live as it were on an island separated from great crowds. The human being seeks concord among his own kind; nature, however, wants discord, in order to provide a constant spur to activity through effort.[138] Friendship from affection is a mere idea. He is sociable who can be an agreeable member of every society. (My dear friends: there is no friend.)[139]

15:434 Humans do the greatest evil among one another. Hence social vexations through formality, reservation, and the desire to make one's value

preeminent. One can only give one's own life a value in the eyes of others through that which one does, not through that which one enjoys; a useful man is at the same time a happy man, the more so as he has confined his selfishness. To seek well-being in other diversions makes the mind empty in its loneliness and open to terrifying abandonment and desertion. Mordaunt.[140] (*Later addition*: – In youth one values gratification only in accordance with its degree, in age more by its duration, even if it is small.)
P. II.

Taste.

That, the existence of which pleases – thus what interests, from wherever it may be given [–] **gratifies**. What also pleases without any interest is **beautiful**. What interests but only insofar as it is produced by the subject himself or can be considered to be possible in this way is **good**.[141]

That which pleases **from objective grounds** but not through concepts is **beautiful**. It must please *a priori* for otherwise one would not impose it upon others as **necessary**. Not empirical precepts, also not *a priori* **precepts**.

1. What pleases in sensation – agreeable⎱ immediate
2. What pleases in reflection – beautiful⎰ immediate
3. What pleases in concepts – good: mediate or immediate
On the deathliness of boredom.
Gratifies – pleases – is approved of.

The superiority of reason over the entire power of the imagination, insofar as one feels this.

992. 1785–89. *LBl* D 22.[142]   15:436
If a judgment is so constituted that it asserts itself to be valid for everyone yet excludes all empirical as well as every other *a priori* proof [*crossed out*: of its correctness] for that necessary consensus, then it relates its [*crossed out*: manner of] representation [*crossed out*: of the object not to a sensible but to a supersensible determination of the subject] to a [*crossed out*: supersensible] principle of the [*crossed out*: supersensible use] supersensible determination of our cognitive faculties. For since the judgment is to be universally valid, it must have a principle; but since it is not capable of any ground of proof nor any rule of the use of the understanding or reason in regard to the objects of the senses, [*crossed out*: our cognitive faculties must have a supersensible principle] it must have a principle of the [*crossed out*: determination of our] use of the cognitive faculties [*crossed out*: in general] which is grounded on or related to some supersensible determination of them; now whether this [*crossed out*: principle] determination is merely assumed or well

grounded, in either case such a judgment can only be made with respect to it.[143]

§ – *A*. Deduction of the aesthetic power of judgment concerning the beautiful in nature;

B. ——— concerning the sublime in nature.

§. The culture of both in nature is preparation for moral feeling: the first with regard to imperfect duties, the second with regard to perfect duties.[144] – For in both there is subjective purposiveness of nature. The first, with respect to its quality, the second, with regard to the magnitude of the purposive determination of the subject.[145]

On the interest in taste – in the common sense – communicability of sensations. *Humanitas.* On the beautiful and sublime in art and the beautiful arts and sciences.

Introduction: on the divisions.

In both aesthetic judgments subjective purposiveness is the content that one would universally **communicate**. In both intuition determines the judgment. Imagination contains the synthesis that is universally communicable for understanding and reason.

993. 1788–89. *LBl* Warda.
P. 1.

Beautiful and Sublime.

The judgment of taste contains something logical, in that it asks for universal consensus, and is to that extent different from another kind of aesthetic judgment, namely that of the feeling that is valid only for the individual.

But it also differs from the logical judgment in this, that this universal validity is not grounded on the agreement of the manner of representation with the object, but rather with the relation of the faculties of representation (which belong to cognition) in the subject, and indeed in every subject.[146]

Hence no rule for judging through taste, in accordance with which it could be decided what accords with taste or is contrary to it, is possible, even if it were itself to be derived from judgments of taste.

The company- or communication-property of taste.

The judgment of taste is thus always a singular judgment,[147] and one can provide no ground whose power of proof another must concede, because it is not a cognitive judgment.

The universal validity of the satisfaction, and yet not through concepts but in the intuition, that is the difficulty.

The cognition of an individual given object, if it is to be communicable, presupposes two faculties: understanding, for the concept, and imagination, for the intuition. – The agreement of the two in

the representation of an object for cognition has universal rules, and thus also this agreement in the subject, although these rules cannot be especially conceived. (The expression "taste" is related to meals, where one may choose among many offerings and hunger is not the incentive.)
P. II.

Taste in company. Women.

The culture of taste is preparation for morals.[148]

On the sublime. It is that in the representation of which (in the imagination) the mind feels its vocation or disposition to extend itself to that which exceeds all measure of the senses.

It is as it were the discovery of a chasm in our own nature stretching itself beyond the bounds of the senses. – Hence the shudder that affects us. – A fear that is always driven away through recollection of our security, and a curiosity which is too great for our power of comprehension.[149]

Mountains and plains. As it were nature in its powerful destruction, hence the fables of giants. – It leads to the raving of the imagination, and then the mind falls victim to fear of tension and madness. Burke – Milton – Klopstock. Aeneas's descent into hell.[150] – The night is sublime, the day is beautiful. Deserts, inhabited by spirits. – Ancient abandoned castles.

– The depth of the mind in the moral is sublime.[151]

3. On the feeling of the good [*end of note*].

15:439

III.
OUTLINES FOR THE COURSE ON ANTHROPOLOGY, 1776–1784.[152]

1487. 1776–78. *LBl* Ha 43.
P. I.

15:717

Gratification and Pain[153]

(*Later addition*: The agreeable for the sense[s]. The beautiful for the power of judgment. The good for reason.)

(*Later addition*: A sensation, insofar as it necessitates that we leave our state, is pain; insofar as it leads us into another state, it is pleasure. Thus simultaneous. The hope of another is pure gratification.)

Physical (*later addition*: sensation) and moral (*later addition*: reflection, concept). Sensation and imagination. Children often cry.

The latter require culture. Hope and fear. An acquired position of honor. Invention.

Genuine moral pains.

Gratification over one's own good conduct.

15:719   Moral gratification: hope of a better state and the disappearance of an evil.[154]

      ....

15:724   P. II.

      Pain is not an evil.

      (*Later addition*: That the existence of which pleases influences our condition.)

      That which (*later addition*: in itself, in intuition, already at home) pleases without gratifying. That which gratifies without pleasing in itself (except in the private relation to our well-being). Finally: that which is approved of without pleasing sense.

      1. That which gratifies (me or an *individuum*) (private sense). 2. That which gratifies communally (where the gratification in each is small, but much multiplied by the assumed sense of community) (*later addition*: pleases through the approval). Communal sense: Taste. 3. That which although to be sure in itself it displeases the senses still pleases as a *principium*.* The cast of mind, *sentiment*, character.

      *(Thus not in relation to everyone's similar sense, but rather to the judgment of every intelligent being. The satisfaction pertains to the rule of satisfaction in general and universal harmony.)

      Agreeable (in sensation). Beautiful (in the proportion of the sensations) (correspondence of the agreeable with the good). Good: relatively or absolutely (moral). We have only one feeling, but different representations and sensations to arouse it.

15:725   Crude gratification.

      Self-feeling, social feeling, moral feeling.

      The sources of judgment are in the first case the private sense, in the second consensus with other, practiced sense in general, in the third with the rule of the consensus of the sensible in general (empirical).

      What pleases in [1.] (private) sensation (enjoyment), 2. intuition, 3. in the mere idea as contained in the *principium* of satisfaction.

      *He who is not readily brought into motion is even-tempered; he who is not quickly brought to sentiment, is indifferent.

      *(Sensitive[a] and even-tempered. Not touchy.[b])

      Pure gratification: 1. with which no pain is combined. 2. What does not derive from the senses: spiritual gratification. To win at play is no pure gratification. Spiritual gratification.

      Sense as well as taste as well as *sentiment* pertain to that which pleases in itself, whether in sensation or in mere viewing or in the concept. They are not interested, neither through utility nor through honor.

[a] *Empfindsam*
[b] *empfindlich*

(*Later addition*: The purposive represented as a free play of sensibility (entertainment of the senses*). Nature, art. Entertainment through taste, not through utility. Style.)

*(The entertainment of the senses as something purposive.)

Nothing can be explained from the feeling, since as something unique it is [not] universal. The lowest feeling is in that which is considered merely in relation to the private sense. More elevated[a] is that which   15:726
pleases the communal sense (taste), and indeed on empirical grounds. The highest is in that which is derived from the unity of the universal satisfaction *a priori*. 1. Sensible feeling. 2. Taste (*sensus communis*). 3. Moral feeling. All three please immediately.

Beautiful or agreeable art. Not science. (what is healthy.) Art like nature and nature like art. The beauty must be merely in the manner and neither constitute nor hinder the end. Refinement of taste. It is mere power of judgment.

The promotion of life in the sensation or through the mere harmony of sensations.

Whether taste has a constant and necessary rule. Fashionable taste. Whether anyone has his particular taste.

(*Later addition*: That all gratification is corporeal and aims at health (laughter). That we immediately understand what another says with the word "agreeable.")

1512. 1780–84. *LBl* Ha 44.   15:834
P. II.[155]

Taste.

The senses of taste. Natural beauty and artistic beauty. Beautiful arts.   15:836
What pleases universally through reason is good. Here reason is legislative.

All satisfaction is:

  1. In the sensation (gratifies) through the sense, the agreeable.
  2. In the universal judgment of the senses (pleases) (*later addition*: in reflection), through taste, the beautiful.*
  3. In the concept (is approved of) through the cast of mind (*sentiment*), the good.

*(What pleases universally through subjective grounds, where each is a law to the other.)

The first has merely private validity, the second universal validity in experience, the third universal validity for everyone through reason. The first in enjoyment; the second in reflection (*later addition*: through

---

[a] *Erhabener*, usually "more sublime," although here, since it is used in contrast with "lowest" (*niedrigste*), the more literal meaning is preferred.

lawfulness), both subjective; the third pleases through universal purposiveness. (*later addition*: 1. Happiness, 2. mannerliness,[a] 3. morality.[b])

Taste is the faculty for the [*crossed out*: investigation] comparison of sensation with the universal sense (which we judge *a priori* from the subjective conditions of cognition). That which gratifies us is also agreeable to others. The faculty for determining the judgment of others *a priori* through one's own satisfaction. What earns approval. Whether one can know prior to experience that something deserves approval. (*Later addition*: Charm and emotion do not belong to the beautiful.) It is therefore sociable. (*Later addition*: gustatory taste.[c]) (*Later addition*: not much appetite, rather without.) (*Later addition*: The judgment about a representation as *schema* of a concept of reason.)

15:837

He who asserts the complete independence of taste from the approval of others (*de gustu non est disputandum**)[d] is without taste. Miserly or selfish people, who are not pleasing, have no taste.** Taste is the culture of gratification. *Luxuries* and *luxus*.[e] The former is an immoderation in gratification that makes one sick; the latter one in taste, that makes one poor. The influence of fashion. (The suitability of good living for sociability is a good manner of life.) Selfishness must not be obvious. Also not wastefulness, but art that seems like nature. *Fastus*[f] (oriental). Boastful. Taste in gardens, in buildings, in furnishings, dress, meals, entertainment of society. In writings.

*(The sensation of the agreeable can never be false, but the judgment of taste to prefer it over others on that account may well be. A beautiful face: there charm is often placed before beauty. He who has much appetite must not judge about taste. (*Later addition*: About the two proverbs of taste.)[156])

**(*Later addition*: Not through concepts, not through sensations. *Quot capita: tot sensus, de gusto non est disputandum.*[g] About the beautiful, everyone must judge for himself, and yet no one can call something beautiful without judging for everyone.[157] – Subjective ground that is at the same time objective. Beauty is not charm. Beauty of nature. Art. On the sublime. Relation to morality.)

To have taste and* to be charmed by that are not the same. The judgment of taste and the judgment of inclination: the latter is a weakness. Taste is the greatest culture of sensibility, the *analogon* of morality. (Not charm and emotion.)

[a] *Gesittetheit*
[b] *Sittlichkeit*
[c] *Gaumengeschmack*, that is, taste in the literal rather than metaphorical sense.
[d] "There is no disputing about taste."
[e] indulgence and extravagance
[f] pride, haughtiness
[g] As many heads [minds], as many senses [as there are]: there is no disputing about taste.

526

*(Society gives the beautiful a charm.)

Agreeableness has more of private satisfaction. Taste less, but it replaces it with universality, as music, gardening, architecture, painting.

One can already see the lack of taste in the clothing, in the manner 15:838 of eating, furnishing, etc. (Beautiful. Sublime.)

Taste is found more in courts than in republics. The inclination of taste (society) extinguishes *sentiments*. The ancient Greeks are originals in taste, because the female sex did not influence them in that.

False taste derives from fashion. Subtle and grovelling or boastful and shimmering.

The judgment of taste is without interest; the interest in taste is in society.

1513. 1780–84. *LBl* Ha 38.   15:838
P. 1.

What gratifies (agreeable); what pleases (beautiful); what is approved (good).

(*Later addition*: in sensation (sense); intuition (imagination); in concept (reason).)

What pleases the senses alone is agreeable; what pleases universally in the correspondence of sensibility to the understanding, is beautiful; what pleases the understanding alone – good.

Formal purposiveness distinguished from ends of nature.*a*

On the basis of taste. The good on the basis of principles.

The beautiful is in natural combination with the good; yet the satisfaction of the senses is the chief end. Beautiful development*b* requires good organs. Whether big ears, which are not beautiful, hear better. (*Later addition*: Virtuosi – dilettantes – fops about taste.) The useful is less beautiful. The strength and lightness of a column contribute to its beauty. Nature is beautiful when it looks like art, and art, when it is recognized as art and yet looks like nature.[158] (*Later addition*: The satisfaction is here 15:839 determined *a priori* through rules.) The increase of needs produces culture. The spread of taste civilizes (promotes sociability); insight (freedom under laws) moralizes, and conversely. Taste demands ideal gratification and weakens the crude. Taste, insofar as it outweighs natural need, is *luxus*. It enlivens the arts, increases the [number of] people, and increases the evil. (*Luxus* is weakening. Driving in coaches.) The appearance*c* of the good belongs together with taste. Courteousness. It prepares for good dispositions. (*Later addition*: Virtue and morals. *conduite*.)

---

a *Naturzwecken*, a term Kant would use in the "Critique of the Teleological Power of Judgment" for "organisms."
b *Bildung*
c *Schein*

The (*later addition*: conditional) good (*later addition*: of things, respectively perfection – likewise skill) does not ask after the consensus of the senses, but of reason. It comes last and is not to be found in primitive times. Culture. He is often called a good (noble) person who lets himself be pleased by everything. The skill of talent is rated higher than the goodness of the manner of thinking. A good or a great prince. The true, the beautiful, the good. (*Later addition*: Strength of soul, goodness of soul, greatness of soul. Moral feeling is different from moral disposition.) The will to make nothing but good use of all talents. *There is a difference between chattering about the good, like Christina, and *sentiment*.[159] The agreeable has private approval, the beautiful public, the good universal. The good includes everything, but does not exclude the previous ones. As long as honorableness receives particular honor there are bad times. Even worse if it is laughed at and met with contempt. Nature does not allow that the good are separated from the evil. The good is invisible, one sees only what brings advantage. Peace of mind without vanity and self-satisfaction is its reward.

15:840

*(Many can, to be sure, judge the good, but without *sentiment*. Likewise the evil, even if it causes them damage. Discourse about morality interests many not at all.

Maxims do not come from nature; they must be thought through. One must make oneself familiar with them in time in order to have them ready.)
.... [160]

IV.
NOTES FROM THE REFLECTIONS ON LOGIC.

16:100 **1748.** 1753–59. *V* 6, at §19.[161]

A sensible [*crossed out*: representation] judging of perfection is called taste. A cognition that is cognized as perfect by the sensible power of judgment is called aesthetic. Gothic taste.

The agreement of the manifold in a thing with a common intention is called perfection. If everything agrees with the rules of the inferior power of cognition, then it is aesthetically perfect. I.e., if the agreement is cognized solely through the powers of sense, and thus the gratification is aroused through the lower powers. E.g., acquaintance with epic poems, with what is painterly in the description. If it is discovered through the higher powers, then it also makes for a gratification, but a distinct one, which is on that account not so charming.

What taste is. The doctrine of taste.

16:101 **1753.** 1753–59. *V* 7, at §22.[162]

In every perfection there is to be found a rule or intention, secondly an agreement with that. There are two preeminent aims with regard to cognition: to instruct, or to gratify, or both. The first is attained solely through distinct insights, the latter in two ways: either through the beauty of the object or the agreeableness of the presentation. The latter, since it cannot be attained through perfectly distinct representations, is the aesthetic perfection of cognition.

16: 102

Without aesthetic assistance, distinct cognition contains a source of gratification solely through the charm of the object through logical perfection, that is, the correctness [*crossed out*: of exposition] and order in which it is considered, which exceeds all aesthetic perfection in both magnitude and duration. Archimedes's gratification in the bath.[163] Kepler's at the discovery of a proposition.[164]

The aesthetic is only a means for accustoming people with too much tenderness to the rigor of proofs and explanations. As when one rubs honey on the rim of a vessel for children.

The natural history of earthquakes [is] an example of a thorough science that awakens gratification. Who has discovered the science of aesthetics.[165]

1780. 1764–68? 1769? *V* 7, at §22.
Logical perfection is related to the object, beauties to the subject.*
*(The matter of cognition in relation to the subject is sensation. The form of cognition in relation to the subject is called appearance.[166] All satisfaction is correspondence and is either subjective, if it rests on correspondence with the subject, or objective, if it rests on correspondence with the object, and is universally valid.)

16: 112

1781. 1764–68? 1769? 1770–71? 1773–75? *V* 7.
The criticism and history of the beautiful belongs to scholarship, but not to art; the talents of genius, e.g., philosophy and fine art, do not belong to scholarship.

16: 112

1784. 1764–68? 1769? *V* 8, at §24.[167]
Rational perfection pertains to subordination, aesthetic perfection to coordination: the former, to considering the *concretum in abstracto*, the latter to considering the *abstractum in concreto*.

16: 113

1786. 1764–68? 1769? *V* 9, at §33.[168]
Logical perfection is partly historical, partly rational: the former is speculative.
The aesthetic perfection of sensation or taste (in itself).
The practical perfection of utility or morality.

16: 114

1787. 1766–68? 1769? *V* 8.
Taste affords no rules *a priori* because it ought to be a sensible judgment, which cannot be made in accordance with such rules, but only in sensible intuition.

16: 114

The rules serve to explain and criticize taste, but not as precepts.

The norm[s] of taste are models, not for imitation (*later addition*: precepts), but for judging.

16: 115   **1789.** 1769–70? 1771–72? *V* 6, at §19.

The pleasure that can be attained only through [*crossed out*: the feeling about] the sensation of the object (consequently matter) constitutes charm and emotion and is called feeling.

The pleasure that can be attained only [*crossed out*: the feeling] concerning the form of the object is called taste, and since the cognition of the form cannot be attained through the effect of the object on the senses but rather arises through the laws of the activity of the subject (es-

16: 116   pecially of the inferior cognition, which coordinates): thus the ground of satisfaction is subjective in regard to the matter and objective with regard to the formal ground.[169]

16: 116   **1791.** 1769–70? (1771–72?) *L* 6.

Taste pertains to the universality of satisfaction[170] and hence pertains precisely to the form of the object that fits with the universal laws of sensibility. But what corresponds with the laws of the powers of our mind is agreeable. If this agreeableness is small in a private relation, insofar as our own condition is concerned, it can by contrast be represented that it is universally valid for sociability. In solitude indifference with regard to the beautiful. Young people have much feeling and little taste. The conditions of the beautiful form of objects are representations in accordance with relations of space and time. Those of beautiful cognition: novelty, contrast, variety.[a]

16: 117   **1793.** 1769–1770? (1771–72?) *V* 7.

Beauty consists in the correspondence of the form – appearance – with the [*crossed out*: universal] laws of sensibility. Order. Unity.

The charm in the correspondence of the object insofar as it alters our condition in accordance with laws of sensibility: novelty.

Taste is the faculty of cognizing that which is universally sensibly pleasing.

Beautiful objects.

Beautiful representations of [*crossed out*: sensation or] imitation or cognition of objects.

Good is that which pleases in concepts, thus universally, and which agrees with the object.

Cognition is logically perfect through correspondence with the ob-
16: 118   ject, thus in accordance with rules of the understanding; aesthetically perfect: what pleases in sensibility, hence subjectively.

---

[a] *Mannigfaltigkeit*, usually translated as "manifoldness."

1794. 1769–70. *V* 7.   16: 118
Logical perfection with regard to form consists in truth (in concepts) and its means. Aesthetic perfection with regard to form consists in graspability in intuition.
The form of sensibility, which facilitates the perfection of the understanding, is the self-subsistently beautiful, which can serve to make general concepts intuitive and prepares appearances for distinctness through general concepts.

1795. 1769–75? (1776–78?) *V* 7.   16: 118
The judging of matter occurs through sensation (*later addition*: relation of the representation to the subject).
The feeling of form is taste. But since the form can only be cognized *reflectendo*[a] [*breaks off*]

1796. 1769–70. *V* 7.   16: 118
The judging of the object through sensation is not universally valid, through true taste it is valid for all human beings, but both are subjective; through reason, however, it is valid for all. If the object is in agreement with the feeling of the subject with regard to matter, then it is agreeable and charms or moves; if it is in agreement with feeling with regard to   16: 119
form, then it is beautiful; but if there is a correspondence with feeling *in abstracto*, then it is good.

1797. 1769–70. *V* 7.   16: 119
The form of beauty consists in two elements. **First**: of graspability (clarity) in the intuition [*crossed out: in concreto*] (correspondence with the rules of the understanding. **Second**: In the [*breaks off*]

1798. 1769–70. *V* 7.   16: 119
The essential form of the beautiful consists in the correspondence of the [*crossed out*: appearance] intuition with the rules of the understanding. Music. Proportion. Maxims in examples.

1799. 1769–1775. *V* 8.   16: 119
Perfect sensibility is beauty. (*Later addition*: All beauty consists in presentation.[b]) Sensibility, however, consists in correspondence with the subjective laws of execution, and the form is the coordination in the case of *obiectis sensuum*, subordination in the case of *obiectis rationis*.[c]

---

[a] in or by reflection, reflectively
[b] *Darstellung*
[c] objects of the senses, objects of reason

Abstraction helps with logical perfection, association, however, with aesthetic perfection. The abstract is isolated, dry, difficult; the concrete that which is hidden,[a] lively, and easy. From the particular no inference to the universal is valid, and the cognition of the particular in the universal is without any intuition.

16:122   **1806.** 1769–70? 1771–72? *V* 8.

The teachers of taste have greatly erred in praising sentiment (charm and emotion) more than intuition in aesthetic perfection; for it is the latter that presents concepts *in concreto*, giving back to them what the understanding has taken from them through abstraction. Essentially beautiful.

There are creative intuitions, which are distinct from [*crossed out*: derivative] empirical ones. There are deceptive or [*crossed out*: dreaming] raving intuitions, which are not really depicted but are added in thought.

16:123   **1807.** 1769–70? 1771–75? *V* 9, opposite §31.[171]

Whether logical or aesthetic perfection must go first?

Aesthetic perfection must bear the mark of contingency, thus must not be sought.

It must not be superfluous with regard to logical perfection, but must carry (*later addition*: intuition) unity with it.

It must [*crossed out*: only serve] never be without simplicity.

16:123   **1809.** 1769–70. *V* 9.

Logical perfection is related to the object (and concerns quality or quantity) and is either truth (perfection with regard to matter or quality) or distinctness (perfection of form) or magnitude (perfection with regard to quantity). Subjective perfection is in relation to feeling (aesthetic) or to the will (practical).

Practical: either with regard to cognition itself or to the objects and their reality.

16:123   **1810.** 1769–70. *V* 9–10.[172]

(*Later addition*: There is no principle of taste (doctrine). Thus also no doctrine of taste (criticism) for the imagination.)

16:124   Aesthetic perfection in relation to cognition or in relation to the mere feeling of pleasure. The former is business, the latter play.

It is very pleasing when business appears like play. It is displeasing when play appears like business. It is, however, a business to bring sensibility and understanding into correspondence for the promotion of

---

[a] *versteckt*. Adickes did not suggest an alternative reading of Kant's handwriting here, although this word does not seem to fit the context.

cognition. By contrast, it is mere play to bring sensibility into unison with the feeling of pleasure in accordance with universal laws (of versification), since that contributes nothing to cognition, like music and aimed-at rhyme or the murmur of sentiment. Thus there can be no aesthetic perfection of cognition, but only the mere perfection of taste. It is very displeasing when we encounter the aim for taste in a discourse that is meant for business.[173]

1811. 1769–75. *V* 10.   16:124

The utility of cognition is not beauty.

1812a. 1770–71? (1772–77?) *V* 6.   16:125

The perfection of cognition in accordance with laws of reason is logical, that in accordance with laws of sensibility aesthetic. The aesthetic perfection of cognition consists either in its relation to the sensibility of the subject, where it excites the play of inner actions, or to the understanding of the subject. The first is feeling, the second taste. E.g., order, unity, etc. To taste there belongs understanding, and it is because it is properly an understanding and a subjective concord that this pleases everyone.

1814. 1770–71? (1772–76?) *V* 6.   16:125

Beauty is self-sufficient where the sensibility harmonizes with perfection regarding reason in accordance with universal laws; self-sufficient beauty thus lies in the understanding insofar as it fits with the subject. Original beauty[a] also cannot be drawn from experience, it is rather the means for judging beauty; but from experience the understanding as it were takes the purpose of nature.

1820. 1771–77. *V* 6.   16:127

Universal validity is either outer or inner: the former pertains to all persons and is subjective and contingent; the second pertains to the object in general, it is objective and necessary.[174]

1820a. 1771–72? (1773–75?) A pencilled remark on the address side of   16:127
the letter from Marcus Herz of 9 July 1771 (10:119 ff.).[175]

Beauty is distinct from agreeableness and utility. Utility, if it is thought of antecedently, yields only a mediate satisfaction, but beauty an immediate one. Beautiful things indicate that the human being belongs in the world and even his intuition of things is an agreement with the laws of his intuition.

---

[a] *Die originalschönheit*

16:127 **1821.** 1772–75? (1769–70?) *V* 5.[176]

All cognition is (contains) intuition or concept (either can be distinct or indistinct). Cognition through concepts is thought. The faculty of
16:128 intuitions is sensibility, the faculty for thinking is understanding (for thinking *a priori*: reason). (*Later addition*: For cognition both together are required.) In the first case it is opposed as a superior (dispositive) faculty to the inferior faculty of sensibility, which provides the matter. (*Later addition*: Thus intuition belongs to sensibility and concept to the understanding.)

The perfection of cognition in accordance with laws of sensibility is aesthetic, that in accordance with laws of understanding is logical. The first is a correspondence with the subject (*later addition*: pleasure or displeasure), the second with the object, both in accordance with universal laws,* logically or empirically universal.

*(In the case of the first: novelty, facility, liveliness, comprehensiveness. (as we are affected in the intuition or sensation). In the case of the second: truth, universality, purity. (To both belong distinctness and universality, but of different kinds.) The faculty for producing both (products) of cognition originally is genius. (It is the origin of rules; to judge of it is called either the power of judgment or taste.) That which is objective in the case of sensibility is intuition; consequently this agrees with the understanding and is by its nature universally valid, for otherwise humans would not understand one another. Feeling has private validity.

(There is no doctrine (*a priori*) of taste, but there is criticism. The rules are not rational.)

16:129 **1823.** 1772–75? (1769–70?) *V* 5.

We do not make the judgment of taste from a rule, but from intuition; for the rules are not *a priori*.

16:130 **1826.** 1772–75. *V* 6.

Because the essential in every representation is the idea of the thing, all aesthetic perfection is a union of the subjective with the objective.

16:130 **1829.** 1772–75. *V* 6.

Two distinctions: what the thing **is** (this relates to the object, the other to the subject), and how it **pleases**. That which pleases pleases either (*later addition*: mediately or immediately. What pleases immediately pleases either) in a private relation or universally; the former gratifies. What pleases universally pleases either in accordance with universal laws of human sensibility* or in accordance with laws of reason; the former is beautiful, the latter good.[177]

*(in the appearance; these judgments are universally valid, those from charm have only private validity. In the judgment whether something

pleases in the appearance one must abstract from all interest[a] of the subject and its well-being; the charm in a beautiful object also fades with time, although the judgment about beauty not only remains but also even manifests the same degree.)

16: 131

1831. 1772–78. *V* 6.

16: 131

Beauty is the harmony of sensations.

1834. 1772–75? (1772?) (1776?) *V* 6, at §17.[178]

16: 132

Understanding and intuitions constitute what is objective in cognition.

The subjective pertains to sensation, the power of judgment, spirit, and taste.[179]

Sensation and spirit belong to content, spirit and taste to form.

The ultimate aim of aesthetic cognition is truth and good-naturedness, hence that it accord with understanding and will through subjective means.

1839. 1775–78? (1773–75?) *V* 5.[180]

16: 133

The purpose of all logical perfection is to bring everything to concepts (to universality) and to bring these to distinctness.

The purpose of all aesthetic perfection is to bring everything to intuition and to bring these to liveliness. Yet in both cases order and agreement in an idea are still necessary.

(*Later addition*: Correspondence with the object – truth. Correspondence with the subject. Agreeableness.)

1840. 1775–78? (1773–75?) 1778–79? *V* 9, opposite §32.[181]

16: 134

The science for the culture of taste, being well-read in the ancient poets and orators[b] is so called[c] because it promotes *humanitatem*, and to promote the dryness of science through what is universally pleasing in sensibility, hence what is sociable in cognition, is likewise to promote the concord of human beings for instruction, through the connection of the doctrines of the ancients with our own. Through this [*breaks off*]

(*Later addition*: Aesthetic perfection for the (promotion) communication of **cognition** is business.)[182]

1844. 1776–78. *V* 6.

16: 135

Sentiment and spirit move. The power of judgment and taste direct and moderate. The former is the wind in a flute, the latter the fingers.

---

[a] *Antheil*

[b] Following Adickes in reading *Redner* instead of *Römer* (Romans).

[c] That is, called "the humanities."

16:135   **1845.** 1776–78. *V* 6.

Perfection consists in general in correspondence with universal laws (what universally necessarily pleases). Either with universal objective laws, through which cognition acquires a correspondence with the object (distinctness, thoroughness), or with subjective ones, through which it agrees with the nature of the subject. The latter is aesthetic. What sets our powers of mind into a light and strong play is agreeable. What sets them into a harmonious play is beautiful. What at the same time sets the higher powers into a play that is in unison with sensibility is good.

16:136   **1847.** 1776–78. *V* 6.

Sentiment and spirit belong to genius. The power of judgment and taste do not produce anything, but only administer either in relation to the object or to each other.

What corresponds with the subjective laws of the understanding has spirit.

What enlivens belongs to sentiment and spirit; what preserves and protects, to the power of judgment and taste.

Genius is architectonic. It creates. The power of judgment and taste administer.[183]

16:137   **1850.** 1776–78. *V* 6.

The capacity to choose with universal validity is taste. The use of universal rules *in concreto* is the power of judgment. Feeling makes distinctions only for oneself; the judgment is not valid for others. Taste is sociable.

16:137   **1851.** 1776–78. *V* 7.

Whether taste has constant and universal rules. But not to be cognized *a priori* (*in abstracto*), but *in concreto*. It is a sensible power of judgment that is valid for all. Sensibility yields no other judgment than *in concreto*, otherwise it would be understanding. All rules leave out much from the *concreto*. The rules are not laws, which, namely, would make aesthetic perfection and be universal.

16:138   **1855.** 1776–78. *V* 7.

The means of the beautiful is art, the rule, nature. Nature is not the model (*later addition*: rather the example) of the beautiful, for the beautiful lies in ideas; yet it is its *substratum*. Nature signifies what is unforced in beauty, art what is purposive and orderly. The artificial,[a]

---

[a] *Gekünsteit*

536

however, what is painstaking. Everything is natural that seems to have arisen in accordance with a universal law of efficient causes.

If art resembles the accidental and the accidental art: this is the unexpected.

(*Later addition*: Beauty is the property of an object or cognition through which the cognitive faculties are set into a harmonious concord.)

1856. 1776–78. *V* 7. 16:138

Taste is the polishedness (*politesse*) of the power of judgment.* One becomes polished only through social intercourse. The sensible power of judgment has its ideal, but not taste: this has examples, but not models.*a* Archetypes [are] not examples. The Venus of Praxiteles[184] is not a model.*b*

(Idea. What can be drawn from many examples.)

*(Taste reveals itself in the moderation of both the strong and the delicate. Taste costs nothing, is pleasing, as it were courteous and humorous, imposes nothing burdensome on anyone, is virtue out of inclination.)

1860. 1776–78. *V* 7. 16:139

*Diiudicatio aesthetica (secundum sensum communem) est gustus. Secundum sensum privatum est appetitus. Gustus est iudicium societatis sive sociale.*c*

(*Later addition*: Barbaric beauty [is] oriental.)

1861. 1776–78. *V* 7. 16:139

The power of judgment, *jugement*, healthy understanding are all the same and are the capacity of understanding in application.

1864. 1776–78. *V* 7. 16:140

Sensation and the power of judgment together constitute sensible intuition. Sensation is different from feeling: the former is the matter of sensible cognition, the latter the subjective in satisfaction and is either emotion or charm.[185] The feelings damage the judgment of the understanding through the interest*d* they arouse. The truly beautiful must please in intuition; he who is thereby interested*e* is corrupted and cannot judge impartially. He who judges according as something charms or moves him no longer judges about the object; that is a *metabasis eis allo genos,*f* such a judgment is not advantageous to the understanding and

---

a *Muster*

b model

c Aesthetic judgment (in accordance with common sense) is taste. In accordance with private sense, it is appetite. Taste is the judgment of society or social judgment.

d *Antheil*

e *interessirt*

f Here Kant writes this Greek phrase in Latin characters; the phrase means a "leap into another kind," or what we now call a category mistake.

does not concern the essentially beautiful. This is the good in intuition (but all intuition is sensible). To the power of judgment there belongs the design, the order, the precision, the natural. It is not the gratification that arises from sensation that constitutes the satisfaction, rather the satisfaction insofar as it arises from all four elements universally constitutes the gratification.

16:144   **1869.** 1776–78. *V* 9.

The production of the beautiful does not belong to precepts (rules), but to models (rules need examples (illustrations)); and these not for imitation, for these would themselves be contrary to beauty, but of analogical conformity. The models of style in writing are the ancients. Just because they are our models they cannot be superseded. Boldness is to want to supersede the first models (of nature), which happens because nature has not made all things for our sensible satisfaction, but rather also for our use. No one of our time can become a true model. The prototype is the model which is not borrowed. It lies only in the idea. Morality requires rules, it does not afford a model, but certainly an example.[186]

16:144   **1871.** 1776–78. *V* 5.

The understanding is in itself already communal (judgment: universally valid, sense has private validity); hence one also does not say *intellectus communis*, rather *vulgaris*, i.e., the empirically capable understanding. But one also calls this *sensus communis*, since that which is first judged by understanding in the case of the senses is reckoned as part of the senses.

Taste can only originate through the comparison of many judgments of the senses.

16:145   **1872.** 1776–78. *V* 5.

The faculty for choosing what is pleasing for the sense of everyone. *Facultas diiudicandi per sensum communem.*[a] The faculty of choosing sensibly and universally validly is taste. This is concerned more with the form than with the matter of sensibility.

Universally valid laws are not general, rather it is asked, how are they valid[?] The understanding judges in accordance with general laws, i.e., in accordance with concepts.

16:146   **1876.** 1776–78? 1790s? *V* 6.

Aesthetic perfection: the subjective correspondence of the cognitive faculties in the representation of a thing.*

---

[a] The faculty of judging by means of the common sense.

*(Hence not a concept, but a feeling of pleasure, but universally valid. Understanding and sensibility.)

Logical perfection: concept (universal). Distinctness.

Understanding: also empirical; the rule objective – reason: *a priori* – the power of judgment: understanding and sensibility in relation. reflecting.

1891. 1776–78? (1790s?) *V* 9. 16: 150

The immediate satisfaction merely in what is formal in the manner of representation is taste, that in the material (for the sense) is the feeling of the agreeable and disagreeable. The mediate satisfaction in the good through reason is the manner of thought.

1892. 1776–78. *V* 9, at §30.[187] 16: 150

In logic there is no concern for practical perfection.

There is no science of the beautiful, rather only art.

Art is a faculty of execution which cannot be learned in accordance with rules. Knowing and being able[a] are here different.[188] For a skilled presentation of cognition is not cognition. The rules of presentation are subjectively universally valid and yet *a priori*.

To choose the beautiful presupposes science. The culture of the power of judgment with regard to the beautiful through cognitions is *humaniora*.[b,189]

1894. 1776–78? (1775–77?) *V* 5. 16: 151

The essential aesthetic perfection is that which contributes to cognition in general, thus not feelings, rather that which as intuition makes the concepts of the understanding concrete.

Ideas of intuition (represented) are the essential and the *substratum*.

Sensation is merely subjective, but intuition is objective.

Sensation: the power of judgment pertains to how the sensation corresponds with the concept.

Spirit (genius): Animation through an idea.[190] Taste compares it with the universal sense.[191]

Animation through associated sensations is different from a universal principle of the association of many sensations.

Instrument of animation or *principium*.

Field for fantasy and the unity thereof.

We act only from the beauty of the cognition, not of the objects.

---

[a] *Wissen und Können*

[b] The humanities. Preceding this word, Kant writes the plural verb *sind* (are) rather than *ist* (is), which could agree with either "cognitions" or *humaniora*, but the actual subject of the verb can only be "the culture of the power of judgment."

16:153   **1904.** 1776–79? (1790s?) *V* 5.[192]
Logical perfection,* formal: distinctness; material: truth (through concepts).
Aesthetic perfection: ** Distinctness and truth of intuition.
Harmony with the subjective conditions of the entire power of cognition is aesthetic, with the objective, logical. (The conditions of appearance are subjective.)
(subjective harmony, objective harmony.)
Universal validity in sensation: aesthetic; in thought: logical. (*Later addition*: Sensation weakens the logical perfection.)

16:154   *(Universality as concept. Rules are empirically universal.)
**(The individual as intuition and sensation. Sensation constitutes the contingent in aesthetic perfection.)

16:154   **1905.** 1776–79. *V* 6.
Objective perfection pertains to the cognition of the object. Intuition also pertains to the object, but only in relation to the subject, the whole of human nature.

16:154   **1907.** 1780–89? (1776–79?) *V* 6.
That in the representation of which sensibility and understanding harmonize into a cognition is beautiful.

16:154   **1908.** 1780–89? (1776–79?) *V* 5.
The ground of a universal satisfaction in accordance with laws of sensibility is beauty, in accordance with laws of a particular satisfaction it is charm; to beauty there belongs understanding. Charm. Sensation.

16:155   **1909.** 1780–89? (1776–79?) *V* 5.
The united *interesse* of imagination and understanding.[193]

16:156   **1918.** 1780s? (1776–79?) *V* 8.
Quality: Distinctness (subjective) (lively, particular). (Aesthetic: clarity of intuition.)

16:157   Relation: Truth. (2. subjective truth in the appearance.) (*Later addition*: 2. The relation to the subject is aesthetic. Charm and emotion.)
Quantity: Universality. (subjective.) (3. The universal in the particular.) (*Later addition*: subjective for all.)
Modality: Certainty, necessity. (*Later addition*: of cognition in general. The customary, usage. It is *coustome*.) (4. empirical necessity. Approval. Universal. The customary. Taste.)[194]

1922. 1780s? (1776–79?) *V* 8.   16:158

That displeases which conflicts with our mental power as a hindrance of its free play. Hence what conflicts with sensibility in accordance with universal (although empirical) laws displeases aesthetically.

1923. 1780–89? (1776–79?) *V* 9.   16:158

Beauty of cognition is the correspondence of the freedom of the imagination with the lawfulness of the understanding in the presentation of concepts. The poetic art has the first as its purpose, oratory, the second, eloquence both.

1926. 1780–89? (1776–79?) *V* 9, at §32.[195]   16:158

Taste affords no precepts and rules,* because the imagination gives the law, namely the universal judgment, and it is free.

*(For it is a subjective power of judgment, which does not determine   16:159
the judgment in accordance with concepts, but rather in accordance with pleasure and displeasure.)

1928. 1780–89. *V* 1.   16:159

Beauty and virtue agree in this, that they both must be judged in accordance with the satisfaction of the commonweal and not in accordance with private gratification. They require an observer who is interested in the gratification of the entirety. Only with this difference, that the grounds of the satisfaction in the first are merely empirical and can have no necessity at all *a priori*, but those of the second are intellectual, and must necessarily arouse the satisfaction of everyone, because they concern the harmony of the ends of rational beings in general. Taste and sentiment*a* (character) are both unselfish, both make for honor. The former can only be preserved through the consensus of the judgment of many people over a long time, the latter, however, through the reason of each. In nature beauty and utility are a joy and an end for the senses and reason; in freedom, morals and virtue. The one prepares for the other.

1931. 1790s? 1776–78? *V* 7.   16:160

Since the beautiful carries no interest with itself, so that its existence is indifferent to us, yet there is nevertheless a satisfaction in it, it must consist in the awakening of the feeling of that in which we do take an interest, i.e., the harmony of the understanding and imagination for a cognition in general.[196]

---

a *Sentiment*

Hence the beautiful does not gratify, rather the harmony of the cognitive powers [does]. For the unification of the two is good in every respect, the promotion of the understanding, e.g., mathematics, only in one. The correspondence of the representations with the laws of sensibility can only be universal when it pertains to cognition.

16: 160 **1932.** 1790s? 1776–78? *V* 7.

The correspondence of sensibility with the understanding in a cognition is beauty. Beauty does not rest on sensation, charm, and emotion, for they contribute nothing to cognition.

(*Later addition*: Sensation does not belong to cognition.)

16: 161 The feeling of this harmony of both cognitive powers constitutes the satisfaction in the beautiful.

16: 161 **1935.** 1790s. *V* 10.

Beauty concerns only one part of cognition, namely the sensible presentation of the concept, not logically *in abstracto* but aesthetically *in concreto*.

Beautiful cognition is an expression without sense; for the more I see to the subjective, the less is the objective in the manner of representation, i.e., the cognition, promoted. But the beautiful manner of representation of an object as a presentation of a concept consists in the subjective correspondence of the two faculties of [*crossed out*: cognition] representation that belong to cognition with each other, in which each follows its own rules for itself. Hence freedom of the imagination with the lawfulness of the understanding. Taste is the sensible, subjective (aesthetic) power of judgment (insofar as it agrees of itself with the logical), either of subsumption under a given concept and thus of the presentation thereof, i.e., that of the delivery for a cognition, or of the object of the senses as a beautiful object (of the correspondence of the imagination with the understanding for a cognition in general prior to all concepts). – Freedom

16: 162 of the imagination in harmony with the lawfulness of the understanding; aesthetic perfection of the manner of representation has no rule that determines (antecedently), since the imagination should harmonize with the understanding in its very freedom. The aesthetic perfection in the immediate relation of a representation through the imagination to feeling (not by means of cognition to it) is not beauty, but charm or emotion.

(N.B. Here we deal not with beautiful objects, but with the beautiful presentation of concepts through the imagination, even if the objects are ugly.)[197]

(Agreement with cognition is logical perfection.)

(*Later addition*: A manner of representation is beautiful in which the correspondence of the free play of the imagination with the lawfulness of the understanding is felt.)

(*Later addition*: Taste is the aesthetic power of judgment.

There is no science of the beautiful as such. One demands a universal satisfaction, which is thus not mere feeling; for the agreeable cannot serve others as a rule of satisfaction; but the satisfaction can still not be grounded on universal rules.)

Notes

Notes to Introduction

1. This is the popular name for *Kant's gesammelte Schriften*, edited by the Royal Prussian Academy of Sciences, successively the Prussian Academy of Sciences (by 1926), the German Academy of Sciences at Berlin (by 1955), the Academy of Sciences of the German Democratic Republic (by 1974), and most recently the Berlin-Brandenburg Academy of Sciences, in conjunction with the Academy of Sciences at Göttingen (by 1997). The edition was originally published by Georg Reimer in Berlin, and the first volume to be published – volume 10, the first volume of correspondence – appeared in 1900. Volume 1 of the whole edition, the first volume of Kant's published works, appeared in 1902; but the edition as a whole should be cited as having commenced publication in 1900. Georg Reimer continued to appear as the publisher through 1917. When the series resumed publication with a second edition of the correspondence volumes in 1922, after the crisis of World War I and the ensuing years of chaos in Germany, the publication credit was given to the "Union of Scientific Publishers, Walter de Gruyter & Co., formerly G. J. Göschen'sche Verlagshandlung, J. Guttentag Verlagsbuchhandlung, Georg Reimer, Karl J. Trübner, and Veit & Comp," but since 1923 to the present the publisher has been simply Walter de Gruyter & Co. Throughout this volume as elsewhere in the Cambridge edition the volume and page numbers of the *Akademie* edition are given in the margins, and citations to all works of Kant except the *Critique of Pure Reason* are located by its volume and page numbers (the *Critique of Pure Reason* is always cited by the pagination of its 1781 first edition ("A") and/or 1787 second edition ("B")). The one exception to this rule is Chapter 1, which uses a different source.
2. These notes have been translated into French and Italian: Emmanuel Kant, *Remarques touchant les Observations sur le Sentiment du Beau et du Sublime*, translated by Brigitte Geonget with a preface by Bernard Bourgeois (Paris: J. Vrin, 1994); and Immanuel Kant, *Bemerkungen: Note per un diario filosofico*, translated by Katrin Tenenbaum (Roma: Meltemi, 2001).
3. Immanuel Kant, *Bemerkungen in den "Beobachtungen über das Gefühl des Schönen und Erhabenen,"* Kant-Forschungen Band III (Hamburg: Felix Meiner Verlag, 1991).
4. Immanuel Kant, *Critique of the Power of Judgment*, edited by Paul Guyer, translated by Paul Guyer and Eric Matthews (Cambridge: Cambridge University Press, 2000).
5. Immanuel Kant, *Theoretical Philosophy after 1781*, edited by Henry Allison and Peter Heath, translated by Gary Hatfield, Michael Friedman, Henry Allison, and Peter Heath (Cambridge: Cambridge University Press, 2002).

6. Immanuel Kant, *Opus postumum*, edited by Eckart Förster, translated by Eckart Förster and Michael Rosen (Cambridge: Cambridge University Press, 1993).

7. Immanuel Kant, *Critique of Pure Reason*, edited and translated by Paul Guyer and Allen W. Wood (Cambridge: Cambridge University Press, 1998).

8. To be edited by Frederick Rauscher and Kenneth Westphal.

9. Adickes mentions that in the 1750s Kant used the third edition of Baumgarten's *Metaphysica* (1750) but that the whereabouts of Kant's copy were unknown. The copy has apparently been discovered in the Gdansk library within the past several years, but no information about it has been published.

10. See the division of his subject in the lectures on moral philosophy transcribed by (or for) Georg Ludwig Collins in 1784–85, at 27:242–471, translated in Immanuel Kant, *Lectures on Ethics*, edited by Peter Heath and J. B. Schneewind (Cambridge: Cambridge University Press, 1997), pp. 37–222.

11. The text of Baumgarten's *Ethica Philosophica* is reprinted in the *Akademie* edition at 27:735–1028.

12. See Werner Stark, *Nachforschungen zu Briefen und Handschriften Immanuel Kants* (Berlin: Akademie Verlag, 1993), p. 88. This work is indispensable for understanding the provenance of Kant's *Nachlaß* and the history of its publication, and I have relied upon it for this introduction.

13. Volume 25 of the *Akademie* edition, selected transcriptions of Kant's lectures on anthropology from 1772–73 to 1788–89, was published only in 1997, and volume 26, lectures on physical geography, is still being edited.

14. See Stark, *Nachforschungen*, p. 40. Some of the material was auctioned after Gensichen's own death, however.

15. *Immanuel Kant's Logic: A Manual for Lectures*, edited by Gottlob Benjamin Jäsche, 9:3–150; translated in Immanuel Kant, *Lectures on Logic*, edited by J. Michael Young (Cambridge: Cambridge University Press, 1992), pp. 519–640.

16. Schubert's organization of the *lose Blätter* as reported by Rudolf Reicke in a letter to Dilthey of 12 January 1889. This information is taken from the transcription of Reicke's letter in Stark, *Nachforschungen*, p. 73.

17. See Stark, *Nachforschungen*, p. 71.

18. These annotations are included as footnotes in the Cambridge edition of the *Critique of Pure Reason*, edited by Paul Guyer and Allen W. Wood (Cambridge: Cambridge University Press, 1998).

19. Modern reprint in one volume with an introduction by Norbert Hinske (Stuttgart-Bad Canstatt: Fromann-Holzboog, 1992).

20. See 13:xiv–xvi. Reicke would complete the publication of the correspondence in volumes 11 and 12 by 1902, but was prevented by age and illness from producing the intended fourth volume of notes; that was completed in 1922, along with revisions of the previous three volumes adding new letters, by Rose Burger and Paul Menzer (see 13:xxxi).

21. See Stark, *Nachforschungen*, pp. 70–1.

22. H. Vaihinger, *Commentar zu Kants Kritik der reinen Vernunft*, two volumes (Stuttgart: W. Speman, 1881, and Stuttgart, Berlin, Leipzig: Union Deutsche Verlagsgesellschaft, 1892). In his 1,069 pages, Vaihinger had not gotten past the "Transcendental Aesthetic," but had demonstrated a profound

knowledge of Kant's development as well as the subsequent reception of his views. Vaihinger's *Commentar* is still the best source for information on the intense nineteenth-century controversy over the interpretation of Kant's transcendental idealism.

23. See Stark, *Nachforschungen*, pp. 76–80.
24. Modern reprint: Erich Adickes, *German Kantian Bibliography* (New York: Burt Franklin, 1970).
25. Stark, *Nachforschungen*, p. 80.
26. Stark, *Nachforschungen*, p. 91.
27. See 14:xxvii. Kant's notes in his own copy of the first edition of the *Critique*, previously published by Erdmann in 1881 (see note 18), were to be saved for the second half of the edition of the *Nachlaß*, and were eventually included in volume 23. Two sketches for the *Critique*, a draft of its table of contents (*LBl* B 2) and a sketch of the argument of the book (*LBl* B 12), also ended up in volume 23, but since these were not notes in Kant's own copy of the *Critique*, they were not included in the Cambridge translation of that work; the latter, the more significant of the two, has been restored to its proper position in Chapter 3 of the present volume.
28. The story of the *Opus postumum* is a fascinating one that does not belong here; see Förster, ed., *Opus postumum*, pp. xvi–xxiii, and Stark, *Nachforschungen*, pp. 100–19.
29. Or almost-published works, since one set of drafts, those for an essay on the Berlin Academy of Sciences competition on *What Real Progress Has Metaphysics Made in Germany since the Times of Leibniz and Wolff?*, had not resulted in a work published by Kant. But they had resulted in a published work – they were edited by Kant's sometime student Friedrich Theodor Rink (1770–1811) and published in 1804 – and were readily datable to the period 1793–95.
30. A list of the materials originally intended to be used for the third division of the *Akademie* edition is given in Stark, *Nachforschungen*, pp. 86–7.
31. Erdmann periodized Kant's development into early "dogmatism," then "critical empiricism" in the mid-1760s, then "critical rationalism" around the time of Kant's inaugural dissertation *On the form and principles of the sensible and intelligible world* of 1770, and finally "criticism" itself beginning several years later. See *Reflexionen Kants zur Kritik der reinen Vernunft*, pp. xii–lx; in the reprint by Hinske, pp. 265–312.
32. The following account is based on Stark, *Nachforschungen*, pp. 90–151.
33. *Kants Ansichten über Geschichte und Bau der Erde* and *Untersuchungen zu Kants physischer Geographie* (both Tübingen, 1911).
34. Adickes's 1911 *Untersuchungen zu Kants physischer Geographie* (see note 33) provides detailed comparisons of the version of the lectures on physical geography that Kant's disciple Friedrich Theodor Rink had published in 1802 with surviving transcriptions of the lectures. Adickes had attempted to persuade the Kant Commission to undertake a new edition of the material based on these transcriptions for volume 9 of the *Akademie* edition division of Kant's published works, but in the end the *Akademie* simply reprinted Rink's edition. The other transcriptions of the lectures on physical geography are now being edited for the missing volume 26 of the *Akademie* edition.

35. Theodor Haering, *Der Duisburgsche Nachlaß und Kants Kritizismus um 1775* (Tübingen, 1910). Some of this material has been translated into French as Emmanuel Kant, *Manuscrit de Duisbourg (1774–75)/Choix de Réflections des Années 1772–1777*, translated by François-Xavier Chenet (Paris: J. Vrin, 1988).

36. See Adickes's preface at 17:v.

37. Stark, *Nachforschungen*, p. 129.

38. Stark, *Nachforschungen*, p. 152.

39. See Stark, *Nachforschungen*, pp. 154–5.

40. Stark, *Nachforschungen*, p. 107.

41. Adickes had been prepared to publish the *Opus postumum* in chronological order, while Buchenau and Lehmann decided to publish the material in the order in which it was found in twelve folders ("convolutes") at some point in the nineteenth century, which was apparently the result of an accident and makes the material extremely difficult to use. They did, however, include a chart showing Adickes's intended ordering as an unnumbered fold-out at the end of volume 22, and Eckart Förster based his ordering of the selections in the Cambridge edition of the *Opus postumum* on Adickes's work. Förster is currently revising the *Akademie* edition of the *Opus postumum*.

42. For the criticism of this work, especially the work of Lehmann, see Stark, *Nachforschungen*, especially pp. 169–205.

43. Unfortunately, the card has long been lost from most library copies of the *Nachlaß* and is not currently supplied with new purchases of the volumes. A handy tabulation of the scheme can be found in Helmut Holzhey, *Kants Erfahrungsbegriff: Quellengeschichtliche und bedeutungsanalytische Untersuchungen* (Basel and Stuttgart: Schwabe & Co., 1970), p. 324.

44. Stark, *Nachforschungen*, pp. 206–7.

45. See *Nachforschungen*, pp. 293–319.

46. Kant sometimes wrote "sentiment" in his Latin hand, and may have regarded that as an English word.

Notes to Chapter 1

1. In this note, as the subsequent reference makes clear, Kant is obviously criticizing the feasibility of the model of education proposed in Rousseau's *Émile*.

2. King Alfonso X of Castile (1221–1284) objected to the idea of a natural order. He was referred to by Leibniz in the *Theodicy*, II. §193. Manes, or Manichaeus, a third-century Persian, taught that there were two gods, a good one and an evil one. (See Ri, p. 201.)

3. Here Kant refers to Alexander Pope's dictum, "Whatever is, is right," from the *Essay on Man* (1733–34), line 294. Ri, pp. 198–211, provides extensive citations of relevant passages in Newton and Rousseau as well as other authors lying behind Kant's present comments.

4. Cf. Ovid, *Ex Ponto* III, 4, 79: "ut desint vires, tamen est laudanda voluntas..."

5. Cf. Propertius, *Elegiae*, II, 10: "in magnis et voluisse sat est."

6. Quintus Fabius Maximus Verruscosus, consul five times from 233 to 209 B.C.E., called "Cunctator" ("Delayer") after his delaying tactics in trying to

wear down rather than overpower the invading Carthaginian forces of Hannibal, a strategy that ultimately enabled Scipio to humble Carthage.

7. Kant here refers to the conclusion of Jonathan Swift's *Tale of a Tub* (1704). What Swift says is "that books must be suited to their several seasons, like dress, and diet, and diversions" (The Oxford Authors, *J. Swift*, 1984, p. 162). And cf. Kant's preceding remarks about lover & bride to Swift's poem "A Beautiful Young Nymph Going to Bed..." (1731).

Notes to Chapter 2

1. Kant's notes on §§1–4 of Meier's text, concerning the "Concept, Task, and Division of Logic", extend from **1562** to **1629**. Parallel material in Kant's own logic textbook, the so-called *Jäsche Logic* (*Immanuel Kant's Logic: A Manual for Lectures*, edited by Gottlob Benjamin Jäsche (1804); translated in Immanuel Kant, *Lectures on Logic*, ed. J. Michael Young [Cambridge: Cambridge University Press, 1992]), is found in the Introduction, section II (9:16–21).

2. Literally, "common sense." But the term has a long history. In late medieval Aristotelianism, it was used to denote a higher cognitive capacity thought necessary to integrate the information delivered by the various particular senses such as sight, hearing, etc. In Kant's *Critique of the Power of Judgment*, §20, it would denote the ability, necessary for aesthetic judgment, to make universally valid judgments on the basis of feeling rather than concepts. His usage here, in an early note, is presumably closer to the traditional sense than to his own later special sense.

3. For further reflections on "healthy reason," see **1580–1582, 1586, 1587,** and **1589**.

4. According to Adickes, Kant is probably thinking of the Marquis d'Argens's *Philosophie du bon-sens, ou réflexions philosophiques sur l'incertitude des connoissances humaines, à l'usage des cavaliers et du beausexe* (The philosophy of good sense, or philosophical reflections on human knowledge, for the use of gentlemen and the fair sex) (1737; new edition in two volumes, 1740).

5. In this note, Kant is discussing what he calls in the *Critique of Pure Reason* "general logic" in contrast to "transcendental logic" (see A 50–7/B 74–82), a term that he does not yet use in the period 1773–75. However, his statement in **1608**, also from 1773–75, that "The *canon* of all real use of the understanding is transcendental philosophy," anticipates his subsequent conception of transcendental logic.

6. See note 5 above.

7. The phrase "title of the understanding" becomes prominent in Kant's crucial sketches of the emerging *Critique of Pure Reason* from 1774–75 (**4674** through **4684**, translated in Chapter 3 below), and anticipates Kant's conception of the "pure concepts of the understanding" or "categories" in the *Critique* (introduced at A 76–83/B 102–9; see also B 128–9).

8. This is one of Kant's earliest references to apperception, the concept of the unity of consciousness that would become central to his deduction of the categories beginning in 1774–75. In the next sentence, however, he equates apperception with apprehension, which he would later distinguish from it,

apprehension providing only the raw material for apperception (see, e.g., A 98–100 and 105–9).

9. §§10–14 in Meier's text concern the concepts of representation, object of representation, kinds of cognition, clarity, and distinctness. Kant's notes on these sections are **1676** through **1715**.

10. Kant will use the notion of "representation" (*Vorstellung*) throughout the *Critique of Pure Reason*, although without attempting to provide any general definition or characterization of it until A 319–20/B 375–7. It is interesting to see that even in the earliest period of his lecturing on logic he felt the need to define this notion at the beginning of the course.

11. This note should also be compared to Kant's classification of representations at A 319–20/B 375–7.

12. As previously noted, much of the intervening material, especially **1747** through **1935**, commenting on Meier's §§19–35, concerns the contrast between logic and aesthetics, under the rubric of logical and aesthetic "perfections of cognition"; a selection from this material will be presented in Chapter 5 below. Meier's §§36–65 and Kant's **1936** through **2064** concern various "imperfections" in cognition. Meier's §§66–91 and Kant's **2065** through **2106** concern the "magnitude" or extent of knowledge. Our selection resumes with Kant's comments on Meier's §§92–98, which concern the essence and criteria of truth and falsehood.

13. **2131** through **2171** discuss the fact that general logic offers only a necessary and not a sufficient condition for the truth of a proposition. To this discussion, compare *Critique of Pure Reason* A 57–62/B 82–8 and A 132–6/B 171–5 as well as *Jäsche Logic*, Introduction, section VII, 9:49–57.

14. Meier's §§109–14 and Kant's notes **2242** through **2274** discuss the nature of error.

15. The notes to this section, **2260** through **2274**, focus on agreement with others as an "external" rather than "logical" mark of error (these terms come from **2272**).

16. §§115–21 of Meier's text concern *Merkmale* or "marks," which we would now call predicates, and Kant's notes on these sections, **2275** through **2326**, give evidence of his thought on concepts and predicates. These notes may be compared to the first section, §§1–16 of the *Jäsche Logic*.

17. §§122–38 in Meier's text concern "clarity" and "distinctness" in cognition; Kant's notes **2327** through **2388** address those concepts. In the *Jäsche Logic*, Kant takes this subject up in the Introduction, section VIII, 9:58–65. Meier's discussion of "degrees of cognition" extends from §139 to §154, and Kant's notes on this subject from **2389** to **2421**.

18. §§155–67 of Meier's text concern "Opinion, belief, and knowledge," as do Kant's notes **2422** through **2514**. These passages should be compared with the section "On having opinions, knowing, and believing" (A 820–31/B 848–59) in the "Canon of Pure Reason" of the "Doctrine of Method" in the *Critique of Pure Reason*, as well as with section IX of the Introduction to the *Jäsche Logic* and to the *Critique of the Power of Judgment*, §§90–1.

19. This passage may be compared with Kant's discussion of a postulate of pure practical reason in the "Dialectic" of *Critique of Practical Reason*, especially 5:119–33 and 142–46, as well as with *Critique of the Power of Judgment*, §91.

20. In §168, Meier begins a discussion of prejudice (pre-judgment), which continues through §170. Kant's notes on these sections are **2505** through **2582**. These notes parallel Kant's treatment of prejudice and its prevention in *Jäsche Logic*, Introduction, section IX, 9:75–81.

21. This brief characterization of the method for securing objectivity in one's judgments should be compared to *Critique of the Power of Judgment*, §40.

22. Meier's §§171–5 and Kant's notes **2583** through **2632** concern "probability, plausibility, and moral certainty"; §§176–78 and the corresponding **2633** through **2654** concern "doubt." **2655** through **2672**, on "dogmatism, skepticism, and skeptical method," primarily state definitions of these terms; **2667**, translated here, is representative of the others.

23. Meier discusses hypotheses in §§181–3; Kant comments on these sections in **2673** through **2694**. See also **2788** below. Kant discusses hypotheses at *Critique of Pure Reason*, A 769–82/B 797–810, *Critique of the Power of Judgment*, §90, 5:466, and *Jäsche Logic*, Introduction, section X, 9:84–6.

24. In §184 Meier discusses "conviction" and in §185 "science" and "system"; Kant's notes on these sections are **2695** through **2709**. §§186–89 concern the "kinds and degrees of certainty"; Kant's notes on these sections are **2710–16**.

25. This remark may be compared to Kant's statement in the *Critique of Pure Reason* that since belief in God can only be based on a postulate of practical reason, "I must not even say '**It is** morally certain that there is a God,' etc., but rather '**I am** morally certain'" (A 829/B 857).

26. In Meier's text, §§191–200 concern "proof"; Kant's notes on these sections are **2720** through **2737**.

27. Meier's §§201–6 concern "experience, reason, and belief"; Kant's notes on these sections are **2738** through **2773**.

28. Meier's §§207–15 deal with "Testimony, Unbelief, and Moral Belief"; the corresponding notes in Kant are **2774–94**.

29. **2789** and **2793–4** should be compared to Kant's published discussions on opinion, belief, and knowledge; see note 18 above. See also **2450–2, 2454, 2460, 2462, 2470**, and **2503** above.

30. This paragraph may be compared with Kant's argument in the *Critique of the Power of Judgment*, §§84, 87.

31. Meier's §§249–53 concern "concept in general" and "idea." This note and **2836** should be compared to *Critique of Pure Reason*, A 320/B 376–7, as well as to **2394**.

32. Compare to Kant's discussion of ideas and transcendental ideas at *Critique of Pure Reason*, A 312–32/B 368–89.

33. There are a number of figure named "Aristides" in antiquity, but presumably Kant refers to the fifth-century Athenian statesman and general in the Persian wars whose life was chronicled by Plutarch. In the *Athenian Constitution*, Aristotle claims he initiated the policy of democratic state socialism, which may be doubtful; but he was considered a paragon of probity and justice, which is presumably why Kant mentions him here.

34. Meier's §§254–67 and Kant's notes **2843–2910** concern concepts and their formation, including their formation by abstraction, comparison, and reflection; see also *Jäsche Logic*, §6, 9:94–5. §§268–84 and Kant's notes **2911–3008**

concern definition, explication, and description; on this, see *Critique of Pure Reason*, A 726–32/B 754–60, and *Jäsche Logic* §§99–109, 9:140–45.

35. These sections, and Kant's notes **2986–3008**, concern nominal and real definition. See also *Jäsche Logic*, §106, 9:143–4, as well as Locke's famous discussion of nominal and real essences in *Essay concerning Human Understanding*, Book III, chapter iii, §§15–18.

36. This note is particularly reminiscent of Locke's distinction between nominal and real essence; see note 35.

37. Meier's §§292–352 and Kant's **3032–3143** concern judgments; the analogous part of the *Jäsche Logic* is §§17–40, 9:101–40. §§292–3 define the concepts of judgment, subject, and predicate. Kant's definition of judgment in the *Critique of Pure Reason* is at A 68–9/B 93–4; see also §19 of the second edition of the "Transcendental Deduction of the Categories," B 140–2.

38. Kant's famous contrast between analytic and synthetic judgments is in the *Critique of Pure Reason*, A 6–10/B 10–14.

39. Compare this note to Kant's division of the functions of relation in judgments at *Critique of Pure Reason* A 70/B 95 and A 73–4/B 98–9.

40. Compare to §§18–19 of the second-edition "Transcendental Deduction," *Critique of Pure Reason* B 139–42.

41. Compare this note to the table of the functions of judgment at *Critique of Pure Reason*, A 70/B 95, as well as to Kant's discussion at *Jäsche Logic*, §§20–30, 9:102–9. In particular, this note and the next two illuminate Kant's conception of "infinite judgment," less well explained at A 72–3/B 97–8.

42. Meier's §§311–12 and Kant's **3113** through **3118** concern the contrast between theoretical and practical judgments. See also *Jäsche Logic*, §32, 9:110.

43. Meier's §§313–18 and Kant's **3119–3137** concern demonstrable and indemonstrable judgments, axioms and postulates, and analytic and synthetic judgments.

44. Meier's §323 concerns the "judgment of experience" (*Erfahrungsurtheil*). **3145** and **3146** should be compared to Kant's famous distinction between judgments of perception and judgments of experience in the *Prolegomena*, §20, 4:300–1.

45. Part 10, §§353–413, of Meier's work concern inferences. Kant's notes on this part of the work are **3190** through **3315**. The corresponding sections of the *Jäsche Logic* are §§41–93, 9:114–36. **3200** should also be compared with Kant's discussion of the distinction between determining and reflecting judgment in the *Critique of the Power of Judgment*, Introduction, section IV, 5:179, and its First Introduction, section V, 20:211–12.

46. **3203** through **3274** are notes on inferences and the figures of the syllogism that do not add materially to Kant's published logic text. At Meier's §401, which concerns induction and analogy (literally, "inference from example"), Kant resumes the discussion of analogy and inference he had started at **3200**.

47. Kant characterizes the "principle of specification" as the principle that for every more general, i.e., genus concept, a more particular, i.e., species concept can be given (*Critique of Pure Reason*, A 654–6/B 682–4). What he seems to have in mind here is that if we have made the general concept more specific on the basis of a particular instance of it that is given to us, then we

will tend to make it specific in the same way for particular instances that are not given. Of course, in the *Critique* he argues that this is a regulative, not a constitutive principle.

48. Compare, again, *Critique of the Power of Judgment*, Introduction, section IV, and First Introduction, section V. That the distinction between reflecting and determining judgment does not appear in Kant's published works prior to the third *Critique* argues for a later rather than earlier date for this note.

Notes to Chapter 3

1. Kant refers of course to Descartes's exposition of the ontological argument for the existence of God in *Meditations in First Philosophy*, Meditation V; see also *Principles of Philosophy*, Part One, section 14. Kant criticized Descartes's argument in his first philosophical work, *A New Elucidation of the First Principles of Metaphysical Cognition* (1755), Proposition VI, 1:394–5, and in *The Only Possible Argument in Support of a Demonstration of the Existence of God* (1763), First Reflection, 2:72–5. His most famous critique of it is in the *Critique of Pure Reason*, "The Ideal of Reason," A 592–602/B 620–30. He also discusses it at length in the *Lectures on the Philosophical Doctrine of Religion*, 28:1004–6, 1013–28; these lectures were published by Karl Heinrich Pölitz in 1817, based on transcriptions from lectures Kant gave in 1783–84 and/or 1785–86, and are translated in Immanuel Kant, *Religion and Rational Theology*, ed. Allen W. Wood and George di Giovanni (Cambridge: Cambridge University Press, 1996), pp. 335–451. Kant discusses the ontological argument throughout the notes on metaphysics, well into the 1790s.

2. The winged horse and the triangle are Descartes's examples; see *Meditation* V, paragraphs 10 and 12.

3. The first three sections of Baumgarten's *Metaphysica*, comprising its "Prolegomena," define metaphysics as the "first science of the principles of human cognition," comprising ontology, cosmology, psychology, and natural theology.

4. §§101–23 concern *Necessarium et contingens*. §109 defines necessary and contingent things as those whose non-existence is not or is possible, respectively.

5. Here Kant uses the word *Critik* not in the sense of a philosophical determination of the principles and limits of a form of thought or knowledge, as he will in the titles of his three main works, but in the sense of an empirically based body of critical judgments; he often uses it in this sense in his earlier notes on aesthetics when he contrasts a critique (or "criticism") to a science. See Chapter 5 below.

6. This will become a central theme of the *Critique of Pure Reason* and the basis for Kant's critique of traditional metaphysics in the "Transcendental Dialectic." See A 305–9/B 362–66, A 333–8/B 390–6.

7. This anticipates Kant's thesis in the *Critique of Pure Reason* that all analysis presupposes synthesis; see for example A 77–9/B 102–4, B 130, and B 133–4.

8. See *Critique of Pure Reason*, A 119, and §15 of the second-edition "Transcendental Deduction," B 129–31.

9. Here of course Kant refers to Socrates's defense that his wisdom consisted only in knowing what he did not know; see *Apology* 21a–23b.

10. This is an allusion to Kant's view that the difference betwen sensible and conceptual representation is a difference in kind, not, as the rationalists from Leibniz to Baumgarten held, a matter of degree in which sense perception is merely a confused form of conceptual representation. The *locus classicus* for the rationalist conception of sense perception is Leibniz's "Meditations on Knowledge, Truth, and Ideas," published in the *Acta Eruditorum* in 1684; the *locus classicus* for Kant's response is in the "Transcendental Aesthetic" of the *Critique of Pure Reason*, A 43–6/B 60–3; see also *Critique of the Power of Judgment*, First Introduction, Section VIII, 20:227.

11. See *Critique of the Power of Judgment*, §17, "The Ideal of Beauty."

12. §§803–62 of the *Metaphysica* comprise the chapter *Existentia Dei*. §803 defines the concept of a perfect being.

13. In this note, Kant recapitulates the argument for the existence of God as the ground of all possibilities that he presents in the *New Elucidation*, Proposition VII, 1:395–6, and *Only Possible Argument*, Second and Third Reflections, 2:77–83. For a related note, see **3809** below. He ultimately rejects this argument in the "Ideal of Pure Reason" in the *Critique of Pure Reason*, saying that "All of this does not signify the objective relation of an actual object to other things, but only that of an **idea** to **concepts**" (A 579/B 607).

14. See *Only Possible Argument*, 2:83–4.

15. See *Only Possible Argument*, 2:84–5.

16. Kant will later call God the highest *original* good, in contrast to the highest *derived* good, namely the combination of maximal virtue and happiness that we can only conceive to be possible through his authorship of the laws of nature as well as morality; see *Critique of Practical Reason*, 5:125.

17. See *Only Possible Argument*, 2:87–8.

18. See *Only Possible Argument*, 2:89.

19. Kant defines the distinction between analytic and synthetic judgments in the Introduction to the *Critique of Pure Reason*, A 6–10/B 10–14. But he also anticipates the distinction in the 1763 *Attempt to Introduce the Concept of Negative Magnitudes into Philosophy*, 2:202, and the 1764 *Inquiry concerning the Distinctness of the Principles of Natural Theology and Morality*, §1, 2:276–8. See also **3743, 3744, 3747**, and **3750** below, and for other notes concerning this distinction prior to the first *Critique*, although later than the present note, see **4674–84** below.

20. Here Kant refers to Locke's distinction between "trifling propositions" that "bring no increase in knowledge," or what he also calls "barely verbal propositions," and those propositions that do increase our knowledge, for which he has no special name. See *Essay concerning Human Understanding*, Book IV, chapter VIII. Kant may also have Locke's distinction in mind when he equates analytic and synthetic judgments with judgments of clarification and amplification, respectively, at *Critique of Pure Reason*, A 7/B 10–11.

21. In the contemporaneous *Inquiry concerning the Distinctness of the Principles of Natural Theology and Morality*, First Reflection, Kant first argues that "mathematics arrives at all its definitions synthetically" because its concepts can and must be based on the construction of their objects (2:276–8).

22. In §448, Baumgarten defines the concept of preestablished harmony. From §448 to §465, he argues for the superiority of the system of preestablished harmony over the systems of physical influx and occasionalism because it is more consistent with the idea of a most perfect world.

23. This is the view that Kant would defend in his 1770 inaugural dissertation, *On the Form and Principles of the Sensible and Intelligible World*, §§16–22.

24. See also **3733** and the texts referred to in note 13 above.

25. In §826, Baumgarten states that the properties of the necessary being can only be known by analogy. Kant uses the occasion of this note and the next, **3819**, to make a remarkably early suggestion of his mature view that positive theology is possible only on moral and not theoretical grounds.

26. Kant would argue that these ontological properties can be attributed to God only as necessary conditions for the moral properties listed on the left at *Critique of Pure Reason*, A 814–15/B 842–3, *Critique of Practical Reason*, 5:139, and *Critique of the Power of Judgment*, "General Remark on the Teleology," 5:481, although in the last work Kant emphasizes more than ever that "our aim in using [these concepts of God] is not that of determining [his] nature, but of determining ourselves and our will in accordance with them" (§88, 5:457).

27. Notes **3855** through **3872** are a series of notes on the concept of freedom written alongside Baumgarten's chapters on *Spontaneitas*, *Arbitrium* (will), and *Libertas*, §§700–732. Further series of such notes are found at **4218–29, 4333–38, 4541–51, 4723–7, 5434–50**, and **5611–20**. Selections from these notes are found in numerical sequence throughout this chapter.

28. This is a thesis that Kant would always maintain and use to argue against a mechanical explanation of life; see for example *Critique of the Power of Judgment*, §73, 5:394, and *Metaphysik L*₁, 28:275.

29. In this confusing note Kant seems to be caught between the Leibnizian compatibilism that he espoused in his first philosophical work, the *New Elucidation*, Proposition IX, 1:398–405, in which freedom is simply determination by an internal rather than external cause, and his later rejection of that, as the mere "freedom of a turnspit" (*Critique of Practical Reason*, 5:97), in favor of the view that we are always free to do what is right no matter what our prior history seems to be. Here he seems to be trying to split this difference by holding that a radically free will of the latter sort is only sometimes active!

30. §708 describes actions whose opposites are equally in the power of the agent as free actions.

31. With this note, Kant already suggests two of his three mature theses about freedom: he does not yet suggest that transcendental idealism is needed to allow for the possibility of freedom, but he does suggest that the reality of freedom is a matter for a practical postulate, not a theoretical proof, and yet that freedom is inscrutable, that is, it cannot be explained why freedom is exercised one way rather than another. Each of these theses is asserted innumerable times in Kant's published works, but see for example *Groundwork*, Section III, 4:461–2; *Critique of Practical Reason*, 5:47–50; and *Religion within the Boundaries of Mere Reason*, Part Two.

32. Here Baumgarten distinguishes between the sensible and the free power of choice.

33. See also **3862**. The distinction between weak and evil will is an anticipation of the distinction among grades of evils that Kant draws much later in the *Religion within the Boundaries of Mere Reason*, Part One, 6:29–30.

34. In the *Religion*, Kant will argue that evil acts are just as much a product of free choice as good ones (e.g., 6:25). But even as late as the *Metaphysics of Morals* he also argues that freedom cannot be defined as the power to choose either good or evil, because we can only know that we have freedom through our power to choose good (Introduction, Section III, 6:226).

35. §723 defines the moral as that which is done through freedom, and conversely that which is morally possible strictly speaking as that which is freely done in conformity with moral laws.

36. Kant typically contrasted Epicurean and Stoic conceptions of the highest good, on the former of which virtue is reduced to happiness and on the latter of which happiness is reduced to virtue, before presenting his own account of the synthetic connection between virtue and happiness, which needs an additional basis in God's common authorship of the laws of morality and of nature; see *Critique of Practical Reason*, 5:111–12, and *Moral Philosophy Collins*, 27:248–52, as well as notes included in Chapter 4 below.

37. See *Critique of Practical Reason*, 5:125–6.

38. This is an allusion to the Platonic doctrine that knowledge of the forms must be by acquaintance (which in turn implies the doctrine of recollection, that we must have been acquainted with the forms prior to birth, and can recover the knowledge of them through dialectic). See for example *Meno* 81c–86c. Kant explicitly alludes to the doctrine of recollection at *Critique of Pure Reason*, A 313–14/B 370–1. He refers to Plato's theory as a theory of "higher intuition" at *Metaphysik Mrongovius*, 29:760; see generally the discussion at 29:759–3. See also *Metaphysik Vigilantius*, 29:950.

39. As one would expect, in 1769 Kant has not yet formulated his mature list of categories on the basis of the logical functions of judgment, so this list of "fundamental rational concepts" is rather inchoate. For a briefer although still not yet organized list, see *On the Form and Principles of the Sensible and Intelligible World*, §8, 2:395. But for a contemporaneous list that comes closer to Kant's mature list, see **3941**.

40. This characterization of analytic judgment would remain constant; see *Critique of Pure Reason*, A 6–7/B 10–11, A 150–3/B 189–93.

41. Of course Kant subsequently rejects this view; see especially *Critique of Pure Reason*, B 14.

42. Kant's expression "Locke's rule" might suggest a reference to Locke's posthumous little treatise on "The Conduct of the Understanding," first published in 1706, although Section V of this essay merely alludes in a general way to the necessity of "getting clear and determined ideas," the expression with which Locke replaced the Cartesian phrase "clear and distinct ideas" in the "Epistle to the Reader" in the fourth edition of the *Essay concerning Human Understanding*, so Kant probably intends only a general reference to Locke.

43. See again Kant's list of metaphysical concepts at §8 of the inaugural dissertation (2:395).

44. This list of "metaphysical concepts" more closely approximates Kant's mature table of categories than the list given in **3927**.

45. See *On the Form and Principles of the Sensible and Intellectual World*, §15A, 2:402, and *Critique of Pure Reason*, A 23/B 38.

46. Kant's suggestion here that the method of metaphysics is merely analytic and that for this reason there are no substantive discoveries in metaphysics looks back to the 1764 *Inquiry concerning the Distinctness of the Principles of Natural Theology and Morality*, Second Reflection, 2:283–6; the claim that the questions of metaphysics cannot be open-ended, however, but must be able to be settled conclusively, would remain in the *Critique of Pure Reason*, A xx, B xxiii–xxiv, as a consequence of the foundation of metaphysical concepts in pure reason itself.

47. See Kant's characterization of "general logic" as independent from all particular "contents of cognition" at *Critique of Pure Reason*, A 130–4/B 169–73.

48. This is of course the role that Kant would subsequently assign to "transcendental logic," e.g., *Critique of Pure Reason*, A 135–6/B174–5.

49. Kant has the same difficulty indistinguishing between the pure intuitions of space and time and the pure concepts of them, which are the concepts *of* those intuitions, which is still reflected in the section titles within the second edition of the "Transcendental Aesthetic," at A 22/B 37, B 40, and A 30/B 46.

50. See Kant's characterization of number, the object of mathematics, at A 142–3/B 182.

51. In the 1786 *Metaphysical Foundations of Natural Science*, Kant would argue that the pure principles of judgment derived from the synthesis of the pure forms of intuition and the pure concepts of the understanding must be supplemented by the empirical concept of matter as the moveable in space in order to yield mechanics and the other parts of "general natural science"; see 4:476, 480, 496, and 536.

52. See *Critique of Pure Reason*, A 20/B 34.

53. For Kant's use of the concepts of coordination and subordination at this period, see *On the Form and Principles of the Sensible and Intelligible World*, §2, 2:390–2, and §5, 2:393–4. See also **3976** below.

54. Kant retains this description of his method for reaching the pure intuitions of space and time at *Critique of Pure Reason*, A 22/B 36.

55. This seems to be the first appearance of this term in Kant's notes.

56. The first of these principles seems to suggest that sensory cognition and judgment are alternative forms of intuition, as Kant may suggest in the inaugural dissertation (§8), but the second seems to point the way to the doctrine of the *Critique of Pure Reason* that all cognition requires intuitions on the one hand and concepts and judgments on the other (see A 51–2/B 75–6, A 68–9/B 92–4).

57. This contrast between the indefinitely extendable syntheses that are possible for our understanding and the completed syntheses that are not will of course become the basis for Kant's diagnosis of the errors of traditional metaphysics in the "Transcendental Dialectic" of the *Critique of Pure Reason*; for a succinct statement see A 308/B 364–5.

58. Once Kant becomes clear that there is no cognition of that which is given by the senses without the application of the concepts of the understanding

and the principles of judgment, he will also recognize that what is given as actual by the senses must also be regarded as necessary under laws in conformity with the general principles of judgment; see *Critique of Pure Reason*, A 230/B 282.

59. Here Kant anticipates the third "Antinomy of Pure Reason"; see *Critique of Pure Reason*, A 444–8/B 472–6.

60. See **3958** and note 53, above.

61. See also the first "Antinomy of Pure Reason," especially A 426–7/B 454–5.

62. This is essentially Kant's solution to the third antinomy; see *Critique of Pure Reason*, A 531–2/B 559–60.

63. §20 gives Baumgarten's proof of the principle of sufficient reason.

64. See Kant's famous statement in the proof of the second "Analogy of Experience" that "The principle of sufficient reason is the ground of possible experience" (*Critique of Pure Reason*, A 201/B 246).

65. §53 maintains that everything possible is determinate through its essence.

66. This is precisely the formulation Kant uses in his critique of the ontological argument at *Critique of Pure Reason*, A 598/B 626. See also the 1763 treatise *The Only Possible Argument for a Demonstration of the Existence of God*, where Kant states that "existence occurs as a predicate in common speech," but then it is a predicate "not so much of the thing itself as of the thought which one has of the thing" (2:72).

67. These sections define the necessary as that whose opposite is impossible and the contingent as that whose opposite is possible.

68. §109 defines a necessary being as one whose non-existence is not possible.

69. §239 defines space as the order of simultaneous things that are *extra se* (outside of one another), and time as the order of successive things. See also **4188–91**.

70. In §392, Baumgarten asserts that the world is either simple or complex, and that one who asserts that it is simple is an "egoist." This must be because such a person assumes his own existence, and then has no choice but to identify the world with himself, since on his hypothesis of the simplicity of the world it can contain only one object.

71. Here Kant alludes to an argument he had made fourteen years earlier in the *New Elucidation of the First Principles of Metaphysical Cognition*, Proposition XII, 1:410. His search for an epistemological rather than ontological basis for this argument would eventually lead to the "Refutation of Idealism" in the second edition of the *Critique of Pure Reason* and after (see especially **5653–4** and **6311–23** below).

72. This otherwise rather peculiar note is included because it suggests that Kant's later position that immortality could only be a postulate of pure practical reason had its roots as early as 1769.

73. In §850, Baumgarten argues that eternity cannot be understood as an infinite succession of contingent things.

74. See Kant's subsequent argument in the first "Analogy of Experience" that we can have empirical knowledge only of the alteration of substances, not of the coming- or ceasing-to-be of substances; *Critique of Pure Reason*, A 188–9/B 231–2.

75. In §942 Baumgarten argues that the highest good is the celebration of the perfection of God. Kant is already trying to reconceive of God as the ground of good human actions.
76. Kant's remark that "ontology is nothing other than a transcendental logic" may be compared to his statement that "the proud name of an ontology...must give way to the modest one of a mere analytic of pure understanding" (*Critique of Pure Reason*, A 247/B 303), while his suggestion that the formal principles of morality are analytic but must be synthetically connected to the human will is the issue throughout Sections II and III of the *Groundwork for the Metaphysics of Morals*.
77. "General phenomenology" is a term that Kant also uses in his letter to Marcus Herz of 21 February 1772 to designate the first section of the first part of his intended work *The Bounds of Sensibility and Reason*, preceding metaphysics. This is presumably what became the transcendental theory of knowledge, called "phenomenology" because it concerns *phenomena* rather than *noumena*, which in turn precedes the special metaphysics of nature eventually worked out in the *Metaphysical Foundations of Natural Science*.
78. See also **4169**.
79. §16 defines hypothetical possibility as possibility relative to something else.
80. See Kant's statement in the introduction to the second edition of the *Critique of Pure Reason* that "although all our cognition commences **with** experience, yet it does not on that account all arise **from** experience" (B 1).
81. §20 contains Baumgarten's attempted proof of the principle of sufficient reason.
82. This note anticipates the second "Analogy of Experience" in the *Critique of Pure Reason*; see the terms of Kant's summary of the proof at A 199/B 244.
83. In these sections Baumgarten argues that the only opposite of the necessary is the impossible.
84. Kant would subsequently criticize any attempt to infer that the self is a genuine substance from the fact that "predicates terminate with me, and I am not one myself"; see the first "Paralogism of Pure Reason," *Critique of Pure Reason*, A 348–51 and B 407.
85. See **4073**, note 71.
86. Compare this note to the inaugural dissertation, §15.A and B, 2:402.
87. In §382 Baumgarten argues that the infinite series of contingent events in time must have a necessary being as its cause. Kant's response in the present note is an anticipation of the first part of the first "Antinomy of Pure Reason," A 426–7/B 454–5.
88. **4218** through **4229** comprise another set of notes on Baumgarten's chapters on *Arbitrium* and *Libertas*. §708 distinguishes between actions that are physically possible for one, or in one's power, and those where one may choose between opposites, with respect to which one is free.
89. Kant will continue to attempt to infer the freedom of the will in the practical context from the spontaneity of thought and judgment in the theoretical context in Section III of the *Groundwork of the Metaphysics of Morals*, 4:452. He does not make this argument in the *Critique of Practical Reason*.

90. §724 argues that necessitation by the moral law is compatible with freedom of the will.

91. In the *Critique of Pure Reason*, Kant will argue that the representation of the "I" is not an intuition at all; see especially the second-edition deduction, §25, B 157–8, and the second-edition "Paralogisms of Pure Reason," B 412–13.

92. **4230–41** are interesting notes on the immateriality and immortality of the soul. Notes on the prolegomena to natural theology, discussing proofs of the existence of God, begin at **4242** and continue through **4269**.

93. Kant subsequently rejects this proof at *Critique of Pure Reason*, A 571–90/B 599–618.

94. This is an anticipation of Kant's argument for the practical postulate of the existence of God as the "highest original good," that is the ground of the possibility of the "highest derived good" in us; see especially *Critique of Practical Reason*, 5:125–6.

95. In the inaugural dissertation, Kant uses the expression "subreptic axioms" to designate *illegitimate* assumptions that the limits of our sensibility imply restrictions on the nature of reality itself (see especially §26, 2:413). Here he seems to be emphasizing the positive, namely that the synthetic principles of reason are valid subjectively.

96. See among other similar passages *Metaphysik L₁*, 28:233; *Metaphysik Mrongovius*, 29:760–4; *Metaphysik Vigilantius*, 29:958–9; and *Critique of Pure Reason*, B 167–8. See also **4446**.

97. See *Critique of Pure Reason*, A 201/B 246.

98. See Kant's definitions of the "Postulates of empirical thinking in general" at *Critique of Pure Reason*, A 218/B 265–6. See also **4302**.

99. See **4073**, note 69.

100. **4333** through **4338** is the next set of notes on Baumgarten's chapters on *Arbitrium* and *Libertas*. See also **4218** through **4229**, many of which are translated above.

101. See also **4341**.

102. §826 maintains that properties may be attributed to the necessary being either by analogy or by the *via negativa*.

103. §865 defines the character of divine intellect.

104. In §870, Baumgarten argues that the divine intellect has distinct cognition of all possible worlds.

105. This paragraph anticipates Kant's subsequent view that freedom is the presupposition of the possibility of acting as morality demands while God and immortality are the conditions of the possibility of the realization of the highest good as the object of moral action. This distinction is not made explicitly in the *Critique of Practical Reason* (see for example 5:132), but is made clearer in subsequent works, such as *Critique of the Power of Judgment*, §91, 5:469, and *On the Common Saying: That May Be Correct in Theory but It Is of No Use in Practice* (1793), 8:279.

106. In §244, Baumgarten argues that the monad is indivisible.

107. In these sections Baumgarten defines the "course" and "order" of nature, in contrast to anything supernatural.

108. Aristippus (fourth century B.C.) was the founder of the Cyrenaic school. His views are known from comments in Cicero, *De finibus*, I. 29–39 and V.17–20, and Diogenes Laertius, 10.136–7. Kant mentions him again in **4449**. In *Metaphysics of Morals Vigilantius*, Kant describes him as holding that "all duty arises from the feeling of pleasure and pain" (27:647), but does not add there, as he claims here, that we are infallible in our judgments of what is pleasurable and painful.

109. See Kant's comment about Aristotle's failure to find a principle for his list of categories at *Critique of Pure Reason*, A 81/B 107. Aristotle discusses the categories of substance, quantity, relation, and quality in *Categories* 5–9, 2a12–11b6, without any explanation for the sequence of his discussion.

110. Here Kant is still defending the position of the inaugural dissertation (e.g., §26), according to which the errors of metaphysics arise from allowing the limits of sensibility to limit all cognition of objects rather than from the failure to recognize that the limits of sensibility do limit all cognition of objects.

111. Kant would reuse the image of an island of truth surrounded by a sea of illusion at the opening of the chapter on the distinction between phenomena and noumena in the *Critique of Pure Reason*, A 235–6/B294–5.

112. This reflection should be compared to Kant's famous letter to Marcus Herz of 21 February 1772; it must have been drafted around the same time Kant wrote that letter. See 10:129–35; in Immanuel Kant, *Correspondence*, translated and edited by Arnulf Zweig (Cambridge: Cambridge University Press, 1999), pp. 132–7. See also **4633** below.

113. The restriction of the task of transcendental philosophy to the discovery of the conditions of synthetic *a priori* cognition that is presupposed is what Kant calls the "analytic" method in the *Prolegomena* and distinguishes from the "synthetic" method, which presupposes no synthetic *a priori* cognition but goes on to prove that we have some, that he claims to have used in the *Critique of Pure Reason* (*Prolegomena*, §4, 4:274–5). Which method he actually uses in the *Critique* is of course a subject of debate.

114. §7 defines the principle of contradiction as the principle that nothing is both *A* and *non-A*.

115. §18 distinguishes between absolute and hypothetical possibility and impossibility.

116. The distinction between merely logical possibility and possibility in accord with the conditions of the possibility of experience introduced in this note underlies Kant's characterization of possibility in the "Postulates of all empirical thinking" in the *Critique of Pure Reason*, A 220–1/B 267–8.

117. §191 defines substance as that which does not exist as the determination of something else.

118. Of course Kant would subsequently reject this claim in the second edition of the "Transcendental Deduction," §25, B 157–8, and in the first "Paralogism of Pure Reason," especially A 350 and B 421–2.

119. See also the exposition and critique of Leibniz's monadology in **4500**.

120. Compare this note to Kant's argument for transcendental idealism at *Critique of Pure Reason*, A 26/B 42.

121. This appears to contradict one of Kant's later arguments for the existence of an *a priori* intuition of space; see *Critique of Pure Reason*, A 24/B 38–9. The more nuanced statement of **4512** may avoid this contradiction.

122. The thesis of this note is discussed at greater length in **4522** and **4524**.

123. In these sections Baumgarten argues that an infinite regress of contingents must have some necessary ground.

124. In this section, Baumgarten maintains that the ultimate parts of the world are simple monads.

125. Compare this note to Kant's approach to the problem of idealism in the fourth "Paralogism of Pure Reason" in the first edition of the *Critique of Pure Reason*, A 367–80.

126. **4541** through **4551** is another series of notes on *Arbitrium* and *Libertas*; see note 27 above.

127. **4565** through **4599** is a series of notes on proofs of God's existence. Only a few are presented here.

128. See the first "Antinomy of Pure Reason," A 426–7/B 454–5.

129. Kant frequently connects number and time because of the time it takes us to count; see *Critique of Pure Reason*, A 142–3/B 182.

130. See Kant's definition of a category at *Critique of Pure Reason*, B 128–9.

131. This passage is the first anticipation of Kant's doctrine that concepts are functions of unity in judgments (*Critique of Pure Reason*, A 68/B 94), which is the premise for his argument in the "metaphysical deduction" that the categories are the pure forms of concepts of objects necessary for applying the logical functions of judgment to them.

132. This note seems to be the next step beyond the question raised in Kant's letter of 21 February 1772 to Marcus Herz; see **4473** and note 112 above.

133. See *Critique of Pure Reason*, A 6–7/B 10–11.

134. Kant uses the same example at A 8/B 12.

135. See B 16–17.

136. This is Kant's first explicit assertion of the principle that will later be the key to the transcendental deduction of the categories; see, e.g., A 93–4/B 126–7.

137. This is the earliest note to enumerate clearly the four main parts of the eventual *Critique of Pure Reason*, assuming that the "transcendental critique" becomes the "Transcendental Dialectic" and the "transcendental architectonic" the "Doctrine of Method."

* *
*

1. This note may be compared to Kant's eventual explanation of the role of the categories at *Critique of Pure Reason*, B 128–9.

2. This comment makes it clear that the characterization of his transcendental idealism that he gives in the *Prolegomena to Any Future Metaphysics*, §13, Note II (4:289), does not represent any change in the conception of this doctrine he had earlier formed.

3. Kant's conception of the function of the understanding in this note thus seems closer to that in the inaugural dissertation on *The Form and Principles of the Sensible and the Intelligible World* (see especially §4, 2:392–3)

than to the one he would shortly begin developing in the "Duis-burg Nachlass" and which would be expounded in the *Critique of Pure Reason*.

4. On Kant's interpretation of Leibniz's and Newton's views of space, see the inaugural dissertation, §15.D (2:403–4) and *Critique of Pure Reason*, A 39–41/B 56–8.

5. The "Duisburg Nachlass" refers to a group of freestanding notes from 1775–76, some of which provide our most extensive evidence about the develop-ment of Kant's thought toward the *Critique of Pure Reason* between the time of his famous letter to Marcus Herz of 21 February 1772 and the publication of the *Critique* in 1781. Those bearing directly on the topics of the eventual *Critique* are included here, except for **4756**, an early outline of the *Critique* that is dated slightly later than these (1775–77). Others bear on the develop-ment of Kant's ethics, and are included in Chapter 4 below. See Theodore Häring, *Der Duisburgsche Nachlaß und Kants Kritizismus um 1775* (Tübingen, 1910).

6. This paragraph is the first in which Kant characterizes the task of explaining the possibility of a synthetic judgment as that of finding the "x" or "third thing" that connects the predicate to the subject concept when it is not analytically contained therein; see *Critique of Pure Reason*, A 9/B 13, A 154–8/B 193–7.

7. See *Critique of Pure Reason*, A 26/B 42 and *Prolegomena*, §§9–10.

8. The date of the letter on which Kant wrote this note is the basis for the dating of the "Duisburg Nachlass."

9. This suggestion of a bond between persistence and externality anticipates Kant's eventual "Refutation of Idealism" in the second edition of the *Critique of Pure Reason*, B 274–9.

10. This paragraph is Kant's first sketch for what would become the second "Analogy of Experience" in the *Critique*, A 188–211/B 232–256.

11. Häring (*Der Duisburg Nachlaß*) and Chenet (*Manuscrit de Duisburg*, p. 31) omit Kant's list of domestic items, assuming that it was some sort of inventory of his own possessions that appeared among his philosophical notes only accidentally. Given the following sentence, however, it appears more likely that his list was meant to illustrate concepts – such as writing perquisites, clothing, and the like, whose extension could not be determined *a priori* in accordance with a rule of construction, but only by some less formal and more practical criterion – in other words, an anticipation of Wittgenstein's concept of family resemblance!

12. Cf. *Critique of Pure Reason*, A 152–3/B 191–2.

13. This passage may be compared to the key footnote in the second-edition "Transcendental Deduction" in the *Critique of Pure Reason* (B 160–1), where Kant argues that the unity of the representations of space and time de-pends upon the understanding and its categories, not just on the faculty of sensibility.

14. Cf. *Critique of Pure Reason*, A 204–5/B 249–50, where Kant, having previously argued that the concept of a substance is the concept of that which endures through change, now argues that the concept of substance is the concept of that which acts.

15. Cf. *Critique of Pure Reason*, A 201/B 246, where Kant writes, "Thus the principle of sufficient reason is the ground of possible experience, namely the objective cognition of appearances with regard to their relation in the successive series of time."

16. Cf. *Critique of Pure Reason*, A 145/B 184: "The schema of actuality is existence at a determinate time."

17. Perhaps this is the first hint of Kant's subsequent idea that the synthetic *a priori* principles of judgment, that is, the synthetic *a priori* principles that are the object of metaphysics rather than mathematics, are yielded by a "schematism" that provides a pure form of sensibility through which pure concepts of the understanding are made "homogeneous" with – i.e., applicable to – their empirical objects. See *Critique of Pure Reason*, A 137–47/B 176–87.

18. Kant's notes in Baumgarten's *Metaphysica* from the period 1773–75 begin with **4688**. The present selection begins with **4708**. This note touches upon a number of themes in Kant's philosophy, but should be particularly compared with the line of thought that would become the third and fourth "Antinomies of Pure Reason" in the *Critique of Pure Reason*; see A 444–60/B 472–88 and A 532–65/B 560–93.

19. See Kant's extended critique of Leibniz in the *Critique of Pure Reason*, under the title of a "Remark to the amphiboly of the concepts of reflection," at A 268–89/B 324–46.

20. This note anticipates Kant's first "Antinomy of Pure Reason" and its resolution; see *Critique of Pure Reason*, A 426–33/B 454–61 and A517–23/B 545–51.

21. See Kant's famous remarks about the impossibility of a science of psychology in the *Metaphysical Foundations of Natural Science*, 4:469–71.

22. To this note on freedom, compare particularly **5434**.

23. Compare this note and the next to Kant's discussion of the "fact of reason" in *Critique of Practical Reason*, 5:29–33. In the same work, Kant discusses the status of freedom as a postulate of pure practical reason (what he here calls a "hypothesis") to the other two such postulates, those of the existence of God and immortality, at 5:132–4. On the incomprehensibility of freedom, see also *Groundwork*, 4:459–60.

24. In this note, Kant seems to be rejecting the view of his 1763 *The Only Possible Basis for a Demonstration of the Existence of God*, arguing contrary to that work that while we must form the concept of a highest reality as the basis of all possibilities, we cannot infer the actual existence of such a being from our concept of it. Thus, in addition to recapitulating Kant's standard critique of the ontological argument in its second paragraph, in its first this note anticipates the critique of the reification of the concept of an "Ideal of Pure Reason" in the *Critique of Pure Reason*, A 577–83/B 605–11.

25. Kant was always concerned that an appeal to the wisdom of God's purposes in the creation of nature could lead to a premature curtailment of scientific investigation into the actual mechanisms of nature: for an early example, see the discussion of teleology in *The Only Possible Argument in Support of an Argument for the Existence of God* (1763), Section 2, Fourth and Fifth Reflections, 2:108–23; for a later example, see *Critique of the Power of Judgment*, §68, 5:381–3.

564

26. Compare to **4708** and the references to the antinomies of pure reason given there.

27. The next five notes, **4756–4760**, which begin the group dated by Adickes from 1775–77, appear to be attempts to outline the emerging *Critique of Pure Reason* as a whole and in particular the "Transcendental Dialectic," although Adickes says they are "presumably lecture notes." **4756** was part of the *Duisburg Nachlaß*, but dated by Adickes, although without any explanation, as later than **4674–4684**, which he assigned to 1774–75. **4765** also belongs in this group of sketches. **4849**, assigned to the next stratum of notes (1776–79), is also a sketch of the emerging book. These sketches touch on so many of the topics of the *Critique* that it would be a distraction to note all of them.

28. In this paragraph, Kant is of course referring to the famous controversy between Leibniz and Newton, the latter represented by his champion, Samuel Clarke. The correspondence was published in English in 1717, the year after Leibniz's death, and was translated into German in 1720; the translation was reprinted later in the century and was readily available to Kant. For a recent study, see Ezio Vailati, *Leibniz and Clarke: A Study of Their Correspondence* (New York: Oxford University Press, 1997).

29. This is the first occurrence of the formula that the conditions of the possibility of experience are also the conditions of the possibility of the objects of experience, which Kant makes central to the argument of the "Transcendental Deduction" in the *Critique of Pure Reason*, A 90–3/B 122–6.

30. The ensuing contrast between the "immanent principles of the empirical use of the understanding" and the "transcendent principles of the pure use of the understanding" is clearly an anticipation of the eventual "Antinomy of Pure Reason," a term that Kant will explicitly use on the next page. But the conflicts are here presented in three rather than four pairs because composition and decomposition are grouped together rather than being separated as they will be in the first and second antinomies; see *Critique of Pure Reason*, A 426–43/B 454–71.

31. This presentation of "rules" by which to avoid antinomies is reminiscent of the approach recommended in Kant's inaugural dissertation on *The Form and Principles of the Sensible and the Intelligible Worlds* (1770), §24, 2:411–12.

32. This note should be compared to the "postulates of empirical thinking in general" in the *Critique of Pure Reason*, A 218–35/B 265–87; it suggests that in their empirical use the modal concepts of possibility, actuality, and necessity do not have different objects, but all apply in different ways to all empirical objects.

33. Kant had frequently used the term "exposition" in the *Duisburg Nachlaß* notes **4674–84** of the previous period to connote the objective experience that results from the application of the "titles of the understanding" to perceptions, but the term disappears from the *Critique of Pure Reason*. Perhaps its replacement here by "intellection" represents the beginning of Kant's change of terminology.

34. This passage appears to anticipate Kant's distinction between productive and reproductive imagination in the *Critique of Pure Reason*; see A 118.

35. This is one of the earliest places where Kant clearly distinguishes between the understanding and reason, and argues that the former yields empirical

cognition and the latter metaphysics. He does not yet say that pure reason has a positive and constitutive role only in its moral use.

36. **4761** is a discussion of the "proof of a future life" and other topics in metaphysics, and **4672** is a list of Latin metaphysical terms followed by a German catalogue of some of Kant's themes with little discussion. These do seem more like notes for lectures than like the sketches for a forthcoming book represented by **4756–60**. **4763** and **4764** are two sentences from the same sheet and page as the following **4765**; Adickes does not say why he assigns them separate numbers, so here they are prefaced to **4765**.

37. This brief note has nothing to do with Baumgarten's text, but is the first suggestion of Kant's division between the "Analytic of Concepts" and "Analytic of Principles" in the *Critique of Pure Reason*, a division which reflects his recognition that the categories derive from pure logic but yield the synthetic *a priori* judgments that metaphysics had always sought only when applied to experience through the schemata.

38. These terms come from the eighteenth-century debate in embryology between preformationism and epigenesis: *educta* would be what develops from completely preformed embryos, while *producta* would be entirely new products formed from the combination of parental germ cells. For evidence of Kant's direct interest in this debate, fundamental to eighteenth-century biological science, see *Critique of the Power of Judgment*, §81, 5:421–4.

39. See note 19 above.

40. **4852** through **5133** are notes written by Kant in and around the introduction to his copy of Baumgarten's *Metaphysica* in 1776–78, and constitute general observations and *aperçus* about the nature of philosophy and Kant's predecessors. They reveal much about Kant's conception of his own approach to philosophy in the years immediately before he finished the *Critique of Pure Reason*. We present a selection of these notes here.

41. Kant always began his lectures on the central subjects of philosophy – logic, metaphysics, and ethics – with a brief review of the history of that part of philosophy from the most ancient times to the times of Descartes, Locke, Leibniz, and Wolff, aimed at showing his students that they had much to learn from a charitable understanding even of the errors of the great philosophers of the past. See, for example, *Jäsche Logic*, 9:27–33; *Metaphysik Mrongovius* (1782–83), 29:757–68 (especially 764, where he describes Epicurus, sympathetically, as the "anti-metaphysician of the ancients"); *Metaphysik Vigilantius* (1794–95), 29:956–9; and *Moral Philosophy Collins*, 27:247–54.

42. For Kant's view of Plato's theory of ideas, see *Critique of Pure Reason*, A 313–19/B 370–5.

43. In restricting the use of pure reason to a "canon" for grounding the fundamental truths of morality and religion, this note anticipates the "Canon of Pure Reason" in the first *Critique*, A 795–31/B 823–59.

44. See also **4893**.

45. See Kant's comment about Locke in the introduction to the transcendental deduction of the categories, *Critique of Pure Reason*, A 86–7/B 118–19.

46. Compare to Kant's remark about Wolff at *Jäsche Logic*, 9:32, where he calls him dogmatic precisely because he failed, in Kant's view, to investigate "the

procedure of reason itself, in analyzing the whole human faculty of cognition and examining how far its *limits* may go." See also **5035** below.

47. Johann Heinrich Lambert (1728–77), author of the *Neues Organon, oder Gedanken über die Erforschung und Bezeichnung des Wahren und dessen Unterscheidung von Irrtum and Scheine* (The new organon, or thoughts on the investigation and designation of truth and its distinction from error and illusion) (Leipzig, 1764) and the *Anlage zur Architektonik* (Foundations of architectonic) (Riga, 1771). During the 1760s, Kant thought that Lambert was coming closer than anyone else in Germany to the proper approach to metaphysics (see the exchange of letters between them from November 1765 to February 1766, in Immanuel Kant, *Correspondence*, ed. Arnulf Zweig [Cambridge: Cambridge University Press, 1999], pp. 77–85). But Lambert criticized Kant's first presentation of transcendental idealism in a letter of 13 October 1770 (Zweig, pp. 113–20), and Kant apparently felt in turn that Lambert had not gone far enough in a critical scrutiny of the cognitive capacities.

48. Christian August Crusius (1715–75) was the leading philosopher of Pietism and the most important critic of Wolffianism before Kant. He particularly rejected Wolff's Leibnizian attempt to derive all the fundamental principles of metaphysics from the two principles of identity and sufficient reason, and instead argued that a larger number of principles had to be self-evident (see especially *Entwurf der nothwendigen Vernunftwahrheiten* [Sketch of the necessary truths of reason] [Leipzig, 1745]). Crusius's critique of Wolff's use of the principle of sufficient reason was crucial in the development of Kant's critical attitude toward rationalism, and he expressed considerable sympathy toward Crusius in the prize essay *Inquiry Concerning the Distinctness of the Principles of Natural Theology and Morality* (1764; see especially 2:293–6); but he eventually came to feel that Crusius's catalogue of self-evident principle lacked an adequate foundation in a critical examination of the human cognitive faculties themselves.

49. Compare this note to Kant's definition of a "transcendental exposition" at *Critique of Pure Reason*, B 40, and to his definition of "transcendental philosophy" at A 13/B 27. See also **5133** below.

50. See also the similar **4894** and notes 45 through 48 to it.

51. On Lambert, see note 47. Johann Nicolaus Tetens (1736–1807) criticized traditional metaphysics in *Über die allgemeine spekulativische Philosophie* (On general speculative philosophy) (Bützow and Wismar, 1775) and presented a threefold division of the higher faculties of mind in his *Philosophische Versuche über die menschliche Natur und ihre Entwicklung* (Philosophical essays on human nature and its development). Tetens's psychology exercised great influence on Kant – some think the need to assimilate it in detail slowed down Kant's work on the *Critique of Pure Reason* in 1777–78, but, as **4901** shows, Kant thought that Tetens failed to see the genuinely constitutive power of human cognitive faculties, and thus remained at the level of empirical rather than transcendental psychology.

52. This suggestion that transcendental freedom is a necessary condition for all thought, not just moral obligation, may be compared to Kant's argument in Section III of the *Groundwork for the Metaphysics of Morals*, 4:452–3.

53. See Kant's similar point in the third "Paralogism of Pure Reason" in the first *Critique*, A 361–6.

54. See **4866** and note 48.

55. Here Kant is presumably referring to the *Système de la nature, ou des Lois du monde physique et du monde moral* (1770) of Paul-Henri Thiry, Baron d'Holbach, which argues that man is entirely a product of natural mechanisms, so that even his moral and intellectual attributes are only products of sensation. Kant thinks that such a naturalistic reduction of the claims of philosophy and especially morality is just as much a stimulus to critical thinking as are the excessive speculations of the rationalists.

56. See *Critique of Pure Reason*, B xxii–xxiv, A 11–14/B 25–8, and A 480–1/B 508–9.

57. For Kant, a postulate of pure practical reason is a theoretical proposition that cannot be disproven by the theoretical use of reason but which can be affirmed only on moral grounds, as something that it is necessary to believe in order coherently to undertake to fulfill one's moral obligations; see, e.g., *Critique of Practical Reason*, 5:126.

58. Cf. Kant's remark in the preface to the first edition of the *Critique of Pure Reason* that his critique is not "a critique of books and systems, but a critique of the faculty of reason in general" (A xii).

59. By "my treatise" here Kant is clearly referring to the emergent *Critique of Pure Reason*; "the idea" that he hopes to salvage from his earlier work is singular rather than plural, so must refer to some general feature of his earlier work but not specifically to the doctrine of ideas of pure reason.

60. This remark points the way toward Kant's 1784 essay "Idea for a Universal History from a Cosmopolitan Point of View," in which he argues for an "end in nature" behind the "senseless course of human events" not as a matter of theoretical fact but like another postulate of practical reason, that is, a belief that will facilitate actual moral and political progress.

61. See *Critique of Pure Reason*, A 160/B 199.

62. Here Kant is obviously referring to his 1770 inaugural dissertation *On the Form and Principles of the Sensible and Intelligible Worlds* and its public defense.

63. This paragraph and indeed the whole note can be compared to Kant's discussions of critical philosophy as the successor to the skeptical response to dogmatism and especially its internal contradictions in the *Critique of Pure Reason*, e.g., the Preface to the first edition, A vii–xiv, and the section on "The discipline of pure reason with regard to its polemical use" in the "Doctrine of Method," A 738–69/B 766–97. Kant's lack of confidence in the present paragraph about the rapid success of his critique is, however, suppressed in the published work.

64. Joseph Priestley (1733–1804), English scientist, philosopher, and Unitarian minister. In natural science, he made significant contributions to the study of electricity and chemistry; in political philosophy, he defended maximal civil liberty and freedom of expression as conducive to the greatest happiness for the greatest number; and in general philosophy, he vigorously defended associationism as a source of first principles against the Scottish "common sense philosophy" of Reid, Beattie, and Oswald, as well as materialism and

determinism. Kant presumably has his associationism in mind in linking him here to Locke.

65. This note may be compared to Kant's similar apology for his adoption of "a dry, merely scholastic manner" in the Preface to the first edition of the *Critique of Pure Reason*, A xvii–xix.

66. See **4866** and **4893** above.

67. See **5031** above.

68. Cf. Kant's remark in the second edition of the transcendental deduction of the categories that all explanation of why we have the forms of intuitions and categories that we do is inexplicable (since they are after all themselves the framework for all explanation) (B 145–6).

69. Compare this to Kant's explanation of how in the first two, "mathematical" antinomies of pure reason, those concerning the extension and division of the material world, both thesis and antithesis can be false, at *Critique of Pure Reason*, A 497–507/B 525–35.

70. On the "logical" concept of personality, see §25 of the second-edition transcendental deduction in the first *Critique*, B 157–9, as well as the "Paralogisms of Pure Reason," e.g., A 355–6, A 398, and B 407–8. On "practical personality," see Kant's definition of personality as the concept of the capacity to be able to be moved by the moral law at *Religion within the Boundaries of Mere Reason*, 6:27–8, as contrasted to his accounts of personality as the locus of moral value, or that which is an end in itself, at *Groundwork*, 4:428, and *Critique of Practical Reason*, 5:87–8.

71. Kant's term "subreption" for metaphysical errors harks back to his diagnosis of them in the inaugural dissertation, Section 5, especially §26. But the present assignment of subreptions to judgment, the faculty that mediates between sensibility and intellect, indicates that he now sees metaphysical illusion as resulting from the failure to see the necessary connection between these two cognitive powers rather than from limiting reason by the conditions of sensibility.

72. See *Critique of Pure Reason*, B xix–xxi, as well as **4945** above.

73. See *Critique of Pure Reason*, A 57–62/B 82–86, "On the division of general logic into analytic and dialectic."

74. This remark is clearly an anticipation of Kant's footnote in the "Transcendental Aesthetic" of the first *Critique* (A 21, only slightly modified at B 35), in which he argues that the name of "aesthetics" should not be used for the theory of taste, which cannot amount to a science, but should be reserved for his own theory of pure intuition and its contribution to cognition generally, which does amount to a science.

75. Kant would develop this thought at length in the Appendix to the Transcendental Dialectic in the *Critique of Pure Reason*, especially in its first half, "On the regulative use of the ideas of pure reason," A 642–68/B 670–96, and return to it, although now assigning the search for systematicity to the faculty of "reflecting judgment" rather than reason in the *Critique of the Power of Judgment*, Introduction, sections III–VI, 5:179–88.

76. See the note to the Transcendental Aesthetic in the *Critique of Pure Reason*, A 21/B 35–6.

77. On morality as the form of the intelligible world that can and should inform the sensible world, see *Critique of Pure Reason*, A 808–11/B 836–9.
78. Johann Georg Sulzer (1720–79) was best known for his ultimately four-volume encyclopedia *Allgemeine Theorie der schönen Künste* (General Theory of the Fine Arts), originally published from 1771 to 1774, and was also the director of the philosophical section of the Berlin academy of sciences after 1755, thus during the period in which Kant entered several of the academy's essay competitions. By "minor writings" Kant presumably means the various essays that Sulzer published in the proceedings of the academy, which were collected in his *Vermischte philosophische Schriften* (Miscellaneous Philosophical Writings), the first volume of which was published in 1773 and the second, posthumously, in 1781. In referring to Sulzer's "vain" hope for a "demonstration," Kant could be referring to Sulzer's essay "Development of the concept of the eternal being" (Vol. I, pp. 377–88), originally published in 1770, or to the series "On the immortality of the soul, considered as an object of physics" (Vol. II, pp. 1–86), which appeared in the yearbooks of the academy in 1775, 1778, and 1779, thus during the same period as the present note of Kant.
79. See Kant's explanation of all dialectical illusion as ultimately arising from the conversion of the principle "when the conditioned is given, then so is the whole series of conditions" from a "logical maxim" to a metaphysical assumption; *Critique of Pure Reason*, A 307–8/B 364.
80. This argument depends on Kant's thesis that action is the fundamental characteristic of substance; see *Critique of Pure Reason*, A 203–5/B 249–51.
81. See Locke, *Essay concerning Human Understanding*, Book II, chapter xxiii, §§15–16, 22–32.
82. That the only properties that can be ascribed to God are those necessary for characterizing him as the ground of the possibility of the realization of the end of morality, that is, the highest good, is a central idea of Kant's moral theology, repeated in each of the three *Critiques*: see *Critique of Pure Reason*, A 814–15/B 842–3; *Critique of Practical Reason*, 5: 13–1, 140–1; *Critique of the Power of Judgment*, "General Remark on the Teleology," especially 5:478–84.
83. Compare this sentence to the opening paragraphs of the Preface to the first edition of the *Critique of Pure Reason*, A vii–viii. This note has all the earmarks of a draft for the Preface to the eventual *Critique*.
84. Compare this paragraph to Kant's argument in the "Paralogisms of Pure Reason" that neither the essential identity of mind and body (materialism) nor their essential difference (dualism) can be proven; *Critique of Pure Reason*, A 384–95.
85. Compare this note to Kant's famous distinction between analytic and synthetic judgments in precisely these terms at *Critique of Pure Reason*, A 7/B 11.
86. Compare this note to **4890** above.
87. Kant's notes on the body of Baumgarten's text from 1776 to 1778 are **5165** through **5551**; our selection begins with **5165**, which is the first that injects any of Kant's own views into his notes.
88. See Kant's contrast between logical and real possibility at *Critique of Pure Reason*, A 220–4/B 267–72.

89. This note succinctly expresses the premise of the second "Analogy of Experience"; cf. *Critique of Pure Reason*, B 233–4, A 192–5/B 237–40.

90. To this paragraph compare *Critique of Pure Reason*, A 200–1/B 245–6.

91. The present reflection **5203** and the subsequent **5208, 5211, 5213, 5216,** and **5221** seem to be Kant's earliest surviving attempts to sketch what would become the "Transcendental Deduction" of the categories in the *Critique of Pure Reason*, that is, the attempt to demonstrate that the categories apply to all the appearances that we can experience without reference to the specifically temporal form of those appearances and their exposition (the strategy that he followed in the period 1775–75, as represented by notes **4674** through **4684**). That these notes toward the "Transcendental Deduction" are found within a group that otherwise point to the "Analogies of Experience" suggests that it was only in this period that Kant began to distinguish the two levels of argumentation from each other.

92. Kant's attempt in this note to distinguish between apprehension and the further activity of the understanding which provides an object for what is given through experience may point the way toward his theory of three-fold synthesis in the first-edition "Transcendental Deduction," *Critique of Pure Reason*, A 99–107, although that theory will insert "reproduction" by the imagination between apprehension by sensibility and recognition of an object under a concept.

93. This sketch may be compared with Kant's discussions of the role of the concept of an object in both editions of the "Transcendental Deduction," *Critique of Pure Reason*, A 104–6 and B 137.

94. This note obviously reflects Kant's long-standing critique of the ontological argument, from his first philosophical writing of 1755 (*A New Elucidation of the First Principles of Metaphysical Cognition*, Proposition VI, 1:394–5) to the *Critique of Pure Reason* (especially A 598–601/B 626–9).

95. This note demonstrates how fluid Kant's terminology remained up until the publication of the first *Critique* (and no doubt afterward as well). What he here refers to as both "anticipations" and "postulates" are in fact what he calls in the *Critique* the "schemata" for the application of the pure concepts of the understanding to intuitions through the forms of sensibility, and the example that he gives, that substance endures forever, is the subject of the first "Analogy of Experience" in the *Critique*, where the "Analogies" are distinguished from both the "Anticipations of Perception" and the "Postulates of Empirical Thinking."

96. This passage is an anticipation of Kant's discussion of the "Ideal of Pure Reason" in the *Critique of Pure Reason*, A 572–83/B 599–611; the penultimate sentence here hints but does not say outright that we are not entitled to infer from the logical idea of a real ground of all determinations to the metaphysical and objective reality of such a ground. For further discussion, see also **5271** through **5274**.

97. Although this note is appended to Baumgarten's discussion of the first principle of the mathematics of intensive magnitudes, it concerns only Kant's more general contrast between the constructability of mathematical concepts and the non-constructability of general concepts in philosophy; see, e.g., *Critique of Pure Reason*, A 712–26/B 740–54.

98. See Kant's discussion of action as the criterion of substance at *Critique of Pure Reason*, A 204–5/B 249–51.

99. See also **5212**.

100. In the "Schematism" chapter of the *Critique of Pure Reason*, Kant says that "The schema of substance is persistence of the real in time" (A 144/B 183), and in the "Second Analogy" he writes that "the ultimate subject of the changeable is therefore **that which persists**, as the substratum of everything that changes, i.e., the substance" (A 205/B 250).

101. In the *Critique of Pure Reason*, Kant does not argue for the transcendental ideality of space and time from the fact that they can be neither substances nor accidents of substances, but rather infers this as a conclusion from independent proofs of their transcendental ideality. See A 22–3/B 37–8, A 26/B 42. See also **5323**.

102. This note and the next, in which Kant struggles with how time can be transcedentally ideal yet "actual," is reminiscent of *Critique of Pure Reason* A 36–8/B 53–4; but since this passage is itself Kant's attempt to answer the objection to his inaugural dissertation that had been raised by Lambert (letter of 13 October 1770 in Zweig, *Correspondence*, pp. 113–19) and Mendelssohn (letter of 25 December 1770, Zweig, pp. 122–4), it is possible that these notes stem from the earlier period (1771) assigned to it by Adickes as least likely.

103. See also **5298**.

104. Kant had raised this objection to Leibniz in the inaugural dissertation, §15.D, and would reiterate it in the *Critique of Pure Reason*, A 39–40/B 56–7.

105. This note demonstrates that Kant was conceiving of the argument of the "Refutation of Idealism" that he added to the second edition of the *Critique of Pure Reason* (B 274–8) well before the publication of the first edition. This note may also be compared to **5653** below.

106. This note and **5400** anticipate the theme that Kant strikes in Note 3 (B 278–9) to the "Refutation of Idealism," as well as many times in the further versions of the refutation from 1788–1790 (**6311** through **6317** below). See also the brief preceding notes on realism and idealism, **5394–5** and **5398**. The notes from **5370** through **5392** that have been omitted concern the concepts of contingency and continuity.

107. The intervening notes **5401–12** concern the concepts of substance and essence.

108. This argument may be compared not just with Kant's general claim in the *Critique of Pure Reason* (5:29–30) and *Religion within the Boundaries of Mere Reason* (e.g., 6:62–3, 66–7) that the fact of our obligation under the moral law makes the otherwise inscrutable fact of our freedom known to us, but also with his argument in the *Metaphysics of Morals* (6:226–7) that *only* our obligation under moral law, not violations of it, can make freedom known to us.

109. Compare Kant's argument, at *Critique of Practical Reason*, 5:29–30, that we do not have an experience of our own freedom although we do have an experience of moral obligation and infer our freedom from that.

110. Cf. Kant's similar definition of the will (*Wille*) at *Groundwork*, Section II, 4:412, 427. But note that at 427 he also maintains the will must have an

end in order to have an "objective ground of its self-determination" in accordance with a law.

111. The argument of this paragraph may be compared to Kant's argument in *Groundwork*, Section III, 4:452–3.

112. **5444** through **5450**, an important series of notes on the good will and the moral law, are to be included in Chapter 4.

113. Compare this paragraph to Kant's argument in the "Paralogisms of Pure Reason" in the first *Critique*, A 386–93.

114. On the concept of the seat of the soul, see also **5459**.

115. In the following note **5458**, Kant briefly categorizes the alleged proofs of the immateriality of the soul without asserting or denying their conclusiveness.

116. Kant does not mention the necessity of having a body for empirical self-consciousness in the second-edition "Refutation of Idealism," but he does make it explicit in at least one of the subsequent reflections on the refutation, namely **6315**.

117. Kant comments on the last two sections of Baumgarten's chapter on rational psychology, concerning the origin of the human soul and its status subsequent to death, in **5462** through **5481**. **5477** is translated in Chapter 4. Kant's notes on the final chapter in Baumgarten, on natural theology, begin with **5482**.

118. This note alludes back to the proof of the existence of God that Kant propounded in his 1763 book *The Only Possible Basis for a Demonstration of the Existence of God*, but which, under the name of the "Ideal of Pure Reason," he would ultimately reject in the *Critique of Pure Reason* (see A 571–83/B 599–611). It is not clear whether he is rejecting it yet in this note or in related notes such as **5502**, **5504**, **5519**, **5522** (translated below), or **5526** and **5527** (both translated below), although he does appear to be casting doubt on it in **5508** (also translated below).

119. As **5505** (translated below) suggests, Kant may be referring here not to Descartes's exposition of the ontological argument in the Fifth *Meditation* but to his argument in the third *Meditation* that any knowledge of imperfection presupposes knowledge of the existence of perfection, and thus the existence of God.

120. Wolff argues from the existence of contingent beings, through the premise of the principle of sufficient reason, to the existence of a necessary being, in the *Vernünfftige Gedancken von Gott, der Welt, und der Seele des Menschen* ("German Metaphysics"), new edition (Halle: Renger, 1751; originally 1719), §§928–31.

121. This may be compared to the conception of the "Ideal of Pure Reason" that Kant ultimately rejects in the *Critique of Pure Reason*, A 571–83/B 599–611. Kant also presents the argument he later rejected in **5508**, **5518**, **5522**, **5526**, and **5527**, although in the first of these with the reservation that the argument is only subjectively valid.

122. This may again be compared to Descartes's argument in the third *Meditation*.

123. Here Kant is clearly referring to Descartes's ontological argument for the existence of God in the fifth *Meditation*. Kant had criticized this argument

on the ground adduced here as early as his 1755 dissertation *On the First Principles of Metaphysical Cognition* and again in 1763 in *The Only Possible Basis for a Demonstration of the Existence of God*, which could explain Adickes's uncertainty about the date of this note. Kant returns to his critique of the ontological argument in **5507** and **5523**.

124. See note 121.

125. Here Kant is obviously thinking of the conflict that would become the first "Antinomy of Pure Reason," *Critique of Pure Reason* A 426–33/B454–61.

126. Kant's notes from 1778–79, the last notes clearly written before the final composition and publication of the *Critique of Pure Reason* in 1781, begin with **5552** through **5555**. The first three of these, "loose sheets," and the last, written on an undated letter but also apparently from 1778–79, appear to be preparatory drafts for the "Transcendental Dialectic" of the *Critique of Pure Reason*. **5552** **is** a sketch of the "Amphiboly of the Concepts of Reflection" as the transition from the "Transcendental Analytic" to the "Transcendental Dialectic," and **5553** is a detailed draft of the "First Book" of the "Dialectic," "On the concepts of pure reason" (A 310/B 366–A 338/B 396).

127. For the identification of the "matter" of a syllogistic inference with its major premise, see the *Jäsche Logic*, §59; in Immanuel Kant, *Lectures on Logic*, ed. J. Michael Young (Cambridge: Cambridge University Press, 1992), p. 616.

128. See the *Jäsche Logic*, §62; *Lectures on Logic*, p. 617.

129. This definition of a paralogism may be compared to Kant's account at *Critique of Pure Reason*, A 396–7.

130. These are what Kant calls the "concepts of reflection" at *Critique of Pure Reason*, A 261–6/B 317–22.

131. This is the gist of Kant's critique of Leibniz's use of the principle of the "identity of indiscernibles," developed more fully in the *Critique* at A 271–2/B 327–8.

132. Cf. *Critique of Pure Reason*, A 274/B 330.

133. Kant presents the same table of negative concepts, although without the helpful examples, at *Critique of Pure Reason*, A 292/B 348.

134. Having finally separated the transcendental deduction of the pure concepts of the understanding from the derivation of the principles of empirical judgment in the period 1776–78, Kant now had to develop the doctrine of schematism to explain the connection between the categories and the principles of judgment; see *Critique of Pure Reason*, A 137–47/B 176–87.

135. Cf. *Critique of Pure Reason*, A 323/B 379, A 334/B 391.

136. Cf. *Critique of Pure Reason*, A 643–4/B 671–2.

137. Cf. *Critique of Pure Reason*, A 335–6/B 392–3.

138. In fact, under each of the three main forms of dialectical inference derived from the categorical, hypothetical, and disjunctive syllogisms – namely, the "Paralogisms of Pure Reason," the "Antinomy of Pure Reason," and the "Ideal of Pure Reason" – Kant does present four more specific fallacious or conflicting arguments. But only in the case of the "Antinomy of Pure Reason" can its four subdivisions be readily associated with the four categorial headings of quantity, quality, relation, and modality.

139. Kant here refers to the organization that we find in "Book Two" of the published "Transcendental Dialectic": the "Dialectic" as a whole is divided into three parts, the "Paralogisms of Pure Reason," the "Antinomy of Pure Reason," and the "Ideal of Pure Reason," and the first two but not the third are officially divided into four parts (although when Kant adds his critique of the traditional ontological, cosmological, and physico-theological proofs of the existence of God to the critique of his own argument for the existence of God as the ground of all possibilities, there will in fact also be four main parts to the "Ideal of Pure Reason" as well).

140. See Kant's treatment of the second paralogism, especially A 354–6 and B 407–8, as well as his general remarks about the paralogisms at A 396–7 and B 406–7.

141. Cf. *Critique of Pure Reason*, A 33–4/B 390–1.

142. This refers to the first two volumes of a translation of Lucian by H. Waser, published in 1769 by Orell, Gessner, and Co. in Zürich. Lucian of Samosata (b. 120 C.E.) was the most famous satirist of the ancient world, lampooning popular religious beliefs, human vanity, and philosophical pretensions. It is not clear why Kant mentions him here: Kant's present diagnosis of the source of metaphysical illusion is surely more than mere satire.

143. See note 141.

144. Cf. Kant's definition of "idea" at *Critique of Pure Reason*, A 320/B 377.

145. Cf. Kant's discussion of Plato's theory of ideas at *Critique of Pure Reason*, A 312–19/B 368–75.

146. See notes 139 and 141.

147. Kant is again referring to the concepts of reflection; see **5552** and note 130.

148. Cf. Kant's 1763 "Attempt to introduce the concept of negative magnitudes into philosophy," 2:165–204; in *Theoretical Philosophy, 1755–1770*, pp. 205–41.

149. This refers to Kant's critique that Leibniz's principle of the identity of indiscernibles generates his monadology because he thinks that numerically distinct things must always have distinct concepts, not merely distinct positions in intuition, i.e., in space and time. See *Critique of Pure Reason*, "The Amphiboly of the Concepts of Reflection," A 260–89/B 316–46. For clear statements of Leibniz's principle, see his 1686 paper "Primary Truths" and the contemporaneous *Discourse on Metaphysics*, §9; for a statement readily accessible to Kant, see *Monadology*, §9.

150. On Kant's account of Leibniz's monadology, the monad is identified with the entirety of the relations in which an object would otherwise be thought to stand, and all of its properties are held to be representations because only representations are entirely internal to the substance that has them. See Leibniz's *Principles of Nature and Grace*, §2, and *Monadology*, §§8–30.

151. Pierre-Louis Moreau de Maupertuis (1698–1759), French scientist and philosopher, president of the Berlin Academy of Sciences from 1746 until his death. He was famous for leading an expedition to Lapland in 1736 that helped prove that the earth is an oblate spheroid, for the law of least action, for a revision of the cosmological argument, for an alternative to preformationism attempting to explain the origin of organic life out of

combinations of desire, aversion, and memory in elementary particles, and for the view that our knowledge of objects is projected from phenomenal fragments that can never yield us a fully determinate conception of the natural world.

152. This may be Kant's first use of this concept, which is prominent in the first-edition "Transcendental Deduction"; see A 109, and Kant's further explanation of the concept at A 250–3.

153. See the chapter "On the ground of the distinction of all objects in general into *phenomena* and *noumena*," especially A 253, B 307–8, and A 253–60/B 309–15.

154. Compare this note to **5552** and *Critique of Pure Reason*, A 321–37/B 378–94.

155. Kant's notes on Baumgarten's text from 1778–79, fewer than those from 1776–78, are **5556** through **5635**. For further brief notes on the concept of possibility, see **5557–5559** and **5565**. These notes may be compared to Kant's discussion of possibility in the first *Critique*'s "Postulates of Empirical Thinking," especially A 220–5/B 267–71.

156. See also **5572**.

157. This note should be compared to Kant's definition of alteration in the first "Analogy of Experience," A 187/B 230–1.

158. This note anticipates the "Axioms of Intuition" and "Anticipations of Perception" in the *Critique of Pure Reason*, but should also be compared to Kant's discussion of continuity in the second "Analogy of Experience," A 207–9/B 253–5.

159. For the contrast between mathematical and dynamical principles of judgment, see *Critique of Pure Reason*, A 160–1/B 199–200.

160. Compare this note with Kant's early distinction between mathematical and philosophical methods in the 1764 prize essay, the *Inquiry concerning the Distinctness of the Principles of Natural Theology and Morality*, especially the First Reflection, pp. 2:276–83, and his mature discussion in the "Doctrine of Method" in the *Critique*, A 712–38/B 740–66.

161. For Kant's use of the term "exposition," see **4674–84**.

162. Compare the discussion of the concept of nature in **5607–8** to Kant's definition in the first-edition "Transcendental Deduction," A 125.

163. Kant makes it clear that these are only regulative principles concerning nature at *Critique of the Power of Judgment*, Introduction, section V, 5:182.

164. See **5608** and note 164.

165. For earlier notes on *Arbitrium*, *Spontaneitas*, and *Libertas*, see **3855–72, 3922, 4033, 4219–29, 4333–9, 4441, 4541–51, 4724–9, 4783–8, 5104, 5121, 5434–50**.

166. See *Metaphysics of Morals*, "Doctrine of Virtue," Introduction, section XIV, 6:407.

167. This account of evil is subsequently amplified in Book I of *Religion within the Boundaries of Mere Reason*, where Kant clarifies that evil actions are not performed without any principle at all, but in the name of the principle of self-love (6:36–7) – a principle which is, to be sure, not "objectively sufficient."

168. Cf. *Groundwork for the Metaphysics of Morals*, Section III, 4:446–7.

169. Adickes subsumes this note under §§800–2, the *Prolegomena* to *Theologia naturalis*, in spite of its apparent location at §336, on *Utilitas*. The opening words of the note make its assignment to *Theologia naturalis* plausible, but Adickes offers no explanation of its relocation.

170. See Kant's explications of the concept of a postulate of pure practical reason at *Critique of Pure Reason*, A 633–4/B 661–2, and *Critique of Practical Reason*, 5:11n., 5:120–1, and especially 5:143n.

* *

*

1. Following the undated *LBl* B 12, which gives every indication of being a sketch of the transcendental "Deduction of the Pure Concepts of the Understanding" for the first edition of the *Critique of Pure Reason*, perhaps prepared very shortly before the composition of the published version, this section includes notes that have been dated to the period 1780–89. **5636** through **5639** appear to come from the beginning of the period, and thus may still be among drafts for the *Critique of Pure Reason*. Beginning with **5642**, these notes appear to follow the publication of the first edition of the *Critique*. Notes dated 1783–84 appear to be connected with Kant's response to the notorious review of the *Critique* that appeared in the *Göttingschen Anzeigen von gelehrten Sachen*, number 3, 19 January 1782, pp. 40–8, revised by its editor, Johann Georg Heinrich Feder, from a draft by Christian Garve, and to Kant's preparation of the *Prolegomena to Any Future Metaphysics* of 1783, which is in part a product of his response to the Garve-Feder review.

2. Cf. *Critique of Pure Reason*, A 84/B 116–17.

3. In the first edition of the "Transcendental Deduction," Kant describes a very similar statement as "a general remark on which one must ground everything that follows" (A 99).

4. Here Kant anticipates the doctrine of threefold synthesis of the first-edition "Transcendental Deduction"; see *Critique of Pure Reason*, A 98–110.

5. On the contrast between "transcendental principles of mathematics" and "principles of mathematics," see *Critique of Pure Reason*, A 160/B 199, A 165–6/B 206–7.

6. Cf. *Critique of Pure Reason*, A 167–8/B 207–10.

7. This note is written on a bureaucratic document concerning the admission of a student who matriculated at the university in Königsberg on 22 March 1780, making a date shortly after that time most probable. See Adickes's note at 18:268–71n.

8. To this paragraph compare Kant's "conclusions from the above concepts" of space and time at A 26/B 42 and A 32–3/B 49–50.

9. In the second edition of the *Critique*, Kant would call this argument from the presupposition of the synthetic *a priori* status of mathematics to the existence of an *a priori* representation of space the "transcendental exposition" of the concept of space, thereby distinguishing it from the other arguments for this conclusion that do not actually presuppose that mathematics is

synthetic *a priori*, which he then calls the "metaphysical exposition"; cf. *Critique of Pure Reason*, B 40–1, as well as *Prolegomena*, 4:268–9.

10. Persius, *Satires* III, 77, 78: *Hic aliquis de gente hircosa centurionum / Dicat: Quod satis est, sapio mihi.* The last phrase is also quoted at the conclusion of the *Critique of Pure Reason*, A 855/B 883.

11. This paragraph is a mystery. Adickes conjectures that the "to 66" might refer to p. 66 of the second edition of the *Critique*, where Kant is arguing that only transcendental idealism can explain the necessary truth of mathematical propositions, and that the "brave mathematical man" could refer to the mathematician Abraham Kästner (1719–1800), thus suggesting a date toward 1790, when Kästner would indeed have been an old man. But he argues that the ink and style point more to the beginning of the 1780s, thus suggesting that this note is a sketch for the *Critique*. It would not have been like Kant to bother repeating in a note a Latin quote that he had already published, so that also suggests that this was a draft preceding the *Critique*.

12. Leibniz's "refutation" of Locke, the *New Essays concerning Human Understanding*, was not published until 1765, long after the deaths of both Locke (1704) and Leibniz (1716); indeed, the death of Locke was the reason why Leibniz felt it would be unfair to publish his just-completed refutation and withheld it. Perhaps Kant thought that if it had been published when written it would then have undermined Locke's reputation and with it the empiricist program. Kant's claim here that mathematics undermines the possibility of empiricism is reminiscent of his argument that if only Hume had recognized the synthetic but *a priori* character of mathematics, even he would have been forced to give up his empiricism (*Prolegomena*, 4:272–3). Kant was obviously not aware of Hume's extended empiricist treatment of mathematics in the *Treatise of Human Nature*, Book I, Part II.

13. This paragraph obviously anticipates the "Canon of Pure Reason" in the *Critique*, particularly its second section, "On the ideal of the highest good" (A 804–819/B 832–47), where Kant presents his first published account of the existence of God and immortality as postulates of pure practical reason.

14. Kant saw Epicurus as rightly rejecting any appeal to final causes within physical science (*Metaphysik* L_2, 28:574), but as failing to appreciate the thoroughly necessitarian character of scientific explanation when he introduced accidental collisions (the *clinamen*) between atoms as the basis of all his explanations (*Metaphysik Dohna-Wundlacken*, 28:664–5). On Kant's view of Epicurus, see also *Critique of Pure Reason*, A 471–2/B 499–500.

15. On Kant's conception of Aristotle as well as Locke as an empiricist, see *Metaphysik* L_1, 28:232–3.

16. That is, the flattening of the earth at its poles, as confirmed by Maupertuis in 1736.

17. For discussion of the antinomies in terms of whether our concepts are too big or too small for the world, see *Critique of Pure Reason*, "Antinomy of Pure Reason," Section Five, A 486–90/B 514–18.

18. See note 17.

19. Kant's use of "absolute freedom of religion" as an example of a concept about which there can be an antinomy may anticipate his attempt to work out a

complex position in which government may have a right to enforce orthodoxy in an established church as a public institution while having no right to
restrict private belief or philosophical inquiry into theological matters; see
his 1798 book *The Conflict of the Faculties*.

20. With **5642**, we come to notes that appear to have been written after the
publication of the first edition of the *Critique of Pure Reason*, and which
represent Kant's efforts to clarify, defend, and where necessary revise his
views, beginning with his preparation for the publication of the *Prolegomena
to Any Future Metaphysics* in 1783. Adickes conjectures that this note, opening
with the phrase "my putative idealism," was written in response to the review
of the *Critique* in the *Göttingischen gelehrten Anzeigen* of 19 January 1782, as
it later turned out written by Christian Garve but substantially altered by
the editor J. H. Feder, which so incensed Kant. For translations of both the
Garve-Feder review and the original Garve review, which was published the
next year in the *Allgemeine deutsche Bibliothek*, see Brigitte Sassen, ed., *Kant's
Early Critics: The Empiricist Critique of the Critical Philosophy* (Cambridge:
Cambridge University Press, 2000), pp. 53–77.

21. In the *Prolegomena*, Kant would write that he called his idealism "transcendental" to signify that it concerns only our manner of representing things,
and does not impugn their reality; but says that if is this occasions misunderstanding, then it would be better to call his view "critical idealism"; §13,
Note III, 4:293–4.

22. In saying that there is a psychological and theological element both within
the antinomies and outside them, Kant is presumably trying to explain why
the simplicity and freedom of the soul are touched upon in the second and
third antinomies, but at least the former also in the second paralogism,
while the existence of a necessary being is at issue in the fourth antinomy
but also in the "Ideal of Pure Reason," specifically in the analysis of the
cosmological argument. As was evident in such notes as **4673** (1773–75) and
4757–60 (1775–77), Kant had earlier attempted to include all of his critique
of metaphysics within the framework of the antinomies, and therefore had
not needed the kind of explanation of apparent duplication offered in this
paragraph.

23. This is Kant's standard account of Berkeley's idealism; see *Prolegomena*, 4:289.

24. "Syncretists" refers to a seventeenth-century sect, founded by George
Calixtus, aimed at reuniting all Protestants and ultimately all Christians.
Pelagians, followers of the fourth-century monk Pelagius, denied original
sin.

25. Compare this paragraph to Kant's account of the "supreme principle of all
synthetic judgments" at *Critique of Pure Reason*, A 154–8/B 193–7.

26. Kant defines an intuition as that representation through which an object is
given to us "directly" at *Critique of Pure Reason*, A 19/B 33, while at *Jäsche
Logic*, §1, 9:91, he defines an intuition as a singular representation. If one
assumes that only particular objects and not universals actually exist to be
given to us, then the former definition implies the latter. Kant defines an
intuition as a representation that is both immediate and singular at *Critique
of Pure Reason*, A 320/B 377.

27. Cf., again, *Critique of Pure Reason*, A 320/B 377.

28. To this paragraph, compare Kant's account of the function of the concept of an object at *Critique of Pure Reason*, A 104 and B 137.

29. Cf. *Critique of Pure Reason*, A 155/B 194.

30. Adickes reports great similarity in ink and handwriting between this note and a letter of recommendation for Johann Behrendt that Kant wrote to Carl Daniel Reusch on 13 June 1785 (10:405). He also conjectures that this may have been a sketch of a popular essay that Kant was thinking of writing at that time. But Kant's reference to Francis Bacon (see note 31) and scientific progress equally suggests that this note might have been a draft for the preface to the second edition of the *Critique of Pure Reason*. See also note 39 below.

31. Here Kant refers to Francis Bacon (1561–1626), whom he regarded as starting natural science on the same path to certainty as the Greeks had found for mathematics (*Critique of Pure Reason*, B xii). For the second edition of the *Critique*, Kant added a motto from Bacon's *Instauratio Magna*, his method for a revolution in science. In this motto, Bacon asks people to consider what he offers not as an "opinion" but as a work for the "foundation of human utility and dignity," and says that "each may well hope from our instauration that it claims nothing infinite, and nothing beyond what is moral; for in truth it prescribes only the end of infinite errors" (B ii). Both the claims that method enables the avoidance of error and that its ultimate objective is not only the utility but also the dignity of mankind are obviously central to Kant's own conception of his philosophical enterprise.

32. See Kant's discussion of opinion, belief, and knowledge in the "Canon of Pure Reason," A 820–31/B 848–59.

33. The tradition of the first seven kings of Rome was questioned by writers in the eighteenth century, beginning with Giambattista Vico. The *Cloaca Maxima* was an open, later canalized watercourse draining northeast Rome to the Tiber by way of the Forum. Tradition ascribed its regulation to Tarquinius Superbus, the last king of Rome (traditionally 534–510 B.C.E.), and branch drains as early as the fifth century B.C.E. do exist; but much of the existing sewer is due to M. Vipsianius Agrippa in 33 B.C.E.. Adam Ferguson, in his *History of the Progress and Termination of the Roman Republic* (1783), speculated that the sewer had been constructed prior to Tarquinius, and indeed prior to Romulus, the legendary first king of Rome, because it seemed suited to a much larger city than those early kings could have ruled. Servius Tullius was the sixth king of Rome (traditionally 578–535 B.C.E.), so the discovery of inscriptions by him that Kant imagines would prove that the sewer had not been constructed by a pre-Roman civilization. Ferguson's work was translated into German in 1784, so Kant's use of this example makes Adickes's assignment of this note to the next year plausible.

34. Cf. *Critique of Pure Reason*, A 822/B 850, where Kant writes that "In judging from pure reason, **to have an opinion** is not allowed at all."

35. Cf. *Critique of Pure Reason*, A 713/B 741, A 736/B 764.

36. As in, for example, *Monadology*, §2.

37. Kant had long argued that the infinitude of the universe in both space and time made the creation of infinitely many worlds like our own in all sorts of respects, thus including intelligent life, possible and indeed probable.

See, for example, his 1755 work *Universal Natural History and Theory of the Heavens*, Third Part, "Appendix on the Inhabitants of the Stars" (2:351–68). He uses the example of inhabitants of other planets as something on which we might reasonably place a bet, thus a matter of belief rather than mere opinion, at *Critique of Pure Reason*, A 825/B 853.

38. On moral belief and moral certainty, see *Critique of Pure Reason*, A 828–30/ B 856–8.

39. In the *Critique of Practical Reason*, Kant greatly expands on the treatment of the postulates of pure practical reason previously given in the "Canon of Pure Reason" in the first *Critique*. Since Kant only decided to publish a separate *Critique of Practical Reason* during the course of his work on the revisions of the first edition of the *Critique of Pure Reason*, the extensive discussion of the postulates in this note is additional evidence that it might have been a draft of a new preface for the new edition of the first *Critique*.

40. See note 35 above.

41. Cf. *Critique of Pure Reason*, A ix–xii.

42. Cf. *Critique of Pure Reason*, B xxxv.

43. In the preface to the first edition of the *Critique*, Kant argues that human nature cannot maintain the "indifference" called for by skepticism, and thus will inevitably relapse into dogmatism unless saved from it by successful critique (A x–xi).

44. In *Religion within the Boundaries of Mere Reason*, Kant argues against the idea that through moral conversion one becomes, in the Christian expression, a "new man" whose previous sins are simply forgotten; see especially 6:66–77.

45. Here Kant may be referring to Rousseau's confession that he had blamed another servant for a ribbon that he himself had stolen upon the death of Mme. de Vercelli; see *Confessions*, Part One, Book II, in Jean-Jacques Rousseau, *The Confessions and Correspondence, including the Letters to Malesherbes*, The Collected Writings of Rousseau, volume 5, edited by Christopher Kelly, Roger D. Masters, and Peter G. Stillman (Hanover: University Press of New England, 1995), pp. 70–3.

46. Here Kant apparently refers to Dietrich Tiedemann, who published two essays in 1785, "*Über die Möglichkeit einer anfangenden Succession*" and "*Über die Natur der Metaphysik: zur Prüfung von Herrn Prof. Kant's Grundsätzen,*" in the *Hessischen Beiträge zur Gelehrsamkeit und Kunst*, pp. 17–30 and 113–30, 233–48, and 464–74. Presumably Kant wrote this note in response to reading Tiedemann's articles after they appeared. Adickes described the second piece as "a wretched piece of work" and "utterly worthless" in his *German Kantian Bibliography* (New York: Burt Franklin, 1970, originally published in *The Philosophical Review* from 1893 to 1896), p. 47), although he contented himself with the milder epithet "somewhat overestimated" in describing Tiedemann's *Theätet oder über das menschliche Wisse* (Frankfurt am Main, 1794) (p. 219). Adickes describes the contents of this work in detail at pp. 219–21.

47. Cf. *Critique of Pure Reason*, A 204–5/B 249–51.

48. Kant assumes this premise throughout his discussion of matter as comprised of attractive and repulsive forces in the "metaphysical foundations of dynamics," the second chapter of the 1786 *Metaphysical Foundations of*

Natural Science (see, e.g., Proposition 4, 4:503–8). This might suggest that the present note is a sketch connected with the composition of this work, and thus that the word "Metaphysics" in the note is used in the sense used in that work, i.e., to designate the results of the application of pure principles of thought to a fundamental empirical concept, such as the concept of matter.

49. Compare this argument and the remainder of the note to Kant's rejection of the inference from the simplicity of the action of the soul (its application of the simple term "I") to the simplicity of the soul as a substance in the second paralogism of pure reason, A 351–61.

50. The next three sketches seem to be attempts at restating the "Refutation of Idealism" that Kant included in the second edition of the *Critique of Pure Reason* (B 274–9). **5653** and **5654** are both explicitly labelled "against material idealism" or "against idealism." These two notes seem to be comments on the second-edition "Refutation of Idealism" written after its publication, perhaps in or soon after October 1788, when Kant made extracts from Johann August Eberhard's treatment of idealism in his *Philosophisches Magazin* (1788–89), Nos. 2–3. Eberhard would shortly become a major opponent of Kant when he attacked Kant's argument for the synthetic rather than analytic status of mathematical propositions. See Henry Allison, *The Kant-Eberhard Controversy* (Baltimore: The Johns Hopkins University Press, 1973). **5655** does not carry this label but continues the same theme. Kant returns to the "Refutation of Idealism" in **6311** through **6317**, from the fall of 1790, translated below.

51. Compare this to Kant's diagnosis of the error of "problematic idealism" at Note 1 to the published "Refutation," B 276–7. He had previously offered a similar diagnosis in the fourth paralogism in the first edition of the *Critique*, A 368. See also **5709** below.

52. This paragraph may be compared to Kant's official statement of the "Refutation" at B 275–6. That he now goes on to try to explain why the representation of space in particular is necessary for the determination of one's own existence in time suggests that he now recognized the proof published in the second edition to be incomplete.

53. To this paragraph, compare Note 3 to the published "Refutation," B 278–9.

54. Cf. Kant's argument to similar effect in the "General Note on the System of Principles," also added to the second edition of the *Critique*, especially B 291–2.

55. The content of the following paragraphs might seem to link them to the *Critique of Practical Reason*, particularly to the "Critical Elucidation of the Analytic of Pure Practical Reason" (5:89–106), where Kant gives an extended account of the reconciliation of freedom and determinism made possible by transcendental idealism. But if the whole of **5653** dates from October 1788, as Adickes conjectures, then this material could only be a draft for a preface to the *Critique of the Power of Judgment*, on which Kant was then working, and which was intended to show how our conceptions of the mechanical lawfulness of nature and the freedom of purposive ends could be reconciled, through the conception of reflecting judgment, *within* the realm of experience.

56. That is, within nature as the object of experience no substance is ever created (or annihilated); this is the thesis of the first "Analogy of Experience" (A 182–9/B 224–33).

57. This note was written on the reverse of a letter dated 13 October 1788. Adickes does not identify the letter, but the only letter of that date in the collection of Kant's correspondence is a letter to Kant from a former student, Simon Schlesier, then living in Warsaw, asking Kant to help him get a book of his own composition published. Presumably Kant used the letter for scrap paper shortly after receiving it, thus in the second half of October 1788.

58. Cf. *Critique of the Power of Judgment*, §1, 5:203–4.

59. A note on a letter from Christian Friedrich Heilsberg of 23 November 1788 (10:554) that reminded Kant about an article on education that Kant had apparently promised him.

60. Cf. the "Axioms of Intuition" in the *Critique of Pure Reason*, A 161–6/B 202–7.

61. This note and the next two, the originals of which had been transcribed in Schubert's edition of Kant but were no longer accessible to Adickes, appear to have been written in conjunction with the visit to Könisgberg in September or October 1790 by Kant's former student, J. C. C Kiesewetter, who had served as the proofreader for Kant's *Critique of the Power of Judgment* when it had been in press in Berlin during the previous winter. The further notes on the "Refutation of Idealism," **6311** through **6317**, also appear to be connected with Kiesewetter's visit; the first of these is in fact in the hand of Kiesewetter rather than of Kant.

62. Compare these definitions to those at *Critique of Pure Reason*, A 320/B 376–7.

63. Cf. Kant's argument in the first "Analogy of Experience," A 188–9/B 231–2.

64. Kant discusses miracles in the "General Remark" to the second book of *Religion within the Boundaries of Mere Reason*, 6:84–8, where he is particularly concerned to prevent any appeal to miracles in practical reasoning. In his "Lectures on the Philosophical Doctrine of Religion," apparently from the winter semester of 1785–86, he argues that providence can only be understood to work through the general laws of nature, not through miracles; see 28:1104–13; in Kant, *Religion and Rational Theology*, ed. Allen Wood and George di Giovanni (Cambridge: Cambridge University Press, 1996), pp. 432–40.

65. Kant's marginal notes in Baumgarten's *Metaphysica* from the 1780s comprise **5664** through **6205**. Our selection from these notes follows.

66. Cf. Kant's statements in the *Critique of Pure Reason* that the dialectical illusions of pure reason are "natural and unavoidable" (A 298/B 354) as well as in the *Groundwork* that there is a completely "natural dialectic" which threatens our commitment to morality (4:405).

67. Compare this note to Kant's contrast between logical and real possibility in the "Postulates of Empirical Thinking in General," A 218–24/B 265–72. **5690** through **5698** continue the discussion of possibility.

68. Cf. *Critique of Pure Reason*, A 201/B 246.

69. This note should be compared to the notes on the "Refutation of Idealism" at **5653–4** and **6311–6317**. See especially **5653** and note 51 thereto.

70. This note may be compared to Kant's critique of the "ideal of pure reason" at *Critique of Pure Reason*, A 571–83/B 599–611, where he argues that even

the idea of a completely determinate object cannot imply its own existence, but rather existence must always be posited on the basis of some evidence independent of the contents of a concept.

71. The discussion of possibility and existence continues through **5724**; from these notes, **5722** and **5723** are translated here.

72. Compare this note to Kant's discussion at *Critique of Pure Reason*, A 218–24/B 265–72.

73. Cf. *Critique of Pure Reason*, A 292/B 348.

74. Cf. again *Critique of Pure Reason*, A 292/B 348.

75. On the contrast between the categories and the "concepts of reflection" noted in this paragraph, see *Critique of Pure Reason*, A 260–8/B 316–24. Kant continues the discussion of quantity in **5727** through **5732**.

76. **5754** through **5787** concern the modal categories of actuality and necessity. Only a small selection of those notes are translated here.

77. Compare this note to Kant's definitions of the postulates of empirical thinking in general at *Critique of Pure Reason*, A 218/B 265–6.

78. On this theme see also **5761**.

79. Kant refers, of course, to Descartes's version of the ontological argument at *Meditation* V and Leibniz's endorsement of this argument, once the initial step of proving that the concept of an *ens realissimum* is not self-contradictory, at, e.g., *Monadology*, §§44–5.

80. Here Kant could have in mind Wolff's view that both the possibility and the necessity of a thing are entirely determined by the relations among its predicates; see *Vernünfftige Gedancken von Gott, der Welt, und der Seele des Menschen*, §§34–6.

81. Here Kant essentially contrasts the cosmological argument, offered as the primary argument for the existence of God by Wolff, at, e.g., *Vernünfftige Gedancken*, §§928–30, with the ontological argument favored by Descartes and Leibniz.

82. Cf. *Critique of Pure Reason*, A 605–6/B 633–4, where Kant denies that the inference from the *ens necessaria* to the *ens realissimi* is legitimate. The discussion of necessary being continues in **5784** through **5787**.

83. **5788** through **5813** are a series of short notes on the concept of alteration; the two most substantial of these notes, the present one and **5811**, are translated here. These notes should be compared to the discussion of alteration in the "First Analogy of Experience" in the *Critique of Pure Reason*, A 187–8/B 230–1.

84. Cf. *Critique of Pure Reason*, B 48.

85. See again *Critique of Pure Reason*, B 48.

86. This paragraph obviously touches upon the themes of the "Paralogisms of Pure Reason" in the *Critique of Pure Reason*, and perhaps represents thoughts toward the complete revision of this chapter that Kant undertook for the second edition of the *Critique* (B 406–32).

87. See the similar characterization of the categories that Kant added to the second edition of the *Critique*, B 128–9.

88. This amplifies Kant's explanations of infinite judgments at *Critique of Pure Reason*, A 72–3/B 97–8, and *Jäsche Logic*, §22, 9:104. The following reflections **5855** through **5862** are brief notes on the concept of substance.

89. This note can be compared to Kant's argument in the "First Analogy of Experience" at A 188/B 231.

90. See also **5926** below.

91. To this note, compare Section Six of the "Antinomy of Pure Reason," "Transcendental idealism as the key to solving the cosmological dialectic," A 490–7/B 518–25.

92. Cf. **5805** and **5811** above, as well as *Critique of Pure Reason*, B 48.

93. Kant refers here to Leibniz's principle of the identity of indiscernibles, that any things that are completely identical qualitatively are also numerically identical. See, e.g., "Primary Truths" (1686?) and *Discourse on Metaphysics*, §9, neither known to Kant, or, what was known to Kant, *Monadology*, §9.

94. See Kant's rejection of the identity of indiscernibles at *Critique of Pure Reason*, A 263–4/B 319–20.

95. **5923** through **5935**, all written in the period 1783–84 around *M* §307 (in *Causa et causatum*), are comments on or drafts for the transcendental deduction of the categories, written, apparently, either in conjunction with the composition of the *Prolegomena to Any Future Metaphysics* in 1783 or else subsequently in preparation for the revision of the deduction in the second edition of the *Critique of Pure Reason*. It is not clear why Kant wrote these notes at §307: transcriptions of his lectures on Baumgarten's *Metaphysica* from this period do not suggest that he discussed his own transcendental deduction in the classroom at this point (see *Metaphysik Mrongovius* (1782–83), 29:843–8, and *Metaphysik Volckmann* (1784–85), 28:428–35). However, since a decade earlier Kant had not separated the transcendental deduction from the analogies of experience, his response to Baumgarten on *Causa et causatum*, he may have become accustomed to thinking about the transcendental deduction at this point in his lectures.

96. Cf. Kant's account of the relation between concepts and judgments at *Critique of Pure Reason*, A 68–9/B 92–3.

97. To this paragraph, compare §19 of the second-edition "Transcendental Deduction," B 140–2.

98. See also **5879** above.

99. To this paragraph, compare §15 of the second-edition "Transcendental Deduction," B 129–31.

100. Cf. Kant's account of the role of the concept of an object in the second-edition "Transcendental Deduction," §17, B 137.

101. In this usage, "transcendental unity of consciousness" clearly means consciousness of the unity of properties as belonging to a single object, not consciousness of representations as belonging to a single self. Used in this sense, the phrase "transcendental unity of consciousness" replaces the term "pure concept of the transcendental object," which Kant used in the first-edition deduction (e.g., A 109), but drops from the second-edition version.

102. Cf. *Critique of Pure Reason*, B 1218–9.

103. This paragraph may be compared to the doctrine of "threefold synthesis" in the first-edition "Transcendental Deduction," A 98–105. But here Kant presents the three moments of intuition (apprehension), connection in empirical consciousness (reproduction), and necessary unity of that connection

(recognition through a concept) as aspects of experience rather than distinct syntheses.

104. In addition to **5931**, see again *Critique of Pure Reason*, B 128–9.

105. See Kant's general characterization of the principles of judgment at *Critique of Pure Reason*, A 132/B 171, which is the basis for the ensuing "Schematism of the pure concepts of the understanding" (A 137–47/B 176–87).

106. Compare this note to Kant's famous remark in the chapter on the distinction between phenomena and noumena that "the proud name of an ontology . . . must give way to the modest one of a mere analytic of the pure understanding" (A 247/B 303).

107. **5937** through **5979** deal with topics from the "Transcendental Dialectic" of the *Critique of Pure Reason*, and several of them present quite general sketches of that section of Kant's work. Adickes dated most of these notes after 1781, but some only quite generally in the 1780s and possibly as early as 1776–79. So it is not clear whether these notes are sketches of the "Dialectic" for the first edition of the *Critique* or sketches for the *Prolegomena* or just further thoughts of Kant on the subject of the "Dialectic." The several notes (e.g., **5959** and **5970**) that organize the discussion around the proposition "*In mundo non datur abyssus, saltus, casus, fatum*" (In the world no gap, leap, accident, or fate is given) (**5970**) might fall into this last category, since Kant does not use this proposition to organize his discussion in the *Critique* itself.

108. This paragraph points back toward Kant's argument in the inaugural dissertation of 1770, *On the Form and Principles of the Sensible and Intelligible Worlds*, §§17–22.

109. **5950** through **5958** are a series of short notes continuing with themes from the "Antinomy of Pure Reason."

110. See Section IX of the "Antinomy of Pure Reason," part IV, A 559–65/B587–93.

111. In the *Critique of the Power of Judgment*, Kant would argue that these principles should be understood as "maxims" or regulative principles applying to the system of natural laws and empirical concepts for the world of appearance, rather than directly to the objects of experience themselves; see Introduction, section V, 5:182.

112. See Kant's contrast between the solutions to the mathematical and dynamical antinomies at *Critique of Pure Reason*, A 528–32/B 556–60.

* *
*

1. This extensive note as well as those through **5979** recapitulate Kant's treatment of the antinomies, especially his contrast between the solutions to the mathematical and dynamical antinomies (e.g., A 528–30/B 556). If Adickes's dating is correct, then these notes postdate the composition of the *Prolegomena* and could not have been written in preparation for that work. Except for the chapter on the paralogisms, Kant did not revise the Dialectic for the second edition of the *Critique*, so these notes would not seem to be preparation for a revised version of the antinomies. But perhaps Kant considered such a revision, sketching it out in these notes, and then did not do it in the end.

2. For statements of this doctrine accessible to Kant, see for example *Principles of Nature and Grace*, §12, and *Monadology*, §§56–8, 78, 80, and (Leibniz's own cross-references) *Theodicy*, §§22, 59–66, 345–6, 354–5.

3. The presentation of the resolution of the antinomies in terms of the following proposition ("There is no gap, leap, accident, or fate in the world") in this note as well as **5973, 5975**, and **5978** is a stylistic but not substantive departure from the published version.

4. This remark may be contrasted to Note 2 to the published "Refutation of Idealism," where Kant claims that "outer experience is really immediate" (B 276–7). Kant's present remark is compatible with the view that the spatial form of outer intuition is immediate, but that the existence of objects in space independent of our representations of them is a posit, more precisely a presupposition of our use of them to determine the temporal sequence of our own consciousness. This is more consistent with Kant's general view that all cognition of objects requires a synthesis of intuition and concept.

5. This remark should be compared to Kant's statement in the Preface to the second edition of the *Critique* that the "Refutation of Idealism" proves that "outer sense is . . . a relation of intuition to something actual outside me" (B xl) as well as to his remark in the "Refutation" itself that "the perception of [a] persistent thing is possible only through a **thing** outside me and not through the mere **representation** of a thing outside me" (B 275). See also **6312** below.

6. In Kant's time, there were commonly held to be three possibilities for explaining interaction or *commercium* between different substances generally and between minds and bodies in particular: physical influx, preestablished harmony, and occasionalism, or as Kant calls it, "supernatural assistance" (*Critique of Pure Reason*, A 390; see Baumgarten, *Metaphysica*, §§448–58, and Kant, *The Form and Principles of the Sensible and Intelligible World*, §22, 2:409). But Kant did not regard the distinction between preestablished harmony, according to which God established the connections between substances at the initial time of creation, and occasionalism, according to which he coordinates the states of substances anew at every moment, as significant, since he did not regard time itself as real. See A 390–1.

7. **5994** and **5995**, though dated as early as 1783–84, seem to be the first notes among the reflections on metaphysics that take up the issue of reconciling a mechanistic view of nature with a teleological conception of it that would become Kant's concern in the second half of the *Critique of the Power of Judgment*, that is, the "Critique of the Teleological Power of Judgment," which Kant would write in 1788 or 1789.

8. Kant's argument that our distinction between possibility and actuality is connected with the fact that intuitions and concepts are distinct representations for us is developed in the *Critique of the Power of Judgment*, §76.

9. This note could be an early thought about the argument of the third *Critique*, which first argues that the idea of an intelligence greater than our own is a presupposition of the rationality of seeking a system of natural laws in science (Introduction, sections IV–V, 5:180, 183–5), and then that the only final end we can ascribe to nature as the product of such an intelligence is our own moral cultivation (§84, 5:434–5).

10. This note could be a preparation for Kant's discussion of moral teleology and moral theology in *Critique of the Power of Judgment*, §87, 5:447–53, to which it should in any case be compared.

11. Kant mentions enthusiasm in the Preface to the second edition of the first *Critique* (B xxxiv), but discusses it more extensively in "What does it mean to orient oneself in thinking?" (1786; 8:145–6), *Religion within the Boundaries of Mere Reason* (1793; especially 6:83–4, 113, and 173–5), and *Lectures on the Philosophical Doctrine of Religion*, 28:1109.

12. For Kant's view of Plato, see *Critique of Pure Reason*, A 313–20/B 370–7 and A 853–4/B 881–2; *Dohna-Wundlacken Logic*, 24:744–5; *Metaphysik Mrongovius*, 29:759–62; and *Metaphysik Vigilantius*, 29:950, 954, and 957–8.

13. This formulation is reminiscent of Kant's famous letter to Marcus Herz of 21 February 1772, 10:129–35, at 130; translation in Kant, *Correspondence*, ed. Arnulf Zweig (Cambridge: Cambridge University Press, 1999), pp. 132–7, at p. 133.

14. This was a view that others also promulgated in the 1780s, notably F. H. Jacobi, who however claimed that the dogmatic metaphysics that inevitably results in Spinozism should be replaced by religious faith rather than the critique advocated by Kant. See Jacobi, *Concerning the Doctrine of Spinoza, in letter to Mr. Moses Mendelssohn* (Breslau: G. Löwe, 1785), translated in George di Giovanni, *The Main Philosophical Writings and the Novel "Allwill"* (Montreal and Kingston: McGill-Queen's University Press, 1994), pp. 173–251, with excerpts from the second edition at pp. 339–78.

15. Here Kant refers to Anthony Ashley Cooper, third Earl of Shaftesbury, who in his widely read *Characteristics of Men, Manners, Opinions, Times* (1711), lampooned the religious enthusiasm associated with dogmatic metaphysics through a variety of literary means rather than refuting it in a systematic way – although he himself was clearly a devotee of a form of neo-Platonism influenced by the Cambridge Platonists. See particularly the "Letter concerning Enthusiasm" and "*Sensus communis*: An Essay on the Freedom of Wit and Humour" (in Shaftesbury, *Characteristics*, ed. Lawrence E. Klein [Cambridge: Cambridge University Press, 1999], pp. 4–69). The *Characteristics* was widely known and admired by Enlightenment thinkers throughout Europe, and German editions were published in 1768 and 1776.

16. For related evidence about Kant's view of Chinese (Taoist) and Tibetan (Buddhist) religious beliefs and their relation to Spinozism, see *Lectures on the Philosophical Doctrine of Religion*, 28:1050, 1052–3.

17. See the preceding note **6050** and note 12 thereto.

18. This is presumably an allusion to the famous doctrine of Malebranche, presented at, e.g., *The Search after Truth*, Book Three, Part 2, chapter six; in the translation by Thomas M. Lennon and Paul J. Olscamp (Columbus: Ohio State University Press, 1980), pp. 230–6. Kant also alludes to this doctrine in the *Metaphysik Mrongovius*, 29:857.

19. See **6050**.

20. On anthropomorphism in religion, see *Religion within the Boundaries of Mere Reason*, Part Three, General Remark, 6:141–4, and Part Four, second part, §1, 6:168–9, and *Lectures on the Philosophical Doctrine of Religion*, 28:1001–2

(where Kant also further discusses his concept of deism), 1046–7, 1089, and 1110. See also **6099** below.

21. Kant distinguishes the agreeable from the good (as well as both from the beautiful) in *Critique of the Power of Judgment*, §§3–5, 5:206–10, and returns to the topic of the agreeable in *Anthropology from a Pragmatic Point of View* (1798), Book II, §60, 7:230–1. The first extensive discussion of the agreeable in his lectures on anthropology seems to be in the Mrongovius notes from the winter semester of 1784–5 (25:1315–16). Thus this note would not appear to originate before the second half of the 1780s.

22. Cf. Kant's famous contrast between negative and positive conceptions of freedom in the *Groundwork for the Metaphysics of Morals*, Section III, 4:446, as well as *Critique of Practical Reason*, Theorem IV, 5:33.

23. Kant does not use the expression "transcendental freedom" in the *Groundwork*, but does so in the "Critical Elucidation of the Analytic of Pure Practical Reason" in the *Critique of Practical Reason*, 5:94, 97.

24. Given the topic of this and the surrounding notes, Kant is presumably referring to Hume's *Dialogues concerning Natural Religion*, which were posthumously published in 1779 and almost immediately translated into German (1781).

25. See also **6165** below.

26. Cf. the famous Second Proposition of Kant's 1784 essay "Idea for a universal history from a cosmopolitan point of view" (8:18–19). The similarity between that proposition and the present argument is consistent with Adickes's ascription of this note to 1783–84.

27. Compare this paragraph to the third proposition of the essay on universal history, where Kant wrote that "Nature has willed that the human being should produce entirely from himself everything that goes beyond the mechanical arrangement of his animal existence and participate in no other happiness or perfection than what he has himself freely created, free from instinct, through his own reason" (8:19).

28. Kant distinguishes happiness, as the satisfaction of desires, from contentment, as satisfaction in having acted as morality requires, at *Critique of Practical Reason*, 5:118–19. But his present contention that happiness is only an abstract idea that cannot be laid out in any determination is consistent with his argument against happiness as the basis for a moral principle at *Critique of Practical Reason*, Theorem II, Remark II, 5:25–6. See also **6116–17** below.

29. Cf. *Lectures on the Philosophical Doctrine of Religion*, Second Part, "Moral Theology," 18:1071–82.

30. See Kant's extended discussion of true and counterfeit service to God in Part Four of *Religion within the Boundaries of Mere Reason*, especially his comments on prayer in the General Remark, 6:190–8.

31. Cf. *Critique of Practical Reason*, 5:110–11.

32. On Kant's concept of conscience, see *Metaphysics of Morals*, "Doctrine of Virtue," Introduction, Section XIIb, 6:400–1, and §13, 6:347–40.

33. This note might be compared to *Metaphysics of Morals*, "Doctrine of Virtue," §27, 450–1, where Kant argues that pure practical reason does not require entirely ignoring one's own happiness, but rather valuing it only on a par with

the happiness of others. See also his contrast between selfish and unselfish attitudes toward happiness in the 1793 essay "On the common saying: That may be correct in theory but it is of no use in practice," 8:279–80n.

34. For these terms of contrast, see *Critique of the Power of Judgment*, §§85–6, 5:436–47.

35. On anthropomorphism, see **6056** and note 20 thereto.

36. See the section "On having an opinion, knowing, and believing" in the *Critique of Pure Reason*, A 820–31/B 848–59, and *Critique of the Power of Judgment*, §§90–1, 5:461–73.

37. Cf. *Religion within the Boundaries of Mere Reason*, Part One, 6:28, 35.

38. Cf. especially "On the common saying," 8:279–84, and *Religion*, Preface to the first edition, 6:4–6. See also **6111** below.

39. Cf. *Critique of Pure Reason*, A 825/B 853.

40. Here Kant is surely endorsing the argument of Hume's *Dialogues concerning Natural Religion*, although as the next paragraph makes clear he also thinks that Hume failed to consider the moral argument for the existence of God.

41. In the *Critique of the Power of Judgment*, Kant will argue that something like this principle is the principle of the reflecting use of judgment (see the first introduction, section V, 20:214, 216, and Introduction, Section V, 5:185–6), thus avoiding the confusion the present passage creates by characterizing the principle that natural occurrences are amenable to our understanding as a practical postulate.

42. For a similar line of thought, see also **6110**.

43. Kant's most famous use of the concept of a realm of ends is of course in the third formulation of the categorical imperative in the *Groundwork*, Section II, 4:433. The explicit connection in this note between the realm of ends and the highest good is unusual but revealing. See also **6132** below.

44. See **6107** above and the texts referred to in note 38.

45. Cf. *Critique of Practical Reason*, 5:125. See also **6132** below.

46. Cf. *Critique of Practical Reason*, 5:118–19. See also **6092** above as well as **6117**.

47. See again **6092**.

48. See **6113** and *Critique of Practical Reason*, 5:125.

49. See **6111** above and note 43 thereto.

50. Cf. *Critique of the Power of Judgment*, §84, 5:434–5.

51. Again, this would seem to be a general reference to the *Dialogues concerning Natural Religion*, which is clearly a target of Kant's critical teleology in the second half of the *Critique of the Power of Judgment*, where he agrees with Hume that we have no right to a theoretical interest that the world exists for our happiness, but must nevertheless make it a regulative principle of both inquiry and conduct that it exists for our moral self-development; cf. Hume's *Dialogues*, Part 10, and *Critique of the Power of Judgment*, §§83–4.

52. Presumably a reference to Hume's arguments against theodicy in Part 11 of the *Dialogues*.

53. See also **6132**.

54. Cf. *Critique of Practical Reason*, 5:110.

55. See **6091** above.

56. The first part of this note should be compared to Kant's discussion of providence in *Lectures on the Philosophical Doctrine of Religion*, 28:1104–13. The

discussion of the moral proof of the existence of God in the second half of the note should be compared to Kant's presentations of the proof in *Critique of Practical Reason*, 5:124–32, and *Critique of the Power of Judgment*, §§87–8, 5:447–59.

57. For a similar statement that the highest good must be thought of as achievable in the natural world, not in some supersensible world, see also *Critique of the Power of Judgment*, §87, 5:450.

58. See *Critique of the Power of Judgment*, §§76–7, 4:401–10.

59. Here Kant refers back to the conception of God as the ground of all possibilities that he had entertained since the *New Elucidation of the First Principles of Metaphysical Cognition* (1755) and *Only Possible Basis for a Demonstration of the Existence of God* (1763), but which in the *Critique of Pure Reason* he had argued cannot be regarded as a demonstrable thesis in theoretical cognition (A 571–83/B 599–611).

60. **6206** through **6310** are notes that Kant made in his copy of Johann August Eberhard, *Vorbereitung zur natürlichen Theologie* (Preparation for natural theology) (Halle: im Waisenhause, 1781) (abbreviated "*Th*"). This work, which is reproduced in its entirety in the *Akademie* edition along with Kant's notes, is a compact presentation of conventional natural theology by the Halle Wolffian who was later to engage Kant in a fierce debate over the nature of synthetic *a priori* cognition and the novelty of the *Critique of Pure Reason* (see Henry E. Allison, *The Kant-Eberhard Controversy* [Baltimore: The Johns Hopkins University Press, 1973]). Eberhard's work is useful as a representative of the kind of theology that Kant wanted to replace with his own "moral theology," a frequent subject of discussion in the notes. Eberhard's bibliographical references also provide a valuable guide to the theological literature available to Kant, and especially to the availability of German translations of leading English works in natural theology of the eighteenth century. Adickes dates Kant's notes to the period from 1783 to 1788, and connects them with Kant's *Lectures on the Philosophical Doctrine of Religion*, originally published by Karl Heinrich Ludwig Pölitz in 1830 (translated in Kant, *Religion and Rational Theology*, edited by Allen Wood and George di Giovanni [Cambridge: Cambridge University Press, 1997]). According to Hamann, Kant gave these lectures in the winter semester of 1783–84 (although they are not listed in the university catalogue for that semester) (see *Religion and Rational Theology*, p. 337). These notes are of considerable importance for any student of Kant's thought about religion; only a selection can be presented here.

61. This is an even more general characterization of the tendency of human reason to assume that the totality of conditions for a given conditioned thing is itself given, which Kant identifies as the source of the dialectical inferences of reason; see *Critique of Pure Reason*, A 323/B 379, A 336–7/B 393–4.

62. Cf. *Critique of Practical Reason*, Theorem II, Remark II, 5:25–6.

63. Kant makes it clear that human beings cannot attain holiness but can only progress toward holiness in *Religion*, Part Two, 6:64–6, and *Metaphysics of Morals*, Doctrine of Virtue, §§21–2, 6:446–7.

64. Presumably Kant means that the Roman chronology (the calendar called "Julian" was reformed during the rule of Julius Ceasar) made the world

532 years older than it was according to the currently accepted Christian chronology.

65. This paragraph and the next should be compared to Kant's analysis of the "Ideal of Pure Reason," A 571–83/B 599–611.

66. Compare the following analysis to Kant's explanation of the dialectical inferences of pure reason at *Critique of Pure Reason*, A 323/B379 and A 333–6/B 390–3.

67. For the thesis that belief in God is not necessary to provide the motivation to be moral but only to strengthen it, see *Religion within the Boundaries of Mere Reason*, 6:183.

68. On the contrast between religion and cult, see *Religion within the Boundaries of Mere Reason*, Part Four, First Part, especially 6:153–63.

69. This reflection can be compared to the section "On having an opinion, knowing, and believing" in "The Canon of Pure Reason" in the *Critique of Pure Reason*, A 820–31/B 848–59.

70. Compare what follows to Kant's discussion of the cosmological argument in the *Critique of Pure Reason*, A 603–14/B 631–42.

71. Cf. Kant's critique of the ontological argument in *Critique of Pure Reason*, A 592–602/B 620–31, especially A 598–9/B 626–7.

72. See Moses Mendelssohn, *Morgenstunden oder Vorlesungen über das Dasein Gottes* (Morning-lessons, or lectures on the existence of God) (Berlin: C. F. Voss und Sohn, 1785), section XII, pp. 95–103, on "The sufficient ground of the contingent in that which is necessary"; in the modern edition by Dominique Bourel (Stuttgart: Ph. Reclam Jun., 1979), pp. 109–19.

73. This is the basis for Kant's contention that the cosmological argument presupposes the (invalid) ontological argument; see *Critique of Pure Reason*, A 607/B 635.

74. Presumably a reference to the neo-Platonism of Plotinus.

75. Cf. *Critique of Practical Reason*, 5:110.

76. For Kant's view that the difference between possibility and actuality is connected with the distinction between concept and intuition, which is necessary for human beings, see *Critique of the Power of Judgment*, §77, 5:405–10.

77. Cf. Kant's similar critique of the "Ideal of Pure Reason," *Critique of Pure Reason*, A 571–89/B 599–611.

78. Cf. Kant's account of conscience in *Metaphysics of Morals*, Doctrine of Virtue, Introduction, Section XIIb, 6:400–1.

79. That truly virtuous observance of the demands of morality is never slavish, done from mere hope of reward or fear of punishment, is Kant's theme throughout the *Religion within the Boundaries of Mere Reason*, beginning with the famous footnote in response to Friedrich Schiller's essay *Anmut und Würde* (Grace and dignity), 6:23–5n.

80. To this paragraph, compare generally Part Four of the *Religion*, "Concerning service and counterfeit service under the dominion of the good principle, or, of religion and priestcraft" (6:151–202).

81. This section presents notes from the 1790s, thus from the period following Kant's completion of the three critiques but including his major work on philosophy of religion, much of his work on political philosophy as well as his long-awaited work on the *Metaphysics of Morals* (1797) that would

include his final statement on ethical as well as political duties, and finally his uncompleted attempt to provide a restatement of the entire critical philosophy. Most of the surviving drafts toward the final project were published in the *Akademie* edition in volumes 21 and 22, and an extensive selection of that material was published in the Cambridge Edition as Immanuel Kant, *Opus postumum*, edited by Eckhart Förster, translated by Eckart Förster and Michael Rosen (Cambridge: Cambridge University Press, 1993). None of that material is included in this volume; the following materials continue to be drawn from volume 18 of Kant's notes on metaphysics. As in the previous chronological strata, Adickes first presented notes found on loose sheets (*lose Blätter*) from various sources (**6311** through **6368**), followed by marginalia in his copy of Baumgarten's *Metaphysica* (**6370–6445**) (**6369** transcribes a few words or brief comments that Kant wrote in 1800 or 1801 in his copy of Georg Christoph Lichtenberg, *Vermischte Schriften* (1801), vol. II; these are omitted here). Obviously Kant felt compelled to write far fewer new notes in the textbook for his metaphysics lectures than he had in previous decades, and of course he retired from lecturing altogether in 1797.

The selection of notes begins with **6311–6316**, which focus on the "Refutation of Idealism" that Kant had added to the second edition of the *Critique of Pure Reason* in 1787 (**6317** and **6323** also concern the refutation of idealism, though they concern much else besides). These notes appear to have been written in the fall of 1790, in conjunction with the visit to Königsberg of Kant's recent student and disciple Johann Gottfried Carl Christian Kiesewetter, who was at that time a private tutor and lecturer on Kantian philosophy in Berlin and who had been the proofreader for the *Critique of the Power of Judgment* the previous winter. During this visit, Kiesewetter met with Kant daily to discuss issues in philosophy; these notes appear to have been made in preparation for these meetings, or to record what was said during them. They are all in Kant's hand except for **6311**, which is in Kiesewetter's, and represents either Kiesewetter's own understanding of the "Refutation," prepared for discussion with Kant, or his attempt to transcribe what Kant said during one of their meetings (Adickes discusses this question in his note at 18:607–10).

Following **6316**, the undated **Leningrad Fragment I** is inserted, which seems to be part of the group of notes attempting to restate and refine the "Refutation of Idealism."

82. Cf. *Critique of Pure Reason*, A 377 and B 274.
83. Cf. *Critique of Pure Reason*, A 368 and B 376–7.
84. Cf. *Critique of Pure Reason*, B 277.
85. For this distinction, see also §§24–5 of the second-edition "Transcendental Deduction," B 153–9, and his amplification of the "Refutation of Idealism" at B xl–xli. See also **6315**, at 18:615, below.
86. Cf. *Critique of Pure Reason*, B 153–4.
87. Cf. Kant's argument in the First "Analogy of Experience," A 187–8/B 230–1.
88. Cf. *Critique of Pure Reason*, proof added in second edition to the general principle of the "Analogies of Experience," B 219, and proof added to the first analogy, B 225.

89. Cf. *Critique of Pure Reason*, B xxxix and B 275.
90. See also **6315** at 18:618 and 621, below.
91. Kant also uses this premise in the third "Analogy of Experience," where he argues that our experience of the simultaneity of the states of any substances requires interaction between them; see A 211, B 257–8. See also **6313**, at 18:614, and **Leningrad Fragment I** and **6323**, P. II, below.
92. At B 275, this is the "theorem" that is to be proven in the "Refutation of Idealism" rather than the "ground" of the proof.
93. Cf. the second-edition "Transcendental Deduction," §24, B 156, and the "General Note on the System of Principles," also added in the second edition of the *Critique*, B 288–94.
94. For this formulation, see also B xl and B 276–7n.
95. Compare this paragraph to Note 3 to the published "Refutation," B 278–9.
96. To this thesis, compare **6312** above as well as **Leningrad Fragment I** and **6323** below and the third "Analogy of Experience," A 211, B 257–8.
97. Cf. **6311** as well as *Critique of Pure Reason*, A 368 and B 276.
98. See also **6311** and note 85 thereto, above.
99. For a similar statement, see the "Schematism of pure concepts of understanding," *Critique of Pure Reason* A 142–3/B 182.
100. In the second edition of the *Critique*, Kant suggests that time must be represented by a line in space because only the *drawing* of the line can represent the *passage* of time (B 156, 292); here he is arguing that only the simultaneously existing multitude of parts of the line can represent the multitude of moments in time. To borrow an analogy from the first edition of the *Critique*, it is as if the second edition sees the line as necessary to represent the apprehension of the moments of time, while the present passage adds that the line is also necessary to represent the reproduction and recognition of the unity of the multitude of moments of time (see A 98–104).
101. See also Kant's characterization of idealism at *Prolegomena*, 4:288–9.
102. See §15 of the second-edition "Transcendental Deduction," B 129–30, as well as the draft essay "What Real Progress has Metaphysics made in Germany since the time of Leibniz and Wolff?" (ca. 1793–95), 20:271. This material is translated in Kant, *Theoretical Philosophy after 1781*, ed. Henry Allison and Peter Heath (Cambridge: Cambridge University Press, 2002), 337–424.
103. Cf. the "Anticipations of Perception," A 168/B 209–10.
104. Cf. the "Transcendental Aesthetic," A 20–1/B 34–5.
105. That our knowledge of the moral law must be independent of revelation and that our recognition of the authenticity of the latter presupposes the former are constant themes for Kant, from the lectures on ethics in the 1770s (see, e.g., *Moral Philosophy Collins*, 27:306–10) to the *Religion within the Boundaries of Mere Reason*, 6:102–9.
106. See Kant's definitions of imagination at *Critique of Pure Reason*, B 151, and *Anthropology from a Pragmatic Point of View*, §28, 7:167. The definition of imagination as the ability to represent an absent object, thus as including recollection and foresight as well as mere fantasy, was standard for the times; see, e.g., Baumgarten, *Metaphysica*, §558 (15:19).

107. See also **6311** and note 83.

108. See also **6311** above as well as 18:621 in the present note.

109. Cf. Note 3 to the published "Refutation," B 278–9.

110. For statements of Leibniz's preestablished harmony with which Kant could have been familiar, see for example *Principles of Nature and Grace*, §§10–15, and *Monadology*, §§51–58, 77–88.

111. This argument can be traced back all the way to Kant's argument that a change of states in one substance is possible only through real interaction with another substance in the 1755 *New Elucidation of the First Principles of Metaphysical Cognition*, Proposition XII, 2:410–12. Even then Kant had claimed that this argument is sufficient to overthrow Leibniz's preestablished harmony (2:412).

112. Cf. again **6311** and note 83.

113. Cf. **6311** and 18:618 in the present note.

114. Compare this paragraph to *Prolegomena*, §13, Note II, at 4:289, and to Kant's concession that he should have called his transcendental idealism "critical idealism" at Note II, 4:293. For the term "*ens imaginarium*," see *Critique of Pure Reason*, A 292/B 348.

115. This is a reference to the ether, an all-pervasive though imperceptible physical substance, the existence of which Kant attempted to prove in the *Opus postumum*; see the selection of "ether proofs" from 21:206–241 translated in Kant, *Opus postumum*, ed. Eckart Förster, trans. Förster and Michael Rosen (Cambridge: Cambridge University Press, 1993), pp. 62–79. On the contrast between the transcendental ideality of space and time and the mere subjectivity of ordinary secondary qualities, see the "Transcendental Aesthetic," A 28–9/B 44–5.

116. Cf. Note 3 in the published "Refutation," B 278–9.

117. **Leningrad Fragment I** is a note that came into the possession of the public library of Leningrad (then and now St. Petersburg) in 1850, from the collection of Friedrich Wilhelm Schubert (1799–1868), the editor of the first collected edition of Kant's works. The note, details about its provenance, and a commentary are published in Reinhard Brandt and Werner Stark, eds., *Kant Forschungen*, vol. 1 (Hamburg: Felix Meiner, 1987), pp. 1–30. The fragment itself is reproduced at pp. 18–21.

118. Cf. *Critique of Pure Reason*, A 33/B 49–50, B 158–9.

119. Cf. *Critique of Pure Reason*, B 157.

120. Cf. the whole of §25 of the second-edition "Transcendental Deduction," B 157–9.

121. See also **6312** and **6313** above and **6323**, P. II, below, as well as the third "Analogy of Experience," A 211–15/B 256–62.

122. See Kant's argument in the "Axioms of Intuition," A 161–6/B 201–7.

123. Kant argues against the Aristotelian conception of virtue as a mean between two vices at *Metaphysics of Morals*, "Doctrine of Virtue," Introduction section XIII, 6:404, and §10, 6:432–3.

124. Kant would stress that we must represent the moral law produced by our own reason as if it were a divine command in the first fascicle, which is the latest material in the *Opus postumum*; e.g., 21:22–3, 28, 37 (Förster, pp. 229, 232, 239).

125. This formulation goes back to the inaugural dissertation of 1770; see *Form and Principles of the Sensible and Intelligible Worlds*, §26, 2:413.

126. See remark IV added to the "Transcendental Aesthetic," §8, in the second edition of the *Critique*, B 71–2.

127. Here of course Kant is using "aesthetic" in the sense of the "Transcendental Aesthetic" of the first *Critique*, that is, he is referring to the critique of sensibility and not to the critique of judgments of the beautiful and sublime provided in the *Critique of the Power of Judgment*.

128. Here Kant alludes to the argument of the "Axioms of Intuition," A 161–6/B 202–7.

129. Here Kant alludes to the argument of the "Anticipations of Perception," A 166–76/B 207–18.

130. See Kant's contrast between the "supreme principles" of analytic and synthetic judgments, *Critique of Pure Reason*, A 150–8/B 189–97.

131. To the following list of the predicates of God, compare *Lectures on the Philosophical Doctrine of Religion*, 18: 1033–47; on the risks of anthropomorphism in such a conception of God, see 28:1046.

132. Kant discusses how we can think of the intelligence of God in *Lectures on the Philosophical Doctrine of Religion*, 10:1047–59.

133. Kant discusses how we can conceive of the will of God in *Lectures on the Philosophical Doctrine of Religion*, 10:1059–62.

134. See *Critique of Practical Reason*, 5:110–11.

135. See the definition of imagination at **6315**, P. I, and note 106 thereto.

136. **6320** through **6322** as well as **6324** through **6326** also concern the cosmological proof. On the cosmological proof, in addition to *Critique of Pure Reason*, A 603–14/B 631–42, see also *Lectures on the Philosophical Doctrine of Religion*, 28:1028–33.

137. **6320**, **6321**, and **6322** also concern the cosmological proof.

138. See *Critique of Pure Reason*, A 607–8/B 635–6.

139. See also **6312**, **6313**, and **Leningrad Fragment I** above.

140. The next series of notes, **6338** through **6359**, from 1794 through the end of 1797, show that Kant continued to be concerned with the ideality of space and time and with the relation between the categories and space and time throughout his productive years, as is also evident in the uncompleted drafts of his intended final work, the *Opus postumum*.

141. Kant of course argued in the "Transcendental Aesthetic" of the first *Critique* that every space and time can be represented only as part of a larger one (A 24–5/B 39–40, A 31–2/B 47–8); but he did not suggest in those passages that this premise alone suffices to prove the transcendental ideality of space and time.

142. Adickes included this note in volume 18 but Gerhard Lehmann did not include it in his edition of the *Opus postumum* in volumes 21 and 22, which he prepared after Adickes's death but at least partly on the basis of materials left by Adickes. It is not clear why Adickes placed this note in volume 18 instead of saving it for the *Opus postumum*.

143. See the "Axioms of Intuition," A 161–6/B 202–6.

144. In order to prove this, Kant would have to prove that any determination of the magnitude of inner sense is dependent upon a determination of

magnitude in outer sense. Of course, it could be argued that this is precisely what he has attempted to do in his argument that time can be represented only in space, at *Critique of Pure Reason*, B 156, B 288–94, and in **6311** through **6323**, *passim*.

145. Here Kant's notion of "aesthetic value" seems to be similar to his notion of "aesthetic comprehension" (*comprehensio aesthetica*) in the treatment of the mathematical sublime in the *Critique of the Power of Judgment* (§27, 5:254), i.e., a feeling rather than a determinate measurement of incomparable magnitude (the latter would be *comprehensio logica*).

146. This section should be compared to the "Anticipations of Perception," A 166–76/B 207–18.

147. Cf. *Critique of Pure Reason*, A 168/B 210.

148. See Kant's discussions of continuity in the second "Analogy of Experience," A 207–11/B 252–6, as well as in the *Metaphysical Foundations of Natural Science*, Second Chapter, Proposition IV, Remark 2, 4:505–8; Proposition 8, Remark 2, 4:521–2; and Third Chapter, "General Remark to Mechanics," 4:552–3.

149. Compare this remark to Kant's argument in the Appendix to the "Transcendental Dialectic" of the *Critique of Pure Reason* that the law of affinity, which would posit precisely such a continuum of forms among natural kinds, is merely a "maxim" or what he would subsequently call a "regulative principle of scientific inquiry" rather than a "constitutive principle of theoretical cognition" (A 657–66/B685–94).

150. Here Kant is referring to his own early work on *The True Estimation of Living Forces* (1747).

151. See for example *Groundwork*, Section III, 4:459, and *Critique of Practical Reason*, 5:93–4.

152. Here Kant invokes the claim of the *Critique of Practical Reason* that we infer the reality of our freedom from our consciousness of our obligation under the moral law, rather than vice versa; see 5:29–30 and especially 5:55. See also **6348** and **6360**.

153. See also **6346**.

154. Johann August Schlettwein, also referred to in **6343**, published an open letter in the *Berlinische Blätter* in September 1797 (12:362–6) calling upon Kant to declare which of his disciples had understood him correctly, to which Kant replied in the *Allgemeine Literatur-Zeitung*, No. 74, 14 June 1797 (12:367–8, translated in Zweig, *Correspondence*, pp. 510–11). There are two people named Hufeland who intersected with Kant: one is Gottlieb Hufeland, who published an *Essay on the Foundation of Natural Right* Kant reviewed in 1786 (8:127–30, translated by Allen Wood in Gregor, *Practical Philosophy*, pp. 115–17); his cousin was Christoph Wilhelm Hufeland, a physician who published a book entitled *Macrobiotics: Or the Art of Prolonging Human Life* (1796), which Kant criticized in the third part of the *Conflict of the Faculties* (1798), in the section entitled "On the power of the mind to master its morbid feelings by sheer resolution" (7:97–115, translated in Wood and di Giovanni, *Religion and Rational Theology*, pp. 313–27). Gottlieb Hufeland was co-director of the journal in which Kant responded to Schlettwein, so Kant's reference here is probably to him.

155. See also **6342** for a contemporaneous statement of this basic Kantian claim.
156. The argument from infinitude to transcendental ideality was not made in the *Critique of Pure Reason*.
157. See **6343, 6360** at 18:690, and *Critique of Practical Reason*, especially 5:29–30.
158. See also **6343–4**.
159. Ordinarily Kant argues from the fact that our experience of the self is temporal to the conclusion that it represents the self merely as it appears, not as it is in itself; e.g., in the second-edition "Transcendental Deduction," §25, B 157–8. Here he states the contrapositive.
160. "*Aenesidemus*," named after an ancient skeptic of the first century c.e., refers to Gottlob Ernst Schulze, *Aenesidemus, oder über die Fundamente der von dem Herrn Professor Reinhold in Jena gelieferten Elementar-philosophie. Nebst einer Vertheidigung des Skepticismus gegen die Anmaaßungen der Vernunftkritik* (n.p., 1792), which argued that Kant had failed to refute Humean skepticism, which it in turn defended. Schulze was later a teacher of Arthur Schopenhauer at Göttingen.
161. Johann Heinrich Tieftrunk, professor of philosophy in Halle, was an admirer of Kant who published Kantian works on the philosophy of religion and law and edited *Kants vermischte Schriften* in 1799. However, he followed Schulze in criticizing Kant's retention of the thing in itself in his philosophy.
162. See also **6343–4** and **6348**.
163. Leonhard Euler (1707–83), renowned mathematician and astronomer, was director of the Russian Academy of Sciences at various times for Peter and Catherine the Great. However, he was long dead by 1797. Adickes refers to a letter of Kant's of 7 July 1797 to Johann Albrecht Euler that is reported but not transcribed in the *Akademie* edition (12:180).
164. See *Critique of Pure Reason*, A 104–5 and B 137.
165. Karl Leonhard Reinhold (1757–1823) became one of Kant's earliest advocates through his "Letters on the Kantian Philosophy," published in the *Teutsche Merkur* in 1786–87. In 1789, he published a *Versuch einer neuen Theorie des menschlichen Vorstellungsvermögens* (Essay toward a new theory of the human faculty of representation), in which he tried to derive all the essential elements of knowledge from the idea of a subject of representations, thus starting down the path of deriving all philosophy from a single principle that would be taken by Johann Fichte but always rejected by Kant. Reinhold also published several later works; it is not clear what work or thesis Kant has in mind here.
166. Christian Gottlieb Selle, trained in both medicine and philosophy in empiricist Göttingen, was a Lockean, but well enough thought of by Kant to have been sent a complimentary copy of the *Critique of Pure Reason*.
167. Jakob Sigismund Beck, a student of Kant's in Königsberg and then of second-generation Kantians at Halle, published the *Erläuternder Auszug aus den critischen Schriften des Herrn Prof. Kant auf Anrathen desselben* (Explanatory excerpt[s] from the critical writings of Prof. Kant, with his own advice), vols. I–II (Riga: Hartknoch, 1793–94), as well as *Grundriss der kritischen Philosophie* (Halle: Renger, 1796), a more independent statement of what he took to be the essence of the critical philosophy. (This work is

described in detail in Adickes's *German Kantian Bibliography*, pp. 173–77.) Kant corresponded extensively with Beck about his philosophical views throughout the 1790s. See letters from 1791 to 1797 in Zweig, *Correspondence*, or Kant, *Selected Pre-Critical Writings and Correspondence with Beck*, ed. G. B. Kerferd and D. Walford (Manchester: Manchester University Press, 1968). On the idea of beginning the whole of the critical philosophy from the categories, see especially Beck's letters to Kant of 17 June 1794 (11:508–11; Zweig, pp. 479–81) and 20 June 1797 (12:164–9; Zweig, pp. 512–15). The publication of Beck's *Grundriß der critischen Philosophie* (Halle, 1796), in which Beck publicly presented the idea, intervened between these two letters.

168. See especially *Critique of Pure Reason*, second-edition "Transcendental Deduction," §24, B 153–4, and "Refutation of Idealism," Note 2, B 277–8.

169. See the second-edition "Transcendental Deduction," §25, B 157–8.

170. Cf. Kant's comment in the "Transcendental Aesthetic," A 29–30/B 45.

171. See **6353** and note 167 thereto.

172. Here Kant refers to his 1762 essay on "The False Subtlety of the Four Syllogistic Figures," translated in Immanuel Kant, *Theoretical Philosophy, 1755–1770*, edited by David Walford in collaboration with Ralf Meerbote (Cambridge: Cambridge University Press, 1992), pp. 85–105.

173. Here Kant refers to the 1788 essay on "The Use of Teleological Principles in Philosophy," 8:157–84, especially pp. 183–84, where Kant tries to explain how the categories can apply to intuitions and still yield pure cognitions.

174. Here Kant is referring to the argument of the "Schematism of the pure concepts of the understanding" that the "third thing, which must stand in homogeneity with the category on the one hand and the appearance on the other," must be time, because "a transcendental time-determination is homogenenous with the **category** (which constitutes its unity) insofar as it is **universal** and rests on a rule *a priori*," "but it is on the other hand homogeneous with the **appearance** insofar as **time** is contained in every empirical representation of the manifold" (A 138–9/B 177–8).

175. See note 167.

176. Kant had maintained from the outset of the *Critique of Pure Reason* that once properly founded on critical principles metaphysics would necessarily be systematic; see A xii, B xxii–xxiii.

177. See the opening section of the second-edition "Transcendental Deduction," §15, B 129–30, and also Kant's important letter to Beck of 16 October 1792 (11:375–7; Zweig, pp. 434–6). See also **6360** at 18:689 and **6443**.

178. Compare these definitions to Kant's definitions of the same terms in the "Transcendental Aesthetic," A 19–20/B 33–4. For the contrast between the transcendental subjectivity of the pure forms of intuition and the ordinary subjectivity of ideas of secondary qualities, see A 29–30/B 45.

179. See *Critique of Pure Reason*, B 156 and B 291–2.

180. For a similar argument, see **6344**.

181. See **6359** at note 178.

182. See also *Critique of Practical Reason*, 5:29–30 and 55, and **6343, 6348** above.

183. Kant's marginalia in Baumgarten's *Metaphysics* from the 1790s are **6370** through **6455**.

184. In this note, Kant offers another statement of his critique of the ontological argument, as well as of the inference from the *ens necessarium* to the *ens realissimum* on which his critique of the cosmological argument depends. See *Critique of Pure Reason*, A 592–620/B 620–48, and *Lectures on the Philosophical Doctrine of Religion*, 28:1013–33.

185. See the first "Analogy of Experience," especially A 184/B 227–8, where Kant argues that the proposition that substance persists is tautological, so what must be proven synthetically is not that substance persists but that time-determination requires something that persists, therefore that it requires substance.

186. For the claim that space itself is what is permanent, see also **5653**, especially 18:308.

187. See *Critique of Pure Reason*, A 200–1/B 246.

188. Compare this note to *Critique of Pure Reason*, A 528–32/B 556–60.

189. See *Critique of Pure Reason*, A 298–309/B 355–66.

190. See *Lectures on the Philosophical Doctrine of Religion*, 28:1043–5.

191. This is of course a general reference to Hume's *Dialogues concerning Natural Religion*. For more on argument from analogy, see also *Lectures on the Philosophical Doctrine of Religion*, 28:1023.

192. See *Critique of Pure Reason*, "On having an opinion, knowing, and believing," A 820–31/B 848–59.

193. Compare to *Critique of Practical Reason*, 5:124–5.

194. See **6359**, at note 178, and **6360**.

195. See also *Groundwork*, Section III, 4:446, where Kant argues that the moral law is the causal law of the noumenal self. This of course raises the question of how the free agent can ever choose to violate the moral law, which Kant is supposed to have recognized and resolved in the *Religion within the Boundaries of Mere Reason*. If that is true, then this note should be dated before 1793. But perhaps the statement in the next sentence that freedom is the *possibility* of acting from reason means that this note is a statement of the solution to the problem, not an expression of a failure to recognize it.

Notes to Chapter 4

1. To the following notes on character, compare *Anthropology from a Pragmatic Point of View*, Part II, "Anthropological Characteristic," A, "The Character of Persons," §§89, especially 7:291–2.

2. The second paragraph of **1113** concerns the physiological bases of temperaments; it is omitted here, having little relevance to moral philosophy.

3. To this paragraph, compare *Critique of Pure Reason*, A 808–9/B 836–7.

4. That is, in a slave market.

5. **3344** through **3358** are a series of notes concerning morality and law that are found in conjunction with §§422–26 of Meier's logic textbook. These sections concern the difference between analytic and synthetic method, and are part of the chapter on "learned" or "scholarly cognition." Kant's motivation for writing these notes at such a location seems to have been the thought that moral principles might be analytic rather than synthetic, as he suggests in **3344**, although the *Groundwork* would subsequently

argue the opposite, and, more importantly, his view, which remains unchanged, that the fundamental principle of morality does not require any "learned cognition," but is accessible to all. This is the point of **3345**, which is the longest of these notes and the most important for Kant's moral philosophy.

6. In the European legal tradition, commutative justice concerns what is fair in a dispute between two parties considered by themselves, while distributive justice concerns what is determined by rules for the larger community.

7. See above all *Groundwork*, 4:435–6.

8. **5444** through **5450**, which concern the sources of moral value and motivation, are part of a set of notes in Baumgarten's section on liberty that begins with **5438**. That note, as well as **5440–1**, which concern free will rather than moral value, were translated in Chapter 3 above. **5444** should obviously be compared to the opening argument of the *Groundwork* that nothing is unconditionally good except a good will (4:393–4).

9. As this note shows, in the 1770s Kant often presented the basis of morality as a contrast between universal and particular ends rather than a purely formal law that gives no weight to any ends whatsoever. See also *Moral Philosophy Collins*, 27:344–6. That passage suggests that the apparent conflict between the idea of a universal end as the basis for moral law and that of a purely formal law may be resolved by equating the universal end of mankind with the formal goal of the preservation and promotion of freedom itself.

10. This note can be compared to the chapter "On the incentives of pure practical reason" in the *Critique of Practical Reason* (5:71–89) and the discussion of moral feeling in section XIIa of the Introduction to the "Doctrine of Virtue" in the *Metaphysics of Morals* (6:399–400). In those passages, Kant seems more willing to allow us to understand moral feeling as a genuine feeling as long as we recognize that it is a product of our underlying commitment to the moral law rather than a stimulus for that commitment. This later approach would also be consistent with his famous claim in *Religion within the Boundaries of Mere Reason* that real feelings of "fear and dejection" at the thought of having to do one's duty are evidence of incomplete commitment to the moral law (6:23–4n.).

11. Adickes gives no explanation for the inclusion of this note here. M 415 would have been at the very end of Kant's copy of Baumgarten's *Metaphysica*, which ends with a discussion of revelation as part of its rational theology. But the present note has nothing to do with that subject.

12. This can be compared to the Kant's treatment of the postulate of immortality in the *Critique of Pure Reason*, where he does suggest that we can only expect happiness in proprotion to virtue in a future world (A 811/B 839). In the *Critique of Practical Reason*, he only argues that the postulate of immortality is necessary to conceive of the possibility of perfect conformity to the moral law, i.e., perfect virtue, and in the *Critique of the Power of Judgment* he makes clear that by then he thinks that the happiness component of the highest good must be realizable in the natural world, not in another world (see e.g., §87, 5:450). See also **6674** below.

13. See also **5445** and note 9 above.

14. This position seems to conflict with that which Kant would later adopt in Part One of *Religion within the Boundaries of Mere Reason*, where he argues that by themselves all natural inclinations are good, and evil arises only from our own free choice to place self-love ahead of the moral law. But the first paragraph of the present note is consistent with the later position.

15. In his mature writings, Kant would reject the Aristotelian idea that a virtue is always the mean between two opposed vices; e.g., *Metaphysics of Morals*, "Doctrine of Virtue," Introduction XIII, 6:403–4. Perhaps in this incomplete early note he was already moving in that direction. **6583** and **6584** also contain interesting evidence of Kant's early view of ancient ethics. See also **6607** below.

16. Here Kant refers of course to the central character of Rousseau's *Émile, or on Education*, a book which he is known to have read very shortly after it appeared in 1762.

17. Here Kant refers to Thomas Hobbes's *Leviathan, or the Matter, Forme, & Power of a Common-wealth Ecclesiasticall and Civill*, first published in 1651. Almost thirty years after writing this note, Kant would explicitly distinguish his conception of the foundation of the state in the requirements of morality from Hobbes's merely prudential foundation of the state in the 1793 essay "On the common saying: That may be right in theory but it is of no use in practice" (see especially 8:289–306).

18. That we have not merely the right but the duty to leave the state of nature and enter political society is central to Kant's argument in the "Doctrine of Right" of the *Metaphysics of Morals*; see §9, 6:256–7, and §§41–2, 6:306–8.

19. Here Kant clearly rejects Hume's doctrine that reason determines only the means to achieving an end but never the end itself. But Kant would not have been familiar with Hume's argument for this thesis in *A Treatise of Human Nature*, Book III, Part I, chapter 1, because the *Treatise* was not available in German at this time, and Hume's discussion of reason in chapter 1 of the *Enquiry concerning the Principles of Morals*, which was already translated, does not clearly assert Hume's thesis. However, the doctrine is more clearly suggested in Appendix I to the *Enquiry*, "Concerning Moral Sentiment," so it is at least possible that Kant has Hume in mind here.

20. See also **5444** above.

21. This could be an allusion to Adam Smith's *Theory of Moral Sentiments* of 1759, which was not translated into German until 1770 but which was referred to by Lessing in his 1766 book *Laoköon* as well as by Herder in the 1769 *Kritische Wälder* (see Adam Smith, *The Theory of Moral Sentiments*, ed. D. D. Raphael and A. L. Macfie [Oxford: Oxford University Press, 1976], introduction, pp. 30–1). Be that as it may, that Kant here describes moral feeling as a response to a "necessary inner law" and reflection upon oneself suggests that he is moving away from Hutcheson's conception of moral sentiment as a primitive on which all moral reasoning is based, which Kant may still have held in **6581**, and toward his mature view of moral feeling, as expressed in the chapter "On the incentives of pure practical reason" in the *Critique of Practical Reason* (5:71–89).

22. Kant would continue to present his own conception of the highest good as an alternative to the Stoic and Epicurean positions in the *Critique of Practical*

Reason, 5:111–12. He considers the question of the *summum bonum* to be the central question of ancient ethics in his review "Of the ethical systems of antiquity" in *Moral Philosophy Collins*, 27:427–52. As with any eighteenth-century writer, his primary source for ancient views of the highest good was presumably Marcus Tullius Cicero, *De finibus bonorum et malorum* (On good and evil ends), Book III, which reports Stoic and Epicurean views in detail. In Book IV, Cicero, as an Academic, argues that virtue alone cannot be the complete end of life, because virtue can only be exercised in the pursuit of particular ends (see especially paragraphs 40–6). This could well have been the model for Kant's ultimate position on the highest good, as represented in the Preface to *Religion within the Boundaries of Mere Reason*, 6:6–8n. See also **6607, 6619, 6621, 6624, 6837**, and **6838** below.

23. Kant would always retain this threefold division of pleasures; for the *locus classicus*, see *Critique of the Power of Judgment*, §§3–5, 5:205–11. Kant maintained the division from the outset of his anthropology lectures in 1772–73; see *Anthropologie Parow*, 26:367.

24. For Kant's mature treatment of duties of love, see *Metaphysics of Morals*, "Doctrine of Virtue," §§23–36, 6:448–61.

25. This refers to the Stoic doctrine of wisdom, which always knows what it is right to do (cf. Cicero, *De finibus*, III.32, and *Tusculan Disputations*, V.81–2) – but for precisely that reason is almost never realized.

26. See also **6601** and note 22 above. On the doctrine of the mean, see **6581** and note 15 above.

27. On Kant's contrast between affects and passions, see *Anthropology from a Pragmatic Point of View*, §74, 7:252–3.

28. **6611** begins with the large addition by Kant on Pr 139 dated 1776–78? 1778–89?? At the end of **6610** Kant added (in Latin) "see page 139"; likewise on Pr 139 he indicated "see Preface," linking back to Pr VII. Therefore it is unclear whether the material from Pr 139 really belongs to the end of **6610** or the beginning of **6611** (if either).

29. On the difficulty of using empirical examples in moral reasoning, see *Groundwork*, section II, 4:407–12.

30. In the "Critique of the Teleological Power of Judgment" in the third *Critique*, Kant will argue that we can only understand organisms such as plants *as if* they were "possible only in accordance with an idea," but also that this is only a limitation of human understanding; see §§65–6, 5:372–7, and §§76–7, 5:401–10.

31. See "Critique of the Teleological Power of Judgment," §65, 5:372.

32. See *Critique of Pure Reason*, A 568/B 596.

33. For Kant's critique of Plato's conception of ideals, see *Critique of Pure Reason*, A 312–20/B 368–77.

34. Of course this is not quite right: the Epicurean ideal required a careful selection among inclinations for the set of those that could be satisfied under all, even adverse conditions; see for example Epicurus, *Letter to Menoeceus*, 127–32.

35. See for example Seneca, *Letters*, 92.3.

36. The Cynic school, founded by Antisthenes and Diogenes of Sinope in the fourth century B.C., was renowned for the moral ideal of self-sufficiency

(*autarkeia*) achieved through both physical training (*askesis*) and freedom in thought.

37. The Cyrenaic school, founded by Aristippus of Cyrene, a disciple of Socrates, described individual feelings of pleasure and pain (*pathē*), and considered such feelings the only things to be pursued for their own sake, and thus the moral end.

38. Julien Offray de la Mettrie (1709–51), a French physician and philosopher, was renowned as both a materialist and an Epicurean hedonist. His main works include the *Histoire naturelle de l'âme* (1745), *L'Homme machine* (1747), *L'Système d'Epicure* (1750), and *Discours sur le bonheur* (1750). *L'Homme machine* (which was translated into English as early as 1749) brought him instant fame as well as opprobrium.

39. Claude-Adrien Helvetius (1715–71), a wealthy French patron of philosophers as well as a philosopher in his own right, was known for *De l'Esprit* (1758) and *De l'Homme, de ses facultés, et de son éducation*, published posthumously in 1772. He was a radical Lockean who considered all human faculties as well as ideas as derived entirely from education and environment, and an equally radical utilitarian whose supreme criterion of morality was the maximum of possible pleasure combined with the minimum of possible pain throughout a society.

40. That is, Epicurus takes pleasure, which is a motive to action, as a sufficient criterion for morally right action, while Zeno takes the rational obligations of morality to be sufficient for our pleasure. By "Zeno" Kant refers not to the pre-Socratic philosopher Zeno of Elea, but rather to Zeno of Citium (ca. 336–265 B.C.E.), the founder of Stoicism. On the distinction between "execution" and "adjudication," see Kant's discussion "Of the supreme principle of morality" in *Moral Philosophy Collins*, 27:274–5; here Kant ascribes the principle of adjudication, or the moral norm, to the understanding, and the principle of motivation to the heart, or moral feeling. Later, of course, he would argue that action is truly morally estimable only if it is the agent's freely chosen commitment to the moral law that itself produces his moral feeling.

41. On the power of examples of virtue in moral education, see the "Doctrine of Method" in the *Critique of Practical Reason*, especially 5:155–61.

42. Compare this paragraph to Kant's argument in the *Groundwork* that the end of reason cannot be the maximization of happiness at all, because reason is no good at that and instinct does a better job of it (4:395–6). Here Kant does not drive such a wedge between reason and happiness.

43. On the comparison between Epicureans and Stoics, see also **6601, 6607, 6619**, and **6624**.

44. See also **6601, 6607, 6619**, and **6621** above.

45. Diogenes of Sinope, fourth century B.C.E., called the "Dog" (*kuon*) from which the term "Cynic" comes. He argued that happiness lies in freeing oneself from dependence on all but a bare minimum of natural needs. See *Moral Philosophy Collins*, 27:248–9, and *Moral Mrongovius* II, 29:603.

46. Kant's manuscript contains a gap at this space, apparently for a name not then recalled. Berger, the editor of volume 19, suggests that Kant might have been thinking of William Wollaston, author of *The Religion of Nature*

Delineated (1722), whose intellectualist view that morality depends simply upon the recognition of certain truths was mercilessly attacked by Hume in the *Treatise of Human Nature*, Book III, Part I, chapter 1. But Werner Stark, appealing to passages in Kant's lectures on ethics (*Moral Philosophy Collins*, 27:277, and *Moral Mrongovius* II, 29:622), suggests that Kant had in mind Richard Cumberland, author of *De Legibus Naturae: Disquisitio Philosophica* (A philosophical disquisition on the laws of nature) of 1672. See Stark, *Nachforschungen zu Briefen und Handschriften Immanuel Kants* (Berlin: Akademie Verlag, 1993), p. 157.

47. Compare this passage to Kant's classification of approaches to moral theory at *Critique of Practical Reason*, 5:39–41.
48. For Kant's attack on perfectionism, see *Moral Philosophy Collins*, 27:263–6.
49. See **6624**, notes 46 and 47.
50. On the contrast between principles of adjudication and motivating principles of application (or execution), see again *Moral Philosophy Collins*, 27:274–5, and note 40 above.
51. Kant refers of course to Hutcheson's view that all moral principles are based on our feelings of approbation and disapprobation; see Francis Hutcheson, *An Inquiry into the Original of Our Ideas of Beauty and Virtue* (1725), Treatise II, *An Inquiry concerning Moral Good and Evil*, particularly Section I, "Of the *Moral Sense* by which we perceive *Virtue* and *Vice*." See also *Critique of Practical Reason*, 5:40, *Moral Philosophy Collins*, 27:253, and *Moral Mrongovius* II, 29:621–2.
52. Christian Wolff argued for perfectionism in *Vernünfftige Gedancken von der Menschen Thun und Lassen* (Halle, 1720), although of course in his lectures Kant criticized Baumgarten's version of perfectionism. For his critique of perfectionism, see **6625** and note 49 above.
53. For Kant's extended argument that it is only our own moral efforts and not divine grace that can bring about a truly moral disposition, see *Religion within the Boundaries of Mere Reason*, Part Four. See also *Moral Philosophy Collins*, 27:320–7.
54. See also **5477** above, where Kant introduces the idea of a "practical absurdity."
55. For Kant's views on imputation, see *Moral Philosophy Collins*, 27:288–98, and *Metaphysics of Morals Vigilantius*, 27:558–72, especially, on degrees of imputation, 27:567–70.
56. For similar definitions of personality, see *Critique of Practical Reason*, 5:87 and 162; *Metaphysics of Morals*, Introduction, 6:223; and *Religion within the Boundaries of Mere Reason*, 6:27–8. Kant also uses the term "person" to connote the embodied human being, or *homo phaenomenon*, however; e.g., *Metaphysics of Morals Vigilantius*, 27:593.
57. This suggestion that the possibility of the categorical imperative needs a ground, and that such a ground must lie in something originally and primitively good, should be compared to Kant's transition from the first to the second formulations of the categorical imperative at *Groundwork*, 4:428.
58. To this note, compare especially *Moral Philosophy Collins*, 27:272, as well as *Religion within the Boundaries of Mere Reason*, Part Three.

59. The *locus classicus* for Kant's argument that moral feeling succeeds rather than produces the moral determination of the will is *Critique of Practical Reason*, Analytic, Chapter III, "On the incentives of pure reason," 5:71–89. See also *Metaphysics of Morals*, "Doctrine of Virtue," Introduction section XIIa, 6:399–400. See also **6760**.

60. See **6757** and note 59 above.

61. Kant's classification of the different forms of evil in this paragraph can be compared to *Religion within the Boundaries of Mere Reason*, 6:29–30. His claim that good principles are actually less reliable than good moral feeling seems to be in conflict with his argument at *Groundwork*, 4:397, where he argues in the famous case of the philanthropist whose feelings of benevolence have been overcome by his own misfortunes that he can still count on being motivated by duty alone.

62. This does not quote a particular recorded saying of Epicurus, but rather seems to be Kant's summary of Epicurus's argument that the wise person (who is the same as the virtuous person) who limits her desires to what is readily obtainable and does not place her happiness in things beyond her control will always be happy; see chiefly the *Letter to Menoeceus*.

63. Chrysippus (ca. 280–206 B.C.E.) was the third leader of the Stoa. He followed Socrates in thinking that the dictates of reason – which for him consisted in living in accordance with nature – are necessarily efficacious for him who knows them. Whether he actually held that all virtue is reducible to a single thing, namely knowledge, is unclear; see Plutarch, *On Stoic Contradictions*, 1034C-E.

64. Compare this remark to *Moral Philosophy Collins*, where Kant says that "Freedom is thus the inner worth of the world. But on the other hand, insofar as it is not restrained under certain rules of conditioned employment, it is the most terrible thing there could ever be" (27:344).

65. This is what Kant calls only a negative definition of freedom at *Groundwork*, 4:446.

66. On the question of whether the essential ends of life restrict freedom or whether freedom itself is the essential end of life, see also *Moral Philosophy Collins*, 27:340–5.

67. This anticipates Kant's account of the duty of truthfulness as a duty to oneself, not to others, in *Metaphysics of Morals*, "Doctrine of Virtue," §9, 6:429–31.

68. Kant discusses the duty not to commit suicide at numerous places, including *Moral Philosophy Collins*, 27:369–78, *Metaphysics of Morals Vigilantius*, 27:628–9, *Groundwork*, 4:421–2 and 429, and *Metaphysics of Morals*, "Doctrine of Virtue," §6, 6:422–4.

69. See Kant's second formulation of the categorical imperative at *Groundwork*, 4:429.

70. See again *Moral Philosophy Collins*, 27:344–7.

71. Here Kant uses the phrase "metaphysics of morals" in the sense of an entirely rational inquiry into the fundamental principle of morality without any empirical elements whatsoever, as he does in the Preface to the *Groundwork*, 4:488–90. In the 1797 *Metaphysics of Morals*, by contrast, the title refers to the doctrine of political and moral duties that is yielded by the application

of the pure concepts and principles of morality to a few very basic but empirical facts about human beings, such as that we are embodied, physically dependent creatures living on the surface of a sphere with no natural borders.

72. For example, in Cicero, *De Finibus*, I, 29–32, Epicurus situates the first and ultimate good "in pleasure, which he wants to be the greatest good with pain the greatest bad"; in Diogenes Laertius, VII, 87, "Zeno in his book *On the nature of man* was the first to say that living in agreement with nature is the end, which is living in accordance with virtue." To this and the next note, compare also **6601, 6607, 6611, 6619, 6621**, and **6624** above.

73. See also **6634** above.

74. For the claim that the greatest happiness occurs in another world, see *Critique of Pure Reason*, A 810–11/B 838–9. This claim is not made in any of the subsequent treatments of the highest good.

75. Compare this note to Kant's analysis of duty at *Groundwork*, 4:399–400, and his derivation of the fundamental principle of morality at *Critique of Practical Reason*, Theorems I–III, 5:21–8. This note seems to be one of the earliest in which Kant infers the formality of the moral principle from its independence from any object of the will.

76. See also **6850** and the passages cited in note 75.

77. This may allude to the table "of the categories of freedom with respect to the concepts of the good and evil" that Kant would present at *Critique of Practical Reason*, 5:66.

78. Kant clearly distinguishes happiness from the self-contentment that is linked immediately with purity of moral motivation at *Critique of Pure Reason*, 5:118–19.

79. This rather confusing paragraph should be compared with Kant's argument at *Groundwork*, 4:395–6, that instinct would be perfectly good at finding happiness, so reason must have an altogether different end. This position, however, itself sits uneasily with Kant's argument, especially prominent in the *Critique of Practical Reason*, that happiness is an indeterminate and even incoherent end unless it is regulated through reason; see 5:25–8.

80. Compare this to passages in the *Critique of the Power of Judgment* where Kant suggests that the feeling of pleasure in the free play of the cognitive faculties in aesthetic experience is the "feeling of life" itself, in particular §1, 5:204, and the "General Remark" following §29, 5:277–8. See also **6871** below.

81. See again *Moral Philosophy Collins*, 27:344–7.

82. Unlike **6858**, this paragraph does not identify moral feeling with happiness, and so is consistent with Kant's distinction of happiness from morally grounded self-contentment at *Critique of Practical Reason*, 5:118–19, and his account of moral feeling in the *Metaphysics of Morals*, "Doctrine of Virtue," Section XIIa, 6:399–400.

83. Here Kant refers to the theory of the "impartial spectator" in Adam Smith's *Theory of Moral Sentiments* (1759). For Smith, the "impartial spectator" is not "one of the participants" in the moral system because he is not a real person at all, but an image of the response of others toward one's own conduct that the agent forms in order to guide his conduct. See especially Part III, "The Foundation of our Judgments concerning our own Sentiments and Conduct,

and of the Sense of Duty," chapter I, "Of the Principle of Self-approbation and Self-disapprobation."

84. Kant discusses autocracy or self-mastery at *Moral Philosophy Collins*, 27:360–9.

85. Our need to be able to assume that the laws of nature are consistent with the laws of freedom, and thus that moral conduct in accordance with the latter can be achieved in nature consistently with the former, is the basis for the postulate of the existence of God as the author of the laws of both nature and freedom; see *Critique of Practical Reason*, 5:124–5.

86. See **6862** and note 80 above.

87. In connection with this note, see also **6874, 6878, 6879, 6880**, and **6894**.

88. In the *Critique of Practical Reason*, Kant makes this point by saying that the ancients thought that the connection between virtue and happiness is analytic, whereas it is in fact synthetic; see 5:111–12. For a long note on this subject, see also **6894**, not translated here.

89. See *Groundwork*, 4:393–4.

90. For this formulation, see also *Critique of Practical Reason*, 5:110.

91. To this note, compare also **6820** below. For clear evidence that at least after the *Critique of Pure Reason* (see A 810–11/B 838–9) Kant understood the happiness of the highest good as something that is to be achieved in the natural world, through the fulfillment of ordinary human desires in an unselfish way ordered by reason, see especially *Critique of the Power of Judgment*, §87, 5:450.

92. To this note compare of course the opening paragraphs of *Groundwork*, Section I, 4:393–4.

93. See *Critique of Practical Reason*, 5:153–7.

94. This rather Hobbesian thesis that everyone is evil unless coerced into being good is more pessimistic than the argument of Parts One and Two of the *Religion*, where Kant's position appears to be rather that (i) everyone has the possibility and disposition to be evil as well as good, (ii) but that anyone can simply choose to be good rather than evil, (iii) although why anyone chooses one way rather than the other must always remain inexplicable, since the choice is noumenal.

95. Here Kant seems to be equating "happiness *a priori*" with the moral self-contentment that he would later distinguish from happiness in its normal sense; see *Critique of Pure Reason*, 5:118–19.

96. The first sentence of this note, although not the second, may be compared to Kant's formulation of the premise for the inference to the necessity of a highest good in the Preface to the *Religion*; see 6:6–7n.

97. This note may be compared to Kant's recognition that duty may sometimes require the sacrifice of one's own life; see *Moral Philosophy Collins*, 27:369–75, and the "Casuistical questions" following §6 of *Metaphysics of Morals*, "Doctrine of Virtue," 6:423–4. The rather confusing final sentence of the note seems to be an allusion to Kant's discussion of the alleged "right of necessity," in which he argues that while it would be unjust to punish someone who saves his own life by depriving another person of the only available means to save his own, one has no positive right to do so; see *Metaphysics of Morals*, "Doctrine of Right," Introduction, Appendix II, 6:235–6.

98. See also *Critique of Practical Reason*, 5:156–7.

99. In connection with this reflection, see also **6992, 6999, 7000, 7002, 7004,** and **7007.**

100. See also **7020,** not translated here.

101. To this note, compare also **7053, 7056,** and *Morality Mrongovius*, 29:618.

102. See *Metaphysics of Morals*, "Doctrine of Virtue," §18, 6:443–4, where Kant argues that we do not have duties *to* God but rather a duty to regard our moral commands to ourselves as if they were divine.

103. The only other place where Kant suggests that the moral law may be regulative rather than constitutive is in the *Critique of the Power of Judgment*, §76, 403–4. His point there is just that the concept of freedom is not part of our concept of the natural world, thus not constitutive of the latter, but rather a concept to which we should attempt to conform our conduct.

104. See also **7064.**

105. The grounds for the distinction between duties of justice or right and duties of ethics is of course a major concern for Kant in the *Metaphysics of Morals*; see Introduction, Section IV, 6:218–21. See also *Morality Mrongovius*, 29:617–19, and *Metaphysics of Morals Vigilantius*, 27:582–4.

106. To this note, compare Kant's derivation of the right to use coercion in the *Metaphysics of Morals*, "Doctrine of Right," section D, 6:231.

107. See also **7059, 7060.**

108. The role of the divine will, given that the moral law is the dictate of our own reason, was a constant question for Kant, even in the final stages of his work on the unfinished *Opus postumum*. There he resolves the question by maintaining that God is nothing but the idea of our own power to give ourselves the moral law. See especially 22:51–3.

109. To this note, compare *Moral Philosophy Collins*, "Of Prayer," 27:323–7, but especially *Religion within the Boundaries of Mere Reason*, Part Four.

110. This seems like an attempt to provide a logical argument for the inextirpability of evil, in contrast to the apparently empirical argument for the existence of radical evil in *Religion within the Boundaries of Mere Reason*, Part One, especially 6:32–9. Of course, Kant's present argument is fallacious: that it is not necessary always to roll a six, or always to act morally, does not mean that it is impossible to do so. For this argument, see also **7171.**

111. This could be the premise that underlies Kant's example of the philanthropist who has lost all benevolent feelings, at *Groundwork*, 4:398.

112. Compare this sentence to the famous third proposition of the 1784 essay "Idea toward a Universal History from a Pragmatic Point of View," 8:19, where Kant makes the paradoxical claim that nature wills that we should make our own happiness freely.

113. See also the essay on "Theory and Practice," 8:279–80.

114. This (crossed out) paragraph may be compared to Kant's argument in the *Critique of Pure Reason* that opinion, as a measure of (subjective) probability, is only possible where knowledge could also be possible, and thus that since moral matters are never a matter of mere probability, they also cannot be a matter of opinion, but instead of rational belief or faith (A 824–5/B 852–3).

115. See also the earlier note **6820** above.

116. See also *Critique of Practical Reason*, Theorem II, Remark II, 5:25–6, and Theorem IV, Remark II, 5:35–6.
117. See *Critique of Practical Reason*, 5:118–19.
118. These generic references to the basic theories of value of Epicureanism on the one hand and Stoicism on the other do not appear to be based on any particular Epicurean or Stoic doctrines about lying.
119. This is what Kant calls the negative characterization of freedom at *Groundwork*, 4:446.
120. See *Groundwork*, 4:393–4.
121. See *Moral Philosophy Collins*, 27:344.
122. Through the second edition of the *Critique of Pure Reason*, Kant denied that judgments of taste can have any *a priori* principle, and therefore argued against the use of the name "aesthetics" for the theory or critique of taste (A 21/B 35–6n.). In the *Critique of the Power of Judgment*, however, he argues from the outset that judgments of taste must have an *a priori* principle, although not one that can be directly and determinately applied to objects; see its First Introduction, Section III, 20:207–8, and published Introduction, Section III, 5:176–9. The change of view suggests a date of 1787 or after for the present note.
123. However, Kant makes it clear that each agent is under the obligation to obey the moral law even if others are not; see *Critique of Pure Reason*, A 810/B 838. That this remains true even in conditions in which it is empirically evident that the actions of the virtuous person will not have their intended outcome is a premise in the argument that the conditions necessary for virtuous actions to have their intended outcome must be postulated by pure reason.
124. So Kant argues in the *Critique of Pure Reason* (A 810–11/B 838–9), but not in any later work. This may suggest a date prior to composition of the *Critique of Practical Reason* (1787) for this note.
125. In the *Critique of Practical Reason*, Kant explicitly argues that self-contentment at one's moral motivation does not compensate for the absence of happiness as a product of virtue (5:118–19). So this too suggests a date prior to the second *Critique* for this note.
126. Kant discusses the idea of our interest in being moral at *Groundwork*, 4:413n., and *Critique of Practical Reason*, 5:119–21.
127. This note may be compared to Kant's classification of imperatives at *Groundwork*, 4:413–16.
128. To these formulations, compare *Moral Philosophy Collins*, 27:346.
129. See *Moral Philosophy Collins*, 27:344.
130. See *Groundwork*, 4:393–4.
131. See **7217** above, *Moral Philosophy Collins*, 27:344, and also *Groundwork*, 4:446–7.
132. Compare this paragraph to Kant's distinction between aesthetic judgments of sense and of reflection in the First Introduction to the *Critique of the Power of Judgment*, Section VIII, 20:223–4.
133. On the concept of perfection, see also **7238**.
134. This note as well as **7251** may be compared to Kant's remark about the need for positive as well as negative duties at *Groundwork*, 4:430; they also

anticipate the distinction between duties of love and duties of respect within the class of duties to others in the *Metaphysics of Morals*, "Doctrine of Virtue," §25, 6:449–50.

135. See *Metaphysics of Morals*,"Doctrine of Virtue," Introduction, Section D, 6:230–1.

136. On moral feeling, see also **7265**.

137. Compare this particularly lucid account of the difference between perfect and imperfect duties to Kant's accounts at *Groundwork*, 4:421n., and *Metaphysics of Morals*, "Doctrine of Virtue," Introduction, Section VII, 6:390–1.

138. This appears to be the first introduction of the formula that Kant would use to divide the duties of virtue in the *Metaphysics of Morals*, "Doctrine of Virtue"; see Introduction, Sections IV–V, 6:385–8.

139. This paragraph from the *Opus postumum* may actually be a draft for the Preface to the *Critique of Practical Reason*, and is included here for that reason.

140. Here Kant refers to §§24–5 of the second-edition "Transcendental Deduction."

141. Here Kant refers to Chapter II of the "Analytic" of the *Critique of Practical Reason*, "On the concept of an object of pure practical reason."

142. If this is indeed a draft for the Preface to the *Critique of Practical Reason*, then of course Kant could not be referring to a review of that book. He could be referring to the review of Johann Schultze, *Elucidations of Professor Kant's Critique of Pure Reason*, by Hermann Andreas Pistorius, which was published in the *Allgemeine deutsche Bibliothek*, number 66 (1786), pp. 92–123; translation in Brigitte Sassen, *Kant's Early Critics* (Cambridge: Cambridge University Press, 2000), pp. 81–92; this review addresses Kant directly and certainly takes issue with his theory of time as a mere form of appearance.

143. See *Critique of Practical Reason*, 5:110–11.

Notes to Chapter 5

1. Modern Latin/German edition: Alexander Gottlieb Baumgarten, *Meditationes philosophicae de nonnullis ad poema pertinentibus/Philosophische Betrachtungen über einige Bedingungen des Gedichtes*, translated and edited by Heinz Paetzold (Hamburg: Felix Meiner Verlag, 1983; Latin/English edition: *Reflections on Poetry: A. G. Baumgarten's Meditationes philosophicae de nonnullis ad poema pertinentibus*, translated by Karl Aschenbrenner and W. B. Holther (Berkeley and Los Angeles: University of California Press, 1954).

2. *Metaphysica Alexandri Gottlieb Baumgarten*, Editio III (Halle: Carl Hermann Hemmderde, 1757). All of this work but the chapter on *Psychologia empirica* is reprinted in Volume 17 of the *Akademie* edition; *Psychologia empirica* is reprinted in Volume 15, pp. 5–54.

3. *Kant's gesammelte Schriften*, edited by the Berlin-Brandenburgischen Akademie der Wissenschaften, Volume XXV: *Kant's Vorlesungen*, edited by the Akademie der Wissenschaften zu Göttingen, Volume II, Parts I and II, edited by Reinhard Brandt and Werner Stark (Berlin: Walter de Gruyter & Co., 1997). In the notes to this chapter, the anthropology lectures will be cited by the titles given to them by Brandt and Stark (in all but one case, the

name of the note-taker or owner of the transcription): *Collins* (1772–73); *Parow* (1772–73); *Friedländer* (1775–76); *Pillau* (1777–78); *Menschenkunde* ("Knowledge of Human Beings") (1781–82); *Mrongovius* (1784–85); and *Busolt* (1788–89).

4. In *Kant's gesammelte Schriften*, edited by the Königlich Preußischen Akademie der Wissenschaften: *Erste Abtheilung: Werke*, Volume 7 (Berlin: Georg Reimer, 1917), edited by Oswald Külpe; English translation: Immanuel Kant, *Anthropology from a Pragmatic Point of View*, translated by Mary J. Gregor (The Hague: Martinus Nijhoff, 1974) (revised version by Robert Louden to appear in the Cambridge Edition volume *Anthropology, History, and Education*, edited by Günter Zöller and Robert Louden).

5. For an account of the development of Kant's treatment of topics in aesthetics in the anthropology lectures, see Paul Guyer, "Beauty, Freedom, and Morality: Kant's *Lectures on Anthropology* and the Development of His Aesthetic Theory," in Brian Jacobs and Patrick Kain, eds., *Essays on Kant's Anthropology* (Cambridge: Cambridge University Press, 2003), pp. 135–63.

6. Georg Friedrich Meier, *Auszug aus der Vernunftlehre* (Halle: Johann Justinus Gebauer, 1752).

7. *Kant's gesammelte Schriften*, edited by the Königlich Preußischen Akademie der Wissenschaften, Volume XV: *Kant's handschriftliche Nachlaß*, Volume II, *Anthropologie*, Parts I and II, new impression (Berlin and Leipzig: Walter de Gruyter & Co., 1923); *Kant's gesammelte Schriften*, Volume XVI: *Kant's handschriftliche Nachlaß*, Volume III, *Logik*, new impression (Berlin and Leipzig: Walter de Gruyter & Co., 1924).

8. For an account of the composition of the *Critique of the Power of Judgment*, see Immanuel Kant, *Critique of the Power of Judgment*, edited by Paul Guyer, translated by Paul Guyer and Eric Matthews (Cambridge: Cambridge University Press, 2000), pp. xxxix–xlvi.

9. See *Metaphysik L₁*, 28:248–51; *Metaphysik Mrongovius*, 29:878, 890–3; *Metaphysik Dohna*, 28:675–6; all selections translated in Immanuel Kant, *Lectures on Metaphysics*, translated and edited by Karl Ameriks and Steve Naragon (Cambridge: Cambridge University Press, 1997).

10. See Kant's letter of 28 and 31 December 1787 to Karl Leonhard Reinhold (10:513–16; translation in Immanuel Kant, *Correspondence*, edited by Arnulf Zweig (Cambridge: Cambridge University Press, 2000), pp. 271–3).

11. Alexander Gerard, *Versuch über das Genie*, translated by Christian Garve (Leipzig: Weidmanns Erben und Reich, 1776).

12. §§589–94 concern the *facultas fingendi*, or "faculty of invention." §§590–2 concern fictions or aesthetic inventions, in contrast to the following two sections, which discuss non-aesthetic phenomena such as dreams and delirium. However, most of the following notes on aesthetics were written on the interleaved blank pages in Kant's copy of Baumgarten's *Metaphysica*, and are not associated with particular sections in Baumgarten's text in this way.

13. See *Parow*, 25:378; *Friedländer*, 25:526–7; *Pillau*, 25:759–60.

14. This thought is central to Kant's contrast between poetry and oratory in the *Critique of the Power of Judgment*, §51, 5:321, and §53, 5:326–7, and was also frequently made in his anthropology lectures, e.g., *Pillau*, 25:760; *Menschenkunde*, 25:983, 986–8; *Mrongovius*, 1779–80; *Busolt*, 25:1465–8.

15. See *Collins*, 25:164, 168–9; *Parow*, 25:378; *Friedländer*, 25:526–7, 560; *Pillau*, 25:759–60, 782; *Menschenkunde*, 25:986; *Mrongovius*, 25:1331; First Introduction to *Critique of the Power of Judgment*, Section VIII, 20:222–5; *Critique of the Power of Judgment*, Introduction, Section VII, 5:189–91; §9, 5:217–19; General Remark following §22, 5:240–1; §35, 5:286–7.

16. On Kant's classifications of the fine arts, see *Pillau*, 25:760–1, 782–3; *Menschenkunde*, 25:981–95, 997–1006; *Critique of the Power of Judgment*, §§51–3, 5:320–30.

17. See *Pillau*, 25:760; *Menschenkunde*, 25:983; *Mrongovius*, 25:1279–80; *Busolt*, 1465–8; *Critique of the Power of Judgment*, §51, 5:321. See also **1810** below.

18. See *Collins*, 25:189–90; *Parow*, 25:384; *Busolt*, 25:1508.

19. §606 is the first section of *Iudicium*. It begins by defining judgment as the perception of the perfection and imperfection of things.

20. In the "Transcendental Aesthetic" in the first *Critique*, Kant states that all thought has intuition as its object and that empirical intuition is that which involves sensation (A 19–20/B 33–4), while in the "Anticipations of Perception" he defines the real in appearance as that which corresponds to sensation (B 207–8).

21. See Kant's definition of appearance as the "undetermined object of empirical intuition" at *Critique of Pure Reason*, A 20/B 34.

22. See Kant's definition of sensibility as "The capacity (receptivity) to acquire representations through the way in which we are affected by objects" (*Critique of Pure Reason*, A 19/B 33).

23. Kant is reported as discussing genius in all the anthropology lectures except for *Parow*; see *Collins*, 26:167–70; *Friedländer*, 25:557–8; *Pillau*, 25:781–4; *Menschenkunde*, 25:991; *Mrongovius*, 25:1310–15; and *Busolt*, 25:1492–9. His published discussion is of course at *Critique of the Power of Judgment*, §§46–50, 5:307–20. His famous argument that fine art requires genius and science does not is in §47, 5:308–9; this is a rejection of the view advanced by Alexander Gerard in his 1774 *Essay on Genius*.

24. That aesthetics permits only a critique and not a doctrine, thus that its judgments are *a posteriori* and not *a priori*, is a frequent theme in Kant's lectures: see *Collins*, 25:179–80, 194, and 197–8, and *Parow*. 25:376–8, 385, 387. Kant famously says the same in the *Critique of Pure Reason*, A 21/B 35–6n. See also **626** and **806** below.

25. On the contrast between science and art, see again *Critique of the Power of Judgment*, §47, 5:308–9; on the difference between merely copying works of genius and imitating the spirit of originality of a genius, see 5:309.

26. See *Collins*, 25:178; *Parow*, 25:374–5; *Friedländer*, 25:577; *Critique of the Power of Judgment*, §5, 5:209–11, and §13, 5:223 (on the independence of the pure judgment of taste from "charm and emotion," *Reiz und Rührung*, a phrase that Kant uses as early as *Parow*, 25:375).

27. Kant argues that one can only make judgments of taste on the basis of experienced consensus with others at *Collins*, 25:179–80, and *Parow*, 25:376. He omits this claim at *Busolt*, 25:1509 (a year before the publication of the third *Critique*), and explicitly rejects it in the *Critique of the Power of Judgment*, e.g., §8, 5:215–16, and §32, 5:282–3.

28. Kant introduces the requirement of the immediacy of the feeling of beauty and judgments of taste at *Collins*, 25:176, and *Parow*, 25:374–5.

29. See especially *Parow*, 25:379–80. See also **630** and **639** below.

30. See *Collins*, 25:175, 181; *Parow*, 25:379–80; and *Menschenkunde*, 25:1098–9.

31. See the similar thought at *Critique of the Power of Judgment*, §33, 5:284.

32. At *Critique of the Power of Judgment*, §§13–14, 5:223–6, Kant notoriously insists upon a rigorous separation between beauty and mere charm; here he rather treats feelings of beauty as one species of charm, though feelings of beauty themselves can be divided into the subspecies "sensible" and "ideal," depending upon whether they arise from sensation alone or also "associated thoughts." Such a distinction could have helped clarify the relation between beauty and aesthetic ideas in the third *Critique*. On "ideal charm," see also **639** below.

33. See *Critique of the Power of Judgment*, §17, 5:231–6.

34. See **622** above and note 24 thereto.

35. See *Critique of Pure Reason*, A 21/B 35–6n.

36. "Voltaire," as François-Marie Arouet (1694–1778) called himself, wrote among his numerous other works a number of now largely forgotten tragedies on Greek and Roman themes, beginning with his own *Oedipe* (1718) and ending with *Irène* in the year of his death; other tragedies of his were the bases for the libretti of Rossini's operas *Semiramide* and *Tancredi*. There is no way to tell whether Kant had any particular work in mind in making the present comment.

37. See *Collins*, 25:179, and *Menschenkunde*, 25:1095.

38. See **625** above and *Parow*, 25:379–80; *Busolt*, 25:1508–9.

39. See **625** and **630** as well as *Parow*, 25:379–80.

40. In characterizing our response to the good as one to "self-sufficient beauty," Kant here uses the term "beauty" more broadly than he usually does in his standard distinction between the agreeable, the beautiful, and the good. For that distinction, see *Critique of the Power of Judgment*, §§2–5, 5:204–11, and *Collins*, 25:167, 175; *Parow*, 25:367; *Pillau*, 25:788; and *Mrongovius*, 25:316. On the immediacy of the experience of beauty, see also *Collins*, 25:176, and *Parow*, 25:374–5.

41. See Jean-Philippe Rameau, *Traité de l'Harmonie reduite à ses Principes naturels* (1722), *Nouveau Système de Musique théorique* (1726), and *Erreur sur la Musique dans l'Encyclopédie* (1755). Kant could well have been familiar with Rameau's views from Jean D'Alembert, *Systematische Einleitung in die Musicalische Setzkunst, nach den Lehrsätzen des Herrn Rameau*, translated by Fr. W. Marpurg (1757). Kant may well also have been familiar with Rousseau's polemic with Rameau in his articles in the *Encyclopédie*, collected as *Dictionnaire de Musique* (1767). For extracts and citations from these works, see Adickes's note at 15:277–79.

42. On "ideal charm," see also **626** above.

43. See also **625** and **630** above.

44. See above all *Critique of the Power of Judgment*, §§7–8, 5:212–16. See also **647** below.

45. Adickes (15:280–81) gives a number of references to the works of Johann Jakob Winckelmann, beginning with his famous *Geschichte der Kunst des*

Altertums (1764), the gist of which is that our sensuous desires cause us to have different conceptions of beauty even though there is a single ideal form of beauty. For a comparable passage, see Winckelmann, *The History of Ancient Art*, translated by G. Henry Lodge (Boston: James Osgood and Co., 1880), Vols. I and II (in one), pp. 304–5.

46. Compare to Kant's example of a palace that might meet with our moral disapprobation but should nevertheless yield aesthetic satisfaction at *Critique of the Power of Judgment*, §2, 5:204–5. The present use of the distinction between the sentiment of charm and the feeling of beauty elaborates the distinction made in the published work.

47. See *Parow*, 25:380.

48. See also **640** above. For this particular formulation, see also *Busolt*, 25:1509.

49. That taste can occur only in society, and sometimes even that the beautiful only pleases in society, are frequent themes in Kant's early materials. See *Collins*, 25:179, and *Parow*, 25:376, as well as *Logik Blomberg*, 24:46 and *Logik Philippi*, 24:354 (both from 1770–71). See also **653, 686, 710, 987**, and **1791**. A hint of this view may still be found in the *Critique of the Power of Judgment*, §41, 5:297. But for an important though undeveloped distinction, namely that beauty "gratifies" only in society but may still "please" in isolation, see **878**.

50. This note does not bear directly on Kant's theory of taste, that is, aesthetics in the normal sense, but is a particularly clear statement of the distinction between intuitions and concepts central to Kant's "transcendental aesthetic," and is included for that reason. For related notes, see also **658** and **695**.

51. Compare this to Kant's definition of sensibility as receptivity or the capacity to be affected by objects at *Form and Principles of the Sensible and Intelligible Worlds*, §3, 2:392, and *Critique of Pure Reason*, A 19/B 33.

52. This definition of reason is similar to that in the contemporaneous inaugural dissertation, *Form and Principles of the Sensible and Intelligible World*, §2, 2:392. Of course Kant subsequently rejects the idea that reason can give us knowledge of objects considered apart from all relation to the sensitivity of the subject, although it allows us to think of such objects for practical (moral) purposes.

53. The distinction made in this paragraph may be compared to the distinction between the logical and real use of the intellect made in the inaugural dissertation, §5, 2:393–4.

54. See *Critique of the Power of Judgment*, §9, especially 5:218, for an expression of a similar view.

55. See **648** and the texts referred to in note 49 thereto, including **686, 710**, and **1791**.

56. On the relation between beauty and utility to the possessor, see also **661**.

57. See also **660**.

58. See Kant's distinction between arts that play with spatial form and those that play with temporal form at *Critique of the Power of Judgment*, §51, 5:322 and 325; see also *Collins*, 25:181, *Parow*, 25:378, and *Menschenkunde*, 25:997–1006.

59. This introduces an important theme of Kant's anthropology that is presupposed but not explicitly stated in his published moral and aesthetic theory, namely that activity as such is intrinsically pleasurable and should not be

hindered or diminished. See especially *Collins*, 25:167–9, *Friedländer*, 25:559–60, and *Menschenkunde*, 25:1068–70.

60. On the trichotomy of aesthetic evaluations (beautiful, ordinary, ugly) see also *Logik Pölitz* (1789), 24:364, and *Metaphysik Vigilantius* (1794–95), 29:1010.

61. While Kant's footnote in the "Transcendental Aesthetic" of the first *Critique* (a 21/B 35–6n.) rejects the idea that aesthetics as criticism can become a science, a view which Kant entirely maintains in the third *Critique*, §34, 5:285–6, it does not reject the possibility of a "scientific" explanation of the phenomena of taste, which is precisely what the third *Critique* offers.

62. See *Critique of the Power of Judgment*, §50, 5:319–20.

63. See also **702** below.

64. Kant's anthropology lectures contain a number of important discussions of the love of freedom; see especially *Friedländer*, 25:581–2, *Menschenkunde*, 25:1142–6, and *Busolt*, 25:1520–1.

65. Compare this paragraph to Kant's classification of the fine arts at *Critique of the Power of Judgment*, §51, 5:319–25, as well as those at *Pillau*, 25:760–1, 782–3, and *Menschenkunde*, 25:981–95, 997–1006.

66. See *Critique of the Power of Judgment*, §51, 5:325. See also *Parow*, 25:378–80.

67. In §651, Baumgarten writes that the intuition of perfections pleases and that of imperfections displeases. This is the basis for rationalist aesthetics in Wolff and Baumgarten; for Kant's critique, see the First Introduction to the *Critique of the Power of Judgment*, Section VIII, Remark, 20:226–30, and in the published text, §15, 5:226–9.

68. See **648, 653, 710**, and **1791**, as well as the texts referred to in note 49 to **648**.

69. See also **672** above.

70. See also **797**.

71. See also **648, 653**, and **686** above, as well as **1791** below.

72. On the free and unhindered activity of the cognitive powers as the source of the pleasure in the beautiful, see above all *Collins*, 25:181, *Parow*, 25:379–80, and *Friedländer*, 25:559–60.

73. See *Critique of the Power of Judgment*, §14, 5:223–6, and §51, especially 5:324–5.

74. In §662, Baumgarten defines beauty (*pulchritudo*) as the observable perfection of a phenomenon and ugliness (*deformitas*) as observable imperfection.

75. See *Critique of the Power of Judgment*, §2, 5:204–5, as well as *Collins*, 25:176–8, *Friedländer*, 25:577, and *Busolt*, 25:1499–1500, 1508–9.

76. **474–59** are notes to *Metaphysica* §§606–7, which concern the definition of judgment (*iudicium*).

77. See *Critique of the Power of Judgment*, §17, 5:231–6. This appears to be Kant's first mention of the concept of an ideal of beauty.

78. This may be contrasted with Kant's usual distinction between the agreeable, the beautiful, and the good (*Critique of the Power of Judgment*, §§2–5), and suggests an emotional element in moral judgment that Kant does not always emphasize.

79. The idea of "artificial emotion" was introduced in one of the seminal works of eighteenth-century aesthetics, the Abbé Jean-Baptiste Du Bos's *Critical Reflections on Poetry, Painting, and Music*, first published in 1719 in French and

frequently reprinted as well as translated into English by 1748. Influential on Gotthold Ephraim Lessing and Johann Georg Sulzer, Du Bos was widely known in Germany as well, and it is quite likely that Kant is here referring to him.

80. Kant refers explicitly to Adam Smith's concept of the ideal observer in **6864**, included in Chapter 4 above.

81. Contrast this note to *Critique of the Power of Judgment*, §50, 5:319–20, where Kant suggests that there can be a conflict between taste and genius, rather than genius depending on good taste, as he suggests here.

82. To this account of moral feeling, compare Kant's account of respect in the *Critique of Practical Reason*, especially 5:75–6, and in *Metaphysics of Morals*, "Doctrine of Virtue," Introduction, Section XIId, as well as his account of moral feeling in Section XIIa, in all of which he argues that moral feeling is the effect of the adoption of the principle of pure practical reason rather than its cause.

83. On this theme, see the discussion of "The uses of the cultivation of taste" at *Collins*, 25:187–96, especially 187–8; *Menschenkunde*, 25:1102; and *Mrongovius*, 25:1332.

84. Compare this formulation to Kant's statement in the *Critique of the Power of Judgment* that "The beautiful prepares us to love something, even nature, without interest" – although there is no hint here of Kant's continuation of that sentence, namely, "the sublime [prepares us] to esteem it, even contrary to our (sensible) interest" (General Remark following §29, 5:267).

85. See *Collins*, 25:175, *Friedländer*, 25:560, and *Menschenkunde*, 25:1068–70.

86. As previously noted, a theme of Kant's from 1769 (see **621–2**) through the *Critique of the Power of Judgment* itself (see especially §34).

87. This is the first reference in these notes to the distinction between reflecting and determining judgment, first introduced in Kant's published work in Section IV of the Introduction to the *Critique of the Power of Judgment*, 5:179 (see also First Introduction, Section V, 20:211) and thought to be a late addition even in the composition of that work. This could argue for a late dating of this note.

88. See *Critique of the Power of Judgment*, §14, 5:225–6.

89. A number of later additions to pp. 1 and 2, of more interest for the interpretation of Kant's anthropology than his aesthetic theory, are here omitted; see 15:355–8.

90. See *Critique of the Power of Judgment*, §47.

91. Such contrasts between the tendencies of the different peoples or nations, including those with respect to their tastes, were a constant in Kant's anthropological writings, beginning with the 1764 *Observations on the Feeling of the Beautiful and Sublime*, Section Four, 2:244–8. The published *Anthropology from a Pragmatic Point of View* focuses more on differences in conduct than in taste (7:311–20). The treatments of "national character" in *Collins* and *Parow* are quite brief, but there are more extensive treatments in *Friedländer*, 25:654–61, *Menschenkunde*, 25:1181–7, and *Mrongovius*, 25:1398–1415. See also **816**.

92. On the connection between spirit and genius, see *Critique of the Power of Judgment*, §49, 5:313.

93. Kant's term *das Vernunftähnliche* is an unmistakable allusion to Baumgarten's characterization of the capacity for the feeling of beauty and taste as an *analogon rationis*; see especially his *Aesthetica* (1750), §38; in the Latin-German selection by Hans Rudolf Schweizer, *Ästhetik als Philosophie der sinnlichen Erkenntnis* (Basel: Schwabe, 1973), pp. 128–9.

94. See *Critique of the Power of Judgment*, §1, 5:204; *Anthropology from a Pragmatic Point of View*, §60, 7:231; **567, 586, 676, 799, 806, 824, 888, 1838**, and **1839**; *Collins*, 25:167–9, *Friedländer*, 25:55961, *Pillau*, 25:786, *Menschenkunde*, 25:1068, and *Busolt*, 25:1501; *Metaphysik L 2*, 28:247, *Metaphysik Mrongrovius*, 29:891, and *Metaphysik L 2*, 28:586.

95. See, for example, Diogenes Laertius 10.121; Cicero, *Tusculan Disputations* III.41–2, or Atheneaus 546F: "Epicurus says: 'The pleasure of the stomach is the beginning and root of all good, and it is to this that wisdom and over-refinement actually occur'."

96. This explicit assertion of the connection between the free play that is the source of aesthetic pleasure is unusual, although Kant is pointing in the same direction when he says that the state of the cognitive powers underlying aesthetic response is "unintentional" (*unabsichtlich*); see for example *Critique of the Power of Judgment*, Introduction, Section VI, 5:187, and Section VII, 5:190.

97. See **823** and the additional texts referred to in note 94.

98. This note may be compared to Kant's unfavorable comments about "virtuosi of taste" at *Critique of the Power of Judgment*, §42, 5:298. To the general content of this note, compare also **1829**.

99. In *Critique of the Power of Judgment*, §45, 5:306–7, Kant distinguishes "mechanical art" from "beautiful art," but at §46, 5:310, he also states that there is no beautiful art without a mechanical basis, that is, a basis in teachable skills and techniques that can be formulated in rules. That is perhaps the point clumsily made in the last sentence of this paragraph. See also **922** and **924**.

100. See above all *Critique of the Power of Judgment*, §49, 5:313–14.

101. See *Critique of the Power of Judgment*, §50, 5:319–20.

102. See also **873–4, 922**, and **1834**.

103. §597 concerns "prevision," which is the form of imagination that is opposite to memory, that is, the ability to picture future objects or states of affairs.

104. Kant's characterization of the "sensible power of judgment" as moving from particular to universal in **841** and **842** and his contrast of this to reason in **842** clearly anticipates his later distinction between the reflecting and determining powers of judgment without yet employing this terminology; see *Critique of the Power of Judgment*, First Introduction, Section V, 20:211, and Introduction, Section IV, 5:179.

105. See *Critique of the Power of Judgment*, §21, 5:238, the only place in the text where Kant describes the free play of the faculties as resting on a particular "proportion" among them.

106. Compare this to Kant's formulation at First Introduction, Section VIII, 20:223–4, where he says that a reflecting aesthetic judgment "perceives a

relation of the two faculties of cognition which constitutes the subjective, merely sensitive condition of the objective power of judgment."

107. See Kant's discussions of the genuine beauty of pure colors, as opposed to the mere charm of combined colors, at *Critique of the Power of Judgment*, §14, 5:224–5, and §51, 5:324–5. The present claim that purity of color is itself a sign of artistry is not made in those passages.

108. Kant's list of the four ingredients of genius in **874** (and his identical list of the four ingredients of taste in **873**) can be compared to his different lists of its components at *Critique of the Power of Judgment*, §46, 5:307–8, and §49, 5:317–18, as well as **1834**. The implication that because these four elements are not teachable the other elements of genius are teachable may be an allusion to the learnable, "mechanical" technical means of expression necessary for the production of art; see **829** above.

109. See *Critique of the Power of Judgment*, §4, 5:207.

110. See also **648** and the texts referred to in note 49, including **653, 686, 710**, and **1791**.

111. Compare this remark to *Critique of the Power of Judgment*, §45, 5:306. Kant's use of the word "naïve" in this remark shows that Friedrich Schiller's use of it in his famous essay "On Naïve and Sentimental Poetry" (1795) was not novel.

112. See especially *Critique of the Power of Judgment*, §49, 5:318, where Kant argues that the capacity to devise appropriate forms for communicating original ideas as well as that for inventing them is a necessary component of genius.

113. Compare this note to *Critique of the Power of Judgment*, §17, 5:233–5, where Kant argues that an ideal of beauty is not simply an "aesthetic **normal idea**" produced by averaging. Kant refers to Johann Kaspar Lavater (1741–1801), who published four volumes of *Physiognomische Fragmente* (Leipzig: Winterthur, 1775–78). After 1785, Kant included a section on physiognomy in his anthropology lectures and frequently referred to Lavater: see *Friedländer*, 25:668–71; *Pillau*, 25:827–30; *Menschenkunde*, 25:1177–81; and *Mrongovius*, 25:1377–82. He also devoted a section to physiognomy in the published *Anthropology from a Pragmatic Point of View*, 7:295–303, again referring to Lavater several times. However, Kant also refers to Lavater in **921** as a genius who is also "an enthusiast who goes far beyond the circle of experiential cognition" (15:406–7). In this note Kant also strikingly refers to Rousseau as "an enthusiast who is worthy of respect" (15:406).

114. Baumgarten's §649 defines genius as an aptitude for a certain kind of cognition, and then distinguishes a variety of forms of genius, such as "empirical, historical, poetic, divinatory, critical, philosophical, mathematical, mechanical, musical, etc." **922** is one of a series of notes on genius and talent extending from **920** to **980**.

115. See **829** and note 99, as well as **924**.

116. See also **829, 873–4**, and **1834**.

117. For the use of the concept of play in Kant's mature classification of the arts, see *Critique of the Power of Judgment*, §51, especially 5:324–5.

118. On mechanism see **829** and note 99 as well as **922**. On imitation, see *Critique of the Power of Judgment*, §47, 5:309–10.

119. This note as well as **933** clearly attempt to provide a premise for the connection between genius and aesthetic ideas which is absent from Kant's account in *Critique of the Power of Judgment*, §49, 5:313–14.

120. See also **938**.

121. See Kant's contrast between fine arts and handicrafts at *Critique of the Power of Judgment*, §43, 5:304.

122. See Kant's famous remark that "The imagination (as a productive cognitive faculty) is, namely, very powerful in creating, as it were, another nature, out of the material which the real one gives it"; *Critique of the Power of Judgment*, §49, 5:314. See also **959**.

123. See Kant's definition of an organized being in the "Critique of the Teleological Power of Judgment," *Critique of the Power of Judgment*, §65, 5:373–4. Kant never explicitly asserts the analogy between a work of art and an organism in his published text, although it would certainly have helped explain the combination of the "Critique of the Aesthetic Power of Judgment" and the "Critique of the Teleological Power of Judgment" into a single work.

124. Compare this note to Kant's brief argument at *Critique of the Power of Judgment*, §52, 5:326, that it is only "if the beautiful arts are . . . combined . . . with moral ideas" that they retain their enduring attraction for us.

125. Alexander Gerard, whose *Essay on Genius* (1774) was translated into German by Christian Garve in 1776 (Alexander Gerard, *Versuch über das Genie* [Leipzig: Weidmanns Erben und Reich, 1776]). The translation of Gerard's work was presumably the stimulus for Kant's numerous reflections on genius around 1776 from which we have here selected. Gerard argued that genius is manifested, although in different form, in science as well as art; Kant obviously still had Gerard in mind when he argued the contrary in the *Critique of the Power of Judgment*, §47.

126. Kant draws on this language in his account of aesthetic ideas at *Critique of the Power of Judgment*, §49, 5:313–14. **958** also points in the direction of the theory of aesthetic ideas.

127. See also **943** and note 122.

128. Compare to *Critique of the Power of Judgment*, §45, 5:306.

129. Compare, of course, to *Critique of Practical Reason*, 5:161–2.

130. See *Critique of the Power of Judgment*, §47, 5:310.

131. See David Hume, "Of the Dignity or Meanness of Human Nature," paragraph seven: "we bestow the epithet of *beautiful* only on such as possess a degree of beauty that is common to them with a few"; in Hume, *Essays Moral, Political and Literary* (Oxford: Oxford University Press, 1963), p. 85.

132. Alexander Selkirk (1676–1721), the stranded English sailor who was the model for Daniel Defoe's *Robinson Crusoe* (1719).

133. To this note compare **648, 653, 686, 710**, and **1791** and the other texts referred to in note 49 to **648**.

134. See especially *Critique of the Power of Judgment*, First Introduction, Section VIII, 20:223–4, and Introduction, Section VII, 5:189–90.

135. To this formulation compare especially *Critique of the Power of Judgment*, §35, 5:286–7.

136. For other reflections and locations in the anthropology lectures bearing on this paragraph, see **823**, note 94.

137. Here Kant seems to be attempting to associate his explanation of aesthetic pleasure with his explanation of moral feeling as an "*a priori*" feeling, that is, one produced by pure reason; see *Critique of Practical Reason*, 5:75–6, 78–9.

138. See the Fourth Proposition of "Idea for a Universal History from a Cosmopolitan Point of View" (1784): "The means which nature employs to bring about the development of innate capacities is that of antagonism within society," or "unsocial sociability" (8:20).

139. Kant subsequently discusses friendship in the "Doctrine of Virtue" of the *Metaphysics of Morals*, where he writes that "friendship is only an idea (although a practically necessary one) and unattainable in practice, although striving for friendship... is a duty set by reason" (6:469). Here he attributes the statement "My dear friends, there is no such thing as a friend" to Aristotle; in his discussion of friendship in the *Nicomachean Ethics*, Book VIII, Aristotle argues that true friendship between good persons who "wish well alike to each other *qua* good" (1156b9) are very rare (1156b25) (translation by W. D. Ross, revised by J. O. Urmson, in Jonathan Barnes, ed., *The Complete Works of Aristotle* [Princeton: Princeton University Press, 1984], volume 2, p. 1827). There is also a lengthy discussion of friendship in *Moral Philosophy Collins*, 27:422–30, where Kant quotes now Socrates as saying "My dear friends, there are no friends" (27:424) and distinguishes the friendship of "sentiment" from that of "taste" and "disposition" (27:426–7). A second extended discussion is in *Metaphysics of Morals Vigilantius*, 27:675–86. The closest source in the Platonic *corpus* for the Socratic saying would seem to be the lengthy discussion of friendship in *Lysis*, where Socrates ends a lengthy but inconclusive discussion of whether friendship can be between like people generally or only between equally good people by saying that "If neither the loved nor the loving, nor the like nor the unlike, nor the good, nor the belonging, nor any of the others we have gone through... if none of these is a friend, then I have nothing left to say" (*Lysis* 222e, translation by Stanley Lombardo, in Plato, *Complete Works*, ed. John M. Cooper [Indianapolis: Hackett Publishing Co., 1997], p. 707). But Socrates never actually says there are no friends. The Stoics took up the theme that true friendship can exist only among the virtuous (see, e.g., Diogenes Laertius, VII, 124), and given their view that virtually no one actually attained the fully virtuous status of a sage, might have inferred that there are no true friends. So perhaps Kant got the "Socratic" saying from a Stoic source.

140. See *Anthropology from a Pragmatic Point of View*, §61: "As a Parisian said of Lord Mordaunt: 'The English hang themselves to pass the time'" (7:233). Adickes conjectures that the source of this remark is the article "*Du Caton, Du Suicide*" in Voltaire's *Dictionnaire philosophique* (see his note to **1513** at 15:841). This makes sense given Kant's reference to Cato in his discussion of suicide in *Moral Philosophy Collins*, 27:370. Kant also refers to the story of "Mordaunt" at *Parow*, 25:404–5. The editors there suggest an identification with one "Philip Merdant," a cousin of Charles Mordaunt, third Earl of

Peterborough (1658–1735), who shot himself in the head "having given no other reason than that his soul had become surfeited with its long occupation of his body." They give no reason for suggesting that the suicide spelled his name differently from his noble cousin.

141. See *Critique of the Power of Judgment*, §§2–5.

142. This note is obviously a draft of an outline for the "Critique of the Aesthetic Power of Judgment," and because of its use of the concept of the "subjective purposiveness of nature" also intimates the basis for Kant's combination of the critique of taste with a "Critique of the Teleological Power of Judgment" to form the *Critique of the Power of Judgment*.

143. See Kant's solution to the "antinomy of taste" at *Critique of the Power of Judgment*, §57, 5:339–40. Kant does not appeal to the "supersensible" as the basis of the free play of the cognitive powers in aesthetic response in either of the introductions or the "Analytic of the Beautiful."

144. See the "General Remark" following the completion of the "Analytic of the Sublime" at §29, 5:267–8. However, Kant does not there correlate the preparatory roles of the experiences of the beautiful and the sublime with imperfect and perfect duties.

145. In the *Critique of the Power of Judgment*, Kant does not explain the experience of beauty solely with respect to the "quality" of the purposive determination of the subject nor that of the sublime solely with respect to its "magnitude." But he does make a point of beginning the discussion of the "four moments" of the beautiful with the discussion of its quality rather than its quantity (§1, 5:202–3n.), while the discussion of the sublime focuses first on the dynamical sublime, which is a response to the apparently infinite magnitude or quantity of natural vistas.

146. See *Critique of the Power of Judgment*, §8, 5:214–15, where Kant distinguishes between the "logical" and "aesthetic quantity of universality."

147. See *Critique of the Power of Judgment*, §8, 5:215: "all judgments of taste are **singular** judgments."

148. See **992** and note 144.

149. Here Kant alludes to his distinction between the dynamical and mathematical sublime, but seems to deny what he says in the published treatment, namely that "we must see ourselves as safe in order to be sensible of this inspiriting satisfaction" (*Critique of the Power of Judgment*, §28, 5:262).

150. Here of course Kant refers to Edmund Burke's *Philosophical Enquiry into the Origin of Our Ideas of the Sublime and Beautiful* (1757; second edition with an introduction on taste, 1759; translated into German by Christian Garve in 1773 after being extensively reviewed by Moses Mendelssohn in 1758); to Milton's *Paradise Lost*; and to his exact contemporary, the German poet Friedrich Gottlieb Klopstock (1724–1803), best known for his epic *Messias* (1755, revised edition, 1766). Aeneas's descent into the underworld is described in Book VI of Virgil's *Aeneid*.

151. See *Critique of Practical Reason*, 5:86–7.

152. Volume 15, pp. 657–899, contains longer sketches for Kant's course on anthropology from the period 1776–84, drawn from various *lose Blätter* rather than from Kant's copy of Baumgarten's *Metaphysica*. Here we present

only some excerpts of particular relevance to the development of Kant's aesthetics. Elisions from the notes selected here will be marked.

153. See also **1512**, 15:830–33.

154. The lower half of 15:717, all of 718, all but the present line of 719, and much of 720 and 721 are occupied with notes containing extracts that Kant made from Christoph Meiner's 1777 translation, *Gedanken über die Natur des Vergnügens*, of Pierro Verri, *Meditazioni sulla felicità* (Livorno, 1763). Kant's own text reproduced from p. 720 to the bottom of 724 is also omitted here.

155. The first page of this note deals with gratification and pain, like **1487** and **1511**.

156. Kant could be referring here either to the two statements that he contrasts in the "antinomy of taste" in the *Critique of the Power of Judgment* (§56, 5:338), viz., "It is possible to argue about taste" and, "Everyone has his own taste," or to Hume's contrast in "Of the Standard of Taste," between the two "proverbs" that "it is fruitless to dispute concerning taste," on the one hand, and, on the other, that "Whoever would assert an equality of genius and elegance between Ogilby and Milton, or Bunyan and Addison, would be thought to defend no less an extravagance, than if he had maintained a mole-hill to be as high as Teneriffe"; in Hume, *Essays Moral, Political and Literary* (Oxford: Oxford University Press, 1963), pp. 234–5. Kant was of course familiar with Hume's essay, which had been translated into German by Friedrich Gabriel Resewitz in David Hume, *Vier Abhandlungen* (Quedlingburg and Leipzig: Andreas Franz Biesterfeld, 1759); the passage about the two *Sprüchwörter* (Kant refers to *den beyden Sprichwörtern*) is translated on pp. 243–4 of that edition.

157. See especially *Critique of the Power of Judgment*, §33, 5:284–5.

158. See *Critique of the Power of Judgment*, §45, 5:306.

159. In his anthropology lectures, Kant said that Queen Christina of Sweden knew how to spout received moral maxims, but had no genuine moral feeling of her own (*sentiment*). See *Menschenkunde*, pp. 294–5; 25:1108.

160. The remainder of this note (15:840–3) is a section entitled "on desire."

161. **1747** through **1936** are notes in §§19–35 in Chapter 1, "On learned cognition," of Georg Friedrich Meier's *Auszug aus der Vernunftlehre* ("*V*"), concerning the difference between logical and aesthetic perfections of cognition. §19 says that "A perfect historical cognition is a **beautiful cognition** (*cognitio pulcra, aesthetica*), and the beautiful sciences concern themselves with the rules through the observation of which historical cognition is beautified." By "historical cognition" Meier means cognition based on the senses and imagination, including memory, as contrasted to cognition based purely in reason. Comments on §§19–35 of Meier's *Vernunftlehre* may also be found in Kant's lectures on logic at *Blomberg Logic* (1770–71), 24:43–63, and *Logik Philippi* (1772), 24:344–72, and in the *Jäsche Logic*, Introduction, Section V, 9:34–9.

162. §22 states that the "perfection of cognition" consists in the coherence or agreement of the manifold in the cognition, and that when the perfection of the cognition is indistinct (*undeutlich*) that is the "aesthetic perfection of cognition."

163. This of course refers to Archimedes's legendary discovery of the principle of displacement by volume rather than mass by observation of the water rising when he settled into his bathtub.

164. In the *Observations on the Feeling of the Beautiful and Sublime*, Kant refers to the pleasure that Kepler took in one of his discoveries, "which he would not have sold for a princedom" (2:208). There is no mention of any particular discovery or proposition.

165. In **1756**, omitted here, Kant discusses how logically perfect cognition can also be presented in a form that is aesthetically unpleasant. In **1765** he observes that false cognition can still be aesthetically pleasing. In **1770** he says that one should always begin from logical perfections, which can be treated without aesthetic perfections, and in **1773** that in case of a conflict between logical and aesthetic perfections, the former must be preferred.

166. Compare to Kant's definitions at *Critique of Pure Reason*, A 19–20/B 33–4, as well as to **1789** and **1864** below.

167. §24 distinguishes between cognition that has only logical perfection and that which has both logical and aesthetic perfection.

168. §33 states that a single cognition can combine several logical perfections, and that a logically perfect cognition can be beautiful or ugly or neither.

169. See *Critique of the Power of Judgment*, §§13–14, as well as **1864** below.

170. See **648** and note 29 above, as well as *Critique of the Power of Judgment*, §9, 5:218.

171. §31 states that learned cognition is all the more perfect the more "extensive, important, correct, distinct, certain and practical" it is, and says that "every rational person" must strive for the greatest perfection in each and all of these dimensions as well as for "beauties of cognition."

172. See also **1841**.

173. Compare this note to Kant's distinction between poetry and oratory at *Critique of the Power of Judgment*, §51, 5:321; to **618**; and to the passages in the anthropology lectures cited in note 17 to **618**.

174. See *Critique of the Power of Judgment*, §8, 5:214–15.

175. See Immanuel Kant, *Correspondence*, ed. Arnulf Zweig (Cambridge: Cambridge University Press, 1999), pp. 128–31.

176. See also **1838, 1839, 1866, 1869, 1876**, and **1884**. See further **1904**, translated below.

177. See *Jäsche Logic*, Introduction, Section V, 9:36.

178. §17 defines rational cognition as cognition based on distinct grounds.

179. For other occurrences of this list of the elements of taste and genius, see **829, 873–4**, and **922**.

180. See also **1838**.

181. In §32, Meier maintains that one should not be content with logical perfection of cognition, but wherever possible should also strive to give cognition aesthetic perfection.

182. See also **1841** and **1892** below.

183. To this note as well as **1844**, compare *Critique of the Power of Judgment*, §50.

184. Praxiteles (fl. ca. 370–330 B.C.E.) has always been considered the supreme Attic sculptor. Critics in antiquity regarded his "Venus of Knidos," a copy of which is in the Vatican, as his finest work.

185. See *Critique of the Power of Judgment*, §§13–14, as well as **1780** and **1789** above.

186. For a lengthy discussion of the theme that Kant introduces here, namely that the models of taste must be in an ancient rather than living language, see also **2569**, a lengthy note from the period 1769–70 (16:420–24). Kant's key claim in that note appears to be this: "It is a well-founded provisional judgment in matters of taste to give the advantage to what comes from antiquity, because time has as it were sifted the writings and only left the good ones . . ."; in other words, Kant's idea is not really that there is anything special about the ancient languages *per se*, but rather that those ancient works that have survived have withstood the test of time. However, he fails to include this explanation in his statement that only works in ancient languages can provide models for taste at *Critique of the Power of Judgment*, §47, 5:310.

187. §30 defines cognition as "practical" when it contributes to the "direction of our free action."

188. See *Critique of the Power of Judgment*, §44, 5:303.

189. See **1840** above.

190. See *Critique of the Power of Judgment*, §49, 5:313.

191. See *Critique of the Power of Judgment*, §50, 5:319–20.

192. See also **1821** and the further references given in note 176 thereto.

193. For the significance of Kant's use of the term *"interesse,"* see **1931** below.

194. Kant gives a similar although not identical analysis of the properties of aesthetic judgment under the headings of the table of categories at *Jäsche Logic*, Introduction, Section V, 9:39. The general strategy of analyzing the properties of the aesthetic by analogy to logical features was used by Baumgarten to structure his discussion in his *Aesthetica*; see for example sections 27–9, §§423–504.

195. See **1840**, note 181.

196. See **1909** above.

197. See *Critique of the Power of Judgment*, §48, 5:312.

Glossary

This is a selective glossary of some of the philosophically significant terms used by Kant in the materials included in this volume. Words in very common usage as well as terms Kant may have used only once or twice are omitted. Obvious cognates, usually Latin in origin, are also omitted from the German-English glossary. Many of Kant's most characteristic philosophical terms (e.g., *absolut, analytisch, Identität, Imperativ, kategorisch, Subjekt, Substanz, synthetisch, Totalität, transzendent, transzendental*) are obvious cognates of the equivalent English terms, which were indeed sometimes first coined as equivalents for Kant's terms, and therefore have not been included. In a few cases, Latinate terms in Kant's vocabulary that do not mean the same as their obvious English cognates have been included. However, Kant often used both Germanic and Latinate terms for the same concept (e.g., *absondern/abstrahiren, Bewegunsgrund/Motiv, zurechnen/imputiren*), and both forms have been included in the English-German glossary. Not all of the different forms of a single word (noun, verb, adjective, adverb, etc.) that Kant uses are included, nor are all compound words included. Nominative forms of words that are also verbs are capitalized here, even though they are not always capitalized in Adickes's transcriptions. Kant's spelling has generally been retained.

To the extent possible, translations of terms have been kept consistent with other volumes in the Cambridge edition; where that is not the case, the translation used in this volume has been indicated below. Where multiple English equivalents for a single German term are listed, the most characteristic comes first.

GERMAN–ENGLISH GLOSSARY

Aberglaube	suspicion
abgeleitet	derived
Abhängigkeit	dependency
Ableitung	derivation
Abscheu	abhorrence, aversion
Absicht	aim, intention
absondern	abstract, separate
Achtung	respect
All	totality

allgemein	universal, general
Allgemeingültigkeit	universal validity
analytisch	analytic
Anfang	beginning
anfangen	begin, initiate
Angelegenheit	concern
Angemessenheit	compatibility, suitability
angenehm	agreeable
Anlage	predisposition
Anmaßung	presumption
Anmüth	grace, charm
Annehmlichkeit	agreeableness
Annehmung	assumption
anschaulich	intuitive
Anschauung	intuition
Anstand	propriety
Antheil	interest, share
Antrieb	impulse
Anwendung	application
Anziehung	attraction
Apperception	apperception
Art	kind, manner, species
Aufklärung	enlightenment
Aufzählung	enumeration
Ausdehnung	extension
außer	outer
äußerlich	external
ausüben	perform, execute
Baukunst	architecture
bedeuten	signify
Bedeutung	significance, meaning
bedingt	conditioned
Bedingung	condition
Bedürfnis	need
befördern	promote
Befreyung	liberation
befriedigen	satisfy
Befriedigung	satisfaction
Begebenheit	event, occurrence
begehren	desire (v.)
Begehren,-ung	desire (n.)
Begehrungsvermögen	faculty of desire
Begeisterung	inspiration
Begierde	desire

begreifen	comprehend, grasp
Begriff	concept
beharren	persist
Beharrlichkeit	persistence
behaupten	assert
Behauptung	assertion, declaration
Beifall (Beyfall)	approval
Bejahung	affirmation
beleben	animate
belebend	animating
Belebung	animation
Belesenheit	learning
beliebig	preferred
Beliebung	preference
Beobachtung	observation
Beredsamkeit	oratory
Beschaffenheit	quality, constitution (metaphysical)
Besitz	possession
besonder	particular
beständig	constant, permanent
Bestimmbarkeit	determinability
bestimmen	determine
bestimmt	determinate
Bestimmung	determination, vocation
Beurtheilung	judging (n.)
Bewegung	motion
Bewegungsgrund	motive, motivating ground
Bewegursache	motivating cause
Beweis	demonstration
Bewußtseyn	consciousness
bezeichnen	designate
Bezeichnung	designation
Beziehung	relation
Bild	image, picture
bildend	pictorial, formative
Bildhauerkunst	sculpture
Bildung	formation
Billigung	approbation
Blendwerk	deception
Bonität	goodness, the good
Böse	evil
Bürger	citizen
bürgerlich	civil
Causalität	causality, causation

construiren	construct
Critik (Kritik)	critique, criticism
Criterien	criteria
Cultur	culture, cultivation
Dasein	existence
Dauer	duration
denken	think, conceive
Denken	thinking, thought
Denkungsart	cast of mind
deutlich	distinct
dichten	create
Dichten	composition
Dichter	poet
Dichtkunst	art of poetry
Dijudication	adjudication
Ding	thing
dunkel	obscure
durchgängig	thorough, thoroughgoing
Ehre	honor
Eigennütz	self-interest
eigennützig	selfish
Eigenschaft	property
Einbildung	image, imagining (n.)
Einbildungskraft	imagination
Eindruck	impression
Einfalt	simplicity
Einfluß	influence, influx
Einheit	unity
einig	unitary
Einsamkeit	solitude
Einschränkung	restriction
einsehen	have insight into, understand
Einsicht	insight
Einstimmung	consensus, concordance, unanimity, unison, agreement
Eintheilung	division
einzeln	individual, isolated
empfinden	sense, feel
Empfindsamkeit	sensitivity
Empfindung	sensation, sentiment
empirisch	empirical
endlich	finite
Endzweck	final end
Entschließung	decision, resolution

entstehen	originate, come to be
Erdichtung	fiction
Erfahrung	experience
erfahrungs-	experiential
Ergötzung	delight
erhaben	sublime
Erhabene	the sublime
erkennen	cognize
Erkenntnis	cognition
erklären	explain
Erklärung	explanation, definition, explication
erlaubt	permitted
Erläuterung	clarification
erleichtern	facilitate
Erscheinung	appearance
Erweiterung	amplification
erzeugen	generate
Erzeugung	generation
Erziehung	education
evident	self-evident
exponieren	expound
Exposition	exposition
Fähigkeit	capacity
Fehler	mistake
Fertigkeit	proficiency
Folge	consequence, result, succession
folgen	follow, succeed
Form	form
Fortdauer	persistence
Fortgang	progress
Fortschreitung	progress
Fortschritt	progress
Freyheit	freedom
freywillig	voluntary
Freude (Freide)	joy
Fürwahrhalten	affirmation, affirming (something) to be true
Ganze	whole (n.)
Gartenbau	landscape design
Gartenkunst	horticulture
Gattung	species, genus
Geboth	command
Gebrauch	use
Gedanke	thought
Gedankenwesen	thought-entity

gefallen	please
Gefühl	feeling
Gegenstand	object
Gegentheil	counterpart, opposite
Geist	spirit
Gelehrsamkeit	scholarship
Gemälde	a painting
gemeinnützig	unselfish
Gemeinschaft	community, communion, interaction
gemeinschaftlich	common, communal, joint
Gemüth	mind, cast of mind
Gemüthsart	cast of mind
Genie	genius
Genüßen	enjoyment
gerecht	just
Gerechtigkeit	justice
Geschlecht	sex, sexuality, race
Geschmack	taste
gesellig	sociable
Geselligkeit	sociability
Gesellschaft	society, company
Gesetz	law
Gesetzgeber	legislator, lawgiver
Gesetzgebung	legislation
Gesetzmäßigkeit	lawfulness
Gesinnung	disposition
gesittet	civilized
Gestalt	shape, figure
Gewalt	power, force
Gewissenhaftigkeit	conscientiousness
Gewissheit	certainty
Gewohnheit	custom, habit, habituation
Glaube	belief, faith
glauben	believe
Glaubenssache	matter or article of faith
gläubig	faithful
Glaubwürdigkeit	credibility
gleichartig	homogeneous
gleichformig	uniform
Gleichheit	equality
Gluck	good fortune, happiness
Glückseligkeit	happiness
Gnugsamkeit	moderation

Gottheit	deity, divinity
Grad	degree
Grenzbegriff	boundary-concept
Grenze	boundary
Größe	magnitude
Großmuth	magnanimity
Grund	ground, basis
Grundbegriff	basic concept, fundamental concept
Grundsatz	principle
gültig	valid
Gültigkeit	validity
Gute	good (n.)
Gutherzigkeit	good-heartedness
gütig	kind
Gütigkeit	kindness, good-heartedness
Handlung	action
Harmonie	harmony
harmoniren	harmonize
Häßlichkeit	ugliness
Heiligkeit	holiness
hernehmen	derive
Herrschaft	dominion
Hochmuth	pride
höchstes Gut	highest good
Hoflichkeit	courtesy
Humanität	humanity
Hypothese	hypothesis
Idealismus	idealism
Idee	idea
Identität	identity
Inbegriff	total, sum-total
Inhalt	content
inner	inner
innerlich	internal
Interesse	interest
irren	err
Irrthum	error
kennen	know, be acquainted with
Kenntnis	knowledge
Kennzeichen	characteristics
Keuschheit	chastity
klar	clear
klug	prudent

Klugheit	prudence
knechtlich	servile
Körper	body
körperlich	corporeal
Kraft	power, force
Kunst	art
künstlich	artificial, artful
Laster	vice
lasterhaft	vicious
Lehre	doctrine
Leib	body
leidend	passive
Leidenschaft	passion
Liebe	love
Lohn	reward
Lust	pleasure
Mahlerey (Malerei)	(art of) painting
mannigfaltig	manifold (adj.)
Mannigfaltige	manifold (n.)
Mannigfaltigkeit	manifold (n.), multiplicity
Materialen	materials
Materie	matter
Menge	group, numerical group, quantity
Mein und Dein	property
meinen	to have or hold an opinion
Meinung	opinion
Mensch	human being, person
Menschenliebe	love of mankind
Menschheit	humankind, mankind
Merkmal	mark
Mißbilligung	disapprobation
mißfallen	displease
Mißvergnügen	lack of gratification
Mitgefühl	sympathy
Mitleid, Mitleiden	compassion, pity
Mittel	means
mittheilen	communicate
mittheilend	communicative
möglich	possible
Möglichkeit	possibility
Moral	morality, morals
moralisch	moral
Moralität	morality
Nachahmung	imitation

nachbildend	imitative
necessitiren	necessitate
Neigung	inclination
nothwendig	necessary
nothwendigerweise	necessarily
Nothwendigkeit	necessity
nötigen	necessitate
Nutzen	utility
oberst	supreme
Object	object
öffentlich	public
Ohngefahr	chance
Partheylichkeit	partiality
Persohn	person
Persöhnlichkeit	personality
Pflicht	duty
Poesie	poesy
Position	positing (n.)
Potenz	potential, potency
Princip	principle
principium	principle
Probirstein	touchstone
Raum	space
Realität	reality
Recht	right (n.)
Rechtmäßigkeit	rectitude
rechtschaffen	upright, righteous
Rechtschaffenheit	rectitude, probity
Redlichkeit	honesty
reflectirend	reflecting
Regel	rule
Regelmäßigkeit	regularity, rule-governedness
Reihe	series
rein	pure
Reiz	charm, emotion
reizen	stimulate
Richter	judge (n.)
Richtigkeit	correctness
rühren	touch (v.)
Rührung	emotion
Sache	thing
Satz	proposition, principle
schätzen	esteem
Schein	illusion

scheinbar	apparent
Schicksal	fate, destiny
schlechthin	absolute, absolutely
Schmerz	pain
schön	beautiful
Schöne	the beautiful
Schönheit	beauty
Schöpfung	creation
Schranke	limit, limitation
Schul-	scholastic
Schuldigkeit	obligation
schwärmen	to be an enthusiast, to rave
Schwärmerei	enthusiasm
Seele	soul
Selbst	self
selbstständig	self-sufficient
Selbstbeherrschung	self-control
Selbstbewußtseyn	self-consciousness
Selbstbilligung	self-approbation
Selbstmord	suicide
Selbsttätigkeit	self-activity
Selbstzwang	self-compulsion
Seligkeit	blessedness
setzen	place, posit
Sinn	sense
sinnlich	sensible
Sinnlichkeit	sensibility
Sitten	morals, ethics, mores
Sittlichkeit	morality
sollen	should, ought to
Sollen	ought (n.)
Spiel	play
Spontaneität	spontaneity
Stand der Natur	state of nature
Stelle	position, location
Stoff	matter
Strafe	punishment
Sympathie	sympathy
synthetisch	synthetic
Tauglichkeit	suitability, adaptedness
Täschung	illusion
That	deed
thätig	active
Theil	part

Theilbarkeit	divisibility
Theilbegriff	partial concept
theilnehmend	sympathetic, participatory
Theilnehmer	participant
Theilnehmung	sympathy
Thünlichkeit	feasibility
Trägheit	inertia
Trieb	drive
Triebfeder	incentive
Tugend	virtue
tugendhaft	virtuous
Übel	ill (n.), ill fortune
übereinstimmen	correspond
Übereinstimmung	correspondence, agreement
Überlegung	reflection
übernatürlich	supernatural
Überredung	persuasion
übersinnlich	supersensible
Überzeugung	conviction
Umfang	domain
Umgang	intercourse, company
Unabhängigkeit	independence
unbedingt	unconditioned
Unbedingt	unconditioned (n.)
Unding	non-entity
Uneigennützigkeit	unselfishness
unendlich	infinite
Unendlichkeit	infinitude
unerklärlich	inexplicable
Ungerechtigkeit	injustice
Ungewissheit	uncertainty
Ungleichheit	inequality
Unglück	misfortune
Unlust	displeasure
unmittelbar	immediate, immediately
unpartheyisch	impartial
Unruhe	unrest
Unschuld	innocence
Unsterblichkeit	immortality
Unterordnung	subordination
Unterscheidung	distinction, discrimination
Unterwürfigkeit	subjection
Unvermögen	incapacity
Üppigkeit	excess

Urbild	archetype
Urheber	author
Ursache	cause, reason
ursprünglich	original
Urtheil	judgment
urtheilen	judge
Urtheilskraft	power of judgment
Urwesen	primordial being
Veränderung	alteration
Verbindung	combination
Verdienst	merit
Vereinigung	union, unification
Verfassung	constitution (political)
vergehen	cease to be
Vergesellschaftung	socialization
Vergnügen	gratification
Vergütung	reward
Verhalten	conduct
Verhältnis	relation
Verheissung	promise
Verkettung	concatenation
Verknüpfung	connection
Vermögen	capacity, faculty, resources
Vermuthung	supposition
Verneinung	negation
Vernunft	reason
vernünfteln	argue sophistically, ratiocinate
Vernunftglaube	rational belief
vernünftig	rational
Vernunftschluß	inference
Verstand	understanding
Verstandeswelt	intelligible world
Volk	nation
vollkommen	perfect
Vollkommenheit	perfection
vollständig	complete
Voraussetzung	presupposition
Vorbestimmung	predetermination
Vorsatz	resolution
Vorschrift	precept
Vorsehung	providence
vorstellen	represent
Vorstellung	representation
Vortheil	advantage

Vortrag	presentation
Vorurtheil	prejudice
Wahl	choice
Wahrheit	truth
Wahrnehmung	perception
Wechsel	change
wechselseitig	reciprocal
Weisheit	wisdom
Welt	world
Weltall	world-whole
Weltganze	world-whole
Werth	worth, value
Wesen	being, entity, essence
wesentlich	essential
Wiederlegung	refutation
Wiederspruch	contradiction
Wiederstreit	conflict, opposition
Wille	will
Willkühr	faculty or power of choice
willkührlich	arbitrary, voluntary
wirken	effect (v.), produce
Wirklichkeit	reality, actuality
Wirkung	effect (n.)
Wissen	knowledge
Wissenschaft	science
Wohl	well-being
Wohlbefinden	well-being
Wohlfahrt	welfare
Wohlgefallen	satisfaction
Wohltun	beneficence
Wohlverhalten	good conduct
Wohlwollen	benevolence
wollen	want, will (v.)
Wunder	miracle
Würde	dignity
Würdigkeit	worthiness
Zahl	number
Zeit	time
Zeitfolge	temporal succession
zergliedern	analyze
zetetisch	problematic, zetetic
zufällig	contingent
Zufälligkeit	contingency
Zufriedenheit	contentment

zugleich	simultaneously, at the same time
Zugleichseyn	simultaneity
Zulänglichkeit	adequacy
Zurechnung	imputation
zureichend	sufficient
zusammengesezt	composite
Zusammenhang	interconnection
Zusammennehmung	aggregation, composition
Zusammenordnung	coordination
Zusammenreimen	coherence
Zusammensetzung	juxtaposition, composition
Zusammenstimmung	agreement, harmony
Zuschauer	observer
Zustand	state, condition
Zwang	coercion, compulsion
Zweck	end, purpose
zweckmäßig	purposive
Zweckmäßigkeit	purposiveness
Zweifel	doubt
zwingen	coerce, constrain

ENGLISH–GERMAN GLOSSARY

Where Kant used both Germanic and Latinate terms for the same concept, both are listed here. The Germanic term is listed first; this does not reflect any estimate of frequency of usage. German synonyms are listed alphabetically. In cases of English homonyms, separate entries are provided.

abhorrence	*Abscheu*
absolute	*schlechthin, absolut*
abstract (v.)	*absondern, abstrahiren*
action	*Handlung*
active	*thätig*
actual	*wirklich*
actuality	*Wirklichkeit*
adaptedness	*Tauglichkeit*
adequacy	*Zulänglichkeit*
adjudication	*Dijudication*
advantage	*Vortheil*
affirmation	*Bejahung, Fürwahrhalten* (or *Vorwahrhalten*)
affirm to be true	*Führwahrhalten* (*Vorwahrhalten*)
agreeable	*angenehm*
agreeableness	*Annehmlichkeit*

agreement	*Einstimmung, Zusammenstimmung*
aggregation	*Zusammennehmung*
aim	*Absicht*
alteration	*Veränderung*
amplification	*Erweiterung*
analytic	*analytisch*
analyze	*zergliedern, analisiren*
animate (v.)	*beleben*
animating	*belebend*
animation	*Belebung*
apparent	*Scheinbar*
appearance	*Erscheinung*
apperception	*Apperzeption*
application	*Anwendung*
approbation	*Billigung*
approval	*Beyfall*
arbitrary	*beliebig, willkührlich*
archetype	*Urbild*
architecture	*Baukunst, Architektur*
art	*Kunst*
art of poetry	*Dichtkunst*
artful	*künstlich*
article of faith	*Glaubsenssache*
artificial	*künstlich*
assert	*behaupten*
assertion	*Behauptung*
assumption	*Annehmung*
attraction	*Anziehung*
author	*Urheber*
aversions	*Abscheu*
basic concept	*Grundbegriff*
basis	*Grund*
beautiful (adj.)	*schön*
beautiful (n.)	*Schöne*
beauty	*Schönheit*
begin	*anfangen*
beginning	*Anfang*
being	*Wesen*
belief	*Glaube*
beneficence	*Wohltun*
benevolence	*Wohlwollen*
blessedness	*Seligkeit*
body	*Körper, Leib*
boundary	*Grenze*

boundary-concept	*Grenzbegriff*
capacity	*Fähigkeit, Vermögen*
cast of mind	*Denkungsart, Gemüth, Gemüthsart*
cause	*Ursache*
causality	*Causalität*
causation	*Causalität*
cease to be	*vergehen*
certainty	*Gewissheit*
chance	*Ohngefahr*
change	*Wechsel*
character	*Charakter*
characteristics	*Kennzeichen*
charm (n.)	*Anmüth, Reiz*
chastity	*Keuschheit*
choice	*Wahl*
choice, power of	*Willkühr*
citizen	*Bürger*
civil	*bürgerlich*
civilized	*gesittet*
clarification	*Erläuterung*
clear	*klar*
coerce	*zwingen*
coercion	*Zwang*
cognition	*Erkenntnis*
cognize	*erkennen*
coherence	*Zusammenreimen*
combination	*Verbindung*
come to be	*entstehen*
command (n.)	*Geboth*
communicate	*mittheilen*
communication	*Mittheilung*
communicative	*mittheilend*
communion	*Gemeinschaft*
community	*Gemeinschaft*
compassion	*Mitleid, Mitleiden*
compatibility	*Angemessenheit*
composite	*zusammengesetzt*
composition	*Dichten, Zusammennehmung, Zusammensetzung*
comprehend	*begreifen*
compulsion	*Zwang*
concatenation	*Verkettung*
conceive	*denken*
concept	*Begriff*
concern (n.)	*Angelegenheit*

concordance	*Einstimmung*
condition	*Bedingung, Zustand*
conditioned	*bedingt*
conduct	*Verhalten*
conflict	*Wiederstreit*
conscientiousness	*Gewissenhaftigkeit*
consciousness	*Bewußtseyn*
consensus	*Einstimmung*
consequence	*Folge*
constant	*beständig*
constitution	*Beschaffenheit*
constitution (political)	*Verfassung*
constrain	*zwingen*
construct	*construiren*
content (n.)	*Inhalt*
contentment	*Zufriedenheit*
contingent	*zufällig*
contingency	*Zufälligkeit*
contradiction	*Wiederspruch*
conviction	*Überzeugung*
coordination	*Zusammenordnung, Coordination*
corporeal	*körperlich*
correctness	*Richtigkeit*
correspond	*übereinstimmen*
correspondence	*Übereinstimmung*
counterpart	*Gegentheil*
courtesy	*Hoflichkeit*
create	*dichten, schöpfen*
creation	*Schöpfung*
credibility	*Glaubenswürdigkeit*
criteria	*Criterien*
criticism	*Critik*
critique	*Critik*
cultivation	*Cultur*
culture	*Cultur*
custom	*Gewohnheit*
deception	*Blendwerk*
decision	*Entschließung*
deed	*That*
definition	*Erklärung, Definition*
degree	*Grad*
deity	*Gottheit*
delight	*Ergötzung*
demonstration	*Beweis*

dependency	*Abhängigkeit*
derive	*ableiten, hernehmen*
derivation	*Ableitung*
derived	*abgeleitet*
designate	*bezeichnen*
designation	*Bezeichnung*
desire (v.)	*begehren*
desire (n.)	*Begehren, -ung, Begierde*
destiny	*Schicksal*
determinability	*Bestimmbarkeit*
determinate	*bestimmt*
determination	*Bestimmung*
determine	*bestimmen*
dignity	*Würde*
disapprobation	*Mißbilligung*
discrimination	*Unterscheidung*
dissatisfaction	*Mißfallen*
displeasure	*Unlust*
disposition	*Gesinnung*
distinct	*deutlich, verschieden*
distinction	*Unterscheidung*
divinity	*Gottheit*
divisibility	*Theilbarkeit*
division	*Eintheilung, Theilung*
doctrine	*Lehre*
domain	*Umfang*
dominion	*Herrschaft*
doubt	*Zweifel*
drive	*Trieb*
duration	*Dauer*
duty	*Pflicht*
education	*Erziehung*
empirical	*empirisch*
emotion	*Reiz, Rührung*
end	*Zweck*
enjoyment	*Genüßen*
enlightenment	*Aufklärung*
enthusiasm	*Schwärmerei, Enthusiasmus*
entity	*Wesen*
enumeration	*Aufzählung*
err	*irren*
error	*Irrthum*
essence	*Wesen*
essential	*wesentlich*

esteem (v.)	*schätzen*
esteem (n.)	*Hochschätzung*
ethics	*Sitten*
event	*Begebenheit*
evil	*Böse*
excess	*Üppigkeit*
execute	*ausüben*
existence	*Dasein, Existenz*
experience	*Erfahrung*
experiential	*Erfahrungs-*
explanation	*Erklärung*
explain	*erklären*
explication	*Erklärung*
exposition	*Exposition*
expound	*exponiren*
extension	*Ausdehnung*
external	*äußerlich*
facilitate	*erleichtern*
faculty	*Vermögen*
faculty of desire	*Begehrungsvermögen*
faith	*Glaube*
faithful	*gläubig*
fate	*Schicksal*
feasibility	*Thünlichkeit*
feel	*empfinden, fühlen*
feeling	*Gefühl*
fiction	*Erdichtung*
figure	*Gestalt*
final end	*Endzweck*
finite	*endlich*
follow	*folgen*
force	*Gewalt, Kraft*
form	*Form*
formation	*Bildung*
formative	*bildend*
freedom	*Freyheit*
general	*allgemein*
generate	*erzeugen*
generation	*Erzeugung*
genius	*Genie*
genus	*Gattung*
good (n.)	*Bonität, Gute*
good fortune	*Gluck*
good-heartedness	*Gutherzigkeit, Gütigkeit*

goodness	*Bonität*
grace	*Anmüth*
grasp (v.)	*begreifen*
gratification	*Vergnügen*
ground	*Grund*
group	*Menge*
habituation	*Gewohnheit*
happiness	*Gluck, Glückseligkeit*
harmonize	*harmoniren*
harmony	*Harmonie*
have an opinion	*meinen*
have insight into	*einsehen*
highest good	*höchstes Gut*
holiness	*Heiligkeit*
homogeneous	*gleichartig*
honest	*Redlichkeit*
honor	*Ehre*
horticulture	*Gartenkunst*
human being	*Mensch*
humanity	*Menschheit, Humanität*
hypothesis	*Hypothese*
idea	*Idee*
idealism	*Idealismus*
identity	*Einerleyheit, Identität*
ill, ill fortune	*Übel*
illusion	*Blendwerk, Schein, Täuschung*
image	*Bild, Einbildung*
imagination	*Einbildungskraft*
imagining	*Einbildung*
imitation	*Nachachmung*
imitative	*nachbildend*
immediate, -ly	*unmittelbar*
immortality	*Unsterblichkeit*
impartial	*unpartheyisch*
impression	*Eindruck*
impulse	*Antrieb*
imputation	*Zurechnung*
impute	*zurechnen, imputiren*
incapacity	*Unvermögen*
incentive	*Triebfeder*
inclination	*Neigung*
independence	*Unabhängigkeit*
individual	*einzeln*
inequality	*Ungleichheit*

inertia	*Trägheit*
inexplicable	*unerklärlich*
inference	*Vernunftschluß*
infinite	*unendlich*
infinitude	*Unendlichkeit*
influence	*Einfluß*
influx	*Einfluß*
injustice	*Ungerechtigkeit*
inner	*inner*
innocence	*Unschuld*
insight	*Einsicht*
inspiration	*Begeisterung*
intelligible world	*Verstandeswelt*
intention	*Absicht*
interaction	*Gemeinschaft, Commercium*
interconnection	*Zusammenhang*
interest (n.)	*Antheil, Interesse*
internal	*innerlich*
intuition	*Anschaung*
intuitive	*anschaulich*
joy	*Freude*
judge (n.)	*Richter*
judge (v.)	*urtheilen*
judging (n.)	*Beurtheilung*
judgment	*Urtheil*
just	*gerecht*
justice	*Gerechtigkeit*
juxtaposition	*Zusammensetzung*
kind	*Art*
kind, kindly	*gütig*
kindness	*Gütigkeit*
know	*kennen*
knowledge	*Kenntnis, Wissen*
landscape design	*Gartenbau*
law	*Gesetz*
lawfulness	*Gesetzmäßigkeit*
lawgiver	*Gesetzgeber*
learning	*Belesenheit*
legislation	*Gesetzgebung*
legislator	*Gesetzgeber*
liberation	*Befreyung*
limit, -ation	*Schranke*
location	*Ort, Stelle*
love	*Liebe*

magnanimity	*Großmuth*
magnitude	*Größe*
manifold (adj.)	*mannigfaltig*
manifold (n.)	*Mannigfaltige, Mannigfaltigkeit*
manner	*Art*
mark	*Merkmal*
materials	*Materialen*
matter	*Materie, Stoff*
meaning	*Bedeutung*
merit	*Verdienst*
mind	*Gemüth*
miracle	*Wunder*
misfortune	*Unglück*
mistake	*Fehler*
moderation	*Gnugsamkeit*
moral	*moralisch*
morality	*Moral, Moralität, Sittlichkeit*
morals	*Moral, Sitten*
mores	*Sitten*
motivating cause	*Bewegursache*
motivating ground	*Bewegungsgrund*
motive	*Bewegungsgrund, Motiv*
multiplicity	*Mannigfaltigkeit*
nation	*Volk*
necessarily	*nothwendig, nothwendigerweise*
necessary	*nothwendig*
necessitate	*nötigen, necessitiren*
necessity	*Nothwendigkeit*
need (n.)	*Bedürfnis*
negation	*Verneinung*
nexus	*Zusammenhang, Nexus*
non-entity	*Unding*
number	*Zahl*
object	*Gegenstand, Object*
obligation	*Schuldigkeit*
obscure	*dunkel*
observation	*Beobachtung*
observer	*Zuschauer*
occurrence	*Begebenheit*
opinion	*Meinung*
opposite	*Gegentheil*
opposition	*Widerstreit*
oratory	*Beredsamkeit*

original	*ursprünglich*
originate	*entstehen*
ought (n.)	*Sollen*
outer	*außer*
pain	*Schmerz*
painting (a)	*Gemälde*
painting (art of)	*Mahlerey (Malerei)*
part	*Theil*
partial concept	*Theilbegriff*
partiality	*Partheylichkeit*
participatory	*theilnehmend*
particular	*besonder*
passion	*Leidenschaft*
passive	*leidend*
perceive	*wahrnehmen*
perception	*Wahrnehmung*
perfect	*vollkommen*
perfection	*Vollkommenheit*
perform	*ausüben*
permitted	*erlaubt*
persist	*beharren*
persistence	*Beharrlichkeit, Fortdauer*
person	*Mensch, Persohn*
personality	*Persöhnlichkeit*
persuasion	*Überredung*
pictorial	*bildend*
picture	*Bild*
pity	*Mitleid*
place (v.)	*setzen*
place (n.)	*Ort, Stelle*
play (v.)	*spielen*
play (n.)	*Spiel*
please (v.)	*gefallen*
pleasure	*Lust*
poesy	*Poesie*
poet	*Dichter*
poetry	*Dichtung*
posit (v.)	*setzen*
positing	*Setzung, Position*
position	*Stelle*
possession	*Besitz*
possibility	*Möglichkeit*
possible	*möglich*

potency	*Potenz*
potential	*Potenz*
power	*Kraft*
power of choice	*Willkühr*
power of judgment	*Urtheilskraft*
precept	*Vorschrift*
predetermination	*Vorbestimmung*
predisposition	*Anlage*
preference	*Beliebung*
preferred	*beliebig*
prejudice	*Vorurtheil*
presentation	*Vortrag*
presumption	*Anmaßung*
presupposition	*Voraussetzung*
pride	*Hochmuth*
primordial being	*Urwesen*
principle	*Grundsatz, Princip, Satz*
problematic	*zetetisch*
proficiency	*Fertigkeit*
progress	*Fortgang, Fortschreitung, Fortschritt*
promise	*Verheissung*
promote	*befördern*
property	*Eigenschaft*
property	*Mein und Dein*
proposition	*Satz*
propriety	*Anstand*
providence	*Vorsehung*
prudence	*Klugheit*
prudent	*klug*
public	*öffentlich*
punishment	*Strafe*
pure	*lauter, rein*
purpose	*Zweck*
purposive	*zweckmäßig*
purposiveness	*Zweckmäßigkeit*
quantity	*Menge, Quantität, Quantum*
race	*Geschlecht*
ratiocinate	*vernünfteln*
rational	*vernünftig*
rational belief	*Vernunftglaube*
rave	*schwärmen*
reality	*Wirklichkeit, Realität*
reason	*Grund, Ursache, Vernunft*

reciprocal	*wechselseitig*
rectitude	*Rechtschaffenheit*
reflecting	*reflectirend*
reflection	*Überlegung*
refutation	*Wiederlegung*
regularity	*Regelmäßigkeit*
relation	*Beziehung, Verhältnis*
represent	*vorstellen*
representation	*Vorstellung*
resolution	*Entschließung, Vorsatz*
resources	*Vermögen*
respect	*Achtung*
restriction	*Einschränkung*
result	*Folge*
reward	*Lohn, Vergütung*
right (adj).	*recht*
right (n.)	*Recht*
righteous	*rechtschaffen*
rule	*Regel*
rule-governedness	*Regelmäßigkeit*
satisfaction	*Befriedigung, Wohlgefallen*
satisfy	*befriedigen*
scholarship	*Gelehrsamkeit*
scholastic	*Schul-*
science	*Wissenschaft*
sculpture	*Bildhauerkunst*
self	*Selbst*
self-approbation	*Selbstbilligung*
self-activity	*Selbstthätigkeit*
self-compulsion	*Selbstzwang*
self-consciousness	*Selbstbewußtseyn*
self-control	*Selbstbeherrschung*
self-evident	*evident*
self-interest	*Eigennütz*
selfish	*eigennützig*
self-sufficient	*selbstständig*
sensation	*Empfindung*
sense (v.)	*empfinden*
sense (n.)	*Sinn*
sensibility	*Sinnlichkeit*
sensible	*sinnlich*
sensitivity	*Empfindsamkeit*
sentiment	*Empfindung, Sentiment*

separate (v.)	*absondern, trennen*
series	*Reihe*
servile	*knechtlich*
sex	*Geschlecht*
sexuality	*Geschlecht*
share (n.)	*Antheil*
signification	*Bedeutung*
signify	*bedeuten*
simplicity	*Einfalt, Einfaltigkeit*
simultaneity	*Zugleichseyn*
simultaneous	*zugleich*
sociable	*gesellig*
social	*gesellschaftlich*
socialization	*Vergesellschaftung*
solitude	*Einsamkeit*
soul	*Seele*
space	*Raum*
spatial	*räumlich*
species	*Art, Gattung*
spirit	*Geist*
spontaneity	*Spontaneität*
state	*Staat, Zustand*
state of nature	*Stand der Natur*
stimulate	*reizen*
stimulus	*Stimulus*
subjection	*Unterwürfigkeit*
sublime	*erhaben*
subordination	*Unterordnung, Subordination*
succeed	*folgen*
succession	*Folge*
sufficient	*zureichend*
suicide	*Selbstmord*
suitability	*Angemessenheit, Tauglichkeit*
sum-total	*Inbegriff*
supernatural	*übernatürlich*
supersensible	*übersinnlich*
supposition	*Vermuthung*
supreme	*oberst*
suspicion	*Aberglaube*
sympathetic	*theilnehmend*
sympathy	*Mitgefühl, Sympathie*
synthetic	*synthetisch*
taste	*Geschmack*
temporal succession	*Zeitfolge*

thing	*Ding, Sache*
think	*denken*
thorough, thoroughgoing	*durchgängig*
thought	*Denken, Gedanke*
thought-entity	*Gedankenwesen*
time	*Zeit*
total	*Inbegriff*
totality	*All, Totalität*
touch (v.)	*rühren*
touchstone	*Probirstein*
truth	*Wahrheit*
ugliness	*Häßlichkeit*
ugly	*häßlich*
unanimity	*Einstimmung*
uncertainty	*Ungewissheit*
unconditioned	*unbedingt*
understand	*einsehen, verstehen*
understanding	*Verstand*
unification	*Vereinigung*
uniform	*gleichformig*
union	*Vereinigung*
unison	*Einstimmung*
unitary	*einig*
unity	*Einheit*
universal	*allgemein*
universal validity	*Allgemeingültigkeit*
unrest	*Unruhe*
unselfish	*gemeinnützig*
unselfishness	*Uneigennützigkeit*
upright	*rechtschaffen*
use (n.)	*Gebrauch*
utility	*Nutzen*
valid	*gültig*
validity	*Gültigkeit*
value	*Werth*
vice	*Laster*
vicious	*lasterhaft*
virtue	*Tugend*
virtuous	*tugendhaft*
vocation	*Bestimmung*
voluntary	*freywilling, willkührlich*
welfare	*Wohlfahrt*
well-being	*Wohl, Wohlbefinden*
whole (n.)	*Ganze*

will	*Wille*
wisdom	*Weisheit*
world	*Welt*
world-whole	*Weltall, Weltganze*
worth	*Werth*
worthiness	*Würdigkeit*

.

Index to Kant's Texts

action, imputation of, 90, 122, 145, 288, 430; *see also* freedom
actuality, 126, 246, 296, 297
Aeneas, 523
Aenesidemus (Gottlob Ernst Schulze), 385
aesthetics, 28, 136, 210, 469–470, 486; *see also* beauty/the beautiful; sublimity/the sublime; taste
agreeableness/the agreeable, contrasted to the good and/or beautiful, 418, 421, 438–439, 484, 491, 495, 500, 509, 510–511, 521, 524, 525–526, 528, 531, 533, 539
alteration, 115, 183, 214, 247, 290–291, 299–300, 301, 356, 398
amphiboly of concepts of reflection, 236–237
analogies of experience, 161–162, 164, 174, 175, 177, 183, 210; *see also* causation; interaction; substance
analogy, 65–67, 93, 402; *see also* analogies of experience
analysis, contrasted to synthesis, 56, 81, 82–83, 97–98, 100, 124–125; *see also* judgments, analytic and/or synthetic
animation, 515–516, 517, 539
anthropomorphism, 329, 348
anticipations, 224
antinomies of pure reason, 184, 188–191, 212, 223–224, 238, 251, 265, 267, 321–322, 369–370, 392, 396, 400; concerning free action (third antinomy), 107–108, 109, 110, 184, 315–316, 317; concerning necessity, 312, 316; concerning space and/or time (first and second antinomies), 119, 147, 177, 178, 180–181, 183–184, 208, 228, 236, 251, 314–316, 399; *see also* dialectic
appearances, 33, 126, 151, 167–168, 182–183, 394, 395; and antinomies, 178; and beauty, 494; contrasted to things in themselves, 115, 119, 132, 144, 198, 249–250, 259–261, 303, 307, 382, 385–386, 391–392, 395; exposition of, 158, 160, 168–170, 179, 184, 187, 203, 211, 213, 216–217

apperception, 33, 160–161, 163, 166, 167–168, 172, 179, 208, 244, 258–259, 260, 266, 268–269, 279, 365–366, 394, 442, 470
a priori, see cognition
appetite, contrasted to taste, 495–496, 497, 500–501
Archimedes, 529
architecture, 492, 504
Aristides, 53
Aristippus, 135
Aristotle/Aristotelianism, 124, 135, 198, 209, 263, 327, 427, 433, 435
art, 483; has rules, 497; has models, not rules, 538, 539; and nature, 497, 506–507, 517–518, 525, 527, 536–537
atheism, 347, 348
autonomy, 329
axioms of intuition, 174

Bacon, Francis, 272
Baumgarten, Alexander Gottlieb, 210, 217
beauty/the beautiful, 10, 14, 15, 80, 83, 483; and appearance, 494; in art, 517–518, 538; contrasted to agreeable and/or good, 421, 484, 491, 495, 500, 509, 510–511, 521, 524, 525–526, 528, 531, 533, 539; contrasted to charm, 485, 487–488, 489–490, 498, 526, 540, 542; and form, 530; and harmony, 518, 535, 536–537, 540, 542; has subjective principle, 485; ideal of, 497; and interest, 507, 541–542; and laws of sensibility, 495, 496; and morality, 501–502, 526, 541; and order, 488, 510; and perfection, 486, 493–494, 529, 533; and play, 511–512; and possession, 494; and rules, 484; as sensible presentation of concept, 542; and sight, 496; and understanding, 531–532; universal validity of, 491, 493, 508; varieties of, 485; *see also* taste
Beck, Jacob Sigismund, 389, 392, 394
being, *see* existence
belief, 43, 44–46, 50–53, 272–273, 274, 346–348, 349; moral or practical, 137, 354–355, 373–374; religious, 38; *see also* faith; opinion
beneficence, 11

655

generosity, 18

genius, 410, 483, 490–491, 492, 497, 499, 503, 505, 512, 516–517, 529; and animation, 515–516; elements of, 510; and spirit, 503–504, 507–508, 514–515, 536; and talent, 512–513, 514; and taste, 505, 518–519

geometry, 98, 201, 238, 489

Gerard, Alexander, 516

God: analogical representation of, 402; arguments for existence of, 74–79, 123–124, 153, 179–180, 233–234, 236, 326, 344–346, 349–353, 375–376, 396–398; belief in, 346–349; cannot be proven or disproven, 200; cognition of, 256–257; concept of, 92, 109, 132, 278; as *ens realissimum*, 53, 146, 224–225, 297–298, 352–353, 396–398; and freedom, 329, 340, 342; goodness of, 331, 338–339; hypostatization of good will, 469; as intuitive intellect, 130; moral concept of, 339, 395; and moral obligation, 360–361, 400–401, 433, 460, 475; moral proof of existence of, 129, 146, 147, 204, 212, 332–335, 337, 341–342, 354, 369, 402, 403–404, 478; as necessary being (*ens necessarium*), 84–85, 115, 238, 296–297, 298, 375–376, 396–398; no theoretical cognition of, 401; not spatio-temporal, 314–317, 369; properties of, 87–88, 360–361, 372–374, 401; and providence, 341–342, 343; *see also* cosmological argument; highest good; moral proof; ontological argument; physiocotheological proof; postulates of pure practical reason

good, highest; *see* highest good

good will, *see* will

goodness/the good: absolute, 406–407, 414, 418; conditional or categorical, 18, 19–20, 429; contrasted to agreeableness and/or beauty, 418, 421, 438–439, 484, 491, 495, 500, 510–511, 521, 524, 525–526, 528, 531, 533, 539

gratification, 446, 475, 523–525

gratitude, 9

ground, concept of, 109, 111

habit, 16

handicraft, 515, 517

happiness: and activity, 331–332, 465; and contentment, 338; definition of, 80; and freedom, 210, 448–449, 465–469, 470–471; and highest good, 333, 422; and inclinations, 422–423; in moral world, 411; no purely moral, 446; only conditionally good, 450; as progress,

335; relation to virtue, 5, 80, 333; self-authored, 462–464, 475; as universal end, 445, 449; and universal rules, 425–426; and welfare, 338; and worthiness to be happy, 125, 137–138, 212, 337, 338–339, 352, 373–374, 411–412, 416, 418, 423, 427, 429, 433, 439, 441, 444, 446–447, 449, 450, 453–454, 455, 457–458, 460–461, 462–464, 465–469, 472–474; *see also* highest good

harmony; *see* beauty; preestablished harmony

heaven and hell, 344

Helvétius, Claude-Adrien, 424

highest good, 51–52, 85, 116, 333, 335–336, 337, 339–340, 343–344, 403, 404, 416, 423–424, 445–446, 466, 470, 477; ancient theories of, 421, 422, 426

history: cognition of, 272–273; use of philosophical, 196

Hobbes, Thomas, 181, 419; *Leviathan*, 419

Holbach, Paul Henri Thiry, baron d', 200

holiness, 423, 428–429, 476, 477

honor, 21, 22, 424, 508

horticulture, 485, 517

Hufeland, Gottlieb, 383

humanities, 535

humanity: conditions of, 419; dignity of, 411, 436–437, 444, 476; ends of, 475–476; rights of, 435–437, 475–476

Hume, David, 207, 330, 339, 519

Hutcheson, Francis, 428

hypotheses, 47–49, 50–53, 256–257, 263, 351–352, 354

ideal: of beauty, 512; definition of, 512; moral, 423–424; of pure reason, 240, 241; *see also* highest good

idealism: dogmatic, 355; formal, 362–363, 364, 376; and monadology, 178; problematic, 355; and realism, 233; refutation of, 114, 161–164, 229, 267, 281–288, 294, 355–366, 370, 374, 376, 383; transcendental, 266

ideas: practical, 423; of pure reason or transcendental, 53–54, 93, 99, 196, 208, 222, 240, 241–244, 245–246, 248, 249, 288–289, 305, 311–312, 326–327, 392–393, 400, 517

identity, of person, 374

illusion, transcendental, 240, 242–243, 267

imagination, 15, 92, 229; and outer sense, 358, 361–363, 364, 366; synthesis of, 258–259, 260

imitation, 497, 513

metaphysics, 24, 28, 31, 81, 82, 83, 92, 93,
100–102, 103, 106, 109, 116–117, 125,
130–131, 134–137, 138, 139, 140, 147,
152, 192–193, 196, 197, 198, 201, 202,
214–216, 270–271, 277, 278–280,
292–293, 376–377, 383; of morals, 438,
439–440, 441
miracles, 290–291, 324–325
monads/monadology, 98, 178, 237,
244–245
Montesquieu, Charles Louis de Secondat,
baron de, 22
moral feeling, *see* feeling
moral incapacity, 461
moral law/principle of morality:
absolute/catgeorical or hypothetical,
429, 431; definition of, 469; and final
end, 341–342, 343; and freedom,
414–415, 437; and happiness, 449;
independent of God, 360–361, 403, 433;
pure rather than sensual, 432–433; and
rights of humanity, 435–437; and
truthfulness, 432; and universalizability,
427, 430, 431–432, 434–436, 443,
451–452; *see also* categorical imperative;
principles
moral proof of the existence of God, 123,
129, 146, 147, 204, 212, 234, 332–335,
337, 341–342, 354, 369, 402, 403–404,
478
moral world, 124
morality: based on feeling or reason,
426–427; and character, 411; contrasted
to legality or right, 242, 475; definition
of, 413, 414, 422, 451, 461–462, 467,
471; and happiness, 411–412, 423–424;
and ideas, 243; laws of, 212; and
personality, 430; and religion, 19, 125,
136, 256–257, 332, 432, 433, 441, 445,
448; and rules, 101; and
self-consciousness, 277; supreme
principle of, 124; and utility, 431; *see also*
ethics; feeling; moral law; principles
Mordaunt (Philip Merdant), 521
motion, 152, 177, 247, 290–291, 324–325,
399
motives: kinds of, 407–408; moral, 4, 9,
415, 417, 418, 421, 427, 431, 447–448,
454
music, 482, 487, 494, 502, 503, 504, 513,
518, 531
Myinda, 387

naïve, the, 481, 512
nature: and art, 497, 506–507, 517, 518,
525, 536–537; contrasted to freedom,
250–251, 257, 389, 415–416, 459, 475;
laws of, 230; and mechanism, 320–321;

as object of possible experience,
249–250; as order, 133; state of, 419; as
sum of appearances, 323–325; as system,
210
necessary being (*ens necessarium*), 80, 99,
115, 153, 177–178, 213, 223, 296–297,
298, 313, 350–351, 375–376, 396–398;
see also God; necessity; ontological
argument
necessity, 82, 84–85, 123, 126, 233,
296–297, 320, 391; categorical and
hypothetical, 429, 436; no cognition of
absolute, 111, 112–113, 118, 223, 233,
325; not presented in experience, 226;
opposed to freedom, 89, 232; of value,
403–404, 407; varieties of, 246; *see also*
necessity; ontological argument
neo-Platonism, 327
Newton, Isaac, 9, 181, 230, 282
noumenon, 244–245; *see also* things in
themselves
number, 148, 359

object: concept of, 125, 149, 152, 285,
380, 387–388; conditions of cognition
of, 126, 171–172, 173–174, 178, 184,
186; representation of, 269;
transcendental, 244–245
obligation, 450, 471; definition of, 474;
rest on maxims, 473; *see also* duty
ontological argument, 74–79, 153,
179–180, 233, 234, 325, 349–350,
396–398; *see also* God; necessary being;
necessity
ontology, 116, 217, 249, 270, 271, 311
opinion, 43, 45–46, 272, 348
oratory, 482, 512, 513, 541
outer sense: as appearance, 395; not
imaginary, 358, 361–363, 366; *see also*
inner sense; refutation of idealism;
space

pain, 524
painting, 504
pantheism, 372
pantomime, 492
paralogisms of pure reason, 199, 234,
236–237, 259
peace, 331
perception, 392
perfection: aesthetic and logical, 529,
532–533, 535, 536, 538–540; and beauty,
486, 493–494, 529, 533; of cognition,
492, 534; concept of, 292, 426; and
form, 531; and freedom, 422; logical
and moral, 21; of person, 19, 80, 116,
418; sensible judgment of, 528–529; of
will, 15, 16, 431; of world, 124